BUSINESS WEEK

Guide to Mutual Funds

Ninth Annual Edition

Jeffrey M. Laderman
Senior Writer, BUSINESS WEEK

McGraw-Hill

New York   San Francisco   Washington, D.C.   Auckland   Bogotá
Caracas   Lisbon   London   Madrid   Mexico City   Milan
Montreal   New Delhi   San Juan   Singapore
Sydney   Tokyo   Toronto

To order a subscription to *Business Week* and gain FREE access to BW's entire Web site—including supplementary information and constantly updated data on mutual funds—call toll free 1-888-878-5151.

International Standard Serial Number:
BUSINESS WEEK Guide to Mutual Funds
ISSN 1060-975x

McGraw-Hill

A Division of The McGraw·Hill Companies

1 2 3 4 5 6 7 8 9 0   MAL/MAL   9 0 4 3 2 1 0 9

ISBN 0-07-134261-3

The editor for this book was Nancy Mikhail, the editing supervisor was Jane Palmieri, and the production supervisor was Tina Cameron. It was set in Century Expanded by North Market Street Graphics.

Printed and bound by Malloy Lithographers, Inc.

CONTENTS

PREFACE

Each and every year, BUSINESS WEEK's annual Mutual Fund Scoreboard issue, *The Best Mutual Funds,* is one of the best-selling single issues of the magazine. It's easy to understand why. Mutual fund assets now stand at $5.5 trillion, up $1 trillion in one year alone. Heck, mutual fund assets just hit the $1 trillion mark in 1990.

Of course, BUSINESS WEEK isn't the only publication that reports on and rates mutual funds. But we think we're the best. So do the mutual fund executives who were asked by *Securities Industry Management* magazine a few years ago to rate those who rate mutual funds. SIM's survey awarded BW's Mutual Fund Scoreboard an A–, the highest grade of seven publications rated. In its comments, SIM gave BW "high marks for being an innovator and for solid editorial comment." The best grade any of the competitors received was a B.

Now the magazine with the best mutual fund scoreboard is proud to bring you the best mutual fund book on the market, BUSINESS WEEK *Guide to Mutual Funds*, Ninth Annual Edition. This slim, easy-to-read volume is your passport into the dynamic world of mutual fund investing. We tell you all you want to know about mutual funds—which funds are beating the market and their competitors, which funds are delivering the highest returns with the least risk, and which funds have the highest and lowest costs. And we also feature the BUSINESS WEEK ratings. These ratings assess the risk-adjusted returns of each fund with at least five years of performance history against all other funds (three years for closed-end funds). The new edition's Scoreboard, in the back of the book, has the latest information on 885 equity, 653 bond, and 470 closed-end funds.

But now there's even more to BW's fund coverage than what's in the back. We're pleased to bring you the Interactive Mutual Fund Scoreboard, now available at BUSINESS WEEK's site on the World Wide Web (www.businessweek.com). Your gateway to the online Scoreboard is the Mutual Fund Corner, where you'll also find a collection of BUSINESS WEEK's mutual fund news and analysis.

The Interactive Scoreboard is not confined by the printed page. There's data on over 4700 equity and bond funds and, better yet, it's updated monthly—we recalculate returns and BW ratings and add new funds. This book draws on that trove of information. You can use the online site in many ways: to screen the database for funds in which to invest or to keep tabs on funds you already own. If you want information that goes beyond what's in the Scoreboard, with one click you can jump to a Morningstar page. Another click will take you to the fund's Web site.

The book is basically composed of two parts. In the first part, we pull together the essentials you need to know about mutual funds: how they work and how you can use them. The second part is the print version of the BUSINESS WEEK Mutual Fund Scoreboard. The Scoreboard provides a wealth of information about mutual fund performance, costs, and risks that helps you to keep track of your own holdings—and prospect for new ones. The ratings are the highlight of the Scoreboard. Funds are rated on the basis of their returns—and their risk.

The book's first chapter is an introduction to mutual funds: why they're popular, what kinds of returns they can provide, and how investors can harness their earning power. Chapter 2 takes a close-up look at the world of mutual funds and discusses how they invest your money. We'll also look into the closed-end funds, the manic first cousins of mutual funds. They often have higher highs and lower lows than their mutual fund kin.

In Chapter 3 we examine how you buy and sell mutual funds. That includes all you need to know about commissions, or the "load." There are funds that are sold with front-end loads, back-end loads, low-loads, hidden loads, and no-loads. And if you're going to pay a load, we'll help you determine which is the most cost-effective way of doing so. And we also explore new ways for investors to buy funds, such as networks or fund marketplaces developed by Charles Schwab & Co. and others and the increasingly popular adviser-based "wrap" programs.

When you've completed Chapters 2 and 3, you will know about the variety of funds and how you buy them. Then the question is what to buy. Chapter 4 asks you the questions you need to answer to help you build your own investment portfolio of mutual funds. And, of course, once you have your funds you can't just forget about them. So in Chapter 5 we cover how to monitor your funds—making sure they do what you want them to do—and some online tools you can use to do it.

If you've made the right moves, you're making money. And if you're making money, you will have to pay taxes. Chapter 6 explains the special tax rules that apply to how mutual funds report their income to you and how you, the shareholder, report to the Internal Revenue Service. We'll show you how to minimize the tax bite when you're cashing in your gains, and how to make the most of your losses by turning them into tax deductions.

In Chapter 7 we take a closer look at the Scoreboard and how to interpret the information in it. Chapter 8 looks at the most recent Scoreboard: which funds are in ascendancy, which are in decline, and what it means for the coming years. What follows is the Scoreboard itself—a cornucopia of information on 2000 funds. Once you have the basics of mutual funds investing under your belt, the Scoreboard is the perfect place to start your search for the funds that will help you reach your financial goals.

Acknowledgments

The Scoreboard itself is produced for BUSINESS WEEK by Morningstar, Inc. This company takes care of gathering the vast amounts of data from the funds—organizing it and analyzing it in a way that allows us to assign ratings to funds. We'd like to thank the folks at Morningstar, especially Carrie Thomas, for their advice and assistance in preparing the Guide.

At BUSINESS WEEK, Senior Writer Jeffrey M. Laderman took charge of writing the book and coordinating the project. Laderman, a Chartered Financial Analyst, has covered mutual funds for over 15 years. He helped to launch the first Mutual Fund Scoreboard in February 1986, and has written the accompanying stories every year since.

Also contributing to the book is Senior Editor Seymour Zucker, who lent his skillful editing and much valued advice. Without his enthusiastic support, and that of Stephen B. Shepard, BW's editor-in-chief, and Mark Morrison, the managing editor, this project would not have been possible.

Mutual Funds: The People's Choice

Over the last decade, investors have embraced mutual funds with a fervor that even the most optimistic fund executive could not have predicted. Since the beginning of 1991, investors have poured more than $1.4 trillion into mutual funds that invest in stocks and bonds. In 1997, a record year for mutual fund investing, funds took in a record $293 billion. In 1998, flows to equity funds fell off after the summer's stock market correction, but investor appetite for bonds picked up. All told, investors spent $243 billion on stock and bond mutual funds. And another $235 billion went to money-market mutual funds, more than double 1997's figure.

Why are people putting billions into mutual funds? Well, nothing sells like success, and for the most part investors have been successful. In the early 1990s, they earned plump returns as interest rates fell, vastly increasing the value of stocks and bonds. In 1994, interest rates shot up, causing losses in bond funds that cut off their growth for several years. But investors never wavered in their support for equity funds, even when the stock market teetered that year.

Investors who stuck it out during tough 1994 were paid off wonderfully in 1995, 1996, and 1997. During that three-year period, perhaps the best three years ever for the U.S. stock market, the average U.S. equity fund delivered a total return of 24.5 percent, including appreciation, dividends, and capital gains distributions. That's a rate at which money doubles every three years.

Even 1998 with its gut-wrenching market swoons—disappointing for mutual fund investors in some ways—was still a double-digit gainer. Indeed, with all the problems, the average U.S. diversified equity fund still managed to post a 14.1 percent total return. The all-equity fund average was 11.4 percent. The 25 funds with the highest returns earned at least 66.9 percent each (Table 1-1). The absolute best was the Internet Fund, up 196.1 percent. The average bond fund earned 5.6 percent. But the top 25 bond funds came in with impressive results—the best was up 24.5 percent (Table 1-2).

Investors have also seen some foibles. Over the last few years, several portfolio managers faced disciplinary actions from regulators for making personal investments that conflicted with their professional duties. One was even dismissed. The actions prompted most companies to tighten up their personnel trading policies, and the fund industry itself developed guidelines about what fund personnel should and should not do with personal trading.

Fund shareholders learned a new 4-letter word with 11 letters: "derivatives." These derivatives—financially engineered investment instruments whose value is "derived" from some other security or index—helped to sink two bond funds and erode principal in dozens more. Money-market mutual funds, which are supposed to be the most risk-averse funds of all, were not untouched by the derivatives mess, either. However, in all but one instance, the funds' management companies absorbed the losses of the handful of money funds adversely affected by derivatives. In early 1997, another fund manager stepped in to bail out a money-market mutual fund that had erred the old-fashioned way—it had made an investment that turned out bad because of "financial irregularities" at the company.

For the most part, investors have a lot of confidence in mutual funds. In a 1994 BUSINESS

TABLE 1-1

EQUITY FUNDS

1998'S TOP RETURNS

Fund ▼	Total return* ▼
INTERNET	196.1%
PROFUNDS ULTRAOTC INV.	185.3
GRAND PRIX	111.8
POTOMAC OTC PLUS	104.2
DREYFUS TECHNOLOGY GROWTH	98.4
MUNDER NETNET A	98.0
FIDELITY SELECT COMPUTERS	96.4
MATTHEWS KOREA I	96.2
RYDEX OTC INVESTORS	86.5
FLAG INVESTORS COMMUNICATIONS A	85.3
VAN WAGONER TECHNOLOGY	85.1
TRANSAMERICA PREMIER AGGRESSIVE GROWTH INV.	84.1
MILLENNIUM GROWTH	84.1
NORTHERN TECHNOLOGY	83.0
TRANSAMERICA PREMIER SMALL COMPANY INV.	80.3
PIMCO INNOVATION C	78.1
FIRSTHAND TECHNOLOGY LEADERS	77.6
FIDELITY SELECT TECHNOLOGY	74.2
JANUS TWENTY	73.4
BERGER SELECT	72.3
WWW INTERNET	70.5
PBHG LARGE CAP 20 PBHG	67.8
FIDELITY SELECT DEVELOPING COMMUNICATIONS	67.7
EXCELSIOR LARGE CAP GROWTH	67.0
WARBURG PINCUS GLOBAL TELECOMMUNICATIONS	66.9

*Appreciation plus reinvestment of dividends and capital gains, before taxes

DATA: MORNINGSTAR INC.

WEEK/Harris Poll of mutual fund investors—a year of sharp volatility in the equity and bond markets—94 percent said they're somewhat or very confident that their investments are safe and only 24 percent said they planned to scale back their holdings. In addition, the poll's respondents showed they had a realistic view of the risks that go with investing. Asked who is to blame if a mutual fund loses money, 60 percent said "no one." Asked what they would expect if one of their funds lost money, 80 percent said they did not expect anyone to make up the losses.

The sentiments expressed in that poll were certainly borne out in subsequent years. Investors continue to stash their savings in mutual funds. In only one month since 1994 was more money withdrawn from equity funds than was deposited. With nearly two out of five U.S. households owning mutual funds, funds have established their place in family finance alongside the savings account, the checkbook, and the credit cards.

And those not familiar with funds are learning about them at the workplace. Mutual funds are a mainstay of a pension program called the 401(k) plan. In these plans, employees—often matched in part by employers—make regular pretax contributions. They choose from a variety of investment options, many of which are mutual funds. A large percentage of the monthly inflows to mutual funds comes through the workplace.

Sure, novice investors have learned through experience that markets—and mutual fund prices—don't always go up. But taking a longer-term view, investors have been rewarded for taking the higher risks of investing. Indeed, over the long haul, the greater risk to investors is in playing it too safe. Investors who keep long-term funds in CDs and U.S. Treasury bills may be taking a big risk that they won't meet their long-term financial objectives, like a college education for their children or a comfortable retirement for themselves.

Mutual funds are not new. They've been fixtures of the investment world since the 1920s. For most of that time, funds offered one sort of investment—stocks. Bond funds were few, and tax-free bond and money-market mutual funds didn't come along until the 1970s. Even equity mutual funds were only a sideshow on Wall Street. First, individual investors and, later, pension funds held much more sway.

Today, because individuals have put their dollars in the hands of mutual fund managers, mutual funds dominate the stock market. They don't dominate in the sense that they "control" companies. But right now the funds are the most active investors, with the most new money to put to work. Market participants follow the funds' moves very closely. Just consider all the publicity surrounding the trading in the gargantuan Fidelity Magellan Fund. In late 1995, portfolio manager Jeffrey Vinik, in shareholder reports and in press interviews, made complimentary remarks about technology stocks around the same time he was selling them. Fidelity critics howled, saying Vinik was trying to talk up the stocks to get a better price on his sales. Company officials said Vinik's statements were his honest opinion at the time they were made but portfolio managers have to be free to change their minds. Indeed, that's what they're paid for. Certainly, portfolio managers must play by the rules, but that doesn't include telling everybody what their next move is going to be. That would be detrimental to fund shareholders to whom every portfolio manager has a fiduciary responsibility.

TABLE 1-2

BOND FUNDS

1998'S TOP RETURNS

Fund ▼	Total return* ▼
VONTOBEL EASTERN EUROPEAN DEBT	24.5%
AMERICAN CENTURY–BENHAM TARGET MAT. 2025 INV.	21.9
NICHOLAS-APPLEGATE CONVERTIBLE C	20.1
MANAGERS GLOBAL BOND	19.3
SEI INTERNATIONAL FIXED-INCOME A	18.5
FFTW INTERNATIONAL FIXED-INCOME	18.4
GUINNESS FLIGHT GLOBAL GOVERNMENT	17.9
AMERICAN CENTURY–BENHAM INTERNATIONAL BOND	17.9
PACIFIC ADVISORS GOVERNMENT SECURITIES A	17.8
CALAMOS GROWTH & INCOME A	17.7
MORGAN GRENFELL INTERNATIONAL FIXED-INCOME	17.4
NORTHERN INTERNATIONAL FIXED-INCOME	17.1
AMERICAN CENTURY–BENHAM TARGET MAT. 2020 INV.	16.8
FIDELITY CONVERTIBLE SECURITIES	16.3
RYDEX U.S. GOVERNMENT BOND	15.8
MUNDER INTERNATIONAL BOND A	15.7
FFTW WORLDWIDE FIXED-INCOME	15.7
STRONG INTERNATIONAL BOND	15.3
ABN AMRO INTERNATIONAL FIXED-INCOME COMMON	15.2
AMERICAN CENTURY–BENHAM TARGET MAT. 2010 INV.	15.1
T. ROWE PRICE INTERNATIONAL BOND	15.0
VAN ECK/CHUBB GLOBAL INCOME	15.0
VONTOBEL INTERNATIONAL BOND	14.9
ROCKHAVEN PREMIER DIVIDEND	14.8
AMERICAN CENTURY–BENHAM TARGET MAT. 2015 INV.	14.7

*Appreciation plus reinvestment of dividends and capital gains, before taxes

DATA: MORNINGSTAR INC.

Mutual funds play a critical role in the fixed-income markets as well. State and local governments increasingly turn to the mutual funds to buy their bonds and provide the financing needed to operate public services and rebuild the aging infrastructure. Through investment in U.S. Treasury securities, mutual funds help to finance the U.S. government. Funds bring fresh capital to the home mortgage market through their purchases of mortgage-backed securities, making it easier and a little cheaper for families to buy homes. And, with investments in high-yield bonds and commercial paper, mutual funds are helping to lower the borrowing costs for corporations.

Mutual funds have only became so important because of the millions of individuals who now entrust their money to fund management companies. It's not always an easy trust to give. Savers who move their money out of a bank or thrift give up federal deposit insurance. Mutual funds have no guarantees. The growth of the mutual fund industry has even surprised industry officials. In 1990, for instance, an industry-sponsored study estimated the funds would have $2 trillion in assets by 1995 or 1996, and at least $3 trillion by 2000. At year-end 1998, fund assets were $5.5 trillion; the number of funds stood at 7343; the number of shareholder accounts was 182.8 million (Figure 1-1). The popularity of the funds is more than a bull market phenomenon. After all, many fund investors could just as easily buy stocks and bonds directly, but choose funds instead. Funds are convenient and efficient investment vehicles that give all individuals—even those with small sums to invest—access to a splendid array of opportunities. Mutual funds are uniquely democratic institutions. They can take a portfolio of giant blue-chip companies like Microsoft, General Electric, and Exxon and slice it into small enough pieces that most anyone can buy.

Mutual funds allow investors to participate in foreign stock and bond markets which they couldn't do on their own—or would find to be a costly, time-consuming, and logistical quagmire if they tried. International equity funds make investing across national borders no more difficult than investing across state lines. Funds even allow investors to target their investments into individual countries like China, South Korea, and yes, even Russia. (A terrific investment for a while, but it came crashing down in 1998).

Mutual funds have opened up a world of bond investing to people who not too many years ago had few choices other than passbook accounts and savings bonds. Through bond funds individuals can tap into the interest payments from any kind of fixed-income security you can imagine and many you can't. The range goes from U.S. Treasury bonds to collateralized mortgage obligations, adjustable-rate preferred stock, floating rate notes, and even other countries' debt—denominated both in U.S. dollars and in other currencies. After the bond market volatility investors experienced in 1994 and, to a lesser degree, in 1996, a boring old bank account may look pretty good to a yield-oriented investor. Funds are not the same as bank deposits. No one guarantees that your assets will remain intact, let alone grow. Some legislators and regulators have pointed to surveys of bank customers who bought mutual funds at the bank—and think they're insured. The only fund that can be considered as safe as a bank deposit is one investing solely in U.S. Treasury bills. No one should use equity funds for money that they're going to need to buy a house or a car in the near future. But the

FIGURE 1-1

THE EXPLOSIVE GROWTH IN MUTUAL FUNDS

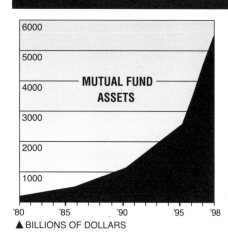

MUTUAL FUND ASSETS

▲ BILLIONS OF DOLLARS

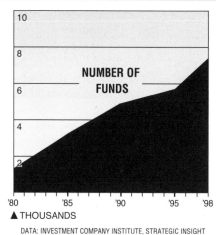

NUMBER OF FUNDS

▲ THOUSANDS

NUMBER OF SHAREHOLDER ACCOUNTS

▲ MILLIONS

DATA: INVESTMENT COMPANY INSTITUTE, STRATEGIC INSIGHT

longer the investment horizon, the lower the risk of losses. Money stashed away for many years instead of months could well go into a mutual fund or a properly constructed portfolio of funds.

How do you find the right funds? BUSINESS WEEK'S *Guide to Mutual Funds, Ninth Annual Edition,* will make it easy for you. In one volume we survey the world of funds, tell you what you need to know about them, help you tailor your own investment plan, and choose the funds that will best fulfill it. Perhaps you would rather invest through a broker or financial planner, relying on their advice. That's fine too. But don't turn to a salesperson without a solid grasp of mutual funds yourself. If you enter the world of mutual funds as an educated consumer and avoid the common mistakes (Table 1-3), you can become a successful investor.

What's a Mutual Fund?

A mutual fund is an investment company that pools the money of many individual investors. When the fund takes in money from investors, it issues shares. The price of a mutual fund share is the total net assets—the fund's assets less liabilities—divided by the number of shares outstanding. This figure is also called the fund's net asset value, commonly referred to as "NAV."

Unlike stocks, whose prices are subject to change at each trade, mutual fund NAVs are calculated at the end of each day. To figure their NAVs, the funds use the closing prices of each of the securities in their portfolios. (Bond funds often own securities that trade infrequently and daily prices are hard to come by. These funds use outside services that estimate the bonds' prices.)

A mutual fund is also an "open-end" vehicle. That means the fund doesn't have a fixed number of shares, but issues new shares as it takes in money and redeems them as investors withdraw. This liquidity—the ability for investors to get in and out of the funds easily and at little or no cost—is one of the most important features the funds bring to the financial system. A smaller number of funds are "closed-end" funds. They raise their capital during offering periods, and, after that, investors can only get into the fund or out of it by buying or selling the shares on a stock exchange or in the over-the-counter market.

Open-end or closed-end, both types of funds are highly regulated entities, governed by a federal law—the Investment Company Act of 1940. Regulators don't dictate investment policy, but they make sure investment managers adhere to prescribed standards of disclosure, record-keeping, and administration. As a practical matter, the fund companies police themselves. The U.S. Securities and Exchange Commission (SEC) has several hundred examiners to check up on thousands of funds. For the most part, the mutual funds have avoided the kind of financial scandals seen on Wall Street and in the thrift business in the 1980s and have a fairly clean record.

A mutual fund is especially good for those just getting started in the investment game. If you only have a few thousand dollars to invest, very few stockbrokers or professional money managers are going to bother with you. Those who do will not give you the attention and research support afforded to their more well-heeled clients—nor should you expect it. They have to make a living, and the commission on a small nest egg isn't worth much of their time. But if you put your money in a mutual fund, the first-string portfolio managers will be working on your mutual fund account. The $2000 investor gets the same attention as the $200,000 investor. That's because the fund's performance is the manager's calling card. Its successes will be chronicled in the media—and so will its failures. That's a powerful incentive for the portfolio manager to give the fund his or her very best efforts.

You might be one of those people who thinks of a mutual fund as an investment for small and unsophisticated investors; that it's okay for investors who are still building their assets, but anyone with an appreciable amount of money moves into direct investment in stocks and bonds. That's not so. Today many investors who could well afford stockbrokers and professional money managers prefer mutual funds. Some fund companies even offer "sector funds," nondiversified funds that invest in a particular industry or group of industries. Such investment vehicles are designed to look more like stocks than mutual funds and to appeal to investors who might otherwise choose to invest in individual stocks.

Service, convenience, and efficiency all help to explain the growth of mutual funds. But no one would invest in mutual funds if they didn't think they would make money. And, indeed, mutual funds have made huge sums of money for those wise enough to have invested in them.

First Encounters with a Mutual Fund

For many investors, the first mutual fund they bought was a money-market fund. Those funds exploded on the financial scene in the late 1970s. It was a time when interest rates were climbing but bank regulators kept rates on consumer deposits artificially low. Those with $10,000 could pull their money out of the bank and buy Treasury bills, but there was no high-interest vehicle for individuals with less money—until the money-market mutual fund.

The money-market funds revolutionized savings in America. They pooled investors' money and bought the kind of higher-yielding money-market investments that individuals could not get on their own. When short-term interest rates soared to almost 20 percent, the money funds made it possible for anyone to take advantage of the enormous yield. Before the advent of these funds, the only choice a small investor had was a passbook account paying 5 percent.

The money-market funds also resuscitated the mutual fund industry, which for years had been suffering from liquidation—investors taking more money out of the funds than they were putting in. By 1982, money-market funds had commandeered about $200 billion in assets. When the great bull market in stocks and bonds got underway, the mutual fund companies had millions of new customers to whom they could pitch their stock and bond funds.

Those early investors were not disappointed. During the 1980s equity mutual funds earned on average an annual total return of 14.9 percent. In one sense, that's terrific. A $1000 investment in the average equity fund at the start of the decade would have grown to a little more than $4000 by the end. But relative to the Standard & Poor's 500 stock index, the yardstick by which money managers are measured, the return is a little thin. The S&P 500, in fact, delivered an average annual total return of 17.5 percent during the decade. But examine those returns more closely. The S&P 500 is an index, "managed" by a computer. A mutual fund is a portfolio of stocks that

TABLE 1-3

FUND INVESTORS' BIGGEST MISTAKES

▶ Buying last year's or last quarter's hottest performer only because it did well.

▶ Ignoring the prospectus—especially the parts on fees and investment policy.

▶ Choosing funds inappropriate for investment goals.

▶ Selecting highest yields without regard for risks.

▶ Losing track of fund performance.

▶ Failure to keep records for investment evaluation and taxes.

needs a manager, who is usually backed up by analysts and some support staff. The fund must keep meticulous records of its own transactions and those of its thousands of shareholders. Account statements need to be prepared and mailed to each of them. There's also the cost of staffing those toll-free phone lines and fees for the auditing and regulatory filings. All this service costs, on average, about 1.44 percent a year of fund assets, or $1.44 per $100 invested. And that comes out of a fund's returns.

Next, consider that most equity mutual funds keep about 5 percent of their assets in cash. In a bull market, cash (Treasury bills and other money-market instruments) has lower returns than stocks. Over the decade, the cash accounted for another half a percentage point in the underperformance.

Finally, remember that the S&P 500 is dominated by large companies—and the average mutual fund owns companies that are much smaller than the General Electrics and Microsofts of the world. In the 1980s, the stock price performance of the larger companies beat the small-to-medium-sized companies. So there was no way that the average fund could top the S&P 500.

This "underperformance" doesn't seem to have dampened investor enthusiasm for mutual funds. Nor should it. The performance of equity funds still beat money-market and bond funds over the decade and probably gave investors a better return than if they had done nothing with their money. In addition, the average return is just that. Hundreds of funds fared better and 64 even beat the S&P during the decade.

In the early 1990s, the tide shifted toward small-to-medium-sized companies—and that played to the benefit of the mutual fund investors. From 1991 through 1993, the average U.S. diversified fund, which has more small and midsized stocks than the S&P 500, beat the S&P by an average of 3 percentage points a year. Since 1994, those smaller companies have had periods of strong performance, but in each of the four calendar years, the S&P 500 topped the average fund. For that reason, many investors are now using index funds that replicate the S&P 500 for at least part of their investment portfolio.

But traditional fund management is far from dead. With some good tools, like this book, the BUSINESS WEEK Online Web site (www.businessweek.com), and a little bit of your time, you don't have to settle for average returns. If you choose your mutual funds carefully and keep abreast of your funds' progress by tracking net asset values, reading shareholder reports, and using the BUSINESS WEEK ratings, you can improve your portfolio performance.

One academic study pondered the question, "Do winners repeat?" The academics examined monthly mutual fund returns over a 12-year period and found that they do indeed, as do losers, and concluded that a review of past performance is useful in differentiating one mutual fund from another. Although it may not be wise to buy only the No. 1 performer in any one year, it is indeed advisable to select from funds that have been among the best year after year.

Another study looked at equity mutual funds over a 14-year period and concluded that there is some "persistence" of performance. The researchers found that funds that excelled during one year continued to excel for as long as eight quarters, or two years, more. More important, they concluded that there are ways to identify these mutual funds so investors can put their money into the funds and enjoy the benefit of the funds' expertise.

One way to find the best funds, the ones that exhibit this persistence of performance, is in the BUSINESS WEEK Mutual Fund Scoreboard. The BW ratings take into account a mutual fund's risk as well as its total return over a five-year period. This longer view of performance screens out the one-year wonders. The funds that rise to the top do so with consistently strong risk-adjusted returns.

The Joys of Compound Growth

If you're ever cornered by a mutual fund salesperson, he or she will whip out the "mountain" chart (Figure 1-2). What's really important is not the mountain, but the top line, which depicts the growth of a one-time investment in a mutual fund. The line rises slowly at first, but soon accelerates and appears to jump off the page. The Templeton funds, for instance, show what would have happened if you had invested $10,000 in the Templeton Growth Fund when it opened for business in November 1954 and instructed the fund to reinvest all dividends and capital gains distributions. Over four decades later, your original $10,000 alone would be worth over $473,044. But with reinvestment of dividends and capital gains, your investment is worth $3.7 million, more than six times as much.

FIGURE 1-2

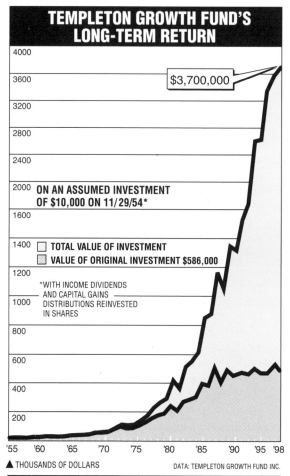

TEMPLETON GROWTH FUND'S LONG-TERM RETURN

$3,700,000

ON AN ASSUMED INVESTMENT OF $10,000 ON 11/29/54*

☐ TOTAL VALUE OF INVESTMENT
▨ VALUE OF ORIGINAL INVESTMENT $586,000

*WITH INCOME DIVIDENDS AND CAPITAL GAINS DISTRIBUTIONS REINVESTED IN SHARES

▲ THOUSANDS OF DOLLARS   DATA: TEMPLETON GROWTH FUND INC.

your returns, and earn, on average, 11 percent, your nest egg grows more than eightfold—to $80,623. Now look at the return in another way. An 11 percent return on $10,000 is $1100. Over 20 years that totals $22,000. So, after two decades you can account for $32,000—your $10,000 initial investment and the annual return earned on it. The other $48,000 is the return on your returns.

Mutual funds don't guarantee a rate of return. The portfolio managers do their best to deliver the highest rate of return they can and live within their investment objectives. And if a fund does earn, on average, 12 percent a year, it's not earning that every year. Some years the fund might earn twice that amount and other years actually lose money. It's only in retrospect that you come up with nice round numbers like a 12 percent or 14 percent annual rate of return. It's simply an average.

If you want to harness the power of compound rates of return, investing in mutual funds is a convenient and efficient way to do it. Suppose you own some bonds and collect $389 in interest twice a year. You want to reinvest the money, but what can you do with it? You can't buy more bonds because it's an odd amount. You can stash it away in a money-market mutual fund until you have enough to buy another bond. But while the money is sitting in a money-market fund, it's probably not earning what it could in a bond.

A mutual fund makes this process much simpler. If a bond fund pays you $389, or any other such amount, you can (in advance) direct the fund to reinvest the money immediately. You don't have to worry about odd amounts of money. There is no check stuck in the mail. Your money is at work all the time. The mutual fund will take whatever the amount is, divide it by the current price per share, and give you that many shares. If it's 17.693 shares, so be it, since the fund can sell you fractional shares down to one-thousandth of a decimal place.

The ability to invest odd sums and buy fractional shares makes mutual funds ideal vehicles for savings programs. Millions of mutual fund shareholders, in fact, invest regularly through automatic investment plans. Suppose you want to save $200 a month and invest it in equities. It's not practical to buy $200 worth of stock at a time. Commissions are high on small orders, and there's no way to invest odd amounts that are left over and buy fractional shares of stock on any exchange.

With a regular savings program the compound growth tables look even more alluring. Remem-

Sales hype? Well, the track record is real. Templeton Growth Fund, which was one of the first international funds (that is, funds that invest in non-U.S. stocks), has had an average annual return of 14.4 percent. What is a little exaggerated is the $10,000 investment. The equivalent in today's dollars is more than $50,000. Even today, that's hardly your average initial mutual fund investment.

The example may be a bit fanciful, but the principle demonstrated in this sort of sales material is simple—the power of compound rates of return. You earn a return on your investment and, if you don't take it out of the fund, you begin to earn returns on your returns. You're probably familiar with a bank certificate of deposit. If you leave the interest in the CD, you earn interest on your interest. Mutual funds don't pay a fixed rate of interest. But if you reinvest profits in more fund shares, you're compounding your returns.

Look at Table 1-4. If you invest $10,000 now, hold on to the investment for 20 years, reinvest

TABLE 1-4

THE WONDERFUL WORLD OF COMPOUND INTEREST

Invest $10,000 in year 1

Rate of return	What your investment would be worth at the end of year...					
	5	10	15	20	25	30
7%	$14,026	$19,672	$27,950	$38,697	$52,274	$76,123
8	14,693	21,589	31,722	46,610	68,485	100,627
9	15,386	23,674	36,425	56,044	86,231	132,677
10	16,105	25,937	41,772	67,275	108,347	174,494
11	16,851	28,394	47,846	80,623	135,855	228,923
12	17,623	31,058	54,736	96,463	170,001	299,599

Invest $2,000 a year

Rate of return	What your investment would be worth at the end of year...					
	5	10	15	20	25	30
7%	$12,307	$29,567	$53,776	$87,730	$135,353	$202,146
8	12,672	31,291	58,649	98,846	157,909	244,692
9	13,047	33,121	64,007	111,529	184,648	297,150
10	13,431	35,062	69,899	126,005	216,364	361,887
11	13,826	37,123	76,380	142,530	253,998	441,826
12	14,230	39,309	83,507	161,398	298,668	540,585

Invest $200 a month

Rate of return	What your investment would be worth at the end of year...					
	5	10	15	20	25	30
7%	$14,402	$34,819	$63,762	$104,793	$162,959	$245,417
8	14,793	36,833	69,669	118,589	191,473	300,059
9	15,198	38,993	76,249	134,579	225,906	368,895
10	15,616	41,310	83,585	153,139	267,578	455,865
11	16,049	43,797	91,772	174,715	318,116	566,046
12	16,497	46,468	100,915	199,830	379,527	705,983

DATA: BUSINESS WEEK

ber, the numbers are greater because you periodically invest new money in the fund. Put $200 a month into a mutual fund and you can really see the money build up. After 20 years you've put in $48,000. If that money earns an 11 percent average annual return for 20 years, your stake grows to about $174,715. That's nearly $127,000 more than you put in.

The ease and efficiency with which investments compound make mutual funds perfect investments for long-term savings programs like college funds or retirement accounts. That's why mutual funds are the investment vehicle of choice for Individual Retirement Accounts (IRAs). According to figures compiled by the Investment Company Institute, mutual funds have about half of all IRA money. Banks and thrifts together have only a little more than half that amount. In

1985 mutual funds had only 12.5 percent of the IRA pie; banks and thrifts together had over 60 percent of the IRA assets.

Be Realistic About Your Expectations

Remember the Templeton Growth Fund, with the hypothetical investor whose $10,000 investment of 40 years earlier made him a millionaire? He didn't become a millionaire instantaneously. Invest $10,000, and even if you earn 20 percent a year, it would still take 26 years to turn it into a million. Mutual funds won't get you rich quick, but if you persist in investing, and you invest with funds that are persistently good, your wealth will grow.

Whatever funds you choose for your investment program, you should be realistic in your expectations. Mutual funds are organized to invest in a specific kind of security or a particular market. So if you choose an equity fund that invests in large-capitalization stocks, you hope it's going to perform better than the S&P 500. But if the S&P is down 20 percent, you can't realistically expect your fund to be up. If your fund was down only 10 percent, you might still be hopping mad at the fund manager, but, in fact, among peers, he or she would be considered a hero. Likewise, if you're investing in a money-market fund when Treasury bill rates are 5 percent, you shouldn't expect a 10 percent return. The returns generated by the fund won't be terribly different from what happens in the market in which it invests. If you did get 10 percent from that very fund, it would be a sure bet that the fund was not living up to the investment guidelines that all money-market mutual funds must follow.

You also need a little perspective on expectations. The last four years, 1995 through 1998, were extraordinary years for the U.S. stock market—a period when the market nearly tripled. The S&P 500 gained an average 30.4 percent a year, nearly three times the long-term average price gain for large-capitalization U.S. stocks. Many market commentators have argued for the last several years that the stock market is overpriced and bound for a crash, or at least a serious correction. We at BUSINESS WEEK believe there are solid fundamental economic reasons for the stock market's advance, and that even with the

Dow Jones industrial average well over 9000, stocks and mutual funds can offer good long-term investment opportunities. However, we recognize—and you should too—that the rate of gain in the last four years cannot continue indefinitely. More important, it doesn't have to continue indefinitely to make investing pay off.

As an investor, you have no control over the stock or bond markets. But you do have control over your own portfolio of mutual funds. We don't advocate buying and selling funds frequently, trying to catch the ups and avoid the downs of the market (what's known as market-timing, see Chapter 4). But if you select funds with the help of the BUSINESS WEEK ratings, monitor their performance, and keep investments matched to your financial objectives, your long-term investment program will be rewarding.

The World of Mutual Funds

You may know you want to invest in mutual funds, but where do you start? At one time, funds pretty much invested in big U.S. corporations. Today, there are funds that specialize in everything from biotechnology to small Asian companies to municipal bonds issued within the boundaries of a single state. The number of funds is so large and investment programs so varied that investors would be overwhelmed without some way to organize the offerings.

This chapter will help you make sense of the thousands of funds—and how they invest your money. To accomplish this, we've broken the chapter into several sections: equity funds, bond funds, and money-market funds. We follow with a section on closed-end funds, the predecessor of the mutual fund that is usually overshadowed by mutual funds and overlooked by investors.

Let's look first at equity funds, those funds that invest in equities, or common stocks. Many of the companies most widely held by equity funds are household names—Microsoft, General Electric, Philip Morris, and IBM (Table 2-1). Find the column, "Percent of net assets." Microsoft, the stock most commonly found in equity mutual fund portfolios, amounts to a little more than 1 percent of the net assets of all equity fund holdings. Even the 25 largest holdings amount to only 15.6 percent of equity funds' net assets. That's a sign of the diversity and variety within mutual fund portfolios.

To get a better understanding of equity funds, you have to look closer. The mutual fund industry has traditionally categorized funds by the fund's investment objective as stated in the prospectus, a legal document required by securities law. These are the investment objectives you will find in most mutual fund publications and advertising: "growth," "growth and income," and "small company."

But now, mutual funds have become so diverse in their strategies that the old nomenclature doesn't work anymore. For example, what is a "growth" fund anyway? It's a fund that seeks "capital growth," and "dividend income is not a significant factor," according to the 1998 *Mutual Fund Fact Book* (which is published by the Investment Company Institute, the fund industry's principal trade association). The problem with that definition is that it's so vague it can be applied to hundreds, if not thousands, of funds.

TABLE 2-1

EQUITY FUNDS

LARGEST HOLDINGS

Stock ▼	Percent of net assets ▼
MICROSOFT	1.14%
GENERAL ELECTRIC	1.11
PHILIP MORRIS	0.92
FANNIE MAE	0.76
MERCK	0.75
IBM	0.72
BRISTOL-MYERS SQUIBB	0.71
PFIZER	0.69
CISCO SYSTEMS	0.67
WAL-MART STORES	0.65
INTEL	0.63
AT&T	0.60
MCI WORLDCOM	0.59
TIME WARNER	0.59
WARNER-LAMBERT	0.58
AMERICAN HOME PRODUCTS	0.54
SCHERING-PLOUGH	0.52
TYCO INTERNATIONAL	0.50
EXXON	0.47
AMERICAN INTERNATIONAL GROUP	0.45
JOHNSON & JOHNSON	0.43
CHASE MANHATTAN	0.42
DELL COMPUTER	0.42
AMERICAN EXPRESS	0.40
HOME DEPOT	0.40

DATA: MORNINGSTAR INC.

The truth is that this definition gives an investor little guidance on exactly how the fund achieves that growth. Vanguard U.S. Growth Fund takes a fairly traditional growth route, buying stocks in blue-chip growth companies such as Microsoft, General Electric, Pfizer, Intel, and Coca-Cola. The median market capitalization (total market value of a company's shares) of all the stocks in the portfolio is $86.5 billion.

At the other end of the growth-fund spectrum is Lindner Growth Investors, which, judged by its portfolio, has little in common with Vanguard U.S. Growth Fund. Among the largest holdings are Alliant Techsystems, Old Republic International, Unisys, and Marine Transport. Recognize any of these names? Perhaps Unisys, if you're in the computer business. By and large, they're not household names, and they're much, much smaller companies. The median market capitalization is only $457 million, less than 1 percent of that of Vanguard U.S. Growth.

Are these two funds at all alike? Other than the fact that both are growth funds that invest in equities, no. It's not even that one invests in very large companies, the other in very small companies. The companies the funds choose differ in more than size. Vanguard U.S. Growth's companies sell, on average, at 11.2 times their "book" value, which, simply put, is the value of the company's assets that are "on the books" less the liabilities. It's what the accountants say the company is worth. That may seem high, but the key here is earnings growth, not book value. On that side, Vanguard U.S. Growth's companies are well above average for large companies—an average 18 percent growth in earnings a year over the last three.

Lindner Growth's companies, on the other hand, sell for just 2.2 times book value. Why so low? Well, these companies are often out of favor with investors. Look at the three-year earnings growth rate—in this case, just 12.6 percent—and you can understand why these stocks are out of favor. So why do the managers of the Lindner Growth fund want to invest in them? They believe that the stocks are undervalued and certain changes are going on in the companies that will result in the market's ultimately recognizing that value. These changes might be an upturn in earnings, an exciting new product, a corporate restructuring, or perhaps even a merger.

In the investment world, Vanguard's stocks would be considered a "growth" portfolio; Lindner's, a "value" portfolio. We can also characterize the funds by the median market capitalization of the stocks they hold. Vanguard U.S. Growth is definitely large-cap, the Lindner fund, small-cap. Use the two characteristics to describe each fund and you get large-cap growth and small-cap value. Those are two very distinct "investment styles," both of which, when executed well, have the capability to make money.

Of course, not all investment styles do equally well all the time. For instance, Vanguard U.S. Growth bested Lindner Growth every year since 1994, but the Lindner fund beat the Vanguard fund in 1992 and 1993. That's one of the reasons it's important to examine mutual funds by their styles. Properly categorized, style tells you more about how the fund invests than the "investment objective."

Investment style also tells you more about what to expect from your fund. Consider the widely varying performances of large-cap growth and small-cap growth funds, many of which are nonetheless categorized as growth funds. Small-cap growth stocks have woefully underperformed large-cap growth stocks since mid-1996, so you would expect a small-cap growth fund to have underperformed as well.

These categories are not entirely new. Several years ago, BUSINESS WEEK started to report investment style in the Scoreboard while still using the old investment objectives for grouping funds. Now we are categorizing funds in the Scoreboard and in this chapter by style. That means it will be easier for investors to compare funds with like investment programs. For example, an investor might decide to switch her money from Growth Fund A to Growth Fund B because the two are growth funds and B has been performing much better than A. But a stylistic analysis reveals an explanation for the disparities in returns: Fund A is a small-cap growth fund, Fund B a large-cap growth fund, and large-caps have been trouncing the small-cap stocks.

There are other good reasons for looking at funds through this stylistic lens. For instance, most fund investors today own more than one fund, with the idea that diversification among funds is a good idea. Suppose an investor owned the Kaufmann, AIM Capital Development, Baron Growth & Income, and Robertson Stephens Emerging Growth funds. Using investment objectives to categorize funds, the investor would have a maximum growth, a growth, a growth and income, and a small company fund and think he's getting diversification. Yet, in a stylistic analysis, all are small-cap growth funds, and it's likely they're making many similar investments. Is that the diversification the fund investor was seeking?

How exactly does a fund "grow" your investment?

A fund investor who is trying to build a diversified portfolio of funds will have an easier time doing it by using stylistic categories than by using the traditional investment objectives.

One more good reason for using style analysis on funds is that it looks beyond labels and marketing hype. For instance, fund companies sometimes give their funds names that track one investment objective when the funds actually pursue another. Look at Robertson Stephens Growth & Income Fund. Most growth and income funds strive to produce some dividend income, so they must invest a good portion of the fund assets in stocks that pay dividends. Such stocks are less volatile than growth stocks that don't pay dividends. Yet the fund's portfolio behaves more like a growth fund than a growth and income fund. The reason: portfolio manager John Wallace does not invest like the majority of growth and income managers. He puts most of the fund's money into high-octane growth stocks that don't pay dividends. For the income component, he invests in convertible bonds and eschews the conservative dividend-paying stocks commonly found in his competitors' funds. Though it hasn't been the case in the last few years, this strategy had long enabled Wallace to outshine the other growth and income fund managers.

Is it right for Robertson Stephens Investment Management to call this a "growth and income" fund? Well, the definition of that investment objective is broad enough and vague enough to allow the Robertson Stephens fund to fit within it. But to call it a growth and income fund might stretch credibility a bit, since it neither invests like most of those funds nor produces returns that look like most of the other growth and income funds. When it outperforms other growth and income funds, do investors really understand it's doing so because it's taking greater risks and investing like a growth fund?

One way of compensating for this sort of unexpected behavior is to ignore the objective listed in the fund's prospectus and put the fund into a different objective group. Morningstar, for instance, has done this on occasion to better describe a fund's behavior. For the last several years, the fund research firm has put Warburg Pincus Growth and Income Common Shares into its growth fund category, even though "income" is in the name. And it seems appropriate. During 1998, the fund paid out only 0.7 percent in yield, which is less than what would be expected in a growth and income fund, even when yields on equities are at record lows.

But moving errant funds into different categories isn't enough if the categories themselves are inadequate for today's investment world. Suppose Robertson Stephens Growth & Income Fund was reclassified as a growth fund. An investor still runs into the same kind of problem described earlier with Vanguard U.S. Growth and Lindner Growth Investors—growth funds encompass a myriad of investment styles. So, comparing growth funds to growth funds isn't always a fair comparison, either. Robertson Stephens Growth & Income is a growth fund investing in midsized companies, while Lindner Growth Investors invests in small-cap value stocks.

Style-based categories give investors much better descriptive information about funds than the traditional investment objectives. The style analysis comes right out of the fund's portfolio. Investment objectives come out of a document written by marketing executives and lawyers. Which would you rather trust?

Investment "style" tells the story.

Determining Style

You don't need an MBA to look at the holdings of a mutual fund and tell whether they're large or small companies. But Morningstar analysts don't eyeball the portfolios to determine their median market caps or whether the stocks fall into the growth or value camp. There's a method to it.

First, what should we consider a large-cap, mid-cap, or small-cap stock? For the last six years, the firm's analysts defined large-cap as companies with a market capitalization (the total market value of all its shares) of $5 billion or more, small-cap as $1 billion or less, and mid-cap, in between.

But the bull market has sent valuations skyward since these parameters were first set. One solution would be just to raise the hurdles, say, to $10 billion for large-caps or $2 billion for small caps. Instead, Morningstar took a different path and switched from fixed to "floating" hurdles. Rather than set a dollar limit, the new definition of a large-cap stock is one with a market capitalization that places it within the 250 largest stocks. As of late 1998, that was a little under $12 billion. Any stock within the next 750 stocks—up to the 1000th, recently about $1.2

billion—becomes a mid-cap stock, and anything below that a small-cap stock.

Okay, now we have the capitalization definitions, but how are they applied to the funds? First, Morningstar ranks the stocks in a fund by each stock's market cap. So if a fund has Microsoft, General Electric, and Intel, those three will show up at the top of the list. Then, the analysts go back and determine how much of the portfolio is represented by each stock.

Suppose Microsoft is 1 percent of the fund, General Electric, 1.5 percent, and Intel, 2.5 percent. Add those three together, and they make up 5 percent of the fund. Well, the analysts don't stop there. They count the fourth, fifth, sixth, and so forth until the sum of the percentages comes to 50 percent.

Suppose the stock at the 50 percent mark was Coca-Cola, most definitely a large-cap stock. That would make the fund a large-cap fund, since at least half the assets are in large-cap stocks. If the stock at the 50 percent mark was T. Rowe Price Associates, the fund would be a mid-cap. That's because the mutual fund company, with a $3.8 billion market cap, is a mid-cap stock. If the median stock were IHOP, Inc., parent of the International House of Pancakes restaurant chain, the fund would be a small-cap, since IHOP has a market cap of less than $400 million.

The second part of identifying a fund's style is to determine whether the fund practices a growth or value approach to investing. Again, the Morningstar analysts turn to the three capitalization categories of stocks—large, small, and mid-sized. First, they determine a median price-to-earnings (p–e) ratio for each group, and a median price-to-book value ratio (p–b) as well. (The p–e is the stock's price divided by the per-share earnings for the last 12 months. The p–b is the stock's price divided by book value per share, or the company's assets less its liabilities).

The next step is to calculate price–earnings ratios and price–book value ratios for every stock in a fund. Then, the process divides the p–e and p–b of every stock in the fund by the median p–e and p–b for that capitalization range. For instance, in late 1998, the p–e for Microsoft was 60 and the median p–e for the large-cap stocks was 31. That gave Microsoft a p–e score of 1.9. At the same time, the p–b ratio for Microsoft was 8.3 and the median p–b ratio for the large caps was 6.6. That gives Microsoft a p–b score of 1.3. Morningstar's system then calculates median p–e and p–b scores for the stocks in the fund and adds the two. If the two numbers together exceed 2.25, the fund has higher than average price–earnings and price–book ratios and is considered a growth-stock investor. If the two numbers come to less than 1.75, the fund portfolio owns stocks that have lower than average p–e and p–b ratios and is considered a value investor. Funds with scores that fall between the two are considered "blend" funds, exhibiting characteristics of both styles.

Since each diversified domestic equity fund is classified in one of three categories of size and style, there are nine categories (Figure 2-1). The BUSINESS WEEK Scoreboard applies this stylistic grouping to diversified funds that invest primarily in the United States. Essentially, all the funds that in the past were categorized as maximum growth, growth, growth and income, equity-income, and small company are now one of the following: large-cap value, large-cap blend, large-cap growth; mid-cap value, mid-cap blend, mid-cap growth; or small-cap value, small-cap blend, small-cap growth. Generally speaking, the large-cap value funds are expected to be the least risky, or volatile; the small-cap growth funds are expected to be the most risky.

There's more to these categories. The three investment objectives that combine stocks and bonds—asset allocation, balanced, and multiasset global—are in two categories: domestic hybrid and international hybrid (Table 2-2). And whether they are domestic or international, hybrids must have on average no less than 20 percent and no more than 70 percent of their assets in equities. Fidelity Puritan Fund, for instance, is a domestic

FIGURE 2-1

A BETTER LOOK AT YOUR FUNDS

BUSINESS WEEK now categorizes U.S. diversified equity funds in two ways: by the median market capitalization of the stocks it owns and by the relative valuation or "style" of those stocks. It's a system developed by Morningstar Inc.

Funds whose stocks have a median market cap of $12 billion or more are considered large-cap funds, $1.2 billion or less are small-cap, and those in between, mid-cap. For large-cap funds, the average price–earnings ratios and price-to-book ratios are calculated and compared with the S&P 500. For mid-cap and small-cap funds, the benchmark is the mid-cap or small-cap fund average. Those with significantly lower-than-average p–e's and p–b's are "value" funds, those higher than average "growth," and those in the middle "blend."

Median Market Capitalization	Investment Style		
	VALUE	BLEND	GROWTH
LARGE	LARGE-CAP VALUE	LARGE-CAP BLEND	LARGE-CAP GROWTH
MEDIUM	MID-CAP VALUE	MID-CAP BLEND	MID-CAP GROWTH
SMALL	SMALL-CAP VALUE	SMALL-CAP BLEND	SMALL-CAP GROWTH

hybrid. Merrill Lynch Global Allocation B is an international hybrid.

As industries, companies, and even stock markets have become more global, so have mutual fund portfolios. Our guidelines allow a domestic fund to have up to 40 percent of its holdings in non-U.S. companies and still be a domestic fund. Funds with more than 40 percent of their holdings in non-U.S. companies are considered international. Thus, SmallCap World Fund, which you might surmise is an international fund investing in small companies, is now considered a domestic small-cap growth fund since it has only 38 percent of its assets abroad.

International funds are cut broadly and regionally. Foreign funds invest almost entirely in non-U.S. markets, though they can have up to 10 percent of their assets in the United States. World funds are just the opposite—they can invest anywhere and must have no less than 10 percent of its assets at home. Diversified emerging markets funds must have at least 50 percent of their assets in the emerging markets. Regional funds—Europe, Latin America, Japan, Diversified Pacific, and Pacific ex-Japan—must have at least 75 percent of their assets invested in their designated region.

Our bond fund line-up also tracks Morningstar's. At BUSINESS WEEK, we no longer use the conventional bond fund objectives that categorize funds mainly by the kinds of bonds they buy—government, corporates, or municipals. Our classification considers both the type of bonds a fund buys and the average maturity or duration of the fund's bonds. A long-term bond fund is one with a duration (a more refined measure of maturity that we'll discuss later in this chapter) greater than 6 years; an intermediate-term fund has a duration of greater than 3.5 years and less than 6 years; a short-term fund, less than 3.5 years but greater than 1 year. There's one ultrashort category that encompasses both government and corporate bonds, with a duration of less than a year. Municipal funds are organized into national and single-state long- and intermediate-term categories, but all short-term muni funds, whether national or single-state, are in the same category. With muni funds, the definitions of long-term, intermediate-term, and short-term are a little different. A long-term fund has a duration greater than 7 years; intermediate, between 4.5 and 7 years; and short, less than 4.5 years.

Shuffling the bond fund categories makes selecting bond funds and tracking their returns much simpler. It's easier to see how well a fund is

TABLE 2-2

THE NEW MUTUAL FUND CATEGORIES VS. THE OLD INVESTMENT OBJECTIVES

New ▼	Old ▼
EQUITY FUNDS*	
Large-cap Value	Maximum Growth
Large-cap Blend	Growth
Large-cap Growth	Growth and Income
Mid-cap Value	Equity–Income
Mid-cap Blend	Small Company
Mid-cap Growth	
Small-cap Value	
Small-cap Blend	
Small-cap Growth	
Domestic Hybrid	Balanced
International Hybrid	Asset Allocation
	Multiasset Global
Diversified Emerging Markets	Diversified Emerging Markets
Foreign	Foreign
World	World
Europe	Europe
Diversified Pacific	Pacific Basin
Pacific ex-Japan	
Japan	
Latin America	
BOND FUNDS	
Long-Term (Gen.)	Corporate—General
Intermediate-Term (Gen.)	Corporate—High-Quality
Short-Term (Gen.)	Corporate—High-Yield
Ultrashort	Government—General
Long Government	Government—Adjustable-Rate Mortgages
Intermediate Government	Government—Mortgage
Short Government	Government—Treasury
Municipal National Long	Municipal—National
Municipal National Intermediate	Municipal—Single-State
Municipal Single-State Long	Municipal—California
Municipal Single-State Intermediate	Municipal—New York
Municipal California Long	Convertibles
Municipal California Intermediate	World Bond
Municipal New York Long	Short-Term World Income
Municipal New York Intermediate	
Municipal Short	
High-Yield	
Convertibles	
International	
Emerging Markets	
Multisector	

*No change in the specialty equity funds.
DATA: MORNINGSTAR INC., BUSINESS WEEK

performing if you compare it to a fund with a similar maturity and duration. On this count, bond funds have always been a little easier to understand than equity funds since many have "long-term" or "intermediate" in their titles. Still, by rating funds in their own categories, investors will be able to see more quickly which long-term U.S. government fund has not only the best return but also the best risk-adjusted return as well.

Not all bond funds fit into these categories. Convertible bonds and high-yield bonds, which in many ways have as much to do with the equity market as interest rates, retain their own categories. There's no further differentiation for intermediate or long-term bonds. Most high-yields (and convertibles, too, since most of them are less than investment grade) fall in the short-to-intermediate-term range. International bonds is a broad category for the funds that invest in mainly investment-grade non-U.S. bonds. Emerging markets bond funds contain securities backed by nations like Thailand, Brazil, and Russia. In other words, the instruments are bonds but they are riskier than many, many stocks.

Equity Funds

We'll start with equity funds and look first at the larger, lower-risk diversified sorts, such as the large-cap value funds, and eventually work our way to the more aggressive small-cap growth funds. Then we'll examine the hybrid and specialty funds.

LARGE-CAP VALUE FUNDS

You know you should invest in equity mutual funds, but somehow the volatility of the stock market and the possibility of losing your money scare the daylights out of you. If this describes you, try a fund that invests in large-cap value stocks. Of the nine categories of domestic equity funds, these funds are the least risky and perhaps the most palatable for the anxious investor. Most of the funds in this category were formerly in the growth and income and equity–income investment objectives. They keep one eye on downside risk and the other on a stock's upside potential. Some of the larger and better-known funds in this category are Fidelity Equity–Income, Fidelity Equity–Income II, Fidelity Destiny I, Fidelity Destiny II, Vanguard Windsor, Vanguard Windsor II, and Washington Mutual Investors.

TABLE 2-3

LARGE-CAP VALUE FUNDS		
BEST RETURNS		
Period	Fund	Total return*
1998	LEGG MASON VALUE PRIMARY SHARES	48.0%
1996-98	LEGG MASON VALUE PRIMARY SHARES	41.1
1994-98	LEGG MASON VALUE PRIMARY SHARES	32.0
1989-98	LEGG MASON VALUE PRIMARY SHARES	20.9

*Average annual, pretax   DATA: MORNINGSTAR INC.

Just because these funds are cautious doesn't mean they can't perform well. During 1997, the funds earned an average 26.7 percent total return—nearly 10 percentage points better than the average fund. In 1996, for instance, the 2 large-cap value funds among the 20 largest equity funds beat the S&P 500. Nineteen ninety-eight, though, was, to put it mildly, a big disappointment for these funds. The average large-cap value fund gained just 12.8 percent, 1.3 percentage points behind the average U.S. diversified equity fund and nearly 16 percentage points less than the S&P 500. The best-performing large-cap value fund in 1998 was Legg Mason Value Trust Primary Shares, up 48.0 percent (Table 2-3). It was also the best performer in the 3-, 5-, and 10-year periods. In some ways, it's an atypical fund—but more about that later.

Why has this category of fund made such a poor showing of late? One is the nature of the stocks these funds buy. No high-flying semiconductor or software stocks here for the most part, but you'll recognize the names: Philip Morris, IBM, Fannie Mae, and AT&T (Table 2-4). To most value investors, what makes a stock attractive is that it's cheap. Don't confuse cheap with a low price, like $5 or $10 a share. A share of stock is said to be cheap only when it's measured by some valuation criteria such as the p–e ratio and/or p–b ratio and then compared to a benchmark, like the p–e or the p–b of the S&P 500.

That a stock is cheap—suppose it has a lower-than-average p–e ratio—is no guarantee against losing money, since a cheap stock can always get cheaper. But think of it this way: If the market gets hit with a downdraft, cheap stocks can fall, but usually not as far or as hard as expensive stocks. Chances are, you're going to lose more money if an expensive stock becomes cheap than if a cheap stock gets cheaper.

That didn't happen in 1998. In fact, conventional wisdom was turned upside down. When the stock market tanked in the summer, the large-cap stocks that did the worst were the financial, natural resource, and energy stocks that these funds tend to own. Even the large-cap value funds' emphasis on dividend-paying stocks didn't help much.

Still, these are all long-term investments, and you shouldn't be deterred by a subpar year. There are many solid funds in this category, and they almost invariably have low or very low risk when compared to those in other categories of funds. Many of them use the term "equity–income" in their name. Look at the Fidelity Equity–Income offerings, which stipulate that at least 65 percent of the stocks in the fund must be dividend payers. There's a reason for this: that a company is able to pay a dividend suggests that it is generating cash above and beyond its needs and is not likely to go broke. Vanguard Equity–Income follows a "relative yield" strategy, buying stocks when their yields are high relative to where they have been over time. That's usually a sign a stock is out of favor at the moment, a true contrarian strategy. If the managers believe the dividend is sustainable and can even grow, they'll buy the stock for the fund. When the stock comes back into favor, the price will go up, and that yield will drop—and eventually it may even drop out of the fund, but at a profit.

In recent years, neither investors nor companies themselves have paid much attention to dividends. Investors preferred to buy stocks that had greater growth potential than is available in most dividend-paying stocks. And companies themselves responded to the market's appetite for share appreciation by deploying excess cash to buy back shares rather than hike dividends.

TABLE 2-4

LARGE-CAP VALUE FUNDS

LARGEST HOLDINGS

Stock ▼	Percent of net assets ▼
PHILIP MORRIS	1.67%
AT&T	1.29
FANNIE MAE	1.19
IBM	1.15
AMERICAN HOME PRODUCTS	0.90
GENERAL ELECTRIC	0.89
CITICORP	0.83
CHASE MANHATTAN	0.83
FIRST UNION	0.83
FORD MOTOR	0.81

DATA: MORNINGSTAR INC.

Some investors argue it's not a bad thing to do. Dividends are considered ordinary income and are taxed at the same rate investors pay on their salary and interest income, which can be as high as 39.6 percent (and that's just the federal tax). When companies buy back shares instead of boosting their dividends, the only shareholders that get taxed are those who sell their shares. If those shares were held for longer than a year, any profits would be taxed at the more favorable long-term capital gains rate, a maximum of 20 percent.

Since these large-cap value funds generate fully taxable dividend income, many advisers counsel high-income investors to use them only in tax-deferred accounts like 401(k)s and IRAs. In such accounts, there's no tax liability until the investor retires and starts drawing the money out.

Be forewarned that many veteran investors take dividends seriously. In bear markets, a situation that many of today's investors have not experienced, a steady dividend stream becomes a primary support of a stock or a portfolio of stocks. After all, the only way to make money in stocks is through capital appreciation and dividends. When the appreciation part is in doubt, the security of a dividend payout starts to look a whole lot better.

Even though they buy many of the same big, cheap, dividend-paying stocks, some funds in this category stand out with their own particular quirks. Vanguard Windsor (which is closed to new investors) is not afraid to concentrate its positions. Its 10 largest holdings amount to some 38 percent of the $18.2 billion portfolio. Unfortunately, that did not work well for the fund in 1998. The total return was just 0.8 percent—the fund's worse showing since 1994.

The Clipper Fund's stocks usually pay dividends, but they're not chosen on a dividend basis alone. What Clipper looks for are companies with solid and sustainable business franchises at cheap prices, and among the current holdings are Philip Morris and Fannie Mae. The managers will sell the stock when it becomes fully valued—as it did with Wal-Mart Stores in 1998. The fund had acquired the giant retailer when its stock was in the 20s, and sold it in the 60s—only to see it go higher. What makes Clipper different from many other funds, both in its category and among all equity funds, is that it will let cash build up rather than lower its investment standards. At the end of 1998, the fund held about 36 percent cash, a significant drag on performance in an up market. Still, the fund is A-rated both when compared to all funds and when compared to other large-cap value funds. (For investors who want Clipper's stocks but not the cash, it just opened the Clipper Focus Fund.) Vontobel U.S. Value takes a similar approach. It concentrates investments in what it believes to be truly undervalued positions and, if necessary, lets cash build up. In 1998, Vontobel's 10 largest positions amounted to 79 percent of the fund, and cash amounted to about 19 percent. Vontobel U.S. Value earned A's both for overall performance and for performance within its fund category.

Then there's Legg Mason Value. In the mid-1990s, portfolio manager Bill Miller loaded the fund with beaten-up financial stocks—a typical move for a value manager—and they paid off. Around the same time, Miller did something atypical for many managers. He bought stakes in America Online and Dell Computer. At the time, Wall Street was wary of both companies. AOL had just gone to flat-rate pricing, subscribers were outraged by an inability to get on the network, and the company's accounting for its huge marketing expenses was under attack. But Miller saw what AOL might become if it could straighten out its problems—and it did. The same happened with Dell Computer, which most pros at the time dismissed as just another PC manufacturer in a cut-throat business. But Dell, by selling direct to customers, building computers to order, and avoiding costly dealer networks, became the most profitable PC company by far.

Still, both companies were unusual buys for a value fund since most shy away from technology companies even when they're out of favor. But perhaps even more unusual is that Legg Mason Value kept the stocks as they went from underpriced to what most professional investors would argue is very high-priced. Miller has sold very few of the stocks, and at the end of 1998, the two companies together comprised nearly a quarter of the portfolio. His argument is that the stocks still have great prospects.

If Legg Mason is so heavily weighted in these richly valued technology stocks, why is this still a value fund? The rest of the portfolio is classic value, with companies like Fannie Mae and Phillip Morris. Under Morningstar's statistical test, it's still a value fund, though one of these days it might well cross over to the "blend" column in the style box.

Some analysts interpret such huge concentrations as Legg Mason's as risky, since there are more eggs in fewer baskets. Managers of these

risk-shy funds see it differently. Good value investments are hard to come by, so when you find them, you have to make the most of them. This buy-and-hold tendency is reflected in the low turnover ratios that are not much more than half the average for equity funds.

A-rated Washington Mutual Investors, part of the American Funds family, has a low turnover as well, perhaps because there aren't that many stocks it can invest in. That's because the fund follows the Prudent Man Rule, a rule for fiduciaries that dictates that every investment in the fund must pass certain quality standards and pay a dividend. According to Morningstar analysts, fewer than 300 stocks are even eligible for investment by the fund.

Lexington Corporate Leaders, another large-cap value fund, also has a rather select portfolio. In fact, it's almost a static portfolio. The fund goes back to 1935 and was set up to invest in 30 stocks its founders thought would prosper for years to come. The portfolio manager has the ability to sell a stock, but cannot add a new name. Still, most of the original 30 survive, and they include such companies as Procter & Gamble, General Electric, AT&T, DuPont, and Exxon. Even more amazing, the fund has been a strong performer over the last 10- and 15-year periods, but in the bottom half of its category in the last few years. Except for Lucent Technologies (the result of an AT&T spin-off), there are no high-tech or pharmaceutical stocks. Although you would not expect to find these kinds of stocks in any great number in a true value fund, this fund is not a value fund by design—just as a result of its unusual investment policy. Had stocks like IBM and Merck been in the original mix, they'd still be there today—and the fund's recent returns would have been a whole lot better.

LARGE-CAP BLEND FUNDS

Some investment managers call themselves *value* investors, and others *growth* investors. But you'd be hard pressed to find investment managers who call themselves *blend* investors. The blend fund, however, is sort of the vast middle—the huge category into which fall all the funds that don't strongly gravitate to either side of the investment world. The blend funds have attributes of both the growth and value styles. What makes them a blend is that when the portfolio statistics are calculated, the numbers fall in the middle. According to Morningstar's criteria, the combined p–e and p–b ratios of these funds can be no more than 12.5 percent greater than or

> "Value" is often in the eye of the portfolio manager.

TABLE 2-5

LARGE-CAP BLEND FUNDS

BEST RETURNS

Period ▼	Fund ▼	Total return* ▼
1998	ALLIANCE PREMIER GROWTH B	48.3%
1996-98	RYDEX NOVA INV.	34.2
1994-98	RYDEX NOVA INV.	28.2
1989-98	FIDELITY CONTRAFUND	24.0

*Average annual, pretax   DATA: MORNINGSTAR INC.

12.5 percent less than the combined p–e and p–b ratios for the S&P 500.

The best performer of 1998 was Alliance Premier Growth B, with a 48.3 percent total return (Table 2-5). Not only is this fund a leader in its category, but in the entire fund universe. Portfolio manager Alfred Harrison powered the fund over the last few years with bets first on financial and later on technology stocks. Top holdings include Dell Computer, Cisco Systems, and Nokia, and Harrison is not afraid to let his winners run. The top 10 holdings comprise 45 percent of the portfolio.

As the Alliance fund demonstrates, blend does not have to be bland. Large-cap blend is a huge category (the largest of the nine categories of U.S. diversified equity funds), and it includes many well-known funds: Fidelity Magellan, Fidelity Growth & Income, Investment Company of America, and T. Rowe Price Blue Chip Growth. While the giant Magellan made a comeback in 1998, it had difficulties for several years before that. Fidelity Growth & Income's returns have remained top-notch, and it still merits A ratings for overall and category performance. If you aren't in it already, it's too late. In 1998, Fidelity closed the fund to new investors and opened Growth & Income II, with a similar investment objective but a different manager. Still, anyone running these funds will work from the same palette of investments. Among the largest holdings of these funds are General Electric, Philip Morris, Microsoft, and Merck (Table 2-6).

Two other Price offerings in this category are also top-rated: T. Rowe Price Blue Chip Growth Fund and T. Rowe Price Dividend Growth Fund. Dividend Growth Fund has a risk profile similar to Equity–Income, but a much smaller asset base. Blue Chip Growth managed to earn a much higher than average return (28.8 percent) in 1998 without gorging on high-priced high-tech stocks. Dividend Growth, while retaining it's double A ratings, had a difficult year and only earned 15

percent. The funds bias for dividends—and the lack of them in the overall market—prompted manager Bill Stromberg to seek them in real estate investment trusts, a type of investment that was cheap when the year started and got even cheaper as the year went on.

But perhaps the most compelling—and sometimes controversial—of the large-cap blend funds are the index funds that replicate the S&P 500. Such funds have been enormously successful in recent years, mainly because the large-cap stocks that account for a large chunk of the S&P 500's performance have done so well. Unlike most "managed" funds, index funds are capitalization-weighted, meaning stocks with larger capitalizations weigh more in the calculation of the index than those with smaller capitalizations. So when large-cap stocks outperform small-cap and mid-cap stocks, S&P 500 index funds do very well. The other way in which index funds differ from most others is that rather than take profits in winners, they let their winners roll. There's no limit on how large Microsoft and General Electric, which move back and forth as the S&P 500's and the U.S. market's largest stocks, will be allowed to become. Index fund managers, unlike managers of conventional funds, never sell a stock too early.

Looking back on the last few years, index funds look like a no-brainer way to riches. Many of our A-rated funds are S&P 500 index funds, in part because of their own strong performance and in part because of the lagging performance of the other mutual funds against which they are judged. The largest index fund, the $74.2 billion Vanguard 500 Index, is one of the fastest growing of the large funds, and during 1999 should overtake the long-time leader, the $83.6 billion Fidelity Magellan Fund.

Index funds have several other attributes that make them winners, such as low expenses. The Vanguard 500 Index has an expense ratio that is one-seventh that of the average fund. Index funds are also low in portfolio turnover, which keeps trading costs down. Low turnover also means little in the way of taxable distributions. In fact, while most funds have failed to beat the S&P on a pretax basis, even fewer do it after taxes. Although most of the money flowing into index funds in recent years came through tax-deferred retirement programs, index funds are perhaps even more effective in a taxable account.

Does this make an S&P index fund a must-buy investment? It's hard to argue against it. Certainly, many investors can benefit by having

TABLE 2-6

LARGE-CAP BLEND FUNDS

LARGEST HOLDINGS

Stock ▼	Percent of net assets ▼
GENERAL ELECTRIC	2.17%
MICROSOFT	2.07
PHILIP MORRIS	1.42
MERCK	1.39
WAL-MART STORES	1.26
INTEL	1.25
BRISTOL-MYERS SQUIBB	1.23
FANNIE MAE	1.19
IBM	1.18
PFIZER	1.08

DATA: MORNINGSTAR INC.

some portion of their equity portfolio in an index fund. But viewing the index fund over the last 5 years alone, or even 10 years, can be misleading. The stock market has had an extraordinarily good run during that period.

But if the market were to fall badly over an extended period (not the three-month pullback of 1998), the index funds might not look so good. For starters, there's no safety net. Index funds don't carry cash, which cushions a fall, and unlike active managers, they can't deploy more of their assets to "defensive" sectors like utilities or food stocks. Although these actions by active managers can hold a fund back during a bull market, when properly deployed, such actions can soften a downturn. So, when you are considering index funds, remember there is that drawback.

Indexing itself does not have to be boring. Look at the Rydex Nova Fund. Though designed for market-timers, Rydex will open the door for anyone with a relatively steep $25,000 minimum investment. By design, the Nova fund seeks investment returns that correspond to 150 percent of the performance of the S&P 500. So if the S&P is up 20 percent, this fund should go up 30 percent. Likewise, if the S&P goes down 20 percent, this fund should go down 30 percent. The fund hasn't been able to hit that 150 percent goal; in 1998, for instance, its return was just 123 percent of that of the S&P 500, and in 1997, 126 percent. For the three-year period, the return was about 121 percent of the S&P. Rydex runs the fund without a share of stock. It's managed with a combination of cash, futures, and call options.

Rydex Ursa Fund is an index fund in reverse. It's managed to move in the opposite direction of the S&P 500, so its fat 19 percent loss in 1997 is neither unexpected nor a sign of portfolio ineptitude. Ursa, the Latin word for bear, is designed to win in a bear market. Its mission is to move in the opposite direction of the S&P 500. (It's run with a combination of cash, options, and futures.) When the stock market dives, Ursa shines. Between July 17, 1998, the summer's peak in stock prices, to August 31, the bottom, the S&P 500 dropped 19.3 percent. Rydex Ursa gained 24 percent.

LARGE-CAP GROWTH FUNDS

For the last several years, Wall Streeters dabbled with small-cap and mid-cap stocks but ultimately fled to the safety of large-cap growth stocks. There was good reason for this. At every hint of a slowing economy, these companies—with a clearly defined, "visible" earnings outlook—seemed more and more attractive in an uncertain economic environment. The major stocks in these funds tended to be larger high-tech companies and defensive consumer stocks like food, drugs, and beverages.

The best fund in this category for the last five years is White Oak Growth Stock Fund (Table 2-7). That fund made enormous gains with high-tech and pharmaceutical stocks, and its largest holding of late is drugmaker Eli Lilly. Over the 10-year period, the winner is Janus Twenty, which in 1998 earned a 73.4 percent total return. That's extraordinary for any fund, but even more remarkable for a fund that already had $6 billion in assets at the start of the year. Janus Twenty, which concentrates most of its portfolio in about two dozen stocks, scored big with high-tech, telecom, and drug stocks. Its high-octane performance is also testament to what a concentrated portfolio can do when most everything goes right.

The best performers for the one- and three-year periods didn't earn their returns quite the same way as the managers of White Oak Growth or Janus Twenty. Profunds Ultra OTC Investors and Rydex OTC Investors are index funds investing in the NASDAQ 100 index, an index of the largest over the counter stocks. You won't find any of the stocks in that index trading on the prestigious New York Stock Exchange, but so what? This index is the home of Microsoft, Intel, Cisco Systems, and Dell Computer. Of course, these stocks are all in the S&P 500, but not in such concentrations. Microsoft is 3 percent of the S&P, but 16 percent of the NASDAQ 100. So just tracking an index dominated by these winning

TABLE 2-7

LARGE-CAP GROWTH FUNDS		
BEST RETURNS		
Period ▼	Fund ▼	Total return* ▼
1998	PROFUNDS ULTRAOTC INV.	185.3%
1996-98	RYDEX OTC INV.	48.1
1994-98	WHITE OAK GROWTH STOCK	30.1
1989-98	JANUS TWENTY	25.8
*Average annual, pretax		DATA: MORNINGSTAR INC.

stocks has been a winning strategy. That's why Rydex OTC was up 86.5 percent in 1998 and an average of 48.1 percent per year for the 1996–1998 period.

But consider the brash new kid on the mutual fund block, ProFunds UltraOTC Investors. Like Rydex OTC, it's designed to replicate the NASDAQ 100—but then goes a step further. Using futures and options, this fund is leveraged two-to-one. That means for every 1 percent move in the NASDAQ 100, this fund should go 2 percent. No wonder it was the best large-cap growth fund in 1998, up 185.3 percent. (Actually, it did *better* than twice the index.) And, of course, that means it would fall twice as much on the downside.

The question to consider when investing in these funds is, how long can these large-cap growth stocks continue their winning streak? The conventional wisdom about successful large companies is that inertia will eventually overtake them. Rapidly growing companies become above-average growers, above-average turns out to be average. The slowdown in growth is predictable—in theory. The art of investing in these companies is getting the timing of that growth right, to buy at a p–e ratio that's fair relative to the growth rate.

Look at Cisco Systems, a principal manufacturer of servers and related equipment to tie together computer networks. It's one of the top holdings of the large-cap growth funds (Table 2-8). The company has gone from annual sales of nearly $70 million in fiscal 1990 to $8.5 billion in fiscal 1998. That's about a compounded annual growth rate of 82 percent a year; during the same time, net income grew at a compounded average annual rate of over 9000 percent. (Is there any doubt why this is such a great company?) Cisco is still growing at a fast clip; the last fiscal year showed 31 percent revenue growth over the previous year. But it's no longer growing at the same torrid pace of five years ago. (At that time, you would have found Cisco not in a large-cap growth

portfolio, but in a small or mid-size fund.) Now the earnings growth rate is forecast to be about 29 percent. That's a far cry from what it was, but it's still four times that of the average big-company stock. At the end of 1998, Cisco sold for about 63 times the estimated fiscal 1999 earnings. While high valuations for top-notch growth stocks can be justified, 63 times earnings—twice the forecasted growth rate—is a price that leaves little room for disappointment.

The apparent risks notwithstanding, there's a reason why the market values these companies highly. They are superb companies. Many of these companies, though based in the United States, are world-class leaders with substantial operations outside the United States. Coca-Cola, for instance, has no equal anywhere on the planet, and most of its profits are generated outside the United States. Nor does any semiconductor company even approach Intel. Mutual funds that identify and invest in these sorts of companies early on can make a bundle for their investors.

The exceptionally strong returns earned by these funds may be masking some unrealized risks. These large-cap growth stocks are the most closely watched on Wall Street (they're the so-called "institutional favorites" you hear about in stock market reports), and they're said to be the most efficiently priced. To stand out in this category, a fund manager has to make some serious sector bets, concentrating holdings in a few areas that he or she thinks will do a lot better than the large growth stocks in general. During 1998, for instance, MFS Massachusetts Growth Stock Investors A had about 29 percent of its assets in technology stocks versus 23 percent for

TABLE 2-8

LARGE-CAP GROWTH FUNDS	
LARGEST HOLDINGS	
Stock ▼	Percent of net assets ▼
MICROSOFT	3.70%
PFIZER	2.54
CISCO SYSTEMS	2.45
GENERAL ELECTRIC	2.40
WARNER-LAMBERT	1.76
MCI WORLDCOM	1.62
DELL COMPUTER	1.59
MERCK	1.58
TIME WARNER	1.55
INTEL	1.40
DATA: MORNINGSTAR INC.	

the large-cap growth funds and 18 percent for the S&P 500. Fortunately, that bet paid off—the fund was up 40 percent in 1998—but it could have been a big depressant on the fund had it not.

Other noteworthy funds in this category include Dreyfus Appreciation, Gabelli Growth, Papp America-Abroad, Vanguard U.S. Growth, and Vanguard Growth Index. Perhaps one of the most interesting of the large company growth funds is Stein Roe Young Investor Fund, a fund with a mission to invest in securities issued by companies that affect the lives of children and teenagers. The idea is perhaps more marketing oriented than market oriented. No doubt Stein Roe marketers thought the fund would be a natural for parents and grandparents to buy for their kids. And, in fact, the company developed sales literature and shareholder reports that even a kid could understand.

The reality is that the fund can invest in almost anything. The largest holding is Cisco Systems. The connection? Well, Cisco builds computer networking equipment, and, well, kids go on the Internet, no? As a practical matter, it's hard to think of a company with a business that couldn't in some way be linked to kids. (A steel company? This company is a supplier to the automakers, who use it to build vehicles that parents use to chauffeur their children.) You don't have to be a young investor to invest in or profit from this fund.

MID-CAP VALUE FUNDS

It's difficult to generalize about mid-cap value funds, or, for that matter, any kind of mid-cap fund. Funds that fit into one of the corners of the nine-category box—large-cap value, large-cap growth, small-cap value, and small-cap growth—are the most discriminating about how they invest. Look inside the portfolio of a small-cap growth or large-cap value fund, and you won't mistake it for anything else.

TABLE 2-9

MID-CAP VALUE FUNDS		
BEST RETURNS		
Period ▼	Fund ▼	Total return* ▼
1998	WEITZ PARTNERS VALUE	29.1%
1996-98	THORNBURG VALUE A	31.1
1994-98	FIRST EAGLE FUND OF AMERICA Y	21.9
1989-98	FPA CAPITAL	20.1

*Average annual, pretax   DATA: MORNINGSTAR INC.

Many mid-cap value funds have long used the term *value* in their names, but only in the last few years have some funds started to call themselves mid-cap or even mid-cap value. Pioneer Three Fund changed its name to Pioneer Mid-Cap Fund in 1996. A few months later, Lord Abbett Value Appreciation Fund was renamed Lord Abbett Mid-Cap Value Fund. What's behind the name changes? One reason is the recognition of investor interest in funds that define their investment style. The other reason may be marketing. Neither the Pioneer nor the Lord Abbett fund had distinguished track records, so there was nothing to lose in changing the names. If nothing else, it might attract money that's looking for a mid-cap home.

Still, many mid-cap funds—including value, blend, and growth varieties—didn't set out to be mid-caps. They sort of backed into it. Take, for instance, Oakmark Select Fund. The fund says nothing about mid-caps in its prospectus, but nearly all the holdings of the fund are unambiguously mid-cap in nature. One explanation for this is that the Oakmark Fund, the Select's big brother, was a mid-cap value fund until 1997, when its holdings became large enough to move into large-cap value. Since the Oakmark family already had a small-cap fund, it made sense for the newest member, Oakmark Select, to troll in mid-cap waters. The other explanation: the fund became a mid-cap value fund as a result of the investments it made, not because it sought to make specifically mid-cap investments.

That's much the case with Weitz Partners Value Fund, the top-performing mid-cap value fund of 1998 (Table 2-9). Weitz Partners Value, along with sister fund Weitz Value Fund, were the only mid-cap value funds to get an A for overall performance for the 1994–1998 period. Portfolio manager Wallace Weitz says his recent success was based on a heavy concentration of cable television and cellular phone stocks. Neither sectors are heavily represented in the value funds, but Weitz said they appeared to be compelling investments. He loaded up, and he turned out to be right in his assessment. The Sound Shore Fund, rated A when compared to other mid-cap value funds, also arrives in this category as a result of what it bought; its prospectus says nothing about sticking to mid-cap investments. However, beyond its three largest holdings, most of the stocks in this concentrated portfolio are mid-cap companies.

Perhaps the best known of the mid-cap value funds are the original Mutual Series Funds—

TABLE 2-10

MID-CAP VALUE FUNDS

LARGEST HOLDINGS

Security ▼	Percent of net assets ▼
CHASE MANHATTAN	1.56%
FNMA DEBENTURE 0% 10/15/98	0.91
GENERAL MOTORS	0.80
INVESTOR CL. B	0.69
MEDIAONE GROUP	0.64
MORGAN STANLEY DEAN WITTER	0.55
RJR NABISCO HOLDINGS	0.54
PHILIPS ELECTRONICS (ADR)	0.54
RAILTRACK GROUP	0.50
CONSECO	0.45

DATA: MORNINGSTAR INC.

Mutual Shares, Mutual Qualified, and Mutual Beacon. (Our Scoreboard reports on the Z-share class, which is the longest standing and largest.) They're three of the five largest funds in this category. Like many mid-cap value funds, these funds include a wide range of investments chosen more for their attractiveness as value plays than to meet any market capitalization target.

One of Mutual Series' biggest successes of recent years was its 1995 foray into Chase Manhattan Corp. Mutual Series management took a large stake, then lobbied the Chase management and the board of directors, into taking action to improve *shareholder value*. That's the buzz word for "get the stock price up—or else." Other large shareholders took note as well, and joined in the chorus. In several months' time, Chase agreed to a merge with rival Chemical Banking Corp. to create a bank holding company larger than Citicorp. Even while participating in the megabanking play, the portfolios remained mid-cap in character.

Mutual Series funds still own a good chunk of Chase Manhattan stock, and because of those funds' size, Chase is the No. 1 holding of the mid-cap value funds, comprising 1.56 percent of total net assets (Table 2-10). Several other of Price's largest holdings also appear on this list: Media-One Group, RJR Nabisco Holdings, and Investor Cl.B. (a Swedish holding company). None of them are particularly mid-cap, but they are value plays.

MID-CAP BLEND FUNDS

Many funds will call themselves mid-cap value or mid-cap growth, but it's unlikely a fund company will ever market a fund as a mid-cap blend. Middle of the road in market cap without a distinct value or growth bent? Sounds like a big yawner—or a marketing challenge.

But consider this: the supersized Fidelity Contrafund became a large-cap fund in 1998. Since Morningstar began tracking investment style, Contrafund has behaved more like a mid-cap blend. Still, Fidelity marketers have never presented this fund as a mid-cap, only as a "contrarian" in nature. With over $30 billion in assets, it's hard to even imagine this as a contrarian. Until 1997, Fidelity Magellan was also a mid-cap blend. After all, the fund's reputation had been built on savvy stockpicking, not stylistic purity. It makes a lot of sense that many of the funds run by star stockpickers wind up in this category—they'll go to all corners of the stock market for a good investment. And when the compositions of those portfolios are calculated, they wind up smack in the middle of the pack.

Mid-cap blends are not easy to categorize, or even easy to spot. The best performer in this category over the last three years is Oak Value Fund (Table 2-11). The top fund for the 5-year period is Mairs & Power Growth Fund. The best for 10 years is CGM Capital Development Fund. Only the 1-year winner Rightime Midcap Fund even gets close to its true nature.

The largest holdings of the mid-cap blend funds certainly don't look very mid-cap at all. That's because the mid-caps are often a blend of large and small, and those large ones tend to dominate such listings. The smallest company of the top 10 holdings (excluding the mutual funds) is Burlington Resources at $6.3 billion market cap, still a little too large to be a mid-cap stock by Morningstar's definitions (Table 2-12). But further down the list, in the No. 11 through No. 20 range, you find companies like Apache Corp. (an oil-and-gas producer) and IMC Global (a fertilizer manufacturer), both with $2.4 billion market caps. You probably wonder why the largest holdings of

TABLE 2-11

MID-CAP BLEND FUNDS

BEST RETURNS

Period ▼	Fund ▼	Total return* ▼
1998	RIGHTIME MIDCAP	37.2%
1996-98	OAK VALUE	28.3
1994-98	MAIRS & POWER GROWTH	22.9
1989-98	CGM CAPITAL DEVELOPMENT	21.1

*Average annual, pretax   DATA: MORNINGSTAR INC.

TABLE 2-12

MID-CAP BLEND FUNDS
LARGEST HOLDINGS

Stock ▼	Percent of net assets ▼
T. ROWE PRICE INTERNATIONAL	0.79%
AMERICA ONLINE	0.69
T. ROWE PRICE NEW HORIZONS	0.66
BERKSHIRE HATHAWAY CL. A	0.59
FANNIE MAE	0.59
FHLMC	0.55
MEDIAONE GROUP	0.53
BURLINGTON RESOURCES	0.51
T. ROWE PRICE GROWTH STOCK	0.49
T. ROWE PRICE BLUE CHIP GROWTH	0.47

DATA: MORNINGSTAR INC.

these funds include some T. Rowe Price funds. That's because the T. Rowe Price Spectrum Growth Fund—a $2.7 billion fund that invests in other Price funds—falls into this category.

Another long-standing mid-cap player is the Nicholas Fund, a $5.8 billion fund run by the man whose name is on the door, Albert Nicholas. By charter, it's supposed to invest in small-cap and mid-cap companies, and it does. Many years ago, the fund had more of a small-cap cast, but with the growth in assets, the fund has tended to own some larger stocks like Berkshire Hathaway, Fannie Mae, and Citigroup. The newer Nicholas II Fund, also run by Albert Nicholas, was for years a mid-cap blend, but has crossed over to the mid-cap growth category.

The Nicholas Fund has an attribute that's a little more common in this category than in most others—portfolio managers with lots of longevity. Nicholas has been running the Nicholas Fund since 1969. George Mairs has been at the helm of Mairs & Powers Growth Fund since 1980. Longleaf Partners' O. Mason Hawkins has been on the job since 1987. Donald Yacktman started the fund that bears his name in 1992. But that came after a long career running other funds, and he was no babe in the business. Mario Gabelli, whose Gabelli Value Fund was the best performer in this category in 1997, is another veteran stockpicker who was a portfolio manager for years before branching out into mutual funds in the mid-1980s.

Another marathoner in this category is Kenneth Heebner of CGM Capital Development Fund. He's been running that fund for 20 years. Heebner, known for making bold bets on particular stocks and industry sectors, has excellent 10- and 15-year records. But interspersed in those

years are some nasty single-year surprises. In the last two years, he lagged the S&P 500 by more than 10 percentage points, and in 1994, the fund was actually down nearly 23 percent.

When big bets go bad, watch out below. Just look at Merrill Lynch Growth B. In 1996, the fund started to load up on energy stocks—especially the volatile energy service firms—in anticipation of stronger demand for oil. The bet worked for a while. But in 1998, the fund held over 50 percent in energy stocks and oil prices, adjusted for inflation, sank to levels not seen in decades. The upshot was that the fund logged a horrendous 24.2 percent investment loss, and assets dropped by another 24 or so percent as investors fled the fund. And in just one year, the fund went from C to D in its overall rating, and from A to F in category rating. (The fund, however, moved from the mid-cap growth to the mid-cap blend category during the year.)

MID-CAP GROWTH FUNDS

Scratch beneath the surface of a mid-cap growth fund and you may just find a successful small-cap growth fund. Many funds, of course, have long plowed the sometimes neglected area of mid-cap stocks, but they never presented themselves as such. Brian W. H. Berghuis, portfolio manager of T. Rowe Price Mid-Cap Growth Fund, recalls that when his fund started in 1992, the term *mid-cap investing* was barely on Wall Street's radar screen. Berghuis seized the ground because, he felt, investors could earn nearly as much money with mid-caps as small-caps but take on a lot less stock-price volatility. Berghuis's strategy is to buy the growth stocks when they are in the $500 million-to-$1.5 billion market cap range and let them roll. If this strategy is successful, they'll grow into mid-caps. If you start with mid-caps, the successful ones eventually graduate to the big leagues.

TABLE 2-13

MID-CAP GROWTH FUNDS
BEST RETURNS

Period ▼	Fund ▼	Total return* ▼
1998	GRAND PRIX**	111.8%
1996-98	DELAWARE AGGRESSIVE GROWTH A	37.5
1994-98	FIDELITY NEW MILLENNIUM	24.6
1989-98	MFS EMERGING GROWTH B	22.9

*Average annual, pretax
**Grand Prix Funds, 800-432-4741; or see Business Week Online

DATA: MORNINGSTAR INC.

There have always been mid-cap growth funds, though, even if they didn't explicitly present themselves that way. The William Blair Growth Fund, for instance, invests in growth stocks of all market capitalizations, but has always balanced the mix so that it falls smack in the middle.

Many mid-cap growth funds never explicitly intended to be mid-cap. They just started as small-cap growth funds and grew into the category. That's what happened with PBHG Growth Fund. The prospectus allows the fund to invest in companies with either revenues or market capitalizations of up to $2 billion. That's the limit. Until 1995, the fund always managed to keep its median market cap well within the small-cap limits. And, of course, the fund excelled in that tough field, especially in the early 1990s. In 1991 and 1995, the fund earned a little better than 50 percent returns.

But in the mutual fund business, success brings in money, and more money can lead to the inevitable "market cap creep." With more and more money, fund managers are simply forced to buy larger- and larger-cap stocks to fill the portfolio. Among those that grew into this category are Alger Small Capitalization, American Century–20th Century Vista Investors, Fidelity OTC, and MFS Emerging Growth B, the fund with the best 10-year record (Table 2-13). Delaware Aggressive Growth A, the fund with the best three-year returns, is a small fund with about $120 million in all its share classes. The fund concentrates its portfolio in just a few sectors, most recently technology, services, and to a lesser extent, financial stocks.

At PBHG Growth, the fund assets grew so much it was remarkable that fund manager Gary Pilgrim could keep the fund focused on small-cap stocks as long as he did. PBHG Growth swelled to $187 million at the end of 1993 from $3 million at the end of 1992. By the end of 1995, the fund had $2 billion in assets, already a sizable fund for one with a small-cap mission. The fund had been closed for awhile in 1995, but reopened at the start of 1996, and the money rushed in again. By year-end, assets were up to $5.9 billion. After that, the fund was weighted down with money at the same time the market for hyperactive emerging growth stocks dried up. In the 1996 through 1998 period, the average annual total return was just 2.2 percent.

Of course, even if a successful small-cap growth fund remains closed to new investors, it still can become a mid-cap fund by virtue of its successes. If enough small-cap stocks flourish,

TABLE 2-14

MID-CAP GROWTH FUNDS	
LARGEST HOLDINGS	
Stock ▼	Percent of net assets ▼
BMC SOFTWARE	1.28%
COMPUWARE	1.23
MICROSOFT	1.19
AMERICA ONLINE	1.04
TYCO INTERNATIONAL	1.04
CISCO SYSTEMS	1.01
EMC/MASS	0.87
CLEAR CHANNEL COMMUNICATIONS	0.83
HBO & CO.	0.80
MCI WORLDCOM	0.77

DATA: MORNINGSTAR INC.

they eventually become mid-caps. Some managers will sell them out of the portfolio at that point, but not all. Hold on to the winners, and the fund becomes a mid-cap. It's just the result of successful investing.

As is much the case with the other mid-cap fund categories, most of the largest holdings are not mid-cap companies (Table 2-14). No. 1 holding BMC Software, with a $9.6 billion market cap, actually is a mid-cap stock, and so is the No. 2 holding, Compuware. America Online was actually a mid-cap at the beginning of 1998, but has since vaulted to the ranks of the megacaps. In fact, about a third of the gain of the S&P MidCap 400 index in 1998 came from America Online. On December 31 of that year, Standard & Poor's Corp. moved AOL to the S&P 500.

SMALL-CAP VALUE FUNDS

When you mention investing in small companies, many people think of an Internet start-up or biotech research firms or faddish specialty retailers or fast-food chains. Consider the major holdings of Longleaf Partners Smallcap Fund, one of the best performing small-cap value funds of the last few years. Among the companies are a machine tool maker, a real estate developer, a cable TV operator, and a community bank. Hardly cutting edge stuff, no?

That doesn't mean you can't make money in these stocks. Indeed, a well-run company in a prosaic business can be a big money-maker. These companies don't usually have to worry too much that their new technology will become obsolete in six months or that new competitors are opening their doors every day. That's usually not the case.

Small-cap value stocks—and the funds that invest in them—often run counter to the faster-paced, highfliers that usually make the headlines. When those "momentum" stocks sputter, as they did in the second half of 1996 and first quarter of 1997, and again late in 1997, the small-cap value stocks usually pick up steam.

There was no steam in 1998 for these funds. In fact, they were dead cold. On average, they ended the year down 5.9 percent. That was the worst showing of any diversified U.S. fund category. But even with a horrible 1998 performance, small-cap value funds beat small-cap growth over the three- and five-year periods.

The last year notwithstanding, small-cap value funds have some advantages. Because the stocks they buy are already "cheap" when measured by traditional yardsticks like p–e ratios, p–b ratios, and dividend yields, the funds tend to be less volatile than the funds that buy the more traditional emerging growth stocks. In effect, these funds are a way to play the small-cap market without wild price swings, a more palatable way to play small-cap stocks for nervous investors.

As a result, small-cap value funds have historically fared a lot better in risk-adjusted ratings than the small-cap growth funds. In the 1999 BUSINESS WEEK Mutual Fund Scoreboard, two small-cap value funds earned A's, the highest rating for risk-adjusted returns. One small-cap growth and no small-cap blend funds made it onto the overall top performers' list.

Small-cap value funds can be a pretty diverse lot, if only because there are so many more companies they can invest in. Large-cap growth funds all build their portfolios from among the same 200 to 300 companies. Even small-cap growth funds tend to be duplicative in their holdings because the managers are mainly seeking the same lightning-like emerging growth companies. But in small-cap value, there are literally thousands of possible investments.

TABLE 2-15

SMALL-CAP VALUE FUNDS
BEST RETURNS

Period	Fund	Total return*
1998	ROYCE GIFTSHARES INV.	21.2%
1996-98	LONGLEAF PARTNERS SMALL-CAP	23.9
1994-98	LONGLEAF PARTNERS SMALL-CAP	18.5
1989-98	SKYLINE SPECIAL EQUITIES	18.3

*Average annual, pretax   DATA: MORNINGSTAR INC.

That doesn't mean it's easy to invest in these companies. Many of the stocks are not liquid. That is, there's little day-to-day trading in the stocks because there are not that many shares to start with. And many of them are "closely held," that is, in the hands of a founder, some family members, or managers (Table 2-15). Because of the limitations of this corner of the market, small-cap value funds sometimes face the choice of closing to new investors or moving up the capitalization ladder. Franklin Balance Sheet Investment, Heartland Value, Longleaf Partners Small-Cap, Skyline Special Equities, and T. Rowe Price Small-Cap Value have dealt with size by closing to new investors, though in 1998, the Heartland and T. Rowe Price funds reopened as the small-cap stocks sank and their assets shrank. Given the difficulty of investing large sums in this corner of the market and the propensity for the funds to close to new investors when performance is strong, there are few megafunds in this category. The giant, of course, is Fidelity Low-Priced Stock Fund, which has been a category-beating performer of $9.1 billion girth. (Heartland Value and T. Rowe Price Small-Cap Value are the next largest funds in the category—each with about $1.6 billion in assets.)

Small-cap is a huge universe of stocks, so many managers find it useful to break it into even smaller segments. Consider the Royce Micro-Cap and Royce Premier Funds. Portfolio manager Charles Royce takes distinctly different approaches to the two. Royce Premier chooses its investments from among 1400 or so small-cap companies with market capitalizations of $300 million to $1 billion. Most small-cap funds and institutional investors stalk that prey, he says, and thus it's a fairly efficient market. So with Royce Premier he makes bigger bets, limiting his holdings to about 50 companies and concentrating them in several sectors. For Royce Micro-Cap, he looks to a universe of some 6500 companies, with market caps of between $5 million and $300 million. Since this micro-market is much less liquid, he owns many more stocks—about 150—in a broadly diversified portfolio. Another Royce-run fund, Pennsylvania Mutual Fund, has a mix of the two strategies.

Perhaps because this universe is so diverse, there is far less concentration in the funds' largest holdings (Table 2-16). For instance, the largest holding of the small-cap value funds is USEC, a processor of uranium fuel for nuclear reactors. It's just 0.29 percent of the category's collective holdings. (It's the second largest in-

TABLE 2-16

SMALL-CAP VALUE FUNDS

LARGEST HOLDINGS

Stock ▼	Percent of net assets ▼
USEC	0.29%
GALLAHER GROUP (ADR)	0.28
FIRST AMERICAN FINANCIAL	0.26
STEWART INFORMATION SERVICES	0.26
KING WORLD PRODUCTIONS	0.26
BJ'S WHOLESALE CLUB	0.25
HYDER	0.25
UNIVERSAL HEALTH SVCS. CL. B	0.24
SHAW COMMS. CL. B (CANADA)	0.24
DALLAS SEMICONDUCTOR	0.24

DATA: MORNINGSTAR INC.

vestment in the Fidelity Low-Priced Stock Fund, the giant in this category.) Compare that to the top name in mid-cap value, Chase Manhattan Corp., which commands 1.78 percent of the mid-cap value funds' aggregate holdings. The tenth-largest holding, Dallas Semiconductor, is about 0.24 percent of aggregate holdings.

SMALL-CAP BLEND FUNDS

If you are only going to invest in one small-cap fund, you may want to go up the middle with a small-cap blend fund. Some funds, for instance, build portfolios with two managers who mix value and growth plays. The value manager buys financial and energy stocks, the growth manager, consumer products and health-care companies. But taken as a whole, the blended funds tend to behave a little more like growth funds than value. So they're not exactly the same as buying 50 percent each of a small-cap growth and a small-cap value fund. Still, these funds can give investors much of the taste of small-cap growth without quite as much hair-raising volatility.

The best performer in 1998, Weitz Hickory Fund, was up 33 percent (Table 2-17). Weitz Hickory is a small-cap version of Weitz Value and Weitz Value Partners, which are A-rated mid-cap value funds, though with a different portfolio manager. During 1998, Hickory's portfolio manager Rick Lawson made big gains in cellular communications and cable TV stocks, much like his associate Wallace Weitz did with the mid-cap funds. The rising valuations for these stocks also pushed the fund over the line from value into blend.

If you're not already in the fund, you can't buy it. Rather than get swamped with money—and suffer PBHG syndrome—Weitz Funds closed the fund to new investors on one day's notice. No doubt that left many prospective investors disappointed, but it should have elated those already in the fund.

Other funds in this category are less specific in their investment objectives. Basically, their portfolio managers are just looking for money-making opportunities in small-cap stocks.

The largest holdings in this category truly are a blend of growth and value stocks, and some aren't even small-cap (Table 2-18). Philip Morris, for instance, isn't even close. The food and tobacco giant ends up on the list because it's a 5 percent holding of Safeco Growth No Load Fund. And when Morningstar analysts crunch Safeco's numbers, the median market cap of its portfolio is $728 million, comfortably in the small-cap range. Safeco Growth, the second largest fund in this category, has a heavy influence on the aggregate holdings. No. 1 holding Green Tree Financial was also its largest, though since Safeco last reported its holdings Green Tree was taken over by Conseco Corp. Chancellor Media, at $6.8 billion in market cap, is a mid-cap company and another large Safeco investment, and it's the No. 2 holding for the category. Still, half of the stocks on the largest holdings list really are small-cap by Morningstar's definition—a market capitalization of $1.2 billion or less.

Safeco No Load Growth Fund is a bit of an oddball for a category in which most fund names incorporate the word "small." Safeco's prospectus makes no mention of market capitalization. It only states that the fund will invest primarily in common stocks. For the 10 years that Thomas Maguire has run the fund, he's found the good opportunities in small-cap stocks, but says he would go up the market capitalization scale if that

TABLE 2-17

SMALL-CAP BLEND FUNDS

BEST RETURNS

Period ▼	Fund ▼	Total return* ▼
1998	WEITZ HICKORY	33.0%
1996-98	WEITZ HICKORY	35.8
1994-98	WEITZ HICKORY	23.8
1989-98	WASATCH GROWTH**	17.3

*Average annual, pretax
**Wasatch Funds, 800-551-1700; or see Business Week Online

DATA: MORNINGSTAR INC.

TABLE 2-18

SMALL-CAP BLEND FUNDS

LARGEST HOLDINGS

Stock ▼	Percent of net assets ▼
GREEN TREE FINANCIAL	0.45%
CHANCELLOR MEDIA	0.40
UNITED STATIONERS	0.32
BANK UNITED CL. A	0.29
PHILIP MORRIS	0.29
APTARGROUP	0.28
DALLAS SEMICONDUCTOR	0.27
ALLIANT TECHSYSTEMS	0.26
EMMIS BROADCASTING CL. A	0.25
VALASSIS COMMUNICATIONS	0.25

DATA: MORNINGSTAR INC.

was what it took to get good investments. The fund does have about 20 percent of its assets in large-cap stocks versus about 60 percent in pure small-cap stocks.

Remember, even in a small-cap fund, managers have a lot of leeway about the companies they will hold. Some just require that the companies be small when purchased; others boot them when they reach a particular size. And some fund commentators have complained that over the last few years none too few small-cap funds bought bigger companies to enhance their returns. Purists were annoyed by that; shareholders probably were glad to have returns higher than they otherwise would have been.

If you definitely want your small-cap fund to stay in small-caps, there's always the Vanguard Small Cap Index. It tracks the Russell 2000 stock index, which for many money managers is the preferred benchmark index for these stocks. The median market capitalization is $671 million, well within the small-cap parameters. While index funds have made mincemeat of most fund managers in the large-cap arena, the case for indexing among small-cap stocks is less clear cut. Active managers argue that these stocks are less efficient than big-caps and they can exploit these inefficiencies through good stock selection. The index funds say the higher costs of operating in the small-cap arena wipe out any gains from stockpicking. New research from Morningstar Inc. comes to two conclusions about small-cap index funds. During bull markets, they edge out actively run small-company funds using the same investment style. During bear markets, they lag, and their overall risk–return profiles are equal to

or slightly worse than those of actively managed rivals. During 1998, which in effect was a bear market for small-cap stocks, the Vanguard Small Cap Stock Index beat about 60 percent of the other small-cap blend managers.

SMALL-CAP GROWTH FUNDS

Strap on your seat belt, put on a crash helmet. Small-cap growth funds are the most volatile of the nine U.S. diversified fund categories. In theory, this should be the most rewarding kind of fund. The fund managers are investing in small, rapidly growing companies. When these high-octane stocks work, they can make big, big bucks for fund investors. When they flop, by failing to meet an expected profit forecast or bungling a new product, look out below. There are few buyers for those busted emerging growth stocks when all the small-cap growth managers want to sell. So they sell what they can and mark down the rest of their holdings.

Still, there's plenty of potential in these stocks and these funds because of some of the simple laws of percentages. There's no limit on how much a successful company can earn or gain in stock value. Just look at Microsoft, which went public in March 1986 at $21 per share—29 cents, adjusted for all the splits since. At the recent price of $167, that's a 57,500 percent gain. Had Microsoft bombed, the maximum loss would have been 100 percent—and fund managers hold on to a losing situation to that point. A few stocks with even one-tenth of Microsoft's gain can make a powerful impact on these funds. A small-cap growth fund doesn't have to hit a home run with every stock; a handful will more than carry the rest of the portfolio to fund stardom in any one year.

This is a category where funds with small asset bases can often stun fund watchers with enormous returns. That's because a few choice small-cap stocks can really make them run. After three years in operation, Jundt U.S. Emerging Growth Fund still has only $12 million in three asset classes, which is surprising considering the performance. The fund was up 37.8 percent in 1998, benefiting from a 43 percent concentration in technology stocks and 28 percent in service industries (media, telecommunications, etc.). That 1998 showing was no fluke. The three-year average annual return is 36.7 percent, making it the best-performing small-cap growth fund for the last three years as well (Table 2-19).

To invest in these funds, investors need to withstand a good deal of volatility. The Jundt

TABLE 2-19

SMALL-CAP GROWTH FUNDS		
BEST RETURNS		
Period ▼	Fund ▼	Total return* ▼
1998	JUNDT U.S. EMERGING GROWTH B**	37.8%
1996-98	JUNDT U.S. EMERGING GROWTH B**	37.6
1994-98	LORD ABBETT DEVELOPING GROWTH A	21.8
1989-98	KAUFMANN	20.9

*Average annual, pretax
**Jundt Funds, 800-370-0612; or see Business Week Online

DATA: MORNINGSTAR INC.

fund, for instance, can really swing. Over its three-year history, two-thirds of the time the fund's monthly return has been within a range of plus or minus 12 percentage points from its average. For small-cap growth funds as a whole, that figure is about 8.5 percentage points. For an S&P 500 index fund, it's 5.9 percent. To make money with these funds, an investor needs to be able to ride out the inevitable downdrafts. Otherwise, investors end up buying after the fund has already done very well—and come to their attention—and selling out at a loss.

Not all funds in this category will take your money on a wild ride. In fact, those which have earned a category rating of A—best risk-adjusted returns—have relatively low volatility and thus give good returns for the risk. Those funds are Baron Asset, Fasciano, Gabelli ABC, Galaxy Small Cap Value Retail, and Nicholas Limited Edition.

Baron Asset has the highest trailing five-year returns, 19.9 percent. But it's a $5.6 billion fund, very large for this category. Its largest holding, the brokerage firm Charles Schwab, is certainly no small-cap stock today, but was when Baron bought it and held on. Since Schwab is a large holding, about 8 percent, of one of the largest funds in the category, Schwab winds up as the largest holding of the small-cap growth funds (Table 2-20). Size is starting to catch up with Baron, though, and its returns are slipping. In 1998, the fund earned just 4.3 percent, a little less than average for the category.

The Fasciano Fund, on the other hand, could be the next Baron Asset Fund. It is still small, just $233.2 million, earned a 7.2 percent return in 1998, and has overall risk that's just average. (Baron is high risk.) Not bad for a small-cap growth fund at all. Gabelli ABC has by far the lowest risk of these, but while it's small-cap growth by the stocks it owns, the fund can also

take steps that are different from most small-caps, like raising cash or buying debt securities. Even with a low-risk profile, the fund's trailing five-year return, 9.9 percent a year, is unlikely to get anyone excited.

Many small-cap growth funds practice an investment strategy called *momentum investing*—buying the stocks of companies with a high earnings growth rate and great prospects that this will continue, companies with "momentum."

Practitioners of this strategy don't believe in buying cheap stocks and selling them when they move up. Their game is to buy what's moving up and sell it when it moves up higher. In other words, "buy high, sell higher." The distinguishing characteristics of the stocks these funds traffic in is their high price-to-earnings ratios. They are also subject to more volatility in their performance.

Among the momentum funds are AIM Aggressive Growth A Fund and the Kaufmann Fund. Kaufmann has the top return funds for the last 10-year period, but in recent years, it has had very little momentum in its returns. Kaufmann earned just 0.7 percent 1998, and has a three-year average annual return of 11.1 percent. Compare that to the 20.9 percent average return over the 10-year period and you can assume that this fund's best days are behind it. Indeed, during 1998, about one-quarter of the fund's assets departed.

Not that any funds that follow small-cap momentum strategies were a whole lot better. AIM Aggressive Growth was up only 5 percent, and American Century–20th Century Giftrust Investors was down 13.1 percent. That one-time high-flier now has a three-year record of –3.2

TABLE 2-20

SMALL-CAP GROWTH FUNDS	
LARGEST HOLDINGS	
Stock ▼	Percent of net assets ▼
CHARLES SCHWAB	0.59%
CENDANT	0.57
SOTHEBY'S HOLDINGS CL. A	0.52
HCR MANOR CARE	0.51
DEVRY	0.37
HEFTEL BROADCASTING CL. A	0.35
AMERICAN TOWER CL. A	0.34
VERITAS SOFTWARE	0.34
DOLLAR TREE STORES	0.34
STERIS	0.33

DATA: MORNINGSTAR INC.

percent a year. That's no doubt made many share-holders unhappy, and there's nothing they can do about it. This unusual fund locks its shareholders in for a minimum of 10 years.

HYBRID FUNDS—DOMESTIC AND INTERNATIONAL

Introduced in 1997, domestic and international hybrid funds are also relatively new investment categories. There's really nothing new here, just reorganization of the funds formerly classified as balanced, asset allocation, or multi-asset global. For the most part, these funds regularly own equities, but may also mix them with bonds, cash, and sometimes gold. Among the leading domestic hybrid funds are Eastcliff Total Return, Value Line Asset Allocation, and Vanguard Asset Allo-cation (Table 2-21).

Because hybrids offer diversification among types of assets as well as diversification among securities, they have become popular vehicles for retirement plans such as individual retirement accounts (IRAs) and employer-sponsored plans like 401(k)s. An asset allocation option can make an appealing choice, both for retirement plans that don't offer a wide variety of funds or for investors who don't want to go through the trou-ble of stitching together a program from a lot of funds.

Outside the retirement plan, investors don't really need the hybrid funds. If fact, if all you want is a fairly straightforward mix of U.S. stocks and U.S. bonds, you can probably get bet-ter performance and perhaps lower costs from putting 60 percent of your money in a large-cap blend fund and 40 percent in an investment-grade bond fund. If you want a richer asset mix, one that includes foreign stocks and bonds, and perhaps real estate and gold, then you need more funds and more money (to meet initial invest-ment hurdles). In that case, a well-diversified

hybrid might be a better option. With many of these hybrids, you can get the diversification and breadth of investment with just a minimum investment of a few thousand dollars.

Before investing in some of these retirement-oriented hybrids, investors are asked to complete a questionnaire that helps to determine their risk-taking ability. Then, depending on the score, investors are pointed toward an aggressive, mod-erate, or conservative asset allocation fund, with the most aggressive usually taking the most risk. Those most aggressive funds are usually recom-mended to the younger investors. Fidelity is the leader in this product, with its Asset Manager series of funds. Putnam, T. Rowe Price, and Van-guard have also introduced their own versions of the Asset Manager approach. Obviously, over time, the investor is going to have to move from the growth to the middle of the road and, eventu-ally, to the most conservative portfolio. Stage-coach Funds, the mutual fund arm of Wells Fargo Bank, takes a different approach. Stagecoach LifePath Funds have different "target maturi-ties" starting with the year 2000. Investors who will be retiring around 2020, for instance, would choose the 2020 fund, which would gradually adjust its portfolio toward a more conservative mix as its shareholders age. Stagecoach also has a 2040 retirement fund, which might make a good choice for someone just getting out of college now. Fidelity's Freedom funds are also a series of time-targeted funds marketed mainly to investors through retirement plans.

The majority of domestic hybrid funds are the old "balanced" funds, which are the "sensible shoes" of the mutual fund business—prudent, practical, and, yes, boring. With these funds you get stocks for growth and bonds for income—and a portfolio manager who gets paid to figure out how much of each you need. There's nothing trendy about balanced funds, either. They are among the oldest funds. Vanguard Wellington Fund opened up shop in 1928, and about a dozen more date back to the 1930s. But new balanced funds are opening all the time.

The original balanced funds were based on the principle that stock prices and bond prices go in opposite directions. In a booming economy, for instance, stocks rise because of improving corpo-rate profitability. The boom creates increasing demand for credit, so interest rates rise and bond prices fall. Then, in a recession, the opposite is supposed to happen: Stocks fall and bonds rise. But in the recession of 1990, both stocks and bonds tumbled. And in 1991, 1993, 1995, 1997, and

TABLE 2-21

DOMESTIC HYBRID FUNDS

BEST RETURNS

Period	Fund	Total return*
1998	EASTCLIFF TOTAL RETURN**	38.7%
1996-98	EASTCLIFF TOTAL RETURN**	29.5
1994-98	VALUE LINE ASSET ALLOCATION	22.1
1989-98	VANGUARD ASSET ALLOCATION	16.7

*Average annual, pretax
**Eastcliff Funds, 800-595-5519; or see Business Week Online

DATA: MORNINGSTAR INC.

TABLE 2-22

DOMESTIC HYBRID FUNDS
LARGEST HOLDINGS

Security ▼	Percent of net assets ▼
PHILIP MORRIS	0.85%
GENERAL ELECTRIC	0.76
FNMA 6.5%	0.66
BRISTOL-MYERS SQUIBB	0.64
CITICORP	0.62
U.S. TREASURY NOTE 5.875% 11/15/05	0.61
IBM	0.61
AT&T	0.60
FIRST UNION	0.58
U.S. TREASURY BOND 6.25% 08/15/23	0.55

DATA: MORNINGSTAR INC.

1998, both stocks and bonds went up together; in 1990 and 1994, they fell side by side. Today, that theory is more the exception than the rule, but balanced funds do have a role to play. They can, at times, deliver much of the return of pure equity funds, but with less volatility in share prices.

As a class, domestic hybrid funds are quite diverse in their results. Their returns depend on how the portfolio managers fill in the stock and bond portions of their portfolios. In 1998, the funds that had large-cap stocks in the equity portion and cash or short-term bonds in the fixed-income portion did best. Of course, these funds are usually pitched to investors as conservative investments and tend to own blue-chip stocks in most cases. Among the largest holdings are familiar blue-chips like Philip Morris, General Electric, Bristol-Myers Squibb, and Fannie Mae, as well as U.S. Treasury and agency securities (Table 2-22).

The balanced funds, with their long histories, may give comfort to investors. Over the last few years, they haven't looked all that appealing compared to all-equity funds that rode the crest of the bull market. But over the long haul, these funds have provided respectable returns with relatively low risk. That's because they tend to live circumscribed lives. For instance, one typical common rule is that the fund have no more than 65 percent of its assets in stocks. It's a good discipline. If rising prices push the stock portfolio up against the limit, the portfolio managers must start unloading stocks in order to balance the holdings. This fits well with an old Wall Street adage, "You can't go broke taking a profit."

The balanced funds have a long history, whereas the asset allocation funds are relative upstarts. Many of them are hyperactive balanced funds. While balanced funds are generally stocks and bonds, asset allocation funds may add other assets into the mix, including gold, real estate, or commodity-linked securities. Many asset allocation funds have the ability to boost a particular class of asset up to 100 percent of the fund. Balanced funds by definition can't take that extreme a position.

Exactly how much of each asset goes into the fund is determined by the fund manager using a sophisticated computer-driven program, and they're not all the same. While equity fund results largely depend on stock selection, the success of asset allocation programs relies on how much of the fund goes into each asset class. Security selection does not play as much of a role in these funds' returns.

Look at Vanguard Asset Allocation Fund, the domestic hybrid with the best 10-year returns. For equities, the managers use an S&P 500 index fund, and for bonds, an index fund based on the Lehman Bros. Long-Term Treasury Bond index. The managers keep shifting the allocation between those two investments, plus a money-market portfolio. It's pure asset allocation, with no particular thought to security selection.

Of course, that's only one flavor of domestic hybrid funds. Value Line Asset Allocation leans more heavily toward equities and does pay attention to which ones it buys. The stocks are those chosen with the help of Value Line's long-time ratings system, which in itself is largely based on earnings momentum.

Eastcliff Total Return Fund, the best-performer in the one- and three-year returns, buys large-cap stocks, but, unlike many hybrid managers, is not afraid to invest in high-growth, high-valuation technology and health-care companies.

In recent years, international hybrid funds haven't appeared all that appealing, mainly because overseas stock markets have either headed

TABLE 2-23

INTERNATIONAL HYBRID FUNDS
BEST RETURNS

Period ▼	Fund ▼	Total return* ▼
1998	MONTGOMERY GLOBAL LONG-SHORT A	53.4%
1996-98	OPPENHEIMER GLOBAL GROWTH & INCOME A	18.6
1994-98	OPPENHEIMER GLOBAL GROWTH & INCOME A	13.3
1989-98	SOGEN INTERNATIONAL A	10.5

*Average annual, pretax   DATA: MORNINGSTAR INC.

TABLE 2-24

INTERNATIONAL HYBRID FUNDS

LARGEST HOLDINGS

Security ▼	Percent of net assets ▼
U.S. TREASURY NOTE 5.875% 11/15/99	5.34%
U.S. TREASURY NOTE 3.625% 4/15/28	1.15
REPUBLIC OF ARGENTINA FRN 4/01/01	0.80
U.S. TREASURY NOTE 3.375% 1/15/07	0.68
GOVT. OF RUSSIA 12.75% 6/24/28	0.57
REPUBLIC OF ARGENTINA 9.75% 9/19/27	0.55
UNITED KINGDOM TREASURY 9.75% 8/27/02	0.55
U.S. TREASURY NOTE 6% 8/15/99	0.51
LANDESBANK HESSEN RESET 6% 11/29/13	0.49
REPUBLIC OF ARGENTINA 11.375% 1/30/17	0.45

DATA: MORNINGSTAR INC.

south or generally lagged U.S. stocks in their gains. Still, there's a strong case to be made for the additional diversification that international securities bring to a fund or to a portfolio.

If the average international hybrid was nothing to sing about, individual funds certainly managed to rise above the crowd. Look at Montgomery Global Long-Short A, the best performer for 1998 (Table 2-23). It's a novel mutual fund, with the ability to sell stocks short. (That means the manager is making a bet that the stock goes down, not up. Of course, you can still lose money if you are wrong and the stock goes up.) The fund has a lot of leeway to go anywhere looking for the best buy and sell opportunities. In 1998, the fund gained 53.4 percent.

Or consider Oppenheimer Global Growth & Income, the best performer in the three- and five-year periods. The portfolio manager has a wide berth in asset mix, country selection, and individual stocks and has generally been at the right places at the right time—until 1998, that is. The fund went heavily into stocks and out of Treasuries just ahead of the summer swoon. Even so, the fund finished the year up 12.8 percent and beat the international hybrid average handily.

Perhaps the fund in this category most admired by investment advisers is SoGen International, the very low-risk but usually rewarding fund managed for nearly 20 years by Jean-Marie Eveillard. The fund has an excellent long-term record, but in the short term it's been a laggard, and that has cost it its usually top-drawer rating.

The New York-based Frenchman runs an eclectic portfolio. There's no elaborate computer model here. Eveillard is an old-fashioned value

investor, and he'll go anywhere in the world to find value. He's not afraid to make unorthodox investments, either. For many years, one of his fund's largest holdings was the Bank of International Settlements, an institution in Switzerland that serves as a clearinghouse for all the central banks (you know, the Federal Reserve, the Bank of England, the Bundesbank). Its shares sell for far less than the amount of cash and gold bullion that backs each share. The bank is still in the portfolio, but it's now a minor investment.

There are clunkers in all fund categories, but in this category you will find two of the real clunkers of the fund universe: the Comstock Partners Capital Value A and Comstock Partners Strategy O funds. Both funds have been prepared for a bear market for 10 years—and the returns show it. The funds play the bearish game through gold stocks, short sales, and put options. Those are good tools, but used at the wrong time they make for a woeful performance.

Perhaps the point of these funds is to be permanently bearish, giving investors a contrarian holding for their portfolios. On that count, the bearish postures worked in the stormy third quarter of 1997. Comstock Capital Value A gained 17.5 percent, and Comstock Partners Strategy O, 14.2 percent. That made them the third and fifth best-performing funds for the quarter. Still, their 1998 returns were just awful—down 22.1 percent and 7.3 percent, respectively. Unless you know how to get in and out at just the right time—and who does—these funds seem like poor choices.

As a group, international hybrid funds only hold about one-third of their assets in bonds. But while their equity investments are quite diverse, their bond holdings are heavily government issues. So these funds' largest holdings tend to be government bonds (Table 2-24).

INTERNATIONAL FUNDS

We pay up for German-made sports cars and luxury sedans. We sip French and Italian wines and bottled water. Many of our favorite electronic toys like compact disc players, video game machines, and camcorders come from the Pacific rim. We Americans are worldly as consumers but, until not so long ago, we've been parochial as investors. United States stocks make up a little less than half the market value of world equities, but U.S. investors have, at most, only about one-sixth of their equity assets abroad.

That's changing thanks to mutual funds that make it easy and convenient to invest abroad. Heck, with funds, buying a portfolio of French,

Brazilian, and Chinese stocks is no more difficult than buying a portfolio of U.S. blue-chips. In 1993, international equity funds captured the imaginations—and the money—of millions of U.S. investors who sent billions abroad. In one year, the number of international equity funds investing abroad shot up from 210 to 344. More important, the assets in those funds rocketed from $42 billion to $104 billion. For many months, one out of every two dollars flowing into equity funds was going international. Today, there are nearly 1400 U.S.-based international mutual funds with some $350 billion in assets.

Because international funds reach into the far corners of the globe, even many sophisticated investors who pick and choose at home opt for mutual funds when investing abroad. Many international funds are associated with organizations having global investment capabilities, and that gives the funds first-hand information on, say, Japanese banks or German machine-tool companies or Spanish utilities. That's awfully hard to get from your desk in Pittsburgh, Peoria, or Paramus—even with a computer, a modem, and the World Wide Web.

Then, too, accounting standards and tax treatments vary across borders, so the financial reports of Germany's Siemens or Sweden's ABB Brown Boveri and General Electric are not going to be comparable, even if their businesses are. Good equity analysis of non-U.S. companies takes some specialized knowledge most U.S. investors just don't have. Finally, the logistics of buying and selling abroad are daunting—and expensive—and may require several brokers, banks, and other services to process trades. That can be vastly simplified by leaving it all to a fund, where the processes are well-established and performed at institutional rates.

One particular type of international fund that really galloped to the forefront during this decade is the so-called "emerging markets" fund—a mutual fund that invests in developing stock markets such as those in Latin America, the Pacific Basin (excluding Japan, Australia, and New Zealand), and even the nascent markets of Eastern Europe. During 1993, for instance, Fidelity Emerging Markets Fund earned an 81.3 percent total return. (Fidelity could not keep up with the demand for prospectuses.) In 1997, that same fund lost 40.8 percent of its value, and in 1998, another 26.6 percent.

In the financial markets, risk and reward are intertwined. Relatively large gains in some years can be expected to result in relatively large losses in others. That's because such funds take large risks just by the nature of the markets they invest in. Investing in developing economies is risky; the skills of corporate managers are usually lacking by U.S. standards; business and politics are hard to separate; corruption and nepotism, while hardly rare in the more mature economies, is often the norm here. Nonetheless, as long as these countries are growing and attempting to develop economic and financial institutions like those of the more developed nations, the stocks of these nations can make alluring investments.

Okay, "investment" is a little strong. "Speculation" is better. South Korea and Thailand are attempting to reform financial and political institutions, and their economies are on the mend. Indonesia and Malaysia are floundering. Russia, whose default on its debts set off a crisis in August 1998, may never develop a true, market-based economy.

While mutual funds have made it cheap and easy to access these emerging markets, the very presence of the funds has changed their nature. The inflows of foreign capital can send stocks to valuations far beyond the level that could be achieved if the stocks were only purchased by local investors. But the influence of outside money cuts both ways. When the foreign investor—that's you or the portfolio manager of an emerging markets fund—wants to sell out, there are precious few buyers for the stock. That causes prices to fall even farther. And once a problem develops in these markets, it spreads quickly.

In 1997, a currency crisis in Thailand spread to neighboring Malaysia, Indonesia, and the Philippines. When the once rock solid Hong Kong market plunged, emerging markets like Brazil and Russia, which had been faring well all year, skidded as well. Fearing redemptions by shareholders and unable to sell many of their Asian stocks, portfolio managers sold holdings elsewhere.

Right now, because of the volatile swings, emerging markets funds make news, but they're a relatively small and recent phenomenon. International mutual funds are hardly a new idea. The Templeton Growth Fund, for instance, started in 1954 and has posted an average annual return of more than 14.4 percent over its four decades. Templeton started investing in Japan in the 1950s when the whole notion that it would become the world's second largest stock market (for a period in the late 1980s, it was the largest) seemed absurd. But for many years, the mutual fund industry left international investing to Templeton and a few others. Today, most fund fami-

International funds help diversify a portfolio.

33

TABLE 2-25

INTERNATIONAL FUNDS
BEST RETURNS

Period ▼	Fund ▼	Total return* ▼
DIVERSIFIED EMERGING MARKETS		
1998	DRESDNER RCM EMERGING MARKETS**	−8.4%
1996-98	NICHOLAS-APPLEGATE EMRG. CNTRY. A	2.8
1994-98	TEMPLETON DEVELOPING MARKETS I	−3.7
1989-98	LEXINGTON WORLDWIDE EMERG. MKTS.	2.3
FOREIGN		
1998	NICHOLAS-APPLEGATE INT. SM. CO. A	35.6%
1996-98	ARTISAN INTERNATIONAL	22.5
1994-98	BT INVESTMENT INTERNATIONAL EQUITY	15.8
1989-98	GAM INTERNATIONAL A	15.6
WORLD		
1998	NICHOLAS-APPLEGATE WORLD GR. C	36.2%
1996-98	DREYFUS PREMIER WORLDWIDE GR. B	24.3
1994-98	DREYFUS PREMIER WORLDWIDE GR. B	19.8
1989-98	NEW PERSPECTIVE	15.7
EUROPE		
1998	WEBS INDEX BELGIUM	52.8%
1996-98	BARTLETT EUROPE A**	29.5
1994-98	WRIGHT EQUIFUND-NETHERLANDS	21.1
1989-98	FIDELITY EUROPE	14.4
LATIN AMERICA		
1998	KEMPER LATIN AMERICA A	−24.3%
1996-98	VAN KAMPEN LATIN AMERICA A	9.6
1994-98	SCUDDER LATIN AMERICA	−0.7
1989-98	NOT APPLICABLE	
DIVERSIFIED PACIFIC		
1998	FIDELITY PACIFIC BASIN	8.3%
1996-98	MERRILL LYNCH PACIFIC B	1.5
1994-98	MERRILL LYNCH PACIFIC B	2.7
1989-98	GAM PACIFIC BASIN A	5.6
JAPAN		
1998	FIDELITY JAPAN SMALL COMPANIES	31.2%
1996-98	WARBURG PINCUS JAPAN GROWTH COMM.	−1.0
1994-98	FIDELITY JAPAN	0.4
1989-98	AIM JAPAN GROWTH A	0.8
DIVERSIFIED PACIFIC EX-JAPAN		
1998	MATTHEWS KOREA I**	96.2%
1996-98	FIDELITY HONG KONG & CHINA	1.3
1994-98	CAPSTONE NEW ZEALAND**	−2.0
1989-98	AIM NEW PACIFIC GROWTH A	0.3

*Average annual, pretax
**Dresdner Funds, 800-726-7240; Bartlett Funds, 800-800-3609; Matthews Funds, 800-789-2742; Capstone Funds, 800-262-6631; or see Business Week Online

DATA: MORNINGSTAR INC.

lies have at least one international fund and many have multiple offerings.

In fact, international funds have become so diverse that we've split the group into eight categories: two broader groups, foreign and world; diversified emerging markets; two regional groups, Europe and Latin America; and three sorts of funds for the Pacific Basin (Table 2-25). Those categories are Diversified Pacific, Diversified Pacific Ex-Japan, and one just for Japan.

If you don't own any international fund, your first should come from the foreign or world categories. Sound the same, don't they? Foreign funds invest mainly in the more industrialized countries and mature capital markets, though some do spice the portfolios with emerging markets securities. What's more, they usually specifically exclude U.S. stocks.

World funds, on the other hand, usually have some of their portfolios in U.S. stocks. (One fund, SmallCap World, has over 60 percent of its portfolio in the United States and has historically kept its U.S. component so high that Morningstar classifies it as a domestic small-cap growth fund.) In fact, 5 of the 10 largest equity holdings in this category are Pfizer, Time-Warner, Microsoft, Cisco Systems, and Philip Morris. They're all U.S. companies, but they all have significant operations around the globe as well. To be a large U.S. company today, you have to be global.

Whether you choose a world fund that includes the United States or a foreign fund that excludes the United States depends on how you construct your portfolio of funds. Suppose you decide you want to invest 25 percent of your total portfolio outside the United States. You should stay clear of the "world" funds, since such funds may have about one-third of their assets in U.S. stocks. So instead of getting 25 percent of your money abroad, you may get only 16 percent. If you don't mind having the U.S. stocks or you don't care about a precise asset allocation, then don't exclude these investment vehicles. World funds have one advantage over foreign funds. If the U.S. stocks look better to the portfolio manager than foreign markets, he or she can take advantage of those opportunities. That was certainly the case in the 1994–1998 period, when U.S. stocks far outpaced the foreign markets.

With international investing, fund managers usually take one of two basic approaches. First, there's the "top-down" method. Portfolio managers look first at the countries, the local economies, and macroeconomic data like growth in Gross Domestic Product, inflation, and employment. Then they look at how that stacks up with the local stock market—is it cheap or dear given the economic backdrop? The funds usually use an international index as a guide and over-weight or underweight countries according to their estimation of the stock market prospects. The managers decide on a country allocation—so much percent of the portfolio to Germany, so much to Japan, and fill in the stocks accordingly, or turn that job over to other managers or analysts. The idea is to get the markets right and all else will follow. Some of the practitioners of this method are Fidelity Diversified International, T. Rowe Price International Stock, and the Scudder International Fund.

The opposite tack is, of course, the "bottom-up" method, one favored by the Templeton Funds. In bottom-up, the portfolio managers first use various stock selection methods to come up with the companies they want to invest in. The resulting country allocation is the result of stock selection. Thus, the returns of these funds can be quite different from the indexes. For instance, Artisan International Fund, with a 34.4 percent total return in 1996 had 11 percent of its assets in Sweden and 10 percent in Norway. The two Scandinavian countries together make up only a few percentage points of any international index. Had the fund stayed close to an index, it would never have earned those kinds of outsized returns. Had the manager been wrong about Scandinavian stocks, the fund would have been near the bottom of the pack.

The sorts of investments made by European, Pacific, and Latin American funds are self-evident. These funds are not substitutes for foreign funds, but supplements. If you want to get even more targeted in your investments, take a look at the WEBS Index funds. No, it's not about the Internet. WEBS stands for World Equity Benchmark Shares. These effectively are index funds that invest in the Morgan Stanley Capital International index for that country. So far, there are 17 WEBS funds: Austria, Belgium, France, Germany, Italy, Netherlands, Spain, Sweden, Switzerland, and the United Kingdom in Europe; Japan, Hong Kong, Malaysia, and Singapore in Asia; Canada and Mexico in North America; and Australia. The advantages of WEBS over, for example, Fidelity France Fund or Scudder Japan are the same as those of any index funds: low cost and low turnover. Fidelity France has a 2 percent annual expense ratio and a 3 percent front-end load. WEBS Index France has a 1.53 percent expense ratio. (WEBS are technically no-load, though the shares have to be purchased on the American Stock Exchange. But equity trading commissions have plunged with the advent of online trading.)

Right now, funds investing in Europe have the best recent returns and perhaps the best near-term prospects. That's because Europe is developing into one megamarket, with economic barriers falling across the continent. That should make it nearly as easy, for instance, for a Spanish company to sell its products in France and Germany as it is for a New Jersey company to sell in Pennsylvania and New York. Perhaps even more significant is the currency union, with the recent introduction of the Euro. The new currency is now used only for financial transactions. But in three years, it will replace marks, lire, francs, and a number of other local currencies. Eventually, this one-market Europe should be a bonanza for businesses and their shareholders.

The last several years have been quite good for U.S. mutual funds that invest in Europe. In 1996, the Europe funds put on their best show since 1993, climbing 24.7 percent and even beating the S&P 500. In 1997, all the major European markets made significant double-digit gains, riding a mergers and acquisition boom not unlike that in the United States. Even after adjusting for the strong dollar, funds investing in Europe delivered 17.8 percent to U.S. investors. In 1998, European markets reverberated from the Russian default and other emerging market crises, but by the end of the year, the returns for funds investing in Europe were virtually the same as 1997's.

On the other side of the globe, Pacific funds have historically had some of the world's worst- and best-performing stock markets. Look at the Japanese stock market. During the 1980s, the market soared, with the Nikkei stock average going from less than 10,000 in 1980 to nearly 40,000 at the end of 1989. But that's not all. Starting in 1985, the value of the dollar versus the Japanese yen has fallen by nearly two-thirds. That means, even if there had been no appreciation in the price of a Japanese stock denominated in yen, it still would have soared for dollar-based shareholders.

Since 1990, the yen price of stocks has more than halved. In the last year, the losses became even worse as the value of the yen sank against the U.S. dollar. The bear market in Japan has been devastating for such one-time high-fliers as the Japan Fund and G. T. Global Japan Growth Fund. (Both funds had good returns in 1993 and 1994, more because of the stronger yen than

"Top-down" funds choose countries first, stocks later.

because of a bull market in stocks.) In 1998, though, Japanese stocks and funds had their best showing in years. Japan's economy was mired in recession, but its legislature finally enacted a bank reform bill that would clean up the trillions in bad loans and get the country moving again—similar to America's savings and loan bailout of the early 1990s. The best-performing fund in the Japan category was Fidelity Japan Smaller Companies, up 31.2 percent. The more mainstream Fidelity Japan Fund earned 13.1 percent. The average Japan fund was up 7.1 percent after being down 16.8 percent in 1997. Still, the 10-year return on Japan funds is dismal. Just 0.1 percent a year. Or look at it this way: every $1000 invested in a Japan fund at the beginning of 1989 was worth about $1010 10 years later.

The rest of Asia is quite another story. Spurred by economic and market reforms in China, the entire region underwent a strong burst of economic growth in the early 1990s. That made a star of the Hong Kong stock market in 1992 and 1993, as Western investors saw it as the door to China. But the China boom spread throughout the region to such nations as Thailand, Indonesia, Singapore, and Malaysia. In 1993, nearly all the stock markets around China's perimeter doubled in local currency terms.

All these markets corrected in 1994, but while Hong Kong rebounded strongly in 1995 and 1996, the other developing Asian markets turned in spotty returns. Then in 1997, these markets melted down, a combination of investor loss of faith in the currency and a sharp economic slowdown. International bankers extended loan packages to South Korea, Thailand, and Indonesia, demanding stiff economic and market reforms in return for loans. The reforms would require big sacrifices such as shutting down and merging many banks as well as high local interest rates that would slow down economic growth and increase unemployment—politically unpopular moves. In 1998, returns in Asia were a mixed bag, but there was still a negative bias in the results. The average diversified Pacific fund was down 4.9 percent; those that exclude Japan were down a little more than twice as much.

Your money does not have to travel halfway around the world to get a wild ride. There's always the Latin America funds, which have opened for business over the last several years as many neighboring nations in our hemisphere started to fight inflation, privatize their economies, and invite foreign investment. In 1997, the average Latin America fund earned a snappy 26 percent

atop 24.3 percent in 1996. Payback time came in 1998, when emerging markets investors, fearing an Asian or Russian style financial calamity in Latin America, started to pull their money out. The capital flight in itself helped to cause problems. All the major markets went into a tailspin, and Brazil, Latin America's largest economy and a major purchaser of U.S. exports, floundered. The United States and the IMF offered a bailout plan in exchange for fiscal and budgetary reform. But when the legislature balked at enacting the plan, the investment community lost faith. The upshot was high interest rates, high unemployment, and a devaluation of the currency, which was what the Brazilians had hoped to avoid all along. So in 1998, the average Latin America fund lost 38.7 percent. That was far worse than the Latin returns in 1994 and 1995, when Mexico's dire financial situation forced it into devaluing the peso—an event that sent investors fleeing from other Latin markets as well.

Sure, international funds are risky. But when they're combined with U.S. funds in a portfolio, they actually lower the overall risk, at least as measured by volatility. That's because U.S. funds have a high degree of correlation. When one goes up or down, they all do, though not to the same extent. But non-U.S. markets and funds that invest in them do not have a high degree of correlation. They're more likely to zig when the U.S. funds zag. So if U.S. funds are in a slump, chances are some non-U.S. funds will be doing well. That's why even when the foreign markets were eclipsed by the United States, mutual fund companies were launching new international funds.

International investing makes sense for another fundamental reason. If other countries are enjoying faster economic growth than the United States, it stands to reason that corporate profits are going to be stronger than in the United States. So by investing abroad you get a chance to capture some of that other growth. And you still have the opportunity to invest in industries that have all but disappeared in the United States, such as consumer electronics.

For some investors, the chief worry about international investing is currency risk. That's an important question to ask when shopping for international funds. Some funds do hedge currencies; some don't. You have to read the prospectus for the fund's hedging policy. Here's how a hedge works: Suppose a fund owned $100 million worth of Japanese stocks and the manager believed the yen would decline against the dollar. One way to protect the yen-denominated investment would be to sell $100 million worth of yen in the currency market. That move has the effect of "neutralizing" the yen in the fund. Then, the fund gains or loses on the stock price movement of the Japanese stock—just as it would with a U.S. stock.

But hedging has a cost, even if it's done right. It can be especially costly if it's done wrong. What if, against the forecasts of the currency experts, the yen went up instead of down against the dollar? (That's exactly what happened in 1994.) That hedge, which is supposed to protect the portfolio, would become a money-loser. That's why many funds—such as Templeton, one of the most experienced in overseas investing—don't explicitly hedge. But they will factor a depreciating foreign currency into their portfolio by investing in companies that benefit from the cheaper currency, like exporters.

Even with currency risk—that the value of your investments will fluctuate because of currency fluctuations—it's still advisable for U.S. investors to place some international funds in their portfolios. Even if you have all your assets in dollars, you're not without risk. What if the dollar is falling in relation to other currencies? You may have to kiss off that European vacation, but you can live without that. A weak dollar could mean you spend more for foreign-made goods, some of which have no domestic substitutions. And a weak dollar can even push up prices for U.S.-made goods. Although you're shopping for a Chevy, your cost for the car can still be affected by currency fluctuations. If the dollar falls against the yen, that would probably lead to higher prices for Japanese cars that compete with Chevrolet. If its competitors' prices are going up, General Motors may try to profit by raising prices too. Putting a portion of your assets abroad is as American as baseball, hot dogs, apple pie, and the 4th of July.

PRECIOUS METALS FUNDS

Incredible? Astounding? No adjectives really do justice to the 1993 performance of the funds specializing in precious metals, or gold funds. Lexington Strategic Investments, the leading precious metals fund and the leading mutual fund of the year, blasted out a 264.9 percent return. That's probably an all-time record for a mutual fund. United Services Gold Shares, at 123.9 percent, was no slouch either, with a double. The top 25 funds of the year were all gold funds, and the average gold fund delivered a whopping 97 percent return.

TABLE 2-26

PRECIOUS METALS FUNDS		
BEST RETURNS		
Period ▼	Fund ▼	Total return* ▼
1998	USAA GOLD	1.1%
1996-98	MONTEREY OCM GOLD**	−5.3
1994-98	IDS PRECIOUS METALS A	−6.5
1989-98	FIDELITY SEL. GOLD	0.3

*Average annual, pretax
**Monterey Funds, 800-251-1970; or see Business Week Online

DATA: MORNINGSTAR INC.

But the subsequent years were not so spectacular. In fact, they were awful. Lexington Strategic Investments was still the leader of the pack in 1994, though it was up only 11.3 percent—the only gold fund to make money that year. By 1995, when the average precious metals fund earned a 1.4 percent return, it lost 14.7 percent. By 1996, it lost another 11 percent. And in 1997, the fund dropped 45.7 percent. U.S. Global Investors Gold Shares, also a hot shot in 1993, lost big chunks of its net asset value every year since. A dollar invested in U.S. Global Investors Gold Shares five years ago is now worth about 15 cents. Even the best fund for the last 10 years, Fidelity Select Gold, was barely profitable—0.3 percent a year average annual gain (Table 2-26).

Why would anyone invest in precious metals funds? For years, the conventional wisdom argued that every investor should place a small portion of his or her assets into gold or gold mutual funds, which mainly buy gold-mining stocks. Gold was seen as a hedge against inflation, a safe haven in times of international upheaval or economic strife. But the conventional wisdom hasn't seemed to work for quite some time. Gold traded for $370 right before Iraq's 1990 invasion of Kuwait. Ten weeks later, after oil prices had nearly doubled, gold sold at about the same price. For the third quarter of 1990, precious metals funds were the best-performing fund category, but they still returned only 4 percent. And for the year, precious metals funds plunged 23.6 percent. Nor did gold prices react much in August 1991, at the time of the abortive Soviet coup. And during the emerging market meltdowns in 1997 and early 1998, investors demanded U.S. dollars, not gold, and prices for the yellow metal remained stuck at or below $300 an ounce. So much for crisis protection.

An inflation hedge? Perhaps. But for many years real interest rates—that is, interest rates after inflation—have been high. An investor who put money in short-term fixed-income securities could earn a rate of return well in excess of the inflation rate. Compare that to owning gold bullion, which must be insured and stored while it produces no income to offset those out-of-pocket expenses.

Gold prices finally started to move up in 1993, from nearly $300 an ounce toward $400. This was the move that helped to spark the tremendous move in gold mutual funds, and that was a period when global inflation was relatively subdued. Since then, gold has rallied to the $400 level several times, but could never sustain it. By early 1997, the price was below $350, and by the end of the year, around $285. The new depressant on gold prices: another wave of gold sales by central banks. Even Switzerland, one of the most economically conservative nations in the world, is considering selling off about half its gold reserves.

The case for having a little money in gold funds is that it's nearly impossible to predict when they're going to zoom. Certainly, the gold market is so beaten up now that a small amount of good news could always spark a rebound. At the end of 1992, on the eve of their spectacular 1993 bull market, the gold funds had a little more than $2 billion in assets, less than half of 1 percent of all the money in equity mutual funds. Clearly, those who profited most in the gold rush of 1993 were investors who had a contrarian bent. They had invested in the doggiest of investments on the chance that the pendulum would swing back the other way.

The advantage of gold funds over gold coins is the mining companies' leverage: a little increase in the price of gold can increase their profits handsomely. Here's why. Suppose a mining company can produce gold at a cost of $325 an ounce, and gold sells at $350 an ounce. That's a profit of $25 an ounce. If gold goes to $375 an ounce, the company's cost is still $325, but the profit is $50 an ounce. That's a 100 percent increase in profits on a 7 percent increase in the price of gold (from $350 to $375). That's why, when gold prices are rising, many traders prefer to play the rally via gold-mining shares. Of course, the same principle works on the way down. If gold is falling, mining company profits can melt away quickly.

This sort of operating leverage is much the same reason that investors buy copper, forest product, or even oil stocks—an investment in a particular commodity market. Indeed, investors are starting to view gold stocks less as inflation plays and more as potential money-making vehicles, the same way they would approach other natural resources like oil, copper, or forest products. In 1996 Bre-X Minerals, a tiny Canadian company that reputedly struck it big in Indonesia, soared 300 percent—and was a major holding of many gold funds. But in 1997, Bre-X stock plunged as serious doubts were raised about its gold find, and regulators launched fraud investigations. But all the junior gold-mining stocks plunged as well, as investors lost faith in a broad swath of the industry.

The largest holdings of the gold funds are larger North American producers, such as Barrick Gold, Newmont Mining, and Placer Dome (Table 2-27). South African shares are no longer off-limits to many funds, as they were during the days of apartheid, but most of the companies there are high-cost producers and not very profitable in an era of low prices.

Putting a little money in precious metals funds is not a bad idea. Most diversified equity funds don't own any gold shares at all, so a precious metals fund helps your total portfolio diversification. And while they are the most volatile of equity funds, precious metals funds live a life of their own. The fluctuations in NAVs have little to do with the ups and downs of the Dow, the S&P 500, or any other stock market indicator. That attribute also improves a portfolio's diversification and lowers its overall risk. It's not easy to find gold funds that shine among the overall universe. But BUSINESS WEEK's category ratings now show SoGen Gold as the best of the precious metals funds. Of course, that's relative. It still lost an average 10 percent a year over the last five years.

TABLE 2-27

PRECIOUS METALS FUNDS

LARGEST HOLDINGS

Stock ▼	Percent of net assets ▼
BARRICK GOLD	7.85%
NEWMONT MINING	5.57
PLACER DOME	5.38
EURO-NEVADA MINING	4.80
FRANCO-NEVADA MINING	4.39
HOMESTAKE MINING	4.20
GETCHELL GOLD	3.89
STILLWATER MINING	3.74
ANGLOGOLD	3.67
NORMANDY MINING	3.01

DATA: MORNINGSTAR INC.

SPECIALTY FUNDS

Specialty funds are really nondiversified mutual funds. They may invest in dozens of companies, but they're all in the same industry or group of industries. When their underlying sectors do well, these funds rise to the top. For a few years, health-care funds led the performance derby. Then it was financial funds, precious metals, technology funds, and, now, real estate and financial funds. (We've separated precious metals from the other specialty funds because they have very different investment characteristics from most specialized portfolios.) Our specialty group also includes a catchall "unaligned" category, which includes such diverse and unrelated sectors as food and agriculture, environmental services, media, and retailing. They're all in the miscellaneous category because there aren't yet enough of any one of them (Table 2-28).

Investment advisers and mutual fund analysts often debate whether fund investors should use specialty funds. After all, if you choose a specialty fund, you are making a choice that's left to professional portfolio managers in the more diversified funds. Are you qualified to make that decision? It's a decision that's more typically made by investors who choose stocks for themselves.

Specialty funds are the middle ground between investing in funds and investing in stocks. In fact, in setting up the vast array of sector funds, Fidelity Investments designed the program to appeal to investors who might otherwise trade stocks. The sector funds are priced every hour during the trading day, and investors can buy or sell at the next hour's prices. (Most mutual funds are priced only after the close of trading, and transactions made before 4 p.m. are executed at the end of the day.)

Though many fund families have some specialty funds in their line-ups, none even approach Fidelity's large menu. For instance, not only is there a financial services fund, but there's a roster of single-industry funds within that: brokerage and investment management, insurance, regional banks, and home finance (savings and loans). There's a fairly broadly chartered technology fund, but Fidelity also manages more narrowly defined funds. Fidelity has separate funds for computers, software, and electronics as well.

If the fund managers are doing their jobs right, the specialty funds should have the same characteristics as the market sectors they represent. Natural resources funds primarily invest in energy and look the best when energy prices are

TABLE 2-28

SPECIALTY FUNDS
BEST RETURNS

Period	Fund	Total return*
COMMUNICATIONS		
1998	FLAG INVESTORS COMMUNICATIONS A	85.3%
1996-98	FLAG INVESTORS COMMUNICATIONS A	42.4
1994-98	FLAG INVESTORS COMMUNICATIONS A	29.2
1989-98	FLAG INVESTORS COMMUNICATIONS A	23.3
FINANCIAL		
1998	FIDELITY SELECT INSURANCE	20.3%
1996-98	FIDELITY SELECT BROKERAGE & INVMT. MGT.	33.8
1994-98	FIDELITY SELECT REGIONAL BANKS	26.6
1989-98	INVESCO FINANCIAL SERVICES	25.1
HEALTH		
1998	INVESCO HEALTH SERVICES	43.4%
1996-98	VANGUARD HEALTH CARE	30.0
1994-98	FIDELITY SELECT HEALTH CARE	30.5
1989-98	FIDELITY SELECT HEALTH CARE	26.4
NATURAL RESOURCES		
1998	AMERICAN GAS INDEX	5.3%
1996-98	AMERICAN GAS INDEX	16.4
1994-98	AMERICAN GAS INDEX	13.2
1989-98	FIDELITY ADVISOR NATURAL RESOURCES T	11.9
REAL ESTATE		
1998	ALPINE INTL. REAL ESTATE Y**	2.6%
1996-98	DELAWARE REIT A	17.7
1994-98	DAVIS REAL ESTATE A	13.0
1989-98	FIDELITY REAL ESTATE INVESTMENT	11.5
TECHNOLOGY		
1998	INTERNET**	196.1%
1996-98	DRESDNER RCM GLOBAL TECHNOLOGY	37.2
1994-98	FIDELITY SELECT ELECTRONICS	37.2
1989-98	FIDELITY SELECT ELECTRONICS	29.8
UNALIGNED		
1998	FIDELITY SELECT RETAILING	45.8%
1996-98	FIDELITY SELECT RETAILING	35.7
1994-98	FIDELITY SELECT RETAILING	21.6
1989-98	FIDELITY SELECT RETAILING	22.5
UTILITIES		
1998	FIDELITY SELECT UTILITIES GROWTH	43.1%
1996-98	FIDELITY SELECT UTILITIES GROWTH	27.6
1994-98	FIDELITY SELECT UTILITIES GROWTH	20.9
1989-98	FIDELITY SELECT UTILITIES GROWTH	18.5

*Average annual, pretax
**Alpine Funds, 888-785-5578; Internet Fund, 516-893-4200; or see Business Week Online

DATA: MORNINGSTAR INC.

rising. They're often considered a hedge against inflation, though they didn't look that way during 1994, when inflation was a concern in the financial markets. Utilities funds should be safe and boring, since they buy stocks to collect the dividends. But in 1994, they were anything but safe and boring. Rising interest rates and increased competition in the utility industry wreaked havoc on the utilities—and funds that invest in them. In 1997 and 1998, lower interest rates sent them climbing.

Specialty funds can only perform as well as the sectors in which they must invest. In 1997, all financial service funds soared, riding the crest of a takeover boom in banks, brokerage firms, and insurance. The companies also climbed on strong profits, the result of a strong economy and buoyant markets, and on lower interest rates. In 1998, the funds started out well, but plunged in the third quarter over concerns about the impact of bad Russian loans on banks and brokerage firms. But these specialty-fund performance returns swing around. Just look at the health-care sector. Funds specializing in health-care stocks were up 22.5 percent in 1990 and 78.3 percent in 1991. Then, the stocks and the funds took to their sickbeds. Health funds slid and earned only an 11.2 percent return in 1992 and 1.7 percent for all 1993. In the 1993–1997 period, an investor would have fared nearly as well in a diversified U.S. equity fund as in the average health-care fund. Are they worth the additional risks of sector investing?

Even within specialty funds, the strategies can vary. As you might expect, technology funds have a high portfolio turnover rate, about 188 percent, twice the turnover rate of the average equity fund. Franklin DynaTech, the only technology fund with A for a category rating, has a turnover rate of less than 10 percent—definitely a buy-and-hold investor. Fidelity Select Technology, on the other hand, is a broker's dream—a turnover rate of over 500 percent. (That means the $1 billion fund did $5 billion in trades last year.) In this sector, however, rapid-fire trading can pay off. The Fidelity fund's five-year average annual return is 28.8 percent; the Franklin fund's, 20.1 percent.

And not all stocks in all funds are pure tech stocks, either. T. Rowe Price Science & Technology Fund invests not only in the creators and producers of technology, but also in companies that employ technology to their benefit. For many years, one of its largest holdings was First Data, a provider of data processing services that relies heavily on the application of computer technology. Among the holdings at Franklin DynaTech are tech-users like Toys R Us and Estee Lauder. Then again, what successful company isn't a tech-user?

Then there are the Internet funds, a subset of the tech funds, which are the hottest categories in years. The fund with the highest return for 1998 was the Internet Fund—up 196.1 percent. That's nearly a triple. Of course, precious few investors actually enjoyed that return since the fund had less than $1 million in assets at the start of 1998. By the end, assets were over $60 million. It's no surprise that other Internet funds were among the year's best performers: Munder Net-Net A earned 98 percent, and WWW Internet Fund, 70.5 percent. There's no doubt that when the Internet stock bubble bursts, these funds will sink quickly—though not as much as many of the individual stocks.

Technology funds have all the hot companies, but tech stocks are not always hot. A few years ago, one of the best-performing specialty categories was real estate. In the 1995–1997 period, they were up an average 22.4 percent a year. But performance started to lag in the second half of 1997 and really sank in 1998, when the funds' returns were negative, down 16.2 percent.

Real estate funds invest mainly in real estate investment trusts (REITs), which are not unlike mutual funds. They pool investors' money to invest in real estate. Some REITs are diversified in the kind of property they buy, but others are specialized—shopping centers, multifamily housing, office buildings, or even nursing homes. Real estate funds may also invest in construction or homebuilding companies, but their principal holdings are REITs.

The real estate fund is one sort of specialty fund that investors could tuck away in their portfolios as a core holding. That's not because they always shoot out the light in performance. Obviously, they don't. But REIT funds really do add diversification to a portfolio. Most diversified equity funds do not invest in REITs, nor do index funds. (In 1996, Vanguard launched a REIT index fund.)

REITs represent a distinctly different asset class from stocks or bonds. Real estate is, of course, cyclical, but it does not have a high correlation with stocks. So a tumble in the stock market does not necessarily presage a fall in REITs. In fact, early in the summer of 1996, when the stock market was going down at a rapid pace, REITs were climbing.

REIT funds make good diversifiers for any portfolio.

The other striking characteristic of REITs and the funds that invest in them is that they are mainly income-oriented vehicles. As such, many fund investors would do well to use them in their tax-deferred retirement accounts rather than in taxable accounts where they'll produce taxable income. The difference between REITs and bonds is that REITs are not fixed-payment instruments. An economic boom that would cause interest rates to rise and bond prices to fall would probably also increase rental income, money that ultimately flows back to REIT owners. So REIT funds can be viewed as an inflation hedge for a fixed-income portfolio.

Whether it's technology funds or health-care funds or financial funds, one thing is clear. When specialty funds are on a hot streak, they attract "hot money." Many professional traders track sector-fund prices, just as they keep tabs on individual stocks, looking for the funds with "momentum." When they spot it, they can really pile into a fund. For instance, at the start of 1992, Fidelity Savings & Loan Fund (since renamed Fidelity Home Finance) had $10 million in assets—it was not even large enough to get into the Scoreboard. But the fund was up 15 percent in the first quarter, while the stock market was down 2.5 percent. By March 31, the fund totaled $134 million in assets. Five very profitable years later, the fund has $800 million in assets, suggesting this sort of fund has limited rather than widespread appeal. If it had wide appeal, the fund would have several billion dollars.

With these specialty funds, the more specific the investment mission, the more risk is in the fund. But there's obviously more potential for big gains. If you think health-care funds have excelled, look at the purely biotech funds. Oppenheimer Global Bio-Tech was up 121.1 percent in 1991, the single best fund for the year. (In 1994, Oppenheimer folded the fund and merged it with Oppenheimer Global Emerging Growth Fund.) Fidelity Select Biotechnology Fund was up over 40 percent in 1989 and 1990 and 99 percent in 1991. The same forces that can bring about big gains can take them away, too. Biotech funds were pummeled in 1992 and 1994 and just broke even in 1993. The Fidelity fund gained 49.1 percent in 1995, but even so, the five-year average annual return was a paltry 3.1 percent, about a third of the return earned by the average health-care fund.

Still, specialty funds can be a good alternative to trying to pick stocks in hard-to-understand industries. For instance, only a handful of biotechnology companies are real operating companies with marketable products and real sales. For those companies, the tools of financial analysis can work. But most biotechnology companies are research and development operations that don't make any money. To find the winners among those, an investor would have to have a Ph.D. in molecular biology to figure out which companies were pursuing the research that would be most likely to result in marketable drugs.

This more specialized service may come at a higher price. Specialized funds tend to have somewhat higher expenses, in part because they're smaller and in part because the fund companies can charge them. Fidelity Select portfolios charge combined loads and redemption fees of 3.75 percent. That's not onerous if it's a long-term investment, but it's a high price if you're looking to capitalize on a short-term move. Watch out. This is one area where fees and expenses can really get you.

INDEX AND SOCIAL INVESTING FUNDS

Index mutual funds have been around for over 20 years, but only in 1996 did they all of a sudden become hot properties. The Vanguard 500 Index, which tracks the Standard & Poor's 500-stock index, took in $8 billion in fresh cash, finished the year with $30.3 billion in assets, and climbed the ladder of size to become the third largest fund. By the end of 1998, the fund had $74.2 billion, second in size only to the Fidelity Magellan Fund and likely to surpass it sometime in 1999.

Indexing is a method for managing investments, not an investment style in itself. The Mutual Fund Scoreboard categorizes index funds like any other funds, by the nature of the portfolio. The Vanguard Index 500 is a large-cap blend fund; Vanguard Small Cap Index, which tracks the Russell 2000 index is a small-cap blend; American Century Global Gold, a precious metals fund (Table 2-29). Fund companies have become very creative in their approach to index funds, too. Vanguard, for instance, splits the S&P into growth and value stocks, and created the Vanguard Growth Index and the Vanguard Value Index. Vanguard also recently introduced mid-cap, small-cap value, and small-cap growth index funds. Small fund companies, such as ProFunds and Rydex, have added a new twist to the index fund—leverage. The leveraged funds use futures and options to amplify the fund's movements, usually 1.5 or 2 times the underlying index.

Index funds try to match, not beat, the market.

TABLE 2-29

INDEX AND SOCIAL INVESTING FUNDS

INDEX FUNDS

AARP U.S. STOCK INDEX*	PRINCIPAL PRES. PSE TECH 100*
AMERICAN CENT. GLOBAL GOLD	PROFUNDS BULL INV.*
AMERICAN CENT. GLOBAL NATURAL RESOURCES*	SCHWAB 1000 INV.
AMERICAN GAS INDEX	SCHWAB INTL. INDEX INV.
ARCH EQUITY INDEX INV. A*	SCHWAB S&P 500 INV.
ARK EQUITY INDEX A*	SCHWAB SMALL CAP INDEX INV.
ASM INDEX 30*	SEI INDEX S&P 500 INDEX E
BLACKROCK INDEX EQUITY INV. B*	SMITH BARNEY S&P 500 INDEX A*
BRIDGEWAY ULTRA-LARGE 35 INDEX*	SSGA S&P 500 INDEX
BRIDGEWAY ULTRA-SMALL INDEX*	STAGECOACH EQUITY INDEX A
BT INVESTMENT EQUITY 500 INDEX	STAR MARKET CAPITALIZATION C*
CALIFORNIA INVESTMENT S&P 500*	STI CLASSIC INTL. EQUITY INDEX*
CALIFORNIA INVESTMENT S&P MIDCAP INDEX*	STRONG DOW 30 VALUE*
CALIFORNIA INVESTMENT S&P SMALLCAP INDEX*	STRONG INDEX 500*
CITIZENS INDEX	T. ROWE PRICE EQUITY INDEX
DEVCAP SHARED RETURN*	TRANSAMERICA PREMIER INDEX INV.*
DFA INTL. SMALL COMPANY	U.S. GLOBAL INV. ALL-AMERICA EQ.*
DFA INTL. SMALL VALUE*	USAA S&P 500 INDEX
DOMINI SOCIAL EQUITY	VANGUARD 500 INDEX
DREYFUS INTL. STOCK INDEX*	VANGUARD BALANCED INDEX
DREYFUS MIDCAP INDEX	VANGUARD EMRG. MKT. STOCK INDEX
DREYFUS S&P 500 INDEX	VANGUARD EUROPEAN STOCK INDEX
DREYFUS SMALL CAP STOCK INDEX*	VANGUARD EXTEND. MKT. INDEX
EVERGREEN SEL. EQUITY INDEX*	VANGUARD GROWTH INDEX
FEDERATED MAX-CAP-INSTL.	VANGUARD MID CAP INDEX*
FEDERATED MID-CAP*	VANGUARD PACIFIC STOCK INDEX
FEDERATED MINI-CAP INSTL.*	VANGUARD REIT INDEX
FIDELITY SPARTAN EXTENDED MKT. INDEX*	VANGUARD SMALL CAP GROWTH INDEX*
FIDELITY SPARTAN INTL. INDEX*	VANGUARD SMALL CAP INDEX
FIDELITY SPARTAN MARKET INDEX	VANGUARD SMALL CAP VALUE INDEX*
FIDELITY SPARTAN TOTAL MKT. INDEX*	VANGUARD TOTAL STK. MKT. INDEX
FIRST AMERICAN EQUITY INDEX A*	VANGUARD VALUE INDEX
FIRSTAR EQUITY INDEX RET.*	VICTORY STOCK INDEX
FORUM EQUITY INDEX*	WACHOVIA EQUITY INDEX A*
GALAXY II LARGE CO. INDEX RET.	WEBS INDEX AUSTRALIA*
GALAXY II SMALL CO. INDEX RET.	WEBS INDEX AUSTRIA*
GALAXY II UTILITY INDEX RET.*	WEBS INDEX BELGIUM*
GATEWAY SMALL CAP INDEX*	WEBS INDEX CANADA*
GREEN CENTURY EQUITY*	WEBS INDEX FRANCE*
HARRIS INS. INDEX A*	WEBS INDEX GERMANY*
IDS SMALL COMPANY INDEX A	WEBS INDEX HONG KONG*
INVESCO S&P 500 INDEX II*	WEBS INDEX ITALY*
KENT INDEX EQUITY INVESTMENT*	WEBS INDEX JAPAN
MAINSTAY EQUITY INDEX A*	WEBS INDEX MALAYSIA (FREE)*
MERRILL LYNCH INTL. INDEX D*	WEBS INDEX MEXICO (FREE)*
MERRILL LYNCH S&P 500 INDEX D	WEBS INDEX NETHERLANDS*
MERRILL LYNCH SMALL CAP INDEX D*	WEBS INDEX SINGAPORE (FREE)*
MSDW S&P 500 INDEX B	WEBS INDEX SPAIN*
MUNDER INDEX 500 A*	WEBS INDEX SWEDEN*
NATIONS EQUITY-INDEX INV. A*	WEBS INDEX SWITZERLAND*
NORTHERN STOCK INDEX*	WEBS INDEX UNITED KINGDOM*
NORWEST ADVANTAGE INDEX I*	WILSHIRE TARGET LARGE GROWTH INV.*
ONE GROUP EQUITY INDEX B	WILSHIRE TARGET LARGE VALUE INV.*
ONE GROUP INTL. EQUITY INDEX A*	WILSHIRE TARGET SMALL GROWTH INV.*
PEGASUS EQUITY INDEX A	WILSHIRE TARGET SMALL VALUE INV.*

*For further information, see Business Week Online

DATA: MORNINGSTAR INC.

TABLE 2-29 *(Continued)*

INDEX AND SOCIAL INVESTING FUNDS

SOCIAL INVESTING FUNDS

AMANA GROWTH*	DREYFUS THIRD CENTURY
AQUINAS BALANCED*	GREEN CENTURY BALANCED*
AQUINAS EQUITY GROWTH*	GREEN CENTURY EQUITY*
AQUINAS EQUITY INCOME*	MEYERS PRIDE VALUE*
ARIEL APPRECIATION	MFS UNION STANDARD EQUITY A*
ARIEL GROWTH	MMA PRAXIS GROWTH*
BRIDGEWAY SOCIAL RESPONSIBILITY*	MMA PRAXIS INTERNATIONAL*
CALVERT CAPITAL ACCUMULATE A*	NEUBERGER BERMAN SOCIAL RESP.*
CALVERT SOCIAL INV. BALANCED A	NEW ALTERNATIVES*
CALVERT SOCIAL INV. EQUITY A*	NOAH*
CALVERT WORLD VALUE INTL. EQ. A	PARNASSUS
CATHOLIC VALUES EQUITY INDIV.*	PARNASSUS INCOME EQUITY*
CITIZENS EMERGING GROWTH*	PAX WORLD
CITIZENS GLOBAL EQUITY*	PAX WORLD GROWTH*
CITIZENS INDEX	RIGHTIME SOCIAL AWARENESS*
CRUELTY FREE VALUE*	SECURITY SOCIAL AWARENESS A*
DELAWARE SOCIAL AWARENESS A*	SMITH BARNEY CONCERT. ALLOC. SOC. A*
DEVCAP SHARED RETURN	TIMOTHY PLAN B*
DOMINI SOCIAL EQUITY	WOMEN'S EQUITY*

*For further information, see Business Week Online

DATA: MORNINGSTAR INC.

ProFunds UltraOTC, run to give its shareholders twice the return of the NASDAQ 100 index, more than met its goal in 1998 when it shot up 185.3 percent. But the leverage cuts both ways. Between February 1 through February 17, 1999, when the NASDAQ 100 slid 11.2 percent, this fund lost nearly 23 percent of its net asset value.

But most index funds are designed to replicate, rather than beat, the performance of a market index. Since they buy a predetermined list of stocks, there are no management decisions to be made. These funds are managed by computers and require little supervision.

Isn't accepting an index return the same as settling for just the average? Not at all. It's better than not beating the index. And every year many funds fail to beat the indexes. The Vanguard 500 Index, which copies the S&P 500, beat the average large-cap blend fund in the 1-, 3-, 5-, and 10-year periods ending in 1998. During the same periods, it also beat the average U.S. diversified fund and the average equity fund. Is it any wonder that index funds are so popular?

In part, the Vanguard Index 500's edge comes from low expenses. The Vanguard 500 fund has an expense ratio of 0.19, or 19 cents per $100. The average large-cap blend fund takes $1.24 per $100 in expenses. Right off the bat, the S&P index fund has more than 1 percentage point edge. But be forewarned. While all S&P 500 index funds have the same stocks, they don't all own the same return. Vanguard 500 has a five-year average annual total return of 24 percent. Fidelity Spartan Market Index and T. Rowe Price Equity Index, also S&P 500 funds, earned just 23.7 percent a year during the same period.

What accounts for the differences in returns? Expenses. Vanguard charges only the cost of running the funds; others charge higher rates. Until 1998, Fidelity charged about 0.45 percent in expenses, though it's since brought the expenses down to Vanguard's 0.19 percent. T. Rowe Price still charges 0.45, and Schwab, 0.38 percent, for their S&P 500 funds.

Index funds also have another advantage that works especially well in bull markets. They are always fully invested in stocks. In fact, one of an index fund manager's main responsibilities at the end of the day is to make sure the net new cash (inflows less outflows) is invested in the index stocks in all the right proportions. That's the only way to insure that all the fund shareholders' money is earning the index returns.

Conventional equity funds don't run fully invested. There's always 4 or 5 percent of their assets in cash, as it sometimes takes awhile to find places for the new money. This is especially a problem with value funds that are picky about where they put their money.

Of course, the main reason index funds look so good now is that the U.S. stock market has been in a bull market for over eight years. In a bear market, cash is a cushion against declining prices. Since index funds don't carry cash, there is no downside protection. If the S&P 500 were to undergo a serious correction, many investors—some of whom have come to think the S&P 500 is riskless—will have a shocking revelation about the dark side of index funds.

There's another reason index funds look so good right now. Index funds don't sell their winners, or their losers for that matter. But in a period when many of the biggest stocks just keep growing and growing, often to ridiculous prices, many conventional managers reduce or eliminate that stock. Indexers don't. By the same token, index funds don't sell losers either. But as losers melt away in value, they have less and less of an impact on the index anyway.

In theory, index funds have just average returns. In practice, of late, they are well above average. In 1998, about 17 percent of the funds in the BW Mutual Fund Scoreboard beat the S&P 500. Over the last five years, only 56 funds—or 4 percent of the funds in the BW Mutual Fund Scoreboard—have actually beaten the S&P 500, and just 36 beat the S&P 500 on an aftertax basis. Index funds, because they don't trade their portfolios, are tax-efficient investors. Because they have done so well in absolute performance, the indexers also have superior ratings. Indexers started to move onto BW's A-list in mid-1988, the result of their strong five-year total returns.

But fund analysts question whether all index funds have such an advantage over managed funds. The S&P 500 fund is successful because the market for big-cap U.S. stocks is very efficient. It's hard for portfolio managers and analysts to add value to an S&P-like fund. Away from the 500, though, markets are far less efficient, and smart stock picking can pay off. Thus, indexing may not be as good an idea in other investment categories, such as small-cap stocks or foreign markets.

In emerging markets, for instance, good stock picking should outperform an index. But Vanguard Emerging Markets Index usually trounces its competitors. For the three years ending in 1998, a difficult time for emerging markets, the Vanguard fund lost, on average, 7.6 percent a year. The average emerging markets fund lost 11.1 percent per year. How could the index beat the average fund? George U. Sauter, the chief of

Vanguard's index funds, says that while it's true that the smaller markets are less efficient, the trading and management costs are much higher. That means the cost of exploiting those inefficiencies wipes out any excess return from those investments.

Bear markets show the ugly side of indexing. Active managers can take some steps to mitigate losses or soften the impact of falling stock prices. Not so an index fund, which must remain fully invested and slavishly adhere to its pertinent index. That same Vanguard emerging markets index fund that did so well in the 1996–1998 period actually trailed its actively managed competitors in 1997. Vanguard International Pacific Stock Index has been a poor performer among the Asian funds for nearly all of the last 10 years because some 75 percent of it, like the Morgan Stanley Capital International Pacific Index, is invested in Japan. Most managed Pacific funds beat it by underplaying or ignoring Japanese stocks.

"Social investing" or "socially responsible" funds, like index funds, cut across a number of categories. The Dreyfus Third Century Fund is a large-cap growth fund; Parnassus Fund is small-cap value; and Pax World Fund, despite its name, is a domestic hybrid. The top-rated Domini Social Fund is both a social investing fund and an index fund. What characterizes these funds is not so much what they do, but what they don't do: They don't invest in defense, tobacco, alcohol, or gaming industries.

And that's not all. Many of these funds screen potential investments for their labor relations, minority employment practices, attitudes toward women, diversity management, and even corporate philanthropy. Companies with questionable track records are also excluded. The same principles carry over to fixed-income investments as well. Pax World won't even invest in U.S. Treasury bonds because the proceeds could be used for military purposes.

In recent years, some of the social investing funds have done well. Pax World and Dreyfus Third Century were top-rated in the early 1990s. That doesn't mean social investing is a superior method of stock picking. It's just that in the 1987–1991 period, drug and health-care companies, which are naturals for social investing funds, performed much better than steel and oil companies, which are much less likely to be part of social investing funds.

Amy Domini, founder of the Domini Social Fund, says the strict screens companies must

"Social investing" funds cut across many categories.

pass before they're approved for the fund result in buying companies with more visionary management. Not surprisingly, the fund's investment criteria tend to pick up a lot of technology companies, which are hot. The same screening process tends to downplay companies in rust bucket industries, which are not.

In recent years, the returns for social investing funds have been all over the lot, suggesting it's more a case of stock selection than social philosophy. Dreyfus Third Century has performed reasonably well in recent years, but Parnassus Fund has not. It earns a D in overall rating and an F when compared to the small-cap value funds. Indeed, social investing screens were never meant to enhance returns, but to assure investors who care about it that their money would not be used to support industries or practices they don't like.

❙ Bond Funds

When interest rates go up, bond prices go down. When rates decline, bond prices shoot up. Understand that, and you're well on your way to understanding bond, or fixed-income, mutual funds.

Look at Table 2-30. Consider a bond that pays a 6 percent coupon and matures in 10 years. If rates go down 1 percentage point to 5 percent, the price of the bond climbs to 7.79 percent. Should rates rise by a like amount, the bond declines 7.11 percent in value. As you can see from the table, the longer the maturity, the more sensitive the bond is to changes in interest rates. If rates on a 30-year bond were to rise 1 percentage point, the bond would drop 12.47 percent in price. The five-year bond would only be nicked 4.16 percent.

The relationship between interest rates and bond prices is one of the most fundamental in all of finance. Yet how many of the millions of investors who flocked into bond funds in the early 1990s understand that? For instance, an investor who purchased Vanguard Long-Term U.S. Treasury Portfolio at the beginning of October 1993 suffered a 17 percent decline in net asset value over the next year. That was softened somewhat by the fund's 7 percent yield, but the bottom line was ugly—a –10 percent total return. Investors may not like it, but will accept that kind of behavior from stocks. But from bonds?

TABLE 2-30

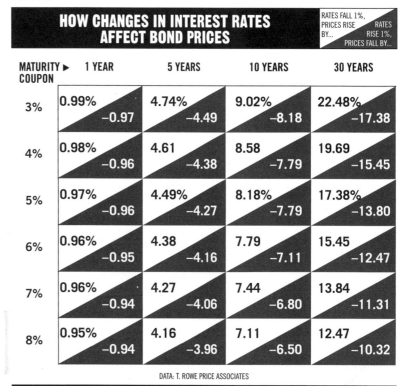

HOW CHANGES IN INTEREST RATES AFFECT BOND PRICES

RATES FALL 1%, PRICES RISE BY... / RATES RISE 1%, PRICES FALL BY...

MATURITY ▶ COUPON	1 YEAR	5 YEARS	10 YEARS	30 YEARS
3%	0.99% / −0.97	4.74% / −4.49	9.02% / −8.18	22.48% / −17.38
4%	0.98% / −0.96	4.61 / −4.38	8.58 / −7.79	19.69 / −15.45
5%	0.97% / −0.96	4.49% / −4.27	8.18% / −7.79	17.38% / −13.80
6%	0.96% / −0.95	4.38 / −4.16	7.79 / −7.11	15.45 / −12.47
7%	0.96% / −0.94	4.27 / −4.06	7.44 / −6.80	13.84 / −11.31
8%	0.95% / −0.94	4.16 / −3.96	7.11 / −6.50	12.47 / −10.32

DATA: T. ROWE PRICE ASSOCIATES

If understanding the inverse relationship between interest rates and bond prices (and bond fund NAVs) isn't hard enough, bond-fund investors also have to grapple with the "D" word, derivatives. These have been around for years but hit the headlines during 1994 when their quickly sinking prices caused big trouble for some corporations, public investment funds, and, yes, a few mutual funds.

Simply put, a derivative is a financial instrument the value of which is derived from some other source. Take, for instance, a "structured note" with an interest payment tied to the price of copper. To price the note you have to know the interest-rate formula, and that's dependent on the price of copper. If the price of copper goes up, so will the interest payments and the price an investor would pay for the note. If copper slides, so will the value of the note.

Derivatives can be used to speculate in stocks, bonds, or commodity-market movements. Options limit the potential loss; futures do not. Most derivatives can be used in a way to hedge portfolio risk. Selling Treasury bond futures, for instance, can protect a bond-fund portfolio from losses related to rising interest rates.

The problem with derivatives comes when they're used to speculate on the direction of the financial markets rather than to hedge against adverse moves—and the portfolio manager's bet turns out wrong. If the derivative is leveraged, too, the loss is further magnified.

The leverage might work like this. During the three years of falling interest rates, many large investors—mutual funds included—bought "inverse floaters," bonds structured so that their interest payments actually increased as rates went down. But because of the way these bonds were engineered, the inverse floater's interest rate may go up 3 or 4 percentage points for every 1 percentage point drop in the regular rate. Naturally, as short-term rates dropped 4 percentage points over the period, some of these bonds were paying out very juicy yields—sometimes in excess of 20 percent. But the flip side is that when interest rates started to rise—as they did in 1994—the bond's interest payments started to decline 3 or 4 percentage points for every percentage point the regular rates went up. Since such securities are valued based on their interest payments, prices for such leveraged derivatives just melted away.

The derivative debacle of 1994 underscored another problem. Many of the derivatives created in the early 1990s from mortgage-backed securities did not behave as the financial engineers' computers had predicted. For instance, Piper Jaffray Institutional Government Income Fund and Managers Intermediate Mortgage Fund—both run by Piper's Worth Bruntjen—plunged and racked up a 25 percent decline in total return in 1994's first quarter. The two funds, chock full of mortgage-backed derivatives, fell, in part, because many of the unusual securities did not behave as expected. For instance, Bruntjen's financial models predicted that the interest-only and principal-only securities would neutralize each other. If one went down, the other would go up in value. Instead, in the chaotic, declining market, both sorts of securities went down in price. The Piper fund ended the year with a –28.8 percent total return, the Managers fund, nearly as bad, went down 25 percent.

Computers can "value" a security, but at the end of the day, when a mutual fund has to price its portfolio, what counts is the market price. When the bond market began to sink, market prices were far below theoretical prices. That's because there were hordes of investors who wanted to unload these derivative securities, but scant few buyers willing to buy them. Losses were so bad in the PaineWebber Short-Term U.S. Government Fund that to preserve its credibility with investors and brokers, Paine Webber spent some $268 million to buy unmarketable securities—known on the Street as "kitchen sink" bonds—from the fund. That, incidentally, did not make the shareholders whole, but simply eased some of their losses. For the year, the fund had a –4.9 percent total return.

What is so daunting to bond-fund investors is that even if they do their homework and study the portfolio, it's hard to spot the derivatives. No portfolio manager is going to point to a security—often the underlying issuer is a government-affiliated issuer like Fannie Mae or Freddie Mac—and say, "This is a derivative security, the price of which can be extremely volatile under rapidly changing market conditions." Usually, investors will look at the credit quality of the issue—which is excellent with these two issuers—and figure the investment is secure. With these derivatives, there's no question that in the end they will pay off at maturity. But the problem is that a portfolio manager may have paid a price based on a five-year payback. However, after rates rose, the estimated payback period might have shot up to 25 years. So the security takes a double price hit because it's now a longer maturity and it's paying a less-than-market interest rate.

TABLE 2-31

WHAT TO ASK A MUTUAL FUND MANAGER ABOUT DERIVATIVES

What percentage of the fund is in derivatives?
Be wary if it's any more than five percent. Most of the funds that ran into trouble had anywhere from 15 to 40 percent.

How are the derivatives used?
Ideally, they're used for hedging. Be wary if the fund is using them to juice the yield. Watch out if interest-only (IO) and principal-only (PO) derivatives are paired off and declared to be perfectly hedged. Experience shows that may not be the case.

Is anyone paying attention to what the fund manager is doing?
The fund management company and the fund's board of directors should be aware of what the portfolio manager is doing and monitoring the use of derivatives.

How are the derivatives priced?
The fund should be using an impartial, third-party service to price derivative securities for purposes of calculating the day's net asset value.

How have the derivatives benefited or hurt the fund in the past?
If the fund hasn't used them before, you might avoid that fund. Do you want the fund manager to get his education in derivatives using your money?

DATA: AMERICAN CENTURY BENHAM FUNDS, BUSINESS WEEK

Of course the derivative minefield can be treacherous for an investor who, until a few years ago, kept most of his or her money in the bank. Fortunately, most bond funds do not—and never have—used the exotic derivatives. But to be sure, Randall Merk of American Century Funds suggests that an investor quiz the broker or fund's sales agent about the use of derivatives in the fund (Table 2-31).

For all the brouhaha over derivatives, most bond funds don't invest in derivatives and, in 1994 and 1996, lost money the old-fashioned way. Interest rates rose, and the price of the bonds went down accordingly. How much they declined depended on the average maturity of the portfolio, a figure that you can find in the BUSINESS WEEK Mutual Fund Scoreboard. But you can also obtain that figure from bond-fund shareholder reports, or just by calling the fund company. The average maturity is nothing more than the weighted average of the maturities of all the bonds held by the fund. And the maturity of the bond is merely the number of years left until the bond will be redeemed by its issuer for its full principal value.

Maturity is a revealing piece of information. The longer the maturity, the more sensitive the bond prices are to changes in interest rates. And buying the golden credit of the U.S. Treasury is no safe haven from fluctuating bond prices. U.S. Treasury bonds, in fact, are considered to have no credit risk, so their values are solely a function of the changes in rates. (High-yield, or junk bond, funds are also affected by interest rates, but less so. When the economy is strong, corporate cash flows increase, and so does the ability for companies to pay their debt. So high-yield bonds usually take a little less of a hit from rising rates than do highly rated investment grade bonds.)

As a rule, the net asset value of a fund comprised of long-term bonds will fluctuate more than a fund of intermediate-term bonds. And a short-term bond fund is the least volatile of the three. Table 2-32, for instance, which comes from the Vanguard Group, sums up how changes in interest rates would affect some of its bond funds. In general, short-term funds like the Vanguard Short-Term Corporate Bond Portfolio keep their average maturities below 3 years; intermediate funds like the Vanguard Total Bond Market Index fund, in the 3- to 10-year range; long-term funds have maturities over 10 years; and many, like the Vanguard Long-Term U.S. Treasury Bond Portfolio, keep the average in the 20- to 25-year range.

TABLE 2-32

HOW INTEREST RATES AFFECT BOND FUNDS

VANGUARD PORTFOLIO ▼	AVERAGE MATURITY ▼	EST. IMPACT OF INTEREST RATE CHANGE ON NET ASSET VALUE			
		−1% ▼	−2% ▼	+1% ▼	+2% ▼
SHORT-TERM CORPORATE BOND	2.7 yrs.	2.4%	4.8%	−2.3%	−4.4%
TOTAL BOND MARKET INDEX	8.8 yrs.	4.3	8.4	−4.5	−9.2
LONG-TERM U.S. TREASURY	20.6 yrs.	11.7	25.3	−9.9	−18.1

DATA: VANGUARD GROUP OF INVESTMENT COS.

Maturity is a good measure of the potential price volatility of a government or general bond fund. But it doesn't tell the whole story. Two bonds, or bond funds, with the same maturity may not necessarily have the same duration, and as such they won't react to interest rate changes in the same way. Bond fund managers pay close attention to duration in running their funds, but the concept is not well-understood by lay investors. Most bond fund managers will give shareholders information on yields and maturities in their funds, but ask a shareholder representative about duration and you might just stump them.

The calculation of duration is complex, but the principle behind it is not. Duration looks at a bond as a series of cash payments (interest payments and the bond redemption at maturity are considered payments). The duration formula calculates a "present value" for each payment, adds them up, and estimates how long it would take the bondholder to recover his or her entire investment in today's dollars.

Suppose Bond Fund A and Bond Fund B have portfolio maturities of 15 years and they yield 6 percent. Fund A owns bonds issued when rates were lower: they have lower interest payments and they sell at a discount to their redemption value, say 90 cents on the dollar. Fund B has bonds that were issued when rates were higher and now sell for 110 cents on the dollar. Fund A has the higher duration because, since it has lower cash payments, it will take longer for the investor to recover his or her money. Fund B, whose bonds pay out more income, has a lower duration.

Is low duration better than high? That depends on your market outlook. When interest rates are falling, high duration bonds and bond funds will do better. The lower interest rate gives all the future cash flows a higher present value. When rates are rising, lower duration is less vulnerable to loss.

Sometimes investors who worry a lot about fluctuations in net asset value choose to keep their money in short-term bond funds or stick with money-market funds. In a money-market fund the principal is steady, but the yield, or interest rate, is very volatile. That's just the opposite of the long-term fund, where the NAV can be volatile, but the interest is steadier. If you depend on your investments to generate a certain amount of income, you will need to use intermediate- or long-term funds. The returns from shorter-term funds may be too unpredictable.

When investing in bond funds, it's also important to note the difference between owning, say, a bond fund and owning bonds directly. Most bonds pay interest twice a year, at predetermined dates and at a predetermined amount. A 20-year, $1000 bond with a 7 percent interest rate will make a $35 payment every six months for the next 20 years. That's not the case with a managed bond fund.

Most bond funds make an income distribution monthly, and it may or may not be the same every month. The funds don't earn the same amount of money every month because they rarely have the interest coming in 12 equal payments. And many bond funds just pass on whatever they've earned during the month, after taking out fund expenses.

But some funds have shareholders that take the income in cash rather than reinvest it. And many of those shareholders like steady payments. In those cases, the fund managers attempt to smooth out the income distributions and pay a set amount. Suppose the fund managers settle on a distribution rate of 10 cents per share per month, which may be reasonable given the interest earnings on the portfolio. Some months the fund earns more, some months less, but on average, the fund can afford to pay out $1.20 over the year.

Now suppose interest rates fall. Thousands of new shareholders are buying into the fund because they heard about the 10 cents per share per month distribution. But the fund can't invest the new money at as high a rate as before, and the earnings of the fund drop. Inevitably, the income distribution must drop too. A mutual fund must pay out its earnings, but it cannot pay what it doesn't earn. If, in a period of falling interest rates, someone tries to sell you a bond fund with an unusually high monthly payment, beware. The

distribution may not be sustainable—or the fund is making the payment out of capital, not income. If that's the case, the fund is chipping away at its net asset value.

This loss of net asset value can be significant. To test just how much, the analysts at Morningstar Inc. looked at the change in fund NAVs for 181 government and high-quality corporate bond funds from November 1, 1986 to September 30, 1994. The significance of those two dates is that the interest-rate environments at the two points were nearly identical, with the long-term interest rate on U.S. government bonds at about 8 percent. If bond funds behaved like bonds, the net asset values in 1994 should have been around the same as in 1986.

But that was not the case at all. The average fund was down 7.6 percent, and with 14 funds, the NAV loss exceeded 15 percent. The reason, concluded Morningstar, was that the funds were stretching to pay the highest possible yields. And in doing that, they emphasized premium bonds—those are bonds whose interest payments were set when rates were higher. So a 20-year government bond with an 11.25 percent coupon will, in a period when a new bond with the same maturity fetches about 8 percent, sell at a "premium"—in this case, $1294 for a bond with a $1000 face value. Even so, the bond pays $112.50 a year, and even on a $1294 investment, that's an 8.7 percent current yield ($112.50 divided by $1294). But here's the catch: Every year, the value of the bond will decline as it gets closer to maturity. So the yield to maturity is much closer to 8 percent—the current rate of interest.

The high-coupon strategy allows a higher current payout, and that's very important to bond funds that are sold by brokers and salespersons, because, as they say in the business, yield sells. Those same bond funds often have much higher than average expenses and so must seek higher yields to be able to pay them and also provide their shareholders a competitive rate of return. Some portfolio managers defend the practice, especially if it has delivered a good total return.

A fund that overachieves on the income side may be okay if it's in an individual retirement account or other tax-sheltered plan. But it doesn't make much sense for taxpaying investors. The interest is taxable in the year it's paid and at ordinary income tax rates. If the high-yield strategy has also delivered capital losses (remember the average 7.6 percent NAV loss over eight years), investors will eventually be able to deduct them. But the future tax sav-

Bond funds are creatures of interest rates.

ings from long-term capital losses will be worth far less than the current tax bite from the higher-yield funds.

There's another major difference between direct ownership of bonds and owning shares in a bond fund. If you own a 10-year bond, you know that next year it will be a 9-year bond; in 2 years, an 8-year; and so forth. In 10 years, it will mature. Though interest rates may go up and down in the interim, the maturity of your portfolio of bonds gets shorter every year. The price volatility should decrease with the shortening of the portfolio's maturity. Bond funds, on the other hand, never mature. If a fund's policy is to keep its maturity around 10 years, it will keep trading the bonds in the portfolio to do just that. Investors can't shorten their maturities without switching to another fund. And that could trigger capital gains taxes, even if the investments are in municipal bond funds.

The basic relationship between average maturity and volatility of bond funds holds true no matter whether your fund is taxable or tax-free, government or corporate. The net asset values of funds that invest in U.S. government securities are almost entirely dependent on interest rate movements.

The creditworthiness of the issuer comes into play—but in a small way—with investment-grade corporate and municipal bonds. Investment-grade corporate and municipal bonds are those rated AAA, AA, A, or BBB by Standard & Poor's, or Aaa, Aa, A, or Baa by Moody's Investor Services (Table 2-33).

Anything less than investment grade is "junk" debt, more charitably known as "high-yield" debt. The junk segment of the bond market is where credit considerations may even overwhelm interest rate movements in the pricing of securities. The highest ratings in the junk sector, sometimes also referred to by the oxymoron "quality junk," are BB and B. Some of the quality junk companies are formerly blue-chips that have taken on enormous amounts of debt in leveraged buyouts, takeovers, or other financial restructurings. Then there's CCC and on down to D for default, or bonds no longer making interest payments. That would include the bonds of companies in bankruptcy.

Since interest rates are the driving force in the bond market, the variations in returns from bond funds are not as dramatic as those from equities. Take, for instance, the municipal bond funds. During 1994, the single worst year in the bond market in 60 years, the best muni fund delivered

TABLE 2-33

A GUIDE TO BOND CREDIT RATINGS

RATING		
S&P	**MOODY'S**	
AAA	Aaa	BellSouth, Exxon, and General Electric are a few of the dwindling number of borrowers in this very exclusive club.
AA	Aa	Here's where you'll find AT&T and many other phone companies. Also Coca-Cola, McDonald's, and Wal-Mart Stores.
A	A	The quality is still high. Among the issuers are Ford Motor, General Motors, IBM, and J.C. Penney.
BBB	Baa	The lowest rating a bond can receive and still be considered an investment-grade security.
BB	Ba	The highest ranking for junk bonds, sometimes known by the oxymoron, "quality junk."
B	B	Many highly leveraged companies are in this category, which suggests some doubt about borrower's ability to pay.
CCC	Caa	"Currently vulnerable," company's ability to pay is subject to current business conditions.
CC	Ca	Just another rung down the credit ladder, with increasing possibility for default.
C	C	The pits. At Moody's this means default.
D	na	Interest and/or principal is in arrears.

DATA: BUSINESS WEEK

a total return of 2.4 percent; the worst, –20.4 percent. That's a range of nearly 23 percentage points. By contrast, equity funds are far more heterogeneous. Interest rates, though they play a role, are only one of many fundamental forces that affect stocks. Returns from equity funds have a much greater variation. During 1994, the best equity fund delivered a 35.3 percent return; the worst, –50.3 percent—a range of nearly 86 percentage points.

The homogeneity in bond-fund returns is even more apparent when you look at funds with similar goals. True, Vanguard Long-Term U.S. Treasury Portfolio, with an average maturity of 20.6 years, is going to get nailed if interest rates rise.

But so will the net asset values of all long-term government bond funds.

So, in a sense, bond funds are much more targeted in their mission than equity funds. Portfolio managers for equity funds typically have far more choice of what stocks to invest in than bond fund managers have choice of bonds. And even in declining stock markets, there are always a few industries or companies that will run counter to the trend. A dramatic breakthrough with a genetically engineered drug will send a biotechnology stock climbing, no matter what's happening to the Dow Jones industrial average. Find enough of the winners and equity fund managers can still buck a downtrend.

But bond fund managers work from a pool of securities that are far more homogeneous. If you manage the Merrill Lynch Federal Securities Fund, you have to invest in U.S. government debt or government-backed debt. How different are the results going to be from other government bond funds?

Bonds and bond funds entail some other risks as well. First, there's call risk. Most corporate and municipal bonds give the issuer the right to redeem the bonds or "call" them after about 5 years in the case of corporates, 10 in the case of long-term municipal bonds. If interest rates have dropped by the time a bond becomes callable, issuers will call the bonds and refinance them at a lower rate. (It's basically the same idea as refinancing your home mortgage to take advantage of lower interest rates.)

Calls can be bad news for bondholders. True, the bondholders collect a premium for their bonds: The issuer may pay $1030 or $1050 for a $1000 bond. But that's small consolation to the bondholders who will have to reinvest the proceeds at a lower rate of interest. A mutual fund with a large number of callable bonds might find itself in that quandary. Part of a bond fund manager's job is to steer around such obstacles. One way around the call problem is to buy bonds whose coupons are so low that they're unlikely to be called. The easiest solution, of course, is U.S. government bonds, which cannot be called.

Whether or not a bond is callable, the bond or bond-fund investor also faces reinvestment risk. Remember, a bond provides the investor a series of interest payments over a set number of years, and the reinvestment of that money is part of the total return from investing in bonds. (If you take the money out when it's paid, there is no reinvestment.) The risk in reinvestment risk is that rates will decline over the life of the bond, and the

cash from the periodic interest payments will be reinvested at lower and lower rates. The antidote to reinvestment risk is to invest in zero coupon bonds. These bonds don't pay interest. Instead they are sold at discount to face value. The difference between the purchase price and the maturity value is the interest. Since there is no cash to reinvest, there is no reinvestment risk.

Another sort of risk is "event risk." There's not too much heard about it nowadays, but it was big back in the 1980s. Event risk was the danger that an investment grade bond would turn into a lower quality bond through an event like a hostile takeover or a management-led leveraged buyout.

In trying to understand bond funds, it helps to think of them as similar to specialty or sector funds found among equity mutual funds. Diversified equity funds have wide latitude in what they can invest in. Specialty funds target particular investments. Bond funds tend to specialize in a certain sector, like a long-term government securities fund or a short-term municipal fund. This specialization puts more responsibility on the investor. If you choose to invest in a long-term bond fund and interest rates shoot up, there isn't much the portfolio manager can do to keep the NAV from falling. The best he or she can do is try to contain the damage.

What's also important to remember when looking at bond funds is the difference between a fund's yield and its total return. Total return includes the yield plus or minus changes in net asset value. Suppose a fund has a 12 percent yield but only a 2 percent total return. You can surmise that the fund lost 10 percent of its asset value during the year. Likewise, in an up market, a fund's total return should exceed the yield owing to an upturn in bond prices. If you're comparing bond funds, be sure to compare yields with yields and total returns with total returns.

Given these caveats, let's look at categories of bond funds in the BUSINESS WEEK Mutual Fund Scoreboard. They're organized by maturity as well as by the issuers of the bonds in the portfolio. The funds in the general bond category mainly invest in investment-grade and government debt. We break them down into four groups by maturity: long, intermediate, short, and ultrashort. U.S. government bond funds are classified as long, intermediate, or short. Among the municipal bond funds, there's one short-term category. Long-term and intermediate-term municipal funds are divided into national (with bonds from all across the country) and single-state (with bonds from a single state, usually of interest only to taxpayers of that state). There are enough state-specific funds for California and New York that we have intermediate-term and long-term categories for them.

The more specialized categories are largely the same as before: high-yield, convertibles, and multisector. International bond funds cover bonds issued in the economically developed nations, while the new emerging markets bond category takes in the bonds of the emerging economies like Mexico, Brazil, Taiwan, and China.

As with the equity funds, the new categories are meant to sort the funds into groups by the way they invest, not necessarily what they say about themselves. As such, you will find funds that, judged by their names, seem to be in the wrong category. For instance, Strong Government Securities is in the general bond intermediate category because it fails to meet the intermediate government fund hurdle of having at least 80 percent of the portfolio in government securities. Despite its name, Fidelity Intermediate Bond Fund falls in the short-term category. That's because its average duration is less than the 3.5 year minimum for intermediate funds.

LONG-TERM FUNDS (GEN.)

If you choose to invest in a general long-term bond fund, you're probably putting your money into one of the most volatile sorts of bond funds. Only long-term government funds are more risky. The risk here, of course, is not credit risk, which comes to mind when most people think about borrowers and lenders. It's interest-rate or market risk, the chance that the fund's net asset value will slide around with fluctuations in interest rates. Funds in this category have an average maturity of 10 years and an average duration of more than 6 years. Roughly speaking, the NAV of a fund whose bonds have an average duration of 6 years will fall 6 percent for a 1 percentage point rise in interest rates, and rise 6 percent for a 1 percentage point decline. The average duration for the funds in this category is 7.8 years and the average maturity is 13.7 years, according to Morningstar, Inc.

That said, why do investors choose these funds? In general, the longer the maturity of a bond, the higher the interest rate. That's one of the underlying principles of investing in bonds. Indeed, though it does not happen every year, over the last five years, the average long-term bond fund topped the intermediates and short-terms.

These funds certainly maintain a high credit quality, so they should hold up relatively well in an economic slowdown or recession. Better than one-quarter of their holdings are U.S. government or government-backed securities. Another sort of blue-chip investment is "sovereign" bonds, or dollar bonds issued by foreign governments with high credit ratings and interest payments in dollars. Only about 10 percent of the holdings are below investment grade. On the other hand, the ability of a general bond fund to dabble in the lower-quality issues can help prop up a fund's results when interest rates are rising.

The short-term performance leader in this category is Vanguard Long-Term Bond Index, up 12.0 percent in 1998 (Table 2-34). The longer-term leader is Vanguard Preferred Stock. Why is a preferred stock fund here? Preferred stocks have higher dividends than common. In fact, like a bond, the dividends are fixed. Unlike a bond, most preferred stocks are issued without a redemption date, though with a call. That gives the stocks characteristics more like bonds than other equities. So Morningstar analysts put this fund in the long-term bond category, where it leads the one-, three-, and five-year periods.

If you wanted a pure long-term bond fund, a good choice would be Invesco Select Income, one of two long-term funds with an A category rating. The Invesco fund also rates an A in the overall bond fund ratings, not an easy task for a bond fund with a long maturity.

Invesco's Jerry Paul keeps the fund's duration shorter than most long-term funds. He prefers to make money through good credit research and savvy trading rather than betting on interest rates. In 1997, for instance, he scored big with utility bonds as many beleaguered electric utility companies worked to improve their finances. Paul also uses his expertise in the high-yield market to the extent he can without compromising the fund's credit standards. Paul manages the Invesco High-Yield Fund as well.

TABLE 2-34

LONG-TERM FUNDS (GEN.)
BEST RETURNS

Period	Fund	Total return*
1998	VANGUARD LONG-TERM BOND INDEX	12.0%
1996-98	VANGUARD PREFERRED STOCK	9.3
1994-98	VANGUARD PREFERRED STOCK	8.7
1989-98	VANGUARD PREFERRED STOCK	11.0

*Average annual, pretax   DATA: MORNINGSTAR INC.

INTERMEDIATE-TERM FUNDS (GEN.)

The general corporate intermediate bond fund category is a broad one, encompassing a wide variety of bond-picking investment styles. What ties these funds together is their focus on a portfolio with an investment-grade credit rating, an average maturity between 4 and 10 years, and average duration of between 3.5 and 6 years. Those duration figures give you a way to assess risk. Simply put, an intermediate fund with an average duration of 5 years has half the interest rate sensitivity as one with a 10-year duration. Since intermediate funds generate yields that are 80 to 90 percent those of the long-term funds, its no wonder that many more investors opt for intermediate maturities. You get most of the yield with much less of the risk.

Intermediate funds don't usually make big bets. Their portfolios tend to revolve around a benchmark, the Lehman Brothers Aggregate Bond Index. That index has a duration of around 5 years, so the portfolio managers who really expect a fall in rates might buy longer-term, higher-yield bonds in order to push their duration out to 6 years. Those who anticipate higher rates might sell longer-term bonds in order to shorten the maturity to 4.5 or even 4 years.

Judging these funds by their largest holdings might have suggested they were government and government-guaranteed bond funds. Prior to 1998, these funds gravitated to government issues because, after a long economic expansion, the yield on investment-grade corporate debt was not much greater than that of governments. In such situations, bond managers might say corporates are "rich" and governments "cheap." What that means is that investors can switch into Treasuries—which have no credit risk—from corporates, without having to give up much yield in return. In a recession, when investors fear corporations may not have the means to pay their debts, that gap is much wider.

In 1998, when the markets went into a spin, investors panicked and feared recession. The demand for governments was high, and these funds, for the most part, already owned plenty of them. At that point, the difference in yields between government and corporate bonds (in bond parlance, they're quality spreads) widened. Many bond managers track these yield differen-tials between many kinds of bonds and often make trades when the historical relationship gets out of whack. In the bond fund world, a manager's compensation can depend on beating the next guy or an index by a couple of one-hundredths of a percentage point. In that context, those trades can be worthwhile.

Strong Corporate Bond Fund, the fund with the highest returns over the last five-year period, rarely gets far away from its duration benchmark (Table 2-35). Instead, the managers add value to the portfolio by paying close attention to those differentials between sectors of the bond market and even unusual gaps between individual issuers. This results in perhaps three times the amount of trading that takes place in the average intermediate fund, but it's been profitable trading nonetheless. The fund earns an A category rating when compared to other intermediate funds.

There's a big line-up of intermediate funds, and there are plenty of others with A category ratings. Take a look at PIMCO Total Return Institutional, PIMCO Total Return III Institutional, and Harbor Bond. They all have A category ratings and are managed by William H. Gross, the chief fixed-income investment officer for Pacific Investment Management Co. Gross, who's been called the Peter Lynch of bonds, has an excellent long-term record. His modus operandi is to move money around the bond market, looking to exploit pricing inefficiencies. The PIMCO institutional funds have the longest track records, but investors buying these funds for the first time now will probably have to buy one of the retail shares classes. (They used to be available in retail-sized pieces through Charles Schwab & Co.) They are now load funds. But Harbor Bond is a no-load with an investment strategy that's the same as PIMCO Total Return.

If you don't want to worry about managers making the right call, this category also includes the Vanguard Total Bond Market Index Portfolio. This fund is managed to replicate the return of the Lehman Bros. Aggregate Bond Index. A bond index fund is a little different than an equity

TABLE 2-35

INTERMEDIATE-TERM FUNDS (GEN.)

BEST RETURNS

Period ▼	Fund ▼	Total return* ▼
1998	PACIFIC ADVISORS INCOME A**	12.1%
1996-98	DREYFUS LIFETIME INCOME R	10.4
1994-98	STRONG CORPORATE BOND	9.4
1989-98	IDEX INCOME PLUS A	10.1

*Average annual, pretax
**Pacific Advisors Funds, 800-989-6693; or see Business Week Online
DATA: MORNINGSTAR INC.

index. While an equity index will buy every one of the stocks in the S&P 500, the bond funds can't. Many of the bonds are locked up and never trade. Instead, the bond index owns about 3100 of the more than 4000 issues in the index. But the fund's correlation with the index is 99 percent.

Indexed bond funds have not caught on in the bond market as in the equity market. Part of the reason is that investors just aren't interested in bond funds these days. The other reason, perhaps, is that with bond funds, people think more about yield than total return, and index funds are total return plays. Still, the numbers are impressive. For the last one-, three-, and five-year periods, the Vanguard Total Bond Market Index Portfolio beat the average taxable bond fund, and it beat the average intermediate funds as well. Vanguard also has separate long-, intermediate-, and short-term bond index funds.

SHORT-TERM FUNDS (GEN.)

As bond funds go, short-term funds are not very volatile. To qualify for this category, the maturities usually must be between 1 and 5 years, and the duration between 1 and 3.5 years. But in absolute terms, they're still pretty safe. Sure, a percentage point increase in interest rates could knock 3 percent off a fund with a duration of 3 years. But in the short maturities, such movements are infrequent.

Since these funds are fairly limited regarding the maturity of the bonds they buy, they try to make their mark through bond selection. These funds generally invest in a wide variety of fixed-income instruments—from Treasuries and investment-grade corporates to high-yield and emerging markets debt. In most cases, the funds are restricted as to the portion of their assets that can go into the less creditworthy issues.

At a time when longer-term bonds are falling in price, these funds can deliver relatively attractive returns. In 1996, for instance, a year that experienced several sharp swings in long-term rates, the short-term funds turned in some attractive returns. The average short-term general bond fund earned a 5 percent total return, which handily beat the intermediate's 3.7 percent return and the long-term's 3.3 percent return. That was the reverse order of 1995 and 1997, both bullish years for bonds in which the longest maturities made the most money.

The best short-term bond fund for the last one-, three-, and five-year periods was BT Investment Lifecycle Short-Term (Table 2-36). Look at the numbers, and you can see it's an atyp-

TABLE 2-36

SHORT-TERM FUNDS (GEN.)

BEST RETURNS

Period ▼	Fund ▼	Total return* ▼
1998	BT INVESTMENT LIFECYCLE SHORT	13.5%
1996-98	BT INVESTMENT LIFECYCLE SHORT	11.7
1994-98	BT INVESTMENT LIFECYCLE SHORT	9.1
1989-98	VICTORY FUND FOR INCOME	8.1

*Average annual, pretax   DATA: MORNINGSTAR INC.

ical short-term fund. The bonds look fairly conventional for a short-term fund, but there's a small slug of equities—15 percent during 1998—that gives it some extra kick that the competition does not get.

Far more conventional choices in this category are Harbor Short Duration Fund, Hotchkis & Wiley Low Duration, and Strong Short-Term Bond among the no-loads, and PIMCO Low Duration among the load funds. They all earned the highest category ratings. The Strong fund keeps an investment grade credit quality, but has the ability to put up to 25 percent of the assets in bonds rated BB. For most of the last few years, the ability to buy the higher yield, lesser credits has helped boost the returns of the fund. That hurt the fund, though, during 1998, when the high-yield market swooned along with the stock market. The fund lost it's A rating. Hotchkis & Wiley Low Duration fared better, because its low-grade limit is 10 percent. The fund's managers look to find extra return in more obscure corners of the bond market, like asset-backed securities. In 1998, at least, it worked.

ULTRASHORT FUNDS

The ultrashort category is the newest addition to the bond fund portion of the BUSINESS WEEK Mutual Fund Scoreboard. This relatively small category takes in ultrashort corporate funds, like Strong Advantage Fund and Neuberger & Berman Ultra-Short Bond, and the adjustable-rate mortgage funds that were previously in the government category. The two types of funds have very different investment programs but they share an important common characteristic—a portfolio duration of less than one year. The idea behind these funds is to earn a higher return than a money-market fund without taking a whole lot more risk.

Strong Advantage Fund is the best performer of the last 10-year period (Table 2-37). To be honest, it's not that great an honor. Ultrashort is a relatively new idea in bond funds, and there are only six other funds with 10-year records. Still, that's not to belittle the fund. With $2.6 billion in assets, it's also larger than the other six combined—and then some. Volatility is kept to a minimum. Portfolio manager Jeffrey A. Koch, who's run the fund since 1991, keeps the duration at six months. That's not a whole lot more than a money-market fund. He seeks the extra yield by venturing out into the lesser credits where money-market funds typically don't go. That's because money-market funds are managed to keep their net asset values (NAVs) constant at $1 per share. Strong Advantage does not have a lot of variation in NAV, but it's not obliged to stay at a fixed rate. During 1998 the fund earned a total return of 4.8 percent and paid out income distributions of 6.0 percent, which means the fund actually lost some NAV.

The winners for one-, three-, and five-year total returns are loan participation funds or floating-rate funds. They're not new, but they are new to the BW Scoreboard this year, and they are definitely worth checking out. These funds invest in senior bank-originated loans—those made to large corporations—and have first claim on assets. And these loans generally pay an interest rate that's anywhere from 0.75 percentage points to 3 percentage points above LIBOR, or the London Interbank Offered Rate, a global benchmark for bank lending. In early 1999, the LIBOR was about 5 percent.

There is almost no interest-rate risk in these funds. That's because the loans reset every 30 to 60 days. If rates go up, so will the income from the loans. These loans do have credit risk, and the job of the funds' portfolio managers is largely that of credit officers. But since the loans are senior-secured debt, there is less credit risk here than in a high-yield bond. In its nearly 10-year history, Eaton Vance Prime Rate Reserves' net asset value has been as high as $10.07 and as low as $9.95. In 1998, the variation in NAV was just

TABLE 2-37

ULTRASHORT FUNDS
BEST RETURNS

Period ▼	Fund ▼	Total return* ▼
1998	EATON VANCE PRIME RATE RESERVES	6.9%
1996-98	MSDW PRIME INCOME TRUST	6.7
1994-98	MSDW PRIME INCOME TRUST	7.6
1989-98	STRONG ADVANTAGE	7.2

*Average annual, pretax   DATA: MORNINGSTAR INC.

two cents, yet the yield was 6.8 percent, nearly two percentage points more than the average taxable money-market fund. Eaton Vance Prime Rate Reserves earned an A-rating when compared to all other taxable bond funds. So did competitors Merrill Lynch Senior Floating-Rate, MSDW Prime Income Trust, and Van Kampen Prime-Rate Income. The MSDW fund also had the highest returns in the ultrashort category over the last three- and five-year periods.

There is a catch with these funds. You can invest in them at any time, but you can only withdraw money once per quarter and on a predetermined date. The reason for these restrictive redemption procedures is that the bank loans are illiquid, and portfolio managers may not be able to raise money for redemptions on a day's notice. With just quarterly redemptions, the portfolio managers can manage the fund in a way so that cash will be available for those who ask for it.

Another type of ultrashort fund invests in adjustable-rate mortgages. In theory, a mutual fund that owns nothing but adjustable-rate mortgages (ARMs) should be a pretty safe, conservative offering. Most of the ARMs are issued by government-sponsored enterprises like Fannie Mae and Ginnie Mae, so credit is not an issue. And since most ARMs reset their interest rates at least once a year, the effective maturity is no more than a year. So even though the net asset values of ARMs funds fluctuate, they shouldn't fluctuate much—and ARMs still provide a higher rate of interest than a money-market mutual fund.

In reality, many of these funds have been disappointments. If anything, these short-maturity funds should have distinguished themselves in 1994's bear market by at least completing the year with a positive total return. But the average ARMs fund fell far short, and, in fact, only 5 of the 12 ARMs funds in the Scoreboard had positive results.

The bear market disappointment might have been more palatable if the funds really outperformed during the bull markets. But in the three-year period of falling interest rates, only in 1991 did the funds—and there were only six at the time—really stand out, earning a 10.5 percent total return and beating the average taxable money-market fund by 5 percentage points.

LONG-TERM GOVERNMENT FUNDS

Long-term government bond funds are not for the faint of heart. Sure, the U.S. government guarantee may comfort the investor worried

TABLE 2-38

LONG-TERM GOVERNMENT FUNDS
BEST RETURNS

Period ▼	Fund ▼	Total return* ▼
1998	AMER. CENT.–BENHAM TARGET MAT. 2025	21.9%
1996-98	WASATCH-HOISINGTON U.S. TREASURY SEC.	12.7
1994-98	AMER. CENT.–BENHAM TARGET MAT. 2020	12.7
1989-98	AMER. CENT.–BENHAM TARGET MAT. 2015	13.1

*Average annual, pretax
**Wasatch Funds, 800-551-1700; or see Business Week Online
DATA: MORNINGSTAR INC.

about the creditworthiness of borrowers. Because government bonds have no credit risk, they are totally creatures of changes in interest rates. And since the long government funds own bonds with average maturities in excess of 10 years and durations of more than 6 years, they are the most sensitive to changes in interest rates. When rates fell in 1995, 1997, and 1998, these funds scored big. In 1994 and 1996, when rates rose, the total returns were negative, even after the interest payments. In 1998, the best performer in this category was American Century–Benham Target Maturities 2025, a zero-coupon bond fund (Table 2-38).

American Century–Benham runs a series of these funds and they are the most volatile in what is a potentially volatile category of fund. These bonds sell at a fraction of their par value, $1000, and mature in their target year at $1000. There are no interest payments in the interim. The "interest" from a zero-coupon bond is just the difference between the purchase price and $1000. There are six of these funds, with maturities in 2000, 2005, 2010, 2015, 2020, and 2025. The last three belong to the long-term government category.

There's no bond more sensitive to changes in interest rates than a zero-coupon bond. Think back to the idea of duration, introduced earlier in this chapter. A 30-year bond with a 7 percent coupon has a duration of around 11 or 12 years. A 30-year zero-coupon bond has a duration of 30 years. There are no interest payments between now and year 30, so the value of the bond is determined by the present value of that redemption payment of so many years away. In 1998, a year in which long-term interest rates declined to the lowest level in decades, the fund maturing in 2025 had gained nearly 35 percent by early October, but then declined to finish the year with a still strong 21.9 percent gain. In 1994, when interest rates shot up quickly, that same fund lost 17.7

percent in net asset value. In 1995, the fund shot up an amazing 61.3 percent.

In periods of falling interest rates, the zero-coupon funds will invariably be the best performers. Of course, they'll likely be the worst when interest rates rise. As short-term trading vehicles, these funds make some sense. They're no-load and can be bought and sold with a telephone call. But as long-term investments, even Benham management admits you're better off in a regular zero-coupon bond.

Suppose you're going to be 65 in 2020, nearly 25 years away. You decide to put your individual retirement account funds into zero-coupon bonds that mature that year, a reasonable thing to do. The best bet would be to pay the broker's commission, for once you do, you won't pay another nickel for the next 25 years. But if you buy the zero-coupon mutual fund, you'll be hit for about 0.6 percent in expenses each year.

(Zero-coupon bonds or bond funds only make sense in a tax-deferred account. Though they pay no cash interest, the Internal Revenue Service says the zero earnings "accrete" interest every year as they get closer to maturity. So you have to pay taxes on the interest every year, though you don't collect it for years to come. Some people use them for children's accounts, and invest in the series that matures when the child is college age. If a child is paying tax at his or her parents' rate—and many now do—the zeros may not be worthwhile for him or her, either. Right now, only minors 14 years and older have their income taxed at their own tax rates.)

The fate of the more conventional long-term government funds, those that buy coupon-bearing bonds, is largely determined by the course of interest rates. Still, there is some room for portfolio managers to maneuver. If the manager believes that interest rates will decline, he or she can move fund assets into longer maturity bonds with higher duration. If it looks like interest rates are heading higher, the manager can sell bonds to shorten the maturity and duration.

One fund that has a flexible maturity policy is Wasatch-Hoisington U.S. Treasury Securities Fund. Portfolio manager Van R. Hoisington invests only in U.S. Treasuries, and then mainly in the long- or short-term varieties. For the last several years, he has stayed with the longer maturities, and it has paid off well as interest rates have trended down. In 1998, the fund was up 14.6 percent total return, which beat the average long-term government fund by nearly 3 percentage points. The five-year average annual

Over time, mortgage funds beat Treasuries.

return, which won the fund an overall A rating and a category A rating, was 10.1 percent.

If the fund is a general government bond fund instead of one restricted to Treasuries, the manager has the ability to pick up some extra return by investment in government-backed mortgages or government-agency issued bonds. As a practical matter, the government stands behind them, but because they are not Treasuries, they tend to pay somewhat higher interest rates.

Not surprisingly, this long-term government fund category is a relatively small one in number of funds and assets under management. Most bond investors are risk-averse anyway, so why invest in bonds that at times can exhibit the same volatility as equity funds? General long-term bonds are risky, too, but they can moderate a little of the interest-rate sensitivity by investing in lower-grade corporates or non-U.S. issues, which also respond to changes in credit quality. Not so for long-term government funds.

INTERMEDIATE-TERM GOVERNMENT FUNDS

If you listen to the business and financial news on television and radio, the announcers will, along with the Dow Jones industrial average, give the bond market a mention: "The interest rate on the benchmark 30-year U.S. Treasury bond declined one-tenth of 1 percent today. . . ." Investors pay a lot of attention to the 30-year government bond, but that's no more the bond market than the price of Coca-Cola or General Electric is the stock market. The government bond market is by and large a market of intermediate-term securities.

There's another good reason for investors to choose intermediate-term over long-term bond funds. They provide nearly as much return for about one-third to one-half less risk. That's certainly the case in the bond market, in which the yield on a 10-year bond is usually around 90 percent or more of that of the 30-year bond. It's not quite the same for mutual fund returns. For the 5 years ending in 1998, the intermediate-term government funds earned 77 percent of the return earned by long-term government funds.

Some of these government funds rely mainly on Treasuries and U.S. agency issues, others emphasize mortgage-backed securities. The advantage of those that have only Treasury and U.S. agency issues is that the income produced by those bonds is exempt from state and local income taxes. Mortgage-backed securities have no such exemption, even those issued by government agencies like Fannie Mae or Freddie Mac.

Mortgage-related funds tend to dominate this category. Many are recognizable as such, with "GNMA" or "Mortgage Securities" in their titles. But not all. The $8.9 billion Franklin U.S. Government Securities I invests solely in government-guaranteed mortgages. But aren't mortgages mainly long-term, like 15 or 30 years?

Indeed they are, but rare is the person who sticks with one mortgage for 30 years and pays it off in its entirety. Most people pay much sooner, either when they sell the house or refinance. Most mortgage-backed securities issued by the Ginnie Mae are backed by pools of individual mortgages, and the average life of a GNMA is about 12 years.

Intermediate-term government funds may sound fairly generic, but they take different approaches to investing. Note, for instance, State Street Research Government Income A does not have "U.S." in front of the word "government." The fund's prospectus says it will usually have at least 65 percent of its assets in U.S. government securities. What about the rest? For part of 1997, at least, it was Australian and Israeli government debt. In all, 25 percent of the portfolio was in something other than U.S. government securities. In 1998, the fund had fewer non-U.S. securities, which, given the summer turmoil, was a smart move. The fund earned a 9.1 percent return in 1998 versus 7.4 percent for the average intermediate government fund.

An investor would also expect a government income fund to preserve capital, but that's not necessarily the case. Some funds say their objective is preservation of capital and current income, or current income consistent with preservation of capital. Some say current income alone, with no mention of capital preservation. There is a difference. To maximize current income, a fund can take steps that put a part of its capital at risk.

That's certainly the case with Franklin U.S. Government Securities I. It's a popular fund because it has one of the highest yields in the bond fund universe, even when compared to high-yield corporate issues with far higher coupons. (The yield in 1998 was 6.5 percent.) The fund achieves this by investing in current coupon GNMA securities (those whose mortgages pay at the going rate at the time of purchase). Most investors recognize that higher interest rates will damage the NAVs. But if mortgage holders prepay higher-rate mortgages too quickly, the fund suffers capital losses, and the NAV drops. During 1998, the fund paid out 6.5 percent in cash, but the total return was 6.6 percent. So the fund made a slight gain in NAV.

Fidelity Mortgage Securities Initial Shares, which earned the best returns over the five-year period, doesn't make bets on the direction of rates (Table 2-39). The fund's duration is usually that of the Salomon Bros. Mortgage Index. The manager tries to earn extra returns by investing in sectors of the mortgage market he thinks are undervalued, like balloon-note mortgages or securities backed by commercial properties.

To understand how mortgage securities work, think of your own situation. Most of these funds invest in home mortgages, just like yours. You make a mortgage payment every month to a bank, thrift, or mortgage company. You don't send your payment to a mutual fund. But it's likely that the original lender has sold your mortgage and is now merely collecting payments and forwarding the proceeds—less a small service charge, of course.

Your mortgage, along with hundreds of others, might be pooled together into a mortgage-backed security—and such investments are the principal holdings of the government-mortgage funds. Mutual funds are among the major buyers of mortgage-backed securities. In that sense, they have a role to play in supporting home ownership. Who knows? You may invest in a mutual fund that owns a security that includes your mortgage.

Either way, Fannie's, Freddie's, and Ginnie's mortgage-backed securities are prized by investors. Their credit quality is considered just a shade under that of pure Treasury securities. If borrowers default, the federal agencies guarantee interest and principal. And the federal government stands behind the agencies. Yet the yields are about 1 percentage point higher than Treasury bonds. In 1989, the yield advantage went as high as 1.7 percentage points, as the ailing thrift industry dumped billions into mortgages to raise capital.

TABLE 2-39

INTERMEDIATE-TERM GOVERNMENT FUNDS
BEST RETURNS

Period	Fund	Total return*
1998	API TREASURIES TRUST**	13.3%
1996-98	LEXINGTON GNMA INCOME	7.8
1994-98	FIDELITY MORTGAGE SECURITIES INIT.	7.8
1989-98	HEARTLAND U.S. GOVERNMENT SECURITIES	9.2

*Average annual, pretax
**API Funds, 800-544-6060; or see Business Week Online

DATA: MORNINGSTAR INC.

Some mortgage-backed securities are bonds, with pools of mortgages serving as collateral. Many are mortgage pass-through certificates and they're like owning the mortgages themselves. A growing segment of this market is collateralized mortgage obligations, better known as CMOs. In a broad sense, all CMOs are derivatives. But not all CMOs are volatile securities that can blow a big hole in a fund's net asset value. However, to understand the mortgage derivatives, you should first understand how the underlying mortgages work.

Despite the sometimes odd behavior of mortgage-backed securities, the mortgage funds are still governed by the immutable laws of fixed-income investing. When interest rates go up, the value of existing mortgages goes down. But there's another dynamic at work, too. The interest and a small part of the principal is paid monthly and is predictable. But mortgages can pay off their principal at any time. A certain amount of prepayment is always figured into the price of a mortgage security. However, what is unsettling to the mortgage market—and to funds that invest in mortgage securities—is when the expectations about principal repayment suddenly change.

Here's why. The mortgage-backed market operates on the assumption that a pool of 30-year mortgages will have an average life of 12 years. Most people move or refinance their homes well before they pay off a mortgage. But a change in interest rates also alters the expected life of a mortgage-backed security. If that life expectancy drops to 10 years—or lengthens to 15 years—the price of the securities can change dramatically.

Suppose you buy a house and finance the deal with an 8 percent mortgage. And that mortgage, in turn, is owned by some investors through a mortgage-backed security with an 8 percent coupon. You plan to trade up to a larger house in five years, but that doesn't change anything because other mortgagers have no plans to move at all.

Five years go by and you're ready to move, but interest rates shoot up to 10 percent. Your plans are now on hold. You can't sell your house, because the higher interest rates have depressed the housing market. In addition, you are reluctant to take on a mortgage at 10 percent. Instead of selling your home and paying back the mortgage, you stay in the house for a few more years.

At the same time, the investors who hold your mortgage are also hurt. Like all fixed-income instruments, the higher interest rate lowers its value. But in addition, you and many others have delayed your moving plans. That means you will be holding on to your 8 percent mortgages longer. So this security, originally assumed to have a 12-year expected life, now has a 15-year expected life. Higher rates and a longer life make the security less desirable.

But suppose interest rates had dropped to 6 percent. The owners of your mortgage are happy because they're getting 8 percent from you while new mortgages are fetching only 6 percent. But then you sell your house, pay off the 8 percent mortgage, and buy another house with a 6 percent mortgage. Other homeowners in your mortgage pool also sell or refinance their homes to take advantage of the 6 percent rate.

That means the principal gets repaid faster than originally expected, and the security with a 12-year life expectancy now looks like a 10-year. If rates were going up, the mortgage holders would like the faster payback. But with rates heading down, the last thing they want is principal coming back to them. That principal was earning 8 percent. Reinvested in a new mortgage-backed security, the principal would fetch only 6 percent. As mortgage rates come down, one of the major problems for mortgage-fund managers is minimizing prepayment risks.

Got it so far? Now let's look at CMOs and mortgage derivatives. To understand this, go back to how CMOs are created. Investment bankers start with a pool of underlying mortgage securities, like GNMAs. Suppose an underwriter has $200 million worth of mortgages. That represents two cash flows. One is a predictable one, the interest and partial principal payment that homeowners make each month. The other cash flow is the prepayments, or principal that gets paid back early, either from homeowners' selling their homes or refinancing their mortgages. The sponsor of the CMO will look at all the cash flows the mortgages produce and then carve them up to suit different investors.

For those investors who want the more predictable stream of payments, the CMO bankers will take half the mortgage pool, or $100 million, and create a series of "planned amortization class" bonds (PACs). These bonds will behave much like conventional bonds, with regular cash flows. Such bonds will work fine for most bond funds. Generally, these funds also carry a lower interest rate than the underlying mortgages. That's the price these investors pay for predictability. Two-to-three-year PACs will work fine in bond funds with two-to-three-year maturities. Seven-year PACs are fine for long-term bond funds.

Then come the PAC II and PAC III bonds. Their cash flows are far less certain (II's are more certain than III's) since they get paid after all the PACs are paid. That makes them inherently more risky than PACs, and as such they have higher interest rates (some of the yield held back from the PAC bonds is assigned to the PAC II's and III's). But PAC II's or PAC III's are also far more volatile than PACs, and probably should be shunned by most bond funds.

Risk-averse investors should also avoid the funds that invest heavily in interest-only securities (IOs) or principal-only securities (POs). Those are mortgage-backed securities that pay either interest from a pool of underlying mortgages or principal from a pool of underlying mortgages, but not both. Both are volatile in periods of rapidly changing interest rates. In addition, the risk-shy should avoid funds that are heavy investors in inverse floaters, which are floating rate securities whose payouts go up when rates go down. Their main problem is that when rates go up, their payouts—and prices—melt away. Finally, cautious fund investors should be wary of "Z" bonds, which have the most erratic payout schedule of all the mortgage-backed securities.

Many of those derivatives—inverse floaters, POs, and Z bonds—were responsible for several of the worst bond fund wrecks of 1994: Piper Jaffray Institutional Government Income, with an ugly 28.8 percent loss for the year, and Managers Intermediate Income Fund, with an almost as ugly 25.1 percent loss. The basic problem was that those derivatives plunged in value when interest rates shot up, far faster than conventional mortgages and bonds would have. Added to that was the fact that many of these securities had been leveraged—purchased with borrowed money—meaning that the funds were even more susceptible to higher rates and falling bond prices.

How good are mortgage funds as investments? That depends on other market conditions. Millions of shareholders poured into government mortgage funds in the mid-1980s as interest rates tumbled. Their government imprimatur and higher yields were appealing. But high-coupon mortgage securities usually lag behind bond market rallies because investors are reluctant to pay up for high-yielding mortgages when the conditions are ripe for homeowners to pay them off. On the other hand, when the bonds are beginning to falter, mortgages often hold up better than bonds

Short-term bond funds have little interest rate risk.

because what principal does come back gets reinvested at higher rates. Held over an "interest-rate cycle"—a period when rates go up, down, and return to the starting point—the mortgage funds should outperform the pure Treasury funds by about 1 percentage point a year.

SHORT-TERM GOVERNMENT FUNDS

Short-term government bond funds fill the gap between the inviolable safety of the money-market fund and the calculated risk-taking of the intermediate-term fund. The market risk of these funds is roughly half that of the intermediates, and a lot less than that of the long-terms. Not a whole lot of market risk, but not a whole lot of reward, either. During 1996, a difficult year for the bond market, they earned a 4.3 percent total return, beating the intermediates and trouncing the long-term government funds. But the yield paid out was over 5 percent, suggesting that even in these low-risk vehicles, you can suffer a capital loss. In 1997 and 1998, strong years for the bond market, these funds returned about half as much as the average long-term fund.

To qualify for this category, the maturities usually must be between 1 and 5 years, and the durations, between 1 and 3.5 years. That, plus the constraints of a government fund, doesn't leave room for funds to differentiate themselves. But leave it to the fund managers. There's a lot more diversity in investment approach than you might think. The Vanguard Group even has two entries in this category: Vanguard Short-Term U.S. Treasury Securities and Vanguard Short-Term Federal Securities. The difference? The Treasury fund invests only in Treasury securities, the Federal, in all U.S.-issued securities except Treasuries. The Federal portfolio has a slightly higher yield and total return.

Some funds earn extra returns by searching for the more out-of-the-way government securities. Look at the Sit U.S. Government Securities, the best performer for the three-year and five-year periods ending in 1998 (Table 2-40). It's a pipsqueak of a bond fund, less than $150 million, but this gives the portfolio manager more flexibility than the managers of a $10 billion fund. This fund, for instance, is able to put 40 percent of its assets into GNMA-backed mobile-home mortgage bonds, which pay 0.80 to 1.5 more percentage points in yield than Treasuries with very little additional risk.

IDS Federal Income takes an approach that's fairly unusual for a short-term fund. The manager doesn't confine himself to the short end of

TABLE 2-40

SHORT-TERM GOVERNMENT FUNDS
BEST RETURNS

Period	Fund	Total return*
1998	HERITAGE INTERMEDIATE GOVERNMENT A**	8.2%
1996-98	SIT U.S. GOVERNMENT SECURITIES	6.6
1994-98	SIT U.S. GOVERNMENT SECURITIES	6.6
1989-98	ALLIANCE MORTGAGE SECURITIES INCOME A	8.2

*Average annual, pretax
**Heritage Funds, 800-421-4184; or see Business Week Online

DATA: MORNINGSTAR INC.

the spectrum, but chooses from a variety of U.S. agency and mortgage-related securities, some with decades to go to maturity. From these securities, he gets a higher yield than he would from a strictly short-term portfolio but he also gets the duration of an intermediate fund, about 4.5 years. To bring the duration down, he uses futures and options. Those derivatives have a "negative duration" of 2.3 years. The result is a fund with a duration of around 2.6 years, well in the range of a short-term fund.

Yet another approach, practiced by AIM Limited Maturity Treasury Retail Shares, is what's called "laddering." (Actually, this strategy can be and is done with intermediate- and long-term bonds as well.) The fund buys two-year Treasury notes and sells them off after owning them for about a year. Then it buys more two-year notes. The duration ends up at around 1.4 years and changes little. The net asset value remains fairly steady, and the fund usually earns good risk-adjusted returns.

The laddering approach is so simple that many investment advisers say there's no point to doing it within a mutual fund, especially a U.S. Treasury fund. The portfolio manager isn't performing any credit analysis or interest-rate forecasting. Why pay a management fee? Investors can buy the Treasuries themselves—they're easily purchased through frequent Treasury auctions—and do much the same as the portfolio manager is doing. With $5000 or less to invest, a short-term government fund might make more sense. But if you would put $20,000 or more into a short-term government fund, you could ladder a portfolio yourself. Divide your money into thirds, buy a one-year, a two-year, and a three-year note. One year from now, replace the note that's about to mature with a new three-year note. A mutual fund is not always the best way to fill an investment need.

HIGH-YIELD FUNDS

High-yield bonds and the mutual funds that invest in them make most other sorts of bonds look like pikers. Even with down years in 1994 and 1998, the 5-year record still beats all but convertible and long-term government bonds. Even looking at 10- and 15-year records, which include a vicious bear market in 1989 and 1990, the high-yield funds still look good. You have to wonder why anyone would ever invest in a government or investment-grade security.

Well, here's the rub. High-yield bonds are legally bonds. The issuer, or borrower, promises to pay interest at particular times and at a particular interest rate. And because of those fixed-rate payments, these bonds have some sensitivity to changes in interest rates. But the truth is, even if these securities look like bonds, they behave more like stocks. With the exception of 1998, every year in this decade when the stock market has been strong, so has the high-yield bond market. And even in 1994, when the stock market was barely profitable, the high-yield bonds beat stocks by a few percentage points. Martin Fridson, chief of high-yield research at Merrill Lynch & Co., confirmed our suspicions about the true nature of high-yield bonds. He looked at the monthly returns of high-yield bonds from 1985 through 1996 and found that the returns on high-yield bonds correlate with the stock market about 52 percent of the time versus a 41 percent correlation with the 10-year U.S. Treasury bond.

If it's not a stock, but doesn't really behave like a bond, what is a high-yield security? It's evolving almost as a separate and distinct asset, the inclusion of which in a portfolio can help to diversify risks and enhance returns. In short, many investors should consider adding one of these funds to their portfolios. The best performer over the last five years has been Fidelity High-Income (Table 2-41). It's a winner on risk-adjusted

TABLE 2-41

HIGH-YIELD FUNDS
BEST RETURNS

Period	Fund	Total return*
1998	STRONG SHORT-TERM HIGH-YIELD BOND	8.4%
1996-98	STRONG HIGH-YIELD BOND	14.9
1994-98	FIDELITY HIGH-INCOME	10.8
1989-98	FIDELITY ADVISOR HIGH-YIELD T	13.0

*Average annual, pretax   DATA: MORNINGSTAR INC.

returns as well, earning an A rating for overall performance and an A rating against other high-yield funds.

How high are the high yields? That's a moving target, depending on the general level of interest rates. When the high-yield, or "junk," bond market was flat on its back in 1990, many big issues traded at yields 10 or more percentage points higher than the comparable Treasury rates. In early 1998, the yields were perhaps 2-to-3 percentage points higher, and high-yield bond funds had yields (after expenses) of about 8 percent. In early October of 1998, during a global flight to quality, high-yield bond prices sank and rates jumped to nearly 5 points over comparable Treasuries. That yield gap has closed to about 4 percentage points by year-end.

Many investors argue that high-yields are too low to make them attractive. Perhaps so, but they are also a lot safer securities now than they were back in the 1980s. It's somewhat analogous to the people who, when the Dow Jones hit 6000, said the stock market was overpriced. When the Dow hit 9000, those who had declined to invest paid a heavy opportunity cost.

One thing is for certain: The returns from high-yield bond funds from here on out cannot match those earned over the last decade. Ernest Monrad, portfolio manager of Northeast Investors Trust, recalls that in 1990 he snapped up R. J. Reynolds bonds at 20 percent yields. So he collected a fat coupon payment to start with, and the bonds eventually appreciated in price as well, giving a substantial total return. But now, rates have fallen considerably and credit quality is much improved. A bond with an 8.5 percent coupon still might go up in value, but it's probably not going to make the gains that can be had when a bond is selling to yield at twice that rate. However, investors might still consider putting some money into these sorts of funds. Says Monrad: "All things being equal, you start off with an 8 percent or 9 percent return. With stocks, the dividend yield is less than 2 percent. You have to depend on appreciation to do better. And income is more reliable than stock price appreciation."

High-yield bond funds were originally pitched to income-oriented investors, who still own large amounts of them. But they should be equally, if not more, attractive to stock market investors as "high-yield equity." At least equity fund buyers would probably take their sometimes volatile performance more in stride. Since these funds pay out a large portion of their profit as income, most investors would probably fare better if they held high-yield bond funds in their tax-deferred accounts, such as IRAs or 401(k)s.

So why do these bonds behave a lot like stocks? They're responding to many of the same forces in the economy. Since the 1990–1991 recession, the economy has been on a relatively slow but steady upward climb. Business conditions improved. Companies got leaner and meaner. Productivity increased. Corporate cash flow and profits zoomed.

All of that is great for stocks—and for high-yield bonds, too. Here's why: The issuers of high-yield bonds are often less mature companies or those with a lot of debt. They pay higher interest rates because they are riskier borrowers. There's a greater chance with these companies that they'll default—or fail to make their interest payments. When business is good and the companies make money, they become stronger financially and more creditworthy borrowers. Fewer issuers default on their bonds. (The average default rate is about 3 percent a year. For the last several years, the rate was about 1 percent—another reason this market has performed so well.) With better credit ratings, the prices of their bonds will also go up. The investors win two ways—bond prices go up and they collect a very healthy interest payment to boot.

A strong economy is good for high-yield bonds. It's not always good for investment-grade bonds, because interest rates often go up. Higher rates do hurt the high-yield bonds somewhat, but that can be offset by improved credit quality. What would really derail the high-yield bond market is a recession (it would be hard on stocks, too). That's when business goes into a tailspin, and that's especially rough on less mature, debt-heavy companies. The reason high-yields have looked so strong in recent years is that we haven't had a recession. But that doesn't mean we won't in the future, either. The last recession hit just as the high-yield market was imploding from the excesses of the 1980s. It wasn't pretty.

The character of the high-yield market has changed a lot over the last 20 years—and it's still evolving. Until the late 1970s nearly all junk bonds were "fallen angels," bonds of once investment-grade companies that had fallen upon hard times. But then, investment banker Michael R. Milken of Drexel Burnham Lambert pioneered the idea of original-issue junk bonds. First, Milken used the bonds to raise money for capital-hungry emerging growth companies. Later, corporate raiders tapped the junk bond market to raise funds to take over big companies or to finance leveraged buyouts—purchases of companies that are made with mostly borrowed money. In the 1990s, there's been little takeover or LBO-related junk bond issuance. Instead, many of the new bonds come from new companies borrowing for the first time or established borrowers refinancing high-interest-rate debt.

The original premise behind junk bond investing is simple. Though these securities were riskier than high-quality bonds, the vast majority continued to make interest payments. So, although investing in a few junk bonds may be a dicey proposition, a well-diversified portfolio of junk bonds would be a tempting dish. In such a portfolio the regular income would more than make up for the losses from the occasional default. So mutual funds made a natural vehicle for investing in junk bonds.

The high-yield funds captured investors' attention—and their dollars—in the mid-1980s when interest rates on government and investment-grade bonds fell into the single digits. While the yields in junk bond funds averaged 3 to 4 percentage points higher than those from high-quality funds, the difference between the total returns on junk funds and investment-grade funds was less striking: 22 percent total return (yield plus capital appreciation) for junk funds in 1985 versus 20.6 percent for high-quality funds. In 1986 and 1987, the total returns were nearly identical. The high-yield funds were paying out more in interest, but the investment-grade funds did a better job of maintaining their net asset values.

Those numbers suggest that investors bought junk bond funds for their yields and were not really looking at total return. Only in 1988 did the total returns from junk bonds beat investment-grade bonds decisively—12.6 percent versus 7.6 percent. That was more than reversed in the junk bond debacle. In 1989, for instance, junk funds had an average return of 1.5 percent versus 11.9 percent for high grades. In 1990, junk bonds had a –12.3 percent return versus 17.4 percent for high-quality funds.

What happened to the junk bond market? For starters, Drexel Burnham Lambert—the investment bank that controlled nearly half the market—started to falter in 1989 and went into bankruptcy in 1990. The empires of some big junk bond issuers teetered or collapsed under mountains of debt. Milken ultimately pleaded guilty to some securities laws violations and spent time in a federal penitentiary. Finally, new federal laws prevented savings and loans from buying junk bonds and forced those that already owned them

High-yield funds can diversify any portfolio.

to divest. That further depressed demand for the bonds and increased supply. And an investor exodus from high-yield funds exacerbated the junk market's woes. To meet redemptions, fund managers often sold their "quality" junk because it could be sold. That left portfolios in even worse shape.

While high-yield bond funds can deliver equity-like returns, they can also have some equity-like changes in their NAVs. For instance, on November 22, 1995, Harrah's Jazz company filed for Chapter 11 bankruptcy, causing bond prices to plunge. Keystone High-Income (B-4) Fund lost 2.6 percent in NAV that day; Paine Webber High-Income Fund, 2.2 percent; and Fidelity High-Income and Fidelity Capital & Income Fund, 1.9 percent each. (That was not severe enough to cost either Fidelity fund its high BW rating.)

Junk bond funds, like equity funds, encompass many investment styles. As a result, their portfolios—and their returns—are far more varied than, say, government or municipal funds. Most high-yield funds now have the lion's share of their assets in B-rated bonds. Some, like Phoenix High-Yield, have also gone into global emerging markets—bonds of such countries as Mexico, Argentina, Morocco, and Thailand—in their search for a high yield. That paid off handsomely in 1993 when the fund earned a 21.5 percent total return. But the fund stayed abroad too long in 1994, and its fund return sank to –28 percent. At least two other junk bond funds damaged by emerging market debt were Keystone America Strategic Income B, down 10.3 percent, and T. Rowe Price High-Yield, down 8 percent.

Then there's the more conservative sort, like Nicholas Income and Vanguard High-Yield Corporate Portfolio, which stress higher-rated bonds and have lower highs and higher lows than the Phoenix fund. The Vanguard fund, by charter, must have 80 percent of its assets in bonds rated B or better. Northeast Investors Trust takes yet another path. It invests in the junkiest junk—the fund is invested almost entirely in credit B or below and unrated bonds. The fund can also boost its income by leveraging the fund, borrowing money to buy bonds on margin, thereby increasing the income.

A more conservative approach isn't necessarily less risky. For instance, when the junk bond market—like most bond markets—fell in October 1992, the total return for Fidelity Capital & Income was –1 percent. The higher-quality Vanguard fund had a 2.5 percent fall. Why the differ-

ence? The prices for the Fidelity fund's bonds are dependent on each company's situation. The prices for higher-quality junk bonds are more interest-rate sensitive. Each approach to junk fund investing carries its own risks. They're not all the same.

The latest wrinkle in the high-yield fund category is short-term funds. One such fund, Strong Short-Term High-Yield Bond, turned in the best performance in 1998—an 8.4 percent total return, including a generous 7.4 percent yield. It almost looks like it totally dodged the bullets of the high-yield market sell-off. The other funds, Dreyfus Short-Term High Yield Securities and Dreyfus Premier Limited-Term High-Income, didn't dodge it. Even with their high yields, their total returns were –0.8 percent and –0.6, respectively. That was worse than the average high-yield fund which held securities with longer maturities and, in theory, should have declined more. Of course, these funds looked steady as a rock compared to the longer-term Dreyfus High-Yield Securities, which lost 15.8 percent and won notoriety as the year's worst-performing high-yield fund.

CONVERTIBLE FUNDS

If high-yield bonds are really stocks in disguise, consider convertible bonds. They are issued as bonds, with a set interest payment schedule and a promise to redeem by a certain date. The interest rate is a lower rate than you might expect the issuer to pay. But there is a sweetener here that should more than compensate for that lower rate—the bondholder has the option to convert the bonds into a specified amount of stock in the issuing company at a specified price. So when stocks do really well, convertibles do too. And if the stock of the issuing company doesn't reach its conversion price, the investor always has some interest income from the investment.

The last five years, a strong period for the stock market, was a sweet time for convertibles. Convertible bond funds were the best-performing category of bond fund—and they were best in three-year performance as well. And Nicholas-Applegate Convertible C was the best performer for 1998, and also for the 1996–1998 period (Table 2-42). Yet even when convertible funds do well, they usually don't attract much investor attention. The funds are rather small, and new start-ups are rare. They suffer perhaps because convertibles, which have attributes of both stocks and bonds, are little appreciated by pure stock or pure bond investors. Yet they seem to have a role to play in an equity portfolio. With dividend yields

The new twist on high yield: short-term funds.

TABLE 2-42

CONVERTIBLE FUNDS		
BEST RETURNS		
Period ▼	Fund ▼	Total return* ▼
1998	NICHOLAS-APPLEGATE CONVERTIBLE C	20.1%
1996-98	NICHOLAS-APPLEGATE CONVERTIBLE C	20.5
1994-98	CALAMOS GROWTH & INCOME A**	16.2
1989-98	PACIFIC HORIZON CAPITAL INCOME A	16.6

*Average annual, pretax
**Calamos Funds, 800-823-7386; or see Business Week Online

DATA: MORNINGSTAR INC.

on stocks so low, they make a good addition to the portfolio of a more conservative equity investor, perhaps supplanting the role once played by equity–income funds. For the bond investor, the convertibles can actually smooth out the volatility of a portfolio that's overly sensitive to interest rates. Convertible bonds have only a 20 percent correlation with investment-grade bonds, so they definitely do bring diversification to an income-oriented portfolio.

Although both high-yield bond funds and convertible bond funds seem to take more of their cues from stocks than from bonds, the two sorts of funds are not duplicative. In theory, at least, the conversion feature to equity gives convertibles an unlimited return. High-yield bonds, on the other hand, are still fixed-income instruments. The gains are limited by the fixed interest payment and the difference between the purchase price and the bond's redemption price. The issuers are not the same, either. Companies that issue convertible bonds are smaller, more rapidly growing concerns, often in growth industries like high technology and health care. They are looking to keep borrowing costs down because they need money for growth. Those that issue high-yield debt tend to be more mature companies that are not growing fast enough to need to expand their shareholder base. So, in effect, an investor bringing convertible funds and high-yield funds into his or her portfolio is adding diversification.

The convertible bond market is not a large one. In fact, it's only about one-quarter the size of the high-yield bond market. Sometimes, even the portfolio managers of the relatively few convertible bond funds have a hard time finding the right bonds. So under certain market conditions, some funds create "synthetic convertibles" by pairing straight debt and call options on the issuer stock. (After all, a convertible bond is merely the combination of a straight bond and a call option on the issuer's stock.) And some funds just park their money in straight debt or equity when they don't like what's happening in the converts market.

INTERNATIONAL AND EMERGING MARKETS FUNDS

Just a dozen years ago, it wasn't too hard to guess which international bond fund would be the best of the year. There were only two, and they both invested in investment-grade foreign debt. Emerging markets debt mutual funds had not yet been invented. Nor had short-term world income funds, a sort of fund that tried—and ultimately failed—to earn high short-term yields without currency risk.

Today, you will find many choices for all these fund types in the mutual fund marketplace. In fact, there are so many emerging markets bond funds now that they have been split off into their own category.

To qualify for the international bond category, a fund must have at least 40 percent of its assets in foreign-issued bonds. But that's it. There's a wide variety of investment strategies. American Century-Benham International Bond Fund used to invest only in the bonds of the major European nations. Since they now have a common currency (at least for business and finance, though not in the wallet), the fund recently expanded its charter (and changed its name from European to International) and decided to expand the list of nations to Canada, Australia, and, on a limited basis, Japan. It rarely hedges currencies. Goldman Sachs Global Income A, on the other hand, goes heavy on hedging. Franklin Templeton Hard Currency Fund is really a foreign money-market fund. The portfolio's average maturity is always around six months, and the fund never hedges currency exposure. The idea behind the portfolio is to buy currencies of low-inflation countries as a hedge against inflation in the United States. Nowadays, the fund holds lots of U.S. securities, which says a lot about inflation in the United States and the strength of the dollar.

The best performer in 1998 was the tiny Vontobel Eastern European Debt Fund, up 24.5 percent in total return (Table 2-43). It sure sounds like it should be an emerging markets fund, but it's not. The fund's mandate says it must invest in debt rated BBB or better, which is the minimum rating to be considered investment grade. It's only allowed to have 10 percent of its assets in lower ratings, where most of the emerging markets bond funds invest.

TABLE 2-43

INTERNATIONAL AND EMERGING MARKETS FUNDS

BEST RETURNS

Period ▼	Fund ▼	Total return* ▼
INTERNATIONAL BOND		
1998	VONTOBEL EASTERN EUROPEAN DEBT**	24.5%
1996-98	ALLIANCE NORTH AMER. GOVT. INCOME B	14.4
1994-98	BT INVESTMENT GLOBAL HIGH-YIELD SECS.	8.7
1989-98	LORD ABBETT GLOBAL INCOME A	8.9
EMERGING MARKETS BOND		
1998	BEAR STEARNS EMERGING MKTS. DEBT A**	−10.8%
1996-98	BEAR STEARNS EMERGING MKTS. DEBT A	12.8
1994-98	BEAR STEARNS EMERGING MKTS. DEBT A	7.4
1989-98	NOT APPLICABLE	

*Average annual, pretax
**Vontobel Funds, 800-527-9500; Bear Stearns Funds, 800-766-4111; or see Business Week Online

DATA: MORNINGSTAR INC.

Ah, the emerging markets. They got nailed something awful in 1998, down 25.5 percent in total return. Net asset value went down even further. The big hit, of course, was Russia, which failed to make good on its bonds. Most banks eventually wrote off their Russian bonds, figuring they'd never pay off. The funds had to mark down whatever they couldn't sell at mark-down prices. Naturally, the Russian repudiation reverberated through all the emerging markets and everything collapsed in price. The best-performing emerging markets bond fund during 1998 was Bear Stearns Emerging Markets Debt, it was down only 10.8 percent in total return. Fidelity New Markets Income Fund, the leader in 1997, suffered a 22.4 percent loss in total return in 1998. Ouch.

Last year was the second bear market for these funds in their relatively short history. The last one was in 1994 and 1995 and was precipitated by the surprise devaluation of the Mexican peso and a quick collapse in the Latin American stock and bond markets. In 1994, these funds were down 16 percent. And even though the crisis spilled over into early 1995, the markets recovered enough so the funds finished the year up 22 percent.

The idea behind investing in emerging markets debt is that these countries have cleaned up their acts economically. They've restructured their economies, allowed for privatization of state-owned industries, lowered trade barriers, and welcomed foreign capital. In short, they became much better borrowers than they had been. Indeed, portfolio managers who run these funds hone in on such factors as inflation, unemployment, and government fiscal and monetary policy before buying only those countries or "credits" that are clearly on the road to economic reform. The profit for emerging markets debt funds is not only in the higher interest rates, but also in price appreciation of the bonds as other investors recognize the improved credit quality and pay up for the bonds. In that sense, they're somewhat analogous to junk bond funds, and, indeed, many junk bond funds also invest in these markets.

Currency changes play a part in these funds, too, but usually not as much as you think. Many emerging nations peg their currencies to the U.S. dollar or issue dollar-denominated debt, so currency-induced fluctuations in the funds may well be less than in traditional international bond funds. But when a Third World currency collapses, like many of those in East Asia did in 1997, watch out below.

With the more conventional international bond funds, currencies count for more than credit quality. The argument for international bond investing is the same as it is for investing in foreign stocks—diversification. But non-U.S. bonds do not always zig while the other markets zag. The 1994 bear market in bonds was a global, not just a U.S., bear market. As such, it was hard to find any short-term world income or world bond funds that excelled in 1994, when a U.S. investor would really have appreciated it. Likewise, in 1995, these funds went up along with U.S. bond funds, but nobody complains about that.

What sometimes makes foreign fixed-income securities alluring is when interest rates are higher abroad than they are at home. That makes the yields attractive in themselves. But you have to factor in whether the dollar is appreciating against either the yen or the euro. What if your fund is earning 9 percent on its German bonds and the euro appreciates 9 percent against the dollar? Your total return is 18 percent.

But what happens if the dollar appreciates or the other countries' currencies depreciate? That's what happened in 1992. U.S. investors in international bond funds earned, on average, total returns of only 2.8 percent—that's after the yield. PaineWebber Global Income Fund, for instance, paid out a yield of nearly 7 percent, but wound up the year with a total return of 1.3 percent. Investors lost nearly 5 percent of their net asset value during the year.

Or, what happens when the dollar falls, making foreign bonds more valuable, yet the international bond fund you own is plodding along because of a hedging strategy? Indeed, that's what happened in early 1995 when the dollar plunged, especially against the German mark and the Japanese yen, yet very few international bond funds were able to profit on that. That's because they had used the foreign exchange market to "convert" their marks into dollars, a strategy that pays off when the dollar goes up against the mark. But if the mark goes up against the dollar, and the fund has sold its marks, there's no money to be made. Yet most international bond funds employ strategies that do just that.

Why? These funds are usually sold as low-risk yield vehicles, not as total return investments. And one way to keep the risk low is to neutralize the foreign currency exposure. But a fund that does that is also undercutting much of the diversification advantage investors get from going global.

MULTISECTOR FUNDS

Can't decide what kind of bond fund you want? Maybe you don't have to. Try a multisector bond fund. By their charters, they are supposed to keep their money in three types of fixed-income investments: U.S. government bonds or government-backed mortgage securities; foreign debt, both government and private issue; and high-yield corporates, or "junk" bonds. Most of the funds have a benchmark or "neutral" allocation of one-third of assets to each of the three sectors. Then, the portfolio manager is permitted to diverge from that depending on the investment opportunities in each.

The mix makes a lot of sense. U.S. government bonds are high in credit quality, but are the most sensitive to interest-rate risk, or the changes in bond prices that come from changes in interest rates. High-yield corporates are less interest-rate sensitive, but more credit-sensitive. A strong economy might send interest rates up on government bonds, but should also improve the cash flow, and, hence, credit quality, of high-yield bonds. Foreign bonds, even if they are dollar denominated, bring diversification to the mix, since the movements of many foreign economies and bond markets do not correlate to that of the United States.

Though these funds try to maintain somewhat of a balance among the bond sectors, the managers do tilt them to take advantage of perceived market opportunities. During 1997, the best

TABLE 2-44

MULTISECTOR FUNDS		
BEST RETURNS		
Period ▼	Fund ▼	Total return* ▼
1998	JANUS FLEXIBLE INCOME	8.2%
1996-98	FRANKLIN STRATEGIC INCOME	10.2
1994-98	JANUS FLEXIBLE INCOME	8.7
1989-98	KEMPER DIVERSIFIED INCOME A	11.1

*Average annual, pretax   DATA: MORNINGSTAR INC.

opportunities were in high-yield and foreign bonds—especially those with emerging markets debt. In 1998, the savvier fund managers ratcheted up their high-quality holdings. The best multisector performer of 1997, Janus Flexible Income (Table 2-44), earned its 8.2 percent total return by largely avoiding emerging markets and stocking up on U.S. government and corporate bonds. Treasuries in particular went up while almost everything else went down. The average multisector fund earned only 1.9 percent in total return during 1998.

Janus' Ron Speaker, the portfolio manager, says the fund has a wide berth in what it can invest in. He says the fund can also exploit opportunities that other more focused bond funds miss. For instance, he mentions "split-rate" bonds, which are bonds rated investment grade by one ratings agency but junk by another. Speaker says such bonds can be a good buy because both high-grade and high-yield investors shun them.

AIM Income A has a different take on the multisector bond fund. It tends to own longer-term securities with higher durations. The average multisector fund looks to earn its money from sector allocations, not interest-rate bets. Most keep their durations around 4 or 5 years, giving them volatility characteristics of intermediate funds. T. Rowe Price Spectrum Income, rated A compared to other multisector funds, takes yet a different approach. It's a fund of funds, investing in other T. Rowe Price bond funds.

One interesting note about the multisector funds: nearly all of them are sold and managed by load-fund companies. The reason is that the funds' investment pitch is more sophisticated than just a government bond or a straight muni fund. So fund executives thought that, to sell the funds, they would need the help of salespeople to explain the product to investors. There are only three pure no-loads in this category: Janus Flexible Income, Strong Short-Term Global Bond, and T. Rowe Price Spectrum Income.

MUNICIPAL FUNDS

No one likes higher taxes. No one, that is, except the people who sell and manage municipal bond funds. When Bill Clinton was first elected, the "muni" market cheered. His tax hikes for upper-income taxpayers make the muni alternative look better than ever. The Internal Revenue Service can't touch the income from muni bond funds as long as the interest income comes from tax-exempt securities issued by state and local governments and authorities. Right after the Republican sweep of Congress in the 1994 elections, muni bond prices slumped. One explanation: the GOP's campaign promises to lower taxes. Lower taxes make munis less attractive. Just about the time munis started to recover from that GOP Congress, millionaire publisher Steve Forbes started campaigning for the Republican presidential nomination. His chief rallying cry was the "flat tax," a "one rate fits all" plan that's anathema to the municipal bond crowd. The lower tax rates go, the higher the yields tax-exempt bonds have to pay to attract investors.

A tax-exempt security typically sports a lower yield than a taxable security of comparable maturity and credit quality. All things being equal, their returns are lower than those on comparable taxable funds, though at times muni funds can outperform taxable funds (Table 2-45). That's because investors will accept a lower rate in return for the tax exemption. In deciding whether to invest in a muni or taxable bond fund, the key question to ask is, "What is the taxable equivalent of the yield on a muni fund?" The answer to that question depends on your marginal tax rate. The higher the rate, the better a muni looks compared to a taxable fund. (If you're talking about a tax-deferred retirement account, always choose the higher yielding taxable bonds.)

When marginal tax rates were first slashed in 1982, some predicted that tax-exempt bonds would lose their attraction. Prior to that, the top tax rate on individual income was 50 percent, so a 7 percent muni bond payout was the same as a 14 percent taxable bond. But after the 1986 tax act, which introduced a 28 percent top rate, the 7 percent coupon was worth only 9.72 percent in a taxable bond.

But the muni never lost its appeal to investors. The 1986 tax bill that cut rates also scotched many of the tax shelters high-income individuals used to cut their tax bills. The muni was the one

TABLE 2-45

MUNICIPAL FUNDS		
BEST RETURNS		
Period ▼	Fund ▼	Total return* ▼
MUNICIPAL NATIONAL LONG		
1998	CITIFUNDS NATIONAL TAX-FREE INCOME	10.1%
1996-98	UNITED MUNICIPAL HIGH-INCOME A	8.5
1994-98	UNITED MUNICIPAL HIGH-INCOME A	7.6
1989-98	EXCELSIOR LONG-TERM TAX-EXEMPT	9.2
MUNICIPAL NATIONAL INTERMEDIATE		
1998	FIRST INVESTORS INS. INTERM. TAX-EX. A	6.9%
1996-98	VAN KAMPEN HIGH-YIELD MUNICIPALS A	7.8
1994-98	VAN KAMPEN HIGH-YIELD MUNICIPALS A	7.4
1989-98	DELAWARE NATIONAL HIGH-YIELD MUNI. A	8.4
MUNICIPAL CALIFORNIA LONG		
1998	FRANKLIN CALIF. HIGH YIELD MUNI. A	7.4%
1996-98	FRANKLIN CALIF. HIGH YIELD MUNI. A	8.4
1994-98	FRANKLIN CALIF. HIGH YIELD MUNI. A	7.3
1989-98	SAFECO CALIF. TAX-FREE INCOME NO LOAD	8.5
MUNICIPAL CALIFORNIA INTERMEDIATE		
1998	FRANKLIN CALIF. INTERM.-TERM TAX-FREE	6.5%
1996-98	SELIGMAN MUNICIPAL CALIF. HIGH-YIELD A	6.8
1994-98	SELIGMAN MUNICIPAL CALIF. HIGH-YIELD A	6.3
1989-98	SELIGMAN MUNICIPAL CALIF. HIGH-YIELD A	7.7
MUNICIPAL NEW YORK LONG		
1998	VAN KAMPEN N.Y. TAX-FREE INCOME A	6.9%
1996-98	VAN KAMPEN N.Y. TAX-FREE INCOME A	7.5
1994-98	LEBENTHAL N.Y. MUNICIPAL BOND A**	6.4
1989-98	ROCHESTER FUND MUNICIPALS A	8.5
MUNICIPAL NEW YORK INTERMEDIATE		
1998	FRANKLIN N.Y. INTERM. TAX-FREE INCOME	6.6%
1996-98	FRANKLIN N.Y. INTERM. TAX-FREE INCOME	6.6
1994-98	PUTNAM N.Y. TAX EXEMPT OPPORTUNITIES A	6.0
1989-98	CHASE VISTA N.Y. TAX-FREE INCOME A	8.0
MUNICIPAL SINGLE-STATE LONG		
1998	FRANKLIN MICH. TAX-FREE INCOME A	7.6%
1996-98	ALLIANCE MUNICIPAL INCOME II MASS. A	9.0
1994-98	DUPREE TENNESSEE TAX-FREE INCOME	7.6
1989-98	DREYFUS PREMIER STATE MUNI. TEXAS A	8.8
MUNICIPAL SINGLE-STATE INTERMEDIATE		
1998	LORD ABBETT TAX-FREE INCOME GEORGIA	7.2%
1996-98	COLORADO BONDSHARES**	8.0
1994-98	COLORADO BONDSHARES**	7.9
1989-98	LORD ABBETT TAX-FREE INCOME TEXAS	8.2
MUNICIPAL SHORT		
1998	STRONG SHORT-TERM HI-YIELD MUNICIPALS	6.3%
1996-98	SIT MINNESOTA TAX-FREE INCOME	6.8
1994-98	SIT MINNESOTA TAX-FREE INCOME	6.5
1989-98	DAVIS TAX-FREE HIGH INCOME B	6.8

*Average annual, pretax
**Colorado Bondshares, 800-572-0069; Lebenthal, 800-221-5822; or see Business Week Online

DATA: MORNINGSTAR INC.

tax haven left. More important, shelters only delay paying taxes. The interest income generated by municipal bonds is always tax-free, and so is the interest income that an investor receives from a muni bond fund. However, not all the income generated by the fund is tax-exempt. If the fund is adept at trading bonds and earns some capital gains, those gains (net of losses) will be passed on to investors as a capital gains distribution, taxable at the capital gains rate.

It's possible that muni funds may start to generate fully taxable ordinary income as well. That's because the 1993 tax act changed the law so that the money earned when bonds bought at discount to par are redeemed at par will be considered ordinary income—taxable at the investor's highest rate. Before the changes, that difference would have been considered capital gains, taxed at a lower rate. Not surprisingly, Wall Street and mutual fund lobbyists are trying to change that law.

Even so, muni bond funds make sense for many investors. The top federal tax bracket is 36 percent, and for an elite few, a millionaire's surcharge raises it to 39.6 percent. Municipal bonds almost always beat taxable bonds for investors in the highest brackets. But muni yields have been so high at times that muni funds are attractive to investors in lower tax brackets too. To get the maximum return, investors need to compare muni and taxable funds, adjusting for the tax exemption. For instance, in February 1998, the Vanguard Long-Term U.S. Treasury Fund was yielding 5.36 percent, while the Vanguard Long-Term Tax-Exempt Fund was yielding 4.46 percent. What's the better buy? Suppose you're in the 31 percent marginal tax bracket. You merely subtract 31 percent of the yield from 5.36 percent and you get 3.7 percent after taxes. Obviously, the muni fund offers a better yield.

There's another way to look at this. Start with the number 1 and subtract your marginal tax bracket from it: 1 minus 0.31 (31 percent is also expressed as 0.31) equals 0.69. Next, divide that number into the tax-exempt yield. Divide 4.46 percent by 0.69 and you get 6.46 percent. So, unless you can get a return of at least 6.46 percent in a taxable investment of like quality, the muni is the better deal.

Though municipal bond income is free from federal taxes, states tax municipal income from bonds issued in other states. Neither the New Yorker investing in a California bond nor the Californian with the New York bond will owe federal tax on the interest, but he or she will owe state income tax. In states with low income tax rates, that may not matter. But in high tax states like California and New York, the extra tax can cut into your returns.

So the mutual fund folks have come up with an antidote for that, too—single-state municipal bond funds. By restricting investment to the investor's home state, these funds generate income that's exempt not only from federal taxes but from state and city income taxes as well. For the tax-weary folks of New York City, a New York bond fund is said to be "triple-tax-exempt." The largest municipal fund of all, in fact, is the Franklin California Tax-Free Income Fund. It's also one of the oldest, dating back to 1977.

No longer do you have to live in a big, heavily populated state to have a single-state fund to call your own. Single-state funds abound in 44 states and Puerto Rico, though New Yorkers and Californians have the most funds to choose from (Table 2-46). If a state isn't represented, it may be because the tax laws are not amenable to it. If there's no state income or personal property assessment that taxes financial holdings, there's no need for a single-state muni fund—though Texas has 21 of them anyway. Illinois, for instance, does have a state income tax, but does not exempt interest earned from most Illinois municipal bonds. So there's no particular advantage for an Illinois taxpayer to invest in most Illinois bonds.

The big drawback of single-state funds is just that: All the bonds come from a single state and rise and fall on the financial condition of the state,

TABLE 2-46

STATES WITH SINGLE-STATE BOND FUNDS

State	Funds	State	Funds	State	Funds
ALABAMA	7	MASSACHUSETTS	61	OREGON	20
ARIZONA	41	MICHIGAN	49	PENNSYLVANIA	67
ARKANSAS	9	MINNESOTA	38	PUERTO RICO	2
CALIFORNIA	170	MISSISSIPPI	12	RHODE ISLAND	7
COLORADO	29	MISSOURI	20	SOUTH CAROLINA	20
CONNECTICUT	28	MONTANA	1	SOUTH DAKOTA	1
FLORIDA	89	NEBRASKA	2	TENNESSEE	28
GEORGIA	35	NEW HAMPSHIRE	1	TEXAS	21
HAWAII	11	NEW JERSEY	53	UTAH	3
IDAHO	21	NEW MEXICO	9	VERMONT	2
INDIANA	1	NEW YORK	124	VIRGINIA	44
KANSAS	9	NORTH CAROLINA	48	WASHINGTON	5
KENTUCKY	20	NORTH DAKOTA	1	WEST VIRGINIA	9
LOUISIANA	13	OHIO	55	WISCONSIN	6
MARYLAND	42				

DATA: MORNINGSTAR INC.

its local governments, and bond-issuing authorities. In December 1994, the muni market in general and the California market in particular were rocked when Orange County disclosed it had what was eventually determined to be about $2 billion in losses in its investment portfolio, a fund (not a mutual fund) in which Orange County and many smaller jurisdictions had money that was needed to service their debt.

Within days, the county filed for bankruptcy, which put all debt service in doubt and sent bond prices into a skid. The NAV of the Franklin California Tax-Free Fund, the largest California muni fund, dropped 1.32 percent. Franklin California Insured Tax-Free Income Fund took the same percentage hit, even though bond insurers would step in to make up any payments Orange County borrowers missed. In contrast, the nationally diversified Franklin Federal Tax-Free Income Fund fell too, but only 0.8 percent.

Insured funds are popular with New York investors as well, since the Empire State for many years seemed to lurch from one fiscal crisis to another. Ironically, in New York as in many other states, high-quality bonds of well-known issuers aren't always a safe harbor. When the muni market gets the shakes, the first bonds to get dumped are those of the highest quality. They're the most liquid. Provided they don't default, the lesser credits and lesser-known names seem to hold up relatively well. They don't go on the auction block. Many muni funds that have "high-yield" in their names achieve that objective just by seeking out the higher interest rates of the little-known issuers.

If you've decided to invest in tax-exempt funds, you still have to make the same kinds of decisions you make with taxable funds. Do you want a fund with short-, intermediate-, or long term bonds? Is there a single-state fund for your home state, and is the yield competitive? The municipal fund categories are organized along maturity and geographic lines. They are municipal national long-term, municipal national intermediate-term, municipal single-state long-term, municipal single-state intermediate-term, and, for California and New York, long-term and intermediate-term categories of their own. The category "municipal short-term" takes in both national and single-state funds. Funds that invest in insured bonds usually say so in their names. Those that invest in junk-rated or unrated municipal bonds generally use "high-yield" in their names.

The menu of municipal bond offerings is broad, so a good fund can make use of it to diversify a portfolio, both geographically and by the type of project the bonds finance. General obligation (GO) bonds—those backed by the credit and taxing power of the issuer—are only a small part of the tax-exempt bond line-up. Far more numerous are revenue bonds, which are paid off by rentals, fees, tolls, and the like from roads, bridges, tunnels, arenas, ballparks, water works, sewage treatment plants, power plants, parking structures, housing, and hospitals.

Revenue bonds are riskier than GOs—after all, the project's revenue can easily fall short. That's a risk with nonessential public projects like arenas and stadiums. Suppose a project runs far over budget or is never completed? That's what happened with the Washington Public Power Supply System in the early 1980s, which failed to complete or build several nuclear power plants that it financed with revenue bonds.

If your fund manager has done some savvy bond trading and racked up some capital gains, the fund will have to make a capital gains distribution too. Sorry, capital gains from tax-free bonds are taxable. But such distributions are infrequent. Still, investors who don't want capital gains should stick to yield-oriented funds that emphasize bonds selling at a premium, or above par. Such funds don't climb as much in a falling rate environment, nor do they melt as quickly if interest rates climb.

Like their taxable counterparts, muni funds are creatures of interest rates. But munis don't move in lock-step with Treasuries either. At times they can be more volatile. In the spring of 1987, when interest rates rose swiftly in the government bond market, investors rushed to pull funds out of the muni bond funds. With insufficient cash on hand to meet them, muni funds had to sell bonds into a falling market in order to meet redemptions. Since the municipal bond market is far less liquid than the Treasury bond market, even big institutional investors must take huge discounts in price in order to sell bonds quickly. Between mid-March and mid-April 1987, the T. Rowe Price Tax-Free Fund lost 9.22 percent of its net asset value.

On the other hand, sometimes the muni market will outperform taxables. In 1988, for instance, government bonds finished the year about where they started. The muni bonds, in contrast, gained about 6 points, or $60 per $1000 bond. Why? A shortage in supply combined with a pickup in demand from shell-shocked equity investors. Supply and demand of muni bonds does have an effect on prices and, in turn, on

Muni funds can generate taxable gains.

yields. In 1992 and 1993, muni funds outdistanced the taxables, even though the muni market was flooded with record new issuance. That's because demand was so strong. In 1994, the supply of new bonds dropped to nearly half. But with rising interest rates and tax-law changes affecting the treatment of market discount bonds, demand—thus prices—dropped even more. As a result, on a total return basis, muni funds did far worse than taxables.

And in 1998, interest rates fell, but muni prices did not rise as fast as those on government bonds. In the flight to quality, many investors wanted Treasuries only, even though state and local government are generally in better financial shape than they have been in years. The other reason for lagging returns: record issuance of new bonds, some $280 billion worth, hit the market at a time when demand was slack. While intermediate government funds earned a 7.5 percent total return in 1998, intermediate municipal funds gained just 5.6 percent. Still, considering that the yield portion of the return is tax-exempt, the intermediate muni funds' return probably beat the government funds' return after adjusting for taxes.

TABLE 2-47

MONEY-MARKET MUTUAL FUNDS: THEY'RE NOT ALL THE SAME

Money-Market Fund	Comments	Yield*
100% U.S. TREASURY	Highest safety, but lowest yields. Interest is subject to federal tax, but is exempt from state and local income taxes in most states.	4.63%
U.S. TREASURY AND REPO'S	Invests in repurchase agreements, in which a bond dealer sells securities, agreeing to buy them back on a certain date at a higher price. Difference between two prices is the interest.	4.83
U.S. GOVERNMENT & AGENCIES	May also invest in securities issued by U.S.-backed agencies such as Federal National Mortgage Assn. Agency paper is highly-rated and has nearly the same credit quality as U.S. Treasuries.	4.91
GENERAL PURPOSE	Can also buy high-quality commercial paper of corporations and non-insured bank-related investments, which adds some credit risk. A few "second tier" funds purchase lower-quality paper for a higher yield (5.23%).	4.98
TAX-FREE	Invests in short-term municipal securities, such as tax anticipation notes. Exempt from federal taxes, but not state and local taxes. State-specific funds avoids taxes for taxpayers of those states (2.81%).	2.93

DATA: IBC MONEY FUND REPORT, BUSINESS WEEK   *1998

Money-Market Funds

Money-market mutual funds are a breed apart from stock and bond funds. Their principal difference is that they keep their share prices at a constant $1 per share. They're able to do this because they invest in very short-term debt instruments. Usually, price fluctuations in those investments are so small that funds can maintain their constant dollar price. Thus, a money-market mutual fund account will look a lot like a bank account.

As with bond funds, there are taxable and tax-free money-market funds. The taxable funds come in several categories, depending on the kind of investments they make (Table 2-47). U.S. Treasury-only funds invest in just Treasury securities. They have the lowest yield but are considered the safest. Then comes those that invest in Treasuries and repurchase agreements, a sort of loan that's backed by Treasuries. The next category invests in U.S. Government agency securities, such as those issued by Fannie Mae and Freddie Mac. The general purpose funds may invest in all of the above, but also seek higher yields from bank-issued instruments and short-term corporate debt. Tax-exempt funds invest in the short-term instruments issued by state and local governments.

TAXABLE FUNDS

In 1981, when short-term interest rates were in the high teens, money-market funds looked like the dream investment. Interest rates on bank deposits were regulated, and passbook accounts—the province of the small investor—paid about 5.5 percent. The average money-market fund paid nearly 17 percent! That's when Americans who never heard of mutual funds got their introduction to them. And it was because of the high yields of the money funds. During the 1980s and into the 1990s, as interest rates headed south, so did the returns from money-market funds (Figure 2-2). And as returns continued to drop, so did investor interest and media attention.

Well, money-market funds are back on investors' radar screens. True, the dramatic rise in short-term interest rates and the consequent volatility in bond funds made money funds look a

FIGURE 2-2

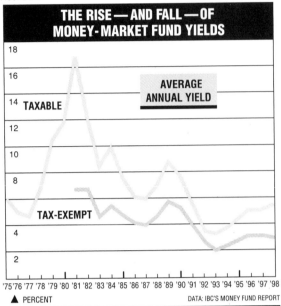

THE RISE — AND FALL — OF MONEY-MARKET FUND YIELDS

AVERAGE ANNUAL YIELD

TAXABLE

TAX-EXEMPT

▲ PERCENT   DATA: IBC'S MONEY FUND REPORT

'75 '76 '77 '78 '79 '80 '81 '82 '83 '84 '85 '86 '87 '88 '89 '90 '91 '92 '93 '94 '95 '96 '97 '98

lot more attractive in 1994 than they had looked in years. But what drew the public attention to money funds again were shocking revelations that some 15 sponsors of 35 money-market funds put up $769 million to avoid "breaking the buck," that is, having to reprice the money-fund shares (kept constant at $1 NAV) because of investments gone bad. Among those bailing out their own funds were Bank of America, Kidder Peabody, United Services, and Value Line. No one came to the rescue of the tiny Community Bankers U.S. Government Money Market Fund, and the fund broke the buck and liquidated for 94 cents on the dollar.

Tax-exempt money-market funds hit the news, too, after Orange County, California, declared bankruptcy. *Money Market Insight*, an industry publication, estimated that sponsors of at least "25 major funds" sought regulators' permission to buy Orange County securities from their funds, lest the securities stop making interest payments. Some sponsors like Franklin and Putnam bought the securities from the funds, while Alliance Capital backed them up with a letter of credit (which would pay off if the securities didn't). Benham and Calvert funds also provided guarantees. In all cases, the fund managers were trying to avoid breaking the buck.

Breaking the buck is the money-fund managers' and the regulators' worst nightmare. Investors recognize that stock and bond funds can fluctuate in NAV, but money funds are not supposed to do so. Usually, the funds invest in instruments that are so short in maturity that the portfolio fluctuations are minute, and thus, the fund can maintain its net asset value at $1 per share. The small profits and losses in the portfolio can be accounted for by varying the payout. If there's a small capital gain, the fund can just pass it along as a little extra yield. By the same token, small losses in principal can be absorbed by the income stream, resulting in a slightly lowered payout. Many funds use an accounting method that allows them to carry the securities on their books at cost. Under those rules, assets don't fluctuate in value at all.

What went wrong in 1994 was that some funds had invested in derivatives such as inverse floaters or "structured notes" which were engineered to pay higher yields in a falling interest-rate environment. When interest rates spiked, these derivatives plunged in price and could no longer be valued at 100 cents on the dollar. These derivatives worked fine for the funds as interest rates fell, since they allowed the funds to pay higher yields than they otherwise would. When rates started climbing, these derivatives' yields fell and the funds could not sell the derivatives without taking a large loss that would break the buck. The SEC later issued rules about what money funds could not invest in, which included the same sort of securities that had caused the problems.

It was not the first time that investments gone sour threatened to break the buck. That happened when a few funds, in stretching for yield, bought "junk" commercial paper that went into default. In both cases, the two sponsors, T. Rowe Price Associates and Value Line, Inc., bought the commercial paper from the funds at the funds' cost, and the parent company, not the money fund, took the loss. In response, the SEC tightened regulations on credit quality of fund investments. Still, credit problems do pop up. In early 1997, Mercury Finance Co., which makes used car loans, had serious financial problems that had not been properly disclosed. One rating agency had rated Mercury's commercial paper (very short-term notes) investment-grade, while nearly all others considered it in the second tier. While many money-market funds will not invest in such "split-rated" securities, Strong Heritage Money Market Fund did. When the depths of Mercury's problems came out, Strong Capital Management stepped in and bought the commercial paper from the fund. Had it not done so, the fund would have "broken the buck."

Since the mutual fund industry and the SEC have long adopted the $1 per share practice for money funds, a money-market fund statement ends up looking a lot like that of a bank account. If you have 15,271 shares, you also have $15,271. Interest earned each day is usually credited daily. The payments are technically "dividends," but they are the functional equivalent of interest. And since the funds behave an awful lot like bank accounts, it's not surprising that many people use them in just that way. There's one big difference, though, and that's the reason for the emphasis on safety—money-market mutual funds are not government-insured.

In general, money-market fund yields have been higher—on average about 1 percentage point more—than bank money-market deposit accounts. As short-term rates shot up in 1994, the yield advantage over bank money-market deposit accounts increased to the point where money funds were paying more than double bank money-market account rates and even more than six-month certificates of deposit. That's because money-market funds pass along to their investors all they earn—less expenses, of course. A bank money-market deposit account is an administered rate. The bank decides what it will pay on deposits. Though they are somewhat linked to the general level and direction of interest rates, banks tend to pay only what they must to maintain the deposits. That is, if they even want or need to maintain them. If loan demand is weak, as it was in the early 1990s, banks can always lower their interest rates enough to encourage depositors to take their money elsewhere.

Most money-market funds offer some kind of checking privileges too. However, since they usually require a minimum check amount of several hundred dollars, you will need a conventional checking account as well. If you want check-writing privileges, be sure to read the portion in the prospectus that describes the program. Not only can there be restrictions on the minimum amount of the check, but also on the number of checks written each month.

But as an investor, you're probably not very concerned with check-writing—though it's handy to have, even if you don't make much use of it. To make your life easier, you'll probably want to have money-market fund accounts with fund groups in which you have other mutual funds.

So, if you have several Franklin, Putnam, or Scudder funds, you might find it convenient to keep a money-market fund there. Suppose you wanted to invest $10,000 in an equity fund, but spread it over a year's time. You might start with $2000 in the equity fund and put the balance in

one of the money-market funds. If you set it up with telephone or online switching privileges, you can gradually shift from the money fund into the stock fund over a period of time. In the same way, the money-market fund is a good parking place for your money. If you're switching out of a stock or bond fund, you can park the cash in the fund group's money fund while you're deciding what to do next with your money. If you like the fund's yield better than the prospects for stock or bond funds, you may decide to let the money sit. With a money-market fund, your assets are not idle. They earn interest every day.

Since there's a great deal of similarity in investment policy and services, investors who spend considerable time shopping for stock or bond funds pay little attention to their money-market funds. Though there are differences in the quality of the money-market instruments in which money funds invest, by and large those differences are not great. If you're otherwise weighing the risks of a growth fund versus a balanced fund, the difference between money funds is trivial.

If you look at money-market-fund yields that are published in the newspaper financial sections every week, it looks like there can be as much as two percentage points of difference in yields. That can be deceptive. In the very short term, yields are volatile and any week's yield will depend on the various maturities of the fund.

The shorter the maturity, the faster the yield will respond to changes in interest rates. Suppose one fund has an average maturity of 30 days and another has 15 days. If interest rates rise in the next two weeks, the yield on the 15-day fund is going to go up faster. That's because the fund has more investments maturing sooner and will be able to roll them over at higher interest rates. But if interest rates fall during the period, the longer maturity fund fares better, because it will hold on to its higher-yielding investments much longer.

As a result of the fluctuations in rates and portfolio maturities, week to week the differentials look big. But over a year's time those differences smooth out. In fact, *Income & Safety*, a newsletter that tracks money-market funds, says that the difference between the highest- and lowest-yielding fund in any year is about 0.9 percentage point. That means that, if you had a $10,000 average balance, and you had the worst-yielding fund, you would receive only $90 less income than from the very highest-yielding fund. Of course, the larger the average balance in your money-market fund, the more you want to focus on the yield.

Most money funds offer checking privileges.

That 0.9 percentage point spread on a $100,000 account is $900—and that's not insignificant.

Still, the search for yield has its limitations. Returns are far more homogeneous in money-market funds than in stock or bond funds. That's because money-market funds must live within fairly narrow strictures set down by industry practice and the Securities & Exchange Commission. Funds mainly invest in U.S. Treasury bills, repurchase agreements, certificates of deposit, bankers acceptances, and commercial paper. But it's also obvious from the events of the last year that perhaps not all funds—at least not the ones that got into trouble—were investing solely in these tried-and-true instruments. Following is a brief description of each.

U.S. Treasury Bills. These are short-term obligations of the U.S. government, which come in three-month, six-month, and one-year maturities. Individual investors can buy these on their own, but there's a $10,000 minimum. Other U.S. government agencies also raise short-term funds in the money-markets from time to time. Their securities are also permissible in many funds. Those include the Farm Credit Bank, Fannie Mae, Freddie Mac, and the Student Loan Marketing Association.

Repurchase Agreements. Repo's, as they're usually known, are short-term borrowings using U.S. government securities as collateral. They work like this. A bank or securities dealer has an inventory of Treasury bonds it needs to finance for, say, 20 days. Sometimes the term of the loan is merely overnight. The dealer borrows from a money-market fund and gives the fund securities as collateral for the loan. The arrangement is called a repurchase agreement because the borrower agrees to "repurchase" the collateral by paying back the loan. The credit on the line is the bank's or dealer's, but as long as the fund can claim the securities in case of default, the credit quality is considered high.

Bank Certificates of Deposit. Most people are familiar with CDs, but the funds invest in "jumbos"—CDs over $100,000 that are not insured by the FDIC. The creditworthiness of the bank is the only thing that backs them up. Sometimes money-market funds invest in Eurodollar CDs, which are dollar-based CDs issued by European, usually London, branches of U.S. banks. The interest rates are usually a little higher than those of domestic CDs. Yankee CDs are issued in the United States by branches of foreign banks.

Banker's Acceptances. These instruments are irrevocable obligations of the banks that issue them, so their quality is similar to that of a bank's certificate of deposit. Acceptances are created as a financing tool for international trade, but holders of the acceptances can raise cash immediately by selling them into the money market. Money-market funds often buy them.

Commercial Paper. As a less costly alternative to bank borrowings, many large corporations raise funds through commercial paper, or short-term IOUs. There is no collateral behind commercial paper. The only backing is the creditworthiness of the issuer.

If you look behind the yields available on these sorts of instruments, you can see why all money-fund yields lie within a tight range. In February 1999, for instance, three-month T-bills yielded 4.38 percent; high-grade commercial paper, 4.82 percent; and CDs, about 4.7 percent. In that interest rate environment, the average taxable money fund yielded 4.6 percent. There's no way a money fund could earn even 7 percent, especially since money funds have management fees and other expenses as well.

With yields in a narrow range, there's not much a portfolio manager can add by actively trading assets. Thus, the major determinant in performance is overhead. All money funds are sold without sales fees, but in choosing a fund be sure there are no hidden sales fees, known in the mutual fund trade as "12(b)-1" fees, coming out of the portfolio. In selecting a fund, also be sure to choose one where the total expenses—management fees and other costs such as printing, mailing, and auditing—come to less than 0.50 percent. That's important because what you earn from the fund is the gross yield less expenses. And when yields are low, expenses play an even greater role. Remember, 0.50 percent on a 5 percent yield is 10 percent of the income. Sometimes fund companies waive all or part of their fund expenses in order to boost the yield. And then they advertise that higher yield as a draw for the fund. If someone's willing to subsidize your investments, why not? Just be sure to ask how long the waiver is expected to continue. Most funds will guarantee a fee waiver through a certain date, but they often extend them. And even when fund sponsors start to implement the fees, they usually don't take

High costs can decimate money fund returns.

them all at once but phase them in over time. Flex-Fund Money Market Fund, part of the Flex Funds Group, takes yet another approach. The fund's goal is to deliver a yield that's in the top 10 percent of all money-market funds, and the fund sponsor will waive all or part of the expenses to assure the fund's place at the top.

All this begs the question, "Should you invest in a money-market fund based on yield and expenses?" Historically, this has been the best way to go, though in the last few years credit and maturity risks have emerged as major concerns as well.

To ward off potential problems in the money funds, the Securities & Exchange Commission has pulled in its reins in recent years. First, the regulators lowered the ceiling on the maximum average maturity of a money-market fund portfolio to 90 days from 120 days. In general, the shorter the maturity of a security or a portfolio, the lower the risk of owning it.

Then, the SEC also came down hard on credit quality. Funds can no longer invest in below-investment-grade commercial paper. And no more than 5 percent of the fund can be invested in the lower tier of investment-grade paper, that which is rated A-2 by Standard & Poor's and P-2 by Moody's.

Finally, in the wake of the 1994 derivatives crises, the SEC banned several sorts of derivatives from money-market funds, mainly because their values can change drastically given a change in interest rates. Those off limits to money funds are inverse floaters, leveraged floaters, CMT (Constant Maturity Treasury) floaters, floaters whose interest rates are capped, and floaters whose resets lag changes in short-term interest rates. All of these instruments gained popularity with money-fund managers as interest rates came down. That's because with these instruments, payouts actually increased or decreased at a slower rate. Of course, when interest rates started moving up, these floaters' payouts sank—and so did their values.

With the banning of the most dangerous derivatives, the most cautious investors can probably sleep comfortably using a U.S. government money-market fund. The securities are free of credit risk but have lower yields than the general purpose funds. Still, in times of economic uncertainty, many fund analysts say going for the governments is advisable, even if you have to settle for a lesser return.

It's not even a certainty that one has to give up any yield. By careful fund shopping it's possible to find some government funds with better yields than those which also include bank CDs and commercial paper. Moreover, even if you switch from a general purpose to a government money-market fund in the same fund family, the difference in yields may not be more than 0.30 or 0.40 percentage point. That's a small price to pay if you're worried about credit quality.

U.S. government funds have another virtue that's sometimes overlooked. Just as the federal government doesn't tax interest earned by investing in state and local government debt, most state and local governments don't tax interest earned on federal government debt. If you are in a high-tax state like New York or California, that exemption can effectively add as much as 1 percentage point to the yield.

Not all government funds qualify for this tax treatment. Interest from repurchase agreements doesn't count because the income is coming not from the government securities but from the borrower who is posting the securities as collateral for a loan. If this is the case, you might consider a money-market fund that holds only U.S. Treasury securities.

TAX-EXEMPT FUNDS

Tax-exempt money-market funds have many of the same characteristics and features as taxable money funds: short-maturity securities, liquidity, and check-writing privileges. What makes these different—and so alluring to many investors—is that the income is out of the Internal Revenue Service's reach.

These funds escape taxes by investing in a variety of short-term instruments that are issued by state, county, and municipal governments and public authorities. For instance, most communities collect taxes several times a year, but their need for cash doesn't totally conform to that tax collection schedule. So they may issue tax anticipation notes, which are short-term borrowings meant to carry the municipality or agency over until the tax receipts roll in. In a like fashion, there are bond anticipation notes—issued as temporary financing until long-term bonds can be sold—and revenue anticipation notes, which may keep a government unit in operation until other revenue such as a federal grant is collected.

The tax-free money funds also rely heavily on "put bonds" and variable-rate demand notes. In either security the interest rate is reset frequently, sometimes in as short a period as seven days. If the fund manager doesn't like the new interest rate, he or she can always give them

Single-state funds can offer high aftertax yields.

back or "put" the bonds back to the issuer for redemption.

Such bonds are rarely put back. The rates are set so that they are competitive with the current rates in the tax-exempt market. These bonds, which are often backed with a bank letter of credit to assure investors the money will be there to redeem them, almost always trade at par. That makes them especially good investments for money-market type funds that strive to hold their net asset values constant at $1. In fact, investment bankers devised these floating-rate securities largely to meet the needs of tax-exempt money-market funds.

When looking at tax-free funds, remember that the income is not necessarily out of the reach of state and local tax officials. States usually exempt income from municipal securities issued in their state, but not from bonds issued by others. Thus, a general purpose tax-exempt money-market fund may not be totally tax-free. The only part of the income that your state income tax authorities will waive is that which is from your own state. If you're a Michigan resident and 5 percent of the income generated by your tax-free fund came from Michigan securities, the Michigan tax folks will still take a bite of the other 95 percent of your supposed tax-free income.

For many people, that may not be much of a bother. If the local tax is minimal, the tax-free fund may still be a great deal. But if you live in California, Connecticut, Massachusetts, Michigan, Missouri, New Jersey, New York, Ohio, or Pennsylvania, you can find tax-free money-market funds that invest in short-term securities of governments and public authorities in those states. All the income passes to the shareholders untaxed by any governmental authority.

In the early 1990s, rates on conventional money funds had dropped so low that they were almost the same as tax-free funds. But in 1998, that was not the case. The average taxable money fund yield was 5.04 percent; for tax-free funds the figure was 2.95 percent. For all but the investors in the very highest tax bracket, the aftertax return on the taxable fund was higher than the tax-exempt returns. But this is not always true. Investors need to monitor the two rates regularly. In general, the closer they are to one another, the more attractive the tax-free fund becomes.

The most important consideration when looking at tax-free money funds is your overall tax bracket. The bigger the bite from the federal,

state, and local taxing authorities, the better a tax-free fund is going to feel. A New York City resident paying the top marginal tax rate is going to find the yield on a "triple-tax-exempt" money-market fund (the "triple" comes from the fact that it's free from federal, state, and city income taxes) attractive. In 1998, some New York tax-exempt money funds were as high as 2.80 percent. That's the equivalent of 5.19 percent for a New York City resident in the highest federal, state, and city income tax brackets.

Single-state tax-free funds suffer some drawbacks, mainly lack of diversification. If the state you live in is undergoing fiscal woes, that will reflect in the marketplace for all municipal securities issued in that state. Remember the Orange County bankruptcy and the effect on California muni bond funds? Though the NAVs did not fluctuate, many California tax-exempt money funds also had Orange County securities. Franklin Resources, for instance, the parent company of Franklin Funds, didn't wait for bad news. It bought $7.1 million in unsecured Orange County debt from two of its California tax-free money-market funds, just in case the securities failed to pay off.

Another problem with single-state funds is a potential shortage of investments. What if money pours in faster than the portfolio managers can find creditworthy investments? Fund managers sometimes have to venture over the border to other states to fill up their funds with quality investments. That means a small portion of the funds' earnings will wind up subject to state income tax.

Closed-End Funds

One of the hottest stocks on the New York Stock Exchange a few years back was not even an operating company. The stock was the Turkish Investment Fund, which shot up 171.3 percent in 1993. The Turkish Investment Fund is one of several hundred closed-end funds. These funds, whose format actually predates mutual funds by more than 100 years, are similar to mutual funds in that they are professionally managed portfolios of securities and are regulated by the same laws.

Many mutual fund management companies run closed-end funds too, and for many of those

TABLE 2-48

CLOSED-END EQUITY FUNDS

BEST RETURNS

Period ▼	Fund ▼	Total return* ▼
1998	FIDELITY ADVISOR KOREA	145.1%
1996-98	EUROPEAN WARRANT	49.6
1994-98	INVESCO GLOBAL HEALTH SCIENCES	26.0
1989-98	FIRST FINANCIAL	22.1

*Average annual net asset value, pretax   DATA: MORNINGSTAR INC.

funds the portfolios look a lot like their mutual fund counterparts. The returns from the best closed-end funds are much like the returns from regular mutual funds (Tables 2-48 and 2-49).

Long overshadowed by mutual funds, closed-end funds had a resurgence over the last 10 years. After the 1987 stock market crash, stockbrokers could not interest their clients in anything much except closed-end bond funds. In 1988, for instance, more than $21 billion went into those funds. And in 1989, as investors became caught up in the sweeping changes in Europe and Asia, they scrambled to buy closed-end equity funds, like the Spain Fund, that were dedicated to investing in single foreign markets. In fact, in 1989, closed-end "single country" funds were 3 of the top 10 performers on the New York Stock Exchange. (The Asia Pacific Fund was No. 4; the Thai Fund, No. 5; the Germany Fund, No. 10.) In 1993, about $17.3 billion was raised for 123 closed-end funds: $15.3 billion for 99 bond funds and $2 billion for 24 equity funds.

In the last few years, however, closed-end funds have all been ignored by investors. Unlike regular mutual funds, mutual fund managers don't usually spend money to promote them. With investors pumping dollars into regular funds, the closed-end funds get no attention. Brokers tend only to recommend them to customers when they're new and pay a higher commission. Once established, the commission drops, so the brokers turn their attention elsewhere. Even when performance is relatively good, these funds are often starved for investor attention.

The big difference between closed-end funds and mutual funds lies in how investors get their money into and out of them. Mutual funds are "open-ended." When investors want to buy into a fund, the fund management company issues new shares at the fund's net asset value plus a sales charge if the fund is a load fund. So if the net asset value is $10 a share, and you invest $10,000,

the fund management company will credit you with 1000 shares. When you want to sell your 1000 shares, the fund management buys them back from you at the prevailing net asset value.

Closed-end funds raise capital differently. Suppose a fund management company wants to start a new venture, the Closed-End Fund. The management company hires an investment bank, which organizes the underwriting and finds buyers for the soon-to-be-issued shares. The investment bank gets commitments from investors for $100 million. So the fund goes public, selling new shares at $10 each (that's the typical starting price), and the fund issues 10 million shares—and that's all. If someone wants to buy or sell shares in the Closed-End Fund after the initial underwriting is completed, he or she has to do it as with any stock: on the stock exchange where it trades.

Is that a big deal? It can be. Suppose the Closed-End Fund portfolio managers are very savvy and the net asset value of the fund goes to $15. An investor decides to take profits and asks her broker to sell the shares. But the broker reports back that he can only get 13½, or $13.50 a share.

True, the shares are worth $15, and $13.50 is 10 percent less than what the stock is worth. But the fund company isn't going to redeem the shares, and the only way to liquidate them is to find a buyer. And there's no law that a seller has to receive NAV. The seller can get only what a buyer will pay.

That's not an unusual case. Closed-end equity funds typically sell at a discount to their underlying net asset value, a discount that in the past has been as large as 40 percent. With closed-end bond funds, the discounts are smaller, but they can still move into the double digits. Right after their initial offerings, closed-end funds tend to trade at modest premiums to their net asset values. But often within four to six months they're trading at discounts to their NAVs. That's why most invest-

TABLE 2-49

CLOSED-END BOND FUNDS

BEST RETURNS

Period ▼	Fund ▼	Total return* ▼
1998	ELLSWORTH CONVERT. GROWTH & INCOME	13.2%
1996-98	ELLSWORTH CONVERT. GROWTH & INCOME	19.0
1994-98	ELLSWORTH CONVERT. GROWTH & INCOME	16.1
1989-98	ELLSWORTH CONVERT. GROWTH & INCOME	14.5

*Average annual net asset value, pretax   DATA: MORNINGSTAR INC.

ment managers counsel investors never to buy initial offerings of closed-end funds.

A close look at the mechanics of the closed-end fund shows why they tend to trade at discounts to their NAVs. Go back to the initial public offering. Suppose Closed-End Fund goes public at $10 a share. Out of each $10, about 75 cents goes for underwriting fees and other selling expenses, leaving only $9.25 of the net asset value. Or, turn it around this way: At $10 a share, the fund is selling at an 8 percent premium to its net asset value. That makes it an overpriced stock from the start. Fees and expenses for bond funds usually eat up about 4 to 5 percent of the initial offering price.

There are two ways for the fund's share price to go up. The obvious way, of course, is through superior management. A winning portfolio will boost the net asset value, and that will more or less carry the fund shares upward (though not necessarily dollar for dollar). The other way is for investors who missed the initial offering to bid up the shares on the market.

But there won't be that many investors to bid up the shares. With most closed-end funds, the size of the offering is a function of how much the brokers can sell. Sure, the underwriters might plan a $100 million offering, but if the sales force brings in $300 million in orders, they'll boost the issue to $300 million. That means nearly all the initial demand for a closed-end fund is met on the offering. After the fact, there are few investors who want to buy shares who haven't already done so.

Then, for a few months, the investment bank that underwrote the fund usually buys shares to keep the price up. But sooner or later, the investment bank goes on to underwrite Closed-End Fund II. The brokers start calling clients to talk up the new fund, not to solicit orders for the Closed-End Fund. They can earn a much larger commission on a new fund than they can earn from taking an order for the existing one.

Meanwhile, some of the original investors in the Closed-End Fund start to sell, and there aren't many buyers for the shares. Prices begin to fall and eventually slip below net asset value. Studies show that after four months the average discount for a domestic equity fund is 10.3 percent, and for a single-country equity fund, 11.4 percent. Bond funds seem to hold up better. They trade at an average discount of only 0.12 percent.

Fund managers don't spend money to promote existing closed-end funds as they do with the open-end mutual funds. If they advertise an open-end fund, the new dollars brought into the portfolio will generate additional management fees. Since closed-end funds can't add new dollars to their portfolios, managers have no incentive to advertise.

Closed-end funds can raise additional capital through "rights" offerings, and many did in 1993. In such offerings, existing shareholders are issued rights to buy new shares at a set price, usually a small discount to net asset value. If shareholders choose not to buy, they can sell the rights to other investors who may want them.

Many fund analysts and investors have been critical of rights offerings for several reasons. First, fund managers usually launch the rights offerings at the wrong time. The closed-end bond funds that did so well in 1993 used the proceeds to buy bonds while interest rates were nearing a low point—thus making bonds "expensive." By adding a lot of newly purchased lower-yielding bonds to a portfolio with a lot of higher-yielding bonds, rights offerings dilute the funds' earnings and thus work to the disadvantage of the shareholder. The best time to be loading up on bonds is when yields are high, not low. However, you rarely see rights offerings in the throes of a bear market.

But shareholders are not the primary concern in a rights offering. The principal beneficiaries of these deals are the investment bankers, who underwrite them, and fund management companies, whose income is based on assets under management. The more money they can lure into the fund, the more money they will make. The other complaint is that the rights offerings are often "coercive." That means that if investors want to maintain their same proportion of ownership in the fund and their share of the income, they have no choice but to invest.

Investor-friendly fund managers are those that take steps to bolster fund share prices if they drop to a large discount to their net asset value. Some funds now have provisions that allow them to buy back their own shares on the market if the discount widens to 10 percent or more. And often the ploy works. For instance, the Franklin Multi-Income Trust, which invests mainly in junk bonds and utility stocks and uses borrowed money to do it, was trading at a 31 percent discount to its NAV near the end of the third quarter of 1990. Then Franklin Resources, the fund's adviser, announced a share buyback. Two weeks later, the shares traded at a slight premium.

And, should the discounts prevail for too long, many funds have new provisions that allow the shareholders to vote to convert to an open-end fund. Once that happens, the discount disappears

Be careful of buying closed-end funds at a premium.

because investors can then take their money out at net asset value. Just look at the T. Rowe Price New Age Media Fund. The fund sold at around a 20 percent discount to net asset value for over two years. Some investors lobbied to convert the fund into a mutual fund. In February 1997, the directors agreed to do it. The stock price jumped immediately, narrowing an 18 percent discount to 5 percent.

At times, some closed-end funds have traded at enormous premiums, too. Stockbrokers will remind you of that if you rebut their closed-end fund sales pitch. After all, remember the Spain Fund, which at one point in time traded at a premium of 144.5 percent of net asset value. What this means is that investors were willing to pay more than $24 a share for every $10 in assets. Such misvaluations don't last for long. Less than a year later, Spain Fund was trading at a discount of 10 percent to net asset value.

Shares of some single-country funds used to command premiums in the marketplace because they had a "franchise" that couldn't be duplicated. Sometimes closed-end funds trade at a premium because the underwriters could not satisfy all the demand for an issue. But most franchises have disappeared as competitive funds start up and many emerging markets open their doors to foreign investors.

Watch out when buying closed-end funds during crisis situations. Suppose you thought the collapse of stock prices in Southeast Asia was way overdone, and you wanted to do some smart contrarian investing. Naturally, a closed-end Asian equity fund selling at a 10 percent discount to NAV might seem better than a similar open-end fund selling at NAV. But individuals, not institutions, dominate the trading in closed-end funds, and they are slow to react. The market price of the country fund shares will sell off, but often they decline at a much slower pace than the underlying portfolios. That might cushion the losses for the investors already in the fund, but the net result is that these funds end up trading at a large premium to their NAVs. Months after Thailand's stock market and currency plunged, the two closed-end Thai funds were selling at premiums of nearly 50 percent. And in early 1998, the closed-end Indonesia funds traded at prices that were more than twice the value of their rapidly depreciating portfolio. So the best bet is to wait until the market stabilizes, or just stops falling, and let the discount settle down.

For all the caveats about closed-end funds, they can be smart buys, especially when you

might otherwise invest in the open-end fund with a similar investment style. As portfolios, view them much like conventional funds and judge their investment savvy by the same criteria.

Like the open-end mutual funds, the closed-end funds break down into the same categories as do equity and bond funds. That allows investors to make better comparisons to see if some closed-end fund might better fulfill a role in a portfolio than an equivalent mutual fund.

Since there are so many open-end analogs of closed-end funds, why bother with the closed-ends? If the closed-end is selling at a large discount to the open-ends, it may offer a better opportunity. Suppose you're interested in a growth fund in health care so you zero in on H&Q Health Care Investors. The portfolio looks good, as does the track record. In addition, the shares sell, for argument's sake, at a discount of 17 percent from net asset value.

To know if a closed-end fund's discount makes it a buy, the discount has to be compared to its historic range. A 17 percent discount may look good, but perhaps the shares have sold at a 35 percent discount as well. As it turns out, H&Q Health Care Investors traded in a range between net asset value and a 19 percent discount to NAV. That fact says the fund is trading relatively cheaply, and it may be a good time to buy.

In fact, an investor who is bullish on health-care stocks may do much better in the specialized closed-end fund than in an open-end portfolio. The closed-end fund gives you more upside potential. And here's how. Suppose you buy H&Q, with an NAV of $12, for $10 a share. (In that case, the fund is selling at nearly a 17 percent discount.) Then the stock market starts to rally, health-care stocks do well, and the health-care portfolio climbs 20 percent. So now the net asset value of the fund is $14.40 ($12 plus 20 percent). If the fund still had a 17 percent discount, H&Q Health Care Investors would trade at $12.45. But if health-care stocks were especially strong, investors would become more willing to bid up for the closed-end fund and the discount on the fund would narrow and perhaps disappear. Suppose that at the end of a year, the discount on H&Q narrows to 5 percent. There's already an appreciation of 20 percent in the portfolio, which brings the NAV to $14.45. Discount that by 5 percent, and the selling price is $13.68. (Since shares trade in sixteenths of a dollar, round that out to $13.6875, or 13^{11}⁄₁₆.) The original investment was $10 a share and selling at $13.63 represents a 36.9 percent return (before commissions). An open-end

> Closed-end bond funds borrow to boost yields.

TABLE 2-50

CLOSED-END FUNDS WITH OPEN-END CLONES

Closed-end ▼	Open-end ▼
GABELLI EQUITY	GABELLI ASSET
ROYCE MICROCAP TRUST	ROYCE MICROCAP FUND
ROYCE VALUE	PENNSYLVANIA MUTUAL INVS.
INVESCO GLOBAL HEALTH SCIENCES	INVESCO STRATEGIC HEALTH
HANCOCK BANK & THRIFT	HANCOCK REGIONAL BANK
COHEN & STEERS TOTAL RETURN	COHEN & STEERS REALTY
TEMPLETON EMERGING MARKETS	TEMPLETON DEVELOPING MARKETS
MFS MULTIMARKET INCOME	MFS STRATEGIC INCOME
PUTNAM PREMIER INCOME	PUTNAM DIVIDEND INCOME
KEMPER MULTIMARKET	KEMPER DIVIDEND INCOME
OPPENHEIMER MULTISECTOR	OPPENHEIMER STRATEGIC INCOME
COLONIAL INTERMARKET INCOME	COLONIAL STRATEGIC INCOME
KEMPER HIGH-INCOME	KEMPER HIGH-YIELD

DATA: MORNINGSTAR INC.

health-care fund might have had only a 20 percent gain. In a bull market the narrowing of a discount on a closed-end fund can give an investor an extra edge.

Of course, if the market turns down, that premium/discount works just the other way. What if the portfolio lost 20 percent of its value and the discount widened to 25 percent? The $12 NAV would then be worth only $9.60—and a 25 percent discount from that is $7.20. The portfolio declined 20 percent, but because of the widening discount the fund price is off 28 percent. In a bear market investors in closed-end funds may be hit harder than regular mutual fund investors.

So much for funds bought at discounts. Let's look at what happens when funds are purchased at a premium. Suppose you buy a fund on the initial offering for $10 a share. After underwriting fees and such, only $9.25 is left for NAV. So, in effect, you pay an 8 percent premium. Let's say the portfolio managers do a good job and the portfolio climbs 20 percent to $11.10. But instead of a premium the fund now sells at a 2 percent discount. If you sell, all you can get is $10.87. So the portfolio went up 20 percent, but the investor could realize less than 9 percent. You're taking an extra risk if you buy closed-end funds selling at a premium to net asset value.

All told, because of differences between share price and NAV in closed-end funds, many fund investors may choose to avoid them altogether and stick with the more familiar and somewhat simpler open-end variety. But there are times when closed-end funds can be the better buy. Mario Gabelli, Charles Royce, and Martin Zweig are just a few investment managers who run both closed- and open-end funds. If you would consider investing in one of their open-end funds, perhaps you should consider a closed-end fund that's selling at a discount.

Look, for instance, at the open-end Royce Value Fund and the closed-end Royce Value Trust. The two have the same portfolio managers and many of the same stocks since they both specialize in value investing in small-to-medium-sized companies. The difference is that the closed-end fund usually sells at a discount. That means that with the closed-end fund you get $1 worth of stock for perhaps 90 or 95 cents. With the open-end fund you get $1 worth of stocks for $1.

If you own closed-end funds, you should also keep your eye on any open-end clones (Table 2-50). Sometimes there's money to be made by trading a closed-end fund at a premium for a similar mutual fund. Templeton Emerging Markets, a closed-end fund, has the same portfolio manager and investment policy as the open-end Templeton Developing Markets Fund. But Templeton Emerging Markets spent most of 1992 trading at an average premium to net asset value of 25 percent. The open-end fund would have been the better buy—even after paying the load. In 1993, in fact, John Templeton himself unloaded his shares of the closed-end Templeton Emerging Markets Fund at a premium of 25 percent over net asset value and reinvested the proceeds in the open-end fund.

Fund companies such as Franklin, Massachusetts Financial Services, Oppenheimer, and Putnam also operate closed-end bond funds with investment goals similar to their open-end bond portfolios. Bond funds can trade at discounts to NAV, but usually not to the extent of equity funds.

Investing in a closed-end bond fund that's selling at a discount to NAV may result in a higher yield than in a comparable open-end bond fund. Suppose there are open-end and closed-end bond funds with the same manager and similar portfolios. Both have NAVs of $10 per share and a 20 cents per quarter payout, or 80 cents a year. The open-end fund has a yield of 8 percent. But the closed-end fund trades at $9.50, a 5 percent discount to NAV. Buy the closed-end fund, and the same 80-cent payout becomes an 8.4 percent yield. Less money for the same payout results in a higher yield.

The other time to consider closed-end bond funds is when interest rates are falling. When short-term interest rates drop, investors seek to maintain their yields by pulling money out of money-market funds or CDs and buying long-term bond mutual funds. But such a strategy is often self-defeating. What money comes pouring into open-end funds during a time of falling interest rates will be invested at a lower interest rate than the "older" money. That lowers the average yield of the fund and dilutes returns for all shareholders. Closed-end bond funds, because they don't take new money into the portfolio, don't suffer from this sort of dilution problem (unless, of course, the management launches a rights offering).

Buying closed-end bond funds in a period of falling interest rates has some pitfalls, too. After all, a falling-rate environment is a bull market for bonds, so the market prices for closed-end bond funds may trade up to a premium to net asset value. In 1993, for instance, the ACM Government Income Fund sold at a premium as high as 10.9 percent to the value of its portfolio. In that case, the buyer paid $1.09 for every $1 worth of bonds. Moreover, the fund is only earning interest on $1 worth of bonds. So the investor, in effect, is buying a bond at a premium.

But there's a big difference between buying a bond at a premium and a bond fund at a premium. With the bond fund, the investor has all the interest rate risk of a bond, but something more. An investor in a U.S. Treasury or investment-grade bond knows what the interest payment is going to be. On the other hand, bond fund "dividends"—they're technically dividends even though the payout is earned from interest—can be cut, and often are, in a period of declining interest rates. Funds that don't cut—and aren't earning the dividend—could end up making a nontaxable distribution. That's not a freebie, like interest on municipal bonds. A nontaxable distribution means the fund never really earned the money it distributed, so the distribution is considered a return of the investor's own capital. That can be especially annoying to investors who paid a premium for their bond funds. The money comes back at net asset value.

Investors in many closed-end bond funds might be lured by high yields that are produced with leverage. Here's how the funds work. Suppose the funds raise $200 million from investors for regular closed-end bond fund shares. The bond fund then sells perhaps $100 million in preferred stocks—typically to corporations or other institutional investors. The preferred shares pay a dividend that can be either a fixed or a variable interest rate.

So now, the leveraged bond fund can invest $300 million instead of $200 million. Suppose the fund can invest the money to produce an 8 percent interest rate, while paying an average 5 percent rate on the preferred shares. The $200 million earns $16 million a year. The $100 million earns $8 million, less $5 million paid to the preferred stockholders. So the $100 million nets an extra $3 million for the common stockholders. Instead of $16 million in income, the fund earns $19 million. So far, so good.

But what happens if the interest rates climb and bond prices tumble? The portfolio losses to the leveraged fund will be magnified. In addition, if the rate on the preferred shares moves up higher than the interest payments on the bonds in the portfolio, the bond fund could be in the position of having to pay the preferred shareholders out of the common shareholders' capital.

The moral of the story: If a closed-end bond fund seems to promise a return that's higher than what the market bears, you have to ask how the fund produced it.

Buying and Selling: The Essentials

Until not too long ago, investing in mutual funds was an "either or" business. You either bought them through a salesperson, a stockbroker, a financial planner, or, sometimes, an insurance agent, or you bought them direct from the mutual fund company. If your investment went through a salesperson, you paid a sales charge or "load," a fee that compensates the salesperson for selling you the fund. If you bought directly from the fund company, there was no salesperson, so the fund was purchased "no load," without that fee. In essence, the load and no-load arrangements represented two ways to distribute funds, and most fund companies followed one or the other. Companies such as Alliance, Franklin, and Putnam are load-fund groups and sell through brokers. The funds are sometimes called "broker-dealer" funds. (These funds also include the brokers' in-house proprietary products, such as Merrill Lynch mutual funds.) Janus, T. Rowe Price, and Vanguard are no-load groups. They sell without an intermediary. Instead, investors reach them through the mail, toll-free telephone lines, walk-in investor centers, and now, through the Internet. A few, like Fidelity and Dreyfus, though mainly no-load, manage and sell load funds as well.

Now, new ways to invest in mutual funds that are neither load nor no-load are emerging. One model is the mutual fund network, or supermarket. The oldest, biggest, and best-known of these supermarkets is Charles Schwab & Co.'s Mutual Fund Marketplace. The network addresses one of the drawbacks of investing in funds of several no-load companies: You must maintain relationships with numerous fund companies and keep track of paperwork for every company with which you deal. The network makes moving money from, say, a Janus to a Scudder fund as easy as moving from one Janus fund to another. Of course, those who run these networks are in it for the money, and with no-load funds, who's going to pay the

firm that runs the network? Many fund companies find this distribution method so compelling that they pay the networks an annual fee, about 0.25 to 0.35 percent of assets under management, for bringing them customers.

The networks make simple what was previously difficult, managing diverse portfolios of funds. The networks also make it possible for many brokers and salespersons to leave the big firms and set up shops on their own. Instead of selling Franklin and Putnam funds with loads attached, they use the networks of no-load funds. Instead of collecting a commission for selling a particular fund, they manage a portfolio of no-load funds, assessing an annual "management fee." Many load-fund companies, not wanting to miss this distribution channel, now make their funds available no-load to investors who buy through advisers who charge fees. The big Wall Street firms, seeing the popularity of fee-based mutual fund investing, are changing their ways as well. Now major brokerage houses like Merrill Lynch, Smith Barney, and Prudential Securities are offering large numbers of funds, load and no-load, on a fee-only basis. And even fund companies like Fidelity, Vanguard, American Express, and Strong have networks that can plug in others' funds besides their own.

A little confusing? First, let's take a few steps back.

What You Need to Know About Loads

For most of their 75-year history, mutual funds were sold by salespeople working for the fund companies, brokerage firms, and insurance companies. And for most of that time, the funds came with a stiff load, or commission. Today, most funds sold by brokers are commonly known as load funds.

Until the mid-1980s, the load was an 8.5 percent up-front sales charge that swallowed a big chunk of money right off the top of an investment. That meant that out of a $1000 investment, $85 would go toward commissions and only $915 into investments. The 8.5 percent charge usually applied to investments of less than $10,000. For large amounts, the sales charge would start to scale back and might even disappear after, say, $1 million. A few fund groups even levied a load on the reinvested dividends and capital gains, though the regulators kept it a tad lower than the initial front-end load. True, the commission seemed high, but salespeople would remind investors that, unlike stocks and bonds, it was only paid on purchase, not again when the fund was sold.

Load funds outnumber the no-loads. That's because many funds need brokers to bring them investors. Some no-loads with excellent track records never really attracted investors until they added loads. That allowed them to pay brokers to sell their funds. In 1992, mutual fund regulators on the U.S. Securities & Exchange Commission staff proposed negotiated loads, allowing fund companies, brokers, and investors to dicker over price. After all, stock commissions have been negotiable since 1975, why not funds? The fund industry howled, and the SEC commissioners didn't press it. The matter died.

NO-LOAD FUNDS

In the early 1970s, the stock market plummeted and so did mutual fund sales. To shake off the slump, some companies started to sell their funds direct to investors without a sales charge. No-load funds weren't brand new then, either. But the early no-loads were started by investment counseling firms like T. Rowe Price for accounts deemed too small for individual management and were not widely marketed.

But along with the no-loads came liberalized rules on mutual fund advertising. Then fund management companies like Dreyfus and Fidelity began dropping the loads from some funds, and when new funds were launched they came without loads. Money-market funds, which drew millions of new investors into mutual funds in the 1970s, were also sold no-load. Their popularity worked to the advantage of the no-load fund families.

Until the mid-1980s the mutual fund universe was split between the loads funds, which stuck with their 8.5 percent sales charges, and the no-loads. Then the load funds, feeling investor resis-

tance to the high costs, started lowering their sales charges. Now, there are only a handful of funds with 8.5 percent loads. Most of the load funds have dropped their fees to the 4 to 6 percent range. Increasingly, they have also offered funds with different methods to pay the sales charge, the "back-end load" and the "level load."

BACK-END LOADS

They call it a back-end load, "redemption fee," "exit fee," or, technically, the "contingent deferred sales charge." The fee starts at 4 or 5 percent of the value of the fund you're selling, depending on the fund. If you sell your shares in the first year, you pay the full charge. In the second year, your exit fee drops by 1 percentage point, and so on. By the fifth or sixth year the redemption fees are usually gone, so if you're truly a long-term investor, you may never pay that fee.

Back-end loads were first introduced in the mid-1980s. But this alternative didn't really take off until the late 1980s, when Merrill Lynch introduced "dual pricing." Dual pricing creates two classes of shares for each fund: "A" shares, which carry a one-time up-front load, and "B" shares, which carry the back-end load. Now dual pricing is widespread among brokerage house proprietary funds, and even among the independent fund managers that sell through brokers. While many use the A and B share method, a few, such as Eaton Vance, offer a separate line-up of funds with back-end loads.

During the 1980s, as the load funds lowered up-front sales charges and introduced back-end loads, some no-load companies were going the opposite way. Fidelity Investments, for instance, slapped "low-loads," 2 or 3 percent sales charges, on funds that were previously sold no-load. Fidelity used the load not to pay brokers, but to pay for its extensive advertising.

By the 1990s, even though the mutual fund industry enjoyed record sales, investors were resisting loads. Strong Funds, which had low-loads on its equity funds, dropped them altogether in late 1992. Fidelity now waives its low-loads on most funds purchased in retirement accounts, and dropped low-loads on several more of its diversified U.S. funds. In recent years, some load funds with hot performance, such as Oberweis Emerging Growth, switched to no-load. And Heartland Value Fund dropped its front-end load in favor of a back-end load and eventually went no-load. (There are still a few funds going in the opposite direction. Evergreen

A no-load fund may have hidden sales fees.

Funds switched to loads after the fund management company was acquired by a bank.)

Just because a fund is no-load does not mean there are no fees. For instance, the Vanguard Group levies "transaction fees" on its index funds ranging from 0.5 percent to 1.5 percent, depending on the fund. The difference between this fee and most loads is that the proceeds go to the fund, not to the fund company. The fee is to offset the transaction costs of investing the money. (In most funds, that cost is not explicit but indirect, and it is reflected in the price that a fund pays for its stocks.) At the same time, the Vanguard index funds levy a $2.50 per quarter "maintenance fee" on accounts with less than $10,000 in them. That takes care of reports, statements, and the like. In most funds, that cost ends up on the line itemized as "other expenses."

Some no-loads charge redemption fees, too, but they're usually meant to discourage short-term trading. Vanguard has a 1 percent redemption charge on some specialty funds for shares held for less than one year. On Vanguard's Aggressive Growth and Capital Opportunity funds, that 1 percent contingent fee extends to shares held less than five years. The Pennsylvania Mutual Investors fund and most of the others in the Royce Fund family levy a 1 percent exit fee on shares redeemed within a year of purchase.

Since the wide variation in loads has so muddled the distinction between load funds and no-loads, the terms don't mean so much anymore. In fact, the Investment Company Institute, the fund industry's trade association, looks at funds by the method used to distribute them, not by the sales charges. There are "sales force" funds, those sold to investors through sales folks, and "direct marketing" funds, those sold by the management companies directly to investors (Table 3-1).

"HIDDEN LOADS"

If the loads, low-loads, and no-loads aren't confusing enough, consider the "12(b)-1" fee, or what some commentators call the "hidden load." The 12(b)-1 charge, named for the U.S. Securities & Exchange Commission rule which enabled funds to levy it, is, like loads, meant to help defray marketing and distribution costs. Sales force fund companies can use the 12(b)-1 revenues to compensate brokers for their selling efforts. Direct marketing companies, on the other hand, use the money to pay for advertising. At least half of all funds levy some sort of 12(b)-1 fee.

What's different about this charge is how it is collected from the shareholders. Instead of paying the charge once when investors buy the fund (front-end load), or when they sell it (back-end load), investors pay this fee from the fund's assets. In that sense, the 12(b)-1 charges are treated just like the fees shareholders pay for portfolio management, administration, auditing, printing, postage, and other expenses.

There are limits on 12(b)-1 fees. The fee, which must be disclosed in the prospectus, has a maximum of 0.75 percent of assets per year, or 75 cents per $100 of assets, plus a 0.25 percent "service fee," for a total of 1 percent. Many funds, in fact, charge less. Many sales-force companies with front-end loads also offer funds with back-end loads and 12(b)-1 fees. Many no-load funds have 12(b)-1 fees, too, but the charge is usually much smaller than with a sales-force fund. The rules say that a fund that calls itself "no-load" can have a 12(b)-1 fee of no more than 0.25 percent. Funds with 12(b)-1 charges are noted in the BUSINESS WEEK Mutual Fund Scoreboard.

TABLE 3-1

THE BIGGEST FUND MANAGERS

Fund management company	Assets Billions*	Direct marketing No-load, low-load, and institutional	Sales force Load and deferred
FIDELITY	$645.5	●	●
VANGUARD	430.2	●	
AMERICAN FUNDS	273.6		●
MERRILL LYNCH	221.4		●
PUTNAM	193.3		●
FRANKLIN TEMPLETON	166.9		●
SMITH BARNEY	122.9		●
DEAN WITTER	107.7		●
FEDERATED	105.8	●	●
AIM MANAGEMENT	102.3		●
DREYFUS	101.8	●	●
T. ROWE PRICE	94.5	●	
OPPENHEIMER FUNDS	89.0		●
AMERICAN EXPRESS	84.8		●
JANUS	82.5	●	
SCHWAB	81.0	●	
AMERICAN CENTURY	77.2	●	
MFS	69.0		●
ALLIANCE	64.2		●
PRUDENTIAL	62.0		●
BLACKROCK/PNC	59.6		●
EVERGREEN INVESTMENT	54.7		●
VAN KAMPEN	53.5		●
KEMPER	52.8		●
GOLDMAN, SACHS	51.2		●

*As of December 31, 1998. Excludes variable annuities and offshore funds.

DATA: STRATEGIC INSIGHT, BUSINESS WEEK

One percent may not sound like much, but think about it this way. On a $10,000 investment, that's $100 in the first year. But you have to pay 1 percent every year you're in the fund. And, providing that the fund is increasing in value, that 1 percent represents more money each year. The SEC's rules cap 12(b)-1 fees in a way so that investors don't pay more than they would have paid with an 8.5 percent load. But that cap pertains to the entire fund and not to any individual investor. According to experts, the 12(b)-1 fee on a fund that is not growing would eventually hit the cap. But a fund that's taking in new money may never hit the ceiling. So investors in those funds may end up paying the 12(b)-1 fee indefinitely.

Confusing enough? It's getting worse. Alliance is one of a number of fund companies that have A, B, and C classes of shares for all its stock and bond funds. (Some companies have more classes than that, but three is usually the largest number of classes offered to the individual investor. For simplicity's sake BUSINESS WEEK Scoreboards just report on the largest share class in multi-class funds.) The A shares carry a 4.5 percent up-front load. The B shares have an ongoing 1 percent annual 12(b)-1 charge and a declining back-end load. For equity funds, the back-end load is 4 percent in the first year, declining 1 percentage point a year, and disappearing in the fifth year. For fixed-income funds, the back-end load starts at 3 percent and disappears in the fourth year.

The C shares charge neither front- nor back-end loads, they just levy a 1 percent a year fee. That's perhaps why it's called the "level-load" fund. Like the 12(b)-1 fee, this level-load comes out of the fund's assets every year. You might call it the "forever load." Introduced in the early 1990s, some fund executives thought they would quickly outpace both front- and back-end shares in new sales, but that hasn't been the case. Perhaps it's because the shares are probably not the best deal for investors or for the commissioned salespeople who sell them.

Although most fund companies call their front-end load shares "A," back-end load shares "B," and level-load shares "C," don't assume all A's, B's, or C's are alike. In some fund groups, for instance, the C shares are for institutional investors or reserved for investors who come to the fund via an employer-sponsored retirement plan. Some fund managers create multiple classes of shares and call them institutional or "trust" shares. In most cases, those are shares that are distributed through bank trust departments. "Retail" shares are for individual investors.

The A, B, and C funds are fairly common, but a few companies have turned to the other end of the alphabet. Neuberger & Berman and Oppenheimer Management use the "Y" designation for institutional shares, but Evergreen Funds uses Y to designate shares purchased when the fund was still a no-load fund company. New shares are in A, B, and C classes. Those investors who owned any of the Mutual Series funds before their 1996 acquisition by Franklin funds now have "Z" shares. Those who've bought since have either "Class I" or "Class II" shares, a structure unique to Franklin. These shares are an alternative to front-end loads and have a totally different payment structure: Investors would pay a 1 percent load at the time of purchase, and another 1 percent of assets if they sell the fund within two years. Class II shareholders also pay higher 12(b)-1 fees—0.65 percent for bond funds and 1 percent for equity funds. Another variant is "Investor" shares for individual investors and "Service" shares for institutional customers, or employee benefit plans.

Mutual fund companies are always coming up with new ways to sell their wares, too. One method is the "hub and spoke" or "master and feeder" fund arrangement, which accounts for about 5 percent of all funds. It works like this: A fund company sets up and manages, for example, a government bond fund. That's the hub. Since this company distributes directly to individual investors, it opens a no-load government bond fund. But instead of owning government bonds, the fund owns shares in the hub, which is a government bond fund. Next, the fund company thinks banks might want to sell this government bond fund to their customers. So it creates another spoke, perhaps with the bank's name on it, sold with a 4 percent load.

The process can go on and on, creating spokes for sales through different distribution channels, institutional investors, retirement plans, and offshore investors, all feeding into the same hub. The advantage of this arrangement is that it's cheaper to run one large, centralized hub portfolio than several smaller funds. That savings should be passed on to the investors in the form of lower expenses.

Investors, for the most part, may not even realize their fund is the spoke of a hub. And, if they're satisfied with results, they may not care. But suppose you paid a load for a spoke fund, while others bought the same hub for a lesser load, or without a load. Right now, a broker selling you a spoke has no obligation to tell you there's another spoke for the same hub with a different pricing scheme. So you may well ask.

Loads, low-loads, hidden loads. Does this mean you forgo all of them and just concentrate on no-load funds? Not necessarily. What is important is that those who invest in mutual funds understand the sales charges, exit fees, and ongoing distribution fees and how they affect the total return from their investments. The U.S. Securities & Exchange Commission, for the most part, has been fairly vigilant on fee disclosure. The agency's philosophy is to provide investors with the information and let the buyer decide. But that puts the burden of fathoming the fee structure on you, the fund investor.

To Load or Not to Load?

Why would anyone buy a load fund? In most cases you can find a no-load analog of most any load fund. True, there are some excellent load funds, but there are also great no-loads. And portfolio performance has nothing to do with whether you paid a broker to sell you the fund. So if you're going to go to the trouble of researching mutual funds at all, you might as well buy no-loads, right?

Perhaps. That's a question only you can answer for yourself. If you're reading this book, it may be because you want to take these decisions into your own hands. You don't want to use a broker, financial planner, or investment adviser. But it's a mistake to dismiss load funds out of hand. If you do, you're cutting yourself off from a large part of the mutual fund universe and many excellent investment opportunities.

When the only alternative to the no-load was an 8.5 percent load, the scales tipped heavily toward the no-load. But today there are former no-load funds that sell with 2 and 3 percent low-loads, and former full-load funds with 4 percent loads. And then there's the back-end load, which many investors never have to pay.

In determining whether to pay a load you have to consider how long you anticipate staying with the fund. Everyone's financial plans are subject to change, of course. And if yours do change, most load fund families have a wide range of port-folios to choose from, just like no-loads. And intrafamily switches, such as moving from a Putnam international bond fund to a Putnam govern-

ment bond fund, can usually be done without paying another load. Increasingly, some load-fund groups, like Fortis and Prudential, will let investors switch funds out of other load funds and into theirs without paying a new load. Of course, that's not going to help you if you will end up owing the fund a redemption fee. So if you want to retain the flexibility of moving to other funds of other managers, consider taking the charge up front.

If your investment is for your retirement nest egg or your toddler's college education, a load should not stand between you and the best possible fund. After all, even an 8.5 percent load, and there are very few of them left, over a 10-year holding period works out to less than 1 percent per year. That kind of sales burden can easily be overcome in the performance of an exceptional load fund versus a mediocre no-load.

But most investors are not faced with a choice of 8.5 percent versus no charge. What about choosing between the A, B, and C shares? Suppose you're interested in a load fund and the A shares have an up-front 5.75 percent load, which is fairly stiff in today's market. The B shares have no up-front load. But there are 12(b)-1 fees amounting to 1 percent a year and a back-end load that's 4 percent in the first and second year, but then declines 1 percentage point a year until it disappears in the seventh year. The C shares charge 1 percent a year forever but levy no redemption charges. What's the best buy? (see Table 3-2). That depends on your assumptions for your holding period and the rate of return on your investment. If you assume a $10,000 investment and an average annual return of 10 percent a year, here's how it works, according to Multiple Class Calculator, a software program developed by Money Marketing Inc. In the early years, the C shares work out best. That's because there is neither a big bite up front, nor one on the back end. For instance, in year 2, the C shares are worth $11,586 versus $11,124 for the A shares and $11,571 for the B shares before redemption, $11,171 after. But the A shares have a much lower expense ratio than the B or C shares. And over time, that gives the advantage to A-share investors. In year 7 and beyond, the advantage swings to the A-share owners; they have a $169 advantage over B-share owners, and a $93 advantage over C-share owners. By year 10, the A-share holders are $427 ahead of the B-share holders, and $706 over the C-share holders.

What is cheapest in the short run is not always cheapest in the long run. The C shares, the least

Differences between load and no-load funds are blurring.

TABLE 3-2

PAY THE LOAD NOW, LATER, OR FOREVER?

Suppose a fund has three classes of shares. "A" shares have a traditional front-end load of 5.75%, and a 1.36% expense ratio. "B" and "C" shares have expense ratios of 2.43% and 2.36%, respectively, because of the higher 12(b)-1 fees. "B" shares have a 4% redemption fee if you cash out in the first or second year, 3% in the third and fourth, 2% in the fifth, and 1% in the sixth year. Assuming a $10,000 initial investment and a 10% average annual return, which shares make most sense?

Year-end	A shares	B shares	B, if redeemed	C shares
1	$10,239	$10,757	$10,357	$10,764
2	11,124	11,571	11,171	11,586
3	12,085	12,447	12,147	12,472
4	13,129	13,389	13,090	13,424
5	14,264	14,403	14,203	14,450
6	15,496	15,493	15,393	15,554
7	16,835	16,666	16,666	16,742
8	18,289	17,928	17,928	18,021
9	19,870	19,477	19,477	19,398
10	21,586	21,160	21,160	20,880

DATA: MONEY MARKETING INC.

costly of the three in the earlier years, could end up costing the most if the investment is truly a long-term one. Perhaps the C shares are appropriate if, at the start, you believe the investment will be redeemed in the first few years. Still, many people have a hard time swallowing that chunky up-front sales load. If that's the case, B shares may make the best choice under certain conditions. MFS, for instance, will automatically convert B shares into A shares after the customer has passed the period in which a back-end charge might be levied, usually six years. That way, the investor is also relieved of the heavier 12(b)-1 fees built into the B shares.

In weighing a load versus a no-load fund, you should also consider the fund's investment parameters. For instance, equity funds generally have broad charters and disparate results. So even if both funds are growth funds, the differences in returns of growth funds are great and having the "right" fund is important. Paying a modest load for an equity fund that's demonstrated superior results may be better than buying just any no-load.

At the other extreme, short-term bond funds all maintain a similar portfolio, and the differences in returns from one fund to the next are small. So it doesn't make sense to pay a load for a short-term bond fund when there's little likelihood that it will show any better performance than a no-load fund.

There is at least one reason to pay a load and that is to compensate a broker or financial planner for the time he or she spends meeting with you and monitoring your investments. Perhaps a recommendation for one equity fund does not merit paying a 5.75 percent load. But if a financial planner takes the time to tailor a portfolio of funds for you, he or she has to be paid. The load is one way to do it.

There are other ways as well. Many financial planners, for instance, put their clients' money into no-load funds and then charge an annual fee for the entire portfolio, perhaps 1 or 2 percent. That's not necessarily a better deal for investors, either. You might be better off paying your planner by investing in load funds, providing the planner still delivers good service long after being paid. Six percent off the top of the initial investment may sound steep, but if the fund managers have sliced off 1 percent a year for 10 years, you've paid a whole lot more.

Keep in mind, too, that while it's common practice to refer to a fund as a "4 percent load" or a "6 percent load," not everyone pays the full freight. If the fund carries a sales charge, there are ways to minimize the costs. Most load-fund groups have fee schedules that slide downward for progressively larger investments. Typically, purchases up to $10,000 carry the maximum load. Before making a large investment in a load fund, ask the broker about the next "breakpoint," the dollar amount necessary to qualify for a lower load. In some cases, it might be worth making an extra $1000 or $2000 investment to qualify for the lower sales charge. At the high end, the sales fee often drops to 1 percent, or even totally disappears on major investments of $1 million or more.

Suppose you plan to invest $15,000, but you won't be able to put the money in all at once. Check with your broker to see if the fund management company will let you sign a letter of intent. In such an agreement you pledge to invest over a 13-month period a specified amount which, if invested at one time, would qualify for a reduced sales charge. If you fail to fulfill the letter of intent, you'll owe the fund the difference between the sales charges you've paid and what you should have paid. The company can take the money from your account.

If you're spreading your investments over several funds in the same load-fund group, many funds will give you the same break as if the investment were made in one fund. And all the funds don't have to be for the same account. If you're investing for your personal funds, your

IRA, a spousal IRA, and some custodial accounts for the kids, you can probably get a discount that takes in the total investment. But you have to ask.

Mutual Fund Networks

If you opened a stock brokerage account and invested in, say, 10 stocks, you could buy, sell, and keep track of them through one account. It used to be nearly impossible to do the same with mutual funds, except if you kept your investments to one fund family. You could mix and match multiple funds in one account using a commissioned broker or financial planner, but you would still be limiting yourself to a little more than half the fund universe. You would not be able to include, say, T. Rowe Price or Vanguard offerings, since they don't pay commissions to brokers.

Mutual funds are not as interchangeable as stocks, but thanks to the mutual fund networks or "supermarkets," they're heading that way. You can think of the networks as sort of a family of fund families. The brokerage firm Charles Schwab & Company originated the supermarket concept more than a decade ago in a program called Mutual Fund Marketplace (MFM) (Table 3-3). MFM has some 1640 funds available to the individual investor and you would recognize nearly all of them as no-load funds. Within the MFM is the OneSource program, with 1024 funds that can be purchased with no fee. With One-Source funds, the fund company pays the broker, often through a 12(b)-1 charge. For the others, there is a small transaction charge.

For the other no-load funds, you pay a transaction fee to Schwab. For trades up to $15,000 in size, the fee is 0.7 percent of the investment. The fee is 0.2 percent on the next $15,001 to $100,000, and 0.08 percent on everything over $100,000. A $10,000 trade costs $70 and a $25,000 trade, $125. Schwab officials say that, on average, clients in the Mutual Fund Marketplace program end up paying commissions of about 0.3 percent of the amount invested. Investors can get a discount by conducting their trades by an automated phone line or over the Internet.

So why would anyone pay Schwab to invest in a fund that doesn't charge commissions? If all you ever planned to do was to buy that one fund, there's no good reason. And the commission struc-

ture makes the purchasing of no-load funds uneconomical for small trades or monthly investing programs. The transaction fee is 0.7 percent for $5000, which is $35. But it will cost you $39 anyway. That's because Schwab, like most stockbrokers, has a minimum transaction charge, and in Schwab's case, it's $39—$35 for trades placed electronically. If you're stashing away a couple of hundred dollars a month in a fund, you would do better to deal directly with the fund. You don't want to spend $35 to invest $200.

Many investors like the convenience of the Schwab program even if they have to pay the fees. Rather than a statement and an account with every fund, Schwab delivers a consolidated statement. At tax time there's one Form 1099. If you want to sell one fund and redistribute the proceeds into three other funds, you can effect the change with one phone call instead of several. If you're switching funds, there's a $15 fee for the fund you're switching out of and the commission for the one you're going into. Within OneSource, investors are permitted 15 free trades a year, as long as the funds have been held more than 90 days.

There's another advantage, too. Some institutional funds, like those managed by Brinson Partners or Jurika & Volyes, are usually off-limits to individual investors, or have very high minimum investments of $250,000 or more. But through Schwab's and other such supermarkets, individual investors can buy in for $2,500 or so. That's because the brokerage firm maintains an "omnibus" account with each fund, and the funds' man-

TABLE 3-3

SHOPPING THE MUTUAL FUND SUPERMARKETS

	Phone	Web address
ACCUTRADE	800-882-4887	www.accutrade.com
AMERICAN EXPRESS FINANCIAL DIRECT	800-658-4677	www.americanexpress.com/direct
AMERITRADE	NA	www.ameritrade.com
DLJ DIRECT	800-825-5723	www.dljdirect.com
E*TRADE	800-786-2571	www.etrade.com
FIDELITY BROKERAGE SERVICES	800-544-9697	www.fidelity.com
BARRY MURPHY & CO.	800-221-2111	www.barrymurphy.com
NATIONAL DISCOUNT BROKERS	800-888-3999	www.ndb.com
QUICK & REILLY	800-221-5220	www.quick-reilly.com
CHARLES SCHWAB & CO.	800-435-4000	www.schwab.com
SCUDDER	800-700-0820	www.scudder.com
STRONG	800-368-1550	www.strong-funds.com
VANGUARD BROKERAGE SERVICES	800-992-8327	www.vanguard.com
WATERHOUSE SECURITIES	800-934-4443	www.waterhouse.com
JACK WHITE & CO.	800-233-3411	www.jackwhiteco.com

DATA: BUSINESS WEEK

Mutual fund
networks
can simplify
investing.

agement companies treat all Schwab customers as one account. Schwab, in turn, keeps track of how many shares of that account belong to each customer. So Schwab can offer lower minimum investments because it is pooling funds from a large number of clients.

Schwab has even extended the Mutual Fund Marketplace program to load funds like American, Colonial, Franklin, Pioneer, Putnam, and Templeton. But they don't discount the loads. Still, buying load funds through Schwab or one of its competitors may appeal to investors who want the funds but do not want to deal with the full-service brokers who usually sell them.

Fidelity Investments' FundsNetwork program is similar to Schwab's, offering 3900 no-load and load funds, 900 of them without a transaction fee. Transaction charges are two-part, a base fee plus a variable fee depending on the size of the transaction. For investments of up to $5000, the fee is a flat $35; for investments over $5000, it's $35 plus 0.2 percent of the amount in excess of $5000. A $10,000 investment works out to $35 plus $10 (0.2 percent of $5000) or $45. Fidelity caps the maximum transaction charge at $150. Those rates are for placing orders through a Fidelity representative. For touch-tone phone service, the minimum drops to $30, the maximum, $120. The biggest bargains are for online trading. The fee is a flat $28.95, regardless of the size of the investment.

Several other discount brokers run broad-based mutual fund programs like Schwab's. Jack White & Company has some 7500 no-load and low-load funds. The minimum charge is $27 per trade on trades of up to $5000 ($24 if you do the trade online), $35 for trades of $5001 to $25,000, and $50 for trades in excess of $25,000. Jack White also has a no-fee service with, at last count, 1300 funds.

Load-fund investors may also check out Jack White's CONNECT System. It allows investors to buy load funds without paying loads. Instead, there's a flat $200 fee, no matter how large the purchase.

Suppose an investor would like to place $25,000 in a fund with a 4.5 percent front-end load. That would take $1125 off the top of the investment. The CONNECT charge for the sale would be a flat $200. CONNECT places the buyer's offer on an electronic bulletin board and looks for a seller. CONNECT pays half the fee, or $100, to the seller as an incentive to sell through the Jack White system instead of cashing out through the fund company. And CONNECT can't

guarantee that it can match up willing buyers and sellers on the spot, or even on the day that the order is placed. But the system is expected to become part of every security broker's electronic bulletin board, which will enable Jack White to attract fund buyers and fund sellers.

Advisers and "Wraps"

The mutual fund supermarkets are doing more than changing the way individuals invest. They're changing the way brokers and investment advisers conduct business. Over the last few years, thousands of brokers have left brokerage firms, where they got paid for their advice through commissions, and have opened up their own firms where, instead of charging commissions, they levy a fee based on the client's assets under management.

Instead of selling traditional load funds from companies like Franklin and Putnam, they channel their clients' money into no-load funds through the networks. They're putting so much money into no-load companies, in fact, that some load-fund companies, not wanting to miss this burgeoning market, make their funds available no-load through the networks to the advisers' clients.

Fee-based advisers don't get paid for selling any particular fund, only for their advice. Of course, in theory, a traditional load fund performs the same function. The difference is that instead of paying the salesperson at the time of sale, the client pays the salesperson over time. Perhaps more important, in a traditional load fund, the salesperson is paid the same amount, no matter how the investment performs, and you may never hear from him or her again. With an asset-based fee arrangement, the salesperson is, in effect, on the "same side of the table" and you're in a long-term relationship. If the advice is good, the assets under management grow, and so does the adviser's annual fee. Conversely, if the client loses money, so does the adviser. Paying an adviser through asset-based fees is not necessarily cheaper than traditional loads, and, indeed, could wind up being more expensive. But it should only be more if the fund performs well. Most people don't mind paying for good advice and good service.

Keep in mind, too, that fee-based arrangements only work out well if the fee is reasonable.

Many independent advisers charge in the range of 1 to 1.5 percent of assets, and, the larger the account, the lower the percentage. Most major brokerage firms have a similar arrangement, called the "wrap" account, so-called because it wraps all costs into one price. But the fees may be as high as 3 percent. For a portfolio of mutual funds, that's much too high since the fee covers fund selection and monitoring. The actual stock selection, which is far more complex, takes place within the mutual funds themselves, and that's paid for through the funds' operating expenses.

The fee-based arrangement isn't for everyone. For starters, do you need or want the help? If you feel comfortable and have the time to do it yourself, you don't need an adviser. If you'd like one, but don't have a minimum of six figures to invest, it may be hard to find an independent adviser to take your account. Some advisory firms, in fact, want a $250,000 minimum investment. If you can't meet the minimum and want an adviser, you will have to pay steep hourly rates or go for traditional load-fund products. If you're successful, you may eventually accumulate enough money to switch to an asset-based arrangement.

Considering hiring an adviser to manage a portfolio of mutual funds? Lots of people are doing it, even those who have the savvy to invest the money themselves. Many of those who have the ability just don't have the time. Most people find investment advisers the same way you find other professionals, through referrals and recommendations from friends, relatives, and coworkers. But don't hand over your money to anyone without a thorough investigation—what's known as "due diligence"—of your own.

All people who give investment advice and manage money must be registered with the U.S. Securities & Exchange Commission. Financial planners, who may give more general advice on investments, tax matters, estate planning, and the like, may not be SEC-registered. Getting an SEC registration assures little about the knowledge of the adviser or the quality of the advice. All it takes to become an SEC-registered adviser is to complete a lengthy form and pay the $150 fee. No examinations are required, and there is no requirement for education in investment theory and practice. The SEC's Form ADV, which advisers must complete, asks about education, professional credentials, work experience, and the like, but having none of that is no bar to getting the registration. That's why it's imperative to ask an adviser for a copy of his or her ADV. The law requires that he or she provide you with Part II,

which describes the investment program, fees, and charges. But ask for Part I as well, which includes the adviser's legal and regulatory history. The SEC can investigate investor complaints against registered advisers, but as far as regular audits, they are few and far between. On average, they occur once every four decades. If an adviser is also selling securities, the adviser must pass a qualifying examination administered by the National Association of Securities Dealers.

Most states require investment advisers to register and many also require that they pass some national examinations. But the tests usually deal with the rules and regulations of dealing with clients. They don't test for the adviser's knowledge and understanding of the investments. There are private organizations and professional associations that do that, such as the Association for Investment Management and Research, which awards the Chartered Financial Analyst designation, and the College of Financial Planning, which grants the Certified Financial Planner certificate. If the adviser has one or more such designation, it's definitely a plus. And don't take the adviser's word for it. You may want to call the professional group yourself to verify the credentials. (For an excellent rundown on who's who in the financial planner/investment adviser field, check out the excellent Web site run by the North American Securities Administrators Association at http://www.nasaa.org.)

Most advisers have a track record they can show you. But it's not necessarily going to be useful information. Putting on the best show, the adviser might show you a sample portfolio with what seems to be a high return. But that portfolio might have been devised for a client with far more risk-taking ability or tolerance than you have. So if you are a conservative investor, ask to see what the adviser has done for someone more like yourself. And a really good adviser won't take your word for it that you're a conservative investor. He or she should ask probing questions and perhaps give you a written quiz to get a better sense of your risk-taking appetite and ability. Most people can take more risk than they think they can, and as a result short-change themselves in the long run. A good adviser will spot that and encourage you to correct it.

Once you have decided on an adviser, make sure you understand what services (such as regular consultations and monthly or quarterly reports) the adviser is going to provide, what it's going to cost, and how payment will be collected. Then, the adviser will open up an account for you,

> Hiring an adviser? Check references carefully.

probably with a brokerage firm that has a mutual funds network. The account must be in your name, not the adviser's. You should give the adviser the power to make buy and sell decisions for the portfolio. After all, that's the point of having an adviser. But make sure you receive the confirmation slips and brokerage statements that show the activity in the account. Do not give the adviser the power to take money out of the account. Only you should be able to do that.

Buying on Margin

The convenience and simplicity of the mutual fund networks have also made them popular with mutual fund "market-timers," investors who move assets around, following rigorous technical formulas, trying to capture upside moves in the stock market while steering clear of downdrafts. For more aggressive investors, the program allows the purchase of mutual funds on margin. Margin buying works this way. Suppose a fund investor believes stocks are about to stage a big rally and thinks highly of the Janus Special Situations Fund. She decides to invest $10,000 in that fund. If the fund goes up 25 percent in the next six months, the investment is worth $12,500, and the investor can cash out at a profit of $2500. But if the investor buys on margin, she could invest $20,000 in the fund: $10,000 is her money and $10,000 is a loan from the brokerage firm. The interest rate on the load is usually the broker's loan rate (a figure similar to a bank's prime rate) plus anywhere from 0.5 to 1.5 percent, depending on the size of the loan.

If the fund goes up 25 percent, the investor's holding climbs to $25,000, and if she sells it, there is a 50 percent return on the original $10,000 investment—a $5000 profit. Well, not quite. Remember, the investor took a loan from the broker to buy the shares. Suppose she borrowed $10,000 for six months at 10 percent interest. That comes out to $500. All told, the investor nets (before commissions) $4500 on her original $10,000. In a cash account that does not use margin, the net profit would be $2500.

But not all margin plays work out so well. What if the value of the investment remained unchanged for six months? Then the margin investor is out the interest. Worse yet, the fund headed south instead of north and declined by 25 percent. So the $20,000 investment is now worth $15,000. What if the margin investor sells at that point? She owes the broker the $10,000 originally

borrowed and $500 interest to boot, leaving her with $4500 out of an initial $10,000 investment. Don't use margin buying unless you know exactly what you're doing and can stand the loss.

Prospecting the Prospectus

Nobody wants to read a prospectus. It's a legal document that describes a mutual fund, often in legal and financial terms that may sound awfully technical. But the language is precise for a reason. The SEC has strict guidelines about what the fund can say about itself and how it must present information on past performance, expenses, and fees. Remember, the SEC's approval of a prospectus is only that. It is not an endorsement of any particular investment.

Read it. Okay, scan it and save it, and refer to it if you are going to try something new. There are Fidelity customers who lost money in October 1997 and would not have if they had read the rules in the prospectus. Here's what happened: The markets in Asia had already closed for the day on October 28, after another day of plunging prices. But the U.S. stock market, after some initial selling, recovered that day. These Fidelity investors, betting that it was highly likely that the Hong Kong market would rally the next day, put in orders for the Fidelity Hong Kong & China Fund. If they bought it at October 28th's depressed price, they could likely sell it much higher on the 29th. But Fidelity had exercised a right that's clearly stated in the prospectus. Instead of calculating the fund's October 28 net asset value based on the closing prices in Hong Kong, they opted for "fair value pricing," a valuation based on what these Hong Kong stocks were worth given the new stronger market on the 28th in the United States. Those traders who tried to exploit this timing discrepancy cried foul, since they had ended up buying the shares at prices much higher than they thought they were going to pay. But Fidelity was well within its rights, as spelled out in the prospectus.

If the prospectus looks daunting today, it's only a shadow of what it was just a few years ago. It's easier to read; its figures are easier to compare; and there's a lot less bulk. Most of the objective information you need is in there: sales charges and fees, investment policy, and administrative matters like the procedure for redeeming shares

Don't let the prospectus scare you.

or switching into other funds. If the fund has an operating history, the prospectus will provide historical data too. What the prospectus won't have is a glowing recommendation from a sales rep or a complimentary article from a financial publication. That may be included in sales literature that's stuffed into the same envelope.

Believe it or not, prospectuses are improving. Direct marketers like Fidelity, who don't have salespeople to explain their funds to investors, are making efforts to both simplify the prospectus and, as much as the lawyers allow, explain things in "plain English." In fact, with the blessings of the SEC, some fund companies are currently providing vastly simplified "plain English" prospectuses that fit neatly on two sides of an 8½- by 11-inch piece of paper, with room to spare.

Simplifying a prospectus is never easy because it's a document that's trying to serve two purposes. One is disclosure, or informing investors how a fund invests and operates. But the prospectus is also a document that mutual fund lawyers design as a litigation shield, making sure the fund managers will be able to run the fund without inviting lawsuits.

STATEMENT OF ADDITIONAL INFORMATION

There's plenty of detail in the prospectus, but the investor can also ask the fund to send the Statement of Additional Information (SAI). This bulkier presentation is more of what prospectuses used to be. There are some nuggets you will find here, if you're interested. For instance, in 1998, the SEC started to require that funds list the names and compensation of their directors—though funds have until December 1, 1999 to comply. That's information that's otherwise hard to get. You may be interested in how much the fund pays in brokerage commissions—and that's in the SAI. Then there are some details like shareholder voting rights that are no longer in the prospectus—but are in the SAI.

However, for the most part, the SAI covers the same ground as the prospectus, but in far more detail, consuming far more paper, with more fine print and fewer graphics. For instance, the prospectus for the Fidelity Growth & Income Portfolio (dated September 25, 1997) is 30 pages, set in double columns, double-spaced, with charts and tables and ample white space. Each page is 8⅜ by 5⅝ inches in size. That's a fairly slim mutual fund prospectus. The SAI for the same fund is 27 8½- by 11-inch pages, single-spaced, and largely unbroken by charts and tables. How do they dif-

fer? A prospectus, for instance, might have a heading worded "Adjusting Investment Exposure," followed by two paragraphs outlining in summary form that the fund can use "various techniques" to increase or decrease its exposure to changes in security prices, interest rates, foreign exchange, and other factors that affect security prices. In contrast, the SAI for the same fund might spend two single-spaced pages of type on the same topic.

For most investors, the prospectus should suffice. But you should be aware of the SAI. In a federal appellate court case in New York, the judges ruled that investors are responsible for knowing what's in the Statement of Additional Information. An investor challenged a fee that he said wasn't in the prospectus. The court said it was, but in the SAI. And since the existence of the SAI was noted in the prospectus and is legally part of the prospectus, he could not claim he was unaware of the charge. Any prospectus should alert investors to the existence of the SAI and instruct them on how to attain it. Many, like Fidelity, even put it on the prospectus's cover page.

State securities administrators (who oversee the activities of securities firms at the state level) have been urging fund investors to request SAIs and urging the SEC to require more detailed information in the prospectuses so investors don't have to read both documents. The SEC's Division of Investment Management, which regulates mutual funds, has resisted any moves that might fatten up the prospectuses. If the prospectus is a little-read document now, it will be even less so if it is a thicker and more detailed document.

TAKING A CLOSER LOOK

Don't let the prospectus unnerve you. The financial matters and investment policies may be unique. But much of the other material is boilerplate and doesn't vary much from fund to fund. And not all of it is pertinent to every investor. As long as your planned investment isn't for your Individual Retirement Account or other tax-deferred program, you don't need to read the IRA section in the prospectus.

When thumbing through the prospectus, look for important statistical nuggets like the fund's results and expenses. The documents plainly enumerate sales charges, deferred sales charges, redemption fees, exchange fees, management fees, 12(b)-1 fees, and other pertinent expenses. There will also be a condensed financial history of the fund. (Most of these data are also available in the BUSINESS WEEK Mutual Fund Scoreboard.)

> Financial statements give a sense of the fund.

Want to take a closer look? Go to Figures 3-1 and 3-2, which are pages four and five from the Fidelity Dividend Growth Fund. (The prospectus is dated September 29, 1998.) Look at the expense summary. You can see there is no sales charge on purchases or reinvested distributions and no deferred sales charge on redemptions. There is a $12 annual account maintenance fee for accounts with less than $2500, and it applies across the Fidelity universe.

Then come the operating expenses. The introductory note explains what goes into the charges. The management fee, which can vary depending on the fund's performance, is estimated to be 0.65 percent, or 65 cents per $100. "Other" expenses, which include such administrative costs as maintaining shareholder records and furnishing reports and financial statements, amount to another 0.24 percent.

FIGURE 3-1

Expenses

Shareholder transaction expenses

are charges you may pay when you buy or sell shares of the fund. In addition, you may be charged an annual account maintenance fee if your account balance falls below $2,500. See "Transaction Details," page 25, for an explanation of how and when these charges apply.

Sales charge on purchases and reinvested distributions	**None**
Deferred sales charge on redemptions	**None**
Annual account maintenance fee (for accounts under $2,500)	**$12.00**

Annual fund operating expenses

are paid out of the fund's assets. The fund pays a management fee to FMR that varies based on its performance. It also incurs other expenses for services such as maintaining shareholder records and furnishing shareholder statements and financial reports. The fund's expenses are factored into its share price or dividends and are not charged directly to shareholder accounts (see "Breakdown of Expenses," page 13).

The following figures are based on historical expenses of the fund and are calculated as a percentage of average net assets of the fund. A portion of the brokerage commissions that the fund pays is used to reduce the fund's expenses. In addition, the fund has entered into arrangements with its custodian and transfer agent whereby credits realized as a result of uninvested cash balances are used to reduce custodian and transfer agent expenses. Including these reductions, the total fund operating expenses presented in the table would have been 0.86%.

Management fee	0.65%
12b-1 fee	None
Other expenses	0.24%
Total fund operating expenses	**0.89%**

Examples: Let's say, hypothetically, that the fund's annual return is 5% and that your shareholder transaction expenses and the fund's annual operating expenses are exactly as just described. For every $1,000 you invested, here's how much you would pay in total expenses if you close your account after the number of years indicated:

1 year	$ 9
3 years	$ 28
5 years	$ 49
10 years	$110

These examples illustrate the effect of expenses, but are not meant to suggest actual or expected expenses or returns, all of which may vary.

Understanding Expenses

Operating a mutual fund involves a variety of expenses for portfolio management, shareholder statements, tax reporting, and other services. These expenses are paid from the fund's assets, and their effect is already factored into any quoted share price or return. Also, as an investor, you may pay certain expenses directly.

Add up all fund operating expenses and the figure comes to 0.89 percent of the fund's net assets. So what does that mean to your bottom line? You can find that right below, where the cumulative impact of sales charges and expenses is shown. If you invest $1000 and earn 5 percent a year, you've spent $9 on sales and operating expenses in the first year, $28 after 3 years, and $110 after 10 years. Actually, a 5 percent assumed rate of return for this fund is absurd, and if that's all you thought you could earn, you certainly would not invest in it. However, that's not the point. The SEC requires funds to use that reporting format account to make it easier for investors to compare fees and expenses.

If the fund is brand new, be sure to check whether the fund's parent company is subsidizing the fund's overhead or waiving management fees. Don't snub these funds; if someone's going to give you a free lunch, take it. But free lunches don't

FIGURE 3-2

Financial Highlights

The financial highlights table that follows has been audited by PricewaterhouseCoopers LLP, independent accountants. The fund's financial highlights, financial statements, and report of the auditor are included in the fund's Annual Report, and are incorporated by reference into (are legally a part of) the fund's SAI. Contact Fidelity for a free copy of the Annual Report or the SAI.

Selected Per-Share Data

Years ended July 31	1998	1997	1996	1995	1994	1993[F]
Net asset value, beginning of period	$ 25.07	$ 17.24	$ 16.04	$ 11.68	$ 10.80	$ 10.00
Income from Investment Operations						
Net investment income	.17[E]	.20[E]	.11	.05	.02	(.01)
Net realized and unrealized gain (loss)	5.21	8.09	2.25	4.47	1.01	.81
Total from investment operations	5.38	8.29	2.36	4.52	1.03	.80
Less Distributions						
From net investment income	(.15)	(.09)	(.09)	(.01)	(.01)	—
From net realized gain	(2.19)	(.37)	(1.07)	(.15)	—	—
In excess of net realized gain	—	—	—	—	(.14)	—
Total distributions	(2.34)	(.46)	(1.16)	(.16)	(.15)	—
Net asset value, end of period	$ 28.11	$ 25.07	$ 17.24	$ 16.04	$ 11.68	$ 10.80
Total return[B,C]	23.81%	49.21%	15.44%	39.14%	9.51%	8.00%

Ratios and Supplemental Data

	1998	1997	1996	1995	1994	1993[F]
Net assets, end of period (In millions)	$ 7,371	$ 4,368	$ 1,220	$ 465	$ 72	$ 18
Ratio of expenses to average net assets	.89%	.95%	1.02%	1.21%	1.43%	2.50%[A,D]
Ratio of expenses to average net assets after expense reductions	.86%[G]	.92%[G]	.99%[G]	1.19%[G]	1.40%[G]	2.50%[A]
Ratio of net investment income to average net assets	.64%	.99%	.86%	.78%	.13%	(.73)%[A]
Portfolio turnover rate	109%	141%	129%	162%	291%	90%[A]
Average commission rate[H]	$ .0437	$ .0419				

[A] Annualized
[B] Total returns for periods of less than one year are not annualized.
[C] The total returns would have been lower had certain expenses not been reduced during the periods shown.
[D] Limited in accordance with a state expense limitation.
[E] Net investment income (loss) per share has been calculated based on average shares outstanding during the period.
[F] For the period April 27, 1993 (commencement of operations) to July 31, 1993.
[G] FMR or the fund has entered into varying arrangements with third parties who either paid or reduced a portion of the fund's expenses.
[H] For fiscal years beginning on or after September 1, 1995, a fund is required to disclose its average commission rate per share for security trades on which commissions are charged. This amount may vary from period to period and fund to fund depending on the mix of trades executed in various markets where trading practices and commission rate structures may differ.

last forever. It's common for fund management companies to subsidize money-market and bond funds when they're trying to build assets, and they'll often do it for equity funds as well. If the parent company absorbs 0.50 percentage point in expenses, it can really make a money-market or bond fund stand out. And, of course, that's the point. The yield looks alluring, and the money flows in.

But watch out. The prospectus must disclose the full fee structure even if shareholders are not paying it. The point is you should be aware of what the fees are and what they would be if they were paid. Without the waiver, some of these funds may not look as attractive as others that have no waiver but lower expenses. You can put the money in and take the free lunch. But be ready to leave if and when full rates are levied.

The financial statements also give you some feeling for the fund. The numbers may look scary, but they're really pretty simple. Go to Figure 3-2. Start with the first column, which is for the fiscal year ending July 31, 1998. The top line, net asset value (NAV) at the beginning of the period, tells you what a fund share was worth on August 1, 1997, the start of the fiscal year. That's $25.07. Seven lines down, you come up with net asset value at the end of the period, $28.11. The steps in between explain how the fund got from the beginning NAV to the end-of-period NAV.

Start with "net investment income." That's 17 cents a share. It's what's left from stock dividends and interest from fixed-income or money-market holdings after paying for fund expenses. Such expenses include fund managers, record-keeping, postage, auditing, and legal fees. That 17 cents is available for distribution to Fidelity Dividend Growth shareholders. That's only a 0.64 percent yield. (You can see that near the bottom of the table on the line "ratio of net investment income to average net assets.") A low yield, for sure, even in a period of low dividend yields.

The big money in equity funds now comes from capital gains. Look at the line "net realized & unrealized gain (loss) on investments." When a mutual fund sells a security at a profit, it has a "realized" gain; when it sells at a loss, it's a realized loss. If a fund continues to hold stocks that are worth more than the fund paid for them, the stocks represent unrealized gains. Likewise, stocks held in a portfolio that are valued at less than cost are unrealized losses. To get "net" gains, the fund tallies the gains and losses, both realized and unrealized. If the

number is positive, as it is here, the fund had net gains. If negative, net losses. In fiscal 1998, Fidelity Dividend Growth had net gains of $5.21 per share. Net gains plus net investment income gives you the next line, "total from investment operations" of $5.38 per share.

Mutual funds must make distributions of income and realized capital gains in order to preserve their unique tax status. (See more on that in Chapter 6.) So go to the next section, "less distributions." The next line tells you there was 15 cents a share in income distributions. But wait! The fund earned 17 cents in net investment income. Well, for tax purposes fund distributions are made on a calendar year basis; for book purposes, on a fiscal year basis. So since Fidelity Dividend Growth keeps a different fiscal year, the distributions aren't usually the same. Nonetheless, that 15 cents came out of each fund share in fiscal 1998, so it's recorded here. Then there was a distribution of $2.19 a share in net realized gains, for a total of $2.34.

The next group of figures, "ratios and supplemental data," should help compare this fund to others. The ratio of expenses to average net assets is 0.89 percent for fiscal year 1998. But the next line, "ratio of expenses to average net assets after expense reductions" is what the shareholders actually pay. The footnote indicates that the fund management company has recaptured part of the brokerage commission rebates (known in the investment business as "soft dollars") to pay for some fund expenses. In this case, it's 0.03 percent. That may not sound like much, but it's $2.2 million on this $7.4 billion fund. So the expense ratio, after these cost reductions, is 0.86 percent. That's below average for equity funds.

Before moving on, look at the expense ratio and how it changes from year to year. The number is trending downward. That's to be expected, for as the fund grows, it should have some economies of scale in its operations that benefit its shareholders. Be wary of funds in which this ratio is moving up.

The last line, "portfolio turnover rate" (109 percent) indicates that securities amounting to 109 percent of the total assets of the fund changed hands during the year. This means that if a fund had $100 million in assets, the value of the securities that "turned over" during the year amounted to $109 million. Fidelity Dividend Growth, whose average assets were $5.9 billion during this fiscal year, had securities trades worth about $6.5 billion. A turnover rate of 109 percent is a little high, as the average equity fund has an 80 turnover rate. (There's more about portfolio turnover in Chapter 7.)

Following the financial highlights, there's a short section on fund performance, showing the average annual total returns and cumulative total returns for the fund over various fiscal year periods. The fund performance is also compared to the S&P 500 and to the Lipper Growth Funds Average. Perhaps more meaningful to investors is another table that shows the fund's returns year by year on a calendar year basis. This table also compares each year's returns to that of the S&P 500, the Lipper average, and the U.S. Consumer Price Index.

INVESTMENT POLICY

After the financials, the prospectus turns to the investment objective. In the Fidelity Dividend Growth prospectus, for instance, the section is called "Investment Principles and Risks." The investment policy section will outline the overall strategy, the permitted investments in the broadest of terms (i.e., stocks or U.S. government or government-guaranteed securities), and restrictions, if there are any.

For a fund with a descriptive name (i.e., a fund that says small company or health care or North America in its name), pay particular attention to what else the fund can do. For instance, in early 1995, a group of shareholders filed a lawsuit against the Alliance North American Government Income Fund, which suffered severe losses during the Mexican currency crisis. The complaint? The fund name said it was North American, but the fund had invested in Argentina, which, of course, is in South America. But the prospectus noted that only 65 percent of the fund had to be in North American debt obligations, and the fund met that condition. (In addition, in reports to shareholders, the fund had advised them of the Argentine holdings. That's another reason to read those shareholder reports.)

Pay careful attention to the investment objective and how the fund managers plan to achieve it, especially the kind of risk they might undertake (with your money). Be forewarned. Most fund prospectuses are written in a way that gives fund managers the widest latitude and discretion.

Some funds try to boost returns by trading futures and options contracts or other derivatives. That must be spelled out. Is preservation of capital the utmost priority? Don't assume it is, even if the investment is a government bond

fund. Some sacrifice net asset value in order to deliver a high payout, and it says so, though not in such blunt language.

The information in this section helps to describe the fund's character. First Eagle Fund of America, for instance, says it will pursue capital appreciation with a flexible investment strategy that may include junk bonds, foreign securities, restricted securities (illiquid securities that are not publicly traded), and "special situations" (opportunities that may arise from liquidations, reorganizations, mergers, material litigation, technological breakthroughs, or new management and management policies). Moreover, First Eagle may buy and sell options and futures contracts and even "leverage its assets for securities purchases." That's another way to say the fund buys on margin. If you'd sleep better with a fund that invests solely in name-brand blue-chip stocks, First Eagle is probably not for you.

SHAREHOLDER SERVICES

Look for services and conveniences. The standard ones are automatic investment and reinvestment of dividends and capital gains distributions. They'll be described in the prospectus. Most money-market funds and many bond funds also offer check-writing privileges. But those that do will often require that you write a check of $500 or $1000 at the least, so don't plan on using these funds to pay at the supermarket. Convenient as they are, such privileges are no substitute for a conventional checking account. (U.S. Global Investors Treasury Securities Cash Fund is a U.S. money-market fund with no minimum check size and no limit on the number of checks written.)

Automatic investing is an arrangement you set up between the fund company and your bank. You can make periodic investments from your checking account to a designated mutual fund. It's an excellent way to accumulate capital, and unlike a contractual arrangement that some funds still market, you can stop or alter the program at your discretion without any penalty.

Most fund groups ordinarily roll over the dividends and capital gains into new shares. That's one of the major benefits of investing in mutual funds. By reinvesting your earnings you have the opportunity to compound the growth rate of the fund. It's the same idea as earning interest on your interest. This is not an irrevocable decision. At any time, you can change your mind and start taking the cash.

The fund's investment goals should match yours.

❙Redemptions

Getting money out of a fund takes planning.

Putting money into a mutual fund is simple. Fidelity Investments' walk-in centers, for instance, make investing easy by having personnel on hand to field questions, take applications, and accept checks. But though you can invest at one of these locations as though you were making a deposit at a local bank, you can't make a "withdrawal" on the spot. The money must come through regular channels, either a check by mail or by bank wire.

Getting money out isn't quite as simple as putting it in. But there's a whole lot less bother getting money out if you plan for it on the way in. Some investors are surprised to find a $5 exchange or redemption fee taken out of their proceeds when they get their account statement. But if you've read about the fund's redemption procedures in the prospectus ahead of time, it should not be a shock. It has to be in the fee table, along with information about sales charges, 12(b)-1 fees, and the like.

Most funds offer telephone redemption privileges. But that's not something to request on the day you want the money. It's best to do it when setting up the account. If you have an existing account that doesn't have telephone switching privileges, request the form that permits it. And don't assume that if some funds in a family of funds offer telephone redemption, all the funds in the group do. Some Vanguard equity funds, for instance, bar telephone switches. Even when a fund offers telephone redemption there may be limits on the amount of money that can be withdrawn or the number of switches within a given period. Plan on following the advice of a mutual fund timing service? Ask if the fund group has any qualms about letting frequent switchers into their funds. (That's something you won't find in the prospectus but will have to ask a fund representative yourself.) Sometimes fund groups per-

mit intrafamily telephone switches from an equity fund to a bond fund or money-market fund, but may restrict telephone withdrawal from the fund group. Depending on the amount of money involved (sometimes it's anything over $5000), the fund company may want written instructions.

Obtaining quick access to your funds is especially important with money-market funds since they're most often used as liquid assets or "rainy day" emergency money. All money-fund accounts should be set up with telephone redemption privileges.

Ask for check-writing privileges too. Even if you don't use the checks for regular bill-paying, the checks provide quick access to your account. Most funds can transmit funds by wire to your bank, but again that's not something to negotiate over the phone on the day you need the money. If you want this service, the fund will ask for the appropriate banking information on the application. There's usually a charge for the service as well as a minimum amount of money that must be wired.

Pay particular attention to a fund group's rules on withdrawals. They're not all the same. For many funds a signature on a redemption letter may not be enough. The company may require that the signature (and that of any other person whose name is on the account) be "guaranteed." A signature guarantee is an endorsement that verifies that the signature is genuine. The guarantor will compare the authenticity of the signature to one already on file. You're supposed to sign the letter in the presence of the guarantor.

Many funds accept guarantees from commercial banks or savings institutions that are members of the Federal Deposit Insurance Corporation or brokerage firms that are members of the New York Stock Exchange. Some may accept others like state-insured thrifts and federally insured credit unions, but ask the fund service personnel first. A notary public's seal is usually unacceptable.

Building an Investment Portfolio

You've seen the ads for some of the new drugs on the market, and you give your doctor a call. "Doc, these new drugs sound great. How about writing me some prescriptions for the two or three that you think are best?" Sounds absurd, doesn't it? First you have to know what ails you before you get a prescription.

Yet many investors choose their investments the same way. They hear about a hot-performing fund, or a fund with a novel investment twist, and jump in. What they need to do first is examine their financial goals and decide what exactly they are trying to achieve through their investments (Table 4-1). Only then can they make a sensible choice from the multitude of investment opportunities. There are hundreds of excellent mutual funds out there, but not every one of them—even those with the highest BUSINESS WEEK ratings—is appropriate for every investor.

Determining Your Financial Goals

The 35-year-old physician with two preschool-aged children needs to build capital—and has time on her side. She would probably benefit from an all-equity portfolio, with the number of funds depending on how much money she is starting with. With $10,000 or so, she might go for five funds: a large-cap blend fund such as the Vanguard Index 500, which tracks the S&P 500; a mid-cap blend fund such as Mairs & Power Growth Fund or a mid-cap value fund like Weitz Value Fund; a small-cap value fund such as Royce

Total Return; a small-cap growth fund such as the Acorn or Fasciano funds; and a foreign fund such as Janus Overseas, BT Investment International Equity, or Templeton Foreign. With, say, $40,000 to $50,000 in assets, she might add large-cap growth and large-cap value funds to supplement or supplant the index fund and a diversified emerging markets fund to supplement the international component.

The 45-year-old computer programmer, having built some savings through aggressive investing, may have to settle for a lower return to steady his investment portfolio. He's about to embark on years of college tuition payments for his children and he wants to be sure the money will be there when he needs it. So he's keeping at least one year's worth of tuition and room and board payments in an ultrashort bond fund like the Strong Advantage Fund. He's lightened up a bit on the more aggressive small-cap and mid-cap growth funds. Now, less volatile funds like Vanguard Windsor II Fund, Fidelity Equity-Income, and

TABLE 4-1

BEFORE INVESTING, CONSIDER...

▶ Do you need current income from your investments?

▶ How soon will you need the proceeds of your investments?

▶ How will inflation affect you?

▶ How much risk are you willing to take?

▶ How will taxes affect your investments?

▶ What kind of temperament do you have for investing?

Third Avenue Value Fund have more appeal to him. He still owns international funds, which make up 25 percent of his portfolio. And, except for the college money that's tucked away in the ultrashort bond fund, it's still an all-equity portfolio.

The 55-year-old lawyer is finished with his children's education and is now socking it away for retirement about 10 years hence. He still has 80 percent of his portfolio in equities, but only about 10 percent is in the volatile small-cap growth funds. As his tolerance for risk has lessened, he's tilting more of his equity investments to the value categories—small-cap value, mid-cap value, and large-cap value. On the international side he also has value-oriented funds, such as Tweedy Browne Global Value.

His friend, also 55, is a corporate executive who fears that cutbacks might cost him his job and force him into early retirement. He too is moving from more aggressive equity funds to tamer funds such as T. Rowe Price Equity–Income. For the fixed-income portion of the portfolio, he chooses less volatile intermediate-term bond funds like American Century–Benham GNMA Income and Harbor Bond.

Mutual funds, like all investments, are only a means to an end, not an end in themselves. They're used to accumulate a down payment for your first home, as an educational fund for your children, or as a nest egg for your retirement. So before you choose the investment vehicle, you need to assess what goal you want to achieve through your investments. If you go to a travel agent, the first question is, "Where do you want to go?" not "Which airline do you want to fly?"

The conventional wisdom says younger people should take on the most risky investments and gradually shift over to less risky investments as they age. By the time they're retired they should be into income-producing vehicles almost entirely. But the conventional wisdom is too general to serve everybody's needs. If you're in your late twenties and saving to buy a home, you don't have decades to wait. You'll need money-market funds and short-term bond funds to help you achieve that objective. You may have a two-track investment plan. Keep taxable assets in the shorter-term investments and keep the long-term investments, like growth-oriented equity funds, in your IRA.

Likewise, many retirees shift too quickly into income-producing investments, whether they need them or not. Younger retirees, in particular, might do best if they stick with equities when

their various pensions and other sources of retirement income suffice. Life expectancy is going up, and retirees in their early sixties may live well into their eighties. That means they need to increase their capital faster than the rate of inflation. They're going to need equity investments to do that.

To help choose the most appropriate funds for an investment program, you should first answer the following series of questions.

DO YOU NEED CURRENT INCOME FROM YOUR INVESTMENTS?

If you're the kind of person who needs to spend the interest from your certificates of deposit, you need current income. Most investors for whom current income is a priority are retirees, but not exclusively. Sometimes families may have some investment capital, obtained perhaps through an inheritance, but need to use it to generate income to meet expenses. A single parent, for instance, may need income from investments to supplement other sources.

Figure how much income you need from your investments. Start with an estimate of how much regular income you need in total, and then subtract all other sources, such as salaries, pension payments, Social Security payments, and the like. Suppose you need $60,000 a year, and all other sources produce $50,000. Your portfolio will have to produce $10,000. Long-term interest rates are around 5 percent, and yields on stocks are, on average, only 1.3 percent. You'll need at least $200,000 invested in long-term bonds (or bond funds) to produce $10,000. But if you have $300,000 you can count on, the other $100,000 could be invested for capital appreciation. That will enable you to build a larger portfolio for the day when $10,000 won't be enough.

If you have a regular income from your job that meets your needs, current income should not even be a consideration. You should emphasize investments that shoot for capital gains, not income. Sure, you balance the two. But remember, investments that maximize current income, like money-market mutual funds, provide no capital gains. And many bond funds that maximize current income will, at times, suffer capital losses.

These guidelines are not inviolable absolutes. When short-term interest rates are high, say 10 percent, a money-market mutual fund is going to be a hard investment to beat. The return would be so large and the risks so minimal that no other investment would look competitive.

The younger you are, the more risk you can take.

HOW SOON WILL YOU NEED THE PROCEEDS OF YOUR INVESTMENTS?

Identifying the right time horizon goes a long way toward finding the right funds. If you're saving for a goal 15 years distant—like college tuition for a preschooler—you can rely on equity funds to carry the weight of reaching your goals. Over long periods of time they outperform bond and money-market funds. For periods of less than 10 years, short- and intermediate-term bond funds have to play a greater role in the portfolio. Cash that's going to be tapped in a year or less should be invested in a money-market fund.

Some people fail to grasp the importance of the time horizon. What is the long term, they say, but a series of short terms back to back? So why not just invest short term and continue to reinvest over and over again?

Here's why. In the 70 years for which good records exist, U.S. Treasury bills—the safest short-term investment around—have delivered an average annual return of 3.8 percent, and long-term government bonds, 5.3 percent. During the same period, the total return on common stocks—capital appreciation plus reinvestment of dividends—averaged 11.2 percent per year. The story is much the same if you look at only 30 years. Fixed-income returns are higher, but they still lag well behind equities.

The time horizon is easy to quantify. If it's 1999 and your child starts college in 2010, his or her education fund has a time horizon of 11 to 15 years. If you're 40 now and have a 401(k) plan at work, the 401(k)'s time horizon is at least 19 years (you can start withdrawing funds at age 59½), but it's more likely to be 27 or 30. Think of the time horizon as a balance sheet: The assets are your investments; the liabilities are the expenses to be funded in future years.

HOW WILL INFLATION AFFECT YOU?

Since your investment dollars will ultimately be used to "purchase" goods or services some time in the future, then inflation, the erosion of purchasing power, is an important matter that must be considered in your investment portfolio. If you don't take the impact of inflation into account in your investment planning, you risk being ravaged by its effects.

Think of it this way. You invest $1000 in a 30-year U.S. government bond paying 5 percent interest. You collect $50 a year (actually, $25 every six months), and in 30 years you get back your $1000. Suppose that for now the $33 semiannual payment buys you and your spouse dinner at

a modestly priced restaurant (and you don't order alcoholic beverages and you skip dessert).

What will it buy in 10 years? If inflation is modest, say only 3 percent—the long-term average—that $33 will be $24.50 in today's money. So, in 10 years, what bought dinner for two now may buy lunch for one—maybe. What about the principal? If inflation averages only 3 percent a year for the next three decades, the $1000 will have only about $412 worth of purchasing power. Maybe dinner for one, if you're lucky.

To get a jump on inflation, you have to buy equity funds. Common stocks and small company stocks have shown over the long haul that they beat the Consumer Price Index hands down. True there are times—like the 1970s—when inflation ravaged the stock market. Stocks in general don't usually beat inflation in periods when inflation is accelerating. But small company stocks can do well in inflationary periods if the companies' growth rates outpace inflation.

International stock and international bond mutual funds should also help guard a portfolio from inflation. In periods of inflation in the United States, the dollar tends to drop in value against foreign currencies. This in itself feeds inflation because U.S. consumers must pay more dollars for imported goods. But when the dollar goes down in value, assets denominated in foreign currencies go up. So to the extent you have money in foreign assets, you have a hedge against the declining value of your dollars.

HOW MUCH RISK ARE YOU WILLING TO TAKE?

As the jocks will tell you, "No pain, no gain." Well, in the investment world the pain is the risk and volatility. We don't seem to mind when the Dow Jones industrial average shoots up 150 points in a day, but we're unhappy when it's down that much. People say they don't like volatility and risk, but what they're really telling you is that they don't want their investments to go down. Nobody ever complained when their investments went up.

Most investors are so risk averse that they fail to make objective judgments. Taking risks isn't easy. Psychologists studying how people make financial decisions have found that most will shy away from risks, even when the odds dictate otherwise. Many people pay a premium in the form of a lower return on their investment for the greater certainty of preserving that capital. That's because most people are more influenced by their fear of losses than by the prospect of

> To best fight inflation, invest in equity funds.

gains. Behavioral psychologists, in fact, find that the pain of a loss looms twice as large as the pleasure of an equivalent gain. Even if the odds are 50–50, the average person will take a risk only if he or she can win twice as much as he or she can lose.

Investors often avoid risks because they're more influenced by recent history than by a long run of events. For most of 1987, investors couldn't get enough of the stock market. From January through August, the Dow industrials gained over 800 points. The fact was, as the Dow climbed, it became very risky. Stocks entered the overvalued zone in terms of corporate earnings, book value, and dividend yields. But as the market went up, people paid little attention to those risks.

Then the market crashed, losing 508 points on October 19, 1987. More than one-fifth of the market value of Corporate America was washed away in six and a half hours. In the following weeks stocks were marked down by more than a third from the summer's high, yet no one wanted the merchandise. They were afraid, or waiting for the 50-percent-off sale. Of course, the month after the crash, in retrospect, was the time to buy. Yet investors were far too scared to do so.

If you're like most investors, you've erred on the side of caution. You have probably underestimated the amount of risk you can take (like having too much in money-market funds relative to your investment goals) and are paying for it dearly in lost opportunities. It's a serious matter when it comes to pension savings. When companies give employees the option of directing how their pension funds are to be invested—the nub of the increasingly popular 401(k) plans—they have tended to choose fixed-income investments. Only in the last few years have participants opted for equity investments. Still, the existing base of 401(k) money is still heavy with interest-bearing investments. Younger employees, in particular, need stocks if they are to have enough on which to retire. When companies direct the pension plan investments, they place 60 to 70 percent of the assets in stocks.

If you have a long time horizon, your ability to take risks is greatly enhanced. Here's why. The long-term return from owning stocks is 11.2 percent, more than twice as much as from bonds. But, of course, stocks don't achieve that return year-in and year-out. In 1995, 1996, 1997, and 1998, for instance, the stocks in the Standard & Poor's 500 stock index racked up total returns (price appreciation plus dividends) of 37.5, 22.9,

33.4, and 28.6 percent, respectively. And 1991 was a banner year as well, with a 30.4 percent gain. In 1992, the return was a more modest 7.6 percent; in 1993, the return was 10.1 percent; and in 1994, only 1.3 percent. Over the last six decades the best year was 1933—in the depths of the depression. Stocks gained 54 percent. The worst year was two years earlier, in 1931, when stocks lost more than 43 percent of their value. Since World War II the best year was 1954, up 52.6 percent; the worst, 1974, down 26.5 percent.

Though any one year's results can be a stunner, over time the law of averages takes over. In any one year, statisticians estimate, the probable return from common stocks is between –10 percent and +30 percent. But over a five-year period, that expected range of returns narrows considerably—from +1 percent to +19 percent. And over 20 years, the range of expected returns is +5.5 to +14.5 percent. Simply put, the more years in your average, the more likely your results will look like the long-term average.

HOW WILL TAXES AFFECT YOUR INVESTMENTS?

Most investment advisers would caution you against making an investment solely because it shelters you from taxes. For many years lots of buildings were built because investors coveted the tax-sheltering attributes of commercial real estate. That they had tenants for the buildings was only a secondary consideration. The best investments are those that make sound economic sense.

But once you've identified a good investment idea, you should see how it stands up to the tax system. To do that, you have to know—or have a good approximation of—what your marginal tax bracket is. And don't forget to include state and local income taxes when you make that calculation.

Suppose your combined federal and state marginal tax bracket is 35 percent. What that means is that for every additional $1 in income, the tax folks siphon off 35 cents. So you have to start asking yourself, "How much do I want to bring in, and how much can I defer?"

When it comes to the taxes, mutual funds don't have a whole lot of leeway. The tax laws say a fund must pay out 98 percent of its net income and realized capital gains each year (that's net after deducting the expenses of running the fund). A fund that yields 5 percent may leave shareholders with only 3.25 percent after they've paid taxes.

If you want to minimize taxes, concentrate on small-cap and mid-cap growth funds. For one, the sorts of stocks these funds buy pay few or no dividends. And if the portfolio manager has a policy of holding stocks for the long term, he or she is not going to do a lot of trading. Trading and, more importantly, profits from trading produce gains that must be passed on to shareholders. On that point, index funds are fairly tax-efficient because of their ultra-low turnover. The only time they sell a stock is when it is removed from the index.

In the matter of bond and money-market funds, it's always wise to examine whether a lower-yielding tax-free fund will provide a greater aftertax return than a taxable one. Table 4-2 walks you through the calculation of how to know whether a tax-free investment will provide a better return than a taxable one.

Of course, if you're investing within the confines of a tax-deferred account, like an IRA, you don't give a hoot about taxation. There's no tax until you start withdrawing from a conventional IRA or a 401(k), and in the case of a Roth IRA, there's no tax on withdrawal. One warning: never put tax-free municipal bonds or bond funds in a tax-deferred plan.

WHAT KIND OF TEMPERAMENT DO YOU HAVE FOR INVESTING?

Looking at income needs, taxes, time horizons, and the like, it's easy to come up with an objective conclusion such as: I should put 70 percent of my money in small-cap and mid-cap growth funds. You understand the rationale and fully accept the notion that, with your time horizon, the riskier, higher-return vehicles should deliver the best results.

But if you're the sort of person who shudders at the thought of losing a piece of your principal, who worries about every twist and turn of the stock market, who would become stressed out if your investment went south for a while, this investment program is not for you. If you like the plan, but your spouse doesn't, it's not worth straining a marriage. If 70 percent is too heavy a concentration in equities, see if you can start with 30 percent in an equity mutual fund. If you (or your spouse) can get comfortable with that, then you can always increase the percentage of your assets in equities. Don't be ashamed to move cautiously. Advice comes from others, but the money that's invested on that advice is yours.

Research on how people make investment decisions has turned up some interesting observations that may help you examine your ability to take investment risks. In her work on the psychological characteristics of individual investors, Marilyn MacGruder Barnewall, a financial consultant, describes the "passive investor" and the "active investor."

Passive investors—and most people fall into this category—have a greater need for security than tolerance for risk. In fact, they usually perceive risks to be greater than they are. These people typically have come by their wealth "passively"—by inheritance or by risking others' capital to achieve their wealth. Included in this

TABLE 4-2

WHAT'S A SINGLE-STATE MUNI BOND FUND WORTH TO YOU?

FEDERAL MARGINAL TAX RATE					FEDERAL MARGINAL TAX RATE				
State ▼	28% ▼	31% ▼	36% ▼	39.6% ▼	State ▼	28% ▼	31% ▼	36% ▼	39.6% ▼
ALABAMA	31.6	34.5	39.2	42.6	MISSOURI	32.3	35.1	39.8	43.2
ARIZONA	30.7	34.3	39.0	42.6	MONTANA	35.9	38.6	43.0	46.2
ARKANSAS	33.0	35.8	40.5	43.8	NEBRASKA	33.0	35.8	40.5	43.8
CALIFORNIA	34.7	37.4	42.0	45.2	N. HAMPSHIRE	31.6	34.5	39.2	42.6
COLORADO	31.6	34.5	39.2	42.6	NEW JERSEY	32.0	35.4	40.1	43.4
CONNECTICUT	31.2	34.1	38.9	42.3	NEW MEXICO	33.7	36.7	41.2	44.6
DELAWARE	32.1	35.4	40.1	43.5	NEW YORK	32.9	35.7	40.4	43.7
DIST. OF COL.	34.8	37.6	42.1	45.3	N. Y. CITY	35.4	38.0	42.5	45.8
GEORGIA	32.3	35.1	39.8	43.2	N. CAROLINA	33.0	36.3	41.0	44.3
HAWAII	35.2	37.9	42.4	45.6	N. DAKOTA	36.6	39.3	43.7	46.8
IDAHO	33.9	36.7	41.2	44.6	OHIO	31.9	35.3	40.4	43.7
INDIANA	31.2	34.0	38.8	42.3	OKLAHOMA	32.9	35.7	40.3	43.7
IOWA	34.5	37.2	41.7	45.0	OREGON	34.5	37.2	41.8	45.0
KANSAS	32.6	35.5	40.1	43.5	PENNSYLVANIA	30.0	32.9	37.8	41.3
KENTUCKY	32.3	35.1	39.8	43.2	RHODE ISLAND	33.3	36.7	42.1	45.9
LOUISIANA	30.9	35.1	39.8	43.2	S. CAROLINA	33.0	35.8	40.5	43.8
MAINE	34.1	36.9	41.4	44.7	TENNESSEE	32.3	35.1	39.8	43.2
MARYLAND	33.6	36.4	41.0	44.3	UTAH	33.0	35.8	40.5	43.8
MASS.	32.3	35.1	39.8	43.2	VERMONT	33.0	36.3	41.8	45.6
MICHIGAN	31.2	34.0	38.8	42.3	VIRGINIA	32.1	35.0	39.7	43.1
MINNESOTA	34.1	36.9	41.4	44.7	WEST VIRGINIA	32.7	35.5	40.2	43.5
MISSISSIPPI	31.6	34.5	39.2	42.6	WISCONSIN	32.9	35.7	40.3	43.7

Suppose you are a Californian with a combined federal and state marginal tax bracket of 42%. What's the tax-equivalent yield for a California municipal bond fund yielding 5%? Here's the calculation:

$$\frac{\text{Tax-free yield}}{1 - \text{Combined marginal tax rate}} = \text{Tax-equivalent yield}$$

$$\frac{5}{1 - (0.42)} = \frac{5}{0.58} = 0.0862 \text{ or } 8.62\%$$

The 5% yield would be the equivalent of an 8.62% taxable yield.

DATA: FRANKLIN RESOURCES, BUSINESS WEEK

group are most corporate executives and most people who are employed by others. This is not to suggest that those who work for salaries do nothing for them, but the investment capital at stake in their enterprise is not theirs—and that's a critical factor. Passive investors are more likely to use brokers, investment advisers, or financial planners.

Active investors, on the other hand, are individuals who have earned their own wealth in their lifetimes. Barnewall says these people understand how to take risks and have a higher tolerance for risk than a need for security. In fact, they often underestimate their risks. Their tolerance for risk is high, she says, because of a strong belief in themselves. They usually feel most comfortable with investments which they "control." So, for some active investors, mutual funds may be unappealing since the funds' portfolio managers are the ones calling the shots on what stocks to buy and sell. On the other hand, the mutual fund universe is diverse enough to offer many choices and timing decisions, so an active investor can still achieve a lot of control. Nonetheless, direct sales funds would probably be more appealing to active investors than those sold through brokers or other intermediaries.

Of course, no one is totally one thing or the other. Passive investors may maintain, say, 70 percent of their investments in relatively secure products like certificates of deposit, money-market funds, and bond funds, with the other 30 percent in more risky ventures like growth funds. Active investors may do just the opposite.

The investment counseling firm of Bailard Biehl & Kaiser takes a different approach. It identifies four sorts of investor profiles: "adventurer," "celebrity," "individualist," and "guardian." Adventurers are just that. They like risk and they often make intuitive judgments. Celebrities are the trendies—fashion followers wanting to do what's hot rather than what's best. Individualists are the entrepreneurial sort and take a rational, methodical approach to most everything they do. Then there's the guardians, who are nervous about preserving their wealth and seek guidance in doing so.

Do you recognize yourself in one of these categories? Are you an adventurer? If so, you may need to practice a little self-restraint. Before embarking on a financial adventure, be sure you have enough of your assets under a fairly conservative investment program. Celebrity? You need restraint too. Your history is probably one in which you've made a lot of investments, but have

Make sure you have a cash stash.

not earned much to show for it. Individualists, as it turns out, often make the best investors.

Putting It All Together

Okay, you now know what you want from your investments and have a good idea of what kind of investor you are. You still need to choose a mutual fund portfolio. And with thousands of funds available, the job is not easy. But don't be overwhelmed by it. Think about your favorite supermarket. There are thousands of items on its shelves and in the refrigerated and freezer cases, but does that fact prevent you from shopping? You choose what you need and virtually ignore most everything else. True, the supermarket is familiar ground, whereas the mutual fund market is not. Yet with a good shopping list and smart shopping skills, it's possible to assemble an ideal portfolio of funds.

What you need is an idea of the categories of funds you want and in what proportions. In theory, the higher-risk funds should provide the higher rewards, though that's over a multiyear period. You certainly can't make that generalization for short-term results. To get an idea of how the various categories of funds stack up on risk, look at Figure 4-1. Keep this chart of relative risk in mind as you design and assemble a portfolio of funds.

The risk spectrum here goes from 0 to 10. Money-market funds, for purposes of this exercise, will be assumed to have zero risk. The riskiest funds here are precious metals funds, which are well ahead of the next two risky funds, technology and Latin America. (These calculations are based on the last five years of performance.) The most volatile of the diversified funds, small-cap growth, is still less risky than precious metals, technology, and Latin America.

Note here that risk is not equated with loss—only with volatility. Precious metals funds and diversified emerging markets funds have been losers during the last five years while technology funds have, of course, been big winners.

The equity funds that mix in bonds and cash, the hybrid funds, have a much lower risk profile, around 3.0. Among the specialty funds, utilities funds are the least volatile, about 3.5. Still, that's more volatile than all but one category of bond fund, emerging markets bonds. Nearly all the categories of bond funds cluster between 1 and 2.

FIGURE 4-1

MUTUAL FUNDS RISK SPECTRUM

Are specialized funds riskier than diversified equity funds? How much risk is there in bond funds compared to equity funds? Here's a chart that can help investors understand the relative risk of various types of mutual funds. The risk scale goes from 0 to 10, with 0 defined as no risk. Money-market funds are not on the chart, since there are no fluctuations in their net asset value (NAV). Some specialized funds, like technology and precious metals, are at the high end of the risk spectrum. The NAVs of these funds can fluctuate sharply.

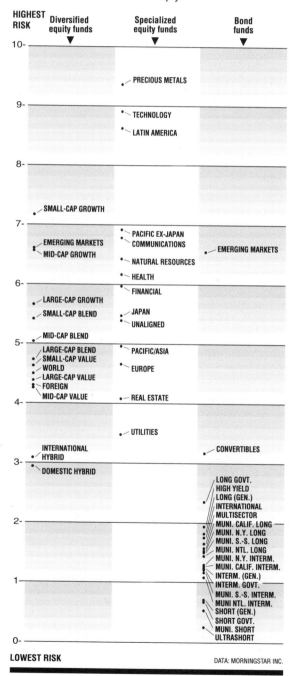

DATA: MORNINGSTAR INC.

First, before making any long-term investment, be sure you have cash in reserve that could cover a minimum of six months' of living expenses. Set it aside in a money-market mutual fund. That's not part of the long-term investment program. It's a rainy-day account, and if you tap into it, be sure to replenish it. If you're in a high tax bracket, you might consider using a tax-free money-market fund instead of a taxable one.

YOUR ASSET ALLOCATION PLAN

When you're ready to invest, you need an "asset allocation" plan. That's just a strategy on how to divvy up your money. A sample asset allocation plan may recommend placing 50 percent of the portfolio in U.S. equities, 30 percent in bonds, 10 percent in foreign stocks, and 10 percent in foreign bonds.

Many money managers devise allocations with elaborate computer models that make the whole process look about as simple as performing the calculations to guide a spacecraft to Mars. Most of the popular personal finance software programs also perform this function. Many mutual fund companies will also give you software that will do the same, usually putting you through a quiz, adding up points, and recommending an asset allocation plan based on your score. Some of the more sophisticated programs will allow you to set minimum or maximum allocations, such as no less than 10 percent or more than 50 percent, for various sorts of asset classes (for our purposes, large company mutual funds, small company funds, international funds, etc.). It then crunches the numbers, spitting out a range of asset mixes that go from the safest to the riskiest.

Some of the programs describe the probability of achieving or exceeding your goal over several time periods. One hint: Don't take the first allocation that pops up. If the program allows it, tinker with the choices and the parameters until you get something that "feels" right. What happens if I add more stocks? Change my time horizon? Once you have a plan, it's easy to implement it through mutual funds. Large-cap funds fit big stocks; small- and mid-cap funds fit little stocks; international funds fit foreign stocks; money-market funds fit Treasury bills, etc.

There are other ways to get help in devising your plan. If you are working with a broker, financial planner, or investment adviser, that's part of his or her job. Even the direct marketing fund companies are now helping investors with asset allocation. Firms like Dreyfus, Fidelity,

T. Rowe Price, Scudder, and Vanguard, to name a few, all offer various worksheets, computer software, consultations, and seminars.

ACHIEVING YOUR FINANCIAL GOALS

The right asset allocation plan starts with the financial goal. Are you trying to accumulate a specific amount of money? Perhaps you want to be able to send your four-year-old to a top-drawer private college, which, in today's dollars, costs about $34,000 a year for tuition, books, and living expenses. How much will you need?

Hold on to your hat. Assume that costs will rise at 8 percent a year, since educational expenses have continued to run far in excess of the Consumer Price Index. Today's $34,000-a-year college costs will be nearly $100,000 a year 14 years hence, when your preschooler starts college.

How are you going to get that money? To fund a $100,000 expense, you'll need 100 zero-coupon Treasury bonds that mature in 2013. In early 1999 such bonds had a yield of 5.66 percent, and would cost $444.70 each, or $44,470 for the lot. (Zeros are sold at a discount to face value and mature at par.) And that would only take care of one year's education. What about the other three? Graduate school? And other children?

But if you could earn a higher rate of return on your investments, you wouldn't need to put as much up front. True, the long-term return from stocks is only 11 percent, but suppose that through savvy mutual fund investments you could earn 2 percentage points more? Then you would only have to put up a little less than $20,000 to get $100,000.

If you don't happen to have a spare $20,000 either, you're going to have to start a regular savings and investment program. The college fund planning kits available from many fund companies and brokerage firms will help you determine how much you'll need and how much you have to save per month or per year to achieve that goal. For instance, if you can earn an average 10 percent return, saving about $250 a month—for the next 14 years—will get you $90,000. But if, through more aggressive and riskier investments, you get an average 12 percent return, your $250 a month should come out to around $107,000. Of course, that only covers one year of college. But look at it this way: As you and your child or children get older, you should be putting more money away each month. The more you put away, the more you'll earn.

SAVINGS FOR RETIREMENT

And what about savings for retirement? Projecting how much you're going to need in 25 years to carry you through another 20 or so after that may seem pointless. But many mutual fund companies, brokerage firms, and financial planners have worksheets or software that can walk you through the exercise. You don't have to be an actuary, nor do you have to know what your grocery bill will be in the year 2025. Expenses are calculated in today's dollars, and they are later multiplied by an inflation factor. Based on your current nest egg and how much you can expect it to grow, the worksheet will tell you how much a year you have to save in addition to reach your retirement goal.

But let's face it. The longer your time horizon, the less accurate specific targets are going to be. You might just approach the investment in a way that would let you earn a rate of return in excess of the inflation rate. That should preserve purchasing power and build some extra capital too.

TABLE 4-3

THE LONG, LONG HAUL

What would have happened to $1000 invested in each of these funds for the 58-year period, January 1, 1940–December 31, 1998?

	Total value ▼	Average annual total return* ▼
EQUITY FUNDS		
FIDELITY FUND	$1,491,085	13.4%
INVESTMENT CO. OF AMERICA	1,477,618	13.4
SELIGMAN GROWTH	1,133,641	12.9
EVERGREEN STRATEGIC GROWTH**	1,306,657	13.2
LORD ABBETT AFFILIATED FUND	1,012,304	12.7
SELIGMAN COMMON STOCK	936,417	12.5
BALANCED FUNDS		
DELAWARE FUND	$589,172	11.6%
AMERICAN BALANCED	312,695	10.4
GEORGE PUTNAM FUND OF BOSTON	283,729	10.2
CGM MUTUAL	260,984	10.1
ALLIANCE BALANCED	219,904	9.7
BOND FUNDS		
EVERGREEN HIGH-YIELD A***	$175,055	9.3%
LORD ABBETT U.S. GOVERNMENT SECS.	111,303	8.5
SCUDDER INCOME	71,602	7.6

*Pretax return, includes reinvestment of dividends and capital gains
**Formerly Keystone Strategic Growth
***Formerly Keystone High-Income

DATA: CDA/WIESENBERGER, MORNINGSTAR INC.

Over the past 70 years, stocks have beaten the inflation rate handily, with an average return that is 8 percentage points higher than the Consumer Price Index. Small company stocks, the sort you find in small-cap funds and some mid-cap mutual funds, did even better, 9 percentage points higher. Over a 58-year period starting in 1940, the Fidelity Fund—yes, the original, before Magellan and all the others—achieved an average annual return of 13.4 percent (Table 4-3). The comparable inflation figure during that time was about 4 percent. According to Wiesenberger Investment Companies Service, five other funds also earned 12 percent or more per year.

Bonds, on the other hand, have only topped the inflation rate by a little more than 1 percentage point. But some bond funds that have been around for 58 years have fared far better: For the period 1940 through 1998, Evergreen High-Yield (formerly Keystone High-Income) averaged 9.3 percent and Lord Abbett U.S. Government Securities, 8.5 percent.

True, bonds in general have not given much inflation protection, but it's quite possible that bonds will provide better returns in the future. That's because a fundamental shift has taken place in the capital markets and the way that interest rates are determined. Prior to 1979 the Federal Reserve—the U.S. central bank and traffic cop for the money that flows through the economy—would look at the economy, decide what the interest rate should be, and then try to manage the money supply in such a way as to achieve that rate.

That approach often fueled inflation since the Fed, though independent, was always under political pressure to keep interest rates down. The central bank often erred by keeping interest rates too low, which, in itself, is a contributing factor to inflation. But since then, the Fed—and the rest of the world's major central banks—changed course, concentrating on the appropriate supply of money for the state of the economy. With tighter controls on the creation of money, the central bankers now let market forces determine interest rates.

The bright side of this more volatile world of bonds is that the "real" rates of return—what you're left with after counting the effects of inflation—have been high for the past decade and are likely to remain so. During the 1980s, for instance, the real rate of return on long-term government bonds was as high as 6 percentage points. While that abnormally high number did not last, it's a good bet the real rates will stay

well in excess of the 1.4 percent rate experienced over the last six decades.

One new development that bears watching is the Treasury's new inflation-indexed bonds. These long-term bonds, first issued in 1997, pay a low interest rate, around 3 percent, which remains the same for the life of the bond. The inflation adjustment is made to the principal. Several mutual fund companies have launched funds to invest in them, but it's too soon to tell if these bonds are a good investment or not. One thing is certain. The upward adjustments in the value of principal will be taxed as income, even though there is no payout. Thus, these sorts of bonds and bond funds should be held in a tax-deferred account only. Otherwise, you end up paying taxes on what some people call "phantom" income.

LOOK TO YOUR HORIZON

Since stocks remain the best long-term investments, mutual fund investors with long time horizons should invest heavily in equity funds. So start with the premise that investors in their twenties and thirties, and perhaps even through their forties, should invest in equity mutual funds. Their investment horizons are 20 years or more.

Those whose horizons are between 10 and 20 years—say the 40- to 50-year-olds—might begin to lower their risks by moving some of their assets into more conservative equity funds and some bond funds. Even at retirement, investors shouldn't shy away from equities. With improved medical care, many persons in their mid-sixties might well live another 20 years. These people are still going to need to keep some equities. If they convert everything to fixed-income investments early in their retirement, they may produce more income now but risk not having enough capital later.

Figure 4-2 lays out five different portfolio mixes for five different decades of life. Suppose you're in your early thirties. Your investment horizon is at least 30 years or so, you can tolerate a good deal of risk, and you need inflation protection. So you split your money into four pieces, putting equal amounts into large-cap, mid-cap, small-cap, and foreign funds. Within those groupings, choose both growth and value funds.

By your forties you may want to come down a notch in the amount of risk you take with your equity funds. Perhaps now you would trim back the equity funds and use that portion of the allocation for high-yield bond funds. These funds

> Your fifties are peak years for investment.

FIGURE 4-2

BUILDING A MUTUAL FUND PORTFOLIO FOR YOUR NEEDS

THE 20s Single or married, the investment horizon calls for growth-oriented funds. Still, if you are yet to purchase a home, you will need some of your assets in a low-risk fund like a short-term bond fund. If you already have a home, consider the sample portfolio for the 30s.

40% MONEY-MARKET OR SHORT-TERM BONDS
20% LARGE-CAP
20% SMALL-CAP OR MID-CAP
20% FOREIGN

25% LARGE-CAP
25% MID-CAP
25% FOREIGN
25% SMALL-CAP

THE 30s Married, with small children, and you already have purchased a home. You're starting on a long-term investment program. College bills are a dozen or more years ahead of you, and retirement is decades away.

THE 40s You're more secure financially, but you have a more cautious investment program now. College may be a near-term expense. Retirement is still 20 or so years away. So the asset mix changes, and you introduce more conservative vehicles like high-yield bond funds, and short- or intermediate-term bond funds. That lowers the portfolio risk, but still provides long-term growth.

20% HIGH-YIELD
20% MID-CAP
20% LARGE-CAP
20% SMALL-CAP OR MID-CAP
20% FOREIGN

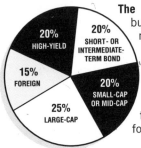

20% HIGH-YIELD
20% SHORT- OR INTERMEDIATE-TERM BOND
15% FOREIGN
20% SMALL-CAP OR MID-CAP
25% LARGE-CAP

The 50s You're still married, but you're empty nesters now. The children are grown, and finished or nearly finished with their educations. You are in your peak earning years, and should take advantage of that to sock it away for retirement.

THE 60s You're retired, but don't run from the equity funds. Hopefully, you have many, many years ahead of you, and will need to grow your capital. Only equities can do that.

DATA: BUSINESS WEEK

20% SHORT-TERM BOND
15% HIGH-YIELD
30% LARGE-CAP
FOREIGN 10%
25% MID-CAP

bridge the stock and bond world, and exhibit characteristics of each (see Chapter 2). They can generate a return close to the long-term return from stocks, but with more income and less volatility. Since these funds' relatively large payouts are subject to ordinary income tax, these funds are best used in the confines of a tax-deferred retirement-type account.

For most people, the fifties are peak years for saving. Your earnings growth may have flattened out at this point, but often children are grown and educated, so your expenses have gone down. Disposable income grows and so does your ability to invest. At this point many people are more interested in socking it away than rolling the dice, so they come to depend more on fixed-income investments. You may keep your equity investments intact, but start to put new investment dollars into tax-free municipal bond funds.

For new retirees, the best investment advice is: Don't shorten your time horizon very much. If you put too much money into current income producers like money-market funds or short-term bond funds, you risk depleting your capital when it should be growing. And remember, too, that although the $1 per share net asset value of money-market funds appears solid, the income produced by those $1 shares is quite volatile.

Suppose you've decided to put 40 percent into large-cap funds, 40 percent into mid-cap and small-cap funds, and 20 percent into international funds. How many funds do you need? One from each category? Two? You may decide that no fund should have more than 20 percent of your assets, so you choose two funds each for the growth and maximum growth portions of the portfolio and one international fund. If your entire stake were, say, $20,000, you might put $4000 each into two growth funds, $4000 in each of two more aggressive funds, and $4000 in one international fund—for five funds in all. If you have $50,000, you might want to introduce a few more funds into your portfolio.

Once you get started in mutual funds there are so many good opportunities that you may be tempted to invest in a lot of different funds. There's no sin in that by itself, but keep in mind that if you own a dozen funds when half a dozen would do, you're also burdening yourself with more work. If you're using load funds, concentrating your investment dollars will allow you to qualify for discounts on the sales charge that aren't available to you if you're always investing small amounts. Finally, except for some specialty funds, most mutual funds are diversified to start with, so piling fund upon fund gives you little added benefit.

If the whole notion of a personalized asset allocation plan seems like overkill, there are alternatives. For instance, there's the "fund of funds" approach to asset allocation. T. Rowe Price has two Spectrum funds. Spectrum Growth divvies up your money among other Price equity funds and Spectrum Income does the same for fixed-income funds. The Vanguard STAR Fund tries to strike a balanced portfolio through investment in other Vanguard stock and bond funds. Fidelity Investments has a worksheet that helps you decide how much risk you can tolerate. The exercise leads you toward one of three asset allocation funds: Fidelity Asset Manager or Fidelity Asset Manager: Income, a slightly more conservative choice; or Fidelity Asset Manager: Growth, the most aggressive of the trio (see Chapter 2).

Several funds companies, such as Fidelity and Stagecoach, offer "life cycle" funds. Rather than your having to make the moves from the more aggressive to the more conservative funds as you age, these funds have a target "maturity." You choose the fund whose target maturity is around the time you want to retire. That way the fund's style of management mellows out with age, and you, in theory, don't have to worry about changing funds as you get older. It's an interesting concept, but there is no long-term record yet with these sorts of funds.

Using the Scoreboard Ratings

The BUSINESS WEEK Mutual Fund Scoreboard will help you to find the funds you need. We've made some changes in the ratings this year, but only in the symbols. In the past, we've rated funds using upward- and downward-pointing arrows in seven categories, from three up-arrows as the best, followed by two-up, one-up, average, one-down, two-down, and three-down, the worst. Now, we've abolished the arrows, using letter grades with plusses and minuses instead. But we still have seven ratings categories, and the methodology for calculating those ratings has not changed. Now, A is superior, B+ is very good, B is above average, C is average, C– is below average, D is poor, and F is

very poor. (Read more about the ratings in Chapter 7.)

You'll notice that lots of funds have no ratings. These funds are too new to be rated. That is, they don't have the five-year track record to qualify for a rating (three years for closed-end funds). Should you invest in them anyway? Many investment pros advise against it. There are enough long-lived funds in most fund categories that you don't need to use a fledgling fund.

If you buy funds through a broker or financial planner, no doubt you'll get a call to invest in a "hot" new mutual fund. There's no hurry. Remember, mutual funds are open-ended, and funds constantly take in new investments and create new shares. (If the broker is soliciting for a new closed-end fund, hang up the phone. Chances are, you'll be able to buy it cheaper six months to a year later. For further information, refer to Chapter 2's section on closed-end funds.)

Suppose you're getting a pitch for a technology fund and the time seems right to invest in technology. But there are already plenty of existing funds to choose from—and these funds have track records. If the fund is so unique that no alternative exists, you should be even more wary of putting your money down. The garbage dump of the investment business is strewn with great concepts that worked in theory—but not in practice.

Fund management companies often start new funds after an investment idea becomes hot. High-tech stocks, for instance, dazzled investors when the 1980s bull market took off in mid-1982. But technology funds that raised large sums during that period stumbled badly in subsequent years. It took until the 1990s for these funds to really shine again. In the late 1980s, many short-term world income funds opened, seeking to capture the high short-term yields from abroad. The funds' high payouts were like manna to yield-starved U.S. investors until the European currency system came unglued in 1992—and chewed up the net asset values of these funds. The same thing happened with emerging markets debt funds in 1994.

One way to avoid problems is to adhere to an old rule of thumb in the fund business: Don't invest in a mutual fund until it has a five-year track record. Paying heed to this dictum would have saved investors from some of the newer "concept" funds—like short-term world income funds—which no doubt came to market when the concept was hot. True, it's nearly impossible for the average investor to look at the prospectus for such a fund and say it won't work. But time is a

Be wary of funds with short track records.

good test. The concept came undone within three years.

There are times to consider a new fund and waive the rule. Suppose the portfolio manager of a fund you already own and like starts a new fund. You may well follow him or her. A mutual fund is only a shell, an investment vehicle, and has no life of its own other than what its manager gives it. So following a respected manager can make sense. For instance, Thomas Marsico, the highly regarded portfolio manager of the Janus Twenty and Janus Growth and Income Funds, left Janus in 1997 to start his own funds. In that sort of situation, following the manager to his other new venue makes good sense. In 1998 the new Marsico Focus Fund gained 51.3 percent and the Marsico Growth & Income Fund, 43.3 percent.

On the other hand, beware of funds run by market "gurus." Some popular market soothsayers have learned the hard way that prognostication and portfolio management are very different skills, and that if you have one skill, you don't necessarily have the other. In mid-1987, for instance, Shearson Lehman Brothers launched a fund managed by its superstar stock market strategist, Elaine Garzarelli. In the first few months, Garzarelli made a brilliant call. She left the market in September and largely steered clear of the October 19, 1987 crash.

That well-publicized fact drew in even more investors. At the end of 1987 the fund totaled $685.5 million. But in 1988 Garzarelli missed the stock market's rebound. In fact, the fund lost 13 percent in net asset value while the S&P was up about 16.5 percent. The fund continued to trail the stock market and investors left in droves. Finally, in June 1994, the fund's sponsor, Smith Barney, Inc. (which had acquired the fund in 1993), proposed to merge it into another fund, without Garzarelli at the helm. The remaining shareholders approved the proposal and the remaining $129 million in assets were folded into another Smith Barney fund.

Even if you limit your shopping list to top-rated funds, you may have a hard time finding B+ and B-rated funds in every category. That's why the BW Scoreboard carries a category rating, one based on risk-adjusted performance of funds in the same fund category. With these category ratings, it's possible to identify the best funds in sectors of the market that are performing poorly relative to other sorts of funds. For instance, most precious metals funds have terrible ratings when compared to all funds. But if you are inter-

> Self-directed investors buy no-load funds.

ested in a precious metal fund, these category ratings allow you to identify the best of the lot.

LOAD OR NO-LOAD?

If you want to work with a broker or a financial planner who's also a broker, you may be restricted to the funds that they sell. You pay the salesperson either through the front-end load, or through higher 12(b)-fees. (See Chapter 3.) A fast-growing alternative to the traditional brokerage arrangement is the fee-only adviser. Even some large brokerage firms are offering this option today. Under these arrangements, you purchase load funds at net asset value. You compensate the adviser through an annual fee based on the amount of assets under management.

If you want to run your account yourself, choose no-loads. Why pay for advice you don't want? You can invest by contacting the fund companies directly. That's fine if you want to invest all in one family, but it's cumbersome if you want to mix and match funds from different families. That's where the mutual fund networks really make sense. You can open an account with Schwab or Fidelity, buy funds from a large number of fund companies, and do it all through the brokerage firm—one account number, one phone number, one statement.

A MINIMUM INVESTMENT?

Suppose you have $2000 to invest in each of five funds. You call the toll-free telephone number for each fund to get a prospectus and sales material. But remember to ask about the initial investment. Direct-sales funds, in particular, usually have higher minimum investments than broker-sold funds. Many direct-sales funds carry minimum initial purchases of $1000 to $3000 for equity funds and often a little higher for bond funds. Broker-sold funds usually have minimum buy-ins in the $250-to-$500 range. Both types of funds usually lower the threshold significantly for IRA or other retirement accounts, or for investors who enroll in a monthly investment plan.

TAXABLE OR
TAX-DEFERRED ACCOUNT?

When assembling a portfolio of mutual funds, it's hard enough to come up with the right mix of funds. To maximize your returns, you also have to be selective about which investments you put into the confines of the IRA or 401(k) plan and which you hold in taxable accounts. "Asset placement picks up where asset allocation ends," says

Joel M. Dickson, an investment strategist for the Vanguard Group. "The idea is to put your money in the place where it will work best for you on an aftertax basis."

Asset placement, or what's also known as "preferred domain," has always been important, especially to high-income investors. But the new tax law (the Taxpayer Relief Act of 1997), which widens the gap between the tax rates on capital gains and on ordinary income and expands the availability of Individual Retirement Accounts, makes asset placement that much more important.

The basic strategy is to put investments that produce interest and dividend income into tax-deferred accounts like IRAs, 401(k)s, and variable annuities; those that produce capital gains should reside in your taxable accounts. This, of course, presumes that you have investments outside your tax-deferred accounts. If you have nothing beyond your 401(k) and don't expect to for some time, asset placement is not yet a concern. Just stick to your optimal asset allocation plan.

If you're an investor nearing retirement, the changes in the tax law might dictate a new look at asset placement as well. William S. Young, a financial adviser with the First Financial Group in Towson, Maryland, says new retirees in higher tax brackets should benefit by keeping income-producing investments in their tax-deferred retirement accounts as long as possible, and instead draw down their taxable equity investments to supplement their pension payments. Some of the money they take from equity funds, for instance, will be taxable, but at the lower capital gains rate. Any money they take in income from IRAs and the like will be fully taxable at ordinary income rates.

To review your asset placement, first look at your holdings by their asset classes. Take government or corporate bond funds. Their chief attribute is that they generate interest income, taxable at ordinary tax rates. If you're in the 31 percent federal tax bracket—for a couple filing jointly, taxable income between $102,300 and $156,100—nearly a third (more if you are also subject to state and local income tax) is lost to taxes.

If you hold taxable bond funds for long-term investment, it's best to do so within the confines of an IRA or 401(k). In a traditional IRA or 401(k), the tax on the interest income is deferred until you withdraw the money in your golden years. In the Roth IRA, which totally flips the retirement account in that contributions are not deductible but earnings are, those dollars will never be taxed.

High-yield bond funds seem especially well-suited for all tax-favored accounts, since they generally throw off the highest payouts. Consider Kemper High-Yield A. Its 1998 distribution yield was 9.9 percent. Held in a taxable account, the net return to the 31 percent bracket taxpayer is only 6.8 percent. In a tax-deferred account, that high yield keeps compounding until it's withdrawn. In a Roth IRA, it's never taxed.

If you have exhausted all your tax-deferred avenues and you have money in taxable accounts, seek funds with a track record of paying out only minimal taxable distributions. One way to identify them is by combing the financial statements in fund prospectuses to look for the funds with the smallest distributions relative to the net asset value in the fund. An easier way is to compare pretax and aftertax returns. (Both are in the BUSINESS WEEK Mutual Fund Scoreboard.) Divide the aftertax by the pretax return, and the higher the number, the more tax efficient the fund.

For the 1996–1998 period, one with relatively high fund returns, we had 244 funds with at least 95 percent tax efficiency. Among them: Baron Asset, Founders Passport, MFS Emerging Growth B, Putnam New Opportunities, and Rydex OTC Investors. As you can tell from the names of the funds, most of these tax-efficient funds invest in smaller, emerging growth companies. Such companies usually pay few or no dividends, so there's no taxable dividend income that the fund has to pay out. Many of the others in the 95 percent group are index funds.

But don't equate all emerging growth funds with high tax efficiency. The aftertax returns of Alger Small Capitalization, Montgomery Small-Cap, Strong Discovery, and Value Line Small-Cap Growth were all about one-third less than that of the pretax returns. It doesn't all come from dividend or interest income. Profits on stocks held less than a year (18 months in the new bill) are taxed at the ordinary income rate, and so a fund with a rapid-fire trading strategy might also generate a lot of unwanted ordinary income.

If your asset allocation plan calls for more conservative equity funds, ones that invest in larger dividend-paying stocks, you may want to put those in tax-favored accounts. Many funds with "growth and income," "equity–income," and "balanced" in their names do well in a retirement account. So do specialty funds that invest in utilities or real estate investment trusts, which

Look at a fund's "tax efficiency."

deliver much of their return through dividend income.

If you decide you need some placement related restructuring in your portfolio, remember to do it carefully. Shifting funds within an IRA or 401(k) is easy and does not carry any tax consequences. But if you make any changes in your taxable accounts, you are creating a "taxable event." If you have a taxable investment with a large unrealized gain, you might move the money out over several years and spread the tax bite rather than move the money all at once. If your investment program is long-term, you have time to get your assets in place.

Building and Rebuilding Fund Portfolios

In assembling your own portfolio, it's worthwhile to examine others' portfolios. The point is not necessarily to use the same funds in the same way, but to see the kinds of funds professionals use for particular purposes and in what proportions. You can also try to understand some of the logic that goes into these decisions.

HEAD START ON A COLLEGE FUND

For example, what about a portfolio for a college-bound toddler? Table 4-4 presents one from Debra B. Silversmith of Sterling Partners in Denver, Colorado. It's for a 3-year-old whose grandparents invest $10,000 in her name. Silversmith recommends a portfolio weighted toward funds that emphasize small and midsize companies whose growth prospects are higher than those of the companies in the S&P 500. "Over time, the higher growth rates should lead to greater fund performance," she says.

That's true, as long as you select funds whose managers are skilled at playing the growth-stock game. As the table shows, for the 40 percent of the portfolio dedicated to smaller company stocks, she chooses Baron Asset Fund and the Kaufmann Fund. Baron, which has outperformed its competitors for nearly 10 years, is light on technology stocks. Kaufmann Fund, on the other hand, carries a heavy complement of tech stocks. Both are run by veteran portfolio managers, not rookies. For mid-cap companies, Silversmith selects the Oakmark and Strong Opportunity

funds. Oakmark, a top-rated fund, is a mid-cap value fund, a good offset to the more growth-oriented Baron and Kaufmann.

Looking abroad, she chooses Janus Worldwide Fund. She used to use Warburg Pincus International Equity, but dropped it because of manager turnover and more Japanese exposure than she liked. Janus Worldwide has a value orientation, and it does have some U.S. exposure as well.

Silversmith thinks this portfolio could earn an average annual return of 14 percent a year. If she's right—and that's an ambitious goal—the $10,000 will grow to more than $70,000 when this preschooler turns college freshman. Private college already costs nearly $30,000 a year, so good fund choices are not enough. Her parents will need to add money over the years. For additional investments, Silversmith would allocate the money in the same proportions.

FUNDS FOR A 401(K)

Employees often freeze when they're asked to choose from five or six investment options in their companies' 401(k) plans. So consider the plight of the General Motors Corp. employees, who can select from among 50 Fidelity mutual funds. That's where adviser James B. Kruzan of Investment Management & Research Inc. in Clarkston, Michigan, spotted a business opportunity. He advises GM employees on fund selection for their 401(k)s.

Take, for instance, a 43-year-old executive who has amassed $50,000 in his 401(k), but has it invested in a haphazard mix of stock and bond funds. He'd like to have a well constructed equity portfolio but hasn't a clue which funds to choose and in what proportions.

Since the employee is 25 years from retirement, Kruzan recommends a fairly aggressive mix that he believes will beat the S&P 500 by an average 2 percentage points a year: 40 percent for funds that buy small-cap stocks, 20 percent for mid-cap, 10 percent for large-cap, and 30 percent for foreign stocks. That's the outline, and it's a plan that could be fulfilled by scores of funds, not just Fidelity's. But for the GM clients, Kruzan selects from the Fidelity menu. For the most aggressive funds, he chooses Fidelity Low-Priced Stock, Fidelity Emerging Growth, and Fidelity OTC. For the mid-cap slot, he picks Fidelity Mid-Cap Stock. The big-stock slice splits between Fidelity Growth & Income and Fidelity Dividend Growth.

Kruzan then divides the international portion into four parts, allocating 9 percent each to

Retirees need equity funds too.

Fidelity Diversified International and Fidelity Emerging Markets. Two regional funds, Fidelity Canada and Fidelity Europe, get 6 percent each. Kruzan says the Canadian fund is as much a natural resource fund as a country fund, since natural resources make up a large part of Canada's economy. He likes the Canadian fund and thinks U.S. investors often overlook their northern neighbor. "The slow growth, low interest rate environment that is so good for our market should benefit our biggest trading partner as well," he says.

For ongoing contributions, Kruzan suggests 25 percent each in the following four funds: Fidelity Low-Priced Stock, Fidelity OTC Fund, Fidelity Mid-Cap Stock, and Fidelity Emerging Markets. "That allows you to use these funds' higher volatilities to your advantage by buying more shares at bottoms and fewer at tops," says Kruzan.

THE ROLLOVER IRA

With companies shrinking their payrolls, long-time employees often walk away with six-figure pension distributions and no idea of how to invest them. "That's the kind of help many of our new clients need," says William S. Young of First Financial Group in Towson, Maryland.

Look at the example of a 50-year-old single woman with $100,000. She's not a gambler, but she is willing to take as much risk as her adviser thinks is appropriate. So Young devised an all-equity portfolio with moderate risk. "With at least 10 years to go before retirement, you can go with an all-stock portfolio," says Young. "In all the 10-year periods since World War II, bonds have beaten stocks less than 10 percent of the time."

Unlike Silversmith, who is paid a percentage of assets under management, Young earns his pay from commissions—and so chooses from the load funds. And when a fund has front-end or back-end shares, he recommends the up-front "A" shares, because they're most cost-effective for long-term investors.

Young's prescription is simple: He eschews the latest highflier funds for those that he believes show "consistency of results." The first two holdings, Putnam Growth & Income A (15 percent) and Guardian Park Avenue (25 percent) are "core" funds, with Putnam having a "value" (higher dividend, low price–earnings ratio) approach, while Guardian is more growth-oriented. He also likes Guardian's quantitatively driven stock selection system. "It's proven and disciplined," he says.

TABLE 4-4

FOUR FUND EXPERTS GO SHOPPING FOR YOU

HEAD START ON A COLLEGE FUND

Investment adviser Debra Silversmith suggests this portfolio for a 3-year-old whose grandparents put $10,000 in her name to launch a college fund. They're all no-load funds, available through the big discount brokers or directly from the fund companies.

FUND	ALLOCATION
OAKMARK	20%
STRONG OPPORTUNITY	15
KAUFMANN	20
BARON ASSET	20
JANUS WORLDWIDE	25

AN ALL-FIDELITY 401(k) PORTFOLIO

Adviser James Kruzan counts many General Motors managers among his clients, and many of them look to him for help in choosing among the 50 Fidelity mutual funds in GM's 401(k) plan. This allocation plan is for a 43-year-old with $50,000 in his 401(k), but could as easily be used by anyone wanting an all-Fidelity line-up.

FUND	ALLOCATION
FIDELITY LOW-PRICED STOCK	16.0%
FIDELITY EMERGING GROWTH	12.0
FIDELITY OTC	12.0
FIDELITY MID-CAP STOCK	20.0
FIDELITY DIVIDEND GROWTH	5.0
FIDELITY GROWTH & INCOME	5.0
FIDELITY DIVERSIFIED INT'L.	9.0
FIDELITY EMERGING MARKETS	9.0
FIDELITY CANADA	6.0
FIDELITY EUROPE	6.0

GAME PLAN FOR A ROLLOVER IRA

Financial planner William Young suggested this portfolio for a 50-year-old single woman who is leaving a job with a $100,000 lump-sum payment that will be rolled over into an IRA. As a commission-based adviser, Young sells load funds. He recommends shares with up-front loads, since they are cheapest in the long run.

FUND	ALLOCATION
PUTNAM GROWTH & INCOME A	15%
GUARDIAN PARK AVENUE A	25
SELIGMAN COMM. & INFO. A	10
SMALLCAP WORLD	20
CAPITAL WORLD GROWTH & INCOME	30

FOR THE GOLDEN YEARS

Madeline I. Noveck recommends this portfolio for a 62-year-old with a $500,000 lump-sum pension payment. This retiree has other income sources, and needs to generate $7500 a year from this nest egg. Noveck uses both load and no-load funds.

FUND	ALLOCATION
TORRAY	16%
T. ROWE PRICE MID-CAP GROWTH	10
NEUBERGER & BERMAN GENESIS	5
UAM FPA CRESCENT	4
BT INVESTMENT INTL. EQUITY	15
CGM REALTY	8
T. ROWE PRICE NEW ERA OR VAN ECK HARD ASSETS	6
HARBOR BOND	18
VANGUARD F/I SHORT-TERM CORP. BOND	6
WARBURG PINCUS GLOB. FIXED-INC. OR PIMCO FOREIGN	7
MONEY-MARKET FUND (YOUR CHOICE)	5

DATA: BUSINESS WEEK

Young's also taken an unusual step for a relatively small portfolio: adding a 10 percent holding in Seligman Communications & Information Fund. "I have come to the conclusion that technology is so important it has to be here, even if it brings more volatility to the portfolio." To offset some of that additional volatility, Young picks up most of his foreign exposure through two American Funds offerings: Capital World Growth & Income and SmallCap World. He had previously used Templeton Foreign Class I in this slot, and that's still a good choice. But using two funds from the American Funds group reduces the sales charges his client would have to pay.

EQUITY FUNDS FOR RETIREMENT

Retirement is no reason to drop equity investments. In fact, the longer you hope to live, the more you're going to need them. That's the approach adviser Madeline I. Noveck of Novos Planning Associates Inc. in New York takes in constructing a $500,000 portfolio for a 62-year-old recent retiree.

Noveck works with a large palette of funds, both no-load and load, since that affords more and better investment options. If she uses a load fund, the portion of the commission paid her is credited against her regular asset-based fees. Noveck's list is long, with 11 funds. But she's working with more money, which usually requires more funds. And the client has two needs: the generation of about $7500 a year to supplement his current retirement income and capital appreciation so there will be enough to fund the next 20 years or so in retirement. She believes her portfolio can beat the S&P 500 return but with less volatility.

Like our other advisers, Noveck covers every segment of the stock market. For large- to mid-cap stocks, she chooses the Torray and the T. Rowe Price Mid-Cap Growth funds. Torray is a large-cap value fund, and T. Rowe Price, more mid-cap growth. They complement rather than duplicate each other. For smaller companies, she chooses Neuberger & Berman Genesis and UAM FPA Crescent funds. She has no recommendation for a small-cap growth fund. She's not comfortable with the level of risk in any small-cap growth funds.

For foreign investments, Noveck suggests BT Investment International Equity, which invests both in major and emerging markets, is currently overweighted in Europe, and manages even to make a little money in Japan. Better yet, she says, the fund is still relatively small and is growing more slowly than some other high-performance international funds.

Noveck also places money in funds that don't correlate to the market in general and thus diversify the portfolio. For instance, she allocates 6 percent to either Van Eck Hard Assets for load investors or T. Rowe Price New Era for no-load investors. Both are natural resources funds and would serve as bulwarks against inflation—though at the moment, of course, it seems unnecessary. For real estate, another low-correlation category, Noveck suggest CGM Realty, a mix of both REITs for income and real estate companies for growth.

For income and diversification, Noveck uses Harbor Bond, a well-managed intermediate-term fund, and Vanguard Short-Term Corporate Bond, a lower risk, low-expense offering. For foreign bonds, she suggests PIMCO Foreign Bond for load investors, or Warburg Pincus Global Fixed-Income as a no-load alternative. Five percent goes to a money-market fund ("choose one with a high yield") both for diversification and liquidity.

RESTRUCTURING A PORTFOLIO

So you have a few funds tucked away in an IRA to which you haven't contributed for years. Several funds are still sitting in a 401(k) at a former employer. Then there's a sheaf of funds you've bought yourself over the last few years, listening to tips from fund fanciers at work and from your own perusing of the covers of the personal finance magazines. Does this describe you or someone you know?

Many people have mutual fund portfolios, but they never planned out their portfolios or chose funds with the idea of covering a particular range of investment styles or asset classes. That doesn't mean they haven't made money. In a bull market, most anything can do well.

Still, even if you have a collection of funds that has done well, it may not be the optimal mix for you. The best portfolio for you depends on your tolerance for risk in the value of your portfolio. Look at the "Cranes," a couple in their early 40s who sought the assistance of Lou Stanasolovich of Legend Financial Advisors Inc. in Pittsburgh for restructuring their portfolio (Figure 4-3). Through IRAs, Keogh plans, and other mutual fund investments, they had over $500,000 in a portfolio that was 80 percent in equities.

Like many investors who came to funds during the 1990s, the Cranes had never seen their investments mauled in a bear market. When Stanasolovich showed them what happened to their funds during the 20 percent market decline in 1990, they decided to slice their equity alloca-

Good funds portfolios come from good plans.

FIGURE 4-3

RESTRUCTURING A PORTFOLIO OF FUNDS

BEFORE

The "Cranes," a couple in their early 40s, held $544,051 in taxable and tax-deferred retirement accounts—more than 80% of it in 15 equity mutual funds. Working with Lou Stanasolovich of Legend Financial Advisors, they decided to scale back their equity holdings about 60%. Stanasolovich analyzed the funds for investment style and performance and developed a new investment plan.

	Allocation (%)	Investment Category
DOMESTIC EQUITIES†		
BERGER 100	2.9	MID-CAP GROWTH
NEUBERGER & BERMAN MANHATTAN	1.0*	MID-CAP BLEND
T. ROWE PRICE CAP. APPREC.	4.4*	MID-CAP VALUE
JANUS TWENTY	2.9	LARGE-CAP GROWTH
AMER. CENT.-20th CENT. ULTRA INV.	8.2	LARGE-CAP GROWTH
GROWTH FUND OF AMERICA	10.0*	LARGE-CAP GROWTH
CGM MUTUAL	6.0	LARGE-CAP VALUE
AMERICAN MUTUAL	11.3*	LARGE-CAP VALUE
WASHINGTON MUTUAL INVESTORS	8.1*	LARGE-CAP VALUE
T. ROWE PRICE EQUITY-INCOME	5.5*	LARGE-CAP VALUE
INVESCO INDUSTRIAL INCOME	3.6	DOMESTIC HYBRID
INTERNATIONAL EQUITIES		
SMALLCAP WORLD	8.8*	SMALL-CAP GROWTH**
MONTGOMERY EMERGING MARKETS	0.7	DIV. EMRG. MKTS.
OAKMARK INTERNATIONAL	0.8	FOREIGN
EUROPACIFIC GROWTH	6.2*	FOREIGN

†Includes 0.4% in stocks   *Funds in tax-deferred retirement accounts   **Advisors considers this an international fund, while Morningstar puts it with domestic funds.

AFTER

Stanasolovich slashed domestic equities to 23%, mainly by cutting large-cap and mid-cap funds. He added small-cap growth and small-cap value funds, and substituted Davis New York Venture for large-cap value. He unloaded all the international equity funds except Oakmark International, and added a foreign fund and an emerging market fund. Eight percent went to short-term bond funds, 21% to long-term bond funds, and 6% for international bonds. For further diversification, he added a 15% holding in real estate, and 11% in a risk-arbitrage and other equity funds which have a low correlation with the market.

	Allocation (%)	Investment Category
SHORT-TERM DOMESTIC BONDS*		
PIMCO LOW DURATION	2%	SHORT-TERM
BLACKROCK 2001**	6	SHORT-TERM
LONG-TERM DOMESTIC BONDS*		
LOOMIS SAYLES BOND	8	LONG-TERM
NORTHEAST INVESTORS	8	HIGH-YIELD
PIMCO COMMERCIAL MORTGAGE**	5	INTERM.-TERM
INTERNATIONAL BONDS*		
PIMCO FOREIGN	6	INTERNATIONAL BOND
DOMESTIC EQUITIES		
BERGER SMALL COMPANY GROWTH	6	SMALL-CAP GROWTH
SKYLINE SPECIAL EQUITIES	6	SMALL-CAP VALUE
DAVIS NEW YORK VENTURE A	11	LARGE-CAP VALUE
INTERNATIONAL EQUITIES		
OAKMARK INTERNATIONAL	5	FOREIGN
HARBOR INTERNATIONAL GROWTH	5	FOREIGN
TEMPLETON DEVELOPING MARKETS I	6	DIV. EMRG. MKTS.
REAL ESTATE		
HEITMAN REAL ESTATE-INSTL.	7	REAL ESTATE
COHEN & STEERS SPECIAL EQUITY	8	REAL ESTATE
OTHER		
MERGER	4%	MID-CAP BLEND
CALDWELL & ORKIN MARKET OPP.	3	DOMESTIC HYBRID
BARR ROSENBERG MARKET NEUTRAL	4	N/A

*Funds in tax-deferred retirement accounts
**Closed-end fund

DATA: LEGEND FINANCIAL ADVISORS INC., MORNINGSTAR INC.

tion. So Stanasolovich reviewed the portfolio, came up with a new asset allocation plan, and chose the best funds to implement it. He was able to work with some of the funds they already had. But he sold many of the equity holdings to make room for bond and real estate funds he thought were necessary to balance out the portfolio. He also placed most of the bond and real estate funds inside the tax-deferred retirement accounts. That way, he minimized the taxes on the income they produce. In a like manner, he tried to do much of the selling that needed to be done in the retirement accounts, thereby dodging capital gains taxes. Keep that in mind if you have restructuring of your own to do.

What Stanasolovich did was to drastically reduce the domestic equity allocation, the part of the Cranes' holdings that was most vulnerable to a decline in the U.S. stock market. He took the allocation down from 64.3 percent to 23 percent. He also reduced the number of domestic equity funds from 11 to 3 and changed them all. He uses

Davis New York Venture A, a large-cap value fund, and 6 percent each in Skyline Special Equities and Berger Small Company Growth. Skyline covers the value side, Berger the growth. The old portfolio was overweighted in large-cap stocks. In restructuring, Stanasolovich introduced small-cap and mid-cap holdings as well.

In the makeover, Stanasolovich also increased the international equity exposure and introduced international bonds. He chose PIMCO Foreign, an institutional fund that's open to clients of investment advisers. That fund buys mainly investment-grade bonds.

The new portfolio got a domestic junk bond fund, Northeast Investors; Loomis Sayles Bond, a long-term fund; and PIMCO Commercial Mortgage, an intermediate portfolio. For short-term bonds, he uses PIMCO Low Duration Fund and BlackRock 2001, a closed-end fund that matures in four years.

To further diversify the portfolio's asset mix, Stanasolovich introduced two real estate funds: Cohen & Steers Special Equity and Heitman Real Estate, an institutional fund. He also put a small amount of money into unique funds with low market correlations: the Merger Fund, the only mutual fund built exclusively on risk-arbitrage; Caldwell & Orkin Market Opportunity Fund, a fund which both buys and short-sells stocks; and Barr Rosenberg Market Neutral Fund, which buys undervalued stocks and short-sells what it considers to be overvalued stock. The Rosenberg fund is relatively new, but the underlying investment strategy has long been used by Rosenberg in institutional portfolios.

Making Your First Investment

You've got your investment goals, you know which funds you want to buy, and you're rarin' to go. But then you hesitate and freeze. Fear and doubt set in. You wait; you do nothing; you miss opportunities.

Here's how to get off the mark. If you're a long-term investor, buying today, next week, or next month may not make much difference to your results. If you could perfectly predict stock market tops and bottoms, it would make a difference. But let's face it, if you could do that, you wouldn't be dabbling in mutual funds. You'd be playing the futures or options markets and making a bundle.

When you choose to plunk down your money can matter. But it's not because you have a hunch about the direction of the market. If you are dealing with a taxable investment, you should avoid a mutual fund or closed-end fund just before a dividend or capital gains distribution. Here's why. Funds are required to distribute nearly all of their income and realized capital gains (more about that in Chapter 6). The funds' distribution policies vary. Some equity funds pay out income dividends quarterly (bond funds often pay monthly) if they earn dividends or interest. Capital gains, if there are any, are usually declared once a year, mostly in December. You can find out distribution dates by calling the fund's toll-free line.

Suppose you invest $10,000 in a fund with an NAV of $10 per share and you get 1000 shares. Then, a few days after your investment, the fund declares a capital gains distribution of $1 per share. What happens is this: Each share pays out $1, so the NAV drops to $9 per share. Your 1000 shares are now worth $9000 (assuming there has been no other change in NAV). You reinvest the distribution and that $1000 gets you another 100 shares. So you still have an investment worth $10,000.

But you also have a tax liability. The $1000 distribution is taxable to you, but did you really earn it? Was your capital invested long enough for the managers to earn that kind of money? The gains were earned on money invested long before your money ever found its way to the fund. By investing in advance of the distribution, you wind up being taxed on something you didn't earn. You would have been better off waiting until after the distribution. Before you make a sizable investment in a fund, it's always smart to call to find out if any dividends or distributions are forthcoming.

So, for tax reasons, it does matter when you invest. For pure investment purposes, the advantages of timing are not so obvious. The question seemed particularly compelling in August 1989, when the Dow Jones industrial average raced past the 2722 point—the highwater mark that had been reached on August 25, 1987. Between August 1987 and August 1989 there was a 1000-point decline—508 of it on October 19, 1987—and a remarkable recovery. (On October 27, 1997, the Dow Jones industrials fell 554 points, though because the market was so much higher, the percentage loss was far less.) Had the investors who bought equity mutual funds on August 27, 1987 bounced back, too?

BUSINESS WEEK asked Morningstar, Inc., which provides the data for the Mutual Fund

For tax reasons, it matters when you invest.

Scoreboard, to measure equity fund performance between August 25, 1987 and September 1, 1989, when the Dow had closed at 2752. The survey covered 727 funds and looked at the total returns generated during a two-year period.

The mutual funds, for the most part, did an admirable job for their shareholders—even those who, in retrospect, had invested on perhaps the worst day of the year, if not the decade. Approximately 80 percent of the funds broke even or better. More than 400 funds, or 56 percent, beat the 9 percent return that could have been earned by investing in the Dow stocks during that time. About 300 funds, more than 40 percent, beat the 13 percent total return of the Standard & Poor's 500 stock index during that period. The average U.S. diversified equity fund returned 11 percent. Counting all equity funds—including international and specialty portfolios—total returns averaged 9.6 percent, slightly above the return on the Dow.

The folks at T. Rowe Price mutual fund group conducted a test to measure the impact of timing. Suppose you were a diligent investor and every year you put $2000 into the stocks of the S&P 500. But you were also the world's worst market timer. It seems that every year you managed to invest your $2000 in the stock market at the high for the calendar year.

Well, even if your timing is lousy, there's still a payoff to your discipline. Between 1969 and 1989, the period of the study, the investor who picked the worst day of each year to invest still did well. From his or her $40,000 in contributions ($2000 a year for 20 years), the hapless market-timer amassed a stake of $175,422, an 11.4 percent average annual return. Of course, the perfect timer—the person who invested two grand at the lowest point of each year—did much better. The perfect investor wound up with $226,365, a 13.5 percent average annual return. Granted, there's a $50,000 difference between the best and the worst timer, but as a practical matter most investors' results would be at neither extreme.

There are other ways to ease yourself into mutual funds. Suppose you have a lump sum of $25,000 to invest, but you're leery of doing it all at once. Why not break the total pie into smaller slices, say, $5000 each, and feed them into your mutual funds gradually over the next year? You put $5000 into the funds at first, and the other $20,000 into a money-market fund. You have four more "payments" to make before you're totally invested. Put the next $5000 slice in three months from now, and another $5000 each at six months, nine months, and one year. That way, if the mar-

ket is lower at some time in the next 12 months, you have an opportunity to get in at lower prices.

Though most investors fear a plunging equity market, the bond market can also give them a jolt. Fixed-income investors usually stampede into bond funds when interest rates are falling, anxious to hold onto yields that are slipping away. But at the same time, as a portfolio's yield is going down, the prices of its bonds are going up. That means investors chasing yields are also buying heavily into a rising market.

It may not be necessary to chase intermediate- and long-term bonds. Odds are you'll see today's prices and yields again in the next few years. Between 1988 and 1998, for instance, the long-term rate on U.S. government bonds has fluctuated between 4.8 and 9.4 percent. At the low end, bond prices were said to be "high"; with the higher yield, bond prices were said to be "low." Stock prices, in theory, have no upside boundary. Stocks have infinite lives and their potential is tied to the success of the company.

But bonds have finite lives and what they can pay investors is fixed. So bond prices are constrained by the level of interest rates. Over time, the range of interest rates will vary, but you can bet there will be a trading range. When the economy is booming, rates go up; when the economy is slumping, rates come down. As long as there is a business cycle, there are going to be fluctuations in interest rates.

Dollar-Cost Averaging

If you're feeding a bankroll into mutual funds over time, what you're really engaging in is a time-honored practice called "dollar-cost averaging." This investment strategy is simple. You invest a fixed number of dollars at periodic intervals, usually monthly or quarterly. When the price of the investment is low, your fixed dollar investment buys more. When prices are high, the same amount of dollars buys less. But so long as the total return of your investment is in a generally rising trend, dollar-cost averaging will almost ensure that your average cost per share will be less than the current price. If you're part of a 401(k) plan or some other savings incentive plan, you're already practicing dollar-cost averaging.

Let's look at this a little more closely. Suppose you want to invest $200 a month in an equity mutual fund. You've arranged with your bank for

Dollar-cost averaging is a contrarian strategy.

an electronic transfer of the money from your checking account once a month on the day of your choice.

To see how this works, let's look back at how a monthly investment program would have fared (Table 4-5). Suppose an investor put $200 a month into American Century–20th Century Ultra Investors starting in January 1994.

At the start of the program, the price per share was $21.18. So in the first month the investor bought 9.443 shares (that's 200 divided by 21.18). By the beginning of February, the NAV had

TABLE 4-5

HOW DOLLAR-COST AVERAGING WORKS FOR FUND INVESTORS

In January 1994, an investor decided to start a program of dollar-cost averaging. He selected American Century–20th Century Ultra Investors, and decided to invest $200 on the first business day of every month, and reinvest any dividends or capital gains if and when they're paid.

1994 SUMMARY Invested $2400, purchased 115.921 shares at an average cost of $20.66 per share

Date	Price/Share	Shares purchased	Total shares
January	$21.18	9.443	9.443
February	22.66	8.826	18.269
March	22.18	9.017	27.286
April	20.71	9.657	36.943
May	21.25	9.412	46.355
June	20.46	9.775	56.130
July	19.24	10.395	66.525
August	19.60	10.204	76.729
September	20.41	9.799	86.528
October	20.16	9.921	96.449
November	21.07	9.492	105.941
December	20.04	9.980	115.921

Dec. 17, paid a capital gains distribution of $0.6452 per share, or $74.79 19.32 3.871 119.793

1995 SUMMARY Invested $2400, purchased 103.391 shares at an average cost of $23.21 per share

Date	Price/Share	Shares purchased	Total shares
January	$19.61	10.199	129.991
February	19.49	10.262	140.253
March	20.26	9.872	150.125
April	20.95	9.547	159.671
May	21.28	9.398	169.070
June	22.19	9.013	179.083
July	24.14	8.285	186.368
August	26.10	7.663	194.031
September	26.55	7.553	201.564
October	27.25	7.339	208.903
November	28.16	7.102	216.005
December	27.86	7.179	223.184

Dec. 16, paid a capital gains distribution of $1.2991 per share, or $289.94 25.00 11.598 234.782

1996 SUMMARY Invested $2941.62, purchased 104.866 shares at an average cost of $28.05 per share

Date	Price/Share	Shares purchased	Total shares
January	$26.20	7.634	242.415
February	26.44	7.564	249.980
March	26.83	7.454	257.434
April	26.73	7.482	264.916
May	27.98	7.148	272.064
June	29.05	6.885	278.949
July	28.68	6.974	285.922
August	26.46	7.559	293.481
September	26.60	7.519	301.000
October	29.20	6.849	307.849
November	29.41	6.800	314.649
December	31.70	6.309	320.959

Dec. 19, paid a capital gains distribution of $1.6875 per share, or $541.62 28.98 18.689 339.648

1997 SUMMARY Invested $5341.23, purchased 186.357 shares at an average cost of $28.66 per share

Date	Price/Share	Shares purchased	Total shares
January	$27.84	7.184	346.832
February	30.50	6.557	353.389
March	29.30	6.826	360.215
April	27.57	7.254	367.469
May	29.09	6.875	374.345
June	32.23	6.404	380.749
July	33.00	6.061	386.809
August	36.18	5.528	392.337
September	35.00	5.714	398.051
October	35.76	5.593	403.644
November	34.50	5.797	409.441
December	34.84	5.741	415.182

Dec. 19, paid an income dividend of $0.0133 per share, or $5.52 and a capital gains distribution of $7.0709 per share, or $2935.71 26.54 110.823 526.005

After four years, the investor has invested $9600 out of his pocket, plus another $3842.06 from reinvestment of dividends and capital gains distributions. He owns 526.005 shares at an average cost of $19.62 per share. On Dec. 31, 1997, the price per share is $25.52. The total investment is worth $13,960.

climbed to $22.66. That means he already has a small paper profit in his first shares, but he gets slightly fewer shares for his next $200—this time, only 8.826. The relationship between share price and shares purchased is simple: the higher the price, the fewer shares purchased; the lower the price, the more shares purchased.

As you can tell from the share price, this fund rocketed from the time of the first purchase in 1994 and peaked in August 1997, at $36.18 a share. Of course, the net asset value did not go up in a straight line. In fact, in 1994, a few months after beginning the investment program, the price went as low as $19.24. But with the discipline of monthly investing and a long-term investment horizon, that worked to the investor's advantage. When the price was $19.24, his $200 bought more shares. When the price finally rebounded, he owned more shares on which to profit. All told, the investor had accumulated 526.005 shares from the monthly investments and distributions. At the end of four years, the investor had an unrealized average profit of $1.02 per share, or $535.53 in an account worth $13,960.

Dollar-cost averaging is a contrarian investment strategy. When the prices are low—indicating that investors are not buying stocks—dollar-cost investors are buying stocks, and they're getting more shares. When the bulls are running, these investors are still buying. But the fixed-investment plan restrains them from any wild excesses, such as stepping up investments when the market is roaring or dropping out entirely when stocks are sagging. Bull market or bear market, they're investing the same amount. As long as you hold on for the long term (the average annual return for stocks is over 11 percent) and you choose a well-managed fund, dollar-cost averaging should pay off handsomely.

For sure, the investor who put in a lump sum of $9600 (the total out-of-pocket cost) back in January, 1994 would have far surpassed the investor who put in $200 a month. But that misses the point. Not everyone has a big lump sum to invest, but most people can come up with some monthly contribution.

Switch Funds! The Timing Game

Mutual fund purveyors have always cultivated the image that their wares are long-term investments. Of course, long-term doesn't mean the same thing to all people, but most of us would agree that long-term is at least more than a year, and probably a few beyond that.

However, during the last decade or so, the fund management companies have also made it quick and simple to purchase and redeem funds. It's become so easy to move large sums of money by telephone that some now use mutual funds for trading, which has a much shorter time horizon than investing. What most of these traders are trying to do is to employ a strategy called "market-timing."

The object of the game is to get your money invested early in a market upswing and to get your profits out before the downturn. Traders have long done this with individual stocks and, more recently, with options, futures, and no-load mutual funds. No-load equity funds seem to be made for market-timing. They already are, like the market, a diversified basket of stocks. And getting in and out is cheap and easy.

The idea of market-timing is appealing. Everyone wants to participate in rallies and dodge the declines. Many newsletter advisers and telephone hotline tipsters run market-timing advisory services, but you have to be skeptical about whether they're worthwhile or if the principle is even sound.

Take a look at the records of the market-timers. One timing system used by the newsletter *Systems and Forecasts* racked up a 17.99 percent average annual total return in the 10-year period ending December 31, 1998, according to the *Hulbert Financial Digest* (Table 4-6). That may sound good, but it's not even as good as the return of the S&P 500 or the Dow Jones industrial average. More important, about 142 mutual funds did better, among them Fidelity Fund, FPA Capital, and Janus Twenty. The Kaufmann and PBHG Growth funds, poor performers for the last few years, also beat the best timer.

The record shows that market-timing is no sure thing. What's perhaps even more surprising is how poorly some of the newsletters—which charge subscribers several hundred dollars a year for "advice"—actually performed. Following the advice of *The Elliot Wave Theorist*, a market-timer would have ended up with less than a 6 percent average annual return. He or she could have done almost as well in a money-market fund with a lot less trouble.

More importantly, market-timing results represent gross returns before taxes. Market-timing with taxable funds—that is, anything outside an individual retirement account or other such tax-

> Few timers ever beat the stock market.

TABLE 4-6

THE MARKET-TIMING GAME

Newsletter	Portfolio/ timing system	Average annual total return*
SYSTEMS AND FORECASTS	"Time Trend"	17.99%
THE CHARTIST	Trader's—timing only	17.91
NO-LOAD FUND INVESTOR	Master Wealth Builder—timing only	17.67
BOB BRINKER'S MARKETIMER	Aggressive Growth Fund Portfolio	17.67
TIMER DIGEST	"5 & 10" Consensus	16.60
FIDELITY INSIGHT GROWTH	Timing only	15.89
THE CHARTIST MUTUAL FUND LETTER	Cash account—timing only	15.75
FABIAN PREMIUM INVST. RESOURCE	Domestic Fund Composite—timing only	15.27
MUTUAL FUND INVESTING	Growth Portfolio—timing only	14.60
THE CABOT MARKET LETTER	Model Portfolio—timing only	14.47
INVESTORS INTELLIGENCE	Fidelity Switch Equity—timing only	14.33
THE SECTOR FUNDS NEWSLETTER	Model Portfolio 1—timing only	13.78
THE BIG PICTURE	Master Key—no shorting	13.62
MARKET LOGIC	Seasonality Timing System	13.04
THE ADDISON REPORT	Aggressive Portfolio—timing only	12.62
THE PETER DAG PORTFOLIO	Vanguard Portfolio	12.17
THE DINES LETTER	100% Cash on Intermediate-tm. sells	11.86
THE MUTUAL FUND STRATEGIST	MIRAT-Rydex Growth—timing only	11.59
FUNDADVICE.COM	U.S. Market Timing Model	11.21
GROWTH FUND GUIDE	Mutual Fund Allocation—timing only	9.92
THE PROFESSIONAL TAPE READER	Short-Term Signals—Cash on sells	8.93
INVESTECH RESEARCH	Mutual Fund Advisor—timing only	7.22
FUTURES HOTLINE	Fund Model—Cash on sells	7.21
GRAPHIC FUND FORECASTER	Growth/Intl. 1—timing only	6.81
STOCK MARKET CYCLES	Fidelity Select—timing only	6.49
THE ELLIOT WAVE THEORIST	Investors—Cash on sells	5.65
SWITCH FUND TIMING	Model Portfolio—timing only	4.56

BENCHMARKS

STANDARD & POOR'S 500	19.10%
DOW JONES INDUSTRIALS	18.76
WILSHIRE 5000	16.68
U.S. TREASURY BILLS	5.47
U.S. DIVERSIFIED EQUITY FUNDS	15.51
ALL EQUITY FUNDS	13.86

*Jan. 1, 1989–Dec. 31, 1998   DATA: *HULBERT FINANCIAL DIGEST,* MORNINGSTAR INC.

percent tax on the gains (prior to 1987). And that's before state and local income taxes, too.

Academic studies of market-timing cast doubt on its efficacy. In the mid-1980s, two University of Calgary professors determined that an investor who accurately predicted every bull and bear market from 1926 to 1983—buying stocks at the beginning of bull markets and switching to Treasury bills at the onset of bear markets—earned an 18.2 percent average annual return, even assuming a 1 percent commission was paid on each trade.

By comparison, the buy-and-hold investors only earned an 11.8 percent average annual return during the same period. But no market-timer has a perfect record. What if your market-timing was right about 50 percent of the time? Too bad. If so, your average annual return would have dwindled to 8.1 percent. To beat the buy-and-hold investor, the professors concluded, the timer would have had to be right 70 percent of the time.

One of the problems with market-timing is that the stock market typically makes large gains in relatively short periods, followed by longer periods when not much seems to happen at all. Rushmore Funds, for instance, looks back at the performance of the S&P 500 index during the 1980s. For the entire decade, the average annual return was 17.6 percent. But if you take out the 10 days when stocks made their largest gains, the average annual return drops to 12.6 percent. Take out the 20 best days for stocks, and the return is only 9.3 percent. The point is, if you're not invested during those short bursts of activity, you can miss a lot of the potential rewards.

Or look at the T. Rowe Price New Horizons Fund, one of the oldest and largest of the funds specializing in small companies. In 1990, the fund's sponsors calculated that 80 percent of the gains over the prior 30 years, or 120 quarters, actually occurred in 12 of the quarters. So to time that kind of fund successfully, you would have had to have been invested in the fund during only 12 of 120 quarters. Unless you can tell with absolute certainty which quarters are the critical ones, buy-and-hold would be a better strategy.

There's no better example of this than the first quarter of 1991. The New Horizons Fund rocketed up 28 percent in just three months. Yet at the end of December 1990, the economy was in recession and war was about to erupt in the Persian Gulf. If your assets had been in a money-market fund then, would you have shifted them into stocks, given the gloomy atmosphere?

deferred retirement plan—would hardly be worth the trouble. Every switch is what the accountants call a "taxable event." Assuming that you were making profitable trades over the last 10 years, you might have paid as much as a 50

Though the numbers suggest the odds are against them, market-timers keep trying. But sometimes market-timing can be downright disruptive and harmful to long-term investors. Suppose you're a portfolio manager running a $100 million fund. You normally keep about 5 percent of your assets in cash to meet redemptions and seize upon new investment opportunities.

Then some market-timers start pumping money into your fund. If the timers are following a variety of trading systems, that might not be so bad since they would not all trade at the same time. But suppose a market-timing adviser who had a wide following among both institutions and individuals moves to a particular mutual fund, bringing along about $10 million in assets. At first you are delighted, as it's a vote of confidence in your abilities. (It also pleases the bosses, since the greater the number of dollars in the fund, the more management fees it generates.) Everything goes along swimmingly, and in six months or so the fund goes up 20 percent. The market-timer's followers see their collective $10 million increase to $12 million.

But one day the market-timer says switch—and all of a sudden his or her followers want their money out. The fund has $6 million in U.S. Treasury bills that can be sold to raise cash, and another $1 million in new money came in that day. But to redeem $12 million, you have to sell $5 million worth of stocks. That may not be all bad, since it never hurts to take a profit. But what if your game plan—successful thus far—had called for buying, not selling? Or what if it isn't a particularly good time to sell? Trading has a cost, too, that comes out of the fund's assets. If timers make excessive switches in and out of a fund, it could hurt the returns left for the other shareholders.

As much as management companies love to "gather assets," from time to time they have quietly invited market-timers or suspected market-timers to take their business elsewhere. For instance, the Kaufmann Fund, which invests in many small, emerging growth companies, once returned a $25 million check to a wealthy investor. Lawrence Auriana, one of the portfolio managers, said he feared what would happen when this investor asked for his money back all at once. Auriana said the fund might have to dump stocks just to redeem that big shareholder's

account, which could be detrimental to the other shareholders. Auriana says there are market-timers in the fund, but they don't have enough fund shares to be disruptive.

So many fund sponsors now discourage market-timers from investing in their funds that a few fund companies have sprung up just to cater to market-timers. The first one, Rydex, started about five years ago with the Rydex Nova Fund, the bullish fund that timers buy when they think stocks will go up. It's a souped up index fund and is designed to go up 1.5 times the S&P 500. Why? Market-timers are trend followers and usually don't pick the bottom. When they buy, the trend is already in place. Rydex Nova buys mainly in stock-index futures and options to keep liquidity high, transaction costs down, and give it the extra kick it needs to move 1.5 times the index.

Rydex Ursa is the bears' fund, designed to rise in NAV as stock prices head south. That's because this fund sells index futures and buys put options, both of which yield gains as stocks stumble. (In that sense, it can be used not only by timers but by anyone looking to hedge against a decline in the market.) To discourage less sophisticated investors, Rydex requires a minimum $25,000 investment for all its funds. Beside Nova and Ursa, there is an OTC fund, a pair of bullish and bearish bond funds, and a slew of equity sector funds.

Of course, it was only a matter of time before some funds would go a step farther. The second best-performing fund of 1998 was ProFunds UltraOTC Investors. It nearly tripled—only the Internet Fund edged it out for first place in the last few days of 1998. ProFunds UltraOTC is designed to double the moves of the NASDAQ 100 index, an index dominated by big tech companies like Microsoft, Intel, and Cisco Systems. The mirror-image fund is ProFunds UltraOTC Short. It managed to go down twice as much as the NASDAQ 100. Why would you use it? You would use it if you became very bearish on big tech stocks. ProFunds has a $15,000 minimum investment on its funds.

Market-timing pays only if you're very, very good at it—and then, only if you don't have to pay taxes on the gains. Mutual funds work best when used as long-term investments. No matter what kind of calendar you use, two days is not the long term.

Some funds may spurn frequent switchers.

Monitoring Your Mutual Funds

So now you have a portfolio of mutual funds, which, in effect, gives you a group of top-drawer professional money managers working for you. And those managers are backed up by scores of staff members who can turn up information and analysis that you could never hope to assemble on your own.

Ah, it would be nice if you could leave your mutual funds on autopilot and watch your fortune just mount up. But nothing is that perfect. Many mutual funds can be buy-and-hold investments, but none of them are buy-and-forget. To keep on top of your mutual fund portfolio takes some of your time. Fortunately, it's not a lot of time. An hour or two a month would probably take care of most investors' needs.

Many people keep tabs on their funds by following them in the financial pages of their daily newspapers. But there are other ways as well. With a computer and modem, you can access mutual fund prices through many online services or on the Internet, including BUSINESS WEEK Online (www.businessweek.com). Many popular online sites, including Morningstar.net, Quicken.com, and Yahoo-Finance, will update your portfolio every day. If you don't want to post your portfolio in a remote site, many portfolio management programs will allow you to download the data directly into your computer. And, of course, all fund companies maintain toll-free phone numbers that allow you to check on prices and your account status, and most have Web sites to do the same.

Tracking Funds in the Financial Pages

Mutual fund prices are quoted daily in *The Wall Street Journal, Investors Business Daily*, and just about any newspaper that carries daily financial tables. In addition, Sunday newspapers usually have the mutual fund tables that summarize the high, low, and last price for the week. Not every fund makes it into the newspapers. To qualify, the fund needs a minimum of 1000 shareholders or $30 million in assets.

In the newspaper, fund tables are organized alphabetically by fund family (from AAL Mutual to Zweig Funds), and then alphabetically within families. Many large fund families are broken into subgroups to make it easier to find funds. For example, Fidelity is so large that its funds are broken into several groups, such as Fidelity Investments (where you'll find Magellan, Puritan, and the best-known Fidelity products), Fidelity Selects (the specialty portfolios), and Fidelity Spartan (a line of low-overhead funds). Load-fund families that have several share classes break their funds into smaller groups, such as Alliance Capital A, Alliance Capital B, and Alliance Capital C. Not all funds are parts of families, but they're still integrated into the tables in alphabetical order.

Each fund is followed by several columns of data expressed as dollars and cents. There's net asset value, followed by the offer price, which is the NAV plus the load for funds sold with front-end loads. The last column is the daily price change, which, for most mutual funds, usually amounts to pennies per day. In addition, single lower-case letters footnote such features as 12(b)-1 plans, redemption fees, or an income or capital gains distribution. Over 600 newspapers still carry this basic table, which is distributed by the Associated Press.

But now, some newspapers are starting to vary their mutual fund tables. *The Wall Street Journal*, for instance, shows three basic features: NAV, NAV net change from previous day, and year-to-date return. Some major newspapers, including *The New York Times* and *Chicago Tri-*

bune, carry a somewhat different presentation developed by Morningstar, Inc. *The New York Times* version, for instance, carries the previous day's NAV only, along with a percentage price change, not the price change in dollars and cents. The remaining data also change daily, such as adding expense ratios on one day, three-month returns on another, and a more comprehensive set of tables on Sundays.

If you're familiar with stock tables, you'll notice that mutual fund tables are different. Mutual fund pricing, for instance, goes down to the penny: $8.71, or $15.46, or $65.03, or whatever. Most stocks are now priced in sixteenths—a unit of 6.25 cents.

Day to day, the movement of mutual funds seems almost glacial. Pick up one of the daily tables and scan the right-hand column, headed by "NAV chg" or "Change in net asset value." The changes are usually small: "–.02, +.03, –.07, +.11." If the stock market has made a big move up or down that day, those numbers will usually show greater changes, but most of the time, movements are small.

There are several reasons for this. First, mutual funds are highly diversified and not all the securities move in the same direction at the same time. For example, if there are 100 stocks in a fund, the change in net asset value is the difference between the 50 that went up that day, the 40 that went down, and the 10 that had no change at all.

Whatever the stock market's move, the mutual fund tables appear to mute the effect. Take a look at the stock market's activity on December 29, 1997. The Dow Jones industrial average went up to 7792.41 from 7679.31 on December 26, a 1.47 percent move. Suppose your mutual fund behaves much like the Dow and has a net asset value of $15. A 1.47 percent gain on $15 is just 22 cents.

Look at the mutual fund table that appeared in *USA Today* on December 30, 1997 which reported results of December 29 (Figure 5-1). The NAV of the Fidelity Blue Chip Growth Fund ("BluCh" in the table under the boldface heading "Fidelity Invest") closed at $38.50, a 68-cents-per-share gain. That's a 1.8 percent gain, which is better than the Dow.

If you scan down a few more lines to check out Fidelity Fifty Fund, you see a 32-cent gain. But Fidelity Fifty did better than Blue Chip because its gain was 32 cents on top of a lower NAV of $14.69. So the Fidelity Fifty gain was 2.2 percent. Don't let those cents fool you. What counts is the

level of the NAV before you measure the change. To get the previous day's NAV, add back the losses or subtract the gains from the current day's NAV. Some newspapers even report the day's percentage change.

Tracking bond funds can be like watching the grass grow. The 30-year U.S. Treasury bond—the benchmark by which the bond market is most commonly measured—was 5.92 percent, up 0.02 percent for the day. So there was very little change in the bond funds. The Vanguard Long-Term U.S. Treasury Fund, which is most sensitive to changes in bond prices, dropped 2 cents in NAV.

INTERPRETING THE FUND TABLES

Many newspapers use the abbreviated presentation shown in Figure 5-1. The first column is the NAV, based on December 29 closing prices. The second column is the change in the NAV from December 26, expressed in dollars and cents. The third column, "YTD%," is the year-to-date performance, which is change in net asset value plus reinvestment of dividends and capital gains distributions.

Note how the fund tables are organized. Most funds are listed within families such as AAL Mutual, AARP Investment, and so on. Then they're alphabetical within those families. The tables include both stock and bond but not money-market mutual funds. Funds not part of large fund groups are listed alphabetically along with the fund families, but they will be listed in regular type while the fund families are in boldface.

Look at the listings and you'll see some single letters after the fund names. A capital letter, usually A or B, attached at the end of the fund name usually denotes a class of share. Under Fidelity Advisory, for instance, you will find A, B, and I shares. A shares have a front-end load, B shares a back-end load with redemption, and I shares are for institutional investors. Or look at Galaxy Funds Retail and Galaxy Funds Trust. Retail shares are for individual investors, trust shares for bank trust customers. Whether the fund family uses a letter, or "retail" and "trust," the underlying portfolios are the same. What's different is how the fund shareholder pays for the fund. When the returns of two classes differ, it's because differing amounts of fees are taken out of the fund. (See Chapter 3 for a discussion of multiple classes of shares.)

Then there are various lowercase letters used throughout the table. The "n" means the fund is

Most funds' daily price changes are small.

FIGURE 5-1

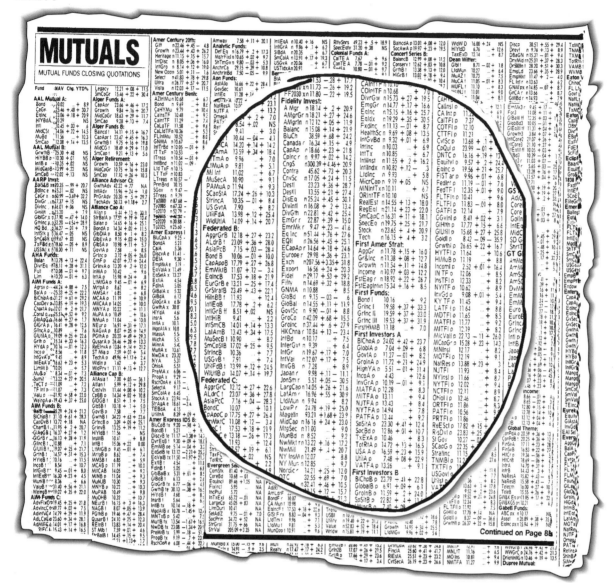

no-load. The "p" indicates that the fund levies a 12(b)-1 fee for distribution expenses. (Need an explanation? See Chapter 3.) Some funds have an "r." That indicates a redemption fee. How much? That's not in the table, but it's an indication that if you sell your fund for the NAV listed in the table, you may not collect the full amount. You'll also see many funds with "t" accompanying them. That footnote tells you that both "p" and "r" apply to this fund.

The footnotes "p," "r," and "t" are there all the time. They describe an ongoing characteristic or policy of the fund. But on occasion you may see an "x," "e," or "s." The "x" may be familiar from the stock tables. It means the fund just paid a dividend. Investors buying after the fund has "gone ex-dividend" do not collect that dividend. Often

the fund appears to decline in net asset value. But the decline may only reflect that money was paid out of the fund. If a fund pays a 10-cents-a-share dividend, and goes down 5 cents a share on the ex-dividend date, that means the fund would have risen a nickel a share had the dividend not been paid.

When a fund pays a capital gains distribution, the symbol is an "e" instead of an "x." No matter, the effect on the fund pricing is the same. The "s" works the same way as an "x," except that it means the dividend is paid in stock instead of cash.

There may be some funds with no NAVs after their names. This usually means the fund company didn't yet have the price available when the National Association of Securities Dealers came to collect it. The day after the October 1987 stock market crash, the fund table was strewn with blanks. That frightened many people, who thought their funds had been wiped out.

Money-market fund quotes are not usually in daily newspapers. They can be found on Thursdays (they're released on Wednesday) and sometimes in Sunday newspapers, too. Net asset value for money funds is held constant at $1 a share, thus there's no point in reporting it. What is reported in the money-market fund table is the annualized yield for the last 7-day period. If it's 4.88 percent, that doesn't mean the fund paid 4.88 percent over the last 7 days, but that the rate paid, held constant over a year, would be 4.88 percent. If the newspaper also includes 30-day yield, compare the two. If the 7-day is higher than the 30-day yield, that's an indication that interest rates have gone up. If the 7-day yield is less than the 30-day yield, rates have come down.

Another useful figure in the money-market fund table is the average maturity. That figure is quoted in days. Consider the Merrill Lynch CMA Money Fund. In early 1999, the fund had a 72-day average maturity. Of course, the money-market funds have billions in securities maturing every day. But a 72-day average maturity means that the average of all the maturities in the fund is 10 weeks. Zurich YieldWise Money Fund had an average maturity of 22 days, about three weeks. The industry average for taxable money funds was 54 days.

Okay, so now short-term interest rates rise. Which fund will deliver more yield to its shareholders? The Zurich fund, for sure, because it will take just several weeks before all the money rolls over and is reinvested at higher rates. In contrast, it will take 2½ months for the Merrill fund to gain full advantage of the higher rates. The Merrill fund's yield will go up more slowly.

Now suppose interest rates come down. The investors in the Merrill fund will hold on to the higher yields longer. The yield from the Zurich portfolio will come down much faster. In fact, the Merrill fund, with what is a long maturity for a money-market mutual fund, was fully expecting a drop in short-term rates.

The maturities of money-market funds are not static either. When portfolio managers anticipate that interest rates will fall, they buy longer-maturity securities for the portfolio, hoping to hold on to the higher rates longer. In like manner, they shorten maturities in anticipation of rising interest rates. Some investors track the ups and

downs of portfolio maturities as market indicators. If the average maturity lengthens, that represents the collective opinion of hundreds of fund managers that rates are heading down. It may not be right, but it tells you what the conventional wisdom is.

Keeping track of closed-end funds is a little trickier. You can find the share prices every day under the appropriate stock market listing: New York Stock Exchange, American Stock Exchange, or the NASDAQ National Market System (over-the-counter market). But what you see is the per-share price, which, as you know, is usually different from net asset value.

The NAVs of closed-end funds are generally reported in the financial pages once a week. Closed-end funds usually report NAVs on Friday and you can find them in the newspapers over the weekend (Mondays in *The Wall Street Journal* and *Investors Business Daily*).

Keeping Score

The whole point of watching your funds' performances is to make sure that they are doing what's expected of them. Fund managers might have all the best intentions, but they're human, too.

The first thing investors want to know about a fund is the total return for the quarter, for the year, or for any other period. The total return—appreciation plus reinvestment of dividends and capital gains—allows investors to compare a fund's performance to that of a benchmark index like the S&P 500, and also to other funds.

Computing the total return is simple (Table 5-1). Suppose you invested your money in a mutual fund on the first business day of the previous year, and the fund had a net asset value of $9.31 per share. On the last day of the year, the NAV was $10.61. And during the year, the fund paid dividends and capital gains distributions amounting to $0.5738 per share.

Here's how to figure the fund's return. Start with the final NAV, $10.61. Add in the distributions of $0.5738. That brings the total to $11.1838. Next, subtract the initial NAV, or $9.31. That amounts to $1.8738 per share, which is the fund's "profit" for the year. Next, divide the $1.8738 profit by the starting NAV, $9.31, which comes to 0.2013. To turn that into a percentage, just multiply by 100. The total return is 20.13 percent.

Closed-end funds report NAVs once a week.

TABLE 5-1

FIGURING MUTUAL FUND RETURNS

Suppose that on the first business day of 1998 you bought a mutual fund at a net asset value of $9.31. Late in the year, the fund distributed $0.5738 per share to investors. At year's end, the NAV was $10.61. What's the fund's return for the year?

$$\frac{\text{Final NAV} + \text{Distributions} - \text{Starting NAV}}{\text{Starting NAV}} \times 100$$

$$\frac{\$10.61 + \$0.5738 - \$9.31}{\$9.31} \times 100$$

$$= \frac{1.8738}{9.31}(100) = 0.2013(100) = 20.13\%$$

HOW TO COMPUTE YOUR TOTAL RETURN

Suppose you invest $2000 in a mutual fund and you reinvest the dividends and capital gains distributions of $325. At the end of the year, your account is worth $2415. In this example, you don't need to add in the distributions—they're already accounted for in the current value. If you take the distributions in cash, you need to add them back as in the first example.

$$\frac{\text{Current value of shares} - \text{initial investment}}{\text{Initial investment}} \times 100$$

$$= \frac{\$2415 - \$2000}{\$2000}(100) = \frac{415}{2000}(100)$$

$$= 0.208(100)$$

$$= 20.8\%$$

DATA: BUSINESS WEEK

Though this calculation covered a one-year period, the method works for any time period. The key to taking an accurate measurement is to remember to include all the dividends and distributions.

But the total return is a measure of how well the portfolio managers performed. That doesn't necessarily tell you how well your own investment is doing. For instance, if you paid a load or sales charge, that won't be reflected in the total return calculation that uses NAV. So here's a way to calculate your own return.

Suppose you invested $2000 in a mutual fund and reinvested dividends and capital gains distributions of $325. At the end of the year, your account is worth $2415. To figure your return, take the value of your shares at the end of the period—$2415. If the fund has a back-end load or redemption fee that applies to you, and you're considering selling the fund, you should subtract that from the current value of the shares.

Next, subtract your initial investment. If you paid a load, that's already figured into the initial investment. If you reinvest dividends and capital gains, there's no need to add them back. They're counted in the current value of your shares. If you don't reinvest and you take distributions in cash, you have to add them back to the current value figure. Then take the difference, $415, and divide that by the initial investment, $2000. That yields 0.208, so multiply that by 100 to come up with 20.8 percent.

Suppose you are investing in a mutual fund on a monthly schedule. Then the calculation starts to get a little stickier. To get an exact return, you need to use a complex method called the internal rate of return, which accounts for the timing of the investments into the fund. Leave that to the professionals, or to a computer program that can provide it. You can get a rough approximation of your return by calculating your average cost per share (see "Dollar-Cost Averaging" in Chapter 4). Do all the numbers have you breaking out in a cold sweat? Calm yourself. With a pocket calculator, a pencil, and paper, you can do it yourself just fine.

Let the Computer Do It

You certainly don't need a computer to keep track of your mutual funds. But if you have one, it can make your job a lot easier. There are a number of money and investment management programs that simplify the "keeping up" process, like Quicken and Microsoft Money. If you're adept at using the spreadsheet programs like Microsoft Excel or Lotus 1-2-3, you can create your own portfolio record-keeping systems.

The computer is particularly handy for investors who make frequent purchases and regular reinvestment of dividends and capital gains. If you invest monthly and reinvest the income and distributions, you will be making 12 to 16 transactions a year. By entering each one into the computer program, the investor knows exactly how many shares of each investment he or she has, what it's worth, and what the average cost is.

More important, the programs show each transaction individually as well as what the profit or loss is on that particular investment. Suppose the overall investment is in the black, but several purchases of funds were made at higher prices and are in the red. One such program that will do that is Mutual Fund Manager by Concepts Software, Inc. Check out a sample at the website, www.conceptsmfm.com.

Mutual Funds at BUSINESS WEEK Online

The online world is emerging as a valuable tool for tracking, researching, and keeping up with mutual funds. We hope BUSINESS WEEK Online (www.businessweek.com) will be the first place to go in cyberspace for the lowdown on mutual funds. BW Online features a Mutual Fund Corner, which collects all the magazine and BW Online stories of interest to fund investors, both from the pages of the magazine and the stories, analyses, and manager interviews that appear only online. But what's even more exciting is that our Web site has an interactive version of the BW Mutual Fund Scoreboard (Figure 5-2). What was one of the magazine's most popular annual features is now updated monthly online. That allows you to better follow your funds and hone in on the BUSINESS WEEK ratings throughout the year.

And that's not all. What's also great about the online Scoreboard is that we're no longer confined to the printed page. We include data on some 4700 equity and bond funds and add more every month as new funds become eligible. In general, we add funds after they've amassed 12 months worth of performance history. For funds with multiple classes of shares (i.e., A, B, and C shares), we report on the largest share class. We also generally exclude institutional funds unless they are also available to retail investors through one of the major mutual fund supermarkets (see Chapter 3).

Trying to find data on specific funds? You can find them alphabetically. Thinking about adding a foreign or a technology fund to your portfolio. You can ask the Scoreboard to give you a list of either. Just want A-rated bond funds? You can do that as well. Want even more info on a fund than we provide? We've included links to Morningstar pages as well. There are also links to Personal Wealth, a Web service from Standard & Poor's Corp. (Both BUSINESS WEEK and S&P are owned by The McGraw-Hill Companies.)

Here's how to use the Scoreboard. Suppose you're tracking several funds and you know their names. Suppose you're looking for the Gabelli Asset Fund. From the first pull-down menu (No. 1, upper left side of the screen), select from "Equity Funds," "Bond Funds," or, if you're not sure whether it's an equity or a bond fund, choose "All Funds." Select "G," and you'll get a listing of the funds starting with G.

FIGURE 5-2

Once you get a listing in the main screen, scroll down the left side of the window until you find the fund you want. Along with the fund name, that window will display the fund's overall rating, category, category rating, and total returns for up to seven different periods. These fund names come into the window 50 at a time. So if you get to the bottom, and you still haven't arrived at your fund, click on the words "Next 50 Funds" which appear at the bottom right of the window.

There's more. If you click on the fund name, a smaller window will open beneath the main window. Here you will find more data specific to that fund: net assets, sales charge, expense ratio, risk, portfolio turnover, and a 12-month distribution yield. You'll also find a toll-free telephone number, a Web site address (if the fund has one), and a five-letter ticker symbol ending in X. You might want to write down the ticker symbol, since you will be able to use this in any stock quote delivery system—BW Online's or others'—to find the latest reported net asset value on your fund. If you click on the ticker symbol in this window, you will jump to a Morningstar "Quick Take" page, which provides further price and more in-depth portfolio information.

Searching for a foreign fund or a technology fund to spice up your portfolio? Go back to "Equity Funds" in the first menu. When you specify equity or bond funds, the second menu box offers up a variety of options: you can ask the scoreboard to display funds alphabetically, by their overall BUSINESS WEEK rating, by total return over one of seven time periods, or by their fund category. Want a foreign fund? Click on "Foreign" in the second box. Then, you have to move on to the third menu box, which offers the choice of viewing the funds either alphabetically or by their category rating.

Perhaps you're not quite sure what kind of fund you want, so you scan the funds by their BUSINESS WEEK ratings. Here's the sequence: first menu, Equity Funds; next menu, click "Overall BW Ratings"; and from the last menu, "A." That will give you a list of all the equity funds whose BW rating is A. Perhaps you want to hunt from the list of the last 12 months' winners. Start with, Equity Funds; next, 1 mo. Return; last menu, 100 Best Rankings.

MUTUAL FUNDS ON THE WEB

The World Wide Web opens vast new resources—and a lot of worthless information as well. We've already screened some of the offerings, and there are excellent sites worth checking out. We've noted some of them (Table 5-2), and there are plenty more. A good jumping off point would be one of the Internet portals, like Yahoo's (http://www.yahoo.com). Go from Yahoo's main page, click on Finance, then Mutual Funds. Another portal, The Mining Company, also has a good mutual funds home page, (http://www.miningco.com). Or go to Invest-O-Rama (http://www.investorama.com), which boasts that it has the largest number of links to other mutual fund–related sites on the Web.

Nearly all investment-related Web sites offer quote services that allow you to look up stock and mutual fund prices. To get the latest net asset value for your fund, you need to know the mutual fund ticker symbol; it's a five-letter sequence that ends in "X," and you can find them in the BW Interactive Scoreboard. For instance, type "FMAGX"—ticker symbol for the Fidelity Magellan Fund—in a quote server, and you will get the most recent net asset value. Remember, mutual funds are priced at the end of the day, so unlike a stock that's trading all through the day, the mutual fund price only changes at the end of the day, after the market has closed and the fund's portfolio is priced.

Closed-end funds, which trade like stocks, generally have two- or three-character symbols, and you can get market prices for them through the day. For most funds, net asset values are still only reported weekly. But about 20 percent of the closed-end funds now make their NAVs available daily through the NASDAQ quotation service, the same outfit that collects mutual fund pricing data. To get a closed-end fund's NAV, type an "X" before and after the fund's ticker symbol. So, for instance, the ticker symbol for the closed-end Gabelli Equity Fund is GAB. That gets you the most recent market price. To obtain the most recent net asset value, type XGABX. Likewise, to get NAV for the Royce Value Trust, type XRVTX. You get the idea.

This system of reporting closed-end fund NAVs is still a work in progress. Most funds do not yet offer it, and not all quote servers carry the data. For most investors, it's trial and error to see if you can find the daily NAV. The best place to check for closed-end funds' NAVs is the Web site operated by the National Association of Securities Dealers (http://www.nasd.com).

The Web sites of the mutual fund supermarkets (Schwab, Fidelity, and Jack White to name a few) often offer fund-screening programs, ability

The Internet opens vast new resources for investors.

127

TABLE 5-2

FUND "SURFING" ONLINE

BUSINESS WEEK Online
Top-drawer news, analysis, and commentary from a world-class business magazine. Features interactive version of the BUSINESS WEEK Mutual Fund Scoreboard that is updated monthly. Also frequent mutual fund commentaries and interviews with managers that appear only online.

http://www.businessweek.com
or keyword:BW on America Online

Quicken.com
Solid offerings for all investors. Mutual fund data from Morningstar and Value Line, fund family directory and interviews with fund managers.

http://www.quicken.com

Mutual Funds Interactive
Well designed, snappy looking pages, with fund news, columnists, and plenty of links to other sites.

http://www.fundsinteractive.com

Morningstar
Classy site, with loads of fund research to help you select and monitor funds. Links with brokerages let you invest as well. There's plenty of free material, but some higher-end services require subscription.

http://www.morningstar.net

Mutual Fund Investor's Corner
Sponsored by the Mutual Fund Education Alliance, a trade association of the direct-marketed (mainly no-load) funds. Fund info is limited to that of member companies, but that's mainly what the do-it-yourself investor would want anyway.

http://www.mfea.com

FundAlarm
Maintains data on 500 funds (mainly those over $500 million), and tracks the fund vs. various benchmarks. Is one of yours a "three alarm" fund, and therefore should be dumped? Listings of portfolio manager comings and goings are also useful.

http://www.FundAlarm.com

FreeEDGAR
An excellent site for accessing the electronic database at the U.S. Securities and Exchange Commission. Look for fund reports as soon as they're filed. You don't have to wait for them to be printed and arrive in the mail. Much easier to use than the SEC's own EDGAR site.

http://www.FreeEDGAR.com

Schwab Online
Long before Internet brokers like E*Trade and Ameritrade, there was Charles Schwab & Co. Now, Schwab is by far the largest—though not the cheapest—online broker. If you're working with Schwab's OneSource and Schwab-managed funds, there aren't any fees or commissions anyhow.

http://www.schwab.com

Fidelity Investments
First thing that catches your eye is legendary fund manager Peter Lynch. But no matter, the site is first-rate. You'll find both Fidelity funds and, through the brokerage arm, thousands of other mutual funds, available both on no-fee and transaction fee bases.

http://www.fidelity.com

Jack White & Co.
If you can't find a fund at Schwab or Fidelity, Jack White probably has it in his line-up. The firm has about 7500 to offer, and it adds more every month. Web site has also done major renovation that brings it closer to those of Schwab and Fidelity. Still, the main draw is selection.

http://www.jackwhite&co.com

Vanguard Funds
Quiz yourself on mutual fund knowledge, but don't worry if you come up short. Enroll in the Vanguard University where you can learn all about funds, fees, and low-cost investing. The site is also the door to the newly invigorated Vanguard Brokerage Services, which is aiming to compete with other mutual-fund supermarkets.

http://www.vanguard.com

IBC Money Fund Monitor
The place to go for the last information on money-market mutual funds. Also includes news and commentary on money-market activity, interest-rate developments, regulatory issues, and fund strategies.

http://www.ibcdata.com

Internet Closed-End Investor
A great online service for an often-overlooked investment vehicle, the closed-end fund. Fund data, charts, screening capability, and more. Some services free, some require subscription.

http://www.icefi.com

Invest-o-rama
Forget the corny 1950's name. Site claims to be the most comprehensive directory of other investment sites on the Web, with over 9000 links in 121 categories. But it's not a way station, either. Plenty of research and reading on hand.

http://www.investorama.com

INVESTools
Besides usual mutual fund screening and reporting features, this site functions as an online marketplace for independent newsletter writers. You can sample their works or sign up for cut-rate sample subscriptions.

http://www.investools.com

IndexFunds.com
Index funds are hot, and this site—a recent merger of two others devoted to index investing—is worth your while. Good basic instructions and advanced series of pages offer plenty of stats for numbers crunchers.

http://www.IndexFunds.com

Scudder Funds
Flashy new Web site that boasts Financial Concierge, which allows visitors to ask questions in plain English—like "What is a variable annuity?"—instead of computerese or scrolling through long menus looking for keywords.

http://www.scudder.com

to download prospectuses, and, of course, online transactions. You can also do all of that at most fund companies' sites, though not all have online buy-and-sell capabilities yet. Sites like Fidelity's, Scudder's, and Vanguard's also have extensive educational material on mutual funds, asset allocation, and investing for retirement and/or your child's education.

If you've used BUSINESS WEEK's Interactive Scoreboard, you may have already visited a Morningstar "Quick Take" page. That's part of Morningstar's excellent Web site, Morningstar .net. Though there's a charge for some services—a monthly subscription fee—there's plenty of good information in the free portion. Be sure to bookmark this page, and also check out FundAlarm (http://www.FundAlarm.com). FundAlarm tracks about 500 of the largest funds and sends out alarms when their share-price is sagging. A "three-alarm" signal is a warning the fund is lagging its peers in share-price performance and may be ripe for a sell. The site also maintains a list of fund manager changes, which may also signal that a fund should be dumped.

While there's plenty of information on equity and bond funds out there, data on closed-end funds and money-market funds is harder to find. That's what makes the Internet Closed-End Fund Investor (http://www.icefi.com) and IBC Money Fund Monitor (http://www.ibcdata.com) good research sites as well. If you're collecting prospectuses and/or semiannual or annual reports, you can find them all in one place if you go right to the source—EDGAR, the U.S. Securities & Exchange Commission's database. The SEC's doorway to the database (http://www.sec.gov/edgarhp.htm) can be difficult to use. A commercial site, Free EDGAR (http://www.freeEDGAR.com), is much easier. Searching through this site is free, though the company that runs it makes money from selling ads and higher-end services (such as the ability to load reports into Excel files).

Fund investors who venture online should also look in on the USENET newsgroup "misc .invest.funds," or one of the myriad message boards and chat rooms at Morningstar or Yahoo. These message boards are where fund folks meet to ask questions, exchange opinions, and gather insight into mutual funds. Want to know why your hot fund was down 2 percent last week when the market fell less than 1 percent? Post the question. Someone might have the answer—and that person may even be from the mutual fund company.

When Your Fund Is Ailing

You're tracking your funds, diligently keeping records of prices, remembering to count distributions in your returns. Then you start to notice that one of your funds is slipping. The stock market is moving up modestly but this fund is heading south.

The long-term record is still exceptional, and you're a long-term investor. So you stick with the fund—and watch it slip away. Now you're not only lagging the market, but you're losing real money. What do you do?

You're facing the most difficult question in all of investing: When do you jettison a fund that's in a funk? Suppose you sell and it turns out to be the bottom of the decline. You might regret it later. Maybe you paid a load to get into the fund, and so are reluctant to leave now. Sometimes people just refuse to admit they made a bad investment; there's too much ego involved. So they're slow to sell when perhaps they should.

Before pushing the "sell" button on a poorly performing fund, ask some questions about it. The most important: How is the fund doing relative to its market sector and peer group? Suppose the S&P 500 delivered a total return of 10 percent over the previous period and your small-cap growth fund gained only half that much. The question is: How much better did the other small-cap growth funds perform? Perhaps your fund, while dragging behind the market, did well among its peers. So besides comparing your fund to the market, compare your fund to similar funds.

If you had owned a high-yield bond fund in 1989 and 1990, you may have been dismayed by plunging net asset values. At that time, no junk fund was going to look good. The question wasn't "Do you want to own this junk fund or another junk fund?" but "Do you want to invest in a junk bond fund at all?" You may have invested in one of the better junk bond funds. But you have to compare yours to others to know that.

Sometimes you make a bet without realizing it, and the failure of the investment is not entirely the manager's. If you buy a long-term government bond fund, the investment won't succeed unless long-term interest rates come down or at least stay flat. If they go up, your fund is going to falter. You may choose to sell out, but don't replace your fund with another long-term

Few funds thrive under all market conditions.

bond fund at the same time. If you're attracted by the long-term results of these sorts of funds, then you just stick with them, through good times and bad.

An investment in narrowly defined funds such as technology or health care or Latin American equities or emerging markets debt is a good bit riskier than in a broad-based fund with a wide menu of portfolio options. If you owned a Southeast Asian equity fund in late 1997 or a Russian fund in 1998, you can't blame the portfolio manager for not beating the S&P 500. You might expect him to beat his peers, but certainly not dodge macroeconomic events.

What was your motivation in choosing this investment? If you were trying to seize upon a trading opportunity, like a big rally in Asian stocks, you might as well sell, since the opportunity didn't materialize. If you bought to diversify your portfolio and to take advantage of a long-term growth opportunity, you should hold on nonetheless—and perhaps even increase your investment. If you bought the fund to diversify your holdings, don't fret. Chances are some of your other funds are doing quite well.

Before you dump a mutual fund, you have to remember that few funds do well under all market conditions. What you should expect is that gains in up periods outweigh the losses in the down periods. The Vanguard Windsor Fund is a case in point. The fund, then managed by John B. Neff, fared only about half as well as the S&P 500 in 1989 and fell more than twice as much as the market during 1990. Neff's "value" style of investing, which has proved successful for years, leads him to buy out of favor, high-dividend-paying stocks like autos, banks, and insurers. Those were among the worst-performing stock groups of the year. But the history of Neff's style of investing is that when the tide turns his way, he more than makes up for downswings—and it happened. In 1992, Windsor more than doubled the returns of the S&P 500; in 1993, it nearly doubled the market index. And even in the difficult year of 1994, the fund finished slightly behind the total return of the S&P 500, but ahead of most mutual funds.

What if large-cap value funds performed well but Windsor didn't? Then you may have good reason to fire the fund. Indeed, it's because the best fund managers run into downdrafts that you diversify your mutual fund investments. That's why you might offset Windsor with, say, the Janus Fund or T. Rowe Price Blue Chip Growth, which choose companies for their earnings growth

When do you sell a laggard fund?

rather than value characteristics. If Windsor tried to boost its returns by loading up on small stocks of fast-growing high-tech companies, that too would be reason enough to dump the fund. Ask the professionals who advise pension funds on selection of investment managers: The only sin worse than underperforming the market is failing to stick to your stated investment discipline.

What if your fund's BUSINESS WEEK rating drops? Don't be too quick to dump. Sometimes funds' ratings fall because the fund manager messed up. Often they drop because other sorts of funds outperformed them and pushed their ratings down. Remember, only 7.5 percent of the rated funds (those with at least five years of performance history) earn an A. So it's not unusual for a fund having a good year to be knocked out of the A rating category by funds having a great year. A few years ago, the A-rated equity funds were dominated by value funds. In 1999, the A-rated equity funds were dominated by the large-cap growth and, to a lesser degree, large-cap blend funds. Does that mean you should sell the value funds? Not at all. Value funds are part of your core holdings. What you want to be sure of is that you have the best value funds, even if value funds are out of favor. So if your value fund dropped to a B+ or B overall rating, it would not be a cause for concern. What would be more worrisome is if a value fund's category rating dropped precipitously. That tells you that your fund is not measuring up very well to the other funds against which it competes.

So when do you get to sell an underperformer? If the fund is in a tax-deferred account—an IRA or a 401(k)—get rid of funds that have performed poorly relative to their peers. If the fund is in a taxable account, the decision is a little trickier. If you have a loss in the fund, or only a small gain, there's little problem in getting rid of the shares. But if you have owned the shares a long time and have amassed long-term capital gains, you have to do some further analysis.

Let's say you're considering selling a fund that would, although it's lagged of late, still trigger a $10,000 long-term capital gain. That means you've got $2000 in taxes to pay (20 percent maximum tax on long-term capital gains).

If you have losses against which you can shelter those gains (see more about that in Chapter 6), go ahead and sell. If there are no losses to offset the gain, the question becomes what are you going to do with the money that's going to earn back the $2000 you paid out in taxes? Perhaps you would be better off sticking with the lagging value fund. If the fund performed well when value funds were in favor before, perhaps this fund has the ability to outperform once again. At least, it's probably worth taking a chance.

Keep in Touch with Your Fund

When you buy a mutual fund you are, in effect, "hiring" an investment manager to do a job for you, such as investing in small- to medium-sized companies. So to oversee your fund portfolio, you have to make sure your managers are doing what they told you they would do. If you invest in a small-cap fund, you don't want the manager spending your money on IBM, AT&T, and GE.

Funds do change gears, but they're supposed to notify you. As a shareholder, you're entitled to get reports twice a year, though many funds report quarterly as well. But the information in a report may be quite dated by the time you see it. Funds have 90 days after the close of their half fiscal and full fiscal year to deliver shareholder reports. Still, even a somewhat dated report can be informative.

Shareholder reports vary in their content and presentation. The Gintel Fund, for instance, has a very simple report, but it's quite informative nonetheless (Figure 5-3). All fund reports will show the market value of a security on the day of the report. But Gintel also discloses the purchase price of the investment. That's a line-by-line report card on how the fund manager is doing.

The Gintel Fund lists its stocks by their value among the holdings in the portfolio. CheckFree Holdings Corp. is by far the largest holding, with 1,650,000 shares. What makes it the largest is not the number of shares, but the market value of those shares (price times the number of shares) which, the statement shows, is $38,568,750. Now compare that to the purchase cost of $27,926,136 and you can also see that the fund has a 38 percent profit in the stock. The biggest winner in the fund is Charter One Financial Corp., with a near 10-fold gain in the stock.

If thinking in millions is a little unwieldy, Gintel reports per-share cost and market value, too. By disclosing cost, this fund also shows its losing positions—stocks whose market value is now below the fund's cost. By comparing cost and market value, you can see that just one of the 12 stocks, Nobel Learning Communities, Inc., is in the red. (Gintel Fund has relatively few stocks because by charter it is a nondiversified fund. A diversified fund would have to have at least 20 stocks.)

But that cost information isn't usually in the reports. Typically, the reports show the security and its market value on the date of the report. The American Funds group, for instance, doesn't provide the shareholder costs, but does a good job in portfolio reporting. Look at Figure 5-4, from the 1997 Annual Report of Growth Fund of America. At the top, there's summary information on major industries in which the fund is invested and the 10 largest holdings. Without reading any further, the shareholder can see how his or her money is deployed. For instance, broadcasting and publishing is the largest indus-

FIGURE 5-3

Gintel Fund Statement of Net Assets			As of December 31, 1998
Number of Shares		Cost**	Market Value
	Common Stocks		
	Technology Related (30.5%)		
1,650,000	CheckFree Holdings Corporation*	$27,926,136	$38,568,750
200,000	C-Cube Microsystems Inc.*	5,101,583	5,425,000
	Insurance (19.1%)		
489,000	Mercury General Corporation	13,915,255	21,424,312
200,000	Conseco Inc.	5,918,750	6,112,500
	Security Protection System (8.1%)		
950,000	Checkpoint Systems, Inc.	10,987,848	11,756,250
	Manufacturing & Service (6.5%)		
660,000	Chart Industries, Inc.	2,082,305	5,032,500
175,000	Ogden Corporation	3,327,434	4,385,937
	Education (1.8%)		
475,000	Nobel Learning Communities, Inc.	3,474,094	2,612,500
	Savings & Loan (1.5%)		
78,750	Charter One Financial Corporation	225,820	2,185,313
	Broadcast Equipment (1.1%)		
100,000	Vertex Communications Corporation*	1,550,000	1,587,500
	Entertainment (1.1%)		
50,000	Imax Corporation*	1,202,950	1,581,250
	Medical Equipment (0.5%)		
700,000	Milestone Scientific Inc.*	769,478	787,500
	Miscellaneous Securities***(3.3%)	3,880,127	4,761,875
	Imputed Brokerage Commissions on Securities Owned	391,000	
	Total Common Stocks (73.5%)	80,752,780	106,221,187

FIGURE 5-4

Investment Portfolio

August 31, 1997

Largest Industry Holdings

Broadcasting & Publishing 13.95%

Electronic Components 12.19%

Data Processing & Reproduction 11.03%

Business & Public Services 8.50%

Health & Personal Care 5.07%

Cash & Equivalents 14.54%

Other Industries 34.72%

Largest Individual Holdings	Percent of Net Assets
Time Warner	4.09%
Federal National Mortgage Assn.	3.06
Philip Morris	2.67
America Online	2.55
Walt Disney	2.04
Intel	1.80
Texas Instruments	1.76
Tele-Communications, TCI Group	1.62
Comcast	1.61
Tele-Communications, Liberty Media Group	1.53

Equity Securities (Common & Preferred Stocks)

	Shares	Market Value (000)	Percent of Net Assets
Broadcasting & Publishing — 13.95%			
Time Warner Inc.	9,250,750	$476,414	4.09%
A leading media and entertainment company. Operations include publishing, film and TV production, recorded music and cable TV. Has acquired Turner Broadcasting System, Inc.			
Tele-Communications, Inc., Series A, TCI Group[1]	10,789,300	188,813	1.62
One of the largest cable operators in the U.S.			
Comcast Corp., Class A special stock	6,339,762	148,588	1.61
Comcast Corp., Class A	1,680,000	39,060	
One of the country's fastest growing cable TV operators. Also owns cellular telephone franchises and QVC, a cable shopping network.			
Tele-Communications, Inc., Series A, Liberty Media Group[1]	6,752,237	178,090	1.53
Owns a controlling stake in Turner Broadcasting System, Inc. and a 50% interest in The Discovery Channel.			
Viacom Inc., Class B[1]	6,000,000	177,750	1.53
Produces feature films and TV shows, operates TV and radio stations and owns several cable channels, the country's largest book publisher, Simon & Schuster, and Blockbuster Entertainment.			
News Corp. Ltd. (American Depositary Receipts) (Australia)	5,400,000	97,537	1.27
News Corp. Ltd., preferred (American Depositary Receipts)	3,363,750	50,876	
Owns broadcasting, newspaper, publishing and entertainment assets in North America, Europe, Australia and Asia.			
E.W. Scripps Co., Class A	1,660,000	65,259	.56
Owns newspapers, television and radio stations, and cable television systems across the U.S.			
Cox Communications, Inc., Class A[1]	2,000,000	54,125	.46
One of the largest cable TV operators in the U.S. and a fully diversified media company.			
Chris-Craft Industries, Inc.[1]	1,050,085	51,520	.44
A television broadcasting company.			

try sector in the portfolio, commanding 13.95 percent of the assets, and the second largest is electronic components, with 12.19 percent.

Then look at "Largest Individual Holdings." The single largest holding in the portfolio is Time Warner, one of the world's major media compa-nies, which alone accounts for 4.09 percent of the fund assets. Four other top 10 holdings come from the broadcasting and publishing, or media, sector—Walt Disney; Tele-Communications, TCI Group; Comcast; and Tele-Communications, Liberty Media Group. Intel and Texas Instruments, the No. 6 and No. 7 holdings, belong to the electronic components group.

If you want more information, there's plenty to follow. Look down the page. The first broad category listed is "Broadcasting & Publishing." Under that heading, the companies are listed according to the market value of the investment. Time Warner Inc., worth $476,414,000 at the time of the report, is first. What's informative about this report and others produced by American Funds is the description of the individual companies, something that is not often provided in mutual fund literature.

Most reports include a letter to shareholders from the president of the management company or from the portfolio manager. The letter typically discusses market conditions, though by the time you get the report the quarter will be long past. Twice a year, the fund is supposed to provide you with a copy of the portfolio. You don't have to second-guess the portfolio manager, but a quick scan might tell you a few things. If the fund is supposed to invest in small, fast-growing companies and you don't recognize many of the companies' names, then the fund manager is probably pursuing what he or she promised to pursue. If you have a high-quality bond fund and you find it's peppered with junk bonds, you ought to ask a few questions. Don't be bashful. Call the fund company and ask for an explanation.

The quality of shareholder reports varies widely. Some fund managers are brutally frank when they have had a period of bad performance; others are elliptical or evasive, and never admit head-on when their results are poor. Charles T. Freeman, portfolio manager of the Vanguard Windsor Fund, includes a report card on his performance by comparing the performance of major fund holdings with their industry group. It's a practice he carried on from his predecessor, John B. Neff. For instance, in the October 31, 1998 annual report, Freeman gave himself A+ based on the performance of his investments in communication service companies (AT&T, Comcast, and MCI Worldcom, the most significant of the lot) and A– for his technology picks (General Instrument was the big hit). But the rest of the grades were awful. Freeman gave himself two F's for his 14 percent positions in both energy and basic materials. Both categories were awful performers, mainly because of global slumps in energy and basic commodities like aluminum, chemicals, and paper. For his financial and health-care stocks, Freeman gave himself D+'s. In his com-

ments, Freeman said the summer sell-off in bank stocks that was related to the emerging markets crisis sank Windsor's holdings, but he argued that the stocks were undervalued and should be held. Indeed, in the weeks after the report was written, these stocks did improve. Few funds are as informative and frank as Windsor, though Vanguard, in general, provides fairly complete reports.

Morningstar analysts also rate mutual-fund reports. They look at the amount of financial information above and beyond what's required by law and the presentation. Is it organized in a reader-friendly manner? Can the shareholder learn something about the investment from the reports?

At one time, Morningstar discovered some correlation between shareholder reports and good returns. In a 1993 study, analysts found that 45 funds with A ratings on their shareholder reports had five-year average annual returns of 20.8 percent. Funds with B-rated reports had an 18.1 percent average annual return for the five-year period. The funds with reports rated B through D all had average annual returns around 15.5 percent. There were only six funds that flunked. But these funds with F-rated reports had nothing much to say for themselves. Their five-year average annual return was a skimpy 4.7 percent. In 1998, we asked Morningstar to revisit the study. This time, there was a similar correlation between quality of reports and the strength of returns. What's more, shareholders don't have to pay a lot more to get a good report. The study found that funds with better-rated reports had lower expense ratios.

There are other times that you hear from a fund. Every time the prospectus is updated, you should get a new copy. That's to keep in your files. If there has been some major change in policy, such as imposition of a load or 12(b)-1 fee, or a change in redemption procedures, it should be highlighted or noted to investors in a separate letter.

Finally, most mutual funds are corporations, registered in various states and governed by the laws of that state. If the state requires annual meetings, your fund will send you a proxy statement, a proxy card, and an invitation to the meeting. At the least, the proxy will have a ballot for election of the fund directors and the hiring of the auditors.

If the fund management contract is up for renewal as well, you'll be asked to approve that, along with any changes in fees or sales charges.

> Shareholder reports vary widely in quality.

Late in 1997, for instance, the shareholders of the Acorn Fund overwhelmingly approved the management company's request for a hike in the management fee schedule that added about 0.25 percentage points to the fund's expenses. Management argued that the costs of hiring top investment talent were climbing and the fund needed to pay more to stay competitive. The fund has an excellent long-term record, said management, and added that even with the increase, the expense ratio, about 0.87 percent, would be well below the industry average.

Shareholders also may be asked to okay mergers and changes in investment management firms and do such routine things as elect directors (from a list of nominees) and ratify the board's choice of auditors. If there is any change in investment policy, it should also be a ballot question. For instance, many domestic equity funds have changed policy to allow investment in foreign securities, usually with a limit on the per-

centage of fund assets that can be invested abroad. If you're against that in principle, then vote no. But the overwhelming chances are that you'll be outvoted.

One of the more unusual proposals that fund shareholders were faced with during 1998 came from the Yacktman Fund. Fund founder and portfolio manager Donald Yacktman initiated a proxy battle to oust four of the six directors. The reason, said Yacktman, was that these directors had turned against him, and he feared they would oust him, leaving the Yacktman Fund without Don Yacktman. True, Yacktman's short-term results were poor at the time, as were those of many funds with like investment policies. Yacktman said he was trying to stay true to his small- and mid-cap value discipline, ostensibly the reason most investors bought the fund.

The dissenting directors, in turn, charged Yacktman was not properly supervising the portfolio. Yacktman won the proxy fight hands down, as might have been expected. No doubt, many investors who had soured on him had already sold their shares, and by the time of the proxy, most of those left who were qualified to vote were Yacktman stalwarts. The irony here is that the directors Yacktman tried to oust spent the fund's (yes, shareholder money) to fight Yacktman, the manager whom most of the shareholders wanted to run their fund.

Still, such battles are rare. Most of the time, proxies are about pretty mundane affairs. You may be disposed to dismiss the proxies as not even being worth your time to read and consider. But don't toss them, not even seemingly innocuous proxies from money-market funds (Figures 5-5 and 5-6). Vote, sign, and return them in the postage-prepaid envelope. You don't have to vote yes, and you can abstain. It's critical to return the proxy because the funds need a quorum to hold a meeting. (In signing the proxy, you give persons named on the statement the ability to vote your shares as you direct.) You have as many votes as you have shares. If a fund fails to obtain enough proxies for a quorum, it will have to conduct another mailing. And shareholders bear the cost of proxy solicitation.

Few funds have meetings anymore. Many conduct votes by proxy without convening a meeting. The meeting is an opportunity to ask questions of fund managers, but there probably isn't anything you're going to learn in person that you can't find out from a phone call or letter to the shareholder services department.

FIGURE 5-5

T.RowePrice
T. Rowe Price Associates, Inc., 100 East Pratt Street, Baltimore, MD 21202

James S. Riepe
Managing Director

Dear Shareholder:

All of the T. Rowe Price mutual funds will hold shareholder meetings in 1994 to elect directors, ratify the selection of independent accountants, and approve amendments to a number of investment policies.

The T. Rowe Price funds are not required to hold annual meetings each year if the only items of business are to elect directors or ratify accountants. In order to save fund expenses, most of the funds have not held annual meetings for a number of years. There are, however, conditions under which the funds must ask shareholders to elect directors, and one is to comply with a requirement that a minimum number have been elected by shareholders, not appointed by the funds' boards. Since the last annual meetings of the T. Rowe Price funds, several directors have retired and new directors have been added. In addition, a number of directors will be retiring in the near future.

Given this situation, we believed it appropriate to hold annual meetings for all the T. Rowe Price funds in 1994. At the same time, we reviewed the investment policies of all of the funds for consistency and to assure the portfolio managers have the flexibility they need to manage your money in today's fast changing financial markets. The changes being recommended, which are explained in detail in the enclosed proxy material, **do not alter the funds' investment objectives or basic investment programs.**

In many cases the proposals are common to several funds, so we have combined certain proxy statements to save on fund expenses. For those of you who own more than one of these funds, the combined proxy may also save you the time of reading more than one document before you vote and mail your ballots. The proposals which are specific to an individual fund are easily identifiable on the Notice and in the proxy statement discussion. If you own more than one fund, please note that **each fund has a separate card. You should vote and sign each one,** then return all of them to us in the enclosed postage-paid envelope.

Your early response will be appreciated and could save your fund the substantial costs associated with a follow-up mailing. We know we are asking you to review a rather formidable proxy statement, but this approach represents the most efficient one for your fund as well as for the other funds. Thank you for your cooperation. If you have any questions, please call us at 1-800-225-5132.

Sincerely,

James S. Riepe
Director, Mutual Funds Division

CUSIP#779572106/fund#065

FIGURE 5-6

T.RowePrice — We Need Your Proxy Vote Before April 20, 1994

Please refer to the Proxy Statement discussion of each of these matters.

THIS PROXY WHEN PROPERLY EXECUTED WILL BE VOTED IN THE MANNER DIRECTED HEREIN BY THE SHAREHOLDER. IF NO DIRECTION IS MADE, THIS PROXY WILL BE VOTED FOR ALL PROPOSALS.

- Please fold and detach card at perforation before mailing. - - - - - - - - - - - - - -

1. Election of directors. FOR all nominees listed below ☐ WITHHOLD AUTHORITY to vote ☐ 1.
    (except as marked to the contrary) for all nominees listed below

(INSTRUCTION: TO WITHHOLD AUTHORITY TO VOTE FOR AN INDIVIDUAL NOMINEE STRIKE A LINE THROUGH THE NOMINEE'S NAME IN THE LIST BELOW.)

Leo C. Bailey   Donald W. Dick, Jr.   David K. Fagin   Addison Lanier   John H. Laporte   John K. Major
Hanne M. Merriman   James S. Riepe   Hubert D. Vos   Paul M. Wythes

2. Approve changes to the Fund's fundamental policies.   FOR each policy listed below (except ☐   ABSTAIN ☐ 2.
    as marked to the contrary)

If you do **NOT** wish to approve a policy change, please check the appropriate box below:

☐ (A) Borrowing	☐ (E) Purchasing Securities	☐ (I) Investment Companies	☐ (M) Ownership of Securities
☐ (B) Commodities & Futures	☐ (F) Real Estate	☐ (J) Purchasing on Margin	☐ (N) Illiquid Securities
☐ (C) Lending	☐ (G) Senior Securities	☐ (K) Oil & Gas	☐ (O) Short Sales
☐ (D) Single Issuer	☐ (H) Control	☐ (L) Options	☐ (P) Unseasoned Issuers

3. Ratify the selection of Coopers & Lybrand as independent accountants.   FOR ☐   AGAINST ☐   ABSTAIN ☐ 3.

4. I authorize the Proxies, in their discretion, to vote upon such other business as may properly come before the meeting.

CUSIP#779572106 / fund#065

- -

T. ROWE PRICE OTC FUND, INC.   MEETING: 8:00 A.M. EASTERN TIME

THIS PROXY IS SOLICITED ON BEHALF OF THE BOARD OF DIRECTORS

The undersigned hereby appoints John H. Laporte and James S. Riepe, as proxies, each with the power to appoint his substitute, and hereby authorizes them to represent and to vote, as designated below, all shares of stock of the Fund, which the undersigned is entitled to vote at the Annual Meeting of Shareholders to be held on Wednesday, April 20, 1994, at the time indicated above, at the offices of the Fund, 100 East Pratt Street, Baltimore, Maryland 21202, and at any and all adjournments thereof, with respect to the matters set forth below and described in the Notice of Annual Meeting and Proxy Statement dated March 9, 1994, receipt of which is hereby acknowledged.

Please sign exactly as name appears. Only authorized officers should sign for corporations. For information as to the voting of stock registered in more than one name, see page 3 of the Notice of Annual Meeting and Proxy Statement.

Dated: _____ , 1994

_____
Signature(s)
CUSIP#779572106 / fund#065

When the Fund Manager Changes

One of the toughest questions in mutual fund investing is what to do when the portfolio manager changes, especially "star" managers like Peter Lynch, who piloted the Fidelity Magellan Fund to tremendous successes and took an early retirement from fund management in 1990. Of course, Lynch's departure was big news. But how do you know if there's been a change in portfolio managers?

For starters, the management company has to tell you in the fund documents. That's a new development in fund regulation. Until a few years ago, funds were under no obligation to tell and many preferred not to. And, in case you haven't picked up on it before, BUSINESS WEEK Mutual Fund Scoreboard also notes when the portfolio manager of an equity fund has changed.

Does a change in leadership matter? It depends on the sort of fund. With a money-market fund and even many bond funds, the manager may not matter much at all. And some fund management companies, such as the American Funds and American Century Investors, take a

Should you sell a fund if the manager leaves?

team approach to investment management, so one portfolio manager may hardly be missed. When Vanguard Windsor's Neff retired a few years ago, he was succeeded by Charles T. Freeman, a deputy who spent 25 years at his side. That fund's investors could be fairly confident that the fund would continue to be managed in a similar style.

That's not always the case. With most equity funds the manager has a lot of latitude. When Peter Lynch retired from the Fidelity Magellan Fund, mutual fund analysts were split over whether to sell. Six months after Lynch's departure, those who sold looked smart. It wasn't that Morris Smith, Lynch's successor, fumbled. Just weeks after he took over the reins, the stock market went into a swoon. True, Magellan underperformed a poorly performing market. But the fund is so large, and owns so many stocks, that it's quite possible that the performance in the second half of 1990 might not have been much different had Lynch remained at the helm.

In 1991, when the stock market rallied, so did Magellan, up 41 percent for the year. But early in 1992, Smith, citing a need for a break, left the fund, too. Jeffrey Vinik, Smith's successor, also trailed the market early in his tenure, and some analysts wondered whether it was time to leave the fund. But Vinik had an excellent track record (he formerly ran Fidelity Contrafund and Fidelity Growth & Income Fund). In 1993, in fact, Magellan posted a 24.7 percent total return, more than doubling the return of the S&P 500—one of the best relative performances since the early 1980s, when the $31.7 billion fund was then less than $1 billion in size. In 1996, Vinik invested 20 percent of the fund in Treasury bonds—and the bond market sank. He left the fund at the end of May. He was succeeded by Robert E. Stansky, another top manager, who has delivered good results since.

Neither Lynch's, Smith's, nor Vinik's departure was fatal for Magellan because Fidelity has an deep pool of managerial talent and an army of talented research analysts. In fact, the company changes fund managers frequently. In 1996, however, the company made a slew of changes in the spring to try to improve sagging performance. Later in the year, manager departures resulted in further shifts. More than half the equity funds got new managers during 1996. The short-term impact, at least, was not good. Most of Fidelity's diversified U.S. equity funds trailed the market through 1997, but by 1998, they were firing on

nearly all cylinders once again. Even Fidelity Magellan delivered a knockout performance—up 33.2 percent versus 28.6 percent for the S&P 500.

Perhaps to protect against the investors' following a star manager out the door, many fund companies have been naming co-managers to funds. The idea, at least, is that if one manager leaves, the second provides continuity and the fund company can say the same management is in place. So when Carlene Murphy Ziegler, co-manager of Strong Opportunity and Strong Common Stock, resigned in 1994, co-manager Dick Weiss was still in place, along with Marina Carlson, who had been named as an additional co-manager earlier in the year.

Even so, many investment managers and financial planners switch funds when a well-regarded fund manager leaves. There have been no definitive studies yet, but Morningstar, for example, uncovered some interesting anecdotal evidence in late 1990. It looked at five managers who switched funds and measured how the old funds had done since the switch versus how the new funds performed under the star managers. In all five cases, investors following the manager to the new fund would have done better.

But there's anecdotal evidence to the contrary as well. Look at Donald Yacktman, who fought to oust some of his own fund's directors in 1998. He left Selected American Fund back in 1992 to set up the Yacktman Fund. The results, so far, have been mixed. But Yacktman's departure from Selected American also spurred an unusual chain of events. Selected Financial Services, the management company, replaced Yacktman with another manager. Unhappy with the performance, the independent directors of the fund—members of the board of directors who were not Selected employees—voted to dismiss Selected as the management company and hired Shelby Davis, the highly regarded manager of the Davis New York Venture Fund, to run the fund. (Davis retired in 1997, but his son runs the fund now.)

Sometimes there's a change when the ownership of a fund management company is taken over. In 1992, for instance, Franklin Resources, which owns Franklin Funds, took over the Templeton fund company but left the Templeton fund managers in place, since Franklin bought Templeton in part for its investment expertise. No need to change. When T. Rowe Price Associates took over the USF&G funds, it folded most of them into existing T. Rowe Price funds. So those fund investors got new managers. In cases like that, investors may want to review the record of the new managers. In late 1993, Pioneering Management, the company that manages the Pioneer family of funds, took over five Mutual of Omaha funds, but did not merge them into its own funds. Instead, in all but one municipal bond fund, Pioneer installed its own portfolio managers. In such a case, find out which other funds your new manager has run and check out his or her records.

Or look at the situation when the management company brings in a new manager to revamp a laggard fund. That's what happened in early 1997 when Warburg Pincus lured Brian Posner away from Fidelity to run its once-golden but then lagging Warburg Pincus Growth & Income Fund. Berger Funds did the same a month later, when it hired Patrick Adams, formerly of Founders and Kemper Funds, to revamp the laggard Berger 100. At the end of 1996 these funds' shareholders were hurting: their trailing three-year records were only half that of the average U.S. diversified funds.

Long-time shareholders applauded both moves, and by the end of the year, the results were mixed. Posner succeeded in repositioning his fund and managed a hefty 30.3 percent total return. Adams overhauled his portfolio as well, but the results were not nearly as good—just a 13 percent total return, about the same as the last year under the previous manager. Worse yet, both new managers traded away much of the portfolios and created large capital gains distributions. Posner's results were strong enough that the aftertax return was still about 23 percent. Under Adams, Berger 100's wan 13 percent pretax return shrank to 4.5 percent aftertax.

What created the large taxable distributions was exactly what the two managers had been brought in to do: overhaul and, hopefully, reinvigorate the funds. To those who had held the fund in tax-deferred accounts, the distributions were nonevents. And to taxable investors who had been in the funds a long time, the tax on the distributions was probably a small price to pay to get their investments back on track—at least the Warburg fund seems like it is.

But any taxable investor who rushed to buy these funds after the new managers were appointed did not get any great deals. Moral of the story: if a lagging fund gets a hot new manager, wait until the portfolio has been overhauled—and the resultant gains distributed. Otherwise, you can end up paying taxes on profits you never made.

Mutual Fund Mergers

For the most part, if a fund does a reasonable job of meeting its investment objectives, the management company isn't going to tinker with success. Most of the time poorly performing funds or funds in poorly performing sectors of the stock market are the ones that get a makeover. Often, the makeover is simply merging the weaker fund into a stronger one.

A mutual fund merger can take place in one of several ways. For instance, several funds within the same family may be combined. That's what is usually done with small, poorly performing funds. Such funds are in a Catch-22 situation. Since they're very small, they tend to have higher overhead and expense ratios, which cut into their total returns. And without strong returns, they are unable to attract new investments—and so they remain small.

For instance, in 1994, Oppenheimer Funds (with shareholder approval, of course) renamed the Oppenheimer Global Bio-Tech Fund—the top-performing fund of 1991—the Global Emerging Growth Fund, giving the fund a much broader investment mandate. Then it merged the smaller Oppenheimer Global Environmental Fund into the Emerging Growth Fund. Oppenheimer officials said the company made the switches to get out of the sector fund business. Because of bear markets in both sectors, neither fund was flourishing or attracting new money. As an emerging growth fund, of course, the fund could invest in biotech and environmental companies, as well as a whole lot more.

Another sort of merger is when a small fund family leaves the business entirely and turns over the funds' management to a major management company. Some of the companies that gave up fund management over the last several years had funds with combined assets of less than $100 million.

Then there's the "rationalization" merger, when two companies combine and try to streamline the fund offerings by merging like funds. That's what happened in 1994, when Smith Barney Inc. merged 12 funds—including five money-market mutual funds—it had picked up in the Shearson acquisition. Among those merged was the underperforming Smith Barney Shearson Sector Analysis Portfolio, run by Wall Street

Investors may benefit from a fund merger.

guru Elaine M. Garzarelli, folded into what is now Smith Barney Strategic Investors.

The best bet is that you will see more fund company mergers in the next few years as industry growth slows and companies combine to achieve more economies of scale. Fund companies are also combining to broaden their product lines. That's some of the motive behind the 1994 merger of Van Kampen Merritt, a fixed-income group, with American Capital, which is more of an equity-fund manager. In 1996, the combined company was purchased by Morgan Stanley, which managed mainly international funds. But in 1997, Morgan Stanley agreed to merge with Dean Witter Discover & Co., and Dean Witter has a wide range of funds.

What does it mean for fund shareholders when the management companies merge? Depends on the merger. After Franklin Resources bought Templeton (1992) and Mutual Series (1996), fees rose somewhat. That's not surprising. Franklin paid handsomely for both and wanted to recoup its investment. Still, investors who owned any of the Mutual Series Funds prior to the merger got "Z" class shares, which gave them the right to continue to invest in their fund and any other Mutual Series Fund on a no-load basis. New shareholders pay a load. The Zurich Group bought Kemper Funds in 1995 and Scudder Stevens & Clark in 1997, but the results of that merger are not yet all that apparent. There have been marginal performance gains at Kemper, and it's too soon to see any changes at Scudder. United Asset Management acquired Pacific Financial (Clipper Fund) in 1997, and there's been no apparent effect on fund performance.

Some of these fund-company linkups will no doubt result in mergers at the fund level. It would be unlikely for a Kemper load fund to merge with a Scudder no-load, but you might find a successful fund on either side cloned for the other one. That's potentially a plus for shareholders.

If the merger is of, say, two no-load companies or two load companies, then you're more likely to see poorly performing funds merged into larger, stronger funds. This can be a blessing. You get new fund shares for the old in a tax-free exchange. The new management company usually folds the acquired funds into its own, trying to match up funds with similar objectives.

Change Objectives, Change Funds

Investors' objectives, their ability to assume risks, and their income needs change over time—usually in a gradual and predictable way. But sometimes the changes are abrupt, such as the loss of a job or the death of a spouse. Should objectives change, investors might find that, while their small-cap growth fund has done a good job, it is no longer an appropriate investment for them.

Likewise, changes in tax status may also dictate a shift in funds. As income increases, so should the relative attractiveness of tax-exempt bond and money-market funds. Once in retirement, an investor might find that taxable bond funds offer more return even after paying taxes. These sorts of shifts don't need to happen all at once, and in fact might best be accomplished in stages. If moving funds results in a capital gains tax liability, the investor might want to spread the move out over several tax years.

Taxes and Record-Keeping

By now, you're gung ho on mutual funds. Good returns, smart management, diversification, low costs, and ease of investing make them wonderful investments. What's the catch? For all the conveniences of investing in mutual funds, there is one big drawback. Depending on the funds you choose, you just may generate a blizzard of paper. Tempted as you may be to ignore or throw away those confirmation statements, don't. At some time you may sell shares of a fund or liquidate all your holdings in the fund. Then you're going to need those records.

Each time you make an investment in a fund, you'll get a statement from the fund management company (Figure 6-1). It will show the date and amount of the investment, the dollar price per share, the number of shares purchased, and the total number of shares in the fund. Redemptions trigger more paper. Switch dollars from, say, a long-term bond fund to a money-market fund, and you may get three statements: one from the bond fund showing the redemption of shares, one from the money-market fund showing a new investment, and another statement indicating an exchange has taken place.

Suppose you are making monthly investments as part of your own dollar-cost averaging program. That's 12 statements a year. And every year the statements should be cumulative. That is, the year's first statement shows a balance forward and the number of shares carried over from the previous year. Then, after the January purchase, you'll get a statement showing the January account activity. In February, it will show February and January. In March, you get all three months, and so forth. By December you should have the entire year's transactions on one statement. So one way to cut down on the file space is to toss out the previous 11 months' statements, as long as you have an up-to-date record of the account activity.

Remember, too, that your investments and redemptions are not the only transactions that generate paper. Every time the fund pays a dividend or capital gains distribution, another statement goes into the mail. Many funds make distributions monthly or quarterly. That can trigger more paper, too. It's enough to make you want to buy growth-oriented equity funds, since most of them make distributions only once a year.

Now, imagine a fund that you bought on several occasions and at various prices, whose shares you sold a few times, also at various prices, and whose earned distributions were reinvested in the funds, also at various prices. You have tons of paper to start with. But your biggest headache isn't paper—it's taxes.

No, even the computer won't stop the blizzard. Good software will help you keep track of the information and make it easier to manage. But the postal service is going to keep on delivering the statements. And the information on each of them has to be entered properly into the program.

Mutual Funds' Special Tax Status

Understanding mutual funds and taxes takes a little extra effort. There's a set of rules that governs how the mutual fund must behave to keep its special tax status. (The rules apply to closed-end funds, too.) And then, once the fund has paid out its earnings, it's up to the shareholders to keep track of them properly. If you miss reporting a dividend or capital gains distribution (the fund sends out 1099-DIVs telling you exactly how much), you're likely to get a letter from the IRS and a bill for the taxes due—plus interest and a penalty.

FIGURE 6-1

December 31, 1997, year-to-date   Page 1 of 2

Vanguard Index Trust-
Total Stock Market Portfolio

||I..I...I...I.I.I.I....II....II.I..I.II.I....I.III......III
SAMPLE SHAREHOLDER
123 ANYROAD ST
ANYTOWN PA 19191-1919

For prompt service when calling please provide your
Statement number: 001234567
(800) 284-7245   –   Voyager Service
(800) 662-6273   –   Tele-Account
Fund number: 85
Account number: 987654321

ACCOUNT VALUE	On 12/31/1996	On 12/31/1997
	$ 44,007.19	$ 66,617.84

Trade date	Transaction	Dollar amount	Share price	Shares transacted	Total shares owned
	Balance on 12/31/1996		$ 17.77		2,476.488
3/25	Income dividend .06	$ 148.59	18.50	8.032	2,484.520
3/25	ST cap gain .01	24.76	18.50	1.338	2,485.858
3/25	LT cap gain .03	74.29	18.50	4.016	2,489.874
6/25	Income dividend .06	149.39	20.76	7.196	2,497.070
9/24	Income dividend .06	149.82	22.58	6.635	2,503.705
12/03	Check purchase	9,000.00	23.10	389.610	2,893.315
12/23	Income dividend .142	410.85	21.89	18.769	2,912.084
12/23	ST cap gain .08	231.47	21.89	10.574	2,922.658
12/23	LT cap gain .15	434.00	21.89	19.826	2,942.484
	Balance on 12/31/1997		$ 22.64		2,942.484

Income dividends	$ 858.65
Short-term gains	256.23
Long-term gains	508.29
Total income year-to-date	$ 1,623.17
Purchases year-to-date	$ 9,000.00

Total cost basis on 12/31/1997	$ 39,467.79
Average cost per share	13.41

The current Fund distribution was payable on
January 2, 1998.

Remember, if you sell shares of a fund, the fund company also has to report the proceeds of the sale to the IRS. That means you will have to account for that transaction as well. You won't forget to do it, since the fund will remind you with Form 1099-B. (Like the 1099-DIV, you get one copy, the IRS gets the other.) There may be taxes due, or you may actually have a loss that can be applied as a deduction against them. Without good records, you could end up paying too little in taxes and get caught, or, worse yet, paying more tax than necessary.

Let's start with the tax status of the mutual fund itself. Remember, most mutual funds are also corporations, and shareholders of corporations, in effect, pay tax twice. The corporation pays taxes on its earnings and, if any of the earnings are paid to shareholders as dividends, they're taxed again as part of shareholders' income. But mutual funds escape this double taxation. The fund is treated as a "conduit"—all the income and responsibility for paying the tax on that income pass through the fund to its shareholders.

To keep their special tax status, mutual funds have to live within rigorous rules. There are requirements about diversification. For instance, a fund can't hold more than 10 percent of the outstanding voting stock in a particular company.

Mutual funds must distribute 98 percent of their income and dividends—and do it in the calendar year in which they are earned. In addition, the funds must distribute 98 percent of their net realized capital gains—both short- and long-term capital gains. (Tax-exempt funds must distribute 90 percent of their tax-exempt income.) A fund that fails to meet this distribution test can be hit with a 4 percent excise tax on the undistributed income.

How much a fund distributes in income and capital gains has direct bearing on its aftertax return. (More on aftertax returns in Chapter 7.) Suppose two mutual funds have the same pretax total return. One made no income or capital gains distributions because it did not buy dividend-bearing stocks and tended to hold rather than trade the stocks in the portfolio. The second fund had the same total return, but about half of it came in the form of distributions. The one that made no distributions would have the higher aftertax return. Of course, if the fund is held in an IRA or other tax-deferred plan, the distributions don't matter. But if the account is taxable, a fund's history and policy of making distributions is a real concern in deciding whether to invest in a particular fund.

When looking at the distributions, remember that not all are taxed equally. Distributions of dividends, interest income, and short-term capital gains are taxed at the same rate at which the shareholder's earned income is taxed—and that can be as high as 39.6 percent. Long-term capital gains—and they're long-term if they were generated by investments held for more than 12 months—get the most favorable tax treatment: The maximum rate is 20 percent, no matter how high the shareholder's regular tax rate is.

Many funds, especially those that practice a buy-and-hold investment strategy, often have huge unrealized and undistributed capital gains in their portfolios. Morningstar, Inc. measures these gains and expresses the magnitude as a percentage of the fund's total holdings. BUSINESS WEEK now includes this number in the Scoreboard under the heading "Untaxed Gains" (see Chapter 7).

Suppose a fund has an untaxed gain of 30 percent. That means 30 percent of the portfolio is unrealized capital gains. If the fund were liquidated tomorrow at $10 a share, the locked-in profits would be unlocked or "realized" in tax terms, and $3 would come back to shareholders as a capital gain. Some investors are wary of funds with high untaxed gains because they think they may be stuck paying tax on the capital gains earned long before they went into the fund.

Sometimes mutual funds have realized net losses, rather than realized gains. But tax rules do not allow mutual funds to distribute their losses to their shareholders. However, the funds can carry the losses forward for eight years and use them to offset future taxable gains. Some Asian funds are in that position right now. As those markets recover, the funds are able to offset their gains with these losses.

That may not assuage those who watched their funds undergo partial meltdowns, but it does suggest an investment strategy. Provided a fund meets all your other criteria, investing in a fund with tax losses makes sense. Some other investors realized the loss, but as a new investor to the fund you can get the benefit of the gains they shelter.

Though fund directors can vote to make the distributions at any time, tax considerations result in distributions piling up toward the end of the year. Some funds have a policy of making quarterly income distributions and some may make capital gains distributions at least once during the year. But if a fund has any income or gains to distribute, you can count on most funds making payouts in December. Sometimes the distribution may even be declared on December 31 and not paid until January. That doesn't get shareholders out of paying taxes on it for the year that ended in December.

Mutual fund companies usually mail Form 1099-DIVs to shareholders by the end of January. This form reports dividend distributions, capital gains distributions—broken out to show those that are short-term and those that are long-term—and, if applicable, taxes paid to foreign governments. (That may come into play in international funds.) Nontaxable distributions should be noted here, too. Check the figures against your own records and make sure they're correct. The numbers you see on the form are the same numbers that the IRS is going to see.

> Mutual fund distributions bunch up at year-end.

Ducking the Distribution

It's a good idea to start checking with funds around Thanksgiving to ask about upcoming distributions. A customer service representative will usually know if a distribution is planned. Sometimes the fund management company will announce the exact date and the per-share distribution rate. Some will give shareholders who ask an estimate of the time and the amount to be paid. You may have to keep calling until you get the information. The funds themselves often don't know the date and size of the distribution until late into the year.

You may recall some brouhaha surrounding the Fidelity Magellan Fund a few years back. What had happened was that Fidelity, as is common practice, told investors in November 1994 that Magellan would make a $4.32 per-share capital gains distribution in December. No doubt some Magellan investors may have made tax-related moves, such as selling Magellan or taking losses in other funds to shelter the Magellan gain. Three weeks later, Fidelity said oops, we made a mistake. There isn't going to be a distribution.

The incident was a stunner, not because anybody lost any real money, but because the large estimation error—in excess of $2 billion—was in the largest equity fund and was made by the largest mutual fund management company. But fortunately, such errors about distributions are rare and, needless to say, Fidelity and others are going to be double, triple, and quadruple checking those estimates in the future.

There are several good reasons to obtain the distribution information near the end of the year. First, if you are planning any new fund investments, you have to be careful about purchasing shares right before the distribution dates. You could end up getting a distribution of profits earned long before you ever invested in the fund (see Chapter 4).

You may also want to get out of a fund ahead of the distribution date, for much the same reason. For instance, just look back at 1997. Suppose you had invested in a small-cap growth fund early in the year. Pretend for a moment you paid $10 a share.

Then move ahead to early December when the fund has lost 20 percent of what you paid for it. But remember that early in the year the market rallied. What if the fund manager had used the rally to take some profits amounting to $1 per share? The fund would have to distribute those profits before the end of the year. If you still owned the fund, you would be hit with a taxable distribution of capital gains. You would be stuck paying taxes on gains, but your investment, so far, is actually showing a loss.

That's why you should consider selling the fund before the distribution. If you do so, you can realize a tax-deductible loss. Then you have one

of two alternatives. If you want to remain fully invested, you can switch to a fund with a similar investment policy—but after that fund has made its distributions for the year. Or, you can stay on the sidelines for 31 days and then return to your fund. The risk in that ploy is that the fund will go up in price a bit before you can get back in. The IRS says you have to wait 31 days before buying back a fund sold for a tax loss—otherwise the loss will be disallowed as a deduction.

Tax Swapping

As the year rolls to a close, some investors like to do "tax swapping." The term comes from the bond market, but can apply to any investment. The idea is to look for a fund in which you may have an unrealized loss and then sell the fund to take the loss and generate a tax deduction. At the same time, you move a like amount of money into a mutual fund with characteristics similar to the one just sold (Table 6-1). The idea is to take advantage of your losses—make the best of a bad situation—while keeping your investment program in place.

Swapping within the same fund family is easiest. In large fund families there is often more than one fund with similar objectives. You may want to switch the Fidelity Contrafund for the Fidelity Dividend Growth Fund. They're both mid-cap blend funds. Fidelity Equity–Income and Equity–Income II, as their names might suggest, are also interchangeable.

Load fund investors should find it most practical to remain within their fund groups. Investors are usually able to switch load funds without paying another load, as long as the load of the new fund is less than or equal to the old one. For instance, if an investor moves her money from a fund on which she paid a 4 percent load into another fund in the same family that has a 5.5 percent load, she will probably have to pay only a 1.5 percent load to make up the difference.

Some advisers discourage investors from swapping funds purely for tax purposes. If a swap triggers redemption fees or new sales charges, that has to be figured in to determine whether there would be any benefit from the trade. If, on the other hand, you can justify selling one fund and buying another as a good investment decision, then the ability to save some money on taxes takes a little of the bite out of the loss.

Avoid the distribution if you can.

TABLE 6-1

SAVING ON TAXES BY SWAPPING FUNDS

If you have a loss in a mutual fund, you may want to sell it for a tax loss. If so, you may want to shift the money into a similar fund so as not to change your investment goals. The funds within each grouping have similar investment policies and risk profiles. They can make suitable swaps.

FUNDS	COMMENTS
FIDELITY CONTRAFUND	Contrafund (or the new Contrafund II) and Dividend Growth make good
FIDELITY DIVIDEND GROWTH	switch candidates under the Fidelity umbrella. Likewise, these Janus funds
JANUS MERCURY	are similar enough to make good switch candidates as well.
JANUS OLYMPUS	
FIDELITY EQUITY-INCOME	Clone funds can make good swap candidates. These Fidelity equity–income
FIDELITY EQUITY-INCOME II	funds are fairly similar. Likewise, the two Vanguard funds don't share the
VANGUARD WELLESLEY INCOME	same name, but they're close in investment style and practice.
VANGUARD WELLINGTON	
FIDELITY EMERGING MARKETS	The two emerging markets funds, though offered by different companies,
LEXINGTON WORLDWIDE EMERGING MARKETS	should be similar enough for tax-swapping. The T. Rowe Price and Scudder
T. ROWE PRICE INTERNATIONAL STOCK	international funds have similar portfolio characteristics.
SCUDDER INTERNATIONAL	
TEMPLETON GROWTH	Many Templeton equity funds are interchangeable. The Developing Markets,
TEMPLETON VALUE	Foreign, Real Estate, and Small Companies funds are unique, and are not
TEMPLETON WORLD	interchangeable with each other nor other Templeton funds.
BABSON ENTERPRISE II	These funds are all from the small-cap value category. Their companies are
FAM VALUE	usually prosaic rather than cutting edge, but that doesn't mean they can't
FIDELITY LOW-PRICED STOCK	make money for mutual fund shareholders.
ROYCE VALUE	
AIM CONSTELLATION	These funds comb the market for companies with earnings momentum, and
AIM SELECT GROWTH	they try to hang on to them as long as earnings growth is accelerating. The
AMER. CENT.–20TH CENT. GROWTH INVESTORS	AIM funds are load, American Century and PBHG, no-load.
ULTRA INVESTORS	
BABSON BOND	Swapping bond funds is easier than equity, since these funds usually have
FIDELITY INVESTMENT GRADE BOND	easily identifiable investment characteristics such as maturity, credit quality,
VANGUARD TOTAL BOND MARKET INDEX	and tax status.
INVESCO HIGH-YIELD	All high-yield, or junk bond funds, are not alike. These all have the reputation
T. ROWE PRICE HIGH-YIELD	for investing in "better quality" junk bonds.
VANGUARD CORP. HIGH-YIELD	

DATA: MORNINGSTAR INC., BUSINESS WEEK

What's My "Cost Basis"?

Mention the term *cost basis*, and eyes glaze over. But it's not a big deal. It's just a measure of how much money you put into an investment. If you bought 100 shares of a stock at $50 per share and paid the broker a $50 commission, your cost basis is $50.50 per share, or $5050.

In just the same way, loads and redemption fees work their way into the cost basis for funds. If you paid a 5 percent load when you bought the fund, that was already figured into your purchase price. So you don't need to adjust for that. Suppose you sell shares and there's a 1 percent redemption fee. If your shares were sold for $5000, a 1 percent exit charge would take $50 out of your proceeds. So your net is $4950, not $5000.

What's complicated about mutual fund record-keeping is that most people don't buy nice round lots, like 100 shares. Many invest a nice round amount, like $1000 or $10,000. Odds are that most shareholders end up with some odd number of shares, with fractional shares rounded off to three decimal places.

Those who reinvest dividends and capital gains must count them when computing their cost basis. Reinvesting a taxable distribution is the same as putting new money into the fund. Forget to include those distributions in the cost basis, and you can wind up paying too much tax. For the most part, investors or their tax advisers are usually on their own when calculating their cost basis. Many companies are providing average cost data—and that's a big help. But hold on to your records, you may need to do it yourself.

What if you don't have good records? Most fund companies will help to reconstruct transaction history records by providing copies of past statements. Depending on the fund, and how many years' worth of data you need, you may be charged a nominal fee for the service.

Suppose you sell all the shares in a mutual fund account. It's easy to compute your cost basis. Add up all the money you invested directly and through dividend reinvestment. That's the total cost. Then, divide that sum by the number of shares you have. That's the average cost per share. To figure your gain or loss, subtract the cost from proceeds of the sale. If you have shares in the account that are both long-term (held for more than 12 months) and short-term (less than 12 months), be sure to note that, even if you use the same cost basis for holdings of various duration. This information is reported on Schedule D of the 1040, the individual's tax return. (This method of computation is also known as the "average-cost" or "single-category" method, and we'll come back to it later.)

You can take this average cost approach a step further, to the "double-category" method. Under this tax treatment, you calculate separate cost bases for the long-term shares and for the short-term shares. This method demands extra work, but may be worthwhile for investors who are in tax brackets of 31 percent or higher. (For single taxpayers, that's taxable income of $51,400 or more; for married persons filing jointly, $102,300 or more.) That's because while the tax rate on short-term gains is the same as on your salary and investment earnings like dividends and interest, the rate on long-term gains is 20 percent. If you have gains, most likely the biggest gains are in the shares held long-term, so you should allocate most of the gains to these shares. If you use the average-cost method, you'll end up putting more of the gain on the short-term shares, and that will result in a bigger tax bite.

The tax situation gets stickier if some but not all the shares are sold. Look at Table 6-2. Suppose

that on November 12, 1998, the fund's NAV is $10.50, your average cost is $10.87 per share, and you're considering selling some shares. You think you have a taxable loss of $0.37 per share. But that's only if you liquidate the entire account.

If you make a partial redemption and don't specify any specific method you wish to use to calculate your gains and losses, the IRS will assume the first shares in are the first shares out. Suppose you ask the fund for a $3000 redemption. That would result in the sale of 285.714 shares ($3000 divided by $10.50). The IRS would assume those shares were from the first 300 shares bought on February 15, 1997, at $10 per share. Even though you have a loss on the entire investment, selling those shares even at November 12's depressed price would result in a small taxable gain.

But there are alternatives. You could sell shares in a way that would generate a tax-deductible loss. Go back to your average cost per share, $10.87. You can use the single- or double-category methods to calculate the tax liability on partial redemptions. (Remember that you have to note which method you're using on your tax return.) Sell $3000 worth of shares by the single-category method and, instead of a gain, you get a tax loss of $105.71.

Finally, there's the "specific shares" method, which is perhaps the best approach. But it takes some planning. You must designate in writing which shares are to be sold, and do so in advance of the transaction. The advantage of this method is you can pinpoint the highest-cost shares, those purchased on June 2 and September 28, 1997, and July 6, 1998. The share prices paid on all three dates are higher than today's NAV. By selling these shares, you can redeem $2675.84, with a tax deductible loss of $324.17.

Don't forget that with the specific shares method—as with all the options—once you choose to redeem shares in a fund under this method, all future redemptions must use the same method. You can't use specific shares this year and the single-category method next year. Investors using the single-category or double-category methods to compute taxes should attach a note to their tax returns saying so. Those using first-in, first-out or the specific shares methods need not do so, but should maintain their records in case of an audit.

Keep in mind that there are rule changes from time to time, so it's best to consult with your accountant or tax adviser. It's also a good idea to call the Internal Revenue Service to get a free

TABLE 6-2

CALCULATING TAXABLE GAINS AND LOSSES

On Nov. 12, 1998, the net asset value, or per-share price, of a fund is $10.50. The total value of your holdings is $7305.51. You are thinking about selling all or part of your shares in the fund. There are several ways to compute tax liabilities. Your goal should be to minimize the tax bite.

Investment Date	Amount Invested	Price/ Share	Shares Purchased	Total Shares
Feb. 15, 1997	$3000.00	$10.00	300.000	300.000
June 2	1000.00	11.75	85.106	385.106
Sept. 28	1000.00	12.25	81.630	466.740
Dec. 15	Distributions of $0.20 per share income, $1 per share capital gains			
Reinvest income	93.35	11.20	8.385	475.075
Reinvest capital gains	466.74	11.20	41.673	516.748
May 10, 1998	1000.00	11.00	90.909	607.657
July 6	1000.00	11.35	88.106	695.763
Total investment	$7,560.09	Average price/share $10.87		

If you are selling all the shares, you can choose from these methods:

SINGLE-CATEGORY Take the average cost of your shares, $10.87, and deduct the $10.50 your shares are worth now. That's a loss of $0.37 per share. With this fund, you have 466.740 shares held more than 12 months for a $172.69 long-term capital loss; and 229.023 held less than 12 months for an $84.74 short-term loss.

DOUBLE-CATEGORY In the prior method, you calculate the average cost and apply it to all shares in both holding periods. In the double-category method, you calculate two average costs—for the long-term and short-term shares—and then deduct that cost from the current net asset value. There are 466.74 long-term shares with an average cost of $10.71 per share. Since the shares are now at $10.50, you have $0.21 per share long-term capital loss. You also have 229.023 shares held less than 12 months with an average cost of $11.18 for a $155.74 short-term loss.

If you are selling some but not all of your shares, you can choose from these three methods:

AVERAGE COST Using the single-category method to redeem $3000, you end up selling 285.714 shares at a loss of $0.37 per share (the average loss per share), for $105.70 long-term capital loss on the lot. It's considered a long-term loss because unless specifically noted (see below), the IRS assumes that the oldest shares are sold first.

SPECIFIC SHARES Direct the fund company to sell the highest-cost shares, those bought on June 2 and Sept. 28, 1997 and July 6, 1998. The June 2 shares are now worth $803.61 for a $106.38 loss; the Sept. 28 shares are worth $857.12, for $142.89 loss. Both are long-term losses. The July 6 shares are worth $925.11, for a short-term loss of $74.89. Specified redemption yield is $2675.84, with $324.17 in tax-deductible losses.

FIRST-IN, FIRST-OUT If you don't tell your mutual fund company which shares to sell, the IRS assumes the oldest shares are sold first. In the above example, the first 300 shares have a cost basis of $10 each. If you sell these shares at $10.50, you have a taxable gain of $150 even though the total investment is in the red. Under the circumstances, this is the least desirable method to use.

DATA: BUSINESS WEEK

---

copy of Publication No. 564, "Mutual Fund Distributions," for the official treatment of the subject.

Tax-Deferred Investing

IRAs

Mutual fund companies make great places to open up individual retirement accounts (IRAs) and other retirement programs. The companies offer professional management, diversification, and a bent for long-term investing. Mutual fund executives love to rake in retirement dollars, since the money tends to stay in place and generate fees for years. Most fund management companies will shower you with plenty of literature on IRAs and the like, and they also have specialists on hand to explain some of the finer, more technical aspects of the programs. Fidelity Investments will even waive sales charges on many of its equity funds for IRA accounts.

Mutual fund companies manage a little more than 47 percent of all IRA assets, according to the Investment Company Institute. That's up from only 33 percent just a few years ago, and it dwarfs the IRA assets held by other financial intermediaries, like banks, savings and loans, and insurance companies. What the IRA holder gets from a mutual fund that he or she doesn't get from a depository institution is an enormous variety of investment options. (Remember, though, that mutual funds are not insured.) The only mutual funds that don't make good IRA investments are tax-exempt funds. If the interest is already free from taxation, what's the point of sheltering it?

IRAs now come in several varieties: the traditional tax-deductible IRA, the nondeductible IRA, and the Roth IRA. In the original IRA, the contribution is tax deductible in the year it's made, all the earnings of the investment are tax-deferred, and the entire proceeds of the IRA become fully taxable when it's withdrawn. In the nondeductible IRA, investors are able to make aftertax contributions to an IRA, enjoy the tax-sheltered buildup of the investment returns, and pay taxes on only the earnings when they start withdrawing from the account at retirement. With the Roth IRA, the contribution is not tax deductible, but all the earnings build up tax free and are not taxed at withdrawal.

One significant difference between the Roth plan and the others is that there is no requirement to start withdrawing the funds at any age, and taxpayers can continue to contribute to them as long as they wish. With traditional tax-deductible and nondeductible IRAs, taxpayers must start withdrawals by age 70½ and are barred from making further contributions beyond that age.

The traditional IRA makes more sense if you expect that your tax bracket in retirement will be lower than your tax bracket is now. The Roth IRA might appeal to investors who already have good pension plans and substantial assets and expect to remain in a high tax bracket when they retire. Of course, Congress seems to revise tax law every few years, so who really knows what your tax bracket will be 20 years hence?

The traditional IRA is always fully deductible for those who are not covered by employer pension plans. But in 1999, it will also be fully deductible for singles with less than $31,000 in AGI and couples with less than $51,000, even if they are covered by an employer's plan. It will be partially deductible up to $40,000 in AGI for individuals and $60,000 for couples. In addition, recent revisions to the tax law raises those limits gradually each year through 2005 for individuals and 2007 for married couples.

The Roth IRA generally allows most taxpayers to participate even if they are in employer-sponsored plans. Singles with AGIs of up to $95,000 and married couples with AGIs to $150,000 can make full contributions of $2000 and $4000, respectively. A partial contribution can be made by singles with AGIs of $95,000 to $110,000 and by married couples with AGIs of $150,000 to $160,000. Those with incomes above these limits can contribute to nondeductible IRAs. In any case, the maximum annual contribution to any sort of IRA is $2000 for individuals and $4000 for married couples.

Education IRA. An IRA for a child? Yup. And junior doesn't have to wait until he's a senior citizen to use the money. Tax law now allows families to establish nondeductible IRAs for their children that can be used to pay for college expenses. Let's face it. Even if you start at birth and invest in the best-performing funds, it's never going to put the little tyke through Harvard. The maximum contribution is $500 per year per child.

But remember there are other ways to save for your child's education. If you establish a custodial account in your child's name, the first $700 in earnings is tax-free. (That's the limit for the 1998 tax year, and it is adjusted annually for inflation.) The income between $701 and $1400 is taxed at the child's rate, and income above $1400 is taxed at the parent's rate. All of this applies to children under 14. Those over 14 pay tax at their own rates.

Transfers. Perhaps you have an IRA at a local bank earning a measly rate of interest. You can move the account to a mutual fund or group of funds. Ask the mutual fund company to send you the applications and the transfer documents and give them to the institution from which you wish to withdraw your IRA. (If you withdraw a certificate of deposit before maturity, you may owe a penalty to the bank.)

The bank will send you the funds, or you can instruct the institution to transfer the funds directly to the new mutual fund company. Make sure the money is reinvested in another IRA within 60 days, or the government will assume you made a premature withdrawal and hit you for tax and a penalty. Moving an IRA from one institution to another is called a "rollover."

Persons who will be receiving their pension benefit in a lump sum distribution because they're either retiring or changing jobs are especially in need of some advance planning. Unless the money is transferred directly from the employer into an IRA or other qualified pension plan, the distribution will be subject to a 20 percent withholding tax. Those hit with the special tax then have 60 days to put the money into an IRA rollover or face additional taxes, including a 10 percent penalty for persons less than 59½ years old. If you need help with a rollover, most any mutual fund company will walk you through it.

Whatever sort of tax-deferred retirement account you have with a mutual fund company, you may have to pay an annual IRA "custodial" or "maintenance" fee. The fee, which takes care of the additional paperwork of an IRA, is typically $10 a year per fund (or much higher at a full-service brokerage firm), but competition for the retirement accounts is so keen that many companies are starting to waive the custodial fee for all accounts over a certain size, say $5000 or $10,000.

Many mutual fund companies send a bill for the annual fee. If the bill's not paid by the due date, the management company will deduct it from the account. If you don't get a bill, ask the fund company when the fee is due. Make plans to pay the fee out of your checkbook and not out of the retirement account. Since contributions to IRAs are limited, you don't want to take anything out of the account if you can avoid it.

KEOGH PLANS

The IRA isn't the only kind of retirement program offered by mutual fund companies. Funds also hold about one-third of the money invested in retirement plans by the self-employed. Commonly known as Keogh plans, these plans are far more generous, allowing the self-employed to stash away as much as 20 percent of their income, up to $30,000, and deduct it from the current year's taxes. These are far more complicated than the simple IRA, and get even trickier when the self-employed person has employees, too. Consult an accountant or tax adviser before starting one of these programs.

There are several varieties of Keogh. The program that allows the largest contribution (and highest deduction) is least flexible, and the contribution must be made every year. Other programs are less demanding, but the maximum contribution is less, too. There's also the Simplified Employee Pension—Individual Retirement Account, otherwise known as SEP or SEP-IRA. The employer can contribute up to $30,000 or 15 percent of the employee's compensation, whichever is less.

401(K) PLANS

Most mutual fund companies offer their funds in 401(k) plans. Unfortunately, as an employee, you cannot start a 401(k) program for yourself; your employer has to do it. You can ask the company to offer a plan with the investment options coming from a mutual fund family. One of the features that makes 401(k)s different from conventional corporate pension plans is that the employee gets to choose how the money is invested. That's why mutual funds make excellent homes for 401(k) plans. Look at the array of choices (though not every fund in every group of funds may be eligible for the program). Mutual funds can also service 403(b) plans, which are similar to the 401(k), except they are exclusively for the employees of certain charitable organizations or public school systems.

In such plans, an employee can choose to place up to a certain percentage of his or her pretax income in the 401(k). How much depends on how a company's plan is structured. The maximum is commonly around 10 percent, but some go as high as 15 percent. Then, too, the law puts a cap on the amount of money you can contribute on a pretax basis, which in 1999 will be $10,000. The amount is subject to inflation adjustments. In addition, employers often "match" employee contributions in part or in full. The earnings of the 401(k) account are also tax-deferred until the money is withdrawn at retirement.

> Mutual funds work well in 401(k) plans.

VARIABLE ANNUITIES

Imagine owning a mutual fund that pays interest, dividends, and capital gains and not having to pay any tax year to year. You can't take the money out until you're at least 59½ or you pay a tax penalty—and perhaps a penalty to the fund company, too. Isn't this a mutual fund IRA? No, but you're close.

It's a variable annuity, and it's growing in popularity. Many fund companies offer variable annuities or manage variable annuity investments for insurance companies. The prime customers for variable annuities are mutual fund investors within 20 years of retirement who have assets they can sock away until then and who can benefit from the tax deferral on investment income. Many babyboomers already fit that category, and more will in coming years.

The variable annuity probably sounds a lot like an IRA or a 401(k) plan, but with several critical differences. For starters, the contributions are not tax deductible. But, unlike any IRA or 401(k), there is no limit to what an investor can put into the annuity.

It's important to know that the costs of investing in a variable annuity can be significantly higher than investing in comparable mutual funds. Depending on the annuity plan, the investor who cashes out before retirement may still pay a load, or a redemption or surrender charge. The redemption charge for some annuity products can be as high as 10 percent—and that's before any tax consequences. Don't invest in these annuities unless you're 99 percent sure you're not going to need the money for at least a decade. In addition, the portfolio management expenses may be higher for annuity funds than they are for comparable mutual funds, since the annuity funds are usually smaller in size and don't enjoy the same economies of scale.

There's an annuity charge or "wrapper," which pays for a guarantee provided by an insurance company. The guarantee, which on average costs 1.27 percent per year, merely assures the investor's heirs that in case he or she dies while the annuity is in force, the annuity will be worth at least as much as what was put in. (That's why variable annuities have to be offered by a life insurance company.)

This feature would have come in handy for the heirs of someone who had invested in a variable annuity with equity funds in July 1998, and died in September, when the investment might have been worth 20 percent less. As a practical matter, this insurance is only worthwhile in the first few years of the investment.

After all, if the annuity is worth less than the investment after 10 or 20 years, you chose the wrong annuity. Annuity buyers can't elect to waive this guarantee. It's the distinguishing feature that makes it an annuity—a life insurance product that allows the earnings to build up on a tax-deferred basis. Some annuities now have a "step-up" provision that keeps raising the guaranteed death benefit. But that isn't free. Such annuities have higher fees.

The variable annuities may look—and behave—much like mutual funds, but the terminology is different. A mutual fund that's connected to a variable annuity is a "subaccount." There are no fund shares in a variable annuity; instead, the worth of the investment is tracked in "accumulation unit value," which, for practical purposes, is the same thing. The average variable annuity has seven subaccount options.

Because of the higher fees and surrender charges, the variable annuity only makes sense as a truly long-term investment. It is often sold as a tax shelter (remember the earnings of the investment are not taxed until withdrawal), but it's really best used as a long-term savings vehicle.

Morningstar classifies the variable annuity subaccounts as it does equity and bond mutual funds. But there are a few exceptions. All the domestic equity categories are the same, except for specialty subaccounts. There are only enough subaccounts to justify natural resources, real estate, and utilities categories. All other specialized funds are lumped into an "unaligned" grouping. For international equity, Morningstar uses the broader foreign, world, diversified emerging markets categories and international hybrid categories and forgoes the regional classifications. Among the bond subaccounts, there's long-, intermediate-, and short-term general bond and government bond categories, plus high-yield, international, and money-market. For yield-oriented investors, most variable annuities also have a "fixed" account option, which works much like a bank CD.

Selecting a variable annuity takes all the same savvy as choosing a mutual fund—and then some. You are not only buying an investment vehicle, but an insurance wrapper as well. And you can often get many of the same investment funds inside different wrappers. For instance, Fidelity Retirement Reserves is a series of variable annuity portfolios that are managed much like their Fidelity mutual fund counterparts. You can call a Fidelity 800 number or drop in at a Fidelity investor center and obtain the prospectus and the application for the Fidelity variable annuity with the insurance wrapper coming from Fidelity's own insurance company. Fidelity recently began offering access to several other fund company subaccounts under the umbrella of the Fidelity annuity.

It's a radical departure for Fidelity to offer its customers other managers' wares, but it's fairly common practice in the variable annuity world. Nearly all the Fidelity-managed subaccounts in Fidelity Retirement Reserves are also available in other insurors' products. The popular Fidelity VIP Fund Equity-Income subaccount is available in over 130 different variable annuity products offered by Aetna Life & Casualty, Life of Virginia Commonwealth, Nationwide Life Insurance, and dozens of other companies. What's different? For one, the service. If you buy the annuity direct from Fidelity, you're pretty much on your own. On the other hand, if you buy the fund through an annuity sold by a life insurance agent, you get the agent to help you choose the fund and monitor performance.

What else is different? The cost. Most annuities are sold without a front-end load. But the redemption fees and insurance costs can vary greatly. (Portfolio expense, the cost of running the investment itself, is the same no matter which insurance company offers the fund.) If you invest in the Fidelity Equity-Income annuity subaccount through Fidelity's Retirement Reserves variable annuity, the insurance expense is 1 percent a year, contract fee $30 a year, and there's a 5 percent declining surrender charge in the first year, declining 1 percent a year for five years. Purchased through Nationwide's Best of America annuity, the contract fee is $30. But the other charges are much higher: 1.30 percent a year for insurance expense and a surrender charge that starts at 7 percent and declines 1 percent a year for seven years.

If you're seriously considering an annuity and don't need a salesperson to help you, look into the low-cost annuity products from Vanguard, Scudder, T. Rowe Price, and Charles Schwab. There are no loads or surrender charges on the policies. Insurance expenses are low, too—0.85 percent in the Schwab plan, 0.70 percent in Scudder, 0.55 percent in T. Rowe Price, and 0.28 percent at Vanguard. Vanguard and Schwab charge a $25 a year contract fee, while Scudder and T. Rowe Price don't charge at all. Minimum investments are $2500 at Scudder, $5000 at Schwab and Vanguard, and $10,000 for T. Rowe Price.

Before investing in any variable annuity, compare the annuity's investment options to a similar, taxable mutual fund. You may find the higher charges and loss of financial flexibility may weigh heavier in your decisions than the opportunity to defer taxes on the fund's earnings. If you would choose a small-cap or mid-cap growth fund for the annuity, the deferral may not be worth it. Those sorts of funds don't earn enough dividend income to distribute, and capital gains distributions are not that frequent. Want a government bond fund for your variable annuity? In that case, don't even bother. Buy municipal bond funds. The income is tax-exempt, there are no annuity charges to pay, and you can get your money out when you want it, without paying a tax penalty.

Variable annuities make most sense for investment options that would generate a lot of income in a taxable account—like high-yield bond and equity–income funds. They're also practical if you are an investor who likes to make frequent shifts between investments—moves that become taxable events when done outside the tax shelter of an annuity or qualified retirement program.

In pitching a costly annuity, some salespersons will play up the annuitizing feature. They'll say that when it's time to swap the nest egg for an annuity—guaranteed stream of payments—their company is the most generous. That may be so, but you don't have to buy their variable annuity. When you're investing for retirement, buy the variable annuity that makes the most investment sense. When it comes time to annuitize, you can always switch the money to another company. And most annuities are never annuitized—people take a lump sum, make periodic withdrawals, or leave the money to their estate.

Because of the higher costs, variable annuities are for most people not the retirement vehicle of first choice. First, if you qualify to make investments in either a conventional or Roth IRA, do that first. And if your company has a 401(k) or other defined contribution plan, be sure you are taking full advantage of that as well, making the full tax-deductible contribution and perhaps maxing out your aftertax contribution option if you have one. If you are self-employed, a Keogh or SEP-IRA should take preference over a variable annuity. Only after you've taken full advantage of more cost-effective retirement investment programs should you embark on the variable annuity.

Watch out for high fees on variable annuities.

CHAPTER 7

Using the BW Scoreboard

The BUSINESS WEEK Mutual Fund Scoreboard works like a road map of the mutual fund world. It provides tons of information about returns, fees, sales charges, and risk that should help you avoid hazards and dead ends on your financial journey. But even with the best of road maps, you still need to have some map-reading skills. That's the point of this chapter.

The equity Scoreboard that appears in the back of the book covers 885 equity funds. That's not every one, by a long shot. But we have all the major funds with assets greater than $200 million. At BUSINESS WEEK Online (www .businessweek.com), we're not confined by paper. We have about 2700 equity mutual funds. Even that's not the whole universe. To keep the numbers more manageable, we don't include funds that are only open to institutional investors. (We do make some exceptions for institutional funds that are available to individual investors through mutual fund supermarkets.) Nor do we include more than one class of shares of funds with multiple share classes. The variation between share classes of the same fund is a function of fees, not portfolio performance. The underlying investments are the same. We also exclude funds with less than 12 months of performance data.

The bond fund Scoreboard in this book has 653 funds, selected by the same process as with equity funds, with some modifications. And we have some 1750 bond funds in the expanse of the online world. The closed-end fund Scoreboard has 120 equity funds and 350 bond funds.

At the start of each Scoreboard, there's a summary description of the sort of data that are under each column heading. In this chapter we'll take a more in-depth look at some of the headings. For a thorough discussion of the investment categories, please refer to Chapter 2.

Ratings

The first column after the fund's name is the overall rating. The best grade is an A, signifying superior performance. B+ is very good, and B, above average. Then comes C, or average, and then the subpar categories: C– for below-average performance, D for poor performance, and F for very poor performance (Figure 7-1).

There are many funds with returns that look very good, yet their ratings are average at best. At the same time, there are highly rated funds with seemingly so-so returns. The reason for this is simple. BUSINESS WEEK ratings don't merely reward funds for winning the year's performance derby. You don't need a ratings system for that because the returns tell all. What the BW ratings system asks is not only how much money a fund made for its shareholders, but also how much risk the fund took in the process.

In rating fund performance we define risk as the potential for losing money. In the strict sense, risk goes both ways. A fund can be said to have high risk if it is volatile—net asset values swing wildly to the upside as well as the down. But as a practical matter, an investor would not complain if a fund appreciated twice as fast as the S&P 500. He or she may accept—but won't like—the fact that the fund has fallen twice as much as the S&P 500. So the ratings, which are calculated by Morningstar, Inc., don't penalize a fund for upside volatility.

To come up with fund ratings, we measure a fund's last five years of returns. (For closed-end funds, we measure the last three years.) For the overall BW rating, the returns are calculated assuming that you paid the maximum sales charge, or load, if applicable. Obviously this gives the no-load funds a head start on the load funds, since an investor who pays a 5 percent up-front

FIGURE 7-1

THE BUSINESS WEEK RATINGS: HOW THE MUTUAL FUNDS STACK UP

EQUITY FUNDS ☐ BOND FUNDS ■

This chart shows how many equity and bond funds earned each of BW's mutual fund performance ratings. The ratings are based on risk-adjusted total returns. The period measured is 1994–98 for both equity and bond funds.

DATA: MORNINGSTAR INC.

| A SUPERIOR PERFORMANCE | B+ VERY GOOD PERFORMANCE | B ABOVE AVERAGE PERFORMANCE | C AVERAGE PERFORMANCE | C– BELOW AVERAGE PERFORMANCE | D POOR PERFORMANCE | F VERY POOR PERFORMANCE |

sales charge has to earn 5.26 percent just to break even. (That's right, 5.26 percent. A 6 percent load would reduce a $1000 investment to $950. To get back to $1000, the investor would have to earn 5.26 percent.)

If a fund has been in operation for more than a year but less than five, we still report on it. We insist on a minimum track record before we rate a fund so we can track the fund's behavior under varying economic conditions. For instance, the 1999 equity fund ratings cover the period 1994 through 1998. We see fund performance under a variety of conditions: years of robust economic expansion and years of slower but steady growth; a bout of rising interest rates; and a long bout of disinflation punctuated by periodic fears of an acceleration of inflation.

To derive the BW rating, we start with the fund's five-year total return. (These numbers are under the column heading "Average Annual Total Returns (%)." We then adjust the pure performance number by subtracting the "risk-of-loss" factor. (See the section, "Risk," later in this chapter.)

The funds are then rated based on a statistical distribution. The top 7.5 percent of the funds get A's. The next 12.5 percent of the funds get B+'s, and the following 17.5 percent, B's. Then there's the group in the middle—the C's. This is the largest group, with 25 percent of all rated funds. The ratings are symmetrical on the negative side: There are as many funds with F's as with A's. There is an exception. To get a B or better rating, an equity fund must also beat the S&P 500 on a risk-adjusted basis.

The risk adjustment can change a fund's place in the line-up considerably. Adjusting high-return funds for their high risks might bring them down to the middle of the pack. Likewise, more modest performers with very low risk profiles often end up a lot higher in the relative standings after the adjustment is made.

The bond fund Scoreboard rates municipal bond funds against other municipal funds rather than comparing them to all the other bond funds, which are taxable. If not for the separation, muni funds would always be at a disadvantage since, as tax-exempts, their yields are lower than those of comparable taxable bonds.

For most of the Scoreboard's history, the highest rated equity funds have tended to have low or very low levels of risk. But in the late 1980s, the Japan Fund and Merrill Lynch Pacific Fund, for instance, captured top honors for several years even with their high risk levels. The same thing happened with some technology and health funds in the 1990s. Their performances were so strong that even the fairly stiff risk-of-loss factor wasn't enough to knock them out of the top ratings group.

Should you invest in only the top-rated funds? It's a good place to start your search. But don't end it there. Suppose your investment plan shows you have a long time horizon and a good tolerance for risk. Then you would want to have some small-cap growth, mid-cap growth, and foreign funds as well. But right now, there are none with A ratings for overall performance.

That's why we have category ratings as well. We approach category ratings the same way as overall BW ratings. The only difference is that the funds are rated against one another within a single category instead of against all other Scoreboard funds. This second layer of ratings makes it easier to identify funds with good risk-adjusted returns compared to their peers, even if they are not particularly good compared to all funds.

The most extreme case of this is, of course, the precious metals funds. Every one of the 26 funds that is rated gets an F. But comparing precious metals funds to each other, just one fund, SoGen Gold, earned an A. Franklin Gold A, Scudder Gold, Lexington Strategic Silver, and Oppenheimer Gold and Special Minerals A earned the next highest rating, B+. Few investors want to buy gold funds these days. But many seek the sorts of funds that have not made the overall A-list, but still are worthy funds. You won't find any foreign or world funds with overall ratings of A, but you still should have international exposure in your investment portfolio.

What if the overall BW rating of one of your funds declines? That's not a sign to dump the fund. Sometimes funds will decline in rating not so much from their own performance, but from the relatively stronger returns of others. That's what happened during 1998, when large-cap value funds were hit with losses in financial and energy stocks. That cost many of them their A ratings. What's more important in assessing a fund's performance is how it compares to other funds in its category. Then, you have to do some investigation as to why the fund underperformed, and you may determine you should sell it.

The one problem with this ratings system is endemic in all performance measurements. They are based on past performance, which is not necessarily the best predictor of the future. But we do know that there is a tendency for winners to repeat and for funds' risk characteristics to stay fairly constant. Depending on the funds, the investment style can be constant as well. In that sense, a thorough assessment of past performance can be useful in investing for the future. The past may not be perfect, but it's the only data we have. What counts is how you use it.

❙Size

For many years the conventional wisdom held that great mutual funds grew into mediocre ones. Here's why. Suppose a fund manager builds an enviable track record with a small fund. The fund gets bigger through appreciation of the assets. But, more important, investors begin to notice it or the fund manager buys big ads to herald his or her success. Money pours in and the fund manager who was a whiz with a $50 million

portfolio now has to find enough attractive stocks to fill a $500 million portfolio.

Rapid growth of assets can sometimes undermine the very success that generated the growth. Perhaps a portfolio manager can keep performing nearly as well at $100 million, but can he or she sustain the pace at $700 million or $1 billion? That depends on the manager and the nature of the stocks invested in. If his or her success has been built on finding little gems and buying them before they're "discovered" by Wall Street, it's going to be difficult. The manager might find enough of them to make an impact on a $100 million or even a $500 million portfolio. But the available supply of great little stocks is not going to expand. If anything, the supply could diminish, as others, seeing the success, rush to buy the same sorts of stocks.

The portfolio manager will usually have to start making investments in companies larger than those on which he or she built this reputation. That isn't necessarily bad, but it does change the nature of the portfolio. Or, to get enough small stocks into the portfolio, it might be necessary to lower the standards for the kinds of stocks bought. That isn't good.

TABLE 7-1

THE LARGEST EQUITY FUNDS

Fund ▼	Net assets* (Millions) ▼
FIDELITY MAGELLAN	$83,552.1
VANGUARD 500 INDEX	74,228.5
WASHINGTON MUTUAL INVESTORS	51,773.8
FIDELITY GROWTH & INCOME	48,639.8
INVESTMENT COMPANY OF AMERICA	48,497.6
FIDELITY CONTRAFUND	38,821.3
VANGUARD WINDSOR II	31,538.2
AMERICAN CENTURY–20TH CENT. ULTRA INV.	27,150.0
VANGUARD WELLINGTON	25,760.9
FIDELITY PURITAN	25,682.3
JANUS	25,490.7
FIDELITY ADVISOR GROWTH OPPORTUNITIES T	24,823.6
FIDELITY EQUITY-INCOME	23,707.4
INCOME FUND OF AMERICA	22,909.0
NEW PERSPECTIVE	21,257.0
EUROPACIFIC GROWTH	20,797.9
PUTNAM FUND FOR GROWTH & INCOME A	20,254.0
FIDELITY BLUE CHIP GROWTH	19,904.1
FIDELITY EQUITY-INCOME II	19,453.7
MSDW DIVIDEND GROWTH SECURITIES B	18,483.2

*December 31, 1998   DATA: MORNINGSTAR INC.

If the fund primarily invests in blue-chip and large-capitalization stocks, a fund's size is less of a problem. A $10 billion blue-chip fund may not be any less nimble than a $1 million one. And over the last several years, a huge part of the stock market's gains came from the superior performance of a handful of large company stocks. In that kind of market, even the Fidelity Magellan Fund—with $63 billion in assets at the start of 1998—was able to find enough stock to earn a mint. And for bond funds, in which the fund's expenses often make the difference between superior or mediocre results, size can be a help rather than a hindrance.

While Fidelity Magellan is still the largest fund, others are on its tail. The assets of Vanguard 500 Index, the second-largest fund at $74.3 billion (Table 7-1), grew by 50 percent in 1998. A little more than half of that came from appreciation of assets, the rest from new money. Bond funds are, on average, smaller than equity funds. Even the largest bond fund, PIMCo Total Return Institutional, with $20.1 billion in assets, looks small compared to all but 3 of the 20 largest equity funds (Table 7-2).

There are some drawbacks to being a small equity fund. Expense ratios for small funds are almost invariably higher. That's because every fund has certain fixed costs like legal, audit, and registration fees that don't vary much with the size of the fund. Since small funds have fewer assets over which to spread these fixed costs, shareholders in the small funds usually bear higher expenses than those in larger funds.

One other note about asset size. Along with the one-year total return figure, asset size can be used to ascertain how much new money has been added to the fund over the last year. Suppose the fund assets grew 50 percent over the last year. If the fund had a 30 percent total return, figure that 30 percent of the growth came from appreciation and 20 percent from new investments.

If the fund had grown only 20 percent, that's an indication that more dollars went out than came in. This rough calculation works pretty well for equity funds, in which most shareholders just reinvest the income and capital gains distributions. However, it may not work so well for bond funds, since investors who use them to supplement their incomes take the distributions in cash.

TABLE 7-2

THE LARGEST BOND FUNDS

Fund ▼	Net assets* (Millions) ▼
PIMCO TOTAL RETURN INSTL.	$20,125.7
FRANKLIN CALIF. TAX-FREE INCOME A	15,523.5
VANGUARD GNMA	10,993.1
BOND FUND OF AMERICA	9,541.5
FRANKLIN U.S. GOVERNMENT SECURITIES A	8,901.4
VAN KAMPEN PRIME RATE INCOME	7,908.5
VANGUARD INTERM.-TERM TAX-EXEMPT	7,895.6
VANGUARD TOTAL BOND MARKET INDEX	7,764.6
FRANKLIN FEDERAL TAX-FREE INCOME A	7,189.4
FRANKLIN HIGH-YIELD TAX-FREE INCOME A	5,897.3
IDS HIGH-YIELD TAX-EXEMPT A	5,728.2
VANGUARD SHORT-TERM CORPORATE	5,427.7
VANGUARD HIGH-YIELD CORPORATE	5,380.5
MSDW U.S. GOVERNMENT SECURITIES B	4,984.7
FRANKLIN N.Y. TAX-FREE INCOME A	4,877.5
MAS FIXED-INCOME INSTL.	4,672.4
FIDELITY SPARTAN MUNICIPAL INCOME	4,638.9
AARP GNMA & U.S. TREASURY	4,535.2
MERRILL LYNCH CORP. HIGH-INCOME B	4,161.1
VANGUARD LONG-TERM CORPORATE BOND	4,152.9

*December 31, 1998   DATA: MORNINGSTAR INC.

Fees

The sales charge is a critical matter for fund investors. Load, no-load, or low-load, it's all here. Some funds have a redemption charge instead of an up-front load. If so, the maximum redemption fee will be under this heading, along with an asterisk noting that it's a redemption fee rather than front-end load. All you need to know about sales charges is in Chapter 3.

Expense ratios are different from sales charges. Whether or not a fund has a sales charge, it still costs to keep it going. Out of the fund's assets come ongoing costs for management, administration, printing, postage, lawyers, auditors, and the like. These costs are totaled and divided by the net assets in the fund. In the case of the Steadman funds—which have been closed to new investors for years—the expenses are extraordinarily high because the funds are so small. Most responsible fund companies would not have allowed that to continue; they would at least have merged the funds to reduce the overhead (Table 7-3). Funds that leverage their portfolios with borrowed money to buy stocks on margin also have high expenses. They end up

TABLE 7-3

EXPENSE RATIOS: EQUITY FUNDS

Fund HIGHEST	Expense ratio*	Fund LOWEST	Expense ratio*
STEADMAN AMERICAN INDUSTRY	22.57%	VANGUARD STAR	0.00%
FRONTIER EQUITY	12.29	T. ROWE PRICE SPECTRUM GROWTH	0.00
STEADMAN SECURITY TRUST	7.34	VANGUARD TOTAL INTERNATIONAL STOCK INDEX	0.00
STEADMAN INVESTMENT	6.48	VANGUARD LIFESTRATEGY MODERATE GROWTH	0.00
AMERICAN HERITAGE	5.85	VANGUARD LIFESTRATEGY GROWTH	0.00
APEX MID-CAP GROWTH	5.26	VANGUARD LIFESTRATEGY CONSERVATIVE GROWTH	0.00
GAMERICA CAPITAL A	5.16	VANGUARD LIFESTRATEGY INCOME	0.00
EAST END CAP APPRECIATION	4.84	AARP DIVERSIFIED GROWTH	0.00
VAN KAMPEN GLOBAL MANAGED ASSETS B	4.42	AARP DIVERSIFIED INCOME WITH GROWTH	0.00
ALLIANCE ALL-ASIA INVESTMENT B	4.15	T. ROWE PRICE SPECTRUM INTERNATIONAL	0.00
BULL & BEAR GOLD INVESTORS	3.88	VICTORY REAL ESTATE INVESTMENT A	0.00
ALLIANCE/REGENT SECTOR OPPORTUNITIES C	3.70	PROFUNDS BEAR INV.	0.00
RAINBOW	3.67	VICTORY LAKEFRONT	0.00
MATTERHORN GROWTH	3.65	FEDERATED INTERNATIONAL GROWTH A	0.07
CENTURION T.A.A. C	3.54	FIDELITY FREEDOM 2010	0.08
BENDER GROWTH C	3.50	FIDELITY FREEDOM 2020	0.08
MERRILL LYNCH ASSET GROWTH B	3.50	FIDELITY FREEDOM 2000	0.08
SMITH BARNEY PACIFIC A	3.37	FIDELITY FREEDOM 2030	0.08
EATON VANCE EMERGING MARKETS B	3.32	FIDELITY FREEDOM INCOME	0.08
CAPSTONE JAPAN	3.30	SEI ASSET ALLOC. DIVERS. GLOBAL GROWTH A	0.12

*1998, funds with few or no expenses may be funds of funds or subsidized by their management companies   DATA: MORNINGSTAR INC.

reporting the interest expense in the expense ratio. International funds also run higher expenses than domestic, just because operating in foreign markets is costlier.

Remember the hidden loads—the 12(b)-1 charges—discussed in Chapter 3? Just to recap, the 12(b)-1 fee—named for the SEC ruling that permitted it—allows fund companies to dip into shareholder assets to pay "distribution" costs. Funds can be used for advertising or marketing expenses, and often they're used to compensate brokers for selling the fund. These charges do find their way into the expense ratio. Chances are, if the fund has an expense ratio of over 2 percent, it's either a very small fund or it levies a 12(b)-1 fee. Those who take such fees are noted in the Scoreboard.

Some funds may show up with 0.00 percent expenses. That could mean the fund is new, and the fund management company is waiving fees and absorbing expenses to help the fund get started. The Vanguard STAR and LifeStrategies funds are funds of funds, investing in other Vanguard portfolios. As such, Vanguard does not charge any fees for these two funds, but collects the fees on the funds these funds invest in. The T. Rowe Price Spectrum funds have the same arrangement with their parent company.

In general, the equity funds with the lowest overhead are index funds. That's because index funds have virtually no management cost. The fund manager merely buys the stocks that are in the index, and sells them if they are dropped from the index. A computer can monitor the portfolio to make sure it's behaving like the underlying index.

The average expense ratio for the funds in the equity Scoreboard varies slightly year to year. (In 1998 it was 1.44 percent.) What this means to you is simple. About $1.44 out of every $100 goes toward expenses. Bond fund expenses, on average, run about 1.01 percent for taxable funds, 0.85 percent for tax-free funds.

All things being equal, a lower expense ratio is better than a higher one. But if an equity fund has built up a strong track record, even with a high-end expense ratio, that's no reason to shun it. Fund performance is reported net of expenses. Thus, if the fund runs up high costs and still turns out impressive results, so be it. The only caveat is that when the fund hits a downdraft—and all do—a high overhead is going to make it even more painful.

Bond fund investors should be especially sensitive to expense ratios, looking first to funds with the lowest ones and steering clear of those with the highest (Table 7-4). That's because bond fund returns are typically in the single-digits. If the fund earns 6 percent and eats up 1 percent in operating expenses, it will only deliver 5 percent to shareholders. That may not sound like much overhead, but one out of every six dollars earned by the fund—17 percent of the earnings—was chewed up in overhead. On the other hand, if an equity fund earns 50 percent, few investors are going to care if the expense ratio was 1.5 or 2 percent.

If the fund manager is subsidizing the fund's overhead in any way, it's useful to know what the expense ratio would be if the fund were paying its way entirely. Such subsidies don't last forever, and one day shareholders will have to pay the full freight. For several years Dreyfus Corp. and Fidelity Investments waged a fierce battle between two big money-market funds, using waivers of management fees to boost yield and make their funds more attractive. If that's the case, the fund prospectus should spell out how much the fees would be without the subsidy. That might give a more realistic picture of the fund.

Total Return: Pretax and Aftertax

Total return is the fund's appreciation, including reinvestment of dividends and capital gains. The equity fund Scoreboard shows pretax and aftertax returns for 1998 and, if applicable, the average annual pretax and aftertax returns for the 3-, 5-, and 10-year periods. In the bond fund Scoreboard, the total returns are reported under the "Performance" heading. If your money was invested for the entire year and you added no new money, only reinvesting the dividends and capital gains, this reported total return should be your actual return too. If the money came in at any other point during the year, or if you made multiple investments in the fund, your own results will be different.

TABLE 7-4

EXPENSE RATIOS: BOND FUNDS

Fund ▼	HIGHEST Expense ratio* ▼	Fund ▼	LOWEST Expense ratio* ▼
NEW YORK MUNI	3.77%	HEARTLAND SHORT DURATION HIGH-YIELD MUNI.	0.00%
FUNDAMENTAL U.S. GOVERNMENT STRATEGIC INCOME	3.53	HEARTLAND HIGH-YIELD MUNICIPAL BOND	0.00
CALIFORNIA MUNI	3.26	CGM AMERICAN TAX-FREE	0.00
ALLIANCE LIMITED MATURITY GOVERNMENT B	3.14	T. ROWE PRICE SPECTRUM INCOME	0.00
PAINEWEBBER STRATEGIC INCOME B	2.63	FRANKLIN STRATEGIC MORTGAGE	0.00
PIMCO GLOBAL BOND II C	2.49	ECLIPSE ULTRA SHORT-TERM INCOME	0.00
FUNDAMENTAL FIXED-INCOME HIGH-YIELD MUNI.	2.49	SCUDDER HIGH-YIELD BOND	0.03
GABELLI GLOBAL CONVERTIBLE SECURITIES	2.48	FRANKLIN ARKANSAS MUNICIPAL BOND A	0.10
VAN KAMPEN STRATEGIC INCOME B	2.44	FRANKLIN WASHINGTON MUNICIPAL BOND	0.10
LEXINGTON CONVERTIBLE SECURITIES	2.38	DELAWARE-VOYAGEUR TAX-FREE CALIF. A	0.13
VAN KAMPEN GLOBAL GOVERNMENT SECS. B	2.33	CITIFUNDS NATIONAL TAX-FREE INCOME	0.14
SUNAMERICA U.S. GOVERNMENT SECS. B	2.26	VANGUARD CALIF. INSURED LONG TAX-EXEMPT	0.16
ALLIANCE GLOBAL DOLLAR GOVERNMENT B	2.26	VANGUARD OHIO INSURED LONG TAX-EXEMPT	0.17
NICHOLAS-APPLEGATE CONVERTIBLE C	2.25	CALVERT MUNICIPAL INTERM. MD. A	0.17
PUTNAM HIGH-YIELD TOTAL RETURN B	2.25	VANGUARD PA. INSURED LONG TAX-EXEMPT	0.18
MAINSTAY INTERNATIONAL BOND B	2.22	VANGUARD N.J. INSURED LONG TAX-EXEMPT	0.18
VAN KAMPEN WORLDWIDE HIGH-INCOME B	2.20	VANGUARD CALIF. INSURED INTERM. TAX-EXEMPT	0.18
MFS INTERMEDIATE INCOME B	2.19	VANGUARD INTERM.-TERM TAX-EXEMPT	0.19
VONTOBEL EASTERN EUROPEAN DEBT	2.19	VANGUARD HIGH-YIELD TAX-EXEMPT	0.19
AIM EMERGING MARKETS DEBT B	2.18	VANGUARD LIMITED-TERM TAX-EXEMPT	0.19

*1998, funds with few or no expenses may be funds of funds or subsidized by their management companies
DATA: MORNINGSTAR INC.

Yield is the fund's dividend payout as a percentage of its assets. It does not include capital gains distributions. This figure will be high in bond funds (it's under the "Portfolio Data" heading) and relatively low for equity funds. Most small-cap growth and mid-cap growth funds often have no yield at all, since the funds invest in companies that reinvest their profits for expansion rather than pay them out as dividends.

Sometimes a bond fund's total return will be less than its payout. That means that the NAV declined during the prior year. If a bond fund is paying out a yield higher than its total return, the fund's income distributions may be a return of your principal. Such payouts, also known as return of capital, are tax-free. Don't cheer about it. It's not a freebie. In effect, you're getting your own money back because the fund couldn't earn a real return on it. Of course, the income distribution just may be a lot higher than the total return because of a loss in principal—not uncommon in years in which interest rates rise and bond prices sag.

In the equity Scoreboard, you will also find aftertax returns. These figures are the same as the total return, less federal income taxes. Of course, not every fund shareholder pays the same tax rate. So for purposes of calculating aftertax returns, we've used the highest tax rate on income and capital gains that was in effect during the period. Since 1991, we have kept the top rate at 31 percent even though rates have gone higher for some shareholders. The number of taxpayers paying higher rates are small enough that it doesn't make much sense to use it for calculations that a large number of mutual fund investors will have to use.

If taxes affected all equity funds equally, there would not be much point to showing these numbers. But exactly how taxes affect funds depends on how the fund earned its returns. As you remember from Chapter 6, mutual funds have to pass along essentially all their net dividend, interest, and realized capital gains during the year in which they are earned. (There is no tax due on income and capital gains generated by funds in qualified retirement programs like IRAs, Keoghs, and 401(k) plans.)

Take a fund that invests in a lot of high-dividend stocks. Those dividends are part of the fund's return, and will be passed along to investors every year. That means those dividends will be part of a taxable distribution even if, like most fund shareholders, you choose to reinvest the dividends in new fund shares. Suppose a fund earns a dividend yield of 6 percent and appreciates 6 percent, for a total return of 12 percent. Assuming the fund makes no capital gains distributions (it wouldn't have to unless it sold stocks at a profit), you could say that one-quarter of the fund's return was taxable to you. If you are in the 31 percent bracket (and for simplicity, set aside state and local income taxes), the aftertax return would be 10.14 percent. How so? After taxes, the 6 percent yield is 4.14 percent. Add that to the 6 percent appreciation, and the return comes to 10.14 percent.

Next, suppose a fund is up 12 percent from capital appreciation, and there is no dividend or income distribution. If half of that return were a capital gains distribution, then, assuming the gains were long-term (held by the fund for more than 12 months), that 6 percent would be taxable at the maximum capital gains rate of 20 percent. That distribution comes out to 4.8 percent after taxes, dropping the aftertax return to 10.8 percent.

Now suppose the fund earned a 12 percent total return, but paid out no taxable dividend or capital gains distributions. In that case, the aftertax return is the same as the pretax return but that doesn't mean you don't pay taxes on your gains. You pay taxes when you or the fund earns income or realizes capital gains. If your fund is able to increase its net asset value without making distributions, that's fine as long as you own the fund. But should you sell the fund, you'll be hit with a taxable gain at that time. Equity mutual funds can help you defer taxes, but not avoid them.

How much attention you have to pay to aftertax returns depends on your tax bracket and investment needs. If you're in the 28 percent bracket, these figures will overstate the tax bite. If you're in the 36 percent or 39.6 percent brackets, the tax impact will be understated. If you're trying to minimize taxes, seek funds whose aftertax returns are fairly close to the pretax results. That means there was little tax impact. You might also steer clear of funds that rely heavily on bonds and dividend-paying stocks. But keep in mind when choosing funds that minimize taxable income that you may be taking on more risk. Funds with higher payouts tend to be more conservative and more stable funds.

> The tax bite may affect your fund choices.

History

This section looks at how a fund performed relative to other funds. For equity funds, there are a total of four boxes, each representing a prior 2½-year period. For bond funds, each box is a 1-year period.

The boxes read from left to right, so, in the equity tables, the box farthest to the left represents the period that runs from 7½ to 10 years past. (For the 10 years ending December 31, 1998, that box covers the period running from January 1989 through June 1991.) The box on the right is the most recent 2½-year period, July 1996 through December 1998. Each box has a number—1, 2, 3, or 4—which indicates which quartile the fund was in during each period.

Suppose the fund's boxes look like this: 3-4-2-1. This means that in the first two periods the fund's performance put it in the bottom half of all funds—in fact, it was in the bottom quartile in the second period. But the fortunes then switched around five years ago. For the third period, the fund jumps to the second quartile, and to the first quartile for the most recent period.

Remember, the "History" figure measures performance relative to all other funds, not the absolute performance discussed under total returns. If the market goes through a few bad years, even the top-quartile funds may have had absolute returns that looked pale. Conservative equity funds are more likely to show up near the top in tough times; the more aggressive funds will show better relative performance in boom times.

History looks behind multiyear returns and lets you examine the consistency of a fund's performance. Is it erratic or does it always stay around the same level? Fidelity Magellan's figures are a 1-1-2-1, telling you performance was strong in all but the January 1994 through July 1996 period. (It was in early 1996 that the former manager mistakenly loaded up on bonds right before they plummeted in price.) Berger 100 Fund, a one-time high flier, is 1-1-4-3. Berger management brought in a new portfolio manager in late 1997, but it has yet to have much impact on the returns of this one-time high flier.

In the bond fund Scoreboard, the relative performance is heavily influenced by the course of interest rates. Look at American Century–Benham Target Maturities 2020, a long-term zero-coupon bond fund. It's a top-drawer performer when rates go down, and a loser when rates go up. Now, for 1995, 1997, and 1998, years in which rates trended down, the fund is a first quartile performer. In 1994 and 1996, when rates went up, the fund was a fourth- or bottom-quartile performer. Strong Advantage Fund, an ultrashort-term bond fund, is just the opposite. It shines when long-term

funds decline, and lags when they rally. Strong Advantage is a fourth-quartile performer in 1995, 1997, and 1998—just the years the long-term funds lead the way, and it's a first-quartile fund when most others run into trouble.

Portfolio Data

The next set of data looks inside each fund's portfolio. The first column, "Turnover," is a measure of trading activity. To arrive at this number, we take the lesser of purchases or sales and divide it by average monthly assets. So if the lesser of the two is $500 million, and the average fund assets are $1 billion, the turnover ratio is 50 percent—which happens to be a moderate figure. (A fund's prospectus will contain its exact turnover ratio.)

The funds are then ranked by those numbers in descending order. Next, the funds are assigned a rating from "very high" down to "very low," using a statistical distribution similar to that for the BW fund ratings.

High turnover could mean higher expenses. High turnover could also mean higher taxes. That's because mutual funds must distribute their net capital gains to shareholders, and funds that trade are presumably taking lots of gains. In contrast, low turnover funds tend to hold onto their winners and let them ride. There's no tax due until the fund sells the holdings. Funds with very high turnover tend to be small-cap growth, mid-cap growth, and even some large-cap blend funds. Funds with "very low" turnover are rather diverse, including precious metals, utilities, and, of course, all sorts of index funds.

While "Turnover" is measured over a period of time, the next three columns are recent snapshots of the portfolio. The item, "% Cash," shows the portion of the fund's portfolio that's not invested in stocks or bonds. A fund with a relatively low cash level, say 2 or 3 percent, is said to be "fully invested." If a fund has a double-digit cash level, it usually indicates the fund manager is wary of the market, or can't find the kinds of investment opportunities he or she likes. On occasion, this figure will be negative. That could mean one of two things. Funds that own stocks purchased on "margin"—that is, with borrowed funds—usually show a negative cash figure. But few funds actually buy on margin. More likely, the fund has just paid out a capital gains distribution.

Next comes "% Foreign." The idea in including this data is that many U.S. diversified funds do own a small measure of foreign stocks. Suppose you had chosen Oppenheimer Quest Capital Value A to fill in the mid-cap blend portion of your portfolio. By looking at this column, you will find the fund has 41 percent of its assets abroad, which could be enough to make you wonder if this fund is the optimal mid-cap growth fund for your portfolio. Likewise, this item of info is a way to check up on how international your international funds really are. SmallCap World, for instance, has only 38 percent of its assets abroad.

Then comes the "P–E Ratio," or price-to-earnings ratio. With equities, the p–e ratio is the price of the stock divided by the last 12 months' earnings per share. A stock that sells at 50 and has earned $2.50 per share has a p–e of 20. Another way to interpret the p–e is, "How many dollars do you have to pay for each $1 of earnings?" In that analysis, a 20 p–e tells you it costs $20 to "buy" every $1 of earnings.

Investment analysts use p–e's as a measure of value. Stocks with low p–e's are said to be "cheap," and high p–e's, "expensive." For the stock market as a whole, the average p–e over time is about 14; in bull markets, that average can climb over 20. At the end of 1998, the p–e on the S&P 500 was a breathtaking 33 times the last year's earnings.

The price–earnings ratio for a mutual fund is simply the average of the p–e's of the stocks in the fund, weighted by the size of the holdings. Suppose a fund has just two stocks: $90 million of bank, with a p–e of 15, and $10 million worth of software company, with a p–e of 45. The average of the two numbers, 15 and 45, is 30. But 90 percent of the fund is in the stock with a p–e of 15, and 10 percent is in the stock with a lofty 45. So take 90 percent of 15, or 13.5, and add to it 10 percent of 45, or 4.5 percent. The weighted average p–e is 18.

Stocks with high p–e's often have no dividends or low dividends because the companies are growing so fast they need to reinvest all their profits. Low-growth companies, like automakers, utilities, and oil producers, pay relatively high dividends. High p–e funds are not going to generate a lot of dividends. Low p–e stocks are often a mainstay of growth and income and equity–income funds.

Stocks and funds with relatively high p–e's are considered riskier than those with low p–e's (Table 7-5). That's because Wall Street has high

TABLE 7-5

EQUITY FUNDS: PRICE–EARNINGS RATIOS

HIGHEST		LOWEST	
Fund ▼	Price–earnings ratio* ▼	Fund ▼	Price–earnings ratio* ▼
JANUS OLYMPUS	54	EVERGREEN LATIN AMERICA B	9
STRONG GROWTH 20	54	DELAWARE EMERGING MARKETS A	9
PIMCO INNOVATION C	53	PRUDENTIAL DISTRESSED SECURITIES B	9
JANUS TWENTY	53	MERRILL LYNCH LATIN AMERICA B	10
PBHG LARGE-CAP 20 PBHG	53	LINDNER INTERNATIONAL INV.	10
JANUS ENTERPRISE	52	MERRILL LYNCH MID EAST/AFRICA B	11
MILLENNIUM GROWTH	52	TEMPLETON LATIN AMERICA I	11
PBHG TECHNOLOGY & COMMUNICATIONS	51	BLACKROCK INTL. EMRG. MARKETS INV. A	11
BLACKROCK SMALL-CAP GROWTH INV. A	51	OAKMARK INTERNATIONAL SMALL-CAP	11
IDEX GROWTH A	51	VONTOBEL EASTERN EUROPEAN EQUITY	11
DREYFUS TECHNOLOGY GROWTH	51	IVY SOUTH AMERICA A	12
APEX MID-CAP GROWTH	50	U.S. GLOBAL INVESTORS CHINA REGION	12
RYDEX OTC INV.	50	FIDELITY EMERGING MARKETS	12
JANUS MERCURY	50	LINDNER/RYBACK SMALL-CAP INV.	12
FIDELITY SELECT COMPUTERS	50	FIDELITY LATIN AMERICA	12
VAN KAMPEN AGGRESSIVE GROWTH B	50	DREYFUS EMERGING MARKETS	12
POTOMAC OTC PLUS	50	CORBIN SMALL-CAP VALUE	12
INFORMATIONTECH 100	50	MONTGOMERY EMERG. MARKETS FOCUS A	12
TRANSAMERICA PREMIER BALANCED INV.	49	KAMINSKI POLAND	12
TCW/DW SMALL-CAP GROWTH B	49	NAVELLIER SMALL-CAP VALUE	12

*1997

DATA: MORNINGSTAR INC.

hopes for such companies and will be quick to dump them if they disappoint. If the investment world assigns a low p–e to a company's stock, expectations are already low. Funds with low p–e stocks have generally been thought to be less risky than those with high p–e stocks.

A low p–e on a fund's stocks may make it look attractive, but these numbers require further analysis. For instance, in the 1999 Scoreboard, the much battered Asian funds show up with the lowest p–e's. How's that? The p–e is based on a current price and the last 12 months' earnings. In the case of many Latin American funds, that price will be much depressed because of all the recent market turmoil. Yet the earnings, the denominator in the ratio, are based on a level of earnings that is unlikely to be repeated in the next 12 months as those nations go through dire financial and economic upheaval. If you could get a reasonable earnings estimate for the next 12 months and recalculate the p–e, you would probably find that it's much higher.

The next column, "Untaxed Gains," is also a revealing feature. This figure shows what percentage of the portfolio is unrealized capital gains and undistributed gains (see Chapter 6). Suppose a $500 million fund acquired its holdings at a cost of $400 million. There's $100 million in unrealized gains. All together, that's 20 percent of the portfolio. Suppose you buy the fund today, and the manager liquidates the entire portfolio tomorrow (that almost never happens). Twenty percent of the money that comes back to you will be capital gains on which you will owe tax.

Just because the figure may be high doesn't mean you should avoid the fund. The figure is very high for Century Shares, 73 percent, but that's because the fund is a long-term investor that holds on to stocks for years. A high untaxed gains figure is also a sign that the fund has been successful. A fast-growing fund will probably have a low figure because the fund assets will likely be increasing much faster than its portfolio profits.

Funds that have suffered large losses often have negative capital gains exposure. That's because although mutual funds have to distribute realized capital gains to shareholders, they're not permitted to distribute realized losses. Instead, the losses are retained within the fund, and used to offset or "shelter" capital gains. Buying a fund with large losses can be a smart move, if you think the fund is poised to make gains. Certainly, investors who bought high-yield bond funds in 1991 had the benefit of

large losses incurred during the 1989–1990 collapse of the junk bond market. And in 1993, many precious metals funds ran up big gains and sheltered them with losses built up over many years. But before buying a fund for the sheltering power of its capital losses, you should be convinced that the fund's fortunes are on the mend. Otherwise, you're just buying another money-losing fund.

Going into 1999, various Asian, Latin American, and diversified emerging markets funds were full of untapped tax losses. Goldman Sachs Asia Growth A has losses amounting to 90 percent of its assets; Excelsior Latin America, 97 percent; and PIMCo Emerging Markets B, 99 percent. When those funds rebound—and they will someday—those losses will shelter a good portion of the early gains.

The column "Largest Holding" is also telling. Though most funds hold dozens, if not hundreds, of stocks, the largest holding often signals the investment style. If the largest holding is Microsoft, Procter & Gamble, or General Electric, you know the fund likes large, strong, and well-established companies. If the largest holding is an obscure high-tech company you've never heard of, that's a tip-off, too. You can bet that the second, third, and other holdings are not Microsoft, P&G, and GE.

Ask the fund to send a shareholder report that has the entire portfolio. Of course, that's only a snapshot of what the portfolio looked like on a particular day. In fact, a portfolio is dynamic. Even if the names don't change much, the numbers do, since the prices of the holdings can change every day. But the "personality" of the fund, as shown through the kind of investments it makes, doesn't change.

The "% Asset" that follows "Largest Holding" tells you how much of the fund is made up of this stock. If it's 10 percent (and that would be high), a 10 percent move in the underlying stock would, all things being equal, show up as a 1 percent move in the fund.

In the bond fund Scoreboard, there's an item called "Maturity." Like p–e's in the equity fund Scoreboard, maturity tells you something about the nature and risk profile of the fund. In the bond business maturity is simply the time until the bond matures or pays back the principal, or face amount. Maturity for a bond fund is simply the average of the maturities of the bonds in the fund, weighted according to the market value of those securities.

As a rule, the longer the maturity of a fund, the more volatile it is, and the greater the risk. Funds with longer maturities fare well when interest rates fall, but they're battered when rates rise. Shorter maturity funds do just the opposite. They may lose a bit when rates rise, but not nearly so much as the longer-term funds.

Keep in mind that there is one major difference between maturity of bonds and maturity of bond funds. The maturity of a bond is declining all the time. A 30-year bond issued 10 years ago is a 20-year bond today, and will be a 5-year security in 15 years. In that sense the riskiness of a bond declines as it gets closer to maturity.

A bond fund, on the other hand, never matures. The maturity does change, but does so by the decision of its portfolio manager. If the goal is to keep the fund's maturity at 15 years, for instance, the manager has to keep juggling the bonds and the mix of bonds so as to produce that average result.

Risk

For our Scoreboard we define risk as the potential for losing money. There are other ways to define it, but for you as an investor it's the most significant way. If your mutual fund is volatile—if its net asset value is subject to sharp fluctuations—it's risky. You're probably not going to get too upset about sharp moves to the upside. But you're not going to like it when the NAV nosedives.

The BUSINESS WEEK ratings focus on downside risk. To determine a fund's risk, we first measure a fund's total return for each month in the five-year measurement period. Total return is the change in net asset value, plus any distributed dividends and capital gains. Suppose the net asset value of a fund drops from $12.50 per share to $12.25 during the month and there were no dividend or capital gains distributions. The fund's total return was –2 percent.

The next step is to calculate that month's Treasury bill rate of return—what you could have earned by taking on no risk at all. If the annualized T-bill rate was 4 percent, the one-month return is 4 percent divided by 12, or 0.33 percent. Then we take 2 percent away from 0.33 percent and get –1.67 percent.

When a fund earns less than the T-bill rate, the result will always be a negative number. Then all the negative numbers are added up and divided by the number of months in the period. So, suppose that in a 60-month period a fund underperforms in 24 months. The negative numbers for each of those months are added up and divided by 60.

The farther fund performance falls below the T-bill rate, the greater the average negative number will be. And the greater the number, the higher your risk of losing money in a mutual fund. This risk-of-loss factor is also subtracted from a fund's total return over the entire period to come up with the BW rating.

For the risk column, the Scoreboard translates these numbers into one of five categories of risk. The funds with the greatest risk-of-loss numbers get the "very high" designation. That classification is followed by "high," "average," "low," and "very low." The funds at each extreme—the very highest and very lowest—are highlighted in Tables 7-6 and 7-7.

We also have a feature in the risk column showing the best and worst quarters of the last five years or 20 calendar quarters. We only include these data for funds with five years of performance history. These figures can show you the range of quarterly results over the last five years, so you get a sense of how volatile the fund can be.

Here's how you might use the best and worst quarter data provided. Consider T. Rowe Price Balanced Fund and T. Rowe Price Blue Chip Growth. (It's an easy comparison because they're next to each other in the Scoreboard.) T. Rowe Price Balanced Fund's best quarter was the fourth of 1998, up 12.2 percent, and its worst, the third of 1998, down 6.5 percent. T. Rowe Price Blue Chip Growth, on the other hand, had higher highs and lower lows: a 24.7 percent gain in the fourth quarter of 1998 and a 12.1 percent loss in the third quarter of 1998. The differences are dramatic. You could also have surmised there was a difference by looking at the risk rating before the best quarter/worst quarter statistics. T. Rowe Price Balanced has a "very low" rating, while T. Rowe Price Blue Chip Growth has a "low" rating for risk.

The best/worst quarterly statistics could help you compare funds with the same risk ratings. Look at Fidelity Low-Priced Stock Fund and the Royce Total Return Fund. Both are small-cap value funds and are low in risk. Royce Micro-Cap Fund has a 9.9 percent best quarter (the fourth of 1998) and a –10.5 percent return in the third quarter of 1998. Fidelity Low-Priced Stock had a higher high, up 13 percent in the third quarter of 1997, and down 16.8 percent in

> "Maturity" is an indicator of a bond fund's risk.

TABLE 7-6

RISKY BUSINESS
FUNDS WITH "VERY HIGH" RISK

ABN AMRO ASIAN TIGERS COMM.	FRONTIER EQUITY	PIONEER GOLD A
AIM EMERGING MARKETS B	GAM PACIFIC BASIN A	PRUDENTIAL NATURAL RESOURCES B
AIM LATIN AMERICA GROWTH A	GOVETT EMERGING MARKETS EQUITY A	PUTNAM OTC & EMERGING GROWTH A
AIM NEW PACIFIC GROWTH A	GOVETT SMALLER COMPANIES A	ROBERTSON STEPHENS CONTRARIAN A
AMERICAN CENT. GLOBAL GOLD	HANCOCK GLOBAL TECHNOLOGY A	ROCKWOOD
AMERICAN CENT.–20TH CENT. GIFTRUST	HANCOCK SPECIAL EQUITIES B	RYDEX PRECIOUS METALS
AMERICAN CENT.–20TH CENT. VISTA INV.	IAI EMERGING GROWTH	SCHRODER ALL-ASIA A
AMERICAN HERITAGE	IDS PRECIOUS METALS A	SCUDDER GOLD
AMERICAN PERFORM AGGR. GROWTH	INVESCO ENERGY	SCUDDER LATIN AMERICA
APEX MID-CAP GROWTH	INVESCO GOLD	SCUDDER PACIFIC OPPORTUNITIES
BT INVESTMENT LATIN AMERICA EQ.	INVESCO PACIFIC BASIN	SEI INSTL. SMALL-CAP GROWTH A
BT INVESTMENT PACIFIC BASIN EQ.	IVY CANADA A	SELIGMAN COMMUNICATIONS & INFORMATION A
BT INVESTMENT SMALL-CAP	IVY CHINA REGION A	SHELBY
BULL & BEAR GOLD INVESTORS	IVY U.S. EMERGING GROWTH A	SMITH BARNEY NATURAL RESOURCES B
BULL & BEAR SPECIAL EQUITIES	JAPAN	SMITH BARNEY SPECIAL EQUITIES A
CAPPIELLO-RUSHMORE EMRG. GROWTH	JP MORGAN EMERGING MARKETS EQUITY	SOGEN GOLD A
CAPSTONE JAPAN	LEXINGTON GOLDFUND	STAGECOACH STRATEGIC GROWTH A
CHESAPEAKE AGGRESSIVE GROWTH	LEXINGTON STRATEGIC INVESTMENTS	STATE ST. RESEARCH GLOBAL RESEARCH A
COMSTOCK PARTNERS CAPITAL VALUE A	LEXINGTON STRATEGIC SILVER	STEADMAN AMERICAN INDUSTRY
DELAWARE NEW PACIFIC A	LEXINGTON WORLDWIDE EMERGING MARKETS	STEADMAN INVESTMENT
DOMINION INSIGHT GROWTH	MERRILL LYNCH DRAGON B	STEADMAN SECURITY TRUST
DREYFUS PREMIER AGGR. GROWTH A	MERRILL LYNCH LATIN AMERICA B	STRONG ASIA PACIFIC
EATON VANCE GREATER CHINA GR. B	MERRILL LYNCH TECHNOLOGY B	T. ROWE PRICE JAPAN
EVERGREEN AGGRESSIVE GROWTH A	MIDAS	T. ROWE PRICE LATIN AMERICA
EVERGREEN LATIN AMERICA B	MONTEREY MURPHY BIOTECHNOLOGY	T. ROWE PRICE NEW ASIA
EVERGREEN PRECIOUS METALS B	MONTEREY MURPHY TECHNOLOGY	TCW/DW LATIN AMERICAN GROWTH B
EVERGREEN SMALL CO. GROWTH B	MONTEREY OCM GOLD	TCW/DW SMALL-CAP GROWTH B
EXCELSIOR LATIN AMERICA	MONTGOMERY EMERGING MARKETS R	TEMPLETON DEVELOPING MARKETS I
EXCELSIOR PACIFIC/ASIA	MOSAIC FORESIGHT	TEMPLETON PACIFIC GROWTH I
EXCELSIOR SMALL-CAP A	MSDW HEALTH SCIENCES B	U.S. GLOBAL INVESTORS GLOBAL RESOURCES
FIDELITY EMERGING MARKETS	MSDW PACIFIC GROWTH B	U.S. GLOBAL INVESTORS GOLD SHARES
FIDELITY JAPAN	MSDW PRECIOUS METALS & MINERALS B	U.S. GLOBAL INVESTORS WORLD GOLD
FIDELITY LATIN AMERICA	NICHOLAS-APPLEGATE SMALL-CAP GROWTH C	UAM ACADIAN EMERGING MARKETS
FIDELITY PACIFIC BASIN	NOMURA PACIFIC BASIN	UNITED GOLD & GOVERNMENT A
FIDELITY SELECT AIR TRANSPORT	OBERWEIS EMERGING GROWTH	USAA AGGRESSIVE GROWTH
FIDELITY SELECT COMPUTERS	OPPENHEIMER GOLD & SPEC. MINERALS A	USAA GOLD
FIDELITY SEL. DEVELOP. COMMUN.	PACIFIC HORIZON AGGRESSIVE GROWTH A	VAN ECK ASIA DYNASTY A
FIDELITY SEL. ELECTRONICS	PARKSTONE SMALL-CAP INV. A	VAN ECK GOLD/RESOURCES A
FIDELITY SEL. ENERGY SERVICE	PARNASSUS	VAN ECK INTL. INVESTORS GOLD A
FIDELITY SEL. GOLD	PATHFINDER	VAN KAMPEN ASIAN GROWTH A
FIDELITY SEL. PREC. METALS & MNLS.	PBHG EMERGING GROWTH	VANGUARD GOLD & PRECIOUS METALS
FIDELITY SOUTHEAST ASIA	PBHG GROWTH PBHG	VANGUARD PACIFIC STOCK INDEX
FIRST AMERICAN EMERG. MARKETS A	PERKINS OPPORTUNITY	WASATCH MID-CAP
FLAG INVESTOR EMERGING GROWTH A	PIMCO OPPORTUNITY C	WPG TUDOR
FORTIS ADVANT. CAPITAL APPREC. A	PIMCO PRECIOUS METALS C	WRIGHT EQUIFUND-HONG KONG
FRANKLIN GOLD A	PIN OAK AGGRESSIVE STOCK	YORKTOWN CLASSIC VALUE

DATA: MORNINGSTAR INC.

the third quarter of 1998—a little wider range of returns than the Fidelity fund, especially on the downside. If you are concerned about downside risk, the Royce fund appears to be the better choice. In five-year average annual return, the Royce fund beats the Fidelity fund, 16.8 percent to 16.2 percent.

Specialized funds usually have bigger swings than the diversified funds. Look at Fidelity Select Computers. Its best quarterly return was 1998's fourth, up 39.4 percent; its worst, the fourth quarter of 1998, down 25.8 percent. But funds that invest in emerging growth companies can also have wide swings. MFS Emerging

TABLE 7-7

NOT SO RISKY BUSINESS
FUNDS WITH "VERY LOW" RISK

ABN AMRO BALANCED COMM.	GABELLI WESTWOOD BALANCE RET.	PHOENIX INCOME & GROWTH A
ADVANCE CAPITAL I BALANCED	GALAXY ASSET ALLOCATION RET. A	PIONEER BALANCED A
AIM ADVISOR FLEX C	GATEWAY	PREFERRED ASSET ALLOCATION
AIM GLOBAL GROWTH & INCOME B	GE STRATEGIC INVESTMENT A	T. ROWE PRICE BALANCED
ALLIANCE CONSERVATIVE INV. B	GEORGE PUTNAM OF BOSTON A	T. ROWE PRICE CAPITAL APPRECIATION
AMERICAN BALANCED	HANCOCK SOVEREIGN BALANCED B	T. ROWE PRICE DIVIDEND GROWTH
AMERICAN DIVERSIFIED GLOBAL VALUE	HERITAGE INCOME-GROWTH A	T. ROWE PRICE EQUITY-INCOME
AMERICAN MUTUAL	HIGHMARK BALANCED FID.	PRIMARY INCOME
ANALYTIC DEFENSIVE EQUITY	HILLIARD LYONS GROWTH A	PRINCIPAL BALANCED A
AQUINAS BALANCED	HOTCHKIS & WILEY BALANCED	PUTNAM BALANCED RETIREMENT A
ARCH BALANCED INV. A	IAA ASSET ALLOCATION	PUTNAM UTIL. GROWTH & INCOME A
ATLAS BALANCED A	IDS MUTUAL A	RIGHTIME
BB&T BALANCED A	INCOME FUND OF AMERICA	RIGHTIME BLUE CHIP
BERWYN INCOME	INVESCO BALANCED	RIGHTIME MIDCAP
BLACKROCK BALANCED INV. A	INVESCO MULTI-ASSET ALLOCATION	RIGHTIME SOCIAL AWARENESS
BOSTON 1784 ASSET ALLOCATION	INVESCO TOTAL RETURN	ROYCE TOTAL RETURN
BT INVESTMENT LIFECYCLE LONG-RANGE	JAMESTOWN BALANCED	SEI INSTL. BALANCED A
BT INVESTMENT LIFECYCLE MID-RANGE	JANUS BALANCED	SELIGMAN INCOME A
CALDWELL & ORKIN MARKET OPPORTUNITY	KEMPER RETIREMENT I	SENTINEL BALANCED A
CAPITAL INCOME BUILDER	KEMPER RETIREMENT II	SIT BALANCED
CARILLON CAPITAL	KEMPER RETIREMENT III	SMITH BARNEY CONC. ALLOC. SOCIAL A
CHASE VISTA BALANCED A	KEMPER RETIREMENT IV	SMITH BARNEY PREM. TOTAL. RETURN B
COLUMBIA BALANCED	LONGLEAF PARTNERS SMALL-CAP	SOGEN INTERNATIONAL A
COUNTRYWIDE UTILITY A	MAIRS & POWER BALANCED	STAGECOACH ASSET ALLOCATION A
DELAWARE A	MAP-EQUITY	STAGECOACH BALANCED A
DODGE & COX BALANCED	MAS BALANCED INSTL.	STEIN ROE BALANCED
DREYFUS BALANCED	MAXUS INCOME INV.	STELLAR A
EATON VANCE BALANCED A	MENTOR INCOME & GROWTH A	STRONG ASSET ALLOCATION
ECLIPSE BALANCED	MERGER	TCW/DW INCOME & GROWTH C
EVERGREEN BALANCED B	MERRILL LYNCH GLOBAL ALLOCATION B	TRIFLEX
EXETER BLENDED ASSET I A	MERRIMAN GROWTH & INCOME	UAM C&B BALANCED
FBP CONTRARIAN BALANCED	MFS GLOBAL TOTAL RETURN A	UAM SAMI PREFERRED STOCK INCOME
FEDERATED STOCK & BOND A	MFS TOTAL RETURN A	UAM SIRACH STRATEGIC BALANCED IS.
FIDELITY ASSET MANAGER: INCOME	JP MORGAN DIVERSIFIED	UAM STERLING BALANCED INSTL.
FIDELITY BALANCED	MOSAIC HILL BALANCED	USAA GROWTH & TAX STRATEGY
FIDELITY PURITAN	NEW CENTURY I	VALLEY FORGE
FIRST AMERICAN BALANCED A	NEW ENGLAND BALANCED A	VANGUARD ASSET ALLOCATION
FIRST AMERICAN EQUITY-INCOME A	NORTH AMERICAN BALANCED C	VANGUARD BALANCED INDEX
FIRST OMAHA EQUITY	NUVEEN DIVIDEND & GROWTH A	VANGUARD STAR
FLAG INVESTORS VALUE BUILDER A	OPPENHEIMER DISCIP. ALLOCATION A	VANGUARD UTILITIES INCOME
FLEX-FUNDS MUIRFIELD	OPPENHEIMER MULTIPLE STRATEGY A	VANGUARD WELLESLEY INCOME
FOUNDERS BALANCED	PACIFIC ADVISORS BALANCED A	VANGUARD WELLINGTON
FRANKLIN ASSET ALLOCATION	PARKSTONE BAL. ALLOCATION INV. A	VICTORY BALANCED A
FRANKLIN EQUITY INCOME A	PAX WORLD	WACHOVIA BALANCED A
FRANKLIN INCOME A	PEGASUS MGD. ASSETS BALANCED A	WM BOND & STOCK A
FUNDMANAGER MGD. TOT. RETURN ADV.	PEGASUS MGD. ASSETS CONSERV. A	ZWEIG MANAGED ASSETS C
GABELLI ABC	PERMANENT PORTFOLIO	

DATA: MORNINGSTAR INC.

Growth B was down 18.1 percent in the third quarter of 1998, and up 28 percent in the fourth.

One thing these "worst quarter" figures don't show you is how the funds behaved in a long bear market. There hasn't been one in the past five years. But as the statistics show, there have been some quarters bad enough to give you a taste of the bear. Take each of your fund's worst quarter returns and double it. If you can live with that kind of one-quarter loss for one of your funds, you're ready for whatever the markets may give you.

1999: Aiming for the Fifth Big Year

Every December for the past few years, the stock market seers made their predictions—and have usually been wrong. Typically, you would expect Wall Streeters to promise investors great riches, only to see the stock market subsequently wobble and fall. But in the latter half of the 1990s, just the opposite was happening. The pundits worked at keeping expectations modest, and the market surprised investors to the upside.

Nineteen ninety-eight was a case in point. At the end of 1997, economists and investment strategists warned investors that stocks would be weak in the first half of 1998. Their rationale: the economic and financial meltdown in Asia that started in the latter half of 1997 would infect and weaken the U.S. economy in 1998, especially in the first half of the year. In early January, the market plummeted, and that looked like a pretty smart prediction. A few weeks later, the market turned around and began a wild and often volatile ride.

When the market closed for the year, the numbers were stunners once again. The Dow Jones industrials, up 1273 points, or 16.1 percent (18.1 percent total return when you add in dividends); the Standard & Poor's 500, up 259 points, or 26.7 percent (28.6 percent total return, adding in dividends). That was the fourth year in a row that the S&P 500 exceeded 20 percent. Compare that to the long-term average, built up over 70 years, of just 11.5 percent.

That's not to say it was easy money. In the course of racking up another strong year, the Dow and S&P 500 suffered corrections of 20 percent. Day-to-day price volatility surged as well. The Dow now makes a daily move of greater than 150 points an average of once a week. And over the year, the gains in the market were made by fewer and fewer large-cap stocks.

Small-cap and mid-cap stocks lagged all year, and small-caps—despite the hoopla and hype around the Internet stocks—were actually down about 2.2 percent for the year as measured by the Russell 2000 stock index. The Internet stocks, companies with little revenue, no profits, and astronomical valuations, provided a lot of entertainment and cocktail party chatter, but there, too, all the action and the money were concentrated in a relatively few stocks. A handful of Internet sector funds soared on the backs of these stocks, and they also gave a lot of lift to the broader technology sector funds. But by and large, these stocks were too small and too illiquid for many mutual funds to buy—and so fund investors were largely left out of their gains.

Micro-cap stocks, the smallest of the small caps, were disastrous. Stocks with market capitalizations less than $250 million were down 24.1 percent in 1998, according to Salomon Smith Barney. That's a far cry from the nearly 26 percent gain earned by all stocks with market caps above $20 billion. Even the gains in the large-cap stocks were not widely distributed. Analysts at Morgan Stanley Dean Witter estimated that 100 of the largest companies in the S&P 500 accounted for 24.2 percent out of the S&P's 28.6 percent return; the other 400 only accounted for about 4.4 percent.

Looking back on 1998, the stock market played out like a three-act play. The first act: a bravura performance by a stock market that wasn't expected to perform very well. Starting the year at 7908, the Dow industrials raced up to 9374 by July 17 (up 18.5 percent), and the S&P 500 climbed 22.7 percent. The NASDAQ Composite, which includes most of the powerhouse technology stocks, was up 28 percent by mid-July.

The second act, starting in midsummer had a very different tone. First slowly, then quickly, stocks ran into trouble. Valuations were high because, during the first half of the year, stocks had made sharp price gains on small gains in corporate earnings, and the profit outlook was deteriorating, even in the face of a strong domestic economy. The economy was so strong, indeed, that some feared the Federal Reserve might raise interest rates, and that would be a major depressant on stocks. In Washington, the President got ever more embroiled in the Monica Lewinsky affair, and the market hates political instability. From abroad, the news was not good. Japan's new government was showing little leadership in trying to turn its mammoth economy around, and the emerging economies of Asia were still bogged down in a funk.

The internal dynamics of the market were signalling trouble, too. Even though major stock market averages were going up and making new highs, the majority of stocks were not. Indeed, the number of losers started to outpace winners on the New York Stock Exchange by May. Small-cap stocks, up 12.5 percent by mid-April, had started to decline. The rally left a good portion of the stock market behind—and mutual fund investors as well. At the end of March, the average U.S. diversified equity fund trailed the S&P 500 by 11.7 percent to 13.9 percent, a 2.2 percentage point performance gap. By mid-year, the average U.S. diversified equity fund return had slipped to 11.4 percent, but the S&P 500 kept on climbing, and the performance gap widened to 6.3 percent. That left many mutual fund shareholders scratching their heads as their funds' returns didn't seem anywhere near as strong as the market's headlines suggested.

Given the deterioration in the fundamentals and technicals—the internal dynamics—a summer sell-off should not have been surprising or unexpected. Federal Reserve chairman Alan Greenspan, a man whose words often move markets, raised the issue of a stock market correction in July 21 comments. And a few weeks later, after the market had begun to fall, analyst Ralph J. Acompora of Prudential Securities, Inc., a longtime bull on stocks, predicted the Dow would fall 1900 points from the July high—to about 7400. That touched off a wave off selling, which was accelerated a short-time later when the cash-strapped Russian government defaulted on its debt.

Why did that prompt investors to dump U.S. stocks? No one knew or could accurately assess the consequences. Would the default cause any bank failure or other financial instability? The Russian default shook one of the underlying assumptions of the bull market, the spread of successful market-based capitalism around the world. In reaction to the Russian situation, investors accelerated their selling in already battered emerging markets, and even took profits in the United States as well. When investors get

nervous, they want to raise cash in a hurry, and the plump gains they had amassed in large-cap U.S. stocks seemed to be the place to get the cash. On August 31, the Dow dropped 513 points, 6.4 percent, the worst one-day loss of the year.

There was turmoil in the bond market as well. Investors also staged a "flight to quality"—they stampeded into U.S. Treasury securities, driving interest rates down. The yield on the long-term U.S. Treasury bond dropped as low as 4.72 percent. The fall in rates did not help other sectors of the bond market. High-yield, emerging market, and some mortgage-backed bonds, all seen as risky, fell behind. Nor did municipal bond prices keep up with Treasuries. That left yields on high-quality municipals, whose interest payments are free from federal taxes, higher than those on U.S. Treasuries, which are not.

Then word got out that Long-Term Capital Management, a large, secretive, and highly-leveraged hedge fund, had made bets that turned bad in a hurry. That set off further consternation, since, like Russia, no one could assess how much damage LTCM would do to its lenders and the other institutions with which it had made trades. If LTCM failed to make good on its obligations, investors worried it could wipe out some major banks as well. In the end, it took the prodding of the Federal Reserve Bank of New York to get a number of Wall Street's largest investment banks to take over the hedge fund.

The crisis subsided somewhat in September, as financial institutions assessed their exposure to Russian bonds and hedge-fund losses. But then investors started to worry about problems in Latin America, especially Brazil, and became concerned that while some Asian countries, like South Korea and Thailand, had started to come back, others, like Malaysia and Indonesia, looked hopeless. And everyone feared that China would devalue its currency, a move that would set Asia back even further. Though investors came back to the U.S. stock market, it was a flight to quality as well. Blue-chips recovered somewhat, but not secondary issues. That left fund investors reeling. At the end of September, the average U.S. domestic equity fund was down 5.2 percent for the nine months of 1998; the S&P 500 was up 6 percent. The performance gap that had plagued the funds all year had only gotten wider.

The stock market started to lose ground again in October, but then the Fed came to the rescue with a surprise cut in short-term interest rates. That launched the third act, the resolution of the conflict. Between October 15 and October 21 alone, the Dow industrials jumped 550 points, regaining half of what they had lost in the summer sell-off. And by mid-November, after further rate cuts, the Dow had recovered about 1000 points; even many small-cap and mid-cap stocks rallied.

In the last three months of 1998, mid-cap growth funds gained 25.6 percent and small-cap growth funds, 24 percent. And the average domestic equity fund gained 20.1 percent in the fourth quarter, a tad below the 21.4 percent gain for the S&P 500. Still, the funds were coming back from a huge deficit in performance, and the total year's returns, while strong in an absolute sense, were poor in a relative sense: a 14.1 percent total return for U.S. diversified equity funds versus 28.6 percent for the S&P 500 (and the index funds that track it). Add in the sector and international funds, and the all-equity fund average drops to just 11.4 percent.

Equity Funds

The stock market has been biased toward large-cap stocks since 1994, but this bias was never more pronounced than in 1998 (and early 1999 for that matter). That made the S&P 500 index funds the big story of the year and the most popular sort of fund, and stodgy Vanguard became the hottest mutual fund company. The S&P 500 is not exclusively a large-cap index, but it has the largest stocks in the market and performs well when large-caps are in favor.

Investors once derided index-fund investing as just "settling for average." Now, investors are looking at S&P 500 index funds in a different light. If the S&P 500's 28.6 percent—24 percent a year over the last five years—is just average, it's still far superior to most other mutual funds. Their outperformance—and everybody's else's relative underperformance—really came to light during 1998. Around the middle of the year, the Vanguard 500 Index and other S&P index funds started to earn A ratings for risk-adjusted total returns over the last five years.

And by year-end, the BUSINESS WEEK A-list was peppered with indexers (Table 8-1). Of the 104 funds on the list, 12 are pure S&P 500 index funds. (Most of them use S&P 500, "Equity Index," or "Market Index" in the fund name. Galaxy II Large Company Index Retail Shares is also an S&P 500 fund.)

Other A-list funds are variations on the large-cap index theme. For instance, Vanguard Growth Index is the growth-stock portion of the S&P 500, and the Wilshire Target Large Company Growth Investors covers similar territory, an index of large-cap growth stocks. Vanguard Balanced Index is a balanced fund comprised of equity and bond market index funds. PIMCo Stockplus Institutional and Smith Breeden U.S. Equity Market Plus mimic the index, but try to earn a little extra using futures and options, while Analytic Enhanced Equity draws from 500 S&P stocks to build a portfolio that hopefully outperforms the index. And Domini Social Equity starts with the S&P 500, but screens out tobacco, alcohol, and gambling stocks to start with, and then tosses companies if their records on labor, environment, or family issues are, by the manager's reckoning, not up to snuff. Sure, that gets rid of a lot of the 500, but Domini adds back non-S&P companies that it believes excel in the values the fund promotes.

But the A-list reaches well beyond the indexers. The variation in the returns are great, from Legg Mason Value Primary Shares, up an astounding 32 percent a year over the last five (and 48 percent in 1998), down to the plodding but steady Fidelity Asset Manager: Income, with just a 9 percent average annual return. What they all have in common is a superior return for the amount of risk they took. Smack in the middle of the list is MFS Massachusetts Investors Trust, with 23 percent a year total return over the last five (and 23 percent in 1998, too). The fund, now with $6.7 billion in three classes of shares, opened for business in July 1924 and it is considered to be the first mutual fund. Lead portfolio manager John D. Laupheimer, who has run the fund since 1993, describes it as a "conservative growth" portfolio looking to invest in blue-chip growth stocks "at the right price." He scored well on that count, last year buying shares of IBM at prices under $100 each. By year-end, it was at $184 and was one of his largest holdings.

Large-cap funds, mainly those that invest in large growth stocks, dominate the A-list. That should not be surprising as large caps have trounced mid-cap and smaller-cap companies every year for the last five years. And growth funds, which emphasize companies with more reliable and sustainable earnings growth, have prevailed over value funds, which often buy more cyclical companies when they are out of favor and bet on the rebound. A few years ago the A-list was dominated by large-cap value

Index funds were stellar performers during 1998.

TABLE 8-1

TOP-PERFORMING EQUITY MUTUAL FUNDS

These equity mutual funds have earned A's
for delivering the best risk-adjusted total returns over the past five years.

Fund	Average annual total return*	Investment category	Risk	Fund	Average annual total return*	Investment category	Risk
ACCESSOR GROWTH**	26.7%	Large-cap Growth	Low	LONGLEAF PARTNERS	19.8%	Mid-cap Blend	Low
AMERICAN CENT. EQUITY GROWTH INV.	23.9	Large-cap Value	Low	LONGLEAF PARTNERS SMALL-CAP	18.5	Small-cap Value	Very low
AMERICAN CENT. INCOME & GROWTH INV.	23.7	Large-cap Value	Low	MAIRS & POWER BALANCED**	17.1	Domestic Hybrid	Very low
ANALYTIC DEFENSE EQUITY**	17.2	Large-cap Blend	Very low	MAP-EQUITY**	21.9	Mid-cap Blend	Very low
ANALYTIC ENHANCED EQUITY**	24.3	Large-cap Blend	Low	MERGER	9.6	Domestic Hybrid	Very low
ATLAS BALANCED A**	13.9	Domestic Hybrid	Very low	MERRIMAN GROWTH & INCOME**	13.0	Large-cap Blend	Very low
BT INVESTMENT EQUITY 500 INDEX	23.9	Large-cap Blend	Low	MFS MASS. INVESTORS TRUST A	23.0	Large-cap Blend	Low
BT INVESTMENT LIFECYCLE LONG-RANGE**	15.6	Domestic Hybrid	Very low	JP MORGAN DIVERSIFIED	15.1	Domestic Hybrid	Very low
BT INVESTMENT LIFECYCLE MID-RANGE**	12.2	Domestic Hybrid	Very low	MOSAIC HILL BALANCED	15.6	Domestic Hybrid	Very low
CALDWELL & ORKIN MKT. OPPORTUNITY	18.4	Domestic Hybrid	Very low	MUNDER INDEX 500 A	23.5	Large-cap Blend	Low
CALIFORNIA INVESTMENT S&P 500 INDEX**	23.8	Large-cap Blend	Low	NATIONWIDE D	24.1	Large-cap Blend	Low
CHASE VISTA BALANCED A**	14.9	Domestic Hybrid	Very low	OPPENHEIMER QUEST BALANCED VALUE A	20.8	Domestic Hybrid	Low
CHICAGO TRUST GROWTH & INCOME	24.0	Large-cap Growth	Average	PAPP AMERICA-ABROAD	24.9	Large-cap Growth	Average
CLIPPER	21.3	Large-cap Value	Low	PAX WORLD	17.9	Domestic Hybrid	Very low
COLUMBIA BALANCED	14.8	Domestic Hybrid	Very low	PEGASUS EQUITY INDEX A	23.7	Large-cap Blend	Low
COLUMBIA COMMON STOCK	20.6	Large-cap Blend	Low	PERFORMANCE LARGE-CAP EQ. CON. SV.**	22.4	Large-cap Blend	Low
DELAWARE DEVON A**	23.7	Large-cap Blend	Low	PIMCO STOCKSPLUS INSTITUTIONAL	24.9	Large-cap Blend	Low
DOMINI SOCIAL EQUITY	24.3	Large-cap Blend	Low	PREFERRED ASSET ALLOCATION	18.0	Domestic Hybrid	Very low
DREYFUS APPRECIATION	24.6	Large-cap Growth	Low	T. ROWE PRICE BLUE CHIP GROWTH	23.9	Large-cap Blend	Low
DREYFUS S&P 500 INDEX	23.4	Large-cap Blend	Low	T. ROWE PRICE CAPITAL APPRECIATION	12.8	Domestic Hybrid	Very low
EASTCLIFF TOTAL RETURN**	21.3	Domestic Hybrid	Low	T. ROWE PRICE DIVIDEND GROWTH	20.5	Large-cap Blend	Very low
FIDELITY ASSET MANAGER: INCOME	9.0	Domestic Hybrid	Very low	T. ROWE PRICE EQUITY INDEX	23.7	Large-cap Blend	Low
FIDELITY DESTINY I	22.8	Large-cap Value	Low	T. ROWE PRICE EQUITY-INCOME	19.9	Large-cap Blend	Very low
FIDELITY DIVIDEND GROWTH	26.5	Large-cap Blend	Low	REGIONS GROWTH INVESTMENT**	22.5	Large-cap Growth	Low
FIDELITY	23.1	Large-cap Blend	Low	RIGHTIME BLUE CHIP	15.3	Large-cap Blend	Very low
FIDELITY GROWTH & INCOME	22.7	Large-cap Blend	Low	RIGHTIME MIDCAP**	15.1	Mid-cap Blend	Very low
FIDELITY SELECT HEALTH CARE	30.5	Health	Low	RIGHTIME SOCIAL AWARENESS**	17.1	Large-cap Blend	Very low
FIDELITY SPARTAN MARKET INDEX	23.7	Large-cap Blend	Low	ROYCE TOTAL RETURN	16.7	Small-cap Value	Very low
FIRST AMERICAN BALANCED A**	14.2	Domestic Hybrid	Very low	SAFECO EQUITY NO LOAD	21.7	Large-cap Blend	Low
FIRST AMERICAN EQUITY-INCOME A **	17.6	Large-cap Value	Very low	SEI INDEX S&P 500 INDEX E	23.8	Large-cap Blend	Low
FIRST FUNDS GROWTH & INCOME III**	22.1	Large-cap Blend	Low	SEQUOIA	28.1	Large-cap Value	Average
FLAG INVESTORS COMMUNICATIONS A	29.2	Communications	Average	SMITH BREEDEN US EQUITY MKT. PLUS**	23.7	Large-cap Blend	Low
FLAG INVESTORS VALUE BUILDER A	19.1	Domestic Hybrid	Very low	SSGA GROWTH & INCOME	23.6	Large-cap Blend	Average
FOUNDERS BALANCED	15.0	Domestic Hybrid	Very low	SSGA S&P 500 INDEX	23.8	Large-cap Blend	Low
GABELLI ABC**	9.4	Small-cap Growth	Very low	STEIN ROE GROWTH & INCOME	18.9	Large-cap Blend	Low
GABELLI EQUITY-INCOME	18.7	Large-cap Value	Low	STRATTON GROWTH**	20.6	Large-cap Value	Low
GABELLI WESTWOOD BALANCED RETAIL**	16.2	Domestic Hybrid	Very low	TORRAY	24.2	Large-cap Value	Average
GABELLI WESTWOOD EQUITY RETAIL**	21.1	Large-cap Blend	Low	TWEEDY, BROWNE AMERICAN VALUE	20.3	Mid-cap Value	Low
GALAXY ASSET ALLOCATION RETAIL A	15.6	Domestic Hybrid	Very low	VALUE LINE ASSET ALLOCATION	22.1	Domestic Hybrid	Low
GALAXY II LARGE CO. INDEX RETAIL	23.6	Large-cap Blend	Low	VANGUARD ASSET ALLOCATION	19.6	Domestic Hybrid	Very low
GAM NORTH AMERICA A**	22.9	Large-cap Growth	Low	VANGUARD BALANCED INDEX	15.8	Domestic Hybrid	Very low
GATEWAY	10.3	Domestic Hybrid	Very low	VANGUARD EQUITY-INCOME	19.6	Large-cap Value	Low
HILLIARD LYONS GROWTH A**	20.8	Large-cap Value	Very low	VANGUARD 500 INDEX	24.0	Large-cap Blend	Low
HOTCHKIS & WILEY BALANCED **	11.5	Domestic Hybrid	Very low	VANGUARD GROWTH INDEX	27.8	Large-cap Growth	Low
INCOME FUND OF AMERICA	14.2	Domestic Hybrid	Very low	VANGUARD HEALTH CARE	28.4	Health	Low
INVESCO BALANCED	19.3	Domestic Hybrid	Very low	VANGUARD U.S. GROWTH	26.2	Large-cap Growth	Low
INVESCO TOTAL RETURN	16.2	Domestic Hybrid	Very low	VANGUARD WELLESLEY INCOME	12.6	Domestic Hybrid	Very low
ISG LARGE-CAP EQUITY A	24.8	Large-cap Growth	Low	VONTOBEL U.S. VALUE**	21.3	Large-cap Value	Low
JANUS BALANCED	18.6	Domestic Hybrid	Very low	WASHINGTON MUTUAL INVESTORS	22.1	Large-cap Value	Low
KENT GROWTH & INCOME INVESTMENT**	20.6	Large-cap Value	Low	WEITZ PARTNERS VALUE	22.2	Mid-cap Value	Low
KENT INDEX EQUITY INVESTMENT**	23.1	Large-cap Blend	Low	WEITZ VALUE	21.6	Mid-cap Value	Low
LEGG MASON VALUE PRIMARY SHARES	32.0	Large-cap Value	Average	WILSHIRE TARGET LGE. CO. GROWTH INV.**	26.7	Large-cap Growth	Low

* 1994–98 pretax returns, appreciation plus reinvestment of dividends and capital gains.
** Fund data in Business Week Online.

DATA: MORNINGSTAR INC.

funds, a period when their returns were more competitive with growth funds but their volatility was much less. In the last year, their returns flagged and their risk increased, forcing many down a notch or two in ratings.

Domestic hybrid funds, which mix mainly large-cap stocks, bonds, and sometimes cash, are also well represented on the list, with 30 funds. In four of the last five years, the bonds added some stability during volatile stock market swings and capital appreciation as interest rates moved downward. These hybrids, by definition, tend to be more conservative than the all-equity portfolios, but you might be surprised: Eastcliff Total Return, an A-rated fund with a 21.3 percent total return for the last five years, climbed 38.7 percent in 1998, thanks to heavy weightings, about 30 percent each, in large-cap technology and health-care companies.

The A-list has just six mid-cap funds (three value, three blend) and three small-cap (two value, one growth). Given the pounding those sectors have gotten of late, their managers did yeoman work. Top-ranked Royce Total Return, for instance, earned a paltry 4.8% last year, which sounds lousy. But it's nearly 9 percentage points better than the average small-cap value fund, which was down 5.9 percent in 1998 (Table 8-2). Longleaf Partners Small Cap Fund did a lot better than Royce, up 12.7 percent last year. But the fund is closed to new investors, a not unusual occurrence among the best-performing small-cap funds.

The one small-cap growth fund on the A-list, Gabelli ABC Fund, is a strange cat for this often high-octane category of funds. Although the equities the fund invests in fit the small-cap growth category, the fund also has a wide charter that lets it buy preferred stocks, convertibles, bonds, or park its assets in cash. That brings the volatility usually associated with these small-cap growth stocks way down. But it also brings the return down as well—the fund was up just 11.1 percent in 1998, and an average 9.4 percent for the last five years. Several other funds on the A-list got there through a similar strategy of keeping the market risk so low that even a so-so return can get it on the A-list: among them are the Rightime Blue Chip, Rightime Midcap, and Rightime Social Awareness funds.

Investors wanting a bigger selection of top-rated small-cap and mid-cap funds should also check Table 8-3, "The Best Performers in Their Categories." In the mid-cap growth area, a good load fund choice is Franklin California Growth A, a fund that invests in companies based in the

TABLE 8-2

EQUITY FUND PERFORMANCE

Only technology, communications, and large-cap growth funds beat the S&P 500 in 1998.

| Category | Average annual total return* | | | |
	1998	1996–98	1994–98	1989–98
TECHNOLOGY	54.3%	22.8%	22.9%	22.0%
COMMUNICATIONS	46.4	25.4	19.7	20.6
LARGE-CAP GROWTH	36.1	26.2	20.8	18.4
LARGE-CAP BLEND	22.1	23.3	19.5	16.3
HEALTH	18.3	17.2	18.4	21.8
MID-CAP GROWTH	18.3	15.5	14.9	15.9
EUROPE	17.7	21.1	17.4	12.3
UTILITIES	17.5	17.2	13.4	13.9
LARGE-CAP VALUE	12.8	19.8	17.9	15.5
FOREIGN	12.0	9.7	7.3	8.5
WORLD	12.0	13.2	11.0	10.9
DOMESTIC HYBRID	12.0	14.6	13.0	12.3
UNALIGNED	10.9	17.0	13.7	16.0
MID-CAP BLEND	9.5	17.7	15.5	14.8
INTERNATIONAL HYBRID	9.1	7.5	6.1	3.9
JAPAN	7.1	–7.0	–2.3	0.1
FINANCIAL	5.1	25.3	23.1	21.9
SMALL-CAP GROWTH	4.6	10.6	11.9	15.5
MID-CAP VALUE	1.5	15.6	14.3	13.5
SMALL-CAP BLEND	–2.4	12.8	11.1	11.0
DIV. PACIFIC/ASIA	–4.9	–11.4	–7.4	2.1
SMALL-CAP VALUE	–5.9	13.8	12.4	12.1
PACIFIC/ASIA EX-JAPAN	–10.4	–12.3	–11.2	0.3
PRECIOUS METALS	–12.7	–18.9	–13.6	–4.0
REAL ESTATE	–16.2	10.8	7.7	8.8
NATURAL RESOURCES	–22.4	2.5	5.8	7.8
DIVERS. EMRG. MKTS.	–26.3	9.0	–11.1	2.3
LATIN AMERICA	–38.7	–1.1	–6.9	NA
U.S. DIVERS. FUNDS	14.1	18.9	16.7	15.6
ALL EQUITY FUNDS	11.4	15.0	13.6	13.9
S&P 500	28.6	28.2	24.0	19.2

*Pretax return, appreciation plus reinvestment of dividends and capital gains.
NA = Not available.

DATA: MORNINGSTAR INC.

Golden State. The fund was one of the few growth funds to earn an A rating in the 1998 Scoreboard. Its overall rating has since slipped back to B+—and it's still a fine fund. Among the no-loads, the standout is Strong Growth, which lives up to its name. The fund beat the S&P 500 over the last five years, and came darn close in

TABLE 8-3

THE BEST PERFORMERS IN THEIR CATEGORIES

Rating funds against their peers, these funds earn A's for five-year risk-adjusted total returns.
Not all categories have ratings, since some lack enough funds to perform a ratings review.

	Average annual total return*
LARGE-CAP VALUE	
AMERICAN CENT. EQUITY GROWTH INV.	23.9%
AMERICAN CENT. INCOME & GROWTH INV.	23.7
CLIPPER	21.3
FIRST AMERICAN EQUITY-INCOME A**	17.6
LEGG MASON VALUE PRIMARY SHARES	32.0
T. ROWE PRICE EQUITY-INCOME	18.8
SEQUOIA	28.1
VANGUARD EQUITY-INCOME	19.6
VONTOBEL U.S. VALUE**	21.3
WASHINGTON MUTUAL INVESTORS	22.1
LARGE-CAP BLEND	
ANALYTIC DEFENSIVE EQUITY**	17.2%
ANALYTIC ENHANCED EQUITY**	24.3
BT INVESTMENT EQUITY 500 INDEX	23.9
DELAWARE DEVON A**	23.7
DOMINI SOCIAL EQUITY	24.3
FIDELITY DIVIDEND GROWTH	26.5
FIDELITY GROWTH & INCOME	22.7
HILLIARD LYONS GROWTH A**	20.8
NATIONWIDE D	24.1
PIMCO STOCKSPLUS INSTITUTIONAL	24.9
T. ROWE PRICE BLUE CHIP GROWTH	23.9
T. ROWE PRICE DIVIDEND GROWTH	20.5
RIGHTIME BLUE CHIP	15.3
RIGHTIME SOCIAL AWARENESS**	17.1
VANGUARD 500 INDEX	24.0
LARGE-CAP GROWTH	
ACCESSOR GROWTH**	26.7%
DREYFUS APPRECIATION	24.6
ISG LARGE-CAP EQUITY A	24.8
PAPP AMERICA-ABROAD	24.9
VANGUARD GROWTH INDEX	27.8
VANGUARD U.S. GROWTH	26.2
WILSHIRE TARGET LARGE CO. GROWTH INV.**	26.7
MID-CAP VALUE	
SOUND SHORE	19.8%
TWEEDY, BROWNE AMERICAN VALUE	20.3
WEITZ PARTNERS VALUE	22.2
WEITZ VALUE	21.6
MID-CAP BLEND	
LONGLEAF PARTNERS	19.8%
MAIRS & POWER GROWTH	22.9
MAP-EQUITY**	21.9
OAK VALUE	21.8
RIGHTIME MIDCAP**	15.1
MID-CAP GROWTH	
WILLIAM BLAIR GROWTH	19.9%
EXCELSIOR INCOME & GROWTH	12.8
FRANKLIN CALIFORNIA GROWTH A	23.5
NICHOLAS II	18.3
T. ROWE PRICE MID-CAP GROWTH	20.6
STRONG GROWTH	24.5
WADDELL & REED GROWTH B	21.7
SMALL-CAP VALUE	
FAM VALUE	16.0%
LONGLEAF PARTNERS SMALL-CAP	18.5
ROYCE TOTAL RETURN	16.7

	Average annual total return*
SMALL-CAP BLEND	
GABELLI SMALL-CAP GROWTH	13.2%
WASATCH GROWTH	16.8
WEITZ HICKORY	23.8
SMALL-CAP GROWTH	
BARON ASSET	19.9%
FASCIANO	17.5
GABELLI ABC**	9.4
GALAXY SMALL-CAP VALUE RETAIL A	15.7
NICHOLAS LIMITED EDITION	15.8
DOMESTIC HYBRID	
CALDWELL & ORKIN MARKET OPPORT.	18.4%
COLUMBIA BALANCED	14.8
EASTCLIFF TOTAL RETURN**	21.3
GABELLI WESTWOOD BALANCED RETAIL**	16.2
INVESCO BALANCED	19.3
JANUS BALANCED	18.6
MAIRS & POWER BALANCED	17.1
MERGER	9.6
PAX WORLD	17.9
PREFERRED ASSET ALLOCATION	18.0
T. ROWE PRICE CAPITAL APPRECIATION	12.8
VALUE LINE ASSET ALLOCATION	22.1
VANGUARD ASSET ALLOCATION	19.6
INTERNATIONAL HYBRID	
MFS GLOBAL TOTAL RETURN A	12.6%
FOREIGN	
BT INVESTMENT INTERNATIONAL EQUITY	15.8%
EUROPACIFIC GROWTH	11.3
FIDELITY DIVERSIFIED INTERNATIONAL	13.2
MANAGERS INTERNATIONAL EQUITY	11.2
SOGEN OVERSEAS A	7.8
UMB SCOUT WORLDWIDE	14.5
WADDELL & REED INTERNATIONAL GROWTH B	14.8
WORLD	
CAPITAL WORLD GROWTH & INCOME	15.4%
DREYFUS PREMIER WORLDWIDE GROWTH B	19.8
JANUS WORLDWIDE	19.3
MUTUAL DISCOVERY Z	15.0
DIVERSIFIED PACIFIC/ASIA	
MERRILL LYNCH PACIFIC B	2.7%
EUROPE	
WRIGHT EQUIFUND-NETHERLANDS	21.1%
NATURAL RESOURCES	
AMERICAN GAS INDEX	13.2%
PRECIOUS METALS	
SOGEN GOLD A	−10.0%
TECHNOLOGY	
FRANKLIN DYNATECH A	20.1%
UNALIGNED	
FIDELITY SELECT FOOD & AGRICULTURE	19.9%
UTILITIES	
MFS UTILITIES B	17.6%
UAM SAMI PREFERRED STOCK INCOME	4.7

*1994–98 pretax returns, appreciation plus reinvestment of dividends and capital gains.
** Fund data in Business Week Online.

DATA: MORNINGSTAR INC.

1998. In addition, the fund's 27 percent total return far outdistanced the average mid-cap growth fund, which earned 18.3 percent. In mid-cap blend, the no-load Mairs & Power Growth Fund still looks good. The fund had an average return for a mid-cap blend in 1998, and that cost its place on the overall A-list that it held for several years. (Its sister fund, Mairs & Power Balanced, remains on the overall A-list). Even so, the fund, specializing in growth companies from the upper Midwest, has only dropped one notch in overall ratings, and gets a B+.

Top-rated small-cap funds are more problematical. A few of them, Weitz Hickory and Longleaf Partners Small-Cap, are closed to new investors. And Baron Asset, a superstar in the category, may have become too successful for its shareholders' own good. The fund grew 50 percent in assets to $5.7 billion last year even though the returns were just 4.3 percent, a little below average for small-cap funds. That suggests the fund is laboring with two much money for too few opportunities. If anything, this fund should have performed a little better because its portfolio makes it look more and more like a mid-cap fund. A better choice would be the Fasciano Fund, which has shown an ability to earn competitive returns with only a small exposure to the technology sector. Instead, Fasciano makes his mark with financial, media, and specialty service companies. At times, the fund also raises cash, an attribute that when executed well, can dampen a fund's volatility considerably. At the end of 1998, the fund had about 20 percent of its assets in cash.

You won't find funds from any of the international categories on this year's A-list. They've been scarce for years. The returns, on average, have lagged the United States in a big way, and the volatility has been greater. Dreyfus Premier Worldwide Growth B and T. Rowe Price European Stock come the closest, both with B+ ratings, and Janus Worldwide and UMB Scout Worldwide have B's. Looking for highly rated foreign or world funds? The best thing is to examine how these funds were rated against others in their category. Table 8-3 has seven A-rated foreign funds and four A-rated world funds. (Foreign funds generally do not own U.S. stocks, while world funds do. For that reason, world funds have done a little better of late.) Some fund analysts like Fidelity's international offerings, especially Fidelity Diversified International, rated A against other foreign funds. The fund returned 14.4 percent last year, a few points ahead of the category average, and the five-year

average annual return, 13.2 percent, is nearly double the category average.

Sector funds also seemed to have missed the mark in earning high, risk-adjusted returns. Just three earned A-ratings when compared to the entire universe of equity funds: Fidelity Select Health Care, Vanguard Health Care, and Flag Investors Communications A. Despite the last year's extraordinary performance by the technology funds—up 54.3 percent in 1998 and 22.9 percent a year for the last five—none of them earned an A when compared to all other equity funds. The closest any of them got was a C-rating. Just two tech funds, Invesco Technology and Franklin DynaTech, get C-ratings. In fairness to the tech funds, only 15 of the 36 in our Scoreboard have been around for the five years needed to get a rating.

NEW FACES AMONG THE TOP-RATED FUNDS

All the studies will tell long-term investors that some of their money should be allocated to international markets. Even when these funds perform well—and they haven't for the last few years—they're often more volatile than their U.S. counterparts. If nothing else, currency fluctuations sometimes send these portfolios on a wild ride. That's a ride that L. Roy Papp says you don't have to take. He has positioned the Papp America-Abroad Fund as a global fund that stays at home, looking to capitalize on growth abroad by investing in U.S. multinationals and exporters. The fund first showed up on the A-list in August 1998 (remember, we rate all the funds every month at our Web site, http://www.businessweek.com) and has remained on it ever since. For the last five years, the fund is up an average 24.9 percent, which makes it one of the 5 percent or so of funds that beat the S&P.

Papp, of Phoenix, Arizona, aims to invest at least 70 percent of the fund in U.S.-based companies with significant revenues coming from abroad. That way, he argues, investors get exposure to the global economy, but in U.S. dollars with U.S. accounting standards and securities regulation. Among the major holdings are U.S.-based global businesses: General Electric, Intel, Microsoft, and Merck. Papp does buy some foreign stocks, but they're large companies with U.S.-traded shares like Hong Kong Telecommunications and L.M. Ericsson. Though Papp himself is a senior citizen, he has trained his daughter-in-law, Rose, the fund's co-manager, in his stockpicking methods.

Many of the best small-cap funds are closed to new investors.

Papp's criteria lead him to large-cap growth stocks, because those are largely the stocks that fit the bill. But many large-cap growth stocks are that way because they're well-managed companies with a huge market, nearly the entire planet. So when you look at top-rated funds like T. Rowe Price Blue Chip and Vanguard U.S. Growth, you see a lot of the overlap in the portfolios. T. Rowe Price Blue Chip has Microsoft, Merck, and General Electric, and they're top holdings in Vanguard U.S. Growth as well. "There were 15 or 20 big stocks last year, and if you didn't own them, you were out of the running," says Parker Hall, chief executive officer of Chicago-based Lincoln Capital Management Co. and portfolio manager of Vanguard U.S. Growth Fund. Fortunately for his shareholders, he owned enough of the right stocks to earn a 40 percent total return last year, beating the S&P 500 and the average large-cap growth fund.

T. Rowe Price's Larry Puglia had many of the same names, but not in quite the same proportion. He backed off some of the highly valued tech stocks, and that cost him some performance; so did his foray into the mid-caps. Still he eked out an S&P-beating return in 1998, 28.8 percent to the S&P's 28.6 percent. Puglia's risk-aversion should help the fund when this winning sector of the market hits a downdraft.

One of the more controversial of the top-rated funds is Legg Mason Value Trust Primary Shares, which jumped to the A-list in February 1998. Who's complaining about its 48 percent return last year? Nobody, really. What's got some investors atwitter is the fund's two largest holdings, America Online (14.7 percent of the fund) and Dell Computer (8.7 percent). What are they doing in a "value" fund at their nosebleed valuations.

The reason is that Legg Mason's William Miller bought them when they were out of favor. Remember a few years ago when America Online went to flat-rate pricing before its system could handle the volume? That was a disaster for the company—and the stockholders. But those who bought then got in on one of the great all-time turnaround investments. The difference between Miller and many other value investors is philosophical. Many would have sold the stock as it became a hot growth property. Miller sold little, arguing the stock was still cheap relative to its long-term prospects. The same goes for Dell. "You have to hand it to [manager] Bill Miller for seeing the value there, and having the prescience to keep them," says Kurt Brouwer of Brouwer & Janachowski, a San Francisco investment advisory firm that puts its clients' money in funds.

But Brouwer would be loathe to buy that fund now, since its net asset value incorporates today's high market prices for AOL and Dell.

One reason why Legg Mason Value Trust has done so well compared to so many others is Miller's flexibility—allowing AOL and Dell to remain in the portfolio while so many others, including growth-stock investors, would have sold them off long ago. Many investors follow strict guidelines, such as selling when a fund reaches certain valuation targets or selling off some shares if a position grows to a certain size within the fund, say 5 or 10 percent.

"By trimming back larger positions, you're controlling risk," says William N. Goetzmann, director of the International Center for Finance at the Yale School of Management. "An equal-weighted portfolio is probably a better-diversified portfolio." So far, the additional risk Miller took by letting the AOL and Dell positions get so large has paid off. In fact, in the first two months of 1999, AOL was up another 15.6 percent, and Dell, 18.3 percent.

Indeed, what's confounding a lot of professional investors right now is that many of their time-proven methods have come up short. "We used to think our sell discipline gave us an advantage," says Samuel C. Harvey of the A-rated Hilliard Lyons Growth Fund A. "But many stocks we've regretted selling even at a good profit, and it's hard to find new ones to buy." Indeed, the fund's been hurting from that. While the five-year average annual return is 20.8 percent, the last year was clearly a disappointment, just 13.6 percent.

Still, many investors with strong, long-term records are loathe to change their ways because of current market conditions. The Clipper Fund, for instance, last year sold off a large position in Wal-Mart Stores because of the huge price rise and a general apprehension about owning stocks with which Wall Street had become enamored. The stake, accumulated several years earlier when it traded in the 20s, was gradually sold off with the stock in the 60s. By early 1999, the stock was in the mid-80s. Michael Sandler, a co-manager of the fund, says the toughest thing about today's market is finding new stocks that fit the fund's value criteria—a stock that sells at a deep discount to the company's intrinsic value, with a long-lived definable business franchise.

FIDELITY'S COMEBACK, JANUS' HOME RUNS

The last year marked a strong comeback for Fidelity mutual funds. And the best news of all was the resurgence in the Fidelity Magellan Fund, still the nation's largest mutual fund. Under portfolio manager Robert E. Stansky, Magellan managed to go neck and neck with the S&P most of the year, but pulled ahead in the final quarter, with a big kick from America Online, up 178 percent in the fourth quarter alone. For the year, Magellan gained 33.2 percent, its best performance since 1995 and the best showing versus the S&P 500 since 1993. Even with a star turn, Magellan's overall rating is still just C, or average. And since Magellan is closed to new investors, most fund watchers expect the Vanguard 500 Index, still taking in money at furious rate, to surpass Magellan in size sometime this fall.

Fidelity's other big winner of recent years, Fidelity Growth & Income, also closed to new investors during 1998. Fidelity opened Growth & Income II under a new manager, but the fund is still untested. (Fidelity also shuttered Contrafund to all but existing investors and launched Contrafund II.) A better choice for large-cap investors would be the A-rated Fidelity Fund or Fidelity Dividend Growth Fund. Fidelity Fund, which dates back to 1930, has a strong record of late under the leadership of Beth Terrana—up 31 percent in 1998 and an average 23.1 percent for the last five years. In the first part of 1998, she made big money by betting on retail, pharmaceutical, and financial stocks but downplaying technology. She took advantage of the third-quarter sell-off to scoop up tech stocks at cheap prices—and it paid off. Charles Mangum, portfolio manager of Fidelity Dividend Growth, earned 35.9 percent in 1998, without gorging on tech stocks. Mangum, former manager of Fidelity Select Health Care, likes the drug and medical care sectors, and placed 20 percent of the fund's assets there. "Technology's fundamentals are great but the relative valuations are very high," says Mangum. "Many [health-care companies] are trading at near-market [price–earnings] multiples with good revenue growth."

Janus' story is not as much a comeback as a giant leap forward. In 1997, start manager Tom Marsico left in a hurry to set up his own firm. That left Janus without its best-known and best-performing U.S. equity manager and raised questions about Janus' results without him. But his successor, Scott Schoelzel, blew out the lights in 1998, with a 73.4 percent return. The Marsico Focus Fund—Marsico's answer to Janus Twenty—was up a not-too-shabby 51.3 percent. What's more, Janus' nine U.S. diversified equity funds had an average gain of 42.8 percent. Compare that to Fidelity's average of 22.7 percent, Putnam's 19.9, and T. Rowe Price's 12.2 percent.

Before you run out and switch all your money to Janus, keep a few things in mind. Janus, the fifteenth largest fund company, is a very different animal from Fidelity, Putnam, and T. Rowe Price. Janus focuses on growth stocks, especially large-cap growth stocks, and 1998 was a great year in which to have that focus. As such, Janus' domestic equity funds have a lot of overlapping holdings, so putting additional Janus funds into your portfolio does not necessarily give you much more diversification. In their defense, Fidelity and Putnam have more funds, more diverse funds, and thus have lower returns. Value stocks had a bad year in 1998 and so did small caps, and that certainly deflated returns at T. Rowe Price, which has a number of small-cap and value funds.

NET STOCK MANIA AND MUTUAL FUNDS

Online bookseller Amazon.com zoomed nearly 1000 percent during 1998, much of that in the last few months. Yahoo!, the leading Internet portal company, climbed almost 600 percent. America Online, the grandaddy of the publicly held online companies, logged a 570 percent gain. And Ebay, Inc., the online auctioneer, logged gains of more than 400 percent between its September 24 initial public offering and the end of the year. Nineteen ninety-eight could well be remembered for Net-stock mania, even more than the summer's terrifying global market meltdown, which involved far more money.

But Net-stock mania is exciting, alluring, and much of the fast and furious trading in these stocks is going on through the online brokerage services of E*Trade, Ameritrade, and even Charles Schwab. The attraction of easy access and cheap commissions has made Net trading in Net stocks an industry in itself—one that offers great potential rewards and a whole lot of risk. What became readily apparent in the last few months of 1998 was that these Net stocks—many of which barely had any revenues, let alone profits—were trading at prices well beyond what tried-and-true financial analysis would argue they could trade. But they did, and went higher.

In early December, for instance, BUSINESS WEEK asked veteran Wall Street analyst Charles R. Wolf of Warburg Dillon Read to evaluate Amazon.com using a method called Economic Value Added. We thought that EVA might uncover some reason for the company's rich valuation that

All the stars were in line for Janus to shine.

other analytical devices had failed to grasped. Wolf's analysis: to justify this stock price, Amazon.com's revenues—already at $587 million—would have to grow nearly 60 percent a year for the next 10 years, taking it to $63 billion.

Is that possible? Possible, yes, probable, no. Anyone who's seen or used it knows Amazon.com's Web site is first rate. But Amazon is still a retailer and distributor and has no hammerlock on a proprietary technology. Retailing profit margins are thin, since competition is fierce.

Still, Amazon.com is a dominant company in its field, so we looked to another dominant firm, Microsoft. Did Microsoft revenues grow at 60 percent a year? Not by a long shot. Since the software giant went public in 1986, its revenues have grown at a compounded growth rate of 43 percent. If Microsoft, with a near-monopoly in its business, only grew 43 percent, what chance does Amazon have to grow at 60 percent? Of course, the argument was persuasive that Amazon was vastly overpriced, but no matter. Three months after the BUSINESS WEEK cover story, the stock was up another 50 percent.

The lesson is this: there's no question that the Internet is transforming many aspects of business and society and is an investment opportunity of enormous magnitude. You can play that opportunity by trading these stocks—and get ready to live with one-day moves, both up or down, of $40 or $80. Or, you can take the mutual-fund approach and get a fund manager to do it for you, spreading the risk across more companies. The earnings might be less than you would have with a few big winners, but a lot more than you would have with a handful of losers.

The fund approach makes a lot of sense. Alberto Vilar, long-time manager of emerging growth and technology stocks, runs concentrated portfolios of only about 20 stocks. And even with the time and energy put into the selection of those stocks, he expects that only five or six of them will hit the jackpot. But, if you own 5 stocks that are up tenfold in a three-year period, you will still make a bundle—even if the other 15 crap out. Vilar's Amerindo Technology Fund gained 84.5 percent in 1998.

But even Amerindo's returns paled next to those of the Internet Fund, up 196.1 percent. The Internet Fund even nosed out ProFunds Ultra-OTC Investors, which uses leverage to double the return of the technology-heavy NASDAQ 100 index. Fund manager Ryan Jacob's investment approach is somewhat akin to Vilar's. Approach these companies as a venture capitalist would: evaluate the companies on their business model, their market, and their management; make some educated estimates of revenues and profits; and accept that many investments will flop. The fund's largest single investment is not Amazon.com or Yahoo!, but CMGI, a firm that takes venture capital stakes in other Internet companies.

The Net-focused funds like Internet, WWW Internet, and Munder NetNet A can be great, but they are also going to be volatile. Since the Internet is the driving force of the technology sector now, a broader-based tech fund might be a better choice: PIMCo Innovation, Northern Technology, or Fidelity Select Technology, to name a few. You don't have to own a pure Internet fund to earn big returns. The tech fund category was up 54.3 percent in 1998.

PLAYING THE SECTORS

Coming fast on the heels of the tech funds are the sector funds specializing in communications stocks. They were up an average 46.4 percent in 1998. Not that many years ago, these funds were only a little more exciting than utility stocks. They were dominated by the phone companies. Today, the phone companies themselves are quickly trying to remake themselves into growth vehicles, turning their efforts toward the Internet and explosive growth in data communications. The communications funds are changing as well. Flag Investors Communications A, one of the few sector funds to get an A-rating for overall fund performance, was up 85.3 percent in 1998. You won't find that fund name in earlier Scoreboards. Until May of last year, it was known by the more prosaic moniker, Flag Investors Telephone Income Trust. Like technology, the communications sector has been energized by the growth of the Internet.

The third best performer in the sector fund category is health. But by tech standards, health fund returns looked pale, up 18.3 percent. The big drug companies certainly gave these funds a lot of lift in the last year, as did biotechnology. Utilities funds, which invest mostly in electric companies, had a 17.5 percent return for the year and waltzed in right behind health funds. They benefited from falling interest rates and some takeover activity as the industry gears up for deregulation. And financial funds, stars for so long, blew up in 1998, largely victims of the fall from the global debt crisis. Don't count them out: as the crisis ebbs, financial stocks have bounced back, and long term, these companies are beneficiaries of tech-

Tech funds are one way to play the Internet.

nology and the Internet, and the industry is ripe for further takeovers and consolidation.

The losers among the specialty funds were precious metals, down 12.7 percent; real estate, down 16.2 percent; and natural resources, down 22.4. Metals and natural resources collapsed as a result of weak global prices for metals, oil, and other natural resources. While the U.S. economy remained strong, most others slowed or were in recession. That meant less demand for gold and especially for oil, which reached 12-year lows. If the global economy rebounds in 1999, returns for natural resource funds should improve. Real estate funds floundered all year in a corrective bear market after three strong years. From 1995 through 1997, real estate funds were up an average 22.4 percent. Even if performance is unexciting now, fund investors should have some real estate exposure in their portfolios. And this is a good time to get it, when prices are down.

INTERNATIONAL SECTORS

The U.S. stock market was the place to be in 1998, but there was money to be made abroad—mainly in Europe. Funds specializing in investing on the Continent earned an average total return of 17.7 percent. That was 3.6 percentage points better than the average U.S. diversified equity fund. The best European funds were several single-country portfolios specializing in Belgium, Spain, and Italy. The best diversified Europe fund was Bartlett Europe A, which gained 41.9 percent. Among the no-load funds, Invesco European delivered the best returns of the year, up 32.9 percent.

What made European stocks so strong was the coming of the euro—the new currency launched on January 1, 1999 by 11 of the Economic Community nations. As nations readied themselves for monetary union, they slashed government spending and privatized the pension systems. And corporations restructured themselves as well, streamlining their businesses and often merging with others. In early 1999, many analysts thought the European economy was slowing down. If so, that will make it a tougher year for the European markets—and the funds which invest there.

Asia was still pretty much an economic disaster area during 1998. A few countries—South Korea and Thailand—did make some progress in the economic, financial, and corporate restructuring needed to get their economies back on track. The Korean stock market was up nearly 100 percent (albeit from very depressed levels). And

Korea Matthews I, which was down 64.8 percent 1997, was up 96.2 percent in 1998. The relatively few funds that invest solely in Japan were up 7.1 percent in 1998, the best showing in years. That came not so much from gains in stock prices; in fact, the Nikkei 225 average fell 7.5 percent over the year. But during the same time, the yen appreciated 15 percent against the dollar. That made Japanese stocks more valuable to dollar-based investors. The strength from Japan gave the Diversified Pacific/Asia funds—which include Japan—a better return than the Pacific/Asia funds that explicitly exclude it. Still, the Pacific/Asia funds that include Japan fell 4.9 percent; excluding Japan, down 10.4 percent.

Diversified emerging markets funds, hard hit by the Asian crisis in 1997, worsened in 1998. By and large, their Asian holdings did not appreciate much, and then Latin American markets, which had been strong in 1997, started to crumble. Although Latin stock prices were weakening earlier in the year, they really got nailed in the latter half following the Russian debt repudiation. Brazil, the largest economy in Latin America and the eighth largest in the world, started to falter, which reverberated through the rest of the region. Latin America funds were down 38.7 percent for the year. Diversified emerging markets funds were down 26.3 percent for the year. That leaves the five-year record at an average 11.1 percent loss per year. That did not hold a candle to the sorry performance of Lexington Troika Russia Fund, the absolute worst fund of the year—down 83 percent, the victim of plunging stock prices and a plunging currency.

Investors came back to bond funds during 1998.

Bond Funds

After ignoring bond mutual funds for years, investors woke up in 1998 and started buying them. In fact, the Investment Company Institute reported that $74.4 billion was invested in bond funds during 1998. That's less than half of what went into equity funds, but it's the strongest inflow in five years.

Why did investors come back to bonds? Certainly not for the yields, which declined from already low levels to even lower levels as the year went on. Of course, low inflation and declining yield meant that there were capital gains to be made in bonds, but nothing approaching what a savvy investor could have earned in the sizzling stock market.

What brought investors back to bonds was fear—fear of falling from great heights in the stock market. When the equities fell in the summer of 1998, those boring old bond funds started to look a whole lot better. For the most part, investors opted for the highest quality: government and investment grade corporate bond funds. That's the usual refuge in uncertain times. If the economy were on the brink of recession—as many thought back then—the credit-sensitive high-yields and equity-linked convertibles would be dead meat. To a lesser degree, fund investors even started to put cash into municipal bond funds—not a bad choice, either. Thanks to a long economic expansion, state and local governments were in the best financial shape they'd been in for several decades. That made the bonds attractive from a safety point of view. And from the summer and well into the next year, yields on municipals were the equivalent of taxable government bonds. That made the muni bond especially attractive for taxable accounts.

THE TOP-RATED FUNDS

For the last few years, the list of top-rated bond funds was dominated by high-yield funds. That's because they take more of their cues from the health of corporate cash flows than from the U.S. budget. When a company's coffers are swelling with cash, its credit rating improves, which makes its bonds more valuable. But the list of A-rated bond funds for the 1994–1998 period (Table 8-4) looks a lot different from previous years. Just 7 of the 98 funds are high-yielders. A year ago, when we examined the 1993–1997 period, 37 of the 83 A-rated funds, or 44.6 percent, were high-yields. That's quite a difference.

Only part of that change came from 1998's subpar returns. After all, high-yield funds were negative, down 0.3 percent on average. That was the first year of negative returns since 1994, when the funds were down 3.4 percent. For the most part, the bond prices didn't fall because companies were defaulting on their debt; investors dumped these bonds in 1998 because of a fear that it might happen.

The other reason for the high-yield funds' fall from grace came from the method by which we measure returns. BUSINESS WEEK ratings are based on the last five years. So when we calculated the 1994–1998 returns, we dropped 1993 and added 1998. That also made a big difference in the performance ratings since 1993 was a strong year for high-yields—the funds were up nearly 19 percent—while adding in 1998 results dragged the five-year averages down.

Look at Northeast Investors, one of the leading high-yield funds and one that still retains its A rating for overall performance. In calculating its rating, we dropped the 23.6 percent earned in 1993 and added in 1998's –0.3 percent. That was enough to cut the five-year average annual return from 15.2 percent at the end of 1997 to 10.4 percent just one year later. And Northeast Investors remained on the A-list because it held up relatively well in 1998. In contrast, AIM High-Yield, an A-list fund a year ago, was down nearly 6 percent in 1998. Adding in a bad 1998 and subtracting a strong 1993 took that fund down to a 6.4 percent average annual return, and a D rating.

Is all this a sign to exit high-yield funds? Probably not, but you should take it as a sign that you need to be a little more selective in your funds. As the interest rates on high-yield bonds came down over the last eight years, some fund managers bought emerging market bonds or unrated debt in an effort to keep yields up. Those who did that were certainly among the most damaged in the 1998 correction. That was the story of Dreyfus High-Yield Securities, which used Latin American telecom bonds to help boost the returns. In 1997, that worked wonders, giving the fund an 11.2 percent yield and a 16.7 total return. In 1998, that strategy came back to haunt the fund. In 1998, the fund's total return was –15.8 percent, even after adding in the 15.3 percent in cash distributions. Ouch.

But it does pay to be selective. Look at Vanguard High-Yield Corporate Fund, one of the more conservatively run high-yield funds. In 1997, it was up 11.9 percent with an 8.5 percent yield, significantly trailing Dreyfus High-Yield Securities. But in 1998, Vanguard's conservatism paid off. The fund held on to its 8.5 percent yield and minimized the damage from falling bond prices. The fund's total return was 5.6 percent. A $10,000 investment in the fund at the beginning of 1997 would have been worth $11,827 two years later; the Dreyfus investment, in contrast, would have turned into $9826. Vanguard High-Yield Corporate, like Northeast Investors, is one of the seven high-yielders that remain on the overall A-list. The others are Columbia High-Yield, Equitrust High-Yield Bond, Fidelity High-Income, Mainstay High-Yield Corporate Bond B, and PIMCo High-Yield Institutional. In addition, the Columbia, Fidelity, Mainstay, and PIMCo funds also earned an A when compared to just other high-yielders (Table 8-5).

The high-yield funds have generally risen to the top ratings mainly through their high returns.

TABLE 8-4

TOP-PERFORMING BOND MUTUAL FUNDS

These 98 funds earned A's, our rating for superior risk-adjusted returns over the past five years.

Fund	Average annual total return*	Investment category	Fund	Average annual total return*	Investment category
AIM TAX-FREE INTERMEDIATE	5.0%	Muni. Short	MONTGOMERY CALIF. T/F INTERMEDIATE BD. R**	5.8%	Muni. Calif. Interm.
AMERICAN CENT.-BENHAM CALIF. MUNI. HIGH-YIELD	6.9	Muni. Calif. Long	MONTGOMERY SHORT-DURATION GOVT. BD. R.	6.4	Short Government
AMERICAN CENT.-BENHAM CALIF. T/F LIM.**	4.3	Muni. Short	MORGAN GRENFELL MUNICIPAL BOND**	6.2	Muni. Ntl. Interm.
ASSET MGMT. ADJUSTABLE RATE	5.7	Ultrashort	MSDW PRIME INCOME TRUST**	7.6	Ultrashort (Gen.)
BOSTON 1784 T/E MED.-TERM INCOME	6.1	Muni. Ntl. Interm.	NATIONS SHORT-TERM MUNI. INV. A**	4.2	Muni. Short
BT INVESTMENT LIFECYCLE SHORT**	9.1	Short (Gen.)	NORTHEAST INVESTORS	10.4	High-Yield
CALAMOS GROWTH & INCOME A**	16.2	Convertibles	ONE GROUP MUNICIPAL INCOME A**	5.6	Muni. Ntl. Interm.
CALVERT TAX-FREE RES. LIMITED-TERM A	4.0	Muni. Short	PAYDEN & RYGEL GLOBAL FIXED-INCOME R	8.1	International
COLONIAL HIGH-YIELD MUNI. B**	6.1	Muni. Ntl. Long	PERMANENT PORTFOLIO VERSATILE BOND**	5.0	Short (Gen.)
COLORADO BONDSHARES**	7.9	Muni. S-S Interm.	PIMCO FOREIGN BOND INSTL.	10.0	International
COLUMBIA HIGH-YIELD**	9.1	High-Yield	PIMCO HIGH-YIELD INSTL.	10.7	High-Yield
DAVIS TAX-FREE HIGH-INCOME B	5.3	Muni. Short	PIMCO LOW-DURATION INSTL.	6.8	Short (Gen.)
DELAWARE NATL. HIGH-YIELD MUNI. A**	6.9	Muni. Ntl. Interm.	PIMCO LOW-DURATION II INSTL.	6.2	Short (Gen.)
DREYFUS PA. INTERM. MUNI. BOND**	6.2	Muni. S-S Interm.	PIMCO SHORT-TERM INSTL.	6.3	Ultrashort (Gen.)
DREYFUS SHORT-INTERM. MUNI. BOND**	4.1	Muni. Short	T. ROWE PRICE MARYLAND SHORT-TERM T/F**	4.1	Muni. Short
DUPREE KENTUCKY TAX-FREE SHORT-MED.	4.2	Muni. Short	T. ROWE PRICE SPECTRUM INCOME	8.6	Multisector Bond
DUPREE TENNESSEE TAX-FREE INCOME**	7.6	Muni. S-S Long	T. ROWE PRICE SUMMIT MUNICIPAL INCOME	7.0	Muni. Ntl. Long
EATON VANCE PRIME RATE RESERVES	7.0	Ultrashort	T. ROWE PRICE SUMMIT MUNICIPAL INTERM.	6.1	Muni. Ntl. Interm.
EQUITRUST HIGH-YIELD BOND**	7.1	High-Yield	T. ROWE PRICE TAX-FREE HIGH-YIELD	6.4	Muni. Ntl. Long
EVERGREEN FLORIDA HIGH-INCOME MUNI. A	7.1	Muni. S-S Long	T. ROWE PRICE TAX-FREE SHORT-INTERM.	4.5	Muni. Short
EXCELSIOR SHORT-TERM TAX-EXEMPT SECS.**	4.0	Muni. Short	SEI DAILY CORP. DAILY INCOME A**	5.7	Ultrashort
FEDERATED SHORT-TERM MUNI. INST.	4.3	Muni. Short	SEI DAILY SHORT-DURATION GOVT. A**	5.9	Short Government
FFTW LIMITED DURATION**	6.1	Short Government	SEI TAX-EXEMPT PA. MUNI. BOND A**	5.3	Muni. S-S Interm.
FFTW U.S. SHORT-TERM FIXED-INCOME	5.1	Ultrashort	SIT MINNESOTA TAX-FREE INCOME	6.5	Muni. Short
FFTW WORLDWIDE FIXED-INCOME HEDGED	10.6	International	SIT TAX-FREE INCOME	6.7	Muni. Ntl. Interm.
FIDELITY HIGH-INCOME	10.8	High-Yield	SIT U.S. GOVERNMENT SECURITIES	6.6	Short Government
FIDELITY MORTGAGE SECURITIES INIT.	7.8	Interm. Govt.	SMITH BARNEY MUNI. LIMITED-TERM A	5.4	Muni. Ntl. Interm.
FIDELITY SPARTAN SHORT-INTERMEDIATE MUNI.	4.4	Muni. Short	SMITH BREEDEN SHORT DUR. U.S. GOV.**	5.5	Ultrashort
59 WALL STREET TAX-FREE SHORT-INTERM.**	3.9	Muni. Short	SSGA YIELD PLUS	5.3	Ultrashort
FIRST AMERICAN LIMITED-TERM INCOME A**	5.5	Short (Gen.)	STEIN ROE HIGH-YIELD MUNIS	6.4	Muni. Ntl. Long
FPA NEW INCOME	6.9	Intermediate (Gen.)	STI CLASSIC INVESTMENT GRADE T/E INV.**	6.5	Muni. Ntl. Interm.
FRANKLIN CALIF. HIGH-YIELD MUNI. A	7.3	Muni. Calif. Long	STRONG ADVANTAGE	5.8	Ultrashort
FRANKLIN CALIF. TAX-FREE INCOME A	6.3	Muni. Calif. Long	STRONG CORPORATE BOND	9.4	Intermediate (Gen.)
FRANKLIN HIGH-YIELD TAX-FREE INCOME A	6.9	Muni. Ntl. Long	STRONG HIGH-YIELD MUNI BOND	7.4	Muni. Ntl. Long
HARBOR SHORT DURATION	5.8	Short (Gen.)	TAX-FREE FUND OF VERMONT	5.5	Muni. S-S Long
HOMESTEAD SHORT-TERM BOND	5.8	Short (Gen.)	U.S. GLOBAL INV. NEAR-TERM TAX-FREE	4.4	Muni. Short
HOTCHKIS & WILEY LOW-DURATION	7.5	Short (Gen.)	UNITED MUNICIPAL HIGH-INCOME A	7.6	Muni. Ntl. Long
HOTCHKIS & WILEY SHORT-TERM INVMT.**	6.1	Ultrashort	USAA TAX-EXEMPT INTERMEDIATE-TERM	6.1	Muni. Ntl. Interm.
HOUGH FL. TAX-FREE SHORT**	4.3	Muni. Short	USAA TAX-EXEMPT SHORT-TERM	4.8	Muni. Short
IDAHO TAX-EXEMPT**	5.6	Muni. S-S Interm.	VAN KAMPEN HIGH-YIELD MUNI. A	7.4	Muni. Ntl. Interm.
INVESCO SELECT INCOME	8.4	Long (Gen.)	VAN KAMPEN PRIME-RATE INCOME	6.9	Ultrashort
JANUS FLEXIBLE INCOME	8.7	Multisector	VANGUARD GNMA	7.4	Interm. Govt.
KENT MI. MUNICIPAL BOND INVMT.**	4.3	Muni. Short	VANGUARD HIGH-YIELD CORP.	8.7	High Yield
LEXINGTON GNMA INCOME	7.3	Interm. Govt.	VANGUARD INTERMEDIATE-TERM TAX-EXEMPT	5.6	Muni. Ntl. Interm.
LIMITED-TERM N.Y. MUNICIPAL A	5.6	Muni. Short	VANGUARD LIMITED-TERM TAX-EXEMPT	4.6	Muni. Short
LOOMIS SAYLES SHORT-TERM BD. INSTL.**	6.1	Short-Term (Gen.)	VANGUARD SHORT-TERM CORPORATE	6.1	Short (Gen.)
MAINSTAY HIGH-YIELD CORPORATE BOND B	9.7	High-Yield	VANGUARD SHORT-TERM TAX-EXEMPT	3.9	Muni. Short
MARSHALL SHORT-TERM INCOME	5.4	Short-Term (Gen.)	WARBURG PINCUS N.Y. INT. MUNI.**	4.9	Muni. Short
MERRILL LYNCH SENIOR FLOATING-RATE**	6.2	Ultrashort (Gen.)	WASATCH-HOISINGTON U.S. TREASURY**	10.1	Long Government

*1994–98 pretax returns, includes appreciation plus reinvestment of dividends and capital gains.
**More fund data on Business Week Online.

DATA: MORNINGSTAR INC.

But there's also a slew of A-rated funds that are more predictably low-yield, but make it to the top because they're also low in risk. That explains why Calvert Tax-Free Reserves Limited Term A, with a 4 percent average annual return over the last five years, is on the A-list again this year. And it's been on the list for many years. That's not a recommendation to buy such a low-yielding fund, but a statement that the fund gives high return for the amount of risk involved.

This year's top-rated funds include a cohort of ultrashort bond funds known as "loan participation" funds. These funds operate under somewhat different rules than other bond funds. Like conventional bond funds, they issue shares whenever an investor wants to buy in. But with these funds, investors can withdraw money only once per quarter and on a predetermined date. The reason for these restrictive redemption procedures is that funds invest in senior secured bank loans, which are illiquid and can't be sold at the drop of a hat to return the money to shareholders.

But the reward for accepting these limitations can be sweet. The loans reset every 30 to 60 days, so the portfolio is well insulated from rising interest rates. Depending on the borrower, the rate ranges from 0.75 to 3 percentage points above the London Interbank Offered Rate (LIBOR), a global benchmark for bank lending. In early 1999, the LIBOR was about 5 percent. The yields on these ultrashort funds compete with those on many intermediate-term funds, which take on much more interest-rate risk. But with ultrashort funds, yield is about all you get.

With longer-term funds, there's an opportunity for a deft manager to earn some capital gains. One A-rated fund that plays that game well is Janus Flexible Income Fund. "We don't have any rules about where we can invest," says portfolio manager Ron Speaker, "so we can take advantage of people who do." For example, "split-rate bonds," bonds that are rated investment grade by one credit agency but junk by another, are often cheap because they're off-limits to both high-quality and high-yield funds. But Speaker can buy them.

Some of our top-rated funds take diametrically opposed views of the economy and bond market. Van R. Hoisington, manager of the Wasatch-Hoisington U.S. Treasury Fund, is sticking with his long-term U.S. Treasury portfolio that served him well in 1998 when the fund earned a 14.6 percent total return. "As long as you have a capacity glut worldwide, countries will compete by driving down the value of their currencies," says Hoisington, who adds that he sees no end to the

> International bond funds are good diversifiers.

deflationary pressure. Taking the other view is Robert L. Rodriguez, who runs the FPA New Income Fund. He believes that inflation bottomed in 1998, a 1.6 percent increase in the consumer price index (CPI). "Even if energy and food prices are stable in 1999, the [consumer price index] will be over 2 percent," says Rodriguez. He has 30 percent of his fund in inflation-indexed bonds. That's a position, he admits, he took too soon. He missed 1998's bond rally, and the fund earned just a 3.9 percent total return. William H. Gross, chief investment officer for the PIMCo bond funds, doesn't expect rates to move dramatically in either direction this year. PIMCo, with $155 billion in assets under management, is the nation's largest bond investor. "Rates should fluctuate around a fulcrum of 5 percent, going a little lower when the economy is weak and a little higher in periods of dollar weakness," says Gross. "This year, I expect most bond investors will just earn the coupon."

INTERNATIONAL BONDS— THE BEAUTIFUL AND THE UGLY

Investment advisers usually recommend international bond funds as well as domestic funds for the same reasons as they tell people to invest in international equity funds: diversification and a chance for higher returns. That wisdom held true in 1998. International bond funds earned average annual returns of 9.8 percent, the second best category after long-term governments (Table 8-6). And the best in the category was the tiny Vontobel Eastern European Debt Fund, up 24.5 percent. Though it sounds like an emerging markets fund, it is not, since the prospectus requires the fund to invest in investment grade bonds—those rated BBB or better—and allows only 5 percent of its assets to be in what might be considered the more speculative emerging markets debt. Of course, that Vontobel fund is not the typical international bond fund, either. Most are much broader and more diversified. American Century-Benham International Bond, one of the oldest in the category, used to be a European investor. Last year it went global and can now invest in Japan, Canada, and Australia, though it still has the vast majority of its assets in Europe. The fund was up 17.9 percent in 1998.

Until last year, the international category included funds that invest in bonds from the major industrial nations as well as those from the emerging markets. But in 1998, Morningstar took out the emerging markets bond funds and created a new category. That, of course, turned out

TABLE 8-5

THE BEST PERFORMERS IN THEIR CATEGORIES

These funds earned A's for risk-adjusted returns when compared with their peers.

Fund	Average annual total return*
ULTRASHORT	
MSDW PRIME INCOME TRUST**	7.6%
SHORT (GENERAL)	
BT INVESTMENT LIFECYCLE SHORT**	9.1%
FIRST AMERICAN LTD.-TERM INCOME A**	5.5
HARBOR SHORT-DURATION	5.8
HOTCHKIS & WILEY LOW-DURATION	7.5
PIMCO LOW-DURATION INSTL.	6.8
INTERMEDIATE (GENERAL)	
BABSON BOND S	6.1%
DREYFUS BASIC GNMA	6.7
FPA NEW INCOME	6.9
FREMONT BOND	8.0
HARBOR BOND	7.6
MONETTA INTERMEDIATE BOND**	7.4
MORGAN GRENFELL FIXED-INCOME	7.4
PIMCO TOTAL RETURN III INSTL.	8.0
PIMCO TOTAL RETURN INSTL.	7.9
STRONG CORPORATE BOND	9.4
WARBURG PINCUS FIXED-INCOME COMM.**	7.1
LONG (GENERAL)	
EQUITRUST HIGH-GRADE BOND**	6.4%
INVESCO SELECT INCOME	8.4
SHORT GOVERNMENT	
FFTW LIMITED DURATION**	6.1%
MONTGOMERY SHORT-DUR. GOVT. BOND R	6.4
SEI DAILY SHORT-DUR. GOVT. A**	5.9
SIT U.S. GOVERNMENT SECS.	6.6
INTERMEDIATE GOVERNMENT	
ACCESSOR MORTGAGE SECURITIES	6.9%
AMER. CENT.-BENHAM GNMA INV.	6.7
FEDERATED INCOME INSTL.	6.7
FIDELITY MORTGAGE SECURITIES INIT.	7.8
FIDELITY SPARTAN GINNIE MAE	7.0
LEXINGTON GNMA INCOME	7.3
SMITH BREEDEN INTERM. DUR. GOV.**	6.9
USAA GNMA	7.3
VANGUARD GNMA	7.4
LONG GOVERNMENT	
WASATCH-HOISINGTON U.S. TREASURY**	10.1%
CONVERTIBLES	
CALAMOS GROWTH & INCOME A**	16.2%
HIGH-YIELD	
COLUMBIA HIGH-YIELD**	9.1%
FIDELITY HIGH-INCOME	10.8
MAINSTAY HIGH-YIELD CORP. BOND B	9.7
PIMCO HIGH-YIELD INSTL.	10.7
INTERNATIONAL	
FFTW WORLDWIDE FIXED-INCOME HEDGED	10.6%
GOLDMAN SACHS GLOBAL A	8.1
PAYDEN & RYGEL GLOBAL FIXED-INCOME R	8.1
PIMCO FOREIGN BOND INSTL.	10.0
MULTISECTOR	
T. ROWE PRICE SPECTRUM INCOME	8.6%
MUNICIPAL SHORT	
DAVIS TAX-FREE HIGH-INCOME B	5.3%
SIT MINN. TAX-FREE INCOME	6.5

Fund	Average annual total return*
MUNICIPAL NATIONAL INTERMEDIATE	
DELAWARE NATL. HIGH-YIELD MUNI. A	6.9%
MORGAN GRENFELL MUNI. BOND	6.2
T. ROWE PRICE SUMMIT MUNI. INTERM.	6.1
SIT TAX-FREE INCOME	6.7
VAN KAMPEN HIGH-YIELD MUNI. A	7.4
MUNICIPAL NATIONAL LONG	
COLONIAL HIGH-YIELD MUNI. B**	6.1%
FRANKLIN FED. TAX-FREE INCOME A	6.0
FRANKLIN HIGH-YIELD T/F INCOME A	6.9
T. ROWE PRICE SUMMIT MUNI. INCOME	7.0
T. ROWE PRICE TAX-FREE HIGH-YIELD	6.4
STEIN ROE HIGH-YIELD MUNIS	6.4
STRONG HIGH-YIELD MUNI. BOND	7.4
UNITED MUNICIPAL HIGH-INCOME A	7.6
MUNICIPAL CALIFORNIA INTERMEDIATE	
MONTGOMERY CALIF. T/F INTERM. BOND R**	5.8%
MUNICIPAL CALIFORNIA LONG	
AMERICAN CENT.-BENHAM CA. MUNI. H-Y**	6.9%
FRANKLIN CALIF. HIGH-YIELD MUNI. A	7.3
FRANKLIN CALIF. TAX-FREE INCOME A	6.3
MUNICIPAL NEW YORK INTERMEDIATE	
BERNSTEIN N.Y. MUNICIPAL	5.0%
MUNICIPAL NEW YORK LONG	
FRANKLIN N.Y. TAX-FREE INCOME A	5.9%
T. ROWE PRICE N.Y. TAX-FREE	6.0
MUNICIPAL SINGLE-STATE INTERMEDIATE	
COLORADO BONDSHARES**	7.9%
DELAWARE-VOYAGEUR T/F MINN. INT. A	4.7
DREYFUS PA. INTERM. MUNI. BOND**	6.2
IDAHO TAX-EXEMPT**	5.6
SEI TAX-EXEMPT PA. MUNI. BOND A**	5.3
THORNBURG N.M. INTERM. MUNI. A	4.9
MUNICIPAL SINGLE-STATE LONG	
DUPREE TENNESSEE TAX-FREE INCOME	7.6%
EVERGREEN FLA. HIGH-INCOME MUNI. A	7.1
FIDELITY SPARTAN PA. MUNI. INCOME	5.9
FRANKLIN FLA. TAX-FREE INCOME A	5.9
FRANKLIN GA. TAX-FREE INCOME A	5.5
FRANKLIN IND. TAX-FREE INCOME**	5.5
FRANKLIN LA. TAX-FREE INCOME A**	5.6
FRANKLIN MASS. INS. T/F INCOME A	5.6
FRANKLIN MICH. INS. T/F INCOME A	5.6
FRANKLIN PA. TAX-FREE INCOME A	5.8
FRANKLIN PUERTO RICO TAX-FREE INC. A	5.8
FRANKLIN TEXAS TAX-FREE INCOME A**	5.9
LEGG MASON MD. T/F INCOME PRIM.	5.5
MONTANA TAX-FREE**	5.2
T. ROWE PRICE MARYLAND TAX-FREE**	5.8
T. ROWE PRICE VIRGINIA TAX-FREE**	6.0
TAX-FREE FUND OF VERMONT**	5.5
USAA VIRGINIA BOND**	6.0
VANGUARD PA. INS. LONG TAX-EXEMPT	5.9

*1994–98 pretax returns, includes appreciation plus reinvestment of dividends and capital gains.

**More fund data on Business Week Online.

DATA: MORNINGSTAR INC.

TABLE 8-6

BOND FUND PERFORMANCE

	Average annual total return*		
	1998	1996–98	1994–98
LONG GOVERNMENT	11.7%	7.6%	7.9%
INTERNATIONAL	9.8	6.6	5.8
INTERMEDIATE (GENERAL)	7.5	6.5	6.5
INTERMEDIATE GOVERNMENT	7.4	6.2	6.1
LONG-TERM (GENERAL)	6.7	7.0	7.2
SHORT-TERM (GENERAL)	6.4	5.8	5.4
MUNICIPAL CALIFORNIA LONG	6.1	6.4	5.8
MUNICIPAL NEW YORK LONG	6.1	6.3	5.5
SHORT GOVERNMENT	6.0	5.5	5.2
MUNICIPAL CALIFORNIA INTERM.	5.7	5.9	5.4
MUNICIPAL SINGLE-STATE LONG	5.6	5.9	5.4
MUNICIPAL NATIONAL INTERM.	5.6	5.7	5.3
MUNICIPAL NATIONAL LONG	5.5	6.2	5.6
MUNICIPAL SINGLE-STATE INTERM.	5.4	5.6	5.2
ULTRASHORT (GENERAL)	5.2	5.7	5.5
MUNICIPAL NEW YORK INTERM.	5.2	5.2	4.6
MUNICIPAL SHORT	4.7	4.6	4.4
CONVERTIBLES	4.4	12.3	10.6
MULTISECTOR	1.9	6.6	6.0
HIGH-YIELD	−0.3	8.5	7.5
EMERGING MARKETS	−25.2	4.8	2.4
ALL BOND FUNDS	5.6	6.2	5.8
TAXABLE BOND FUNDS	5.7	6.6	6.3
TAX-FREE BOND FUNDS	5.5	5.8	5.3

*1994–1998 pretax returns, includes appreciation plus reinvestment of dividends and capital gains.

DATA: MORNINGSTAR INC.

to be a far different story. The emerging market debt crisis blew up these funds just as they went off on their own. The results were disastrous: the best of them, Bear Stearns Emerging Market Debt A, was down 10.8 percent. The worst, Kemper Emerging Markets Income A, was down 36.4 percent. The average fund was down 25.2 percent, a far worse showing than the diversified emerging markets equity funds. Of all categories of funds, only the Latin American equity funds did worse. You can't blame the poor results on currency devaluation, either, as is much the case with emerging markets equities. Most emerging market debt is dollar-denominated.

Judging these funds is difficult, since track records are short as is the history of the entire asset class of emerging markets bonds. Morningstar analysts note that poor country selection and high expenses have left most of these funds lagging the J.P. Morgan Emerging Markets

Bonds Index, down 14.4 percent in 1998. Only one of the 15 emerging markets bond funds in the BW Scoreboard beat that. Perhaps a better way to access the emerging markets bonds is through multisector bond funds. Most of them have the ability, though not the requirement, to invest in this sector. So they can move in when it's ripe, and out when it's not. Of course, that, too, is a judgment call.

COMING BACK TO MUNI FUNDS

Municipal bond funds have had a good story to tell for the last several years. It was just that no one was interested in hearing it. But after volatility in the equity market surged last summer, investors were all ears. During 1998, net cash flow into muni funds of $15.2 billion—an average month for equity funds—looked pretty good compared to 1997, when the funds took in, on balance, less than $1 billion.

Still, muni funds are not getting their fair share. Muni fund assets make up about 35 percent of all bond fund assets, and in 1998, they only got 25 percent of the cash flow. There are some reasons for this. Tax-deferred accounts are the faster growing part of the fund industry, and they don't invest in muni funds. But the muni funds can likely beat the aftertax returns of a government or investment grade corporate fund in a taxable account. Indeed, in 1998, there wasn't even much difference in the average returns. Tax-free funds on average had a 5.5 percent total return versus a 5.7 percent total return for the taxable funds. That suggests that, for many investors, the tax-free funds earned higher aftertax returns.

Among tax-free funds, no one fund company dominates the ratings. Vanguard, of course, has a big line-up of muni bond funds. Given its excellent management and rock-bottom expenses, Vanguard muni funds are always well represented on the A-list. This year, Vanguard has three: intermediate-, short-, and limited-term funds. And T. Rowe Price is also gaining in this market, placing a short-, an intermediate-, and two long-term funds on the list. Fidelity, in contrast, only has one muni fund on the best performers' list. Franklin, by far the largest in the business, comes up relatively short, with just three funds on the overall A-list. Franklin does better in the category ratings, with 15 out of 47 funds in nine muni bond categories.

One advantage of our ratings system is that it identifies winners without the big advertising budgets to tell you how great they are. On that count, take a look at Sit Tax-Free Income, a national intermediate-term fund with a 6.7 percent return over the last five years, a full percentage point better than the category average. In 1998, the fund earned a 6.3 percent total return versus a 5.6 percent average for its category. Portfolio manager Michael Brilley says the fund stresses high-coupon bonds with high current income over a more trading-oriented total return strategy. "If you trade a lot and go for total return, you spend a lot of time trying to forecast interest rates," says Brilley. "We think the main determinant of bond fund return is income. If you get that right, you win over the long term."

Closed-End Funds

If it were a mutual fund, the Korean Investment Fund would have been one of 1998's top performers; its net asset value (NAV) soared 85.3 percent. But anyone who had owned this closed-end fund would have been disappointed. Closed-ends trade like stocks, and last year, shares in this fund rose just 11.8 percent.

Such is the lot of closed-end funds. Unlike mutual funds, where investors always buy and sell for the net asset value of the fund's holdings, these funds trade in the stock market, a place where investment sentiment and portfolio behavior sometimes depart. A year ago, Korean Investment traded at a 33 percent premium over its NAV, even though the fund's portfolio had, in previous months, been decimated by the Asian contagion. That premium was the result of the fund's NAV having dropped faster than the price of shares. As the fund's holdings recovered in 1998, the share prices moved little, so the premium disappeared and eventually went to a discount. In early 1999, the fund traded at a 10.7 percent discount to its NAV.

Then why even bother with closed-ends? One investor's disappointment may be another's opportunity. That Korean Investment Fund may be a great buy at a 10.7 percent discount because the Korean economy, unlike many others in economically ravaged Asia, is on the mend.

The opportunity in these funds is usually a shot at buying a portfolio of securities at a discount to its NAV. Look at the A-rated Hancock Bank and Thrift Opportunity Fund, which trades at a 13 percent discount to NAV. Gregg Wolper, closed-end analyst at Morningstar, Inc. says the fund is a clone of Hancock Regional Bank Fund B, which sells at NAV—and has a 2 percent expense ratio. The closed-end fund's expenses are just 1.45 percent. Or consider the A-rated Salomon Brothers Fund, for instance, which earned an average of 24.4 percent a year on its portfolio over the last three years and trades at a discount of 6 percent. The fund looks a lot like the open-end Salomon Brothers Investors Fund. Both are large-cap blend funds with nearly identical three-year records (the NAV performance of the closed-end fund is actually a little better). The mutual fund charges loads, which can add as much as 5 percent to the cost. Other closed-ends with look-alike mutual funds include Gabelli Equity Trust, Invesco Global Health Sciences, Royce Value Trust, and just about all the muni bond funds. So if you are considering investing in a mutual fund with a closed-end cousin, take a look at these overlooked relatives.

Do-it-yourself fund investors might have balked at buying the closed-ends in the past, not wanting to deal with a broker and pay commissions when they usually buy no-loads. But with the rock-bottom costs of the Net-based brokers, put these funds on your radar screen. If you spend $5000 on closed-end fund shares, even paying Schwab's $29.95 commission comes to just 0.6 percent in additional costs.

As with all funds, it's important to consider the ratings on the closed-end funds. But these ratings are done on the basis of the portfolio performance and address neither the market performance of fund shares nor whether the shares sell at premiums or discounts to the NAV (Table 8-7). During 1998, most of our A-rated equity funds traded at discounts to net asset value, and in early 1999, all of them did. There's money to be made if the NAV goes up and the discount narrows and even goes to a premium. That's a play you might get from Hancock Bank & Thrift Opportunity, which in its past has traded at a double-digit premium to NAV.

But many excellent funds never trade at premiums. Just look at General American Investors, another A-rated closed-end equity fund. It opened its doors in 1927 and makes capital preservation a high priority. Not surprisingly, it's a fund with very low risk. Yet General American Investors, with a large-cap blend investment style, still earns excellent returns: a 34.6 percent NAV return in 1997 (beating the S&P 500 by 6 percentage points) and an average 28.4 percent return for the 1996–1998 period. The discount in early 1998 was 11.2 percent. Though buying Gen-

Most of the A-rated equity funds trade at discounts.

TABLE 8-7

TOP-PERFORMING CLOSED-END FUNDS

These closed-end funds earned A's for risk-adjusted total return

	Average annual total return*		Average annual total return*
EQUITY FUNDS			
GENERAL AMERICAN INVESTORS	28.4%	NATIONS BALANCED TARGET MATURITY	12.7%
HANCOCK BANK AND THRIFT OPPORT.	28.8	SALOMON BROTHERS FUND	24.4
HANCOCK PATRIOT GLOBAL DVD.	12.1	SCUDDER NEW EUROPE	29.6
HANCOCK PATRIOT PREF. DVD.	11.2	SPAIN FUND	40.4
HANCOCK PATRIOT PREMIUM DVD. I	12.6		
BOND FUNDS			
AMERICAN SELECT	10.5%	MUNICIPAL HIGH-INCOME	7.1%
AMERICAN STRATEGIC INCOME	9.4	NATIONS GOVERNMENT INCOME 2003	11.9
AMERICAN STRATEGIC INCOME II	9.3	NATIONS GOVERNMENT INCOME 2004	11.9
APEX MUNICIPAL	8.5	NUVEEN CALIFORNIA MUNICIPAL VALUE	7.0
COLONIAL MUNICIPAL INCOME	7.1	NUVEEN MUNICIPAL INCOME	6.5
DREYFUS CALIFORNIA MUNICIPAL INCOME	6.6	PREFERRED INCOME	11.6
ELLSWORTH CONVERTIBLES GROWTH & INCOME	19.0	PREFERRED INCOME MANAGEMENT	12.6
KEMPER STRATEGIC MUNICIPAL INCOME	6.7	PREFERRED INCOME OPPORTUNITY	12.5
MSDW MUNICIPAL INCOME OPPORTUNITY	8.2	PUTNAM DIVIDEND INCOME	9.9
MSDW MUNICIPAL INCOME OPPORTUNITY II	7.7	PUTNAM HIGH YIELD MUNICIPAL	6.5
MSDW MUNICIPAL INCOME OPPORTUNITY III	7.5	PUTNAM TAX-FREE HEALTH CARE	7.7
MORGAN STANLEY HIGH-YIELD	13.1	STRATEGIC GLOBAL INCOME	10.5
MUNIASSETS	7.7		

*1996–98, pretax return, NAV appreciation plus reinvestment of dividends and capital gains.

DATA: MORNINGSTAR INC.

eral American at a discount can be a smart move, don't buy it with the expectation that the discount will disappear. The discount can narrow or widen, but don't expect it to disappear. There could be a short-term trading opportunity if the discount goes from 11.2 percent to 6.3 percent, which happened to be the smallest discount at which the fund traded in 1998.

In newer funds, the management may take steps to eliminate the discount such as a share repurchase. Consider the case of Scudder New Europe. Despite a 34.9 percent NAV return in 1998, nearly twice that of the average European mutual fund, the fund traded at discounts between 13.7 percent and 27.3 percent. So finally, in late January 1999, the fund directors voted to convert to an open-end mutual fund, a process that will eliminate the discount. Still, you can't count on a closed-end fund's becoming an open-end fund, so the only reason to buy the fund is because you believe it will be a good investment.

For closed-end bond funds, those with the highest payouts generally trade at premiums to NAV. With interest rates having fallen so much in recent years, "yield is scarce, and investors will pay up for it," says Wolper. In 1997 and 1998, most of the rate drop was in the longer-term maturities, not in the short. For much of that

time, there was little difference between short- and long-term interest rates. That made it difficult for funds to boost yields by leveraging the portfolio. In that sort of transaction, the fund borrows money in the short-term market and buys longer-term bonds. Two A-rated funds that sell at large premiums are Morgan Stanley High-Yield Fund and Putnam High-Yield Municipal Trust.

Is it a good idea to buy them? Well, we know the portfolio management is good, but what about that premium? Take the Morgan Stanley fund at a 12 percent premium. At the recent price of 15⅜, the $1.38 a year distribution rate comes out to an 8.9 percent current yield. That's about 1.5 percentage points higher than you can get on the average high-yield mutual fund. That fund may be a good buy, but it's not compelling if you could get 2.5 or 3 percentage points more. What about Putnam High-Yield Municipal Trust, with a hefty 17 percent premium? Do the same analysis, and you come up with a 6.4 percent current yield. That's nearly 2 percentage points over a high-yield tax-exempt bond fund. That's probably a more compelling buy, even though it's a higher premium. The one caveat here is the sustainability of the yield. If the fund has a lot of bonds subject to a redemption, then the juicy distributions that produce that yield might well come down. So before you buy at a premium, you should ask the fund management company about it.

For most of our A-rated bond funds, you don't have to pay a premium. In fact, 18 of the 25 were still selling at discounts in early 1999. That gives you plenty of opportunity to find funds with good portfolio management at a discount. Still, you do need to ask questions. For instance, why does Preferred Income Management sell at a 21.3 percent discount? In recent months, a large shareholder wrested control of the fund, which invests mainly in income-producing preferred stocks. This shareholder plans to change the objective of the fund and invest in common stocks for long-term capital gains. That's why analyst Kevin McNally of Salomon Smith Barney put the fund on the firm's "avoid" list. He expects the dividend to be severely cut or eliminated, leading the yield-conscious shareholders who own it to dump the shares.

The BUSINESS WEEK
Mutual Fund Scoreboard

Equity Funds

MUTUAL FUND SCOREBOARD

How to Use the Tables

BUSINESS WEEK RATINGS

Overall ratings are based on five-year, risk-adjusted returns. They are calculated by subtracting a fund's risk-of-loss factor (see RISK) from historical pretax total return. To get a positive rating, the fund must beat the S&P 500 on a risk-adjusted basis. Category ratings are based on risk-adjusted returns of the funds in that category. The ratings are as follows:

A	SUPERIOR
B+	VERY GOOD
B	ABOVE AVERAGE
C	AVERAGE
C–	BELOW AVERAGE
D	POOR
F	VERY POOR

MANAGEMENT CHANGES

⬤ indicates the fund's manager has held the job at least 10 years; ◻ indicates a new manager since Dec. 31, 1997.

S&P 500 COMPARISON

The pretax total returns for the S&P 500 are as follows: 1998, 28.6%; three-year average (1996-1998), 28.2%; five-year average (1994-98), 24.0%; 10-year average (1989-98), 19.2%.

CATEGORY

Each U.S. diversified fund is classified by market capitalization of the stocks in the portfolio and by the nature of those stocks. If the median market cap is greater than $12 billion, the fund is large-cap; from $1.2 billion to $12 billion, mid-cap; and less than $1.2 billion, small-cap. "Value" funds are those whose stocks have price-to-earnings and price-to-book ratios lower than the average of the stocks in their market capitalizations. "Growth" funds have higher than average p-e and p-b ratios. "Blend" funds are those in which the ratios are about average. Hybrids mix stocks and bonds, and possibly other assets. World funds generally include U.S. stocks; foreign funds do not. Sector and regional foreign funds are as indicated.

FUND	OVERALL RATING	CATEGORY	RATING	SIZE		FEES		1997 RETURNS (%)		
(COMPARES RISK-ADJUSTED PERFORMANCE OF EACH FUND AGAINST ALL FUNDS)		(COMPARES RISK-ADJUSTED PERFORMANCE OF FUND WITHIN CATEGORY)		ASSETS $MIL.	% CHG. 1997-98	SALES CHARGE (%)	EXPENSE RATIO (%)	PRE-TAX	AFTER-TAX	YIELD
AARP BALANCED STOCK & BOND		Domestic Hybrid		773.5	16	No load	0.84	6.4	4.0	3.5
AARP CAPITAL GROWTH	C	Large-cap Blend	D	1550.2	27	No load	0.87	23.7	21.1	0.4
AARP GROWTH & INCOME ⬤	B	Large-cap Value	B	6933.0	4	No load	0.67	6.1	3.3	2.2
ACCESSOR SMALL TO MID CAP	C	Mid-cap Blend	C	257.4	106	No load	1.15	15.3	13.4	0.0
ACORN ⬤	C–	Mid-cap Growth	B	3585.0	–3	No load	0.56	6.0	4.6	0.2
ACORN INTERNATIONAL	C–	Foreign	B	1726.1	6	No load	1.19	15.4	14.9	0.7
ACORN USA		Small-cap Blend		281.5	53	No load	1.35	5.8	4.0	0.0
AIM ADVISOR FLEX C ⬤	B+	Domestic Hybrid	B	669.0	11	1.00**	2.20†	12.4	10.1	1.1
AIM ADVISOR MULTIFLEX C	C	Mid-cap Blend	C	312.6	–17	1.00**	2.42†	–0.3	–1.4	1.1
AIM AGGRESSIVE GROWTH	D	Small-cap Growth	C	3069.3	–17	5.50‡	1.06†	5.0	4.8	0.0
AIM BALANCED A	B	Domestic Hybrid	C	1319.2	93	4.75	0.98†	12.5	11.6	2.3
AIM BLUE CHIP A	B+	Large-cap Blend	B	1366.1	140	5.50	1.31†	30.4	30.3	0.1
AIM CAPITAL DEVELOPMENT A		Small-cap Growth		828.7	34	5.50	1.32†	4.5	4.5	0.0
AIM CHARTER A	C	Large-cap Blend	C–	4260.5	21	5.50	1.09†	26.8	25.6	0.9
AIM CONSTELLATION A	C–	Mid-cap Growth	C	14304.0	2	5.50	1.11†	18.9	18.3	0.0
AIM EUROPE GROWTH A (a) ◻	C–	Europe	F	416.6	–5	5.50	1.75†	16.6	14.5	0.0
AIM GLOBAL AGGRESSIVE GROWTH B		World		1011.6	–16	5.00**	2.30†	3.4	3.4	0.0
AIM GLOBAL GROWTH & INCOME B (b)	B	International Hybrid	B	504.0	7	5.00**	2.15†	19.6	15.5	1.6
AIM GLOBAL GROWTH B		World		314.5	36	5.00**	2.29†	21.4	20.7	0.0
AIM GLOBAL HEALTH CARE A (c)	C–	Health	C	396.3	–6	4.75	1.77†	18.4	18.4	0.0
AIM GLOBAL TELECOMMUNICATIONS A (d)	D	Communications	F	783.2	–9	4.75	1.79†	18.1	17.4	0.0
AIM INTERNATIONAL EQUITY A	C–	Foreign	C	1806.2	13	5.50	1.47†	13.4	13.0	0.6
AIM SELECT GROWTH B (e)	C–	Mid-cap Growth	B	315.4	–11	5.00**	1.99†	26.1	25.4	0.0
AIM SUMMIT	C	Mid-cap Growth	B+	2242.0	36	8.50	0.68	34.4	32.9	0.2
AIM VALUE B	B	Large Blend	C	9678.3	42	5.00**	1.85†	31.7	29.9	0.0
AIM WEINGARTEN A ⬤	C	Large Growth	C	7276.2	24	5.50	1.07†	33.1	31.4	0.1
ALGER CAPITAL APPRECIATION B	C–	Large Growth	D	261.7	22	5.00**	2.38†	37.4	34.9	0.0
ALGER GROWTH B ⬤	C	Large Growth	C–	426.2	50	5.00**	2.08†	44.1	41.3	0.0
ALGER MIDCAP GROWTH B	C–	Mid-cap Growth	B	205.8	25	5.00**	2.19†	31.1	26.8	0.0
ALGER SMALL CAPITALIZATION B ⬤	D	Mid-cap Growth	D	483.2	–15	5.00**	2.14†	9.9	7.5	0.0
ALLIANCE A	C–	Large Blend	F	1006.2	–13	4.25	1.03†	–2.7	–4.0	0.0
ALLIANCE GROWTH & INCOME A	B	Large Blend	C	1091.0	33	4.25	0.91†	21.2	18.3	1.1
ALLIANCE GROWTH B ⬤	C	Large Blend	D	4894.8	30	4.00**	1.95†	27.2	24.9	0.0
ALLIANCE PREMIER GROWTH B	B	Large Blend	C–	3440.6	278	4.00**	2.25†	48.3	47.6	0.0
ALLIANCE QUASAR B	C–	Small Growth	B	750.6	36	4.00**	2.38†	–5.3	–6.3	0.0
ALLIANCE REAL ESTATE INVESTMENT B		Real Estate		244.1	–17	4.00**	2.26†	–20.8	–22.0	4.3
ALLIANCE TECHNOLOGY B	C–	Technology	C	1846.4	80	4.00**	2.38†	62.0	59.6	0.0
ALLIANCE WORLDWIDE PRIVATIZATION A		Foreign		362.3	–25	4.25	1.73†	8.9	4.8	1.0
AMCAP ⬤	B	Large Growth	B	5830.0	29	5.75	0.68†	30.0	26.5	0.7
AMERICAN BALANCED ⬤	B+	Domestic Hybrid	B	5881.4	17	5.75	0.65†	11.1	8.6	3.3
AMERICAN CENTURY BALANCED INV.	B	Domestic Hybrid	C–	998.6	7	No load	1.00	16.3	13.1	2.1
AMERICAN CENTURY EQUITY GROWTH INV.	A	Large Value	A	2018.8	162	No load	0.69	25.5	24.1	0.9
AMERICAN CENTURY EQUITY INCOME INV.		Mid-cap Value		326.1	10	No load	1.00	13.0	7.7	3.0
AMERICAN CENTURY GLOBAL GOLD	F	Precious Metals	C–	228.5	–8	No load	0.67	–12.2	–12.4	0.9
AMERICAN CENTURY INCOME & GROWTH INV.	A	Large-cap Value	A	4284.7	140	No load	0.66	27.7	25.9	1.2

*Includes redemption fee. **Includes deferred sales charge. †12(b)-1 plan in effect. ‡Not currently accepting new accounts. §Less than 0.5% of assets. NA=Not available. NM=Not meaningful. (a) Formerly GT Global Europe Growth A. (b) Formerly GT Global Growth & Income B. (c) Formerly GT Global Health Care A. (d) Formerly GT Global Telecommunications A. (e) Formerly AIM Growth B.

SALES CHARGE
The cost of buying a fund. Many funds take this "load" out of the initial investment, and for ratings purposes, returns are reduced by these charges. Loads may be levied on withdrawals.

EXPENSE RATIO
Expenses for 1998 as a percentage of average net assets, a measure of how much shareholders pay for management. Footnotes indicate if the ratio includes a 12(b)-1 plan, which spends shareholder money on marketing. The average is 1.44%.

PRETAX TOTAL RETURN
A fund's net gain to investors, including reinvestment of dividends and capital gains at month-end prices.

AFTERTAX TOTAL RETURN
Pretax return adjusted for federal taxes. Assumes ordinary income and capital gains taxed at highest rate applicable in each year; uses 31% tax rate on income since 1993. Capital gains are assumed to be long-term.

YIELD
Income distributions as a percent of net asset value, adjusted for capital-gains distributions.

HISTORY
A fund's returns relative to all other funds for four periods, which from left to right are: Jan., 1989-June, 1991; July, 1991-Dec., 1993; Jan., 1994-June, 1996; July, 1996-Dec., 1998. The numbers designate which quartile the fund was in during the period: **1** for the top quartile; **2** for the second quartile; **3** for the third quartile; **4** for the bottom quartile. No number indicates no data for that period.

TURNOVER
Trading activity, the lesser of purchases or sales divided by average monthly assets.

% CASH
Portion of fund assets not invested in stocks or bonds. A negative number means the fund has borrowed to buy securities.

% FOREIGN
Portion of funds assets invested in non-U.S. securities.

PRICE-EARNINGS RATIO
The average, weighted price-earnings ratio of stocks in a fund's portfolio, based on last 12 months' earnings.

UNTAXED GAINS
Percentage of assets in portfolio that are unrealized and undistributed capital gains. A negative figure indicates losses that may offset future gains.

LARGEST HOLDING
Comes from the latest available fund reports.

RISK
Potential for losing money in a fund, or risk-of-loss factor. For each fund, the three-month Treasury bill return is subtracted from the monthly total return for each of the 60 months in the ratings period. When a fund has not performed as well as Treasury bills, the monthly result is negative. The sum of these negative numbers is divided by the number of months. The result is a negative number, and the greater its magnitude, the higher the risk of loss. This number is the basis for BW ratings, category ratings, and the RISK column.

BEST & WORST QUARTERS
The fund's highest and lowest quarterly returns of the past five years.

AVERAGE ANNUAL TOTAL RETURNS (%)						HISTORY	PORTFOLIO DATA						RISK		BEST		WORST		TELEPHONE
3 YEARS		5 YEARS		10 YEARS		RESULTS VS.	TURNOVER	CASH %	FOREIGN %	P-E RATIO	UNTAXED GAINS (%)	LARGEST HOLDING	LEVEL						
PRETAX	AFTERTAX	PRETAX	AFTERTAX	PRETAX	AFTERTAX	ALL FUNDS						COMPANY (% ASSETS)		QTR	%RET	QTR	%RET		
13.6	11.6	NA	NA	NA	NA	3	Average	6	14	25	12	Ford Motor (2)			NA		NA	800-322-2282
26.3	23.5	18.8	16.9	16.3	14.2	3 2 3 1	Average	7	8	31	38	Schering-Plough (3)	Average	IV 98	25.8	III 98	-15.4	800-322-2282
19.1	16.3	18.1	15.6	16.4	14.3	2 2 1 2	Low	2	15	25	22	Ford Motor (3)	Low	II 97	15.5	III 98	-13.8	800-322-2282
25.1	20.8	19.9	17.0	NA	NA	High		2	NA	27	16	Berkshire Hathaway Cl. A (3)	Average	IV 98	23.6	III 98	-18.6	800-759-3504
17.5	15.0	12.7	10.3	16.3	14.2	3 1 3 3	Low	8	10	27	42	Liberty Media Cl. A (4)	Average	IV 98	17.9	III 98	-19.5	800-922-6769
11.7	10.8	7.9	7.3	NA	NA	4 4	Low	19	94	30	30	Tieto Cl B (5)	Average	I 98	18.2	III 98	-16.1	800-922-6769
NA	NA	NA	NA	NA	NA		Low	10	1	23	13	CalEnergy (6)			NA		NA	800-922-6769
16.5	14.5	15.1	13.2	13.6	11.7	3 3 3 2	Very low	1	10	23	30	American Home Products (1)	Very low	II 97	11.5	III 98	-7.3	800-554-1156
11.4	9.8	10.7	9.5	NA	NA	3 3	Average	1	27	23	0	CarrAmerica Realty (1)	Low	II 97	11.3	III 98	-14.5	800-554-1156
10.5	9.5	17.4	16.7	20.8	19.4	2 1 1 4	Average	10	2	33	35	Veritas Software (1)	High	IV 98	25.3	III 98	-22.8	800-347-4246
18.6	17.1	15.3	15.0	15.6	14.4	3 2 2 2	Average	8	4	34	16	S&P 500 Index (Fut.) (Long) (4)	Low	IV 98	13.5	III 98	-8.9	800-347-4246
28.7	26.3	24.1	22.1	18.4	17.0	1 4 1 1	Low	7	4	36	25	S&P 500 Index (Fut.) (7)	Average	IV 98	24.5	III 98	-11.0	800-347-4246
NA	NA	NA	NA	NA	NA	2	Low	7	2	34	10	SunGard Data Systems (1)			NA		NA	800-347-4246
23.7	21.2	19.7	17.0	18.8	16.5	1 4 2 1	High	1	4	35	33	Philip Morris (4)	Average	IV 98	26.1	III 98	-11.9	800-347-4246
16.0	14.8	16.5	15.3	20.6	19.3	1 1 1 3	Average	7	4	38	38	BMC Software (1)	High	IV 98	24.8	III 98	-15.6	800-347-4246
15.8	14.9	9.9	9.3	8.6	8.2	4 4 4 3	High	3	99	34	21	Nokia Cl. A (4)	High	I 98	23.3	III 98	-21.0	800-347-4246
9.5	9.5	NA	NA	NA	NA	4	Average	12	67	33	20	WM-Data Cl. B (1)			NA		NA	800-347-4246
17.7	15.6	12.4	10.6	NA	NA	4 2	Average	3	58	26	29	Bristol-Myers Squibb (4)	Very low	IV 98	12.0	III 98	-7.9	800-347-4246
17.9	17.5	NA	NA	NA	NA	2	High	10	66	33	26	MCI Communications (2)			NA		NA	800-347-4246
16.6	13.1	16.8	13.4	NA	NA	4 1 2	High	12	25	41	12	Pfizer (7)	High	IV 98	21.6	III 98	-11.3	800-347-4246
12.1	10.4	7.9	6.2	NA	NA		Low	2	55	36	33	Nokia Cl.A (5)	High	IV 98	26.8	III 98	-24.0	800-347-4246
12.6	12.0	9.9	9.2	NA	NA	3 3	Average	14	100	29	24	Renault (2)	Average	I 98	14.7	III 98	-14.6	800-347-4246
20.7	18.9	17.1	15.3	NA	NA	2 2	High	7	2	40	44	Dell Computer (3)	High	IV 98	29.2	III 98	-14.5	800-347-4246
26.0	23.4	21.3	18.9	18.9	16.4	1 3 2 1	Average	4	4	36	41	Dell Computer (3)	High	IV 98	29.9	III 98	-12.3	800-347-4246
22.5	20.3	20.3	18.5	NA	NA	2 1	High	8	9	35	30	American Intl. Group (4)	Average	IV 98	27.1	III 98	-12.3	800-347-4246
25.4	21.9	21.5	17.6	18.8	16.4	1 4 2 1	High	7	9	38	25	MCI Communications (3)	Average	IV 98	28.0	III 98	-12.2	800-992-3863
23.4	22.0	26.8	25.7	NA	NA	1 2	High	13	2	45	30	Tyco Intl. (3)	High	I 95	29.5	III 98	-12.5	800-992-3863
25.8	23.1	22.1	19.9	21.8	19.7	1 1 2 1	High	19	1	44	30	Safeway (3)	High	IV 98	25.0	III 98	-8.3	800-992-3863
19.1	16.2	20.0	17.8	NA	NA	1 2	High	12	4	38	16	Elan ADR (3)	High	IV 98	27.3	III 98	-14.5	800-992-3863
7.7	4.7	12.2	9.9	18.9	16.2	1 2 1 4	High	10	2	37	21	MedImmune (3)	High	IV 98	24.1	III 98	-20.2	800-992-3863
15.9	10.9	15.4	10.3	15.5	11.2	2 2 2 2	High	0	5	22	2	MBNA (6)	High	IV 98	23.7	III 98	-24.3	800-227-4618
24.7	20.4	20.7	16.9	16.5	12.5	2 4 2 1	Average	3	1	27	19	Bristol-Myers Squibb (5)	Average	IV 98	23.3	III 98	-13.8	800-227-4618
25.2	23.4	19.9	18.5	21.0	18.6	1 1 3 1	Average	1	10	30	33	MCI WorldCom (6)	Average	IV 98	28.6	III 98	-16.4	800-227-4618
34.1	32.3	27.0	24.8	NA	NA	1 1	Average	4	9	42	27	Nokia Cl. A ADR (7)	High	IV 98	30.8	III 98	-12.3	800-227-4618
13.2	10.4	14.4	9.9	NA	NA	4 1 4	High	4	6	24	-6	Budget Group (4)	High	I 96	18.7	III 98	-28.6	800-227-4618
NA	NA	NA	NA	NA	NA		Low	4	5	25	-17	Equity Office Properties Tr. (5)			NA		NA	800-227-4618
25.9	25.1	29.8	28.0	NA	NA	1 1	Average	10	6	45	41	Dell Computer (8)	High	IV 98	39.6	IV 97	-16.6	800-227-4618
14.9	10.7	NA	NA	NA	NA	3	Average	4	95	24	6	Viag (3)			NA		NA	800-227-4618
24.7	21.0	20.0	16.5	17.3	14.1	2 3 3 1	Low	22	NA	36	42	Philip Morris (4)	Average	IV 98	22.0	III 98	-8.6	800-421-4120
15.0	12.0	14.2	11.5	13.4	10.7	3 3 3 2	Low	13	10	26	14	Hewlett-Packard (1)	Very low	II 97	10.0	I 94	-3.7	800-421-4120
15.3	12.2	13.2	10.4	13.4	11.4	2 4 3 2	High	4	NA	45	17	S&P 500 Index (Fut.) (4)	Low	II 97	12.3	III 98	-6.9	800-345-2021
29.5	25.9	23.9	20.8	NA	NA	3 1 1	High	1	2	27	17	BellSouth (3)	Low	IV 98	23.1	III 98	-13.9	800-345-2021
21.3	15.8	NA	NA	NA	NA	2	High	3	NA	21	1	Mercantile Bancorp. (4)			NA		NA	800-345-2021
-20.6	-21.5	-14.6	-15.2	-3.5	-3.9	4 2 4 4	Low	0	78	30	-78	Barrick Gold (17)	Very high	I 96	19.0	IV 97	-31.4	800-345-2021
28.7	25.6	23.7	20.9	NA	NA	2 1 1	High	1	1	28	19	Microsoft (3)	Low	IV 98	22.2	III 98	-11.3	800-345-2021

DATA: MORNINGSTAR, INC., CHICAGO, IL.

MUTUAL FUND SCOREBOARD

FUND	OVERALL RATING	CATEGORY	RATING	SIZE ASSETS $MIL.	% CHG. 1997-98	SALES CHARGE (%)	EXPENSE RATIO (%)	PRE-TAX	AFTER-TAX	YIELD
AMERICAN CENT. STRAT. ALLOC.: MOD. INV.		Domestic Hybrid		271.7	32	No load	1.10	12.8	11.2	2.1
AMERICAN CENTURY UTILITIES	B	Utilities	B	307.2	49	No load	0.72	27.4	23.5	2.1
AMERICAN CENTURY VALUE INVESTOR	B	Mid-cap Value	B+	2082.6	−14	No load	1.00	5.0	−0.1	1.2
AMERICAN CENTURY-20THC. GIFTRUST	F	Small-cap Growth	D	920.3	−7	No load	1.00	−13.1	−13.1	0.0
AMERICAN CENTURY-20THC. GROWTH INV. ⚹	C	Large-cap Growth	D	6493.2	26	No load	1.00	36.8	32.0	0.0
AMERICAN CENTURY-20THC. HERIT. INV. ⚹	D	Mid-cap Growth	C−	1070.7	−16	No load	1.00	−0.2	−0.2	0.2
AMERICAN CENTURY-20THC. INTL. DISC. INV.		Foreign		799.2	28	2.00*	1.70	17.9	17.8	0.2
AMERICAN CENTURY-20THC. INTL. GR. INV.	C−	Foreign	B	2640.0	48	No load	1.38	19.0	18.6	0.2
AMERICAN CENTURY-20THC. SELECT INV.	C	Large-cap Blend	D	6498.3	30	No load	1.00	35.7	30.6	0.3
AMERICAN CENTURY-20THC. ULTRA INV.	C−	Large-cap Blend	D	27150.0	21	No load	1.00	34.6	32.1	0.0
AMERICAN CENTURY.-20THC. VISTA INV.	F	Mid-cap Growth	F	954.9	−42	No load	1.00	−14.3	−14.3	0.0
AMERICAN GAS INDEX	C	Natural Resources	A	230.4	−6	No load	0.85	5.3	3.6	2.7
AMERICAN MUTUAL ⚹	B+	Large-cap Value	B+	10629.5	9	5.75	0.58†	14.8	11.8	2.5
AMERICAN NATIONAL INCOME	B	Large-cap Value	C	202.1	2	5.75	1.05	6.5	5.7	2.2
AMSOUTH BALANCED PREMIER		Domestic Hybrid		328.6	7	No load	NA	13.6	10.6	2.8
AMSOUTH EQUITY PREMIER ⚹		Large-cap Value		958.6	9	No load	NA	18.4	15.2	1.2
ARIEL APPRECIATION	B	Mid-cap Blend	B+	283.8	39	No load	1.26†	19.6	17.4	0.1
ARIEL GROWTH ⚹	B	Mid-cap Blend	B	201.8	16	No load	1.21†	9.9	7.9	0.2
ARTISAN INTERNATIONAL		Foreign		504.7	68	No load	1.45	32.2	31.6	0.2
ATLAS GROWTH & INCOME A	B	Large-cap Blend	C	224.6	53	No load	1.10†	26.1	24.3	0.5
BABSON GROWTH	B+	Large-cap Growth	B+	512.1	29	No load	0.80	32.2	28.4	0.2
BABSON VALUE ⚹	C	Large-cap Value	C−	1453.8	4	No load	0.97	6.1	4.8	1.2
BARON ASSET ⚹	C	Small-cap Growth	A	5672.3	50	No load	1.32†	4.3	4.2	0.1
BARON GROWTH & INCOME		Small-cap Growth		343.7	−17	No load	1.37†	0.1	0.1	0.1
BARON SMALL CAP		Small-cap Growth		470.0	65	No load	1.39†	2.2	2.2	0.0
BERGER 100	D	Large-cap Growth	F	1566.5	−9	No load	1.30†	16.2	14.7	0.0
BERGER GROWTH & INCOME ⚹	C	Large-cap Growth	C−	347.3	2	No load	1.44†	22.5	17.3	0.2
BERGER SMALL COMPANY GROWTH ⚹	D	Small-cap Growth	C	670.2	−15	No load	1.48†	3.2	−0.4	0.0
BERNSTEIN EMERGING MARKETS VALUE		Diversified Emerging Mkts.		422.7	25	2.00*	1.75	−21.1	−21.4	1.0
BERNSTEIN INTERNATIONAL VALUE	C	Foreign	B+	5147.5	10	No load	1.27	11.0	8.2	5.0
BNY HAMILTON LARGE CAP GROWTH INST.		Large-cap Blend		417.6	12	No load	NA†	23.5	21.2	0.8
BOSTON 1784 GROWTH & INCOME	B	Large-cap Growth	C	579.1	15	No load	0.90†	22.7	22.1	0.2
BOSTON 1784 GROWTH		Mid-cap Growth		203.4	−31	No load	0.91†	1.4	0.7	0.0
BOSTON 1784 INTERNATIONAL EQUITY		Foreign		446.2	2	No load	1.24†	12.5	12.2	0.2
BRAMWELL GROWTH		Large-cap Growth		248.5	66	No load	1.66†	34.5	33.0	0.0
BRANDYWINE BLUE	C−	Mid-cap Growth	C	356.8	−40	No load	1.06	−1.0	−1.5	0.8
BRANDYWINE ⚹	C−	Mid-cap Growth	C	4890.0	−42	No load	1.04	−0.7	−1.0	0.9
BRAZOS/JMIC SMALL CAP GROWTH		Small-cap Growth		382.6	314	No load	1.35	13.6	13.6	0.0
BRINSON GLOBAL (EX-U.S.) EQUITY I (f)	C	Foreign	B+	487.5	20	No load	1.00	14.4	13.9	0.8
BRINSON GLOBAL N		International Hybrid		578.5	−7	No load	1.19†	8.0	5.3	3.6
BRINSON U.S. EQUITY I		Large-cap Blend		691.2	36	No load	0.80	18.6	16.6	0.9
BT INVESTMENT EQUITY 500 INDEX	A	Large-cap Blend	A	873.3	35	No load	0.25	28.6	27.7	1.2
BT INVESTMENT INTL. EQUITY	C	Foreign	A	1400.2	144	No load	1.50	20.8	20.7	0.2
CALDWELL & ORKIN MARKET OPP.	A	Domestic Hybrid	A	374.6	166	2.00*‡	1.17	22.4	20.7	1.9
CALVERT SOCIAL INV. BALANCED A (g)	B	Domestic Hybrid	C−	674.1	9	4.75	1.12†	17.5	14.5	2.1
CALVERT WORLD VALUE INTL. EQUITY A	C−	Foreign	C	221.5	10	4.75	1.76†	16.1	14.3	0.3
CAPITAL INCOME BUILDER ⚹	B+	Domestic Hybrid	B	9238.7	18	5.75	0.65†	11.8	9.1	3.9
CAPITAL WORLD GROWTH & INCOME ⚹	B	World Stock	A	8696.9	18	5.75	0.82†	16.2	13.4	2.0
CCB EQUITY (h)		Large-cap Blend		227.4	14	4.50	1.00†	24.4	22.1	0.4
CENTURY SHARES ⚹	C	Financial	D	415.3	0	No load	0.82	7.0	5.5	0.8
CGM CAPITAL DEVELOPMENT ⚹	D	Mid-cap Blend	F	657.0	−19	No load‡	1.07	10.3	6.9	0.4
CGM MUTUAL ⚹	C−	Domestic Hybrid	F	942.0	−21	No load	0.98	8.2	6.7	3.7
CGM REALTY		Real Estate		435.0	−11	No load	1.00	−21.2	−22.6	6.5
CHASE VISTA CAPITAL GROWTH A (i)	C	Mid-cap Blend	C−	769.8	−12	5.75	1.31†	5.5	3.6	0.0
CHASE VISTA GROWTH & INCOME A (j)	C	Large Value	C−	1602.0	4	5.75	1.27†	14.1	11.6	0.4
CHESAPEAKE AGGRESSIVE GROWTH	D	Mid-cap Growth	F	375.2	−33	3.00‡	1.42	−3.4	−3.4	0.0
CHICAGO TRUST BALANCED ⚹		Domestic Hybrid		241.1	25	No load	1.07†	25.7	23.3	2.4
CHICAGO TRUST GROWTH & INCOME	A	Large-cap Growth	B+	428.2	48	No load	1.07†	35.5	33.8	0.0
CITIFUNDS BALANCED (k)	C	Domestic Hybrid	D	236.4	4	No load	1.02†	7.8	3.2	2.3
CITIFUNDS LARGE CAP GROWTH (l)	B+	Large-cap Growth	B	487.0	87	No load	1.05†	37.2	35.0	0.0
CITISELECT FOLIO 300		Domestic Hybrid		337.7	−3	No load	1.50†	6.6	4.4	2.5
CITISELECT FOLIO 400		Domestic Hybrid		396.3	−16	No load	1.65†	4.5	2.4	1.8
CITIZENS INDEX		Large-cap Growth		437.9	70	No load	1.59†	42.8	42.4	0.0
CLIPPER ⚹	A	Large-cap Value	A	1234.2	50	No load	1.08	19.2	14.2	1.9
COHEN & STEERS REALTY SHARES	C−	Real Estate	B	2145.6	−38	No load	1.05	−18.1	−19.7	4.8
COLONIAL A	B	Domestic Hybrid	C−	993.4	7	5.75	1.14†	13.1	11.3	2.4
COLONIAL SELECT VALUE A	C	Mid-cap Blend	B	421.3	19	5.75	1.03†	14.4	13.5	0.0
COLONIAL SMALL CAP VALUE A	C−	Small-cap Blend	C	405.4	45	5.75	1.42†	−6.2	−6.2	0.0
COLONIAL U.S. GROWTH & INCOME B (m)	B	Large-cap Blend	C−	782.2	62	5.00**	2.16†	19.2	18.1	0.0
COLONIAL UTILITIES B ⚹	B	Utilities	C	777.3	9	5.00**	1.97†	21.3	19.9	1.7

*Includes redemption fee. **Includes deferred sales charge. †12(b)-1 plan in effect. ‡Not currently accepting new accounts. §Less than 0.5% of assets. NA=Not available. NM=Not meaningful.
(f) Formerly Brinson Non-U.S. Equity I. (g) Formerly Calvert Social Investment Mgd. Grth. A. (h) Formerly 111 Corcoran Equity. (i) Formerly Vista Capital Growth A. (j) Formerly Vista Growth & Income A. (k) Formerly Landmark Balanced A. (l) Formerly Landmark Equity A. (m) Formerly Colonial U.S. Stock B.

Equity Funds

AVERAGE ANNUAL TOTAL RETURNS (%)						HISTORY	PORTFOLIO DATA						RISK					TELEPHONE
3 YEARS		5 YEARS		10 YEARS		RESULTS VS. ALL FUNDS	TURNOVER	CASH %	FOREIGN %	P-E RATIO	UNTAXED GAINS (%)	LARGEST HOLDING COMPANY (% ASSETS)	LEVEL	BEST		WORST		
PRETAX	AFTERTAX	PRETAX	AFTERTAX	PRETAX	AFTERTAX									QTR	%RET	QTR	%RET	
NA	NA	NA	NA	NA	NA	3	High	6	20	31	10	Microsoft (1)		NA		NA		800-345-2021
21.9	19.1	17.2	15.0	NA	NA	4 1	Average	1	5	24	24	MCI WorldCom (7)	Low	IV 97	18.0	I 94	−8.7	800-345-2021
18.0	13.0	17.8	13.5	NA	NA	1 2	High	4	1	24	−5	Mercantile Bancorp. (5)	Low	II 97	12.9	III 98	−10.9	800-345-2021
−3.2	−3.7	7.4	6.0	17.7	15.8	1 1 1 4	High	8	1	38	9	Nova (GA) (3)	Very high	IV 98	22.7	III 98	−30.3	800-345-2021
26.7	23.3	19.3	15.2	18.7	15.9	1 3 3 1	Average	4	1	44	29	S&P 500 Index (Fut.) (4)	High	IV 98	20.5	IV 95	−8.4	800-345-2021
11.2	8.4	10.3	7.9	13.7	11.6	2 1 3 3	Average	5	15	35	12	Mylan Laboratories (6)	High	IV 98	17.7	III 98	−21.2	800-345-2021
22.1	20.8	NA	NA	NA	NA	2	High	10	93	36	26	Marschollek Lautenschlager (4)		NA		NA		800-345-2021
17.7	14.7	11.7	9.6	NA	NA	1 4 2	High	9	99	35	18	Novartis (Reg.) (2)	Average	I 98	18.0	III 98	−17.9	800-345-2021
28.8	24.1	19.3	15.1	17.1	13.9	1 4 4 1	Average	5	0	40	26	General Electric (4)	Average	IV 98	22.4	III 98	−7.4	800-345-2021
23.6	19.8	20.1	17.4	24.0	22.1	1 1 2 1	High	2	3	41	30	MCI WorldCom (3)	High	IV 98	23.0	III 98	−11.8	800-345-2021
−5.6	−6.7	5.2	4.0	11.5	9.9	1 3 1 4	High	8	2	35	9	Ascend Communications (4)	Very high	III 94	18.4	III 98	−27.5	800-345-2021
16.4	15.0	13.2	11.9	NA	NA	3 3 2	Very low	3	NA	23	42	Duke Energy (5)	Low	IV 97	12.9	I 94	−6.5	800-343-3355
19.0	15.9	17.3	14.3	15.2	12.3	2 3 2 2	Low	24	2	26	33	Ameritech (3)	Very low	IV 98	12.4	III 98	−5.7	800-421-4120
15.0	13.1	14.2	11.7	14.0	11.2	2 3 2 3	Low	17	3	22	30	Schering-Plough (5)	Low	I 98	10.8	III 98	−12.2	800-231-4639
NA	NA	NA	NA	NA	NA			4	3	31	NA	Pharmacia & Upjohn (2)		NA		NA		800-451-8382
NA	NA	NA	NA	NA	NA			6	2	30		Wal-Mart Stores (3)		NA		NA		800-451-8382
26.8	24.6	18.3	16.0	NA	NA	3 4 1	Low	3	NA	25	40	Century Telephone Entprs. (6)	Low	IV 98	23.4	III 98	−12.9	800-292-7435
22.8	20.7	16.0	13.3	13.5	11.4	3 3 4 1	Low	1	NA	23	40	Specialty Equipment (6)	Low	IV 98	20.1	III 98	−15.6	800-292-7435
22.5	21.0	NA	NA	NA	NA	2	High	2	96	31	16	Union Bank Switz. (Reg.) (4)		NA		NA		800-344-1770
24.0	21.2	20.2	17.5	NA	NA	3 1 1	High	8	NA	41	29	Tyco Intl. (4)	Average	IV 98	20.4	III 98	−9.5	800-933-2852
27.3	23.4	21.9	18.6	16.3	13.5	3 4 2 1	Low	1	1	39	51	Cardinal Health (5)	Low	IV 98	26.2	III 98	−9.5	800-422-2766
18.1	16.9	17.3	16.1	15.6	14.2	3 2 1 2	Very low	1	9	22	23	Chase Manhattan (3)	Average	IV 98	14.1	III 98	−17.8	800-422-2766
19.4	19.4	19.9	19.6	16.9	16.2	4 1 1 3	Low	2	4	38	20	Charles Schwab (8)	High	IV 98	26.6	III 98	−23.5	800-992-2766
18.8	18.6	NA	NA	NA	NA	3	Low	0	3	38	31	Choice Hotels Intl. (10)		NA		NA		800-992-2766
NA	NA	NA	NA	NA	NA			2	10	33	−5	Iron Mountain (6)		NA		NA		800-992-2766
14.5	9.3	11.2	7.8	19.5	16.9	1 1 4 3	Very high	8	1	37	20	Cadence Design Systems (6)	High	IV 98	30.4	III 98	−19.4	800-333-1001
20.2	15.6	14.4	11.5	16.3	14.2	3 1 4 1	Very high	11	6	39	19	Microsoft (3)	Average	IV 98	20.9	III 98	−7.9	800-333-1001
11.9	9.3	16.3	14.7	NA	NA	1 4	High	14	5	43	23	TSI Intl. Software (2)	High	IV 98	26.6	III 98	−29.2	800-333-1001
−13.7	−14.1	NA	NA	NA	NA	4	Low	5	99	16	−67	EDP (5)		NA		NA		212-756-4097
12.5	9.9	9.8	7.8	NA	NA	3 3	Low	2	100	24	−1	Banca Commerc. Italiana (4)	Average	I 98	18.6	III 98	−17.7	212-756-4097
NA	NA	NA	NA	NA	NA			5	6	37	NA	Pfizer (4)		NA		NA		800-426-9363
22.0	21.2	18.8	18.1	NA	NA	1 2	Low	9	16	41	50	Microsoft (5)	Average	IV 98	17.3	III 98	−12.8	800-252-1784
NA	NA	NA	NA	NA	NA	4	Average	6	22	39	24	Aspect Development (6)		NA		NA		800-252-1784
8.2	7.8	NA	NA	NA	NA	4	High	9	100	33	21	Glaxo Wellcome (4)		NA		NA		800-252-1784
26.6	25.4	NA	NA	NA	NA	1	Average	6	4	41	40	Computer Sciences (4)		NA		NA		800-272-6227
13.3	11.6	14.5	13.1	NA	NA	1 1 3	Very high	2	5	44	10	Ascend Communications (6)	High	III 97	19.9	III 98	−19.9	800-656-3017
11.6	9.4	13.6	10.9	18.2	15.5	1 1 1 3	Very high	3	6	43	12	Ascend Communications (6)	High	III 97	19.0	III 98	−18.9	800-656-3017
NA	NA	NA	NA	NA	NA			4	3	42	12	Bright Horizons Family Sol. (3)		NA		NA		800-426-9157
10.9	9.3	9.7	8.4	NA	NA	4 3	Low	2	100	27	12	Royal Dutch Petroleum (2)	Average	IV 98	17.2	III 98	−13.7	800-448-2430
NA	NA	NA	NA	NA	NA		Average	1	30	28	0	Brinson Emg. Mkt. Debt (5)		NA		NA		800-448-2430
23.0	20.6	NA	NA	NA	NA	1	Low	1	1	29	16	Lockheed Martin (5)		NA		NA		800-448-2430
28.1	26.9	23.9	22.7	NA	NA	1 1	Low	8	2	33	54	Microsoft (3)	Low	IV 98	21.4	III 98	−9.9	800-730-1313
19.8	19.2	15.8	14.9	NA	NA	3 2	Average	9	98	31	14	Credito Italiano (2)	Average	I 98	19.4	III 98	−16.6	800-730-1313
26.3	23.3	18.4	16.2	NA	NA	1 3 1	Very high	54	2	37	13	Viacom Cl. B (4)	Very low	IV 95	11.0	I 95	−1.2	800-237-3073
15.1	11.9	12.8	9.7	11.5	9.0	3 4 4 2	Very high	3	4	35	−10	Cardinal Health (2)	Low	IV 98	12.4	III 98	−6.5	800-368-2748
11.5	9.9	8.6	7.1	NA	NA	4 3	Average	8	99	26	15	Zurich Allied (3)	Average	IV 98	18.0	III 98	−14.8	800-368-2748
17.5	15.0	14.7	12.4	14.7	12.6	2 2 3 2	Low	26	41	19	25	First Union (3)	Very low	IV 96	9.8	I 94	−5.8	800-421-4120
18.6	15.8	15.4	13.2	NA	NA	3 2	Low	17	64	25	19	Deutsche Telekom (2)	Low	IV 98	15.0	III 98	−9.7	800-421-4120
25.3	23.8	NA	NA	NA	NA	1	Average	3	5	32	33	General Electric (3)		NA		NA		800-422-2080
23.5	21.8	19.6	17.9	18.2	16.3	1 2 3 1	Very low	2	NA	21	73	Progressive (9)	Average	II 97	19.9	III 98	−17.4	800-321-1928
20.0	13.9	13.5	9.3	21.1	16.4	1 1 3 2	Very high	0	10	22	8	Nokia Cl. A ADR (6)	High	IV 98	29.4	III 98	−21.7	800-345-4048
13.1	9.0	10.2	7.1	13.8	10.7	2 1 4 3	Very high	0	18	31	0	Philip Morris (7)	Average	IV 98	19.3	III 98	−13.8	800-345-4048
12.9	10.0	NA	NA	NA	NA	3	High	1	NA	20	−18	SL Green Realty (8)		NA		NA		800-345-4048
17.4	14.2	14.3	12.0	19.9	18.2	1 1 3 2	Average	3	3	29	25	Liberty Media Cl. A (3)	Average	IV 98	17.5	III 98	−19.6	800-348-4782
20.8	17.4	16.8	14.2	21.6	19.1	1 2 3 2	Average	11	2	31	25	Philip Morris (2)	Average	IV 98	16.6	III 98	−12.2	800-348-4782
7.2	5.5	11.4	9.9	NA	NA	2 4	High	3	4	28	22	Jones Apparel Group (3)	Very high	IV 98	24.7	III 98	−29.3	800-525-3863
21.0	18.9	NA	NA	NA	NA	1	Low	4	3	39	28	Freddie Mac (2)		NA		NA		800-992-8151
29.1	27.6	24.0	23.0	NA	NA	1 1	Low	6	NA	38	40	EMC/Mass. (4)	Average	IV 98	23.7	III 98	−9.0	800-992-8151
11.9	7.9	11.0	8.0	NA	NA	3 4 3	High	1	2	24	4	AT&T (3)	Low	II 97	12.3	III 98	−8.6	800-721-1899
27.1	22.6	21.1	17.9	NA	NA	3 2 1	Average	7	1	44	26	Microsoft (7)	Average	IV 98	22.6	III 98	−7.7	800-721-1899
NA	NA	NA	NA	NA	NA	3		3	24	25	9	National Rural Utils. Coop. (1)		NA		NA		800-846-5200
NA	NA	NA	NA	NA	NA	3		4	34	23	9	National Rural Utils. Coop. (1)		NA		NA		800-846-5200
33.3	32.7	NA	NA	NA	NA	1	Very low	1	0	39	47	Microsoft (8)		NA		NA		800-223-7010
22.9	19.2	21.3	18.0	17.6	14.7	3 2 1 1	Low	36	5	23	14	Philip Morris (12)	Low	II 97	14.2	I 94	−4.8	800-776-5033
11.2	9.0	10.6	8.8	NA	NA	3 3	Low	4	NA	23	0	Vornado Realty Trust (7)	Average	IV 96	19.7	III 98	−11.9	800-437-9912
18.5	15.8	15.9	13.0	14.2	11.8	3 3 3 2	Average	3	17	22	27	Bristol-Myers Squibb (2)	Low	II 97	15.6	III 98	−7.5	800-426-3750
22.4	19.9	19.8	16.9	16.7	13.7	2 3 1 2	Average	3	NA	28	33	Kroger (3)	Average	IV 98	19.9	III 98	−15.6	800-426-3750
11.2	10.4	15.0	14.1	11.4	10.9	4 2 1 3	Low	11	0	19	2	Qlogic (2)	High	IV 98	18.7	III 98	−26.1	800-426-3750
23.9	21.4	19.3	16.8	NA	NA	2 1	Average	5	NA	29	26	Citigroup (3)	Average	IV 98	21.4	III 98	−14.2	800-426-3750
17.6	16.4	14.1	12.8	NA	NA	4 2	Very low	1	13	26	38	GTE (4)	Low	IV 97	14.7	I 94	−9.2	800-426-3750

DATA: MORNINGSTAR, INC., CHICAGO, IL.

MUTUAL FUND SCOREBOARD

FUND	OVERALL RATING (COMPARES RISK-ADJUSTED PERFORMANCE OF EACH FUND AGAINST ALL FUNDS)	CATEGORY (COMPARES RISK-ADJUSTED PERFORMANCE OF FUND WITHIN CATEGORY)	RATING	SIZE ASSETS $MIL.	SIZE % CHG. 1997-98	FEES SALES CHARGE (%)	FEES EXPENSE RATIO (%)	1997 RETURNS (%) PRE-TAX	1997 RETURNS (%) AFTER-TAX	1997 RETURNS (%) YIELD
COLUMBIA BALANCED	A	Domestic Hybrid	A	925.8	17	No load	0.68	20.1	17.1	2.9
COLUMBIA COMMON STOCK	A	Large-cap Blend	B+	754.5	−4	No load	0.77	26.3	23.0	0.5
COLUMBIA GROWTH	B	Large-cap Growth	B	1588.2	20	No load	0.71	30.3	29.0	0.2
COLUMBIA SPECIAL	C− ⚖	Mid-cap Growth	B	869.0	−30	No load	0.98	16.6	16.6	0.0
CONCERT INVMT. GROWTH & INCOME B (n)		Large-cap Blend		1191.4	−1	5.00**	1.88†	18.1	17.1	0.0
CONCERT INVESTMENT GROWTH B (o) ⚖		Large-cap Blend		4105.5	2	5.00**	1.88†	27.3	25.3	0.0
CRABBE HUSON EQUITY A (p)	C−	Mid-cap Value	F	205.7	−46	No load	1.42†	−8.8	−9.6	0.6
DAVIS FINANCIAL A	B+	Financial	B	460.7	60	4.75	1.07†	14.2	14.2	0.0
DAVIS N.Y. VENTURE A	B	Large-cap Value	C−	6820.3	47	4.75	0.91†	14.7	14.1	0.4
DELAWARE A	B+	Domestic Hybrid	B	640.6	12	5.75	0.97†	17.4	15.3	2.0
DELAWARE DECATUR INCOME A	B	Large-cap Value	C	1947.0	0	5.75	0.88†	9.9	5.4	2.5
DELAWARE DECATUR T/R A	B	Large-cap Value	C	1014.4	13	5.75	1.13†	10.6	7.4	1.4
DELAWARE DELCAP A	D	Mid-cap Growth	C	674.4	−10	5.75	1.36†	17.7	14.1	0.0
DELAWARE SMALL CAP VALUE A	C	Small-cap Value	C	282.2	0	5.75	1.39†	−5.1	−5.3	0.6
DELAWARE TREND A	D	Small-cap Growth	B	446.8	−11	5.75	1.34†	13.6	10.1	0.0
DFA INTERNATIONAL SMALL COMPANY		Foreign		272.7	34	No load	0.75	8.2	7.5	1.9
DODGE & COX BALANCED	B+	Domestic Hybrid	B	5770.0	14	No load	0.55	6.7	4.4	3.2
DODGE & COX STOCK	B	Large-cap Value	C	4458.4	9	No load	0.57	5.4	3.2	1.6
DOMINI SOCIAL EQUITY	A	Large-cap Blend	A	635.8	111	No load	1.17†	33.0	32.6	0.0
DREYFUS	C−	Large-cap Value	F	2591.1	−1	No load	0.71	17.2	16.8	0.9
DREYFUS APPRECIATION	A	Large-cap Growth	A	4168.9	111	No load	0.87	30.9	30.6	0.5
DREYFUS BALANCED	B+	Domestic Hybrid	B	321.1	−13	No load	0.96	9.7	7.3	2.8
DREYFUS DISCIPLINE STOCK ⚖	B+	Large-cap Blend	B	2817.6	71	No load	0.90†	26.6	25.3	0.6
DREYFUS GROWTH & INCOME	C	Large-cap Value	D	1777.5	−9	No load	1.01	12.8	11.2	0.9
DREYFUS GROWTH OPPORTUNITY	C	Large-cap Value	D	469.4	−6	No load	1.06	16.1	14.9	0.7
DREYFUS MIDCAP INDEX	C	Mid-cap Blend	C	273.0	6	1.00*	0.50	18.4	12.9	1.1
DREYFUS NEW LEADERS	C−	Mid-cap Blend	C−	691.5	−20	1.00*	1.12	−4.0	−4.5	0.0
DREYFUS PREMIER CORE VALUE A (q)	C	Large-cap Value	D	556.2	−5	5.75	1.14†	7.1	5.0	0.5
DREYFUS PREMIER WORLDWIDE GROWTH B	B+	World	A	658.5	121	4.00**	2.00†	27.7	27.6	0.0
DREYFUS S&P 500 INDEX	A	Large-cap Blend	B+	2153.1	50	1.00*	0.50	28.1	27.7	1.0
DREYFUS SMALL COMPANY VALUE	C	Small-cap Value	C	327.4	−19	1.00*	1.21	−6.3	−6.3	0.0
DREYFUS THIRD CENTURY	C	Large-cap Growth	C	1049.0	30	No load	0.97	30.2	27.3	0.0
DRIEHAUS INTERNATIONAL GROWTH		Foreign		222.3	22	No load	2.11	15.2	14.0	0.0
EATON VANCE BALANCED A (r)	B+	Domestic Hybrid	C	271.2	3	5.75	0.97	13.4	9.1	2.3
EATON VANCE TAX-MGD. GROWTH B ⚖		Large-cap Blend		2194.1	205	5.00**	1.50†	24.5	24.5	0.0
EATON VANCE UTILITIES A (s)	C	Utilities	D	409.3	12	5.75	1.13	23.6	22.6	2.3
ENTERPRISE GROWTH A ⚖	B+	Large-cap Growth	B	827.6	95	4.75	1.43†	30.9	29.7	0.0
EUROPACIFIC GROWTH ⚖	C	Foreign	A	20797.9	10	5.75	0.86†	15.5	14.1	1.2
EVERGREEN B		Mid-cap Blend		727.7	32	5.00**	2.19†	6.2	6.1	0.0
EVERGREEN BALANCED B (t) ⚖	B+	Domestic Hybrid	C	557.9	360	5.00**	1.35†	12.7	7.7	2.6
EVERGREEN FOUNDATION B		Domestic Hybrid		1372.2	47	5.00**	2.04†	11.1	10.5	1.4
EVERGREEN GROWTH & INCOME B		Mid-cap Blend		1014.0	41	5.00**	2.21†	4.4	3.7	0.2
EVERGREEN SMALL CO. GROWTH B (u)	D	Small-cap Growth	D	218.7	−84	5.00**	1.36†	−17.0	−20.2	0.0
EVERGREEN TAX STRATEGIC B		Domestic Hybrid		248.0	88	5.00**	2.18†	5.0	4.6	1.4
EVERGREEN VALUE A ⚖	C	Large-cap Value	C−	467.7	18	4.75	1.01†	9.5	6.0	0.8
EXCELSIOR BLENDED EQUITY A	B	Large-cap Blend	C	665.0	23	No load	0.99	28.7	28.2	0.3
EXCELSIOR INTERNATIONAL	D	Foreign	C−	230.1	29	No load	1.43	7.9	7.7	0.6
EXCELSIOR VALUE & RESTRUCT. A	B	Mid-cap Blend	B+	597.1	160	No load	0.89	10.3	10.0	0.5
EXECUTIVE INVESTORS BLUE CHIP	B+	Large-cap Blend	B	419.5	0	4.75	0.75†	17.8	17.1	0.5
EXPEDITION EQUITY INSTITUTIONAL		Large-cap Blend		319.0	28	No load	1.09	28.5	26.6	0.3
FAM VALUE ⚖	B	Small-cap Value	A	357.7	8	No load	1.24	6.2	4.1	0.5
FASCIANO ⚖	B	Small-cap Growth	A	233.2	318	No load	1.30	7.2	6.3	0.1
FEDERATED AMERICAN LEADERS B		Large-cap Value		1620.7	72	5.50**	1.89†	16.6	13.2	0.1
FEDERATED EQUITY-INCOME B ⚖		Large-cap Value		1224.1	47	5.50**	1.84†	14.9	12.9	0.9
FEDERATED GROWTH STRAT. A	C−	Mid-cap Growth	B	601.5	23	5.50	1.14	16.3	16.3	0.0
FEDERATED SMALL CAP STRAT. B		Small-cap Blend		234.2	22	5.50**	2.19†	0.9	0.9	0.0
FEDERATED STOCK & BOND A	B+	Domestic Hybrid	B	206.2	23	5.50	1.21†	11.2	8.7	3.3
FEDERATED STOCK ⚖	B+	Large-cap Value	B+	1534.2	26	No load	0.99	17.3	14.4	0.9
FEDERATED UTILITY A	C	Utilities	C	809.8	4	5.50	1.14	13.7	8.8	2.4
FIDELITY ADVISOR BALANCED T ⚖	C	Domestic Hybrid	D	2997.2	0	3.50	1.17†	15.5	12.5	2.5
FIDELITY ADVISOR EQUITY GROWTH T	B	Large-cap Growth	B	5194.8	25	3.50	1.29†	38.7	35.2	0.0
FIDELITY ADVISOR EQUITY INCOME T	B	Large-cap Value	B	2637.0	17	3.50	1.21†	16.1	14.8	0.6
FIDELITY ADVISOR GROWTH & INCOME T		Large-cap Blend		399.6	176	3.50	1.59†	30.3	30.2	0.2
FIDELITY ADVISOR GROWTH OPP. T ⚖	B+	Large-cap Value	B+	24823.6	18	3.50	1.27†	24.0	22.8	0.7
FIDELITY ADVISOR MIDCAP T		Mid-cap Blend		367.2	8	3.50	1.44†	14.4	13.7	0.0
FIDELITY ADVISOR NATURAL RES. T	D	Natural Resources	C	279.5	−45	3.50	1.39†	−16.3	−17.0	0.1
FIDELITY ADVISOR OVERSEAS T.	C−	Foreign	B	1138.1	3	3.50	1.65†	11.3	11.0	0.2
FIDELITY ADVISOR STRAT. OPP. T	C−	Small-cap Blend	C	444.8	−15	3.50	1.23†	0.8	0.3	0.0
FIDELITY ASSET MANAGER	B	Domestic Hybrid	C−	12879.2	6	No load	0.74	16.1	11.4	2.9
FIDELITY ASSET MANAGER: GROWTH	B	Domestic Hybrid	D	5119.9	10	No load	0.80	18.1	14.5	1.6

*Includes redemption fee. **Includes deferred sales charge. †12(b)-1 plan in effect. ‡Not currently accepting new accounts. §Less than 0.5% of assets. NA=Not available. NM=Not meaningful.
(n) Formerly Common Sense Growth & Income B. (o) Formerly Common Sense Growth B. (p) Formerly Crabbe Huson Equity Prim. (q) Formerly Dreyfus Core Value Inv. (r) Formerly EV Traditional Investors. (s) Formerly EV Traditional Total Return. (t) Formerly Keystone Balanced K-1. (u) Formerly Keystone Small Company Growth S-4.

AVERAGE ANNUAL TOTAL RETURNS (%) HISTORY							PORTFOLIO DATA						RISK					TELEPHONE
3 YEARS		5 YEARS		10 YEARS		RESULTS VS.	TURNOVER	CASH	FOREIGN	P-E	UNTAXED	LARGEST HOLDING	LEVEL	BEST		WORST		
PRETAX	AFTERTAX	PRETAX	AFTERTAX	PRETAX	AFTERTAX	ALL FUNDS		%	%	RATIO	GAINS (%)	COMPANY (% ASSETS)		QTR	%RET	QTR	%RET	
16.8	13.6	14.8	12.2	NA	NA	3 2	High	1	2	37	17	Microsoft (3)	Very low	IV 98	12.9	III 98	-4.8	800-547-1707
24.1	20.3	20.6	17.7	NA	NA	1 1	Average	2	1	37	29	Microsoft (4)	Low	IV 98	23.3	III 98	-11.5	800-547-1707
25.8	22.3	21.3	18.2	18.8	15.4	2 2 1 1	High	1	NA	42	39	Microsoft (4)	Average	IV 98	25.6	III 98	-14.6	800-547-1707
14.1	11.1	14.5	11.4	16.8	14.1	2 1 1 3	High	16	2	41	30	American Stores (5)	High	IV 98	23.2	III 98	-12.8	800-547-1707
19.2	15.5	NA	NA	NA	NA	2	Average	1	7	29	7	Dell Computer (3)			NA		NA	800-544-5445
23.4	19.9	NA	NA	NA	NA		High	5	4	36	6	MCI WorldCom (3)			NA		NA	800-544-5445
8.6	5.5	10.0	7.6	NA	NA	1 3 4	High	5	1	24	0	Amgen (4)	High	II 97	18.8	III 98	-19.9	800-541-9732
29.5	28.6	25.5	23.9	NA	NA	1 1 1	Very low	1	4	23	74	American Express (7)	Average	IV 98	20.1	III 98	-15.9	800-279-0279
24.7	23.5	21.8	20.1	20.4	18.0	1 1 1 1	Very low	4	5	25	26	American Express (6)	Average	IV 98	21.4	III 98	-14.4	800-279-0279
18.5	15.2	15.6	12.7	14.4	11.6	2 3 3 2	Average	3	4	28	24	Rite Aid (4)	Very low	IV 98	15.1	III 98	-5.5	800-523-4640
19.7	14.7	17.7	13.5	13.9	10.2	4 3 2 2	Average	2	10	27	5	Bestfoods (3)	Low	II 97	13.7	III 98	-9.8	800-523-4640
20.3	16.5	18.8	15.3	15.2	12.0	4 3 2 2	Average	4	10	27	12	Bestfoods (3)	Low	II 97	15.3	III 98	-10.9	800-523-4640
15.2	11.1	13.4	9.6	14.7	12.4	1 3 2 3	High	9	NA	43	24	Staples (5)	High	IV 98	24.7	III 98	-16.3	800-523-4640
15.5	13.0	12.1	10.2	15.4	13.6	2 1 4 3	Average	4	NA	20	21	Trigon Healthcare (2)	Average	II 97	15.3	III 98	-16.0	800-523-4640
14.5	11.4	14.0	11.3	19.0	15.7	1 1 1 3	High	6	3	45	24	EMC/Mass. (4)	High	IV 98	22.9	III 98	-15.8	800-523-4640
NA	NA	NA	NA	NA	NA			4	NA	NA	21	NA			NA		NA	310-395-8005
14.1	12.0	14.2	12.2	14.1	12.1	2 3 2 3	Low	4	9	24	13	ALCOA (2)	Very low	II 97	11.0	III 98	-7.9	800-621-3979
18.3	16.3	18.3	16.5	16.1	14.3	2 3 1 2	Low	5	4	24	18	Pharmacia & Upjohn (3)	Average	IV 98	15.4	III 98	-14.3	800-621-3979
30.1	29.8	24.3	23.8	NA	NA	3 1 1	Very low	1	0	34	32	Microsoft (6)	Low	IV 98	24.6	III 98	-9.8	800-762-6814
14.6	11.4	12.2	7.9	11.8	8.5	3 4 3 3	Very high	3	4	25	22	General Electric (3)	Average	IV 98	20.3	III 98	-12.9	800-373-9387
28.1	27.8	24.6	24.1	18.5	17.5	2 4 1 1	Very low	4	6	31	32	Pfizer (6)	Low	IV 98	20.5	III 98	-10.2	800-373-9387
12.9	9.8	13.3	10.6	NA	NA	3 3	Very high	12	3	27	7	Biogen (2)	Very low	IV 98	10.8	III 98	-7.1	800-373-9387
27.8	25.2	23.1	21.0	19.9	17.9	1 3 1 1	Average	1	4	32	25	Microsoft (3)	Average	IV 98	22.6	III 98	-12.2	800-373-9387
14.4	10.4	12.2	9.2	NA	NA	3 3	High	14	3	26	14	Biogen (3)	Average	IV 98	18.5	III 98	-11.7	800-373-9387
17.8	14.1	14.5	10.0	12.0	8.6	4 4 3 2	High	4	5	26	24	Coastal (3)	Average	IV 98	20.5	III 98	-11.4	800-373-9387
22.7	19.2	18.2	15.4	NA	NA	1 2 1	Low	8	0	31	15	America Online (3)	Average	IV 98	27.8	III 98	-14.6	800-373-9387
10.4	8.7	11.8	9.6	14.2	11.7	2 1 2 4	Average	11	4	29	26	Metromedia Fiber Net Cl. A (2)	High	II 97	17.8	III 98	-20.4	800-373-9387
17.7	12.5	17.2	12.6	13.6	9.6	4 3 1 2	Average	2	8	23	13	Waste Management (2)	Average	IV 98	15.3	III 98	-14.6	888-338-8084
24.3	24.2	19.8	19.6	NA	NA	2 1	Very low	8	38	30	25	Pfizer (5)	Low	IV 98	19.9	III 98	-13.0	800-554-4611
27.6	26.6	23.4	21.8	NA	NA	3 1 1	Very low	3	2	33	38	Microsoft (3)	Low	IV 98	21.3	III 98	-10.1	800-373-9387
16.6	15.0	16.4	14.3	NA	NA	1 3	High	1	2	23	-7	Emmis Broadcasting Cl. A (2)	Average	IV 98	24.6	III 98	-27.2	800-373-9387
27.9	24.3	21.4	17.6	16.8	14.2	2 4 2 1	Average	4	NA	36	35	Merck (4)	Average	IV 98	24.3	III 98	-11.4	800-373-9387
NA	NA	NA	NA	NA	NA			6	100	36	7	Nokia Cl. A ADR (3)			NA		NA	800-560-6111
16.2	12.0	14.8	11.4	13.3	9.9	3 3 3 2	Low	3	13	33	21	Sofamor/Danek Group (3)	Very low	II 97	11.2	III 98	-5.2	800-225-6265
NA	NA	NA	NA	NA	NA	1	Very low	6	6	36	16	Automatic Data Processing (2)			NA		NA	800-225-6265
15.5	12.1	11.5	8.8	12.8	9.6	2 2 4 2	High	3	30	26	33	Energis (17)	Low	IV 98	14.4	I 94	-7.7	800-225-6265
31.8	30.4	26.0	24.5	20.3	18.1	2 2 1 1	Low	4	NA	40	31	Bristol-Myers Squibb (4)	Average	IV 98	26.8	III 98	-14.0	800-432-4320
14.4	12.5	11.3	9.6	13.3	11.9	3 1 3 3	Low	14	100	27	24	Mannesmann (3)	Average	IV 98	17.9	III 98	-13.6	800-421-4120
16.8	16.3	NA	NA	NA	NA	2	Very low	18	1	27	44	Clear Channel Communs. (4)			NA		NA	800-343-2898
15.8	12.1	13.5	10.7	12.1	9.5	3 4 3 2	Average	4	1	33	24	Johnson & Johnson (2)	Very low	II 97	10.4	I 94	-4.4	800-343-2898
15.1	14.1	NA	NA	NA	NA	2	Very low	11	3	29	24	Intel (3)			NA		NA	800-343-2898
18.5	17.7	NA	NA	NA	NA	2	Low	15	3	28	21	Webster Financial (1)			NA		NA	800-343-2898
-1.7	-5.2	5.3	1.9	13.6	10.3	1 1 2 4	High	8	1	30	-13	DeVry (2)	Very high	II 97	17.9	III 98	-29.4	800-343-2898
12.9	12.1	NA	NA	NA	NA	3	Average	1	4	25	8	Perkin-Elmer (1)			NA		NA	800-343-2898
17.9	14.0	17.1	13.7	14.8	11.9	2 4 2 2	Average	9	3	30	28	General Electric (3)	Average	II 97	11.7	III 98	-9.2	800-343-2898
26.1	24.6	20.9	19.2	18.1	16.6	3 2 2 1	Low	0	4	33	55	Pfizer (5)	Average	IV 98	22.4	III 98	-12.1	800-446-1012
8.2	7.5	5.9	5.1	6.9	6.1	4 4 4 4	High	6	99	27	13	Brambles Industries (3)	High	IV 98	16.3	III 98	-14.9	800-446-1012
22.6	21.8	21.3	20.5	NA	NA	1 1	Low	-2	12	28	15	Philip Morris (3)	Average	IV 98	22.9	III 98	-20.5	800-446-1012
21.5	19.7	19.3	17.2	NA	NA	4 1 2	High	12	3	33	9	General Electric (3)	Low	IV 98	19.7	III 98	-13.1	800-423-4026
NA	NA	NA	NA	NA	NA			1	NA	36	25	McKesson (4)			NA		NA	800-922-2085
18.0	16.6	16.0	14.8	16.0	15.0	1 3 2 2	Very low	12	NA	18	38	Conmed (6)	Low	III 97	17.0	III 98	-15.2	800-932-3271
18.1	17.1	17.5	16.0	15.6	14.1	1 4 1 3	Average	20	NA	27	5	Pulitzer Publishing (4)	Average	II 97	14.3	III 98	-13.4	800-848-6050
21.8	18.6	NA	NA	NA	NA	1	Average	1	5	26	13	PECO Energy (3)			NA		NA	800-341-7400
20.1	17.8	NA	NA	NA	NA	2	Average	4	5	27	16	Bristol-Myers Squibb (2)			NA		NA	800-341-7400
22.2	19.0	17.6	14.0	15.8	12.8	1 4 2 2	High	3	3	42	25	America Online (3)	High	IV 98	27.3	III 98	-20.3	800-341-7400
15.3	15.2	NA	NA	NA	NA	4	High	3	2	30	12	S&P 500 Index (Fut.) (6)			NA		NA	800-341-7400
16.1	12.4	13.9	10.8	11.8	9.0	3 4 3 2	Average	4	6	26	13	Federated High-Yield (4)	Very low	II 97	10.5	III 98	-5.2	800-341-7400
24.1	19.9	20.9	17.4	16.2	13.0	3 2 1 1	Average	1	6	26	24	Lexmark International Cl. A (2)	Low	IV 98	16.5	III 98	-11.3	800-341-7400
17.2	13.2	13.2	10.2	14.0	11.2	2 2 4 2	High	11	3	22	19	PECO Energy (3)	Low	IV 97	12.9	I 94	-7.2	800-341-7400
15.3	12.8	10.6	8.8	13.4	11.1	2 2 4 2	Average	5	9	29	21	American Home Products (2)	Low	II 97	12.6	III 98	-5.9	800-522-7297
26.0	23.2	22.5	20.4	NA	NA	1 1	High	6	2	38	36	Johnson & Johnson (3)	Average	IV 98	24.1	III 98	-6.0	800-522-7297
18.8	17.1	18.8	17.3	NA	NA	1 2	Average	3	8	24	29	Citicorp (3)	Low	IV 98	17.8	III 98	-12.3	800-522-7297
NA	NA	NA	NA	NA	NA		Average	10	6	33	15	Time Warner (3)			NA		NA	800-843-3001
23.3	21.5	20.8	19.1	20.2	18.3	1 1 2 1	Low	7	12	29	2	Fannie Mae (5)	Low	IV 98	20.5	III 98	-7.7	800-522-7297
NA	NA	NA	NA	NA	NA	2	Very high	8	1	30	16	McKesson (3)			NA		NA	800-522-7297
2.7	0.4	6.4	4.6	11.9	9.8	1 1 1 4	High	5	29	23	-24	Total Cl. B ADR (6)	High	III 98	14.2	IV 97	-13.2	800-522-7297
11.7	10.3	9.1	8.2	NA	NA	2 4 3	Average	8	98	24	-2	Alcatel Alsthom (2)	Average	III 98	17.3	III 98	-17.8	800-522-7297
8.9	6.3	10.6	8.6	13.0	10.6	2 2 3 3	High	1	6	20	17	Whole Foods Market (8)	High	III 97	18.1	III 98	-18.0	800-522-7297
17.0	13.4	12.1	9.5	13.9	11.6	2 2 4 2	High	13	2	34	14	Philip Morris (2)	Low	IV 98	14.1	III 98	-5.8	800-544-8888
20.6	17.2	14.3	12.0	NA	NA	4 2	High	6	NA	31	16	BellSouth (5)	Low	IV 98	16.1	III 98	-8.2	800-544-8888

DATA: MORNINGSTAR, INC., CHICAGO, IL.

MUTUAL FUND SCOREBOARD

FUND	OVERALL RATING (COMPARES RISK-ADJUSTED PERFORMANCE OF EACH FUND AGAINST ALL FUNDS)	CATEGORY (COMPARES RISK-ADJUSTED PERFORMANCE OF FUND WITHIN CATEGORY)	RATING	ASSETS $MIL.	% CHG. 1997-98	SALES CHARGE (%)	EXPENSE RATIO (%)	PRE-TAX	AFTER-TAX	YIELD
FIDELITY ASSET MANAGER: INCOME	A	Domestic Hybrid	B+	940.8	37	No load	0.69	10.3	7.9	4.3
FIDELITY BALANCED	B	Domestic Hybrid	C	5316.4	24	No load	0.67	20.2	17.1	2.6
FIDELITY BLUE CHIP GROWTH	B+	Large-cap Blend	B	19904.1	48	No load	0.70	34.8	33.2	0.2
FIDELITY CAPITAL APPRECIATION	C	Mid-cap Blend	C	2602.3	23	No load	0.67	17.0	16.3	0.4
FIDELITY CONTRAFUND	B+	Large-cap Value	C	38821.3	26	3.00‡	0.67	31.5	29.5	0.5
FIDELITY DESTINY I ⚓	A	Large-cap Value	B+	7365.3	20	8.67	0.33	25.6	23.1	1.4
FIDELITY DESTINY II ⚓	B+	Large-cap Value	B+	4997.0	31	8.67	0.48	28.1	23.1	0.7
FIDELITY DISCIPLINED EQUITY ⚓	B	Large-cap Blend	C−	3145.4	23	No load	0.64	21.8	20.0	0.7
FIDELITY DIVERSIFIED INTERNATIONAL	C	Foreign	A	2156.9	40	No load	1.23	14.4	13.3	1.3
FIDELITY DIVIDEND GROWTH	A	Large-cap Blend	A	10368.6	131	No load	0.86	35.9	32.9	0.4
FIDELITY EMERGING GROWTH	C−	Mid-cap Growth	B	2897.0	46	0.75*	1.05	43.3	41.3	0.0
FIDELITY EMERGING MARKETS	F	Diversified Emerging Mkts.	F	270.4	−39	4.50*	1.35	−26.6	−26.6	0.0
FIDELITY EQUITY-INCOME	B	Large-cap Value	C	23707.4	12	No load	0.65	12.5	11.0	1.5
FIDELITY EQUITY-INCOME II	B+	Large-cap Value	B	19453.7	15	No load	0.68	23.0	20.4	1.0
FIDELITY EUROPE CAPITAL APPREC.	C	Europe	C−	689.9	86	4.00*	1.07	21.7	21.7	0.0
FIDELITY EUROPE ⚓	B	Europe	B	1622.6	71	4.00*	1.18	20.8	18.9	0.8
FIDELITY EXPORT & MULTINATIONAL ⚓		Mid-cap Growth		411.9	−11	3.75*	0.88	22.4	21.3	0.0
FIDELITY FREEDOM 2000		Domestic Hybrid		502.1	517	No load	0.08	15.2	13.7	3.2
FIDELITY FREEDOM 2010		Domestic Hybrid		914.3	642	No load	0.08	19.3	17.8	2.6
FIDELITY FREEDOM 2020		Large-cap Blend		859.6	923	No load	0.08	21.7	20.4	2.0
FIDELITY FREEDOM 2030		Large-cap Blend		282.4	395	No load	0.08	22.0	20.6	1.7
FIDELITY	A	Large-cap Blend	B+	10563.2	62	No load	0.56	31.0	29.3	0.8
FIDELITY GROWTH & INCOME	A	Large-cap Blend	A	48639.8	33	No load‡	0.68	28.3	26.5	0.8
FIDELITY GROWTH COMPANY	C	Large-cap Growth	C−	11440.4	9	No load	0.68	27.2	25.3	0.2
FIDELITY INTL. GROWTH & INCOME ⚓	C−	Foreign	B+	871.0	−15	No load	1.15	10.0	9.2	0.4
FIDELITY INTERNATIONAL VALUE		Foreign		435.8	12	No load	1.28	11.7	11.6	0.4
FIDELITY JAPAN ⚓	F	Japan		312.5	45	4.50*	1.40	13.1	13.0	0.3
FIDELITY LARGE CAP STOCK ⚓		Large-cap Growth		317.0	127	No load	0.84	36.5	32.7	0.1
FIDELITY LATIN AMERICA	F	Latin America	C−	307.0	−64	4.50*	1.29	−38.3	−38.8	2.4
FIDELITY LOW-PRICED STOCK	B	Small-cap Value	B+	9194.9	−14	4.50*‡	0.95	0.4	−1.9	0.8
FIDELITY MAGELLAN	C	Large-cap Blend	C−	83552.1	31	3.00‡	0.61	33.6	32.2	0.5
FIDELITY MID-CAP STOCK		Mid-cap Blend		1784.5	1	No load	0.86	15.2	13.6	0.0
FIDELITY NEW MILLENNIUM	C	Mid-cap Growth	B+	1683.7	8	3.00‡	0.94	27.7	25.8	0.0
FIDELITY OTC	C	Mid-cap Growth	B+	5476.4	42	No load	0.75	40.4	38.0	0.0
FIDELITY OVERSEAS	C−	Foreign	B	3846.5	4	No load	1.20	12.8	12.3	0.6
FIDELITY PACIFIC BASIN ⚓	F	Diversified Pacific/Asia	B	227.4	6	4.00*	1.31	8.3	8.2	0.2
FIDELITY PURITAN	B+	Domestic Hybrid	B	25682.3	13	No load	0.63	16.6	13.4	3.1
FIDELITY REAL ESTATE INVESTMENT ⚓	C−	Real Estate	C	1239.3	−48	0.75*	0.90	−18.6	−20.2	4.8
FIDELITY RETIREMENT GROWTH	C	Large Blend	D	4946.2	26	No load	0.59	35.9	32.7	0.6
FIDELITY SEL. BIOTECHNOLOGY ⚓	D	Health	C−	704.4	28	3.75*	1.47	29.7	27.9	0.0
FIDELITY SEL. BROKERAGE & INVESTMENT ⚓	C−	Financial	F	550.5	−15	3.75*	1.29	5.7	5.3	0.0
FIDELITY SEL. COMPUTERS	C−	Technology	B	1514.4	166	3.75*	1.34	96.4	96.4	0.0
FIDELITY SEL. DEVELOP. COMMUN. ⚓	D	Communications	D	445.3	119	3.75*	1.55	67.7	67.5	0.0
FIDELITY SEL. ELECTRONICS	C−	Technology	B	2722.8	18	3.75*	1.12	51.1	51.1	0.0
FIDELITY SEL. ENERGY SERVICE ⚓	F	Natural Resources	D	394.1	−65	3.75*	1.22	−49.7	−50.5	0.0
FIDELITY SEL. FINANCIAL SERVICES ⚓	C	Financial	C−	597.3	9	3.75*	1.29	14.1	11.3	0.2
FIDELITY SEL. FOOD & AGRICULTURE	B+	Unaligned	A	233.6	−24	3.75*	1.48	15.6	12.7	0.3
FIDELITY SEL. GOLD (v)	F	Precious Metals	C	201.7	−5	3.75*	1.48	−8.6	−8.6	0.0
FIDELITY SEL. HEALTH CARE	A	Health	B+	3032.1	86	3.75*	1.18	41.2	39.6	0.1
FIDELITY SEL. HOME FINANCE	C	Financial	D	990.3	−40	3.75*	1.19	−14.8	−15.4	0.2
FIDELITY SEL. LEISURE	C	Unaligned	B+	315.4	38	3.75*	1.39	37.9	36.0	0.0
FIDELITY SEL. REGIONAL BANKS ⚓	B	Financial	C	1178.5	−13	3.75*	1.24	11.7	10.2	0.6
FIDELITY SEL. RETAILING	C	Unaligned	B	362.1	89	3.75*	1.55	45.8	45.2	0.0
FIDELITY SEL. SOFTWARE & COMPUTERS	C−	Technology	C−	656.2	54	3.75*	1.42	45.8	44.9	0.0
FIDELITY SEL. TECHNOLOGY ⚓	C−	Technology	C	1061.3	102	3.75*	1.30	74.2	74.2	0.0
FIDELITY SEL. TELECOMMUNICATIONS ⚓	C	Communications	C	810.6	84	3.75*	1.48	41.0	39.0	0.0
FIDELITY SEL. UTILITIES GROWTH ⚓	B+	Utilities	B+	504.1	40	3.75*	1.30	43.1	38.6	0.4
FIDELITY SMALL CAP SELECTOR (w)	D	Small-cap Blend	C−	748.0	−9	1.50*	0.97	−7.4	−8.1	0.2
FIDELITY SOUTHEAST ASIA	F	Pacific/Asia ex-Japan	C	235.2	−11	4.50*	1.32	−5.8	−5.9	0.2
FIDELITY SPARTAN MARKET INDEX	A	Large-cap Blend	B+	7149.9	85	0.50*	0.19	28.5	27.6	0.9
FIDELITY STOCK SELECTOR	C	Large-cap Blend	D	1747.0	−8	No load	0.69	14.7	12.8	1.0
FIDELITY TREND ⚓	D	Mid-cap Blend	F	1198.4	−16	No load	0.59	2.8	2.8	0.0
FIDELITY UTILITIES ⚓	B+	Utilities	B+	2128.5	25	No load	0.85	28.5	26.3	1.4
FIDELITY VALUE	C	Mid-cap Value	C	5522.6	−30	No load	0.61	0.2	−3.1	1.0
FIDELITY WORLDWIDE	C−	World		1013.6	−12	No load	1.16	7.2	6.4	0.6
FIFTH THIRD CARDINAL A (x)	B	Large-cap Blend	C	253.1	−15	4.50	1.06†	24.2	21.7	0.8
FIRST AMERICAN MID CAP GROWTH A (y)	C−	Mid-cap Growth	C	213.0	−19	4.00	1.18†	10.6	6.8	0.0
FIRST AMERICAN STRATEGIC GROWTH & INC.		Domestic Hybrid		212.6	9	No load	0.25	7.7	5.4	3.5
FIRST EAGLE FUND OF AMERICA Y ⚓	B+	Mid-cap Value	B+	456.5	70	No load	1.70	21.0	19.0	0.0
FIRST INVESTORS BLUE CHIP A		Large-cap Blend	C−	418.2	19	6.25	1.44†	18.1	17.3	0.2

*Includes redemption fee. **Includes deferred sales charge. †12(b)-1 plan in effect. ‡Not currently accepting new accounts. §Less than 0.5% of assets. NA=Not available. NM=Not meaningful. (v) Formerly Fidelity Select American Gold. (w) Formerly Fidelity Small Cap Stock. (x) Formerly Cardinal Inv. (y) Formerly Piper Emerging Growth A.

3 YR PRETAX	3 YR AFTERTAX	5 YR PRETAX	5 YR AFTERTAX	10 YR PRETAX	10 YR AFTERTAX	RESULTS VS. ALL FUNDS	TURNOVER	CASH %	FOREIGN %	P-E RATIO	UNTAXED GAINS (%)	LARGEST HOLDING COMPANY (% ASSETS)	RISK LEVEL	BEST QTR	BEST %RET	WORST QTR	WORST %RET	TELEPHONE
10.2	7.8	9.0	7.0	NA	NA	4 3	High	33	12	31	6	BellSouth (1)	Very low	II 97	5.7	I 94	-2.0	800-544-8888
17.5	14.6	12.0	9.9	13.1	10.5	2 2 4 2	High	7	3	28	17	Unisys (3)	Very low	IV 98	12.7	III 98	-4.4	800-544-8888
25.5	23.4	22.7	20.8	23.2	21.3	1 1 1 1	Average	4	3	38	37	Microsoft (3)	Average	IV 98	23.4	III 98	-8.1	800-544-8888
19.4	16.6	15.7	12.7	14.3	11.3	4 2 3 2	High	3	6	30	22	Electronic Data Systems (6)	Average	IV 98	24.8	III 98	-15.8	800-544-8888
25.4	22.4	21.6	19.2	24.0	21.7	1 1 1 1	High	13	7	40	37	WorldCom (3)	Average	IV 98	23.7	III 98	-9.4	800-544-8888
24.9	21.7	22.8	19.1	21.2	17.4	1 1 1 1	Low	5	10	29	43	Fannie Mae (7)	Low	IV 98	20.8	III 98	-7.1	800-752-2347
25.1	21.5	22.7	19.2	21.6	18.1	1 1 1 1	High	8	4	36	25	Time Warner (4)	Low	IV 98	25.6	III 98	-10.9	800-752-2347
23.2	20.2	20.0	17.1	19.4	17.0	1 2 2 1	High	1	1	26	29	Microsoft (3)	Average	IV 98	21.0	III 98	-13.1	800-544-8888
16.0	14.8	13.2	12.0	NA	NA	3 3	Average	15	97	29	16	Novartis (Reg.) (2)	Average	IV 98	15.3	III 98	-14.5	800-544-8888
31.3	28.8	26.5	24.4	NA	NA	1 1	High	5	4	30	21	American Home Products (5)	High	IV 98	19.5	III 98	-6.2	800-544-8888
25.6	22.3	21.9	19.6	NA	NA	1 1 1	Very high	3	4	45	28	McKesson (3)	High	IV 98	26.1	I 94	-10.2	800-544-8888
-21.8	-22.1	-17.6	-17.9	NA	NA	1 4 4	Average	7	99	12	NA	Telebras (ADR) (5)	Very high	III 94	24.2	III 98	-24.4	800-544-8888
21.0	18.9	18.5	16.1	15.7	13.4	4 1 2 2	Low	2	11	24	36	General Electric (4)	Low	IV 98	16.2	III 98	-12.9	800-544-8888
22.9	20.0	19.3	16.9	NA	NA	1 2 1	Average	8	9	27	35	Citicorp (5)	Low	IV 98	20.6	III 98	-12.0	800-544-8888
24.2	21.2	18.6	16.7	NA	NA	3 1	Very high	4	100	25	20	Alcatel Alsthom (2)	Average	I 98	22.7	III 98	-19.9	800-544-8888
23.1	20.6	18.7	16.9	14.4	13.2	4 3 2 1	Average	4	99	31	25	Novartis (Reg.) (3)	Average	I 98	19.0	III 98	-17.4	800-544-8888
28.0	25.0	NA	NA	NA	NA	1	Very high	9	4	45	23	MCI Communications (5)			NA		NA	800-544-8888
NA	NA	NA	NA	NA	NA		Low	17	20	24	6	Fidelity Money: Retire. M (17)			NA		NA	800-544-8888
NA	NA	NA	NA	NA	NA		Low	9	21	26	8	Fidelity Govt. Income (11)			NA		NA	800-544-8888
NA	NA	NA	NA	NA	NA		Very low	0	19	28	10	Fidelity Growth Company (10)			NA		NA	800-544-8888
NA	NA	NA	NA	NA	NA		Low	0	19	28	5	Fidelity Growth Company (11)			NA		NA	800-544-8888
27.5	24.9	23.1	20.4	18.6	15.7	2 3 1 1	Average	10	6	33	32	General Electric (3)	Low	IV 98	23.8	III 98	-10.8	800-544-8888
26.1	24.3	22.7	20.7	20.3	17.7	1 2 1 1	Low	7	6	32	41	General Electric (3)	Low	IV 98	20.5	III 98	-8.3	800-544-8888
20.9	18.7	19.3	17.3	20.7	18.5	1 2 1 2	Average	6	4	40	36	Microsoft (3)	Average	IV 98	21.2	III 98	-8.3	800-544-8888
9.9	8.7	7.7	6.5	8.9	8.1	4 3 4 3	Average	10	99	24	9	Credit Suisse Group (Reg.) (1)	Average	IV 98	16.5	III 98	-17.4	800-544-8888
9.7	9.1	NA	NA	NA	NA	4	Average	3	99	25	16	Alcatel Alsthom (2)			NA		NA	800-544-8888
-3.6	-3.8	0.4	0.1	NA	NA	4 4	Average	13	100	31	-19	Fuji Photo Film (3)	Very high	II 97	23.5	IV 97	-15.5	800-544-8888
27.3	24.4	NA	NA	NA	NA	1	High	6	5	40	20	General Electric (3)			NA		NA	800-544-8888
2.3	1.8	-7.2	-7.6	NA	NA	4 4	Average	9	99	12	-62	Telebras (ADR) (12)	Very high	III 94	29.8	III 98	-30.8	800-544-8888
17.3	14.6	16.2	13.1	NA	NA	1 2 2	Average	10	28	16	15	Gallaher Group ADR (1)	Low	III 97	13.0	III 98	-16.8	800-544-8888
23.6	20.3	20.5	17.8	19.9	16.8	1 1 2 1	Low	6	5	37	44	General Electric (4)	Average	IV 98	27.2	III 98	-11.1	800-544-8888
20.0	17.3	NA	NA	NA	NA	2	High	6	1	32	23	Medtronic (2)			NA		NA	800-544-8888
25.1	22.7	24.6	22.4	NA	NA	1 1	High	3	11	28	35	Best Buy (3)	High	IV 98	32.5	III 98	-14.7	800-544-8888
24.1	20.9	20.8	18.4	19.5	16.4	1 2 1 1	High	9	1	40	33	Microsoft (9)	High	IV 98	28.9	IV 97	-11.0	800-544-8888
12.3	10.9	9.4	8.3	8.7	7.1	4 3 4 3	Average	9	99	24	24	Alcatel Alsthom (2)	Average	IV 98	17.9	III 98	-17.4	800-544-8888
-3.7	-3.9	-4.0	-4.8	1.2	0.5	4 2 4 4	Low	6	100	28	-30	Toyota Motor (3)	Very high	IV 98	21.6	IV 97	-17.2	800-544-8888
18.0	14.6	15.2	12.3	14.8	11.7	3 2 3 2	Average	6	9	28	20	Citicorp (3)	Very low	IV 98	12.7	III 98	-6.7	800-544-8888
10.4	8.5	8.8	7.0	11.5	9.7	3 2 4 3	Average	5	4	25	6	Starwood Hotels & Resorts (8)	Average	IV 96	19.0	III 98	-11.5	800-544-8888
20.4	15.8	16.8	12.6	17.5	13.8	3 1 3 1	Very high	1	14	35	19	Wal-Mart Stores (4)	Average	IV 98	21.8	III 98	-9.5	800-544-8888
16.5	13.3	14.0	12.1	21.8	19.8	1 3 4 2	High	17	2	45	27	Genentech (15)	High	IV 98	26.1	I 94	-13.3	800-544-8888
33.8	32.9	19.6	18.5	20.9	20.0	3 1 4 1	High	11	12	21	25	PaineWebber Group (6)	High	IV 98	29.1	III 98	-33.1	800-544-8888
36.7	31.7	36.1	32.1	28.4	26.0	1 1 1 1	Very high	23	NA	50	40	Dell Computer (16)	Very high	IV 98	39.4	IV 97	-25.8	800-544-8888
26.6	24.0	22.3	18.4	NA	NA	1 1 1	Very high	11	19	47	36	Intel (10)	Very high	IV 98	48.9	I 97	-15.5	800-544-8888
34.7	30.8	37.2	33.2	29.8	27.3	1 1 1 1	Very high	8	4	46	32	Intel (12)	Very high	IV 98	56.8	IV 97	-22.3	800-544-8888
4.4	2.7	10.1	8.4	9.6	8.8	1 4 1 4	Average	9	10	14	-66	Baker Hughes (11)	Very high	III 97	36.9	III 98	-34.8	800-544-8888
28.9	25.4	24.9	21.9	22.2	19.8	4 1 1 1	Average	8	4	21	28	BankAmerica (New) (4)	Average	IV 98	20.2	III 98	-19.8	800-544-8888
19.5	16.3	19.9	17.0	20.4	17.4	1 3 1 2	Average	7	10	31	26	Philip Morris (8)	Low	IV 98	16.8	III 98	-8.1	800-544-8888
-12.8	-13.4	-9.0	-9.4	0.3	0.0	4 1 4 4	Average	5	69	40	-52	Euro-Nevada Mining (10)	Very high	I 96	25.4	IV 97	-32.1	800-544-8888
28.8	24.0	30.5	26.5	26.4	23.0	1 4 1 1	Average	15	2	44	35	Warner-Lambert (5)	Low	II 97	21.3	I 94	-7.0	800-544-8888
19.3	16.8	21.8	18.8	23.5	21.4	3 1 1 2	Average	1	3	16	21	Washington Mutual (5)	High	II 97	19.4	III 98	-25.8	800-544-8888
30.3	27.3	21.2	18.0	19.1	17.0	4 1 2 1	Very high	7	4	37	29	Microsoft (6)	Average	IV 98	32.2	III 98	-15.3	800-544-8888
30.2	28.4	26.6	24.6	24.5	22.1	3 1 1 1	Low	5	3	21	37	US Bancorp (7)	Average	IV 98	18.7	III 98	-16.4	800-544-8888
35.7	35.3	21.6	21.4	22.5	21.0	1 1 3 1	Very high	7	NA	39	26	Federated Dept. Stores (8)	High	IV 98	34.8	III 98	-14.8	800-544-8888
26.8	23.4	24.5	21.5	24.4	21.3	2 1 1 1	High	9	2	46	37	Microsoft (15)	High	I 98	24.3	II 94	-17.5	800-544-8888
30.5	25.9	28.8	24.6	26.1	23.3	1 1 1 1	Very high	11	11	48	37	Intel (11)	High	IV 98	46.0	IV 97	-19.9	800-544-8888
23.1	19.2	20.3	17.2	20.1	17.7	2 1 2 1	High	9	12	30	27	WorldCom (10)	High	IV 98	30.7	III 98	-15.4	800-544-8888
27.6	23.4	20.9	18.0	18.5	15.7	1 2 3 1	Average	6	2	26	30	MCI Communications (10)	Low	IV 98	23.0	I 94	-6.1	800-544-8888
10.2	8.8	10.4	9.1	NA	NA	3 4	Average	2	4	17	8	Ross Stores (2)	High	II 97	17.4	III 98	-24.5	800-544-8888
-14.1	-14.5	-11.1	-11.4	NA	NA	4 4	High	7	100	19	-58	Hutchison Whampoa (7)	Very high	IV 98	25.5	IV 97	-28.6	800-544-8888
28.0	26.7	23.7	22.6	NA	NA	3 1 1	Very low	0	9	32	30	General Electric (3)	Low	IV 98	21.4	III 98	-10.0	800-544-8888
20.1	17.1	18.9	16.1	NA	NA	2 1 2	High	2	6	24	28	Lucent Technologies (2)	Average	IV 98	19.7	III 98	-15.9	800-544-8888
9.3	7.1	8.3	5.4	12.5	9.9	2 1 4 4	Very high	4	22	33	16	Anchor Gaming (6)	High	IV 98	21.7	III 98	-27.0	800-544-8888
23.5	20.7	18.5	15.7	16.6	14.0	3 2 3 1	Average	7	10	23	38	MCI Communications (9)	Low	IV 98	18.5	I 94	-3.7	800-544-8888
12.3	8.5	14.2	11.1	14.6	12.1	3 1 1 3	Low	3	3	22	2	Browning-Ferris Industries (4)	Average	IV 98	14.8	III 98	-20.1	800-544-8888
12.6	11.1	9.5	8.2	NA	NA	1 4 3	Average	18	60	25	18	Telecom Italia (Risp) (2)	Average	IV 98	16.9	III 98	-21.2	800-544-8888
24.7	20.9	19.0	15.4	15.5	12.6	2 4 3 1	Very low	8	2	36	55	Microsoft (5)	Average	IV 98	22.7	III 98	-12.2	800-334-0483
15.1	11.9	15.1	12.5	NA	NA	1 1 3	Low	7	5	41	37	Elan ADR (4)	High	IV 98	25.9	III 98	-19.3	800-637-2548
NA	NA	NA	NA	NA	NA		High	97	4	32	2	First American Fixed-Inc. (37)			NA		NA	800-637-2548
26.5	21.8	21.9	18.0	18.0	14.7	4 1 2 1	High	16	NA	31	21	Biogen (4)	Average	IV 98	16.8	III 98	-13.5	800-451-3623
21.5	19.7	18.5	16.3	14.3	12.7	3 4 2 2	Average	12	4	33	37	General Electric (3)	Average	IV 98	20.0	III 98	-12.9	800-423-4026

DATA: MORNINGSTAR, INC., CHICAGO, IL.

MUTUAL FUND SCOREBOARD

FUND	OVERALL RATING (COMPARES RISK-ADJUSTED PERFORMANCE OF EACH FUND AGAINST ALL FUNDS)	CATEGORY (COMPARES RISK-ADJUSTED PERFORMANCE OF FUND WITHIN CATEGORY)	RATING	SIZE ASSETS $MIL.	SIZE % CHG. 1997-98	FEES SALES CHARGE (%)	FEES EXPENSE RATIO (%)	1997 RETURNS (%) PRE-TAX	1997 RETURNS (%) AFTER-TAX	1997 RETURNS (%) YIELD
FIRST INVESTORS GLOBAL A	C−	World	C	292.8	6	6.25	1.82†	16.8	16.5	0.0
FIRST INVESTORS GROWTH & INCOME A ♜	B	Large-cap Blend	C	295.8	40	6.25	1.39†	23.4	23.3	0.4
FIRST OMAHA EQUITY	B+	Large-cap Value	B+	271.2	−6	No load	1.04†	7.8	5.6	1.7
FIRSTAR GROWTH & INCOME RET. (z)		Large-cap Blend		215.3	53	4.00	1.12†	22.4	20.4	0.8
FLAG INVESTORS COMMUNICATIONS A (aa) ♜	A	Communications	B+	1250.8	101	4.50	1.11†	85.3	83.3	0.4
FLAG INVESTORS EQUITY PARTNERS A		Large-cap Value		246.2	64	4.50	1.35†	25.3	24.9	0.1
FLAG INVESTORS VALUE BUILDER A	A	Domestic Hybrid	B+	610.3	49	4.50	1.14†	18.5	17.2	2.4
FORTIS CAPITAL A	C	Large-cap Growth	C−	421.8	27	4.75	1.13†	29.6	22.9	0.0
FORTIS GROWTH A ♜	D	Mid-cap Growth	C−	654.3	−7	4.75	1.05†	19.0	12.8	0.0
FOUNDERS BALANCED	A	Domestic Hybrid	B+	1254.1	34	No load	0.99†	14.0	12.1	2.4
FOUNDERS BLUE CHIP	B+	Large-cap Blend	B	542.4	0	No load	1.09†	17.8	14.5	1.3
FOUNDERS DISCOVERY	D	Small-cap Growth	C−	239.4	−3	No load	1.52†	14.2	12.1	0.0
FOUNDERS GROWTH ♜	C	Large-cap Growth	C	2377.3	35	No load	1.10†	25.0	23.5	0.1
FOUNDERS SPECIAL ♜	D	Mid-cap Growth	C−	252.3	−21	No load	1.30†	−1.7	−2.3	0.0
FOUNDERS WORLDWIDE GROWTH	C−	World	C	275.3	−11	No load	1.45†	9.6	8.5	0.4
FPA CAPITAL ♜	C	Mid-cap Value	C−	673.7	−8	6.50‡	0.83	−0.4	−3.5	1.8
FPA PARAMOUNT ♜	D	Mid-cap Value	F	354.7	−49	6.50	0.92	−24.4	−26.9	2.2
FRANKLIN BALANCE SHEET INVESTMENT	B	Small-cap Value	B+	1516.6	18	1.50‡	1.08†	−0.6	−1.9	1.6
FRANKLIN CALIFORNIA GROWTH A (bb)	B+	Mid-cap Growth	A	754.8	32	5.75	0.99†	10.7	9.9	0.6
FRANKLIN DYNATECH A (cc) ♜	C	Technology	A	287.5	59	5.75	1.04†	27.3	26.9	1.2
FRANKLIN EQUITY A (dd) ♜	C	Large-cap Blend	D	627.7	20	5.75	0.90†	13.2	11.7	0.2
FRANKLIN EQUITY INCOME A (ee) ♜	B	Large-cap Value	C	446.7	17	5.75	0.97†	6.7	4.5	3.1
FRANKLIN GLOBAL UTILITIES A (ff)	C−	Utilities	F	206.0	−1	5.75	1.03†	6.5	4.9	1.1
FRANKLIN GROWTH A (gg) ♜	B+	Large-cap Blend	B+	1898.6	26	5.75	0.89†	18.5	17.8	1.4
FRANKLIN INCOME A (hh) ♜	C	Domestic Hybrid	D	7783.9	−3	4.25	0.72†	1.0	−1.4	7.6
FRANKLIN MICROCAP VALUE A (ii)		Small-cap Value		224.1	16	4.50‡	1.22†	−6.8	−8.5	0.0
FRANKLIN REAL ESTATE SEC. A (jj)	C	Real Estate	B	295.3	−3	5.75	1.00†	−15.4	−16.9	5.2
FRANKLIN RISING DIVIDENDS A (kk) ♜	C	Mid-cap Blend	B	470.4	13	5.75	1.39†	6.0	4.0	0.4
FRANKLIN SMALL CAP GROWTH A (ll)	C−	Small-cap Growth	B	3723.7	35	5.75	0.89†	−0.0	−0.4	0.6
FRANKLIN UTILITIES A (mm) ♜	C−	Utilities	F	2103.9	−4	4.25	0.75†	7.6	5.4	4.6
FREMONT GLOBAL ♜	C	International Hybrid	C	646.9	−2	No load	0.85	10.0	7.8	2.1
FUNDAMENTAL INVESTORS ♜	B+	Large-cap Value	B	12712.9	21	5.75	0.63†	16.7	14.3	1.3
GABELLI ASSET ♜	B+	Mid-cap Blend	B+	1593.6	19	No load	1.38†	15.9	15.0	0.1
GABELLI GROWTH	B+	Large-cap Growth	B+	1864.0	96	No load	1.43†	29.8	28.6	0.0
GABELLI SMALL CAP GROWTH	C	Small-cap Blend	A	321.3	10	No load	1.62†	−0.0	−0.5	0.0
GABELLI VALUE	C	Mid-cap Blend	B	797.6	34	5.50	1.42†	23.2	20.7	0.0
GALAXY ASSET ALLOC. RET. A	A	Domestic Hybrid	B+	361.4	86	3.75	1.37	17.7	16.3	2.2
GALAXY EQUITY GROWTH RET. A	B+	Large-cap Growth	B+	361.7	50	3.75	1.37	25.7	23.8	0.1
GALAXY EQUITY INCOME RET. A	B+	Large-cap Blend	B	220.3	20	3.75	1.39	15.6	13.1	1.2
GALAXY EQUITY VALUE RET. A	B	Large-cap Value	C	270.7	40	3.75	1.38	23.8	22.9	0.1
GALAXY GROWTH & INCOME RET. A ♜	B+	Large-cap Value	B	238.3	51	3.75	1.27	15.7	14.1	0.7
GALAXY II LARGE CO. INDEX RET. ♜	A	Large-cap Blend	B+	747.0	37	No load	0.40	28.1	27.4	1.0
GALAXY II SMALL CO. INDEX RET. ♜	C−	Mid-cap Blend	C−	310.8	−18	No load	0.40	−1.8	−4.0	0.5
GAM INTERNATIONAL A	C−	Foreign	B	2681.2	50	5.00	1.68†	6.8	6.3	0.2
GATEWAY (nn)	A	Domestic Hybrid	B+	464.2	82	No load	1.07	12.3	12.0	0.6
GOLDMAN SACHS CAPITAL GROWTH A	B	Large-cap Blend	C	1893.1	56	5.50	1.40†	33.9	33.0	0.0
GOLDMAN SACHS CORE U.S. EQUITY A	B	Large-cap Blend	C	552.5	44	5.50	1.27†	21.3	20.7	0.1
GOLDMAN SACHS GROWTH & INC. A ♜	C	Large-cap Value	C−	1175.1	1	5.50	1.25†	−5.4	−5.7	0.9
GOLDMAN SACHS INTL. EQUITY A	C−	Foreign	C	912.9	33	5.50	1.67†	18.0	16.8	0.0
GOLDMAN SACHS SM. CAP VAL. A	D	Small-cap Value	F	280.6	−24	5.50	1.54†	−16.9	−18.4	0.0
GRADISON ESTABLISHED VALUE ♜	B	Mid-cap Value	B	518.2	−1	No load	1.10†	6.1	4.5	1.0
GRIFFIN GROWTH & INCOME A ♜	B	Large-cap Value	C−	310.3	27	4.50	0.84†	7.8	6.6	0.9
GROWTH FUND OF AMERICA ♜	C	Large-cap Blend	D	16246.9	33	5.75	0.70†	31.8	29.2	0.4
GUARDIAN PARK AVENUE A ♜	B+	Large-cap Blend	B	2995.7	29	4.50	0.79†	21.3	19.4	0.6
HANCOCK EMERGING GROWTH B	D	Small-cap Growth		435.0	−3	5.00**	2.02†	11.6	11.0	0.0
HANCOCK FINANCIAL INDUSTRIES B		Financial		2782.2	66	5.00**	1.90†	4.0	4.0	0.3
HANCOCK GLOBAL TECHNOLOGY A ♜	D	Technology	D	246.3	45	5.00	1.51†	49.2	48.9	0.0
HANCOCK GROWTH B ♜	C−	Large-cap Growth	D	285.0	28	5.00**	2.13†	25.5	22.4	0.0
HANCOCK GROWTH & INCOME B	C	Large-cap Blend	D	548.0	61	5.00**	1.87†	15.0	14.0	0.1
HANCOCK INDEP. EQUITY B		Large-cap Blend		347.0	157	5.00**	2.12†	27.9	27.3	0.0
HANCOCK REGIONAL BANK B ♜	B+	Financial	B+	4907.0	−10	5.00**	2.00†	0.7	−0.1	0.6
HANCOCK SOVEREIGN INVESTORS A ♜	C	Large-cap Blend	C	1884.5	8	5.00	1.06†	15.6	13.9	1.2
HANCOCK SPECIAL EQUITIES B ♜	D	Mid-cap Growth	F	519.6	−43	5.00**	2.19†	−6.0	−6.4	0.0
HARBOR CAPITAL APPRECIATION	C	Large-cap Growth	C	4696.7	62	No load	0.70	36.8	35.2	0.2
HARBOR INTERNATIONAL ♜	C−	Foreign	B+	5373.9	2	No load‡	0.97	10.4	8.5	1.5
HARBOR INTERNATIONAL GROWTH	C−	Foreign	C	1323.2	40	No load	1.02	23.5	23.0	0.6
HARTFORD ADVISERS A		Domestic Hybrid		315.5	222	5.50	1.40†	21.1	20.0	1.5
HARTFORD CAPITAL APPRECIATION A		Small-cap Growth		365.3	57	5.50	1.45†	3.3	3.1	0.0
HARTFORD STOCK A		Large-cap Blend		267.0	311	5.50	1.45†	31.3	31.0	0.0
HEARTLAND VALUE ♜		Small-cap Value	C−	1666.0	−22	No load	1.12†	−11.5	−11.9	0.2

*Includes redemption fee. **Includes deferred sales charge. †12(b)-1 plan in effect. ‡Not currently accepting new accounts. §Less than 0.5% of assets. NA=Not available. NM=Not meaningful. (z) Formerly Portico Growth & Income Ret. (aa) Formerly Flag Investors Telephone Income A. (bb) Formerly Franklin CA Growth I. (cc) Formerly Franklin DynaTech I. (dd) Formerly Franklin Equity I. (ee) Formerly Franklin Equity Income I. (ff) Formerly Franklin Global Utilities I. (gg) Formerly Franklin Growth I. (hh) Formerly Franklin Income I. (ii) Formerly Franklin MicroCap Value I. (jj) Formerly Franklin Real Estate Securities I. (kk) Formerly Franklin Rising Dividends I. (ll) Formerly Franklin Small Cap Growth I. (mm) Formerly Franklin Utilities I. (nn) Formerly Gate-

3 YEARS PRETAX	3 YEARS AFTERTAX	5 YEARS PRETAX	5 YEARS AFTERTAX	10 YEARS PRETAX	10 YEARS AFTERTAX	RESULTS VS. ALL FUNDS	TURNOVER	CASH %	FOREIGN %	P-E RATIO	UNTAXED GAINS (%)	LARGEST HOLDING COMPANY (% ASSETS)	RISK LEVEL	BEST QTR %RET	WORST QTR %RET	TELEPHONE
13.0	10.5	10.4	8.4	10.5	9.0	3 4 4 3	Average	6	63	30	24	Bayer (2)	Average	IV 98 18.3	III 98 −15.7	800-423-4026
23.5	22.8	19.5	18.8	NA	NA	2 1	Low	12	4	32	37	General Electric (3)	Low	IV 98 19.4	III 98 −10.8	800-423-4026
14.2	11.6	15.2	12.7	NA	NA	2 3	Low	16	NA	28	23	Rite Aid (4)	Very low	II 97 12.3	III 98 −10.4	800-662-4203
26.7	24.4	NA	NA	NA	NA	1	Low	12	NA	33	35	Tyco Intl. (4)		NA	NA	800-228-1024
42.4	39.7	29.2	26.6	23.3	20.9	1 2 2 1	Low	5	6	42	76	America Online (19)	Average	IV 98 51.2	I 94 −5.9	800-767-3524
26.1	25.7	NA	NA	NA	NA	1	Low	4	6	26	35	America Online (6)		NA	NA	800-767-3524
21.9	20.7	19.1	17.8	NA	NA	2 1	Very low	7	8	29	30	Conseco (4)	Very low	IV 98 17.9	III 98 −9.7	800-767-3524
23.9	18.7	18.9	15.4	17.1	14.2	1 3 2 1	Average	13	8	41	26	Microsoft (3)	Average	IV 98 22.0	III 98 −11.1	800-800-2638
16.6	12.5	12.8	9.9	16.4	13.9	1 2 3 3	Average	11	1	42	32	Cisco Systems (4)	High	IV 98 22.1	III 98 −16.4	800-800-2638
16.5	14.0	15.0	12.3	14.3	11.6	3 2 2 3	Very high	3	24	31	10	Rhone-Poulenc Cl. A (2)	Very low	II 97 10.1	III 98 −3.0	800-525-2440
20.5	15.3	17.8	13.2	16.3	11.8	1 3 1 2	Very high	10	22	30	16	Bristol-Myers Squibb (3)	Low	II 97 12.6	III 98 −7.2	800-525-2440
15.7	12.9	13.4	10.5	NA	NA	1 2 3	Average	17	3	36	26	Applied Micro Circuits (2)	High	IV 98 36.6	III 98 −22.7	800-525-2440
22.7	19.5	21.0	18.0	20.3	17.3	1 1 1 2	Very high	7	4	36	23	MCI WorldCom (5)	Average	IV 98 21.1	III 98 −13.6	800-525-2440
9.7	7.4	9.5	6.6	15.0	11.4	1 1 3 4	High	4	7	37	19	Total Renal Care Holdings (4)	High	IV 98 23.4	III 98 −29.9	800-525-2440
11.4	9.4	10.3	8.7	NA	NA	1 3 4	Average	14	75	28	23	MCI WorldCom (4)	Average	IV 98 14.4	III 98 −16.8	800-525-2440
17.3	13.8	19.8	16.9	20.1	17.0	1 1 1 3	Low	1	NA	19	27	Conseco (8)	Average	IV 98 17.0	III 98 −23.6	800-982-4372
−1.3	−5.1	3.4	−0.2	9.3	5.3	1 3 1 4	Average	14	16	21	−46	Placer Dome (10)	High	I 98 12.9	III 98 −17.8	800-982-4372
13.7	11.5	14.2	12.3	NA	NA	1 2 3	Low	20	7	19	8	Entergy (2)	Low	II 97 11.5	III 98 −13.6	800-342-5236
18.7	17.5	23.5	21.1	NA	NA	1 2	Average	8	2	32	13	Cisco Systems (2)	Average	IV 98 22.0	III 98 −15.3	800-342-5236
23.4	22.3	20.1	19.1	18.5	17.0	1 4 2 1	Very low	46	1	45	46	Intel (9)	Average	IV 98 16.6	IV 97 −5.7	800-342-5236
21.0	18.7	18.4	15.8	13.5	11.0	3 4 2 2	Low	13	16	33	31	Cisco Systems (3)	Average	IV 98 24.1	III 98 −19.3	800-342-5236
15.2	13.0	13.9	11.7	14.0	11.7	3 2 3 2	Low	9	11	23	16	Atlantic Richfield (3)	Very low	II 97 9.1	III 98 −5.8	800-342-5236
15.9	12.8	12.5	10.0	NA	NA	4 2	Average	3	29	24	21	AirTouch Communications (4)	Average	IV 98 12.6	III 98 −12.9	800-342-5236
17.9	17.2	18.5	17.9	15.2	14.4	2 4 1 2	Very low	31	1	34	45	Schering-Plough (5)	Low	IV 98 12.3	I 94 −6.5	800-342-5236
9.2	6.5	8.2	5.3	11.6	8.3	3 1 4 3	Very low	6	6	19	4	Philip Morris (2)	Very low	II 95 7.3	I 94 −5.2	800-342-5236
14.8	13.3	NA	NA	NA	NA	3	Low	5	2	21	0	United Retail Group (3)		NA	NA	800-342-5236
10.4	9.0	11.7	10.4	NA	NA	3	Very low	8	4	23	−11	Archstone Communities Tr. (4)	Low	IV 96 14.5	III 98 −11.3	800-342-5236
20.1	17.4	16.4	14.6	14.0	12.7	1 4 3 2	Low	2	1	24	23	Family Dollar Stores (5)	Average	IV 98 19.1	III 98 −14.7	800-342-5236
13.7	12.7	17.9	16.1	NA	NA	1 3	Low	12	4	34	1	Wind River Systems (2)	High	IV 98 23.3	III 98 −23.6	800-342-5236
11.1	8.5	9.6	7.2	11.7	9.3	3 2 4 3	Very low	4	0	20	22	FPL Group (4)	Average	IV 97 15.0	I 94 −9.9	800-342-5236
11.3	8.0	9.5	7.0	10.4	8.3	4 3 4 3	Average	3	43	27	9	Xilinx (1)	Low	IV 98 12.1	III 98 −8.9	800-548-4539
21.1	18.1	19.3	16.8	17.3	14.3	2 2 2 1	Average	6	12	31	25	Time Warner (3)	Low	IV 98 15.5	III 98 −10.4	800-421-4120
22.0	19.4	17.8	15.4	16.2	14.2	3 2 3 1	Low	5	7	30	47	Time Warner (4)	Low	IV 98 18.2	III 98 −14.2	800-422-3554
30.3	27.2	23.2	19.3	19.8	17.3	1 3 2 1	Average	1	NA	38	32	Home Depot (4)	Average	IV 98 30.2	III 98 −14.5	800-422-3554
15.2	12.6	13.2	10.7	NA	NA	3 3	Very low	2	5	23	24	Liberty (3)	Average	II 97 16.3	III 98 −20.3	800-422-3554
25.7	22.3	19.5	15.8	NA	NA	1 2 1	Low	0	3	33	37	Media General Cl. A (10)	Average	II 97 21.3	III 98 −13.2	800-422-3554
17.5	15.4	15.6	13.9	NA	NA	3 2	Average	10	1	39	16	Cisco Systems (2)	Very low	IV 98 11.7	III 98 −3.8	800-628-0414
25.5	22.7	21.6	19.6	NA	NA	4 1 1	Average	2	4	38	30	MCI WorldCom (3)	Average	IV 98 24.0	III 98 −11.7	800-628-0414
19.1	16.2	17.9	15.4	NA	NA	4 2 2	Low	13	NA	32	25	Automatic Data Processing (4)	Low	II 97 13.3	III 98 −8.4	800-628-0414
24.1	20.6	20.4	16.9	15.9	13.1	3 3 2 1	High	2	NA	28	22	Carnival Cl. A (3)	Average	IV 98 27.2	III 98 −15.3	800-628-0414
21.5	18.1	19.4	16.4	NA	NA	1 1	Average	9	3	29	15	Office Depot (2)	Low	IV 98 20.7	III 98 −13.5	800-628-0414
27.7	26.4	23.6	22.2	NA	NA	3 1 1	Very low	3	2	33	43	Microsoft (3)	Low	IV 98 21.2	III 98 −10.0	800-628-0414
13.3	8.7	13.3	9.8	NA	NA		Very low	3	0	26	−9	Russell 2000 Index (Fut.) (1)	Average	IV 98 17.4	III 98 −20.9	800-628-0414
14.5	13.8	11.9	9.7	15.6	13.1	4 1 4 2	Average	4	96	22	18	Barclays (5)	Average	I 95 17.5	III 98 −10.8	800-426-4685
11.7	10.8	10.3	9.1	11.1	9.1	2 4 4 3	Average	4	1	34	19	Microsoft (7)	Very low	IV 98 7.2	I 94 −2.6	800-354-6339
30.3	26.7	22.4	18.4	NA	NA	1 3 1	Average	5	NA	35	38	Warner-Lambert (3)	Average	IV 98 24.3	III 98 −11.4	800-526-7384
24.7	23.1	21.6	19.9	NA	NA	4 1 1	Average	2	3	32	31	Microsoft (4)	Average	IV 98 21.4	III 98 −14.7	800-526-7384
15.1	12.9	16.6	14.6	NA	NA	1 3	Average	14	5	19	6	Aetna (4)	Low	II 97 15.2	III 98 −17.0	800-526-7384
13.5	12.3	10.2	8.6	NA	NA	3 3	Low	1	100	28	17	Securitas Cl. B (4)	Average	I 98 16.9	III 98 −14.4	800-526-7384
9.7	7.5	4.1	2.5	NA	NA	4 4	Average	3	5	19	−17	Quest Diagnostics (4)	High	I 96 15.6	III 98 −32.2	800-526-7384
15.8	13.3	14.5	12.3	13.1	11.1	4 2 2 3	Low	26	NA	21	33	Household International (4)	Low	IV 98 14.1	III 98 −13.2	800-869-5999
18.3	15.9	18.4	16.5	NA	NA	1 2	Average	2	5	23	9	Waste Management (3)	Average	IV 98 15.5	III 98 −14.3	800-676-4450
24.3	21.8	20.0	17.6	17.9	15.6	2 2 2 1	Low	10	7	38	44	Time Warner (5)	Average	IV 98 27.2	III 98 −9.5	800-421-4120
27.4	24.2	22.3	19.7	19.3	16.5	3 1 2 1	Average	8	1	32	32	Microsoft (4)	Average	IV 98 22.2	III 98 −12.8	800-221-3253
15.4	12.5	16.5	14.8	19.2	18.0	1 1 1 3	High	2	2	40	34	Metromedia Fiber Net Cl. A (1)	High	IV 98 32.7	III 98 −21.8	800-225-5291
NA	NA	NA	NA	NA	NA		Very low	9	13	22	12	Fannie Mae (3)		NA	NA	800-225-5291
21.4	20.1	23.5	21.7	17.6	15.3	4 1 1 1	High	8	1	49	57	America Online (7)	Very high	IV 98 43.0	IV 97 −14.2	800-225-5291
20.3	16.7	15.4	13.0	NA	NA	3 2	High	4	NA	42	3	IBM (5)	High	IV 98 22.2	III 98 −9.7	800-225-5291
23.7	21.4	18.5	16.9	NA	NA	3 1	High	11	5	25	34	S&P Index (Fut.) (7)	Average	II 97 18.2	III 98 −13.1	800-225-5291
25.5	24.6	NA	NA	NA	NA	1	Average	4	2	31	20	Microsoft (3)		NA	NA	800-225-5291
25.5	24.7	23.8	23.0	23.0	21.2	3 1 1 1	Very low	9	1	20	50	First Union (4)	Average	IV 98 15.4	III 98 −16.5	800-225-5291
20.6	18.2	17.4	15.4	15.6	13.4	1 4 2 2	Average	10	NA	29	35	Emerson Electric (3)	Low	IV 98 15.6	III 98 −7.9	800-225-5291
0.2	0.1	8.8	8.6	NA	NA	1 4	Low	6	5	41	48	S&P 500 Index (Fut.) (5)	Very high	IV 98 26.4	III 98 −27.0	800-225-5291
29.2	27.0	25.2	23.7	21.7	19.4	2 1 1 1	Average	6	4	41	31	MCI WorldCom (5)	High	IV 98 30.0	III 98 −13.2	800-422-1050
15.3	13.8	13.4	12.1	15.1	13.9	2 2 2 3	Very low	6	100	24	39	Swiss Reinsurance (Reg.) (3)	Average	IV 98 18.3	III 98 −16.6	800-422-1050
19.1	18.2	14.1	13.5	NA	NA	3 2	Average	8	100	31	23	UniCredito Italiano (7)	High	IV 98 22.4	III 98 −15.2	800-422-1050
NA	NA	NA	NA	NA	NA		Low	3	5	36	13	Microsoft (3)		NA	NA	888-843-7824
NA	NA	NA	NA	NA	NA		High	2	11	33	−2	Genzyme-General Division (2)		NA	NA	888-843-7824
NA	NA	NA	NA	NA	NA		Low	4	5	35	16	Microsoft (3)		NA	NA	888-843-7824
9.7	7.8	11.7	10.0	14.6	12.5	4 1 1 4	Average	11	9	18	10	ICN Pharmaceuticals (4)	Average	III 97 14.8	III 98 −18.6	800-432-7856

way Index Plus.

DATA: MORNINGSTAR, INC., CHICAGO, IL.

MUTUAL FUND SCOREBOARD

FUND	OVERALL RATING (COMPARES RISK-ADJUSTED PERFORMANCE OF EACH FUND AGAINST ALL FUNDS)	CATEGORY (COMPARES RISK-ADJUSTED PERFORMANCE OF FUND WITHIN CATEGORY)	RATING	SIZE ASSETS $MIL.	SIZE % CHG. 1997-98	FEES SALES CHARGE (%)	FEES EXPENSE RATIO (%)	1997 RETURNS (%) PRE-TAX	1997 RETURNS (%) AFTER-TAX	1997 RETURNS (%) YIELD
HIBERNIA CAPITAL APPRECIATION A (oo)	B+	Large-cap Blend	C	343.5	17	4.50	1.21†	26.3	23.3	0.2
HIGHMARK BALANCED FID.	B+	Domestic Hybrid	C	458.2	12	No load	0.79	10.1	8.3	2.6
HIGHMARK GROWTH FIDUCIARY	B	Large-cap Growth	B	572.2	80	No load	0.92	31.8	29.7	0.0
HIGHMARK INCOME-EQUITY FID.	B	Large-cap Value	B	658.1	84	No load	0.99	15.1	11.8	1.3
HOMESTEAD VALUE	B	Mid-cap Value	B+	445.6	21	No load	0.79	8.3	7.3	1.5
HOTCHKIS & WILEY INTERNATIONAL	C-	Foreign	B+	1409.5	35	No load	0.89	6.4	5.4	2.1
IAI REGIONAL	C-	Mid-cap Blend	C-	331.2	-34	No load	1.22	-1.4	-3.9	0.0
ICAP DISCRETIONARY EQUITY		Large-cap Value		205.4	31	No load	0.80	10.2	9.1	1.6
ICAP EQUITY		Large-cap Value		717.3	93	No load	0.80	11.4	11.0	1.3
IDEX GLOBAL A	C	World	B+	350.2	54	5.50	1.91†	24.9	24.9	0.0
IDEX GROWTH A	C	Large-cap Growth	C-	1010.2	62	5.50	1.61†	64.0	63.6	0.0
IDS BLUE CHIP ADVANTAGE A	B	Large-cap Blend	C	1757.4	51	5.00	0.78	22.9	22.2	0.6
IDS DISCOVERY A	D	Mid-cap Growth	D	898.8	-2	5.00	1.13	2.1	0.6	0.0
IDS DIVERSIFIED EQUITY-INCOME A	B	Large-cap Value	C-	2059.1	12	5.00	0.88†	11.8	8.9	1.9
IDS EQUITY SELECT A	C	Large-cap Blend	D	1159.3	17	5.00	0.83	19.5	17.1	0.2
IDS EQUITY VALUE B	C	Large-cap Value	C-	1701.3	-1	5.00**	1.61†	8.5	5.5	0.8
IDS GLOBAL GROWTH A	D	World	D	1081.2	22	5.00	1.37	26.0	24.6	0.5
IDS GROWTH A	C	Large-cap Growth	C-	3936.6	28	5.00	0.87	22.5	21.5	0.0
IDS INTERNATIONAL A	D	Foreign	D	854.3	4	5.00	1.18	15.4	15.0	0.5
IDS MANAGED ALLOCATION A	C	Large-cap Blend	F	2365.5	-7	5.00	0.84	8.4	5.1	3.4
IDS MUTUAL A	B	Domestic Hybrid	C	3258.7	1	5.00	0.83	9.3	5.9	3.1
IDS NEW DIMENSIONS A	B	Large-cap Growth	B	11919.6	34	5.00	0.82	28.3	26.8	0.2
IDS PROGRESSIVE A	C	Mid-cap Blend	C	509.6	2	5.00	1.02	-1.5	-4.7	0.5
IDS RESEARCH OPPORTUNITIES A		Large-cap Blend		382.8	47	5.00	NA	23.3	21.6	0.0
IDS SMALL COMPANY INDEX A		Small-cap Blend		599.9	60	5.00	1.00	-2.3	-3.2	0.0
IDS STOCK A	C	Large-cap Blend	D	3257.6	13	5.00	0.78	19.3	17.1	1.1
IDS STRATEGY AGGRESSIVE B ☖	C-	Mid-cap Growth	C	822.0	1	5.00**	1.77†	18.4	18.0	0.0
IDS UTILITIES INCOME A	B	Utilities	B	1180.1	37	5.00	0.86	22.7	20.2	2.2
INCOME FUND OF AMERICA ☖	A	Domestic Hybrid	B+	22909.0	13	5.75	0.59†	9.5	6.5	4.8
INDEPENDENCE ONE EQUITY PLUS		Large-cap Blend		260.0	39	No load	0.39	31.6	30.3	0.9
INVESCO BALANCED	A	Domestic Hybrid	A	260.3	55	No load	1.22†	17.3	15.5	1.6
INVESCO DYNAMICS	C	Mid-cap Growth	B+	1549.6	38	No load	1.08†	23.3	20.4	0.0
INVESCO EUROPEAN	C	Europe	D	770.7	133	No load	1.25†	32.9	29.8	0.2
INVESCO FINANCIAL SERVICES (pp)	B	Financial	C	1522.9	17	No load	0.99†	13.5	11.4	0.8
INVESCO GROWTH	C	Large-cap Growth	C	1220.1	62	No load	1.04†	41.7	38.4	0.3
INVESCO HEALTH SCIENCES (qq)	B	Health	B	1567.9	66	No load	1.08†	43.4	39.4	0.2
INVESCO INDUSTRIAL INCOME	B+	Large-cap Blend	B	4927.9	1	No load	0.9†	14.1	11.0	2.2
INVESCO LEISURE (rr)	C	Unaligned	B	276.9	24	No load	1.41†	29.8	28.1	0.0
INVESCO SMALL COMPANY GROWTH	D	Small-cap Growth	B	316.8	1	No load	1.48†	14.9	11.4	0.0
INVESCO TECHNOLOGY (ss) ☖	C	Technology	B+	1147.7	12	No load	1.05†	30.1	30.1	0.0
INVESCO TOTAL RETURN ☖	A	Domestic Hybrid	B+	3040.8	41	No load	0.79	13.6	12.1	2.5
INVESCO VALUE EQUITY	B	Large-cap Value	C	432.1	14	No load	1.15†	15.1	13.0	0.8
INVESCO WORLDWIDE COMMUNICATIONS		Communications		323.5	287	No load	1.32†	41.0	40.4	0.0
INVESTMENT CO. OF AMERICA	B+	Large-cap Blend	B	48497.6	22	5.75	0.56†	22.9	20.1	1.5
ISG LARGE CAP EQUITY A (tt)	A	Large-cap Growth	A	806.1	24	3.50	0.99†	37.9	36.5	0.2
IVY GROWTH A	C-	Mid-cap Blend	D	304.8	-5	5.75	1.38†	14.1	13.6	0.1
IVY INTERNATIONAL A ☖	C-	Foreign	C	1618.0	-5	5.75‡	1.59†	7.3	6.9	0.8
JANUS ☖	B+	Large-cap Growth	B+	25490.7	32	No load	0.86	38.9	38.1	0.2
JANUS BALANCED	A	Domestic Hybrid	A	1136.6	192	No load	1.10	31.2	30.3	1.8
JANUS ENTERPRISE	C-	Mid-cap Growth	B	728.0	27	No load	1.04	33.8	30.8	0.0
JANUS EQUITY-INCOME		Large-cap Growth		349.2	409	No load	1.45	40.1	39.6	0.3
JANUS GROWTH & INCOME	B+	Large-cap Growth	B	3504.1	75	No load	0.96	34.9	32.9	0.3
JANUS MERCURY	B	Large-cap Growth	B	3111.6	63	No load	0.96	58.4	55.6	0.0
JANUS OLYMPUS		Large-cap Growth		1288.1	105	No load	1.03	57.0	57.0	0.1
JANUS OVERSEAS		Foreign		4329.0	34	No load‡	1.01	16.0	15.9	0.5
JANUS SPECIAL SITUATIONS		Mid-cap Growth		893.7	130	No load	1.18	25.3	25.2	0.0
JANUS TWENTY	B+	Large-cap Growth	B+	15797.2	163	No load	0.91	73.4	73.1	0.3
JANUS VENTURE	C-	Small-cap Growth	B+	1246.2	1	No load‡	0.92	23.2	21.4	0.0
JANUS WORLDWIDE	B	World	A	16322.7	54	No load	0.95	25.9	25.7	0.4
JAPAN ☖	F	Japan		348.3	29	No load	1.21	24.3	23.9	0.9
KALMAR "GROWTH/VAL." SMALL CAP		Small-cap Growth		222.3	-2	No load	1.25	-7.7	-7.7	0.0
KAUFMANN ☖	C-	Small-cap Growth	B+	4456.1	-26	0.20*	1.88†	0.7	-1.7	0.0
KEMPER BLUE CHIP A	B	Large-cap Blend	C-	420.0	28	5.75	1.19	14.4	13.7	0.4
KEMPER GLOBAL DISCOVERY S (uu)	C-	World	C	301.7	-11	No load	1.63	16.4	16.4	0.0
KEMPER GROWTH A	C-	Large-cap Growth	F	2097.6	15	5.75	1.04	14.2	14.1	0.0
KEMPER INTERNATIONAL A	C-	Foreign	C	433.5	5	5.75	1.57†	7.9	4.9	0.0
KEMPER SMALL CAP VALUE A	C-	Small-cap Value	C-	500.1	-21	5.75	1.32	-12.8	-12.8	0.0
KEMPER SMALL CAP EQUITY A ☖	D	Small-cap Growth	C	659.8	-6	5.75	0.90	-3.1	-4.4	0.0
KEMPER TECHNOLOGY A ☖	C-	Technology	C-	1359.5	34	5.75	0.89	43.6	41.5	0.0
KEMPER TOTAL RETURN A	C-	Domestic Hybrid	D	2606.2	22	5.75	1.01	15.9	13.5	2.6

*Includes redemption fee. **Includes deferred sales charge. †12(b)-1 plan in effect. ‡Not currently accepting new accounts. §Less than 0.5% of assets. NA=Not available. NM=Not meaningful. (oo) Formerly Tower Capital Appreciation A. (pp) Formerly Invesco Strategic Financial Services. (qq) Formerly Invesco Strategic Health Sciences. (rr) Formerly Invesco Strategic Leisure. (ss) Formerly Invesco Strategic Technology. (tt) Formerly DG Equity. (uu) Formerly Scudder Global Discovery.

AVERAGE ANNUAL TOTAL RETURNS (%) — HISTORY — PORTFOLIO DATA — RISK — TELEPHONE

3 YEARS PRETAX	3 YEARS AFTERTAX	5 YEARS PRETAX	5 YEARS AFTERTAX	10 YEARS PRETAX	10 YEARS AFTERTAX	RESULTS VS. ALL FUNDS	TURNOVER	CASH %	FOREIGN %	P-E RATIO	UNTAXED GAINS (%)	LARGEST HOLDING COMPANY (% ASSETS)	RISK LEVEL	BEST QTR	BEST %RET	WORST QTR	WORST %RET	TELEPHONE
27.0	23.7	22.4	19.7	18.2	15.7	2311	Average	1	2	32	43	General Electric (4)	Average	IV 98	23.2	III 98	-12.1	800-999-0124
15.2	12.9	13.9	11.9	NA	NA	333	Low	2	6	27	25	IBM (1)	Very low	IV 98	11.3	III 98	-7.2	800-433-6884
28.4	24.8	21.6	19.0	NA	NA	21	High	2	1	40	23	IMS Health (4)	Average	IV 98	26.0	III 98	-14.4	800-433-6884
19.3	15.8	18.1	15.0	15.4	12.4	3322	Average	1	1	28	11	Baxter International (4)	Low	IV 98	16.7	III 98	-10.2	800-433-6884
17.4	16.2	17.3	16.0	NA	NA	312	Very low	6	3	24	29	Maytag (3)	Low	II 97	13.5	III 98	-11.6	800-258-3030
9.8	8.9	9.1	8.0	NA	NA	144	Low	2	100	17	5	Creative Technology (3)	Average	IV 98	15.5	III 98	-18.4	800-236-4479
10.7	7.0	12.6	9.1	13.7	10.2	1414	Average	10	NA	30	18	Abbott Laboratories (3)	Average	II 97	17.0	III 98	-17.9	800-945-3863
21.2	18.1	NA	NA	NA	NA	2	High	17	19	27	13	NationsBank (4)			NA		NA	888-221-4227
22.0	20.1	NA	NA	NA	NA	1	High	2	18	27	12	BankAmerica (New) (1)			NA		NA	888-221-4227
24.0	21.7	18.2	16.4	NA	NA	22	Average	18	71	43	26	Cisco Systems (3)	Average	IV 98	18.5	III 98	-16.0	888-233-4339
30.9	28.0	24.8	22.0	21.9	19.0	1311	Average	12	12	51	52	Dell Computer (10)	High	IV 98	27.9	III 98	-6.4	800-233-4339
23.5	21.2	21.1	18.4	NA	NA	311	High	1	2	35	23	Microsoft (3)	Average	IV 98	20.2	III 98	-10.6	800-328-8300
14.9	11.5	10.6	7.1	14.7	12.1	1233	High	2	5	40	9	FINOVA Group (3)	High	IV 98	24.7	III 98	-21.8	800-328-8300
16.8	13.3	14.0	11.1	NA	NA	132	Average	7	6	25	10	IBM (3)	Low	IV 98	15.4	III 98	-10.7	800-328-8300
24.6	20.3	17.9	14.5	16.9	13.7	1231	Average	10	6	39	32	Tyco Intl. (5)	Average	IV 98	27.6	III 98	-15.8	800-328-8300
17.3	13.2	14.6	11.5	14.3	11.3	3232	High	2	6	25	11	BankAmerica (New) (3)	Low	IV 98	16.2	III 98	-12.4	800-328-8300
15.8	14.0	8.9	7.6	NA	NA	243	High	9	68	36	20	Mannesmann (4)	High	IV 98	21.0	III 98	-16.9	800-328-8300
22.6	21.7	21.8	20.2	20.6	16.8	1211	Low	4	2	40	44	Microsoft (5)	High	IV 98	27.1	III 98	-17.5	800-328-8300
8.8	7.6	6.8	5.5	7.9	6.4	4344	Average	17	95	32	22	Mannesmann (5)	High	IV 98	19.5	III 98	-19.9	800-328-8300
11.7	7.4	9.6	6.1	14.6	11.2	1143	High	16	20	33	3	General Electric (2)	Average	IV 98	12.0	III 98	-11.1	800-328-8300
13.8	10.1	12.3	9.1	12.4	9.0	3333	Average	6	6	25	6	Washington Mutual (2)	Very low	IV 98	10.2	III 98	-6.6	800-328-8300
25.8	24.1	21.2	19.6	20.7	18.6	1211	Low	8	3	39	45	Cisco Systems (3)	Average	IV 98	24.3	III 98	-11.5	800-328-8300
13.8	10.7	12.8	10.1	10.9	8.3	4333	High	4	4	25	4	Allmerica Financial (4)	Average	IV 98	16.6	III 98	-19.0	800-328-8300
NA	NA	NA	NA	NA	NA			1	1	35	NA	MCI WorldCom (4)			NA		NA	800-328-8300
NA	NA	NA	NA	NA	NA		Low	0	1	26	0	Vitesse Semiconductor (1)			NA		NA	800-328-8300
21.3	18.3	16.9	13.9	16.4	12.8	1232	Average	10	6	37	30	General Electric (3)	Average	IV 98	19.3	III 98	-11.5	800-328-8300
17.1	14.6	15.1	13.1	15.7	13.8	1231	High	12	4	46	52	Cisco Systems (3)	High	IV 98	22.3	III 98	-19.1	800-328-8300
21.9	18.8	15.8	13.1	15.5	12.7	2241	Average	3	4	23	27	MCI WorldCom (5)	Low	IV 97	13.7	I 94	-6.4	800-328-8300
15.5	12.1	14.2	11.3	13.9	11.0	3232	Low	15	15	22	13	Atlantic Richfield (2)	Very low	IV 98	8.2	III 98	-4.9	800-421-4120
28.2	27.0	NA	NA	NA	NA	1		3	5	33	44	General Electric (7)			NA		NA	800-334-2292
17.5	14.2	19.3	16.4	NA	NA	12	High	5	4	32	14	Merck (2)	Very low	IV 98	13.7	III 98	-6.6	800-525-8085
21.2	17.6	19.2	14.7	20.0	16.7	2112	Very high	7	7	39	19	J.D. Edwards (2)	High	IV 98	26.7	III 98	-17.8	800-525-8085
25.7	21.9	18.1	15.1	13.6	11.8	4431	Average	4	100	39	18	TNT Post Group (3)	Average	I 98	26.3	III 98	-17.7	800-525-8085
28.9	25.3	23.0	20.2	25.1	22.1	1121	High	11	7	22	21	Hertz Cl. A (3)	Average	IV 98	19.9	III 98	-18.2	800-525-8085
29.7	23.9	20.8	15.6	19.1	15.3	1231	High	1	2	36	26	Philip Morris (5)	Average	IV 98	26.9	III 98	-5.9	800-525-8085
23.7	19.3	24.9	21.6	25.1	22.6	1411	High	10	8	46	27	Merck (7)	Average	III 95	19.5	II 94	-7.5	800-525-8085
19.0	15.5	15.6	12.6	16.8	13.8	1232	Average	5	4	30	29	Bank of New York (3)	Low	II 97	13.3	III 98	-7.4	800-525-8085
21.4	19.6	14.5	12.3	20.0	17.1	1142	Low	4	23	33	36	Liberty Media Cl. A (6)	Average	IV 98	24.8	III 98	-12.6	800-525-8085
14.9	10.7	13.7	9.5	NA	NA	23	High	13	7	37	9	Sunrise Assisted Living (2)	High	IV 98	26.3	III 98	-16.9	800-525-8085
19.9	16.0	21.5	17.6	23.8	20.5	1112	Very high	5	2	44	16	IBM (5)	High	IV 98	25.1	IV 97	-12.9	800-525-8085
17.1	15.7	16.2	14.8	14.5	12.7	3322	Very low	2	11	23	23	British Telecom ADR (1)	Very low	II 97	11.9	III 98	-5.3	800-525-8085
20.4	18.4	18.8	16.8	15.6	13.4	2412	Average	6	6	26	32	State Street (5)	Low	IV 98	16.7	III 98	-11.7	800-525-8085
29.0	26.8	NA	NA	NA	NA	1	Average	4	21	40	22	MCI WorldCom (5)			NA		NA	800-525-8085
24.0	21.3	20.0	17.6	17.2	14.9	1321	Low	16	8	32	42	Philip Morris (4)	Low	IV 98	17.3	III 98	-7.4	800-421-4120
30.2	29.2	24.8	23.6	NA	NA	11	Very low	3	NA	39	63	Schering-Plough (4)	Low	IV 98	24.8	III 98	-6.0	800-748-8500
14.3	12.2	13.0	11.0	13.3	10.6	2333	Low	3	27	30	35	Cisco Systems (3)	High	IV 98	21.6	III 98	-17.0	800-456-5111
12.4	11.8	10.7	10.0	12.4	11.5	3133	Very low	7	98	24	21	Imperial Tobacco Group (3)	Average	IV 98	16.4	III 98	-15.7	800-456-5111
26.8	23.2	21.2	18.5	20.4	17.8	1221	High	6	5	47	25	Microsoft (7)	Low	IV 98	28.4	III 98	-11.0	800-525-8983
22.6	19.7	18.6	16.0	NA	NA	31	High	8	6	46	15	Dell Computer (3)	Very low	IV 98	18.8	III 98	-4.5	800-525-8983
18.3	16.4	18.1	16.2	NA	NA	13	High	2	10	52	36	Vitesse Semiconductor (8)	High	IV 98	34.2	III 98	-14.6	800-525-8983
NA	NA	NA	NA	NA	NA	1	Very high	2	6	45	16	Comcast Special Cl. A (4)			NA		NA	800-525-8983
31.8	28.8	24.3	21.6	NA	NA	211	High	14	9	45	24	Time Warner (4)	Average	IV 98	21.5	III 98	-9.0	800-525-8983
27.8	24.1	26.3	23.1	NA	NA	11	High	4	10	50	30	Time Warner (6)	Average	IV 98	30.0	III 98	-6.9	800-525-8983
34.3	33.6	NA	NA	NA	NA	1	Very high	17	8	54	42	America Online (6)			NA		NA	800-525-8983
20.9	20.2	NA	NA	NA	NA	2	Average	16	97	36	17	Wolters Kluwer (3)			NA		NA	800-525-8983
NA	NA	NA	NA	NA	NA			1	4	40	12	Time Warner (9)			NA		NA	800-525-8983
42.2	38.0	29.6	25.9	25.8	23.6	1221	High	10	5	53	39	Dell Computer (12)	Average	IV 98	29.7	II 94	-6.4	800-525-8983
14.4	11.1	14.9	11.6	17.0	14.2	1213	High	5	5	43	19	Wind River Systems (4)	High	IV 98	25.0	III 98	-14.1	800-525-8983
24.2	22.6	19.3	17.6	NA	NA	112	Average	17	70	41	23	Microsoft (3)	Average	IV 98	20.2	III 98	-16.1	800-525-8983
-1.8	-2.5	-1.1	-2.0	-0.6	-2.4	4444	High	6	100	37	-17	Murata Manufacturing (5)	Very high	IV 98	27.0	III 97	-18.1	800-535-2726
NA	NA	NA	NA	NA	NA			8	1	24	11	Applied Power Cl. A (4)			NA		NA	800-282-2319
11.1	9.5	15.4	14.2	20.9	20.1	1114	Average	18	9	32	33	Cendant (6)	High	IV 98	17.1	III 98	-18.7	800-237-0132
22.6	18.5	18.2	15.0	16.1	13.7	1422	Very high	6	4	31	17	Abbott Laboratories (2)	Average	IV 98	19.2	III 98	-13.0	800-621-1048
15.8	14.4	11.1	10.0	NA	NA	33	Average	6	51	38	36	Network Appliance (5)	Average	IV 98	20.3	III 98	-16.6	800-621-1048
15.8	11.2	14.0	10.5	15.9	13.3	1333	High	1	2	38	21	Sun Microsystems (3)	High	IV 98	27.6	III 98	-22.2	800-621-1048
11.2	9.0	8.3	6.5	8.7	6.9	4343	Average	5	100	30	8	Viag (4)	Average	IV 98	15.5	III 98	-17.9	800-621-1048
10.7	10.1	14.6	13.4	NA	NA	14	Low	7	2	17	-4	S&P Midcap 400 (2)	High	II 95	16.4	III 98	-24.1	800-621-1048
10.0	7.7	11.1	8.2	14.8	12.1	1124	High	8	3	34	19	Sofamor/Danek Group (3)	High	IV 98	22.5	III 98	-22.9	800-621-1048
22.9	19.0	24.2	19.4	19.4	15.3	2211	Very high	5	3	43	33	Cisco Systems (4)	High	IV 98	37.5	IV 97	-13.8	800-621-1048
17.1	12.8	12.9	9.7	13.9	11.0	2342	High	1	2	32	14	General Electric (2)	Low	II 97	13.1	III 98	-6.7	800-621-1048

DATA: MORNINGSTAR, INC., CHICAGO, IL.

MUTUAL FUND SCOREBOARD

FUND	OVERALL RATING (COMPARES RISK-ADJUSTED PERFORMANCE OF EACH FUND AGAINST ALL FUNDS)	CATEGORY (COMPARES RISK-ADJUSTED PERFORMANCE OF FUND WITHIN CATEGORY)	RATING	SIZE: ASSETS $MIL.	% CHG. 1997-98	FEES: SALES CHARGE (%)	EXPENSE RATIO (%)	1997 RETURNS (%): PRE-TAX	AFTER-TAX	YIELD
KEMPER VALUE S (vv)	B+	Large-cap Value	B+	468.8	33	No load	1.23	11.9	10.7	0.8
KEMPER-DREMAN HIGH RETURN EQUITY A	B	Large-cap Value	B	2505.2	67	5.75	1.22	12.0	10.0	2.4
KEYPREMIER ESTABLISHED GROWTH		Large-cap Blend		260.9	22	4.50	0.44	19.5	18.7	0.5
KOPP EMERGING GROWTH A ☖		Small-cap Growth		304.4	7	3.50	NA†	0.3	0.3	0.0
LEGG MASON AMER. LEADING PRIMARY	B	Large-cap Blend	C–	238.8	39	No load	1.95†	21.3	20.2	0.0
LEGG MASON INTERNATIONAL EQUITY PRIM.		Foreign		258.5	13	No load	2.17†	8.5	8.1	1.1
LEGG MASON SPECIAL INVESTMENT PRIM. ☖	C–	Mid-cap Blend	F	1730.2	27	No load	1.86†	23.3	21.4	0.0
LEGG MASON TOTAL RETURN PRIMARY	C	Mid-cap Value	C	635.8	6	No load	1.88†	–0.4	–2.1	1.7
LEGG MASON VALUE PRIMARY ☖	A	Large-cap Value	A	8079.2	119	No load	1.73†	48.0	47.2	0.0
LEXINGTON CORPORATE LEADERS	B	Large-cap Blend	C	482.7	–8	No load	0.62	9.9	8.6	4.3
LEXINGTON GROWTH & INCOME	B	Large-cap Blend	C	245.7	8	No load	1.17†	21.4	18.7	0.0
LINDNER DIVIDEND INVESTOR ☖	C	Domestic Hybrid	F	1162.9	–35	2.00*	0.61	–4.0	–6.7	8.2
LINDNER GROWTH INVESTOR ☖	D	Small-cap Value	D	617.2	–55	2.00*	0.44	–15.8	–18.7	1.7
LKCM SMALL CAP EQUITY		Small-cap Blend		246.4	–4	No load	0.95	–6.3	–6.4	0.4
LONGLEAF PARTNERS	A	Mid-cap Blend	A	3688.0	42	No load	0.94	14.3	10.0	0.9
LONGLEAF PARTNERS REALTY		Real Estate		776.3	5	No load	1.20	–13.0	–14.0	3.7
LONGLEAF PARTNERS SMALL-CAP	A	Small-cap Value	A	1351.0	48	No load‡	1.09	12.7	9.8	0.7
LOOMIS SAYLES SM. CAP VAL. INST.	C–	Small-cap Value	C–	346.3	41	No load	0.94	–1.1	–1.5	0.7
LORD ABBETT AFFILIATED A	B	Large-cap Value	C	8051.3	4	5.75	0.65†	14.4	12.4	1.5
LORD ABBETT DEVELOPING GROWTH A	C–	Small-cap Growth	B+	825.7	85	5.75	1.06†	8.5	8.2	0.0
LORD ABBETT MID-CAP VALUE A	C	Mid-cap Value	C–	367.8	10	5.75	1.25†	–0.5	–0.5	0.0
LORD ABBETT RESEARCH SMALL CAP A		Small-cap Growth		221.2	5	5.75	1.17†	–7.4	–7.4	0.0
MAINSTAY CAPITAL APPREC. B	C	Large-cap Growth	C	2753.0	47	5.00**	1.61†	38.2	36.9	0.0
MAINSTAY EQUITY INDEX A	B+	Large-cap Blend	B	797.1	83	3.00	0.80†	27.7	27.1	0.5
MAINSTAY TOTAL RETURN B ☖	B	Domestic Hybrid	C	1482.4	24	5.00**	1.65†	26.0	23.9	0.8
MAINSTAY VALUE B ☖	C	Large-cap Value	D	1174.6	–16	5.00**	1.63†	–7.3	–10.6	1.2
MAIRS & POWER GROWTH ☖	B+	Mid-Cap Blend	A	554.8	34	No load	0.84	9.4	8.8	0.8
MANAGERS INTL. EQUITY ☖	C	Foreign Stock	A	552.8	46	No load	1.45	14.5	12.9	0.7
MANAGERS SPECIAL EQUITY ☖	C–	Small-cap Growth	B+	956.5	33	No load	1.35	0.2	0.2	0.0
MARSHALL EQUITY-INCOME	B+	Large-cap Value	B	537.9	2	No load	1.22	10.5	8.3	1.9
MARSHALL INTERNATIONAL STOCK		Foreign		235.4	4	No load	1.59†	3.3	2.7	2.0
MARSHALL LARGE-CAP GROWTH & INCOME	C	Large-cap Blend	C–	360.7	25	No load	1.23	26.2	24.9	0.3
MARSHALL MID-CAP GROWTH	C–	Mid-cap Growth	C	262.6	21	No load	1.24	15.7	14.1	0.0
MARSICO FOCUS		Large-cap Growth		1204.5	NM	No load	1.56†	51.3	51.3	0.0
MARSICO GROWTH & INCOME		Large-cap Growth		373.7	NM	No load	1.51†	43.4	43.4	0.0
MAS BALANCED INSTITUTIONAL	B+	Domestic Hybrid	B	406.4	21	No load	0.56	15.4	12.0	2.9
MAS EQUITY INSTITUTIONAL ☖	B	Large-cap Value	C	904.5	–28	No load	0.59	19.7	12.9	0.9
MAS INTERNATIONAL EQUITY INST.	D	Foreign	C–	509.0	–10	No load	0.63	10.1	7.6	1.7
MAS MID CAP GROWTH INSTITUTIONAL	C–	Mid-cap Growth	B	509.2	17	No load	0.61	37.4	32.9	0.0
MAS MID CAP VALUE INSTITUTIONAL		Mid-cap Blend		501.2	96	No load	0.88	16.1	14.0	0.3
MAS SMALL CAP VALUE ☖		Small-cap Value	C	788.2	–10	No load‡	0.86	–1.4	–4.4	0.4
MAS VALUE INSTITUTIONAL ☖	B	Mid-cap Value	B	2461.9	–26	No load	0.61	–2.9	–6.5	1.5
MASTERS' SELECT EQUITY ☖		Large-cap Value		384.5	30	No load	1.47	14.9	14.8	0.2
MENTOR GROWTH B ☖	D	Small-cap Growth	B	387.8	–20	4.00**	2.03†	0.9	0.1	0.0
MERGER	A	Domestic Hybrid	A	346.0	–21	No load	1.33†	5.4	2.5	1.5
MERIDIAN ☖	C	Mid-cap Growth	B	227.9	–31	No load	0.95	3.1	–1.8	0.5
MERRILL LYNCH BASIC VALUE B ☖	B	Large-cap Value	C	4695.9	7	4.00**	1.56†	10.5	8.7	1.1
MERRILL LYNCH CAPITAL B	B	Domestic Hybrid	C	5390.4	–1	4.00**	1.57†	5.1	3.8	2.3
MERRILL LYNCH DRAGON B	F	Pacific/Asia ex-Japan	C–	219.0	–42	4.00**	2.39†	–17.1	–17.2	0.6
MERRILL LYNCH EUROFUND B	C	Europe	C	840.5	9	4.00**	2.06†	23.8	17.4	2.7
MERRILL LYNCH FUNDAMENTAL GR. B		Large-cap Growth		927.8	229	4.00**	2.16†	33.4	32.4	0.0
MERRILL LYNCH GLOBAL ALLOCATION B	C	International Hybrid	B	6716.8	–30	4.00**	1.85†	–0.4	–2.9	3.0
MERRILL LYNCH GLOBAL GROWTH C		World		292.3	54	1.00**	NA†	31.0	30.5	0.0
MERRILL LYNCH GLOBAL UTILITY B	C	Utilities	C–	327.6	6	4.00**	1.59†	24.7	22.2	1.3
MERRILL LYNCH GLOBAL VALUE B		World		1893.6	51	4.00**	1.99†	25.8	22.5	1.4
MERRILL LYNCH GROWTH B	D	Mid-cap Blend	F	2307.7	–48	4.00**	1.79†	–24.2	–24.4	0.9
MERRILL LYNCH HEALTHCARE B ☖	B	Health	C	223.8	26	4.00**	2.44†	31.8	26.2	0.0
MERRILL LYNCH PACIFIC B ☖	D	Diversified Pacific/Asia	A	505.4	–35	4.00**	1.90†	7.3	6.2	3.3
MERRILL LYNCH PHOENIX B	C–	Mid-cap Blend	F	239.1	–22	4.00**	2.26†	3.7	–0.9	0.1
MERRILL LYNCH S&P 500 INDEX D		Large Blend		375.8	139	No load	NA†	28.0	26.5	0.9
MERRILL LYNCH SPECIAL VALUE B	C–	Small Value	D	471.4	–10	4.00**	2.13†	–6.6	–7.6	1.3
MFS CAPITAL OPPORTUNITIES A (ww)	B+	Mid-cap Blend	B+	1020.5	64	5.75	1.29†	27.1	25.6	0.0
MFS EMERGING GROWTH B ☖	C–	Mid-cap Growth	C	6905.2	37	4.00**	1.97†	23.6	23.3	0.0
MFS GLOBAL EQUITY A (xx)	C	World	B	301.0	66	5.75	1.63†	17.4	16.3	0.0
MFS GLOBAL GROWTH B (yy)	C–	World	C	288.9	–5	4.00**	2.28†	11.4	9.6	0.0
MFS GROWTH OPPORTUNITIES A	C–	Large-cap Growth	D	1111.5	17	5.75	0.84†	29.2	26.2	0.0
MFS LARGE CAP GROWTH B	B+	Large-cap Blend	C	475.9	11	4.00**	2.05†	31.3	28.4	0.0
MFS MANAGED SECTORS A ☖	C–	Mid-cap Blend	D	299.1	8	5.75	1.38†	11.5	8.4	0.0
MFS MASSACHUSETTS INVESTORS A	A	Large-cap Blend	B+	7141.8	66	5.75	0.74†	23.0	21.4	0.7
MFS MASSACHUSETTS INVESTORS GROWTH A	B	Large-cap Growth	B	3312.0	89	5.75	0.71†	40.0	37.3	0.0

*Includes redemption fee. **Includes deferred sales charge. †12(b)-1 plan in effect. ‡Not currently accepting new accounts. §Less than 0.5% of assets. NA=Not available. NM=Not meaningful. (vv) Formerly Scudder Value. (ww) Formerly MFS Value A. (xx) Formerly MFS World Equity A. (yy) Formerly MFS World Growth B.

3 YEARS PRETAX	3 YEARS AFTERTAX	5 YEARS PRETAX	5 YEARS AFTERTAX	10 YEARS PRETAX	10 YEARS AFTERTAX	HISTORY RESULTS VS. ALL FUNDS	TURNOVER	CASH %	FOREIGN %	P-E RATIO	UNTAXED GAINS (%)	LARGEST HOLDING COMPANY (% ASSETS)	RISK LEVEL	BEST QTR %RET	WORST QTR %RET	TELEPHONE
23.0	20.9	19.8	18.0	NA	NA	2 1	Average	14	13	23	12	S&P 500 Index (Fut.) (5)	Low	IV 98 17.1	III 98 –15.3	800-621-1048
23.9	22.0	22.5	21.0	19.2	17.0	2 2 1 1	Very low	6	2	21	10	S&P 500 Index (Fut.) (18)	Average	IV 98 14.2	III 98 –7.7	800-621-1048
NA	NA	NA	NA	NA	NA			0	3	32	52	Schering-Plough (7)		NA	NA	800-766-3960
NA	NA	NA	NA	NA	NA			NA	5	38	NA	Rational Software (9)		NA	NA	612-841-0400
24.4	22.7	17.8	16.7	NA	NA	3 1	Average	1	4	26	28	IBM (5)	Average	IV 98 24.0	III 98 –11.9	800-577-8589
8.8	8.0	NA	NA	NA	NA	4	Average	3	100	20	6	Telecom Italia (2)		NA	NA	800-577-8589
24.7	22.9	15.6	14.4	18.5	17.1	1 1 4 1	Low	2	7	33	34	America Online (15)	High	IV 98 40.1	III 98 –20.5	800-577-8589
21.6	19.2	16.8	14.7	14.5	12.8	4 1 3 2	Low	4	12	20	22	IBM (8)	Average	III 97 13.8	III 98 –15.8	800-577-8589
41.1	39.5	32.0	30.6	20.9	19.7	4 2 1 1	Very low	6	11	30	54	America Online (15)	Average	IV 98 35.9	III 98 –11.6	800-577-8589
18.3	16.0	18.0	15.7	16.4	13.8	2 2 1 2	Low	1	2	28	29	General Electric (7)	Average	II 97 13.5	III 98 –9.5	800-526-0056
26.0	22.5	18.9	15.5	15.8	12.4	3 2 3 1	Average	1	4	36	33	Safeway (3)	Average	IV 98 22.0	III 98 –12.3	800-526-0056
6.9	3.6	7.5	4.4	10.3	7.2	4 1 3 4	Low	2	12	15	–6	CSC Hldgs. (4)	Low	IV 95 6.7	III 98 –7.9	314-727-5305
3.5	–0.2	5.7	2.4	9.0	6.3	4 2 3 4	Low	6	18	16	6	Alliant Techsystems (5)	High	III 97 13.3	III 98 –19.5	314-727-5305
13.6	11.0	NA	NA	NA	NA	3	Low	19	3	24	18	Kirby (3)		NA	NA	817-332-3235
21.1	17.2	19.8	16.7	17.9	15.1	3 1 1 2	Low	2	32	21	14	FDX UK (9)	Low	IV 98 18.5	III 98 –18.4	800-445-9469
16.7	15.7	NA	NA	NA	NA	3	Low	1	7	24	–2	Host Marriott (10)		NA	NA	800-445-9469
23.9	21.7	18.5	16.3	13.5	12.0	4 3 2 1	Very low	8	29	24	11	Shaw Comms. Cl. B (Can.) (12)	Very low	IV 98 14.5	III 98 –13.4	800-445-9469
17.6	14.1	14.5	11.7	NA	NA	1 2 3	Average	12	1	21	5	Intl. Multifoods (1)	Average	IV 98 18.1	III 98 –18.6	800-633-3330
19.8	16.9	18.7	15.3	15.7	12.4	3 2 2 2	Average	2	4	27	33	IBM (4)	Low	IV 98 17.1	III 98 –11.6	800-874-3733
20.1	17.4	21.8	18.0	17.2	14.6	3 3 1 2	Low	6	4	32	25	Plantronics (4)	High	IV 98 28.3	III 98 –22.0	800-874-3733
16.7	12.9	14.1	10.4	13.8	10.7	3 2 3 2	Average	3	4	21	24	Tricon Global Restaurants (4)	Average	II 97 13.8	III 98 –17.3	800-874-3733
18.2	17.2	NA	NA	NA	NA	3	Average	3	NA	26	–9	Electronics for Imaging (7)		NA	NA	800-874-3733
26.5	25.7	21.9	21.4	22.4	20.9	1 1 2 1	Low	7	2	43	52	Tyco Intl. (3)	Average	IV 98 26.9	III 98 –8.3	800-624-6782
27.2	26.0	22.9	21.7	NA	NA	4 1 1	Very low	1	3	33	38	Microsoft (3)	Low	IV 98 21.2	III 98 –10.1	800-624-6782
18.7	16.7	15.8	14.4	14.7	13.2	2 3 3 2	Very high	2	2	45	38	Tyco Intl. (2)	Low	IV 98 16.9	III 98 –4.3	800-624-6782
10.8	7.7	11.7	9.3	14.3	11.9	2 1 2 3	Average	6	4	21	–5	Texas Utilities (3)	Average	II 97 11.2	III 98 –16.6	800-624-6782
21.6	20.7	22.9	21.8	20.5	18.9	1 1 1 1	Very low	5	NA	27	28	Medtronic (4)	Average	II 97 19.0	III 98 –13.2	800-304-7404
12.7	11.2	11.2	9.9	11.6	10.4	4 1 3 3	Low	9	100	26	14	Hoechst (2)	Average	III 98 13.9	III 98 –14.3	800-835-3879
15.9	14.8	15.4	13.6	16.8	14.2	2 1 1 3	Average	11	3	31	15	XTRA (1)	High	IV 98 19.8	III 98 –21.0	800-835-3879
19.5	16.8	17.7	15.5	NA	NA	2 2	Average	6	4	24	16	Exxon (3)	Low	IV 98 11.7	III 98 –7.8	800-236-8560
11.1	10.2	NA	NA	NA	NA	3	Low	7	95	17	15	Zurich Allied (2)		NA	NA	800-236-8560
22.2	19.2	18.1	15.8	NA	NA	3 1	Low	12	3	34	39	General Electric (3)	Average	IV 98 22.7	III 98 –10.1	800-236-8560
19.7	16.9	16.7	14.5	NA	NA	1 3	Very high	9	4	45	26	America Online (4)	High	IV 98 30.6	III 98 –22.9	800-236-8560
NA	NA	NA	NA	NA	NA			1	3	38	5	EMC/Mass. (10)		NA	NA	888-860-8686
NA	NA	NA	NA	NA	NA			2	7	37	13	Time Warner (5)		NA	NA	888-860-8686
16.8	12.7	14.7	11.5	NA	NA	3 2	High	23	5	29	7	Microsoft (2)	Very low	IV 98 12.2	III 98 –6.8	800-354-8185
22.0	15.1	19.4	14.0	17.5	13.6	1 3 1 2	Average	1	5	29	–2	Microsoft (4)	Average	IV 98 21.3	III 98 –14.4	800-354-8185
11.1	9.0	5.6	3.5	8.8	7.2	4 2 4 3	Average	3	97	22	13	Lafarge (France) (3)	High	IV 98 14.9	III 98 –14.1	800-354-8185
29.5	24.3	22.9	17.9	NA	NA	1 1 1	High	1	7	40	29	Health Mgt. Assoc. Cl. A (2)	High	IV 98 36.0	III 98 –19.1	800-354-8185
31.6	29.0	NA	NA	NA	NA	1	Very high	9	2	26	9	Allmerica Financial (3)		NA	NA	800-354-8185
20.3	16.0	16.6	12.2	17.8	15.0	3 1 2 2	High	9	5	23	–5	CalEnergy (2)	Average	III 97 18.3	III 98 –18.3	800-354-8185
15.2	11.9	17.0	13.4	16.2	12.1	2 2 1 3	Average	13	1	18	0	S&P Index 500 (Fut.) (5)	Average	II 97 14.6	III 98 –19.1	800-354-8185
NA	NA	NA	NA	NA	NA		High	3	17	24	18	Media One Group (3)		NA	NA	800-960-0188
12.8	10.4	13.9	11.0	14.9	12.6	3 1 1 4	Average	12	2	35	28	Markel (3)	High	IV 98 22.6	III 98 –22.7	800-382-0016
9.0	6.2	9.6	7.2	NA	NA	3 3 4	Very high	–12	7	28	–5	Allied Group (9)	Very low	IV 98 7.3	III 98 –6.0	800-343-8959
11.0	7.0	11.0	8.1	15.7	13.2	1 1 3 3	Low	2	NA	31	9	Kohl's (3)	Average	IV 98 17.3	III 98 –18.8	800-446-6662
18.2	16.2	17.0	15.1	13.8	12.0	4 2 2 2	Low	15	12	20	35	IBM (3)	Low	II 97 14.2	III 98 –11.5	800-637-3863
12.1	9.9	13.1	10.5	12.5	10.2	3 4 3 3	Low	4	18	29	21	Williams Companies (2)	Low	IV 98 10.8	III 98 –11.7	800-637-3863
–18.2	–19.3	–13.5	–14.4	NA	NA	4 4	Low	18	100	20	–56	Hong Kong Telecom ADR (7)	Very high	IV 98 22.7	IV 97 –30.2	800-637-3863
23.8	17.8	17.0	12.2	14.0	11.5	3 3 3 1	Average	6	100	27	3	Telecom Italia (5)	Average	IV 98 22.6	III 98 –18.7	800-637-3863
27.1	24.4	NA	NA	NA	NA	1	Average	5	9	40	26	Wal-Mart Stores (4)		NA	NA	800-637-3863
8.1	5.1	8.5	5.8	NA	NA	2 3 4	Average	5	49	24	–7	Nikkei 225 Index (Fut.) (3)	Very low	IV 98 9.3	III 98 –13.2	800-637-3863
NA	NA	NA	NA	NA	NA			NA	68	33	NA	SAP (3)		NA	NA	800-637-3863
20.3	18.0	13.8	12.0	NA	NA	2 4 2	Very low	3	64	25	46	Telefonica (6)	Average	IV 98 15.1	I 94 –7.5	800-637-3863
NA	NA	NA	NA	NA	NA		Average	7	45	26	22	Cadbury Schweppes (5)		NA	NA	609-282-2800
4.5	3.1	9.3	7.7	13.6	11.9	1 2 1 4	Low	14	5	28	9	Burlington Resources (7)	High	III 97 19.2	III 98 –19.5	800-637-3863
23.2	17.5	21.3	17.0	14.3	10.2	3 4 1 1	High	4	16	47	20	Pfizer (7)	Average	IV 98 19.7	II 94 –8.9	800-637-3863
1.5	–0.9	2.7	1.0	5.0	3.2	4 4 4 4	Low	7	100	30	–16	Lend Lease (8)	High	IV 98 19.6	IV 97 –19.0	800-637-3863
12.1	7.1	9.5	5.5	11.8	7.9	4 1 3 3	Average	9	10	31	–13	Novell (3)	High	I 98 16.9	III 98 –19.1	800-637-3863
NA	NA	NA	NA	NA	NA			2	3	32	NA	General Electric (3)		NA	NA	609-282-2800
12.4	8.9	12.1	9.0	9.7	7.9	4 2 2 3	High	12	4	23	5	VISX (5)	High	II 97 19.1	III 98 –26.0	800-637-3863
23.3	20.5	21.4	18.5	18.0	14.4	4 1 1 1	High	8	14	34	22	Tyco Intl. (8)	Average	IV 98 24.0	III 98 –14.1	800-637-2929
19.0	18.8	19.7	19.4	22.9	22.5	1 1 1 2	Low	1	4	42	44	Cisco Systems (7)	High	IV 98 28.0	III 98 –18.1	800-637-2929
18.1	16.0	13.7	11.3	NA	NA	3 2	Average	9	61	26	18	Rite Aid (3)	Average	IV 98 19.2	III 98 –13.5	800-637-2929
12.2	10.3	10.7	8.9	NA	NA	3 3	High	6	55	35	15	Cisco Systems (3)	Average	IV 98 20.7	III 98 –17.0	800-637-2929
24.7	21.3	20.1	16.6	16.8	13.1	2 3 2 1	Average	4	2	42	38	Microsoft (7)	High	IV 98 24.2	III 98 –13.6	800-637-2929
23.6	18.2	21.1	16.5	17.1	14.0	2 4 1 1	High	4	2	41	25	Tyco Intl. (4)	Average	IV 98 24.2	III 98 –12.2	800-637-2929
17.9	13.6	16.2	11.8	NA	NA	2 2	High	1	1	32	34	Tyco Intl. (10)	High	IV 98 23.7	III 98 –19.1	800-637-2929
26.8	24.2	23.0	19.9	19.2	15.2	1 3 1 1	Low	7	6	31	29	Philip Morris (2)	Low	IV 98 18.6	III 98 –10.9	800-637-2929
36.6	30.6	25.0	19.9	21.7	17.4	1 1 3 1	Average	8	2	39	30	Microsoft (6)	Average	IV 98 25.5	III 98 –10.1	800-637-2929

DATA: MORNINGSTAR, INC., CHICAGO, IL.

FUND	OVERALL RATING (COMPARES RISK-ADJUSTED PERFORMANCE OF EACH FUND AGAINST ALL FUNDS)	CATEGORY (COMPARES RISK-ADJUSTED PERFORMANCE OF FUND WITHIN CATEGORY)	RATING	SIZE ASSETS $MIL.	SIZE % CHG. 1997-98	FEES SALES CHARGE (%)	FEES EXPENSE RATIO (%)	1997 RETURNS PRE-TAX	1997 RETURNS AFTER-TAX	1997 RETURNS YIELD
MFS RESEARCH A	C	Large-cap Blend	C−	3200.7	36	5.75	0.96†	22.9	22.0	0.0
MFS STRATEGIC GROWTH B		Large-cap Growth		359.9	596	4.00**	2.08†	44.2	43.1	0.0
MFS TOTAL RETURN A	B+	Domestic Hybrid	B+	3810.8	17	4.75	0.93†	11.9	7.8	3.5
MFS UTILITIES B	B+	Utilities	A	442.1	269	4.00**	1.87†	17.0	14.6	1.9
MONTAG & CALDWELL GROWTH N		Large-cap Growth		1157.2	111	No load	1.23†	31.9	31.0	0.0
MONTGOMERY EMERGING MARKETS R	F	Diversified Emerging Mkts.	C	338.1	−66	No load	1.60	−38.3	−38.3	0.0
MONTGOMERY GLOBAL COMMUN. R	D	Communications	C−	282.1	107	No load	1.90	55.0	51.1	0.0
MONTGOMERY GROWTH R	C	Mid-cap Blend	B	1047.8	−23	No load	1.19	2.1	0.4	0.4
MONTGOMERY U.S. EMERG. GROWTH R (zz)		Small-cap Growth		410.4	11	No load‡	1.56	7.9	6.7	0.0
J.P. MORGAN DIVERSIFIED	A	Domestic Hybrid	B+	241.0	140	No load	0.98	18.3	16.9	2.2
J.P. MORGAN U.S. EQUITY	B	Large-cap Blend	C	428.7	8	No load	0.78	24.5	19.4	0.8
J.P. MORGAN U.S. SMALL CO.	C−	Small-cap Blend	C	203.4	−23	No load	0.97	−5.5	−8.2	0.3
MSDW AMERICAN VALUE B (aaa) ♣	C	Large-cap Growth	C	5748.7	41	5.00**	1.46†	31.1	26.0	0.0
MSDW CAPITAL APPRECIATION B (bbb)		Small-cap Growth		219.5	−38	5.00**	NA†	−1.3	−2.8	0.0
MSDW CAPITAL GROWTH SECURITIES B (ccc)	C	Large-cap Growth	D	500.6	0	5.00**	1.84†	17.0	14.3	0.0
MSDW DEVELOPING GROWTH B (ddd)		Small-cap Growth	C	709.4	−12	5.00**	1.68†	7.8	7.5	0.0
MSDW DIVIDEND GROWTH SECURITIES B (eee) ♣	B+	Large-cap Blend	C	18483.2	18	5.00**	1.14†	17.8	16.7	1.2
MSDW EUROPEAN GROWTH B (fff) ♣	B	Europe	B	2226.9	29	5.00**	2.42†	22.5	20.3	0.0
MSDW FINANCIAL SERVICES B (ggg)		Financial		421.9	48	5.00**	NA†	17.2	14.1	0.0
MSDW GLOBAL DIV. GROWTH SECURITIES B (hhh)	C	World		3544.2	0	5.00**	1.71†	11.5	9.1	0.7
MSDW GLOBAL UTILITIES B (iii)		Utilities		521.6	41	5.00**	1.8†	37.6	34.5	0.6
MSDW GROWTH B (jjj) ♣	C−	Large-cap Blend	F	867.8	6	5.00**	1.64†	21.5	16.8	0.0
MSDW HEALTH SCIENCES B (kkk)	D	Health	D	367.8	−7	5.00**	2.26†	18.3	13.4	0.0
MSDW INCOME BUILDER B (lll)		Domestic Hybrid		431.0	6	5.00**	NA†	1.7	−0.8	4.2
MSDW INFORMATION B (mmm)		Communications		386.8	64	5.00**	2.05†	54.8	51.2	0.0
MSDW MID-CAP GROWTH B (nnn) ♣		Mid-cap Growth		581.3	−4	5.00**	1.99†	4.4	0.2	0.0
MSDW PACIFIC GROWTH B (ooo) ♣	F	Diversified Pacific/Asia	F	426.0	−32	5.00**	2.44†	−10.5	−10.5	0.0
MSDW S&P 500 INDEX B (ppp)		Large-cap Blend		932.5	221	5.00**	NA†	26.8	26.8	0.1
MSDW SPECIAL VALUE B (qqq)		Small-cap Value		331.2	−8	5.00**	NA†	−7.3	−9.9	0.0
MSDW STRATEGIST B (rrr) ♣	B	Domestic Hybrid	C−	1704.7	14	5.00**	1.56†	15.4	13.1	1.3
MSDW UTILITIES B (sss) ♣	B	Utilities	C	2751.6	13	5.00**	1.67†	22.0	19.8	2.1
MSDW VALUE-ADDED MARKET EQ. B (ttt)	C	Large-cap Value	D	1481.4	−1	5.00**	1.36†	11.2	9.5	0.3
MUNDER INDEX 500 A	A	Large-cap Blend	B+	246.2	86	2.50	0.39†	28.0	27.3	1.0
MUTUAL BEACON Z ♣	B+	Mid-cap Value	B+	4039.5	−29	No load‡	0.74	2.4	0.1	3.2
MUTUAL DISCOVERY Z	B	World	A	2523.9	−35	No load‡	0.98	−1.9	−3.5	2.7
MUTUAL EUROPEAN Z ♣		Europe		484.0	−11	No load‡	1.02	4.7	3.4	2.6
MUTUAL QUALIFIED Z	B+	Mid-cap Value	B+	3962.3	−24	No load‡	0.75	0.5	−1.8	2.5
MUTUAL SHARES Z ♣	B	Mid-cap Value	B+	6289.6	−21	No load‡	0.72	0.5	−1.6	2.5
NATIONWIDE D (uuu) ♣	A	Large-cap Blend	A	2320.9	50	4.50	0.60	30.3	28.6	0.8
NATIONWIDE GROWTH D (vvv) ♣	B	Large-cap Blend	C−	944.7	13	4.50	0.64	23.8	22.3	0.1
NEUBERGER & BERMAN FOCUS ♣	C−	Large-cap Value	F	1369.6	0	No load	0.84	13.2	12.0	0.2
NEUBERGER & BERMAN GENESIS	C	Small-cap Blend	B+	1210.5	−3	No load	1.11	−7.0	−7.7	0.8
NEUBERGER & BERMAN GUARD	C−	Large-cap Value	F	4502.6	−25	No load	0.79	2.4	−0.9	0.6
NEUBERGER & BERMAN MANHATTAN	C−	Mid-cap Growth	C	563.7	−1	No load	0.95	16.4	14.8	0.0
NEUBERGER & BERMAN PARTNERS ♣	C	Large-cap Value	D	3239.4	0	No load	0.80	6.3	4.4	0.0
NEW ECONOMY ♣	C	Large-cap Blend	D	6530.6	31	5.75	0.81†	28.8	26.0	0.6
NEW ENGLAND BALANCED A	B	Domestic Hybrid	C−	223.4	−4	5.75	1.29†	8.2	5.2	2.2
NEW ENGLAND GROWTH A	C	Large-cap Blend	F	1826.2	25	5.75	1.12†	33.4	27.3	0.1
NEW ENGLAND GROWTH OPPORT. A	B	Large-cap Value	B	300.7	36	5.75	1.25†	24.0	20.0	0.1
NEW ENGLAND STAR ADVISERS B		Mid-cap Growth		508.4	10	5.00**	2.41†	18.2	15.9	0.0
NEW ENGLAND VALUE A ♣	C	Large-cap Value	D	318.40	−9	5.75	1.25†	7.1	4.7	0.2
NEW PERSPECTIVE ♣	B	World	B+	21257.0	31	5.75	0.77†	28.5	26.4	1.1
NEWPORT TIGER B (www)		Pacific/Asia ex-Japan		280.7	−23	5.00**	2.48†	−12.9	−13.2	1.1
NICHOLAS ♣	B	Mid-cap Blend	B+	5823.5	11	No load	0.71	13.1	10.9	0.6
NICHOLAS II	C	Mid-cap Growth	A	1109.5	8	No load	0.61	9.2	6.9	0.3
NICHOLAS LIMITED EDITION	C	Small-cap Growth	A	367.2	12	No load	0.86	1.7	0.6	0.1
NICHOLAS-APPLEGATE GROWTH EQ. B	D	Mid-cap Growth	C−	235.9	−17	5.00**	2.19†	11.9	10.2	0.1
NORTHERN GROWTH EQUITY		Large-cap Growth		594.7	41	No load	1.00	33.2	31.7	0.1
NORTHERN INTL. GROWTH EQUITY		Foreign		206.9	26	No load	1.25	23.9	22.7	1.0
NORTHERN SMALL CAP		Small-cap Value		314.3	−7	No load	1.00	−5.9	−6.8	0.1
NORTHERN TECHNOLOGY		Technology		227.8	182	No load	1.25	83.0	82.0	0.1
NORTHSTAR INTL. VALUE A		Foreign		231.8	278	4.75	1.80†	13.5	11.6	0.8
NUVEEN GROWTH & INCOME STOCK A		Large-cap Value		715.1	5	5.25	1.20†	9.9	6.8	0.8
OAK VALUE	B+	Mid-cap Blend	A	560.8	301	No load	1.22	18.9	18.6	0.3
OAKMARK	B	Large-cap Value	C	7779.3	7	No load	1.08	3.7	0.3	1.1
OAKMARK INTERNATIONAL	D	Foreign	D	815.6	−34	No load	1.32	−7.0	−9.2	2.1
OAKMARK SELECT		Mid-cap Value		1315.3	34	No load	1.22	16.2	15.2	0.2
OAKMARK SMALL CAP		Small-cap Value		747.7	−50	No load	1.45	−13.2	−15.3	0.0
OLSTEIN FINANCIAL ALERT		Mid-cap Value		273.4	26	2.50**	2.25†	15.0	13.9	0.0
ONE GROUP EQUITY INDEX B		Large-cap Blend		412.4	71	5.00**	1.35†	27.0	25.9	0.2

*Includes redemption fee. **Includes deferred sales charge. †12(b)-1 plan in effect. ‡Not currently accepting new accounts. §Less than 0.5% of assets. NA=Not available. NM=Not meaningful. (zz) Formerly Montgomery Micro Cap R. (aaa) Formerly Dean Witter American Value B. (bbb) Formerly Dean Witter Capital Appreciation B. (ccc) Formerly Dean Witter Capital Growth Secs. B. (ddd) Formerly Dean Witter Developing Growth Secs. B. (eee) Formerly Dean Witter Dividend Growth Secs. B. (fff) Formerly Dean Witter European Growth B. (ggg) Formerly Dean Witter Financial Services B. (hhh) Formerly Dean Witter Global Dividend Gr. Secs. B. (iii) Formerly Dean Witter Global Utilities B. (jjj) Formerly TCW/DW Core Equity B. (kkk) Formerly Dean Witter Health

3 YEARS PRETAX	3 YEARS AFTERTAX	5 YEARS PRETAX	5 YEARS AFTERTAX	10 YEARS PRETAX	10 YEARS AFTERTAX	RESULTS VS. ALL FUNDS	TURNOVER	CASH %	FOREIGN %	P-E RATIO	UNTAXED GAINS (%)	LARGEST HOLDING COMPANY (% ASSETS)	RISK LEVEL	BEST QTR %RET	WORST QTR %RET	TELEPHONE
22.6	21.2	20.7	18.6	18.4	15.8	[3112]	Average	2	8	33	25	Microsoft (5)	Average	IV 98 22.0	III 98 -15.0	800-637-2929
NA	NA	NA	NA	NA	NA		Average	6	2	40	16	Microsoft (8)		NA	NA	800-637-2929
15.7	11.8	13.8	10.6	13.5	10.6	[3332]	High	10	10	26	9	British Petroleum ADR (1)	Very low	II 97 9.3	III 98 -3.9	800-637-2929
22.1	18.1	17.6	14.6	NA	NA	[31]	High	6	18	24	9	KN Energy (3)	Low	IV 96 11.8	III 98 -3.8	800-637-2929
32.1	31.7	NA	NA	NA	NA	[1]	Low	3	3	40	26	Bristol-Myers Squibb (5)		NA		800-992-8151
-12.4	-12.7	-10.8	-11.3	NA	NA	[44]	High	7	97	17	NA	Liberty Life Assn. of Africa (2)	Very high	III 94 17.6	III 98 -24.7	800-572-3863
24.7	21.3	14.4	12.5	NA	NA	[41]	Average	3	67	33	26	Global TeleSystems Group (9)	High	I 98 38.7	III 98 -20.2	800-572-3863
15.1	11.9	17.9	15.3	NA	NA	[13]	Average	5	8	26	16	Avid Technology (3)	Average	IV 98 17.0	III 98 -19.3	800-572-3863
17.8	16.0	NA	NA	NA	NA	[3]	Low	2	NA	29	31	Duane Reade (4)		NA		800-572-3863
16.7	14.8	15.1	13.4	NA	NA	[32]	Average	2	21	31	15	Intel (1)	Very low	IV 98 13.4	III 98 -6.2	800-221-7930
24.6	19.7	20.6	16.0	18.6	15.1	[1321]	High	1	2	31	16	BankAmerica (New) (3)	Average	IV 98 21.3	III 98 -11.2	800-221-7930
11.9	8.5	11.7	8.2	13.3	10.9	[4123]	High	2	4	25	-5	RenaissanceRe Holdings (2)	High	IV 98 15.9	III 98 -21.6	800-221-7930
24.0	19.0	20.4	16.6	19.7	16.7	[1121]	Very high	11	4	40	21	Comcast Special Cl. A (2)	Average	IV 98 17.9	III 98 -7.3	800-869-6397
8.8	7.9	NA	NA	NA	NA	[4]		6	6	44	NA	CGI Group (2)		NA		800-869-3326
17.5	13.0	15.6	13.0	NA	NA	[422]	High	2	5	47	15	MCI WorldCom (5)	Average	IV 98 19.8	III 98 -15.0	800-869-3863
11.1	8.5	14.1	11.8	15.0	13.6	[3114]	High	17	3	36	21	BISYS Group (1)	High	IV 98 24.5	III 98 -20.4	800-869-6397
20.9	19.8	18.2	17.2	16.1	14.9	[2322]	Very low	5	5	29	53	Schering-Plough (3)	Low	II 97 15.7	III 98 -9.1	800-869-3863
21.8	19.3	19.2	16.7	NA	NA	[212]	Low	3	100	30	27	British Telecomm. (2)	Average	I 98 19.9	III 98 -15.8	800-869-3863
NA	NA	NA	NA	NA	NA			10	3	29	NA	Providian Financial (4)		NA		800-869-6397
13.3	10.5	13.3	11.0	NA	NA	[23]	Average	4	64	22	11	Northrop Grumman (1)	Low	IV 98 16.6	III 98 -12.6	800-869-3863
22.8	21.2	NA	NA	NA	NA	[1]	Very low	25	41	28	41	BellSouth (3)		NA		800-869-3863
20.8	17.0	15.2	13.0	NA	NA	[32]	Average	3	NA	37	39	United Technologies (8)	High	IV 98 25.1	III 98 -14.2	800-869-3863
8.1	5.3	13.9	11.6	NA	NA	[14]	High	8	3	48	22	Allegiance (4)	Very high	IV 95 19.0	I 97 -13.5	800-869-3863
NA	NA	NA	NA	NA	NA	[3]		2	1	19	NA	Loral Space & Communications (1)		NA		800-869-6397
21.4	20.5	NA	NA	NA	NA	[2]	Very high	7	2	48	37	America Online (5)		NA		800-869-3863
16.0	12.8	NA	NA	NA	NA	[3]	Very high	3	1	44	7	Citrix Systems (3)		NA		800-869-3863
-16.9	-17.2	-13.2	-13.8	NA	NA	[144]	Low	3	100	23	NA	Hong Kong Telecomm. (5)	Very high	IV 98 26.6	IV 97 -28.6	800-869-3863
NA	NA	NA	NA	NA	NA			4	2	33	NA	Microsoft (3)		NA		800-869-3863
NA	NA	NA	NA	NA	NA			10	9	17	NA	Paxar (4)		NA		800-869-6397
15.5	13.1	13.4	11.0	13.8	11.8	[1333]	High	14	1	29	22	Media One Group (2)	Low	I 98 10.2	III 98 -8.8	800-869-3863
17.2	15.0	13.4	11.5	12.9	11.0	[3342]	Very low	5	9	24	47	SBC Communications (3)	Low	IV 97 13.2	I 94 -6.5	800-869-3863
18.2	16.9	16.3	15.4	14.6	13.7	[3322]	Low	0	2	27	41	MCI WorldCom (§)	Average	IV 98 16.5	III 98 -14.1	800-869-3863
27.6	25.9	23.5	21.7	NA	NA	[11]	Very low	3	2	33	35	S&P 500 Index (Fut.) (3)	Low	IV 98 21.1	III 98 -10.0	800-553-4578
15.1	11.9	15.2	12.3	14.5	11.9	[4113]	Average	21	38	21	17	Chase Manhattan (3)	Low	IV 98 12.6	III 98 -17.5	800-342-5236
14.6	11.9	15.0	12.4	NA	NA	[13]	Average	18	66	20	10	Kansas City Southern Inds. (2)	Low	I 98 11.2	III 98 -19.4	800-342-5236
NA	NA	NA	NA	NA	NA		High	21	97	18	16	Suez Lyonnaise Des Eaux (3)		NA		800-342-5236
15.0	12.0	15.3	12.1	14.3	11.2	[4123]	Average	19	29	21	17	Chase Manhattan (3)	Low	IV 98 12.6	III 98 -17.7	800-342-5236
15.3	12.3	15.7	12.2	14.3	11.1	[4123]	Average	23	22	21	21	Chase Manhattan (3)	Low	IV 98 13.3	III 98 -17.0	800-553-3014
31.1	28.9	24.1	21.6	18.9	16.4	[1421]	Very low	1	NA	28	48	Warner-Lambert (9)	Low	I 97 18.5	III 98 -9.7	800-848-0920
22.2	19.7	18.9	16.4	15.1	12.9	[4221]	Average	2	2	37	41	MCI WorldCom (7)	Average	II 97 18.3	III 98 -10.7	800-848-0920
17.8	15.6	17.6	15.4	17.0	14.3	[3122]	Average	6	3	23	44	Citigroup (8)	High	IV 98 34.5	III 98 -27.5	800-877-9700
17.7	17.1	15.3	14.3	14.1	13.1	[3223]	Low	8	0	19	5	Alliant Techsystems (3)	Average	III 97 20.1	III 98 -16.4	800-877-9700
12.5	9.5	13.6	11.3	14.9	12.6	[2123]	Average	7	7	23	23	Countrywide Credit Industry (5)	High	IV 98 23.1	III 98 -26.2	800-877-9700
18.2	13.9	15.8	12.3	15.4	12.0	[2232]	Average	3	5	39	27	Staples (3)	High	IV 98 27.5	III 98 -21.2	800-877-9700
20.2	16.4	18.2	14.5	16.2	12.8	[3222]	High	5	5	24	15	SLM Holding (3)	Average	IV 98 16.4	III 98 -14.7	800-877-9700
23.3	20.7	16.5	14.2	17.5	15.0	[3141]	Low	14	25	35	39	Viacom Cl. B (3)	Average	IV 98 22.1	III 98 -10.8	800-421-4120
14.2	10.8	12.9	10.0	11.8	9.4	[4233]	Average	1	6	24	13	BellSouth (2)	Very low	II 97 10.1	III 98 -6.4	800-225-7670
25.8	19.8	20.7	15.5	18.3	14.3	[1331]	Very high	1	20	30	19	Nokia Cl. A ADR (8)	High	IV 98 28.5	III 98 -18.1	800-225-7670
24.7	19.1	21.5	16.9	17.4	14.0	[2321]	High	3	1	30	22	Wal-Mart Stores (3)	Average	IV 98 19.2	III 98 -12.3	800-225-7670
18.5	14.8	NA	NA	NA	NA	[2]	High	6	4	34	18	Philip Morris (2)		NA		800-225-7670
17.8	14.1	16.4	13.1	14.5	11.7	[3222]	Average	0	6	24	22	Exxon (4)	Average	IV 98 17.5	III 98 -15.2	800-225-7670
20.1	18.1	16.5	14.5	15.7	13.7	[3232]	Low	16	57	33	35	Pfizer (3)	Low	IV 98 20.7	III 98 -10.2	800-421-4120
-14.3	-14.4	NA	NA	NA	NA	[4]	Very low	5	100	18	-55	Cheung Kong Holdings (8)		NA		800-426-3750
22.9	20.4	19.6	16.9	17.2	15.2	[1321]	Very low	13	2	31	50	Freddie Mac (5)	Average	IV 98 19.3	III 98 -15.9	800-227-5987
21.3	18.1	18.3	15.2	15.3	13.1	[2422]	Low	4	9	32	40	Health Mgmt. Assoc. Cl. A (5)	Average	IV 98 16.0	III 98 -15.6	800-227-5987
18.1	15.6	15.8	12.9	15.9	13.6	[2213]	Low	9	3	32	30	Intl Speedway Cl. B (6)	Average	IV 98 19.6	III 98 -17.0	800-227-5987
14.6	10.3	12.0	9.0	NA	NA	[133]	Very high	2	4	36	35	Robert Half International (3)	High	IV 98 24.8	III 98 -18.4	800-225-1852
26.8	24.8	NA	NA	NA	NA	[1]	Average	4	4	40	38	Microsoft (3)		NA		800-595-9111
11.4	10.1	NA	NA	NA	NA	[3]	High	7	100	36	17	Novartis (Reg) (4)		NA		800-595-9111
13.2	11.9	NA	NA	NA	NA	[3]	Low	0	3	19	12	Earthgrains (1)		NA		800-595-9111
NA	NA	NA	NA	NA	NA	[1]	Average	3	2	49	43	Dell Computer (7)		NA		800-595-9111
15.5	14.4	NA	NA	NA	NA	[2]	Low	6	100	24	12	Hutchison Whampoa (5)		NA		800-595-7827
NA	NA	NA	NA	NA	NA		Very high	6	20	25	15	BankAmerica (New) (4)		NA		800-351-4100
28.3	27.4	21.8	20.7	NA	NA	[21]	Very low	2	NA	28	14	E.W. Scripps Cl. A (9)	Low	IV 98 24.4	III 98 -18.6	800-622-2474
16.9	14.4	17.3	15.0	NA	NA	[12]	Low	12	3	23	15	Philip Morris (10)	Low	II 97 15.2	III 98 -13.8	800-625-6275
7.2	4.4	3.9	1.3	NA	NA	[44]	Low	6	100	15	-32	Quilmes Industrial ADR (5)	High	IV 98 14.5	III 98 -19.4	800-625-6275
NA	NA	NA	NA	NA	NA		Average	12	19	23	12	Cablevision Sys. Cl. A (14)		NA		800-625-6275
19.5	18.0	NA	NA	NA	NA	[3]	Low	8	2	21	6	Peoples Bank (CT) (8)		NA		800-625-6275
24.5	21.0	NA	NA	NA	NA	[1]	Very high	27	NA	26	16	Texas Instruments (3)		NA		800-799-2113
26.5	25.7	NA	NA	NA	NA	[1]	Very low	2	2	33	36	Microsoft (3)		NA		800-480-4111

Sciences B. (lll) Formerly Dean Witter Income Builder B. (mmm) Formerly Dean Witter Information B. (nnn) Formerly Dean Witter Mid-Cap Growth B. (ooo) Formerly Dean Witter Pacific Growth B. (ppp) Formerly Dean Witter S&P 500 Index B. (qqq) Formerly Dean Witter Special Value B. (rrr) Formerly Dean Witter Strategist B. (sss) Formerly Dean Witter Utilities B. (ttt) Formerly Dean Witter Value-Added Market Eq. B. (uuu) Formerly Nationwide. (vvv) Formerly Nationwide Growth. (www) Formerly Colonial Newport Tiger B.

DATA: MORNINGSTAR, INC., CHICAGO, IL.

FUND (COMPARES RISK-ADJUSTED PERFORMANCE OF EACH FUND AGAINST ALL FUNDS)	OVERALL RATING	CATEGORY (COMPARES RISK-ADJUSTED PERFORMANCE OF FUND WITHIN CATEGORY)	RATING	SIZE ASSETS $MIL.	% CHG. 1997-98	FEES SALES CHARGE (%)	EXPENSE RATIO (%)	1997 RETURNS (%) PRE-TAX	AFTER-TAX	YIELD
ONE GROUP LARGE CO. GROWTH B		Large-cap Growth		382.8	108	5.00**	1.99†	43.2	39.8	0.0
OPPENHEIMER CAPITAL APPREC. A	B	Large-cap Growth	B	1722.5	42	5.75	1.00†	24.0	22.2	0.2
OPPENHEIMER DISCIPLINED ALLOCATION A	B	Domestic Hybrid	C	314.5	27	5.75	1.11†	10.9	9.3	2.8
OPPENHEIMER DISCIPLINED VALUE A	C	Large-cap Value	D	490.1	27	5.75	1.07†	8.5	7.5	0.8
OPPENHEIMER DISCOVERY A	D	Small-cap Growth	C-	1098.0	-12	5.75	1.22†	-2.0	-2.7	0.0
OPPENHEIMER EQUITY-INCOME A	B	Domestic Hybrid	C	3259.8	9	5.75	0.87†	10.3	7.5	3.2
OPPENHEIMER GLOBAL A	C-	World	C	3427.5	6	5.75	1.13†	12.7	10.7	0.9
OPPENHEIMER GLOBAL GROWTH & INCOME A	C	International Hybrid	C-	256.7	37	5.75	1.43†	12.8	7.8	2.1
OPPENHEIMER GROWTH A	B	Large-cap Blend	C-	1633.5	3	5.75	1.00†	11.0	8.7	1.3
OPPENHEIMER MAIN ST. GROWTH & INC. A (xxx)	B	Large-cap Blend	C	6525.2	35	5.75	0.90†	25.2	23.9	0.6
OPPENHEIMER MULTIPLE STRATEGIES A	B	Domestic Hybrid	C-	672.2	-3	5.75	1.16†	7.1	4.1	3.5
OPPENHEIMER QUEST CAPITAL VALUE A	C	Mid-cap Blend	C-	278.4	0	5.75	1.11†	20.2	19.3	0.1
OPPENHEIMER QUEST GLOBAL VALUE A	C	World	B+	299.3	12	7.75***	1.73†	12.3	10.8	0.4
OPPENHEIMER QUEST OPPORTUNITIES B	B	Large-cap Value	C	2059.6	13	5.00**	2.03†	7.2	6.0	0.4
OPPENHEIMER QUEST VALUE A	B	Large-cap Value	B	1012.0	35	5.75	1.60†	9.5	8.4	0.7
OPPENHEIMER TOTAL RETURN A	C	Large-cap Blend	C-	2602.3	16	5.75	0.89†	21.2	19.0	1.2
PACIFIC HORIZON BLUE CHIP A		Large-cap Blend		400.1	58	5.50	1.18	27.9	26.3	0.3
PAINEWEBBER BALANCED A	B	Domestic Hybrid	C-	212.7	18	4.50	1.34†	17.9	15.0	1.0
PAINEWEBBER FINANCIAL SERVICES GROWTH A	B+	Financial	B+	223.0	34	4.50	1.17†	2.3	1.7	0.9
PAINEWEBBER GLOBAL EQUITY A	C-	World	C-	253.6	-11	4.50	1.44†	11.8	10.7	0.1
PAINEWEBBER GROWTH A	C-	Mid-cap Growth	B	276.6	29	4.50	1.27†	32.5	30.4	0.0
PAINEWEBBER GROWTH & INCOME A	C	Large-cap Blend	C	872.0	58	4.50	1.07†	18.1	16.6	0.7
PAINEWEBBER TACTICAL ALLOCATION C	B+	Large-cap Blend	B	555.2	87	1.00**	1.70†	26.7	26.1	0.0
PAPP AMERICA-ABROAD	A	Large-cap Growth	A	342.8	19	No load	1.11	23.8	23.8	0.1
PARNASSUS	D	Small-cap Value	F	274.7	-19	3.50	1.11	1.4	1.4	0.0
PAX WORLD	A	Domestic Hybrid	A	837.6	33	No load	0.91†	24.6	22.8	2.1
PAYDEN & RYGEL GROWTH & INCOME R		Large-cap Value		265.8	41	No load	0.54	18.1	17.1	1.4
PBHG EMERGING GROWTH	D	Small-cap Growth	C-	1043.8	-31	No load	1.27	3.0	2.9	0.0
PBHG GROWTH PBHG	D	Mid-cap Growth	D	3939.5	-28	No load	1.26	0.6	0.6	0.0
PBHG LARGE CAP 20 PBHG		Large-cap Growth		545.2	368	No load	1.41	67.8	67.3	0.0
PBHG SELECT EQUITY		Mid-cap Growth		289.9	-17	No load	1.35	19.0	19.0	0.0
PBHG TECHNOLOGY & COMMUNICATIONS		Technology		396.3	-28	No load	1.30	26.0	25.6	0.0
PEGASUS EQUITY INDEX A	A	Large-cap Blend	B+	321.6	66	3.00	0.57†	27.9	26.0	0.7
PEGASUS GROWTH & VALUE A	B	Large Blend	C-	268.6	65	5.00	1.09†	13.1	10.8	0.4
PEGASUS MID CAP OPPORTUNITIES A	C-	Mid-cap Blend	C-	278.3	19	5.00	1.09†	4.3	2.8	0.0
PENNSYLVANIA MUTUAL INVESTORS	C	Small-cap Value	B	458.9	-10	1.00*	1.05	4.2	2.0	0.6
PHOENIX AGGRESSIVE GROWTH A	C-	Mid-cap Growth	B	291.0	17	4.75	1.20†	29.6	29.6	0.0
PHOENIX BALANCED A	B	Domestic Hybrid	C-	1684.2	0	4.75	0.98†	18.5	16.6	2.3
PHOENIX GROWTH A	B	Large-cap Blend	C	2818.5	13	4.75	1.10†	29.5	27.2	0.0
PHOENIX INCOME & GROWTH A	B	Domestic Hybrid	C-	584.9	27	4.75	1.13†	11.0	7.8	3.6
PHOENIX MID CAP A	C-	Mid-cap Growth	C	308.0	-13	4.75	1.33†	19.5	13.6	0.0
PHOENIX STRATEGIC ALLOCATION A	B	Domestic Hybrid	C-	319.0	3	4.75	1.17†	20.2	17.1	1.3
PHOENIX-ENGEMANN GROWTH A	C	Large-cap Growth	D	441.7	15	4.75	1.60†	36.7	35.4	0.0
PHOENIX-ENGEMANN NIFTY FIFTY A	C	Large-cap Growth	C	235.0	33	4.75	1.60†	35.1	34.7	0.0
PILGRIM BANK & THRIFT B (yyy)		Financial		391.1	422	5.00**	1.95†	-2.5	-3.1	0.2
PILGRIM MAGNACAP A (zzz)	B+	Large-cap Blend	C	340.3	6	5.75	1.37†	16.1	13.8	0.2
PIMCO GROWTH C	C	Large-cap Growth	C	1942.1	25	1.00**	1.91†	38.9	34.9	0.0
PIMCO INNOVATION C		Technology		327.1	95	1.00**	2.06†	78.1	76.5	0.0
PIMCO MICRO CAP GROWTH INSTITUTIONAL	C-	Small-cap Blend	B	255.6	21	No load	1.51	-3.9	-4.5	0.0
PIMCO OPPORTUNITY C	F	Small-cap Growth	D	369.8	-33	1.00**	2.06†	1.3	-2.5	0.0
PIMCO RENAISSANCE C	B	Large-cap Blend	C	429.1	15	1.00**	2.01†	10.7	6.8	0.0
PIMCO STOCKSPLUS INSTITUTIONAL	A	Large-cap Blend	A	453.5	36	No load	0.65	28.3	23.2	6.0
PIMCO TARGET C	C-	Mid-cap Growth	B	889.4	-6	1.00**	1.96†	23.3	21.1	0.0
PIONEER A	B+	Large-cap Blend	B	5395.2	35	5.75	1.03†	29.1	28.0	0.5
PIONEER BALANCED A	C	Domestic Hybrid	D	257.6	-6	4.50	1.19†	1.2	-0.5	3.0
PIONEER CAPITAL GROWTH A	C	Mid-cap Value	D	1321.7	-17	5.75	0.98†	-4.7	-5.7	0.1
PIONEER EQUITY-INCOME A	B+	Large-cap Value	B	638.7	29	5.75	1.11†	17.4	16.2	1.6
PIONEER EUROPE A	C	Europe	C	346.1	115	5.75	1.78†	20.8	20.2	0.3
PIONEER GROWTH A	B	Large-cap Growth	C	1404.5	139	5.75	0.99†	33.6	31.7	0.0
PIONEER II A	C-	Mid-cap Value	D	6233.5	-13	5.75	0.90†	-8.0	-8.4	0.8
PIONEER INTERNATIONAL GROWTH A	D	Foreign	F	313.6	-18	5.75	1.67†	-6.2	-6.7	1.1
PIONEER MID-CAP A	D	Mid-cap Growth	D	891.1	-4	5.75	0.85†	10.0	8.2	0.0
PREFERRED ASSET ALLOCATION	A	Domestic Hybrid	A	203.8	47	No load	0.92	27.1	24.1	2.6
PREFERRED GROWTH	C	Large-cap Growth	C-	506.6	13	No load	0.84	35.9	30.2	0.0
PREFERRED INTERNATIONAL	C-	Foreign	B	266.0	10	No load	1.20	10.6	9.6	1.1
PREFERRED VALUE	B+	Large-cap Value	B+	389.3	14	No load	0.84	14.4	13.1	1.0
T. ROWE PRICE BALANCED	B+	Domestic Hybrid	B	1649.8	35	No load	0.81	16.0	14.9	2.8
T. ROWE PRICE BLUE CHIP GROWTH	A	Large-cap Blend	A	4330.1	85	No load	0.95	28.8	28.3	0.4
T. ROWE PRICE CAPITAL APPRECIATION	A	Domestic Hybrid	A	1003.7	-5	No load	0.66	5.8	2.1	3.3
T. ROWE PRICE DIVIDEND GROWTH	A	Large-cap Blend	A	1337.7	79	No load	0.80	15.0	13.6	2.0

*Includes redemption fee. **Includes deferred sales charge. †12(b)-1 plan in effect. ‡Not currently accepting new accounts. §Less than 0.5% of assets. NA=Not available. NM=Not meaningful. (xxx) Formerly Oppenheimer Main St. Income & Growth A. (yyy) Formerly Pilgrim America Bank & Thrift B. (zzz) Formerly Pilgrim American MagnaCap A.

3 YEARS PRETAX	3 YEARS AFTERTAX	5 YEARS PRETAX	5 YEARS AFTERTAX	10 YEARS PRETAX	10 YEARS AFTERTAX	HISTORY RESULTS VS. ALL FUNDS	TURNOVER	CASH %	FOREIGN %	P-E RATIO	UNTAXED GAINS (%)	LARGEST HOLDING COMPANY (% ASSETS)	RISK LEVEL	BEST QTR	BEST %RET	WORST QTR	WORST %RET	TELEPHONE
29.8	26.8	NA	NA	NA	NA	1	High	0	1	41	35	Microsoft (7)			NA		NA	800-480-4111
26.1	23.0	22.1	18.6	17.7	15.4	2311	Average	12	4	34	26	Microsoft (4)	Average	IV 98	26.7	III 98	-16.6	800-525-7048
12.7	9.7	11.7	9.0	13.3	10.3	2243	High	1	1	26	11	US West (1)	Very low	IV 98	12.1	III 98	-6.6	800-525-7048
16.8	14.5	16.6	14.3	17.4	14.4	2122	High	11	NA	27	16	IBM (3)	Average	IV 98	18.3	III 98	-15.4	800-525-7048
7.5	6.3	8.6	7.0	15.1	13.5	2124	Average	6	4	39	24	Serologicals Holding (2)	High	II 97	18.5	III 98	-21.4	800-525-7048
19.8	17.0	16.4	13.9	13.6	11.2	3332	Low	26	1	23	27	First Union (3)	Low	II 97	11.3	III 98	-7.9	800-525-7048
17.3	14.8	12.8	10.2	14.3	12.0	2242	Average	8	66	29	20	Canal Plus (5)	Average	IV 98	20.5	III 98	-17.1	800-525-7048
18.6	14.6	13.3	9.8	NA	NA	242	Average	0	61	25	2	National Semiconductor (5)	Average	IV 98	20.7	III 98	-17.5	800-525-7048
17.4	14.3	17.5	14.0	16.1	13.7	2312	Low	32	3	23	21	Compaq Computer (2)	Low	IV 98	17.7	III 98	-13.6	800-525-7048
22.4	20.3	18.8	17.2	23.4	20.9	2121	Average	7	2	34	30	Microsoft (4)	Average	IV 98	22.1	III 98	-11.0	800-525-7048
13.9	10.8	12.3	9.2	11.7	9.3	3333	Average	6	23	26	16	NationsBank (2)	Very low	IV 98	11.2	III 98	-10.4	800-525-7048
15.3	12.4	15.6	13.8	19.6	18.3	1113	Low	7	41	23	23	Security Capital Realty (11)	Average	IV 98	19.3	III 98	-11.6	800-525-7048
14.4	13.2	13.3	11.4	NA	NA	233	Low	2	55	30	22	FHLMC (5)	Low	IV 98	14.8	III 98	-14.4	800-525-7048
16.1	15.1	18.2	17.2	NA	NA	13	Low	13	5	28	17	FHLMC (6)	Low	II 95	14.3	III 98	-13.1	800-525-7048
20.3	18.8	19.2	17.2	16.2	14.3	3212	Low	15	14	24	23	EXEL Cl. A (6)	Low	II 97	13.5	III 98	-13.6	800-525-7048
22.7	19.3	17.3	14.5	16.8	13.9	3131	Average	3	0	35	30	Tyco Intl. (2)	Average	IV 98	18.3	III 98	-10.8	800-525-7048
28.1	25.9	NA	NA	NA	NA	1	Average	4	1	32	12	Microsoft (4)			NA		NA	800-332-3863
19.0	15.3	13.4	9.6	NA	NA	342	High	6	5	30	20	MCI WorldCom (1)	Low	IV 98	15.2	III 98	-8.1	800-647-1568
24.1	21.5	22.9	19.9	22.4	20.2	2111	Low	11	5	21	21	Ambac Financial Group (2)	Low	II 97	16.5	III 98	-15.8	800-647-1568
10.9	9.2	8.7	6.9	NA	NA	43	Average	3	75	30	13	AirTouch Communications (3)	Average	IV 98	19.4	III 98	-19.4	800-647-1568
21.0	17.2	16.1	13.3	16.9	14.7	1232	Average	6	3	43	34	Dell Computer (3)	High	IV 98	30.6	III 98	-13.7	800-647-1568
24.4	21.5	19.3	16.5	15.1	13.4	2421	Average	8	3	30	27	United Technologies (2)	Average	IV 98	20.9	III 98	-14.0	800-647-1568
26.1	25.7	21.6	20.2	NA	NA	21	Low	0	2	33	26	Microsoft (3)	Average	IV 98	20.8	III 98	-10.3	800-647-1568
27.1	26.5	24.9	24.3	NA	NA	11	Very low	1	6	31	27	American Power Conversion (9)	Average	IV 98	27.8	III 98	-12.6	800-421-4004
13.7	11.4	10.6	8.5	12.6	10.7	4142	Average	7	NA	34	15	Intel (9)	Very high	IV 98	44.6	III 98	-24.3	800-999-3505
19.8	17.2	17.9	15.7	14.2	11.8	1421	Very low	15	NA	37	30	AirTouch Communications (5)	Very low	IV 98	14.2	I 94	-3.7	800-767-1729
NA	NA	NA	NA	NA	NA			6	NA	28	18	S&P 500 Dep. Rec. (46)			NA		NA	800-572-9336
5.1	4.7	16.4	15.8	NA	NA	14	High	17	2	41	24	Medicis Pharm. Cl. A (3)	Very high	II 94	21.8	I 97	-20.5	800-433-0051
2.2	2.2	11.0	11.0	18.8	16.0	2114	Average	7	5	47	23	Citrix Systems (4)	Very high	IV 98	27.5	III 98	-26.2	800-433-0051
NA	NA	NA	NA	NA	NA		High	18	NA	53	22	BMC Software (7)			NA		NA	800-433-0051
17.6	17.5	NA	NA	NA	NA	3	Average	6	3	47	44	J.D. Edwards (7)			NA		NA	800-433-0051
26.2	25.2	NA	NA	NA	NA	2	Very high	9	2	51	39	Compuware (8)			NA		NA	800-433-0051
27.8	26.2	23.7	22.1	NA	NA	11	Very low	0	2	33	37	Microsoft (3)	Low	IV 98	21.1	III 98	-10.0	800-688-3350
20.0	17.0	17.3	14.9	NA	NA	422	Low	2	2	27	19	Norwest (3)	Average	IV 98	15.8	III 98	-9.7	800-688-3350
18.5	16.4	14.0	12.1	NA	NA	132	Low	3	NA	23	25	Charter One Financial (3)	Average	IV 98	22.6	III 98	-20.7	800-688-3350
13.7	9.8	11.6	7.8	11.8	8.8	3343	Low	6	3	19	35	Ash Grove Cement (2)	Low	III 97	12.7	III 98	-14.9	800-221-4268
19.8	15.4	20.2	15.9	16.2	12.9	2312	Very high	7	NA	43	25	Cendant (7)	High	IV 98	40.2	III 98	-19.6	800-243-4361
15.0	11.0	12.4	9.2	13.1	10.3	2442	Very high	2	2	42	15	IBM (2)	Low	IV 98	13.5	III 98	-5.5	800-243-4361
22.3	17.5	19.3	15.5	16.4	13.3	1421	Very high	1	1	41	24	IBM (4)	Average	IV 98	22.3	III 98	-8.8	800-243-4361
13.6	9.6	11.1	7.7	12.3	9.3	3243	High	2	4	27	7	Microsoft (1)	Very low	IV 98	9.7	III 98	-6.0	800-243-4361
13.7	9.5	13.1	9.2	NA	NA	233	High	20	NA	41	14	Outdoor Systems (4)	High	IV 98	28.4	III 98	-16.1	800-243-4361
16.4	12.0	12.8	9.4	13.5	10.2	2342	Very high	7	2	42	17	IBM (3)	Low	IV 98	15.9	III 98	-5.7	800-243-4361
24.8	21.8	18.9	17.1	17.0	15.9	1421	Average	2	NA	44	68	Cendant (7)	High	IV 98	34.6	III 98	-14.6	800-243-4361
26.8	25.3	21.4	20.6	NA	NA	421	Average	3	NA	40	56	MCI WorldCom (5)	Average	IV 98	30.7	III 98	-12.1	800-243-4361
NA	NA	NA	NA	NA	NA		Low	8	NA	18	21	Charter One Financial (5)			NA		NA	800-334-3444
20.7	15.3	19.9	16.1	15.8	13.0	2411	Average	4	3	31	33	Schering-Plough (3)	Low	IV 98	18.9	III 98	-11.1	800-334-3444
25.8	21.2	20.3	16.4	18.7	15.5	1321	High	6	NA	43	33	HBO (4)	Average	IV 98	25.1	III 98	-12.6	800-426-0107
33.2	31.8	NA	NA	NA	NA	1	High	10	5	53	53	America Online (9)			NA		NA	800-426-0107
17.6	15.2	17.5	15.9	NA	NA	13	Average	8	NA	20	14	Atlantic Coast Airlines (3)	High	III 97	21.6	III 98	-20.7	800-927-4648
2.5	-0.8	7.7	4.1	17.8	14.7	1114	Average	16	1	28	10	Veritas DGC (6)	Very high	III 98	24.6	III 98	-25.8	800-426-0107
22.9	17.6	17.6	13.9	13.9	11.2	4231	Very high	3	2	28	-15	Philip Morris (4)	Average	IV 98	18.4	III 98	-16.8	800-426-0107
28.0	22.1	24.9	19.2	NA	NA	11	Low	78	NA	NA	-6	NA	Low	IV 98	21.5	III 98	-9.8	800-927-4648
18.1	13.0	17.2	13.3	NA	NA	12	Very high	7	NA	39	19	Providian Financial (5)	High	IV 98	21.0	III 98	-13.3	800-426-0107
28.9	26.8	21.9	19.4	16.9	14.1	3321	Very low	0	7	30	54	Schering-Plough (6)	Low	IV 98	22.3	III 98	-8.5	800-225-6292
8.2	5.5	8.1	5.5	9.6	6.9	3443	High	4	1	32	3	Conseco (4)	Very low	III 97	8.6	III 98	-6.9	800-225-6292
7.7	6.0	13.4	11.2	NA	NA	1114	Average	9	5	28	4	NCR (4)	Average	IV 98	11.7	III 98	-21.4	800-225-6292
21.4	19.5	18.4	16.7	NA	NA	231	Low	1	NA	26	35	Schering-Plough (6)	Low	IV 98	14.4	III 98	-6.6	800-225-6292
23.0	21.3	19.1	17.0	NA	NA	321	Low	5	97	27	23	Raisio Group (3)	Average	I 98	24.3	III 98	-19.9	800-225-6292
34.6	32.4	25.3	20.9	21.0	18.0	1231	Low	10	1	40	25	Monsanto (7)	Average	II 97	24.1	I 94	-12.8	800-225-6292
11.6	9.3	11.7	8.8	11.8	8.9	4233	Average	8	10	21	21	Ambac Financial Group (5)	Average	II 97	15.5	III 98	-22.3	800-225-6292
3.3	0.3	2.3	0.2	NA	NA	44	High	3	98	21	-33	Telecom Italia (7)	High	II 98	18.9	III 98	-22.4	800-225-6292
10.2	7.1	8.5	5.6	11.7	8.9	3143	Average	8	4	37	21	Wind River Systems (3)	High	IV 98	20.1	III 98	-21.8	800-225-6292
20.9	18.0	18.0	15.3	NA	NA	31	Low	41	3	32	26	General Electric (1)	Very low	IV 98	16.0	I 94	-4.6	800-662-4769
28.6	23.2	22.0	18.6	NA	NA	21	Average	3	3	41	35	MCI WorldCom (4)	High	IV 98	28.8	III 98	-12.4	800-662-4769
11.5	10.0	9.5	8.2	NA	NA	43	Very low	11	97	26	18	British Telecomm. (4)	Average	I 98	16.0	III 98	-16.1	800-662-4769
22.4	21.3	20.5	19.4	NA	NA	11	Very low	10	12	27	51	Citigroup (7)	Low	IV 98	17.2	III 98	-15.8	800-662-4769
16.5	15.1	14.1	12.6	14.0	11.9	2332	Very low	2	20	31	30	General Electric (1)	Very low	IV 98	12.2	III 98	-6.5	800-638-5660
28.1	27.7	23.9	23.4	NA	NA	11	Low	5	4	34	28	MCI WorldCom (2)	Low	IV 98	24.7	III 98	-12.1	800-638-5660
12.8	9.1	12.8	9.5	12.9	9.8	2333	Average	10	9	23	7	Amerada Hess (5)	Very low	II 97	8.3	III 98	-3.0	800-638-5660
23.6	21.6	20.5	18.5	NA	NA	21	Low	9	10	25	17	Mobil (2)	Very low	IV 98	13.1	III 98	-7.1	800-638-5660

MUTUAL FUND SCOREBOARD

FUND	OVERALL RATING (COMPARES RISK-ADJUSTED PERFORMANCE OF EACH FUND AGAINST ALL FUNDS)	CATEGORY (COMPARES RISK-ADJUSTED PERFORMANCE OF FUND WITHIN CATEGORY)	RATING	SIZE ASSETS $MIL.	SIZE % CHG. 1997-98	FEES SALES CHARGE (%)	FEES EXPENSE RATIO (%)	1997 RETURNS (%) PRE-TAX	1997 RETURNS (%) AFTER-TAX	1997 RETURNS (%) YIELD
T. ROWE PRICE EQUITY INDEX	A	Large-cap Blend	B+	3347.5	75	0.50*	0.40	28.3	27.8	1.0
T. ROWE PRICE EQUITY-INCOME ⚖	A	Large-cap Value	A	13495.1	6	No load	0.79	9.2	7.2	2.2
T. ROWE PRICE EUROPEAN STOCK	B+	Europe	B+	1548.6	52	No load	1.06	25.8	22.8	1.2
T. ROWE PRICE FINANCIAL SVCS.		Financial		224.3	26	No load	1.25	11.6	10.7	0.9
T. ROWE PRICE GROWTH & INCOME ⚖	B+	Large-cap Blend	B	3563.2	3	No load	0.78	10.0	7.6	1.9
T. ROWE PRICE GROWTH STOCK	B+	Large-cap Blend	B	5041.3	26	No load	0.75	27.4	24.0	0.7
T. ROWE PRICE HEALTH SCIENCE ⚖		Health		316.6	17	No load	1.18	22.4	21.2	0.0
T. ROWE PRICE INTL. STOCK ⚖	C-	Foreign	C	10141.8	4	No load	0.85	16.1	15.0	1.4
T. ROWE PRICE MEDIA & TELECOMMUNICATIONS	C	Communications	C-	246.1	84	No load	1.21	35.1	34.0	0.0
T. ROWE PRICE MID-CAP GROWTH	C	Mid-cap Growth	A	3310.2	80	No load	0.95	22.0	21.4	0.0
T. ROWE PRICE MID-CAP VALUE		Mid-cap Value		221.3	2	No load	1.25	1.4	-0.4	1.3
T. ROWE PRICE NEW AMERICA GROWTH ⚖	C	Mid-cap Growth	B+	2064.5	17	No load	0.96	17.9	15.9	0.0
T. ROWE PRICE NEW ASIA	F	Pacific/Asia ex-Japan	C	622.3	-20	No load	1.10	-11.1	-11.6	1.8
T. ROWE PRICE NEW ERA	C-	Natural Resources	B+	996.6	-33	No load	0.74	-9.9	-12.8	1.7
T. ROWE PRICE NEW HORIZONS ⚖	C-	Mid-cap Growth	C	5228.5	2	No load‡	0.88	6.3	5.0	0.0
T. ROWE PRICE PERSONAL STRATEGY BALANCED		Domestic Hybrid		421.4	50	No load	1.05	13.9	12.2	2.8
T. ROWE PRICE PERSONAL STRATEGY INCOME		Domestic Hybrid		213.2	117	No load	0.95	11.5	10.1	3.7
T. ROWE PRICE SCIENCE & TECHNOLOGY	C-	Technology	C	4695.6	33	No load	0.94	42.4	41.5	0.0
T. ROWE PRICE SMALL CAP STOCK	C	Small-cap Blend	B+	1152.6	41	No load	1.02	-3.5	-4.1	0.5
T. ROWE PRICE SMALL-CAP VALUE	C	Small Value	B	1631.9	-22	1.00*	0.87	-12.5	-13.9	1.2
T. ROWE PRICE SPECTRUM GROWTH ⚖	B	Mid-cap Blend	B	2768.2	6	No load	0.00	13.6	11.4	1.0
T. ROWE PRICE VALUE		Mid-cap Value		774.5	42	No load	1.05	6.9	5.3	1.0
PRINCIPAL CAPITAL VALUE A (aaaa)	B	Large-cap Value	C	565.1	7	4.75	0.70†	12.1	10.2	1.6
PRINCIPAL GROWTH A (bbbb) ⚖	B	Large-cap Blend	C-	396.0	17	4.75	1.03†	20.4	20.2	0.5
PRINCIPAL INTERNATIONAL A (cccc)	C-	Foreign	C	302.8	6	4.75	1.39†	8.5	7.0	1.2
PRINCIPAL MIDCAP A (dddd) ⚖	C	Mid-cap Blend	C	332.9	-5	4.75	1.26†	-0.2	-0.2	0.0
PROFUNDS ULTRAOTC INVESTOR		Large-cap Growth		239.0	NM	No load	1.07	185.3	185.3	0.0
PRUDENTIAL BALANCED B	C	Domestic Hybrid	F	508.3	-11	5.00**	1.94†	7.4	5.2	1.7
PRUDENTIAL EQUITY B	C	Large-cap Value	C-	2925.3	-6	5.00**	1.63†	7.6	5.8	0.5
PRUDENTIAL EQUITY-INCOME B ⚖	C	Mid-cap Value	C-	1262.3	-4	5.00**	1.69†	-3.6	-5.3	1.5
PRUDENTIAL JENN. GROWTH B		Large-cap Growth		986.1	127	5.00**	1.84†	36.7	35.8	0.0
PRUDENTIAL SMALL CO. VALUE B	C-	Small-cap Value	C-	532.1	-21	5.00**	1.96†	-11.6	-13.7	0.0
PRUDENTIAL UTILITY A	C	Utilities	C-	2741.8	6	5.00	0.82†	8.0	5.6	2.5
PRUDENTIAL WORLD GLOBAL B	C-	World	C	303.3	-4	5.00**	2.07†	22.5	21.5	0.1
PUTNAM ASSET ALLOCATION: BAL. A		Domestic Hybrid		944.9	30	5.75	1.27†	11.7	10.7	1.8
PUTNAM ASSET ALLOCATION: CONS. A		Domestic Hybrid		397.8	27	5.75	1.38†	9.1	7.6	3.8
PUTNAM ASSET ALLOCATION: GROWTH A		Large-cap Blend		675.3	25	5.75	1.39†	13.7	13.0	0.7
PUTNAM BALANCED RETIREMENT A	B+	Domestic Hybrid	B	658.7	10	5.75	1.15†	9.2	6.6	3.9
PUTNAM CAPITAL APPRECIATION B		Mid-cap Blend		1643.7	47	5.00**‡	1.78†	7.9	7.3	0.0
PUTNAM DIVERSIFIED EQUITY B		World		350.0	14	5.00**	2.00†	17.1	15.0	0.0
PUTNAM EQUITY INCOME A	B+	Large-cap Value	B	1115.1	24	5.75	1.06†	12.7	9.8	1.6
PUTNAM EUROPE GROWTH A	B	Europe	C	858.1	105	5.75	1.32†	23.6	22.0	0.9
PUTNAM FUND FOR GROWTH & INCOME A	B	Large-cap Value	C	20254.0	17	5.75	0.86†	15.2	12.8	2.1
GEORGE PUTNAM OF BOSTON A	B+	Domestic Hybrid	B	3472.8	21	5.75	1.00†	10.6	7.9	3.1
PUTNAM GLOBAL GROWTH A	C	World	B	3085.1	16	5.75	1.24†	28.8	28.0	0.4
PUTNAM GROWTH & INCOME II B		Large-cap Value		1480.9	16	5.00**	1.75†	11.6	9.4	0.9
PUTNAM GROWTH OPPORTUNITIES B		Large-cap Growth		454.2	390	5.00**	2.00†	46.3	46.3	0.0
PUTNAM HEALTH SCIENCES A	B+	Health	B	2686.6	41	5.75	1.00†	27.1	25.2	0.0
PUTNAM INTL. GROWTH & INCOME A		Foreign		396.8	22	5.75	1.36†	11.6	9.7	2.1
PUTNAM INTL. GROWTH A	C	Foreign	B+	2065.3	87	5.75	1.36†	19.0	18.1	1.1
PUTNAM INTL. NEW OPPORTUNITIES B		Foreign		872.3	-7	5.00**	2.50†	15.0	15.0	0.0
PUTNAM INVESTORS A	B	Large	B	3694.5	90	5.75	0.95†	35.5	34.8	0.0
PUTNAM NEW OPPORTUNITIES A	C-	Mid-Cap	C	9465.0	12	5.75‡	0.98†	24.4	23.5	0.0
PUTNAM NEW VALUE B		Large-cap Value		412.2	-11	5.00**	1.91†	4.7	2.7	0.1
PUTNAM OTC & EMERGING GROWTH A	D	Mid-cap Growth	D	2239.6	-2	5.75	1.00†	11.0	10.2	0.0
PUTNAM UTIL. GROWTH & INCOME A	B+	Utilities	B	857.8	15	5.75	1.05†	14.8	13.1	3.2
PUTNAM VISTA A	C-	Mid-cap Growth	B	3071.4	10	5.75	0.98†	19.5	17.7	0.0
PUTNAM VOYAGER A	C	Large-cap Growth	C-	13901.2	18	5.75	0.96†	24.1	22.2	0.0
PUTNAM VOYAGER II A	C-	Mid-cap Growth	B	659.4	24	5.75	1.22†	23.5	22.6	0.0
RAINIER CORE EQUITY		Large-cap Blend		901.1	81	No load	1.14†	20.7	19.0	0.3
RAINIER SMALL/MID CAP EQUITY		Mid-Cap Blend		542.4	54	No load‡	1.26†	3.0	1.8	0.0
RIGHTIME BLUE CHIP ⚖	A	Large-cap Blend	A	286.6	11	4.75	2.09†	33.9	31.2	0.0
ROBERTSON STEPHENS EMERGING GROWTH A	D	Small-cap Growth	B	394.4	58	No load	1.50†	28.0	26.4	0.0
ROBERTSON STEPHENS VALUE + GROWTH A	C-	Large-cap Growth	F	678.3	-10	No load	1.44†	27.4	24.3	0.0
RODNEY SQUARE LG. CAP. GRTH. EQ. (eeee) ⚖	C	Mid-cap Growth	B+	204.1	123	4.00	1.43	23.6	20.9	0.0
ROYCE PREMIER	B	Small-cap Value	B+	556.2	4	1.00*	1.24	6.7	6.3	0.5
ROYCE TOTAL RETURN	A	Small-cap Value	A	240.0	99	1.00*	1.25	4.8	3.6	1.9
RYDEX NOVA INVESTOR	C	Large-cap Blend	D	941.2	21	No load	1.11	35.1	34.6	1.2
RYDEX OTC INVESTOR		Large-cap Growth		1109.4	438	No load	1.13	86.5	86.0	0.0
RYDEX URSA INVESTOR		Large-cap Blend		420.4	11	No load	1.34	-19.0	-19.1	0.3

*Includes redemption fee. **Includes deferred sales charge. †12(b)-1 plan in effect. ‡Not currently accepting new accounts. §Less than 0.5% of assets. NA=Not available. NM=Not meaningful. (aaaa) Formerly Princor Capital Accumulation A. (bbbb) Formerly Princor Growth A. (cccc) Formerly Princor World A. (dddd) Formerly Princor Emerging Growth A. (eeee) Formerly Rodney Square Multi-Manager Growth.

3Y Pretax	3Y Aftertax	5Y Pretax	5Y Aftertax	10Y Pretax	10Y Aftertax	Results vs. All Funds	Turnover	Cash %	Foreign %	P-E Ratio	Untaxed Gains %	Largest Holding Company (% Assets)	Risk Level	Best QTR	Best %RET	Worst QTR	Worst %RET	Telephone
27.9	26.9	23.7	22.5	NA	NA	3 1 1	Very low	0	2	33	36	Microsoft (3)	Low	IV 98	21.3	III 98	-10.0	800-638-5660
19.2	16.6	18.8	16.1	15.2	12.7	3 3 1 2	Low	5	5	24	24	Amoco (2)	Very low	II 97	11.4	III 98	-7.5	800-638-5660
22.8	20.9	18.6	17.2	NA	NA	3 2 2	Low	4	100	29	29	Wolters Kluwer (3)	Low	I 98	17.9	III 98	-14.0	800-638-5660
NA	NA	NA	NA	NA	NA		Average	8	10	19	19	First Union (4)			NA		NA	800-638-5660
19.5	17.3	17.4	15.2	15.0	12.9	3 2 2 2	Very low	5	4	27	33	Pfizer (3)	Low	II 97	12.9	III 98	-9.6	800-638-5660
25.2	21.8	21.0	18.0	17.7	15.0	2 2 2 1	Low	6	17	33	44	FHLMC (3)	Low	IV 98	23.1	III 98	-11.4	800-638-5660
22.8	21.2	NA	NA	NA	NA	2	High	9	9	44	22	Eli Lilly (5)			NA		NA	800-638-5660
11.4	10.3	8.9	7.6	10.5	8.9	4 2 4 3	Very low	3	100	29	25	Wolters Kluwer (3)	Average	IV 98	18.3	III 98	-13.7	800-638-5660
22.0	18.1	21.1	18.2	NA	NA	1 1	Low	10	8	43	41	MCI WorldCom (3)	High	IV 98	34.0	III 98	-18.6	800-638-5660
21.7	21.0	20.6	19.7	NA	NA	1 2	Low	11	5	34	27	U.S. Foodservice (2)	Average	IV 98	26.8	III 98	-17.5	800-638-5660
NA	NA	NA	NA	NA	NA		Very low	6	7	22	10	Valassis Communications (2)			NA		NA	800-638-5660
19.7	17.5	18.0	16.2	19.2	17.9	1 1 1 2	Low	5	1	33	43	Waste Management (3)	High	IV 98	27.7	III 98	-21.3	800-638-5660
-14.1	-14.4	-11.9	-12.7	NA	NA	1 4 4	Low	15	100	20	-64	Hutchison Whampoa (10)	Very high	IV 98	18.4	IV 97	-27.1	800-638-5660
7.5	4.5	9.6	6.9	9.2	6.7	3 4 2 4	Low	4	23	27	14	Mobil (6)	High	III 97	11.3	III 98	-12.4	800-638-5660
10.9	9.2	16.3	13.8	17.4	14.6	2 1 1 4	Average	4	3	36	33	Paychex (2)	High	IV 98	24.6	III 98	-21.0	800-638-5660
15.3	13.5	NA	NA	NA	NA	2	Low	5	26	27	13	Philip Morris (1)			NA		NA	800-638-5660
12.8	10.2	NA	NA	NA	NA	2	Low	11	22	28	5	S&P 500 Dep. Rec. (1)			NA		NA	800-638-5660
18.3	15.8	24.4	21.7	25.6	22.8	1 1 1 2	High	3	3	45	38	EMC/Mass. (4)	High	IV 98	47.9	III 98	-17.3	800-638-5660
14.6	12.9	15.1	12.4	13.6	10.7	4 1 1 3	Low	12	4	24	13	U.S. Foodservice (2)	Average	II 97	15.5	III 98	-19.4	800-638-5660
11.7	9.9	12.2	10.3	14.1	12.2	3 1 2 4	Very low	4	1	19	16	Poe & Brown (2)	Average	III 97	14.9	III 98	-20.2	800-638-5660
17.2	14.7	16.2	13.7	NA	NA	2 2 2	Low	4	5	31	21	T. Rowe Price International (22)	Low	IV 98	18.6	III 98	-13.4	800-638-5660
21.1	18.3	NA	NA	NA	NA		Average	3	11	24	6	Amoco (2)			NA		NA	800-638-5660
21.2	17.8	18.7	15.8	14.5	12.0	3 3 2 2	Low	6	NA	25	30	First Union (5)	Low	II 97	13.3	III 98	-10.4	800-451-5447
20.2	19.6	19.0	18.2	17.8	16.6	1 2 2 1	Very low	8	5	31	50	Microsoft (3)	Average	IV 98	19.1	III 98	-15.6	800-451-5447
14.6	13.2	9.8	8.4	10.9	9.8	4 1 4 3	Low	4	98	20	18	Nokia Cl. A ADR (3)	Average	IV 98	15.5	III 98	-17.8	800-451-5447
13.5	12.9	15.1	14.5	16.2	15.5	2 1 1 3	Very low	7	3	29	34	EVI Weatherford (3)	Average	IV 98	17.0	III 98	-21.2	800-451-5447
NA	NA	NA	NA	NA	NA			2	NA	16	32	Nasdaq 100 (Fut.) (97)			NA		NA	888-776-3637
12.2	9.0	9.7	7.1	10.8	8.3	3 3 4 3	High	0	4	27	8	Duke Energy (1)	Low	II 97	10.9	III 98	-8.6	800-225-1852
15.7	13.2	15.5	13.2	15.9	13.6	1 3 2 2	Very low	9	9	24	32	Chubb (3)	Low	IV 98	14.0	III 98	-15.5	800-225-1852
16.5	14.0	13.6	11.2	13.4	11.3	3 2 3 2	Low	2	11	17	17	Lehman Brothers Holdings (5)	Average	II 97	16.3	III 98	-18.5	800-225-1852
26.4	25.4	NA	NA	NA	NA	1	Average	3	5	42	32	MCI WorldCom (4)			NA		NA	800-225-1852
13.0	9.2	11.3	8.2	13.4	11.0	3 1 3 3	Average	6	1	16	-2	Financial Security Assurance (3)	Average	III 97	15.8	III 98	-23.3	800-225-1852
19.0	15.8	14.3	11.5	NA	NA	2 4 2	Very low	4	23	22	34	Williams (3)	Low	IV 96	12.4	I 94	-4.8	800-225-1852
14.7	12.4	10.3	8.5	9.1	8.1	4 2 4 3	Average	9	55	30	35	Credito Italiano (3)	High	IV 98	21.5	III 98	-14.9	800-225-1852
15.1	13.0	NA	NA	NA	NA	3	High	0	22	30	13	U.S. Treasury (Fut.) (7)			NA		NA	800-225-1581
10.7	8.7	NA	NA	NA	NA	3	Very high	1	22	30	8	U.S. Treasury (Fut.) (10)			NA		NA	800-225-1581
16.9	15.3	NA	NA	NA	NA	2	High	0	18	33	16	General Electric (1)			NA		NA	800-225-1581
13.7	10.5	13.0	10.3	12.7	9.8	3 3 3 3	High	6	4	26	10	Exxon (1)	Very low	II 97	8.6	III 98	-5.5	800-225-1581
21.6	20.3	NA	NA	NA	NA	2	Low	6	8	30	15	General Electric (3)			NA		NA	800-225-1581
18.5	15.7	NA	NA	NA	NA	2	High	1	53	32	20	Schering-Plough (2)			NA		NA	800-225-1581
20.0	18.1	18.7	17.1	14.4	12.1	3 3 1 2	Average	4	4	26	13	DuPont (2)	Low	IV 98	13.9	III 98	-9.6	800-225-1581
22.7	20.5	19.0	17.4	NA	NA	2 2 1	Average	2	99	23	12	Nestle (3)	Average	I 98	20.0	III 98	-18.3	800-225-1581
20.3	17.2	18.9	16.0	16.2	13.2	2 3 1 2	Average	1	1	27	19	General Electric (3)	Low	IV 98	16.7	III 98	-10.1	800-225-1581
15.9	12.9	15.1	12.2	13.8	10.7	2 4 2 2	High	4	4	24	11	Citicorp (1)	Very low	II 97	9.6	III 98	-6.1	800-225-1581
19.4	16.5	14.2	11.8	13.1	11.3	3 2 4 2	High	2	51	42	19	Microsoft (2)	Average	IV 98	21.9	III 98	-12.3	800-225-1581
18.5	15.9	NA	NA	NA	NA	2	Average	2	3	27	11	Xerox (3)			NA		NA	800-225-1581
NA	NA	NA	NA	NA	NA		Average	2	NA	44	13	Warner-Lambert (5)			NA		NA	800-225-1581
23.7	21.6	26.2	24.5	21.5	19.5	1 4 1 1	Low	3	11	46	34	Pfizer (5)	Average	II 97	20.3	III 98	-6.4	800-225-1581
NA	NA	NA	NA	NA	NA		Average	3	95	21	7	Generale des Eaux Minls. Vit. (3)			NA		NA	800-225-1581
17.6	16.5	13.2	12.3	NA	NA	2 4 2	Average	7	96	23	10	ING Groep (3)	Average	IV 98	22.5	III 98	-19.1	800-225-1581
10.4	9.5	NA	NA	NA	NA	4	High	2	99	39	16	Equant (3)			NA		NA	800-225-1581
30.3	27.6	24.1	20.9	20.2	16.5	1 3 1 1	Average	5	1	39	31	Tyco Intl. (3)	Average	IV 98	25.3	III 98	-12.0	800-225-1581
19.1	18.6	20.6	20.2	NA	NA	1 1 2	Average	3	4	42	42	America Online (3)	High	IV 98	29.4	III 98	-18.9	800-225-1581
NA	NA	NA	NA	NA	NA	3	High	2	3	27	13	Philip Morris (3)			NA		NA	800-225-1581
8.6	7.5	15.3	13.3	17.4	15.2	2 1 1 4	High	5	3	40	24	Compuware (6)	Very high	IV 98	29.6	III 98	-26.6	800-225-1581
19.0	16.0	15.5	13.1	NA	NA	3 3 2	Average	1	10	23	28	Duke Energy (4)	Very low	IV 97	12.2	I 94	-14.5	800-225-1581
21.7	19.6	19.3	17.4	18.4	15.4	2 1 1 2	High	2	1	36	27	Costco (2)	High	IV 98	23.8	III 98	-17.4	800-225-1581
20.8	18.9	19.9	18.1	20.3	18.1	1 1 1 2	Average	3	7	38	37	Tele-Comm.-TCI Ventures Cl. A (2)	High	IV 98	26.7	III 98	-16.2	800-225-1581
18.0	17.7	19.9	19.1	NA	NA	1 2	Average	3	9	41	32	CBS (2)	High	IV 98	28.4	III 98	-17.7	800-225-1581
25.8	22.5	NA	NA	NA	NA	1	High	1	3	31	15	Microsoft (2)			NA		NA	800-248-6314
18.6	15.8	NA	NA	NA	NA		High	2	2	25	5	New Century Energies (2)			NA		NA	800-248-6314
15.6	13.4	15.3	12.4	13.0	10.8	2 4 2 2	Low	100	3	33	42	S&P 500 (Fut.) (13)	Very low	IV 98	15.6	II 97	-1.9	800-242-1421
22.6	17.6	19.1	14.8	20.2	17.0	1 3 1 2	Very high	8	7	35	22	ECsoft Group ADR (3)	High	IV 98	38.4	III 98	-23.4	800-766-3863
18.3	14.8	23.8	21.5	NA	NA	1 1	Very high	0	NA	41	35	Merrill Lynch (4)	High	IV 98	24.1	IV 95	-14.7	800-766-3863
25.1	21.7	20.2	16.9	17.7	15.3	2 2 2 1	Low	1	NA	38	27	Merck (3)	Average	IV 98	25.3	III 98	-12.4	800-336-9970
14.3	12.8	12.7	11.2	NA	NA	3 3	Low	1	2	22	19	National Computer Systems (4)	Low	IV 98	15.1	III 98	-14.5	800-221-4268
17.6	15.2	16.7	14.3	NA	NA	1 3	Low	14	4	18	5	Lincoln Electric Hldgs. (2)	Very low	II 97	9.9	III 98	-10.5	800-221-4268
34.2	34.0	28.2	27.3	NA	NA	1 1	Very low	0	1	33	15	S&P 500 Index (Call) @550 (37)	High	IV 98	31.7	III 98	-16.9	800-820-0888
48.1	48.0	NA	NA	NA	NA	1	Very high	0	1	50	40	Microsoft (24)			NA		NA	800-820-0888
-17.6	-17.6	NA	NA	NA	NA	4	Very low	0	NA	NA	-58	NA			NA		NA	800-820-0888

DATA: MORNINGSTAR, INC., CHICAGO, IL.

MUTUAL FUND SCOREBOARD

FUND	OVERALL RATING (COMPARES RISK-ADJUSTED PERFORMANCE OF EACH FUND AGAINST ALL FUNDS)	CATEGORY (COMPARES RISK-ADJUSTED PERFORMANCE OF FUND WITHIN CATEGORY)	RATING	SIZE ASSETS $MIL.	SIZE % CHG. 1997-98	FEES SALES CHARGE (%)	FEES EXPENSE RATIO (%)	1997 RETURNS (%) PRE-TAX	1997 RETURNS (%) AFTER-TAX	1997 RETURNS (%) YIELD
SAFECO EQUITY NO LOAD	A	Large-cap Blend	B+	2024.9	37	No load	0.73	24.9	23.6	0.9
SAFECO GROWTH NO LOAD	C−	Small-cap Blend	B	1394.2	118	No load	0.85	4.4	3.5	0.0
SAFECO INCOME NO LOAD	B	Large-cap Value	C	373.4	−7	No load	0.85	6.3	4.4	2.6
SALOMON BROS. INVESTORS O	B+	Large-cap Value	B	650.9	7	No load ‡	0.69	15.4	13.0	1.0
SALOMON BROS. OPPORTUNITY ⚖	B	Large-cap Value	C−	202.3	0	No load	1.12	4.9	2.6	0.8
SCHWAB INTERNATIONAL INDEX INV.	C−	Foreign	B+	469.0	44	0.75*	0.61	15.9	15.5	0.9
SCHWAB MARKETTRACK BALANCED (ffff)		Domestic Hybrid		297.7	84	No load	0.78	13.7	12.7	2.4
SCHWAB MARKETTRACK GROWTH (gggg)		Large-cap Blend		311.4	69	No load	0.75	15.2	14.6	1.5
SCHWAB 1000 INVESTOR	B+	Large-cap Blend	B	3820.4	35	0.50*	0.47	27.2	26.9	0.8
SCHWAB S&P 500 INVESTOR		Large-cap Blend		2145.1	108	No load	0.38	28.1	27.7	0.8
SCHWAB SMALL CAP INDEX INVESTOR	C−	Small-cap Blend	C	548.5	28	0.50*	0.52	−3.6	−4.7	0.3
SCUDDER BALANCED	B+	Domestic Hybrid	C	262.0	66	No load	1.02	21.1	19.1	1.8
SCUDDER DEVELOPMENT ⚖	D	Small-cap Growth	C−	782.9	−9	No load	1.41	8.0	6.0	0.0
SCUDDER GLOBAL ⚖	C	World	B	1613.9	3	No load	1.34	12.6	10.1	1.7
SCUDDER GREATER EUROPE GROWTH		Europe		1268.0	455	No load	1.66	29.2	29.1	0.2
SCUDDER GROWTH & INCOME ⚖	B	Large-cap Value	C	7633.9	12	No load	0.76	6.1	3.8	2.2
SCUDDER INTERNATIONAL	C−	Foreign	B+	2945.1	13	No load	1.18	18.6	16.2	0.0
SCUDDER LARGE COMPANY GROWTH	B	Large-cap Growth	B	626.9	104	No load	1.21	33.2	31.9	0.0
SCUDDER LARGE COMPANY VALUE	C	Large-cap Value	D	2355.5	6	No load	0.93	9.5	7.8	0.6
SCUDDER LATIN AMERICA ⚖	F	Latin America	B	462.3	−52	No load	1.89	−29.7	−30.6	2.0
SCUDDER PATHWAY BALANCED		Domestic Hybrid		242.9	17	No load	NA	7.6	6.0	3.0
SCUDDER SMALL COMPANY VALUE		Small-cap Value		279.0	32	1.00*	1.50	−5.5	−5.8	0.2
SECURITY EQUITY A ⚖	B+	Large-cap Blend	B	942.4	25	5.75	1.03	26.5	24.7	0.3
SEI INDEX S&P 500 INDEX E	A	Large-cap Blend	B+	1449.2	29	No load	0.25	28.3	27.5	1.2
SEI INSTITUTIONAL LARGE CAP GROWTH A		Large-cap Growth		1890.4	106	No load	0.85	38.8	38.3	0.1
SEI INSTITUTIONAL LARGE CAP VALUE A	B+	Large-cap Value	B	1749.4	82	No load	0.85	11.4	9.6	1.3
SEI INSTITUTIONAL SMALL CAP GROWTH A	D	Small-cap Growth	C−	723.9	38	No load	1.10	5.6	5.5	0.0
SEI INSTITUTIONAL SMALL CAP VALUE A		Small-cap Value		511.8	44	No load	1.11	−3.2	−3.3	0.3
SELECTED AMERICAN	B	Large-cap Value	C	2905.1	31	No load	0.96†	16.3	15.9	0.5
SELIGMAN CAPITAL A ⚖	C−	Mid-cap Growth	C	271.8	−4	4.75	1.05†	19.1	18.3	0.0
SELIGMAN COMMON STOCK A	C	Large-cap Blend	C−	740.4	1	4.75	1.13	17.4	13.4	1.6
SELIGMAN COMMUNICATIONS & INFO. A	D	Technology	D	3362.2	8	4.75	1.53†	33.9	33.6	0.0
SELIGMAN FRONTIER A	D	Small-cap Growth	B	411.3	−25	4.75	1.52†	−2.2	−2.2	0.0
SELIGMAN GROWTH A ⚖	C	Large-cap Growth	C	868.9	19	4.75	1.16†	35.2	32.6	0.1
SELIGMAN HENDERSON GLOBAL SMALL B		World		369.0	55	5.00**	2.43†	4.9	4.9	0.0
SELIGMAN HENDERSON GLOBAL TECHNOLOGY A		Technology		512.0	−5	4.75	1.67†	30.7	29.9	0.0
SELIGMAN INCOME A	B	Domestic Hybrid	C	256.7	−5	4.75	1.14†	7.3	4.6	4.3
SENTINEL BALANCED A ⚖	B	Domestic Hybrid	C	336.4	5	5.00	1.16†	11.9	9.4	2.6
SENTINEL COMMON STOCK A	B	Large-cap Value	C	1637.3	7	5.00	1.04†	14.0	11.8	0.9
SEQUOIA ⚖	A	Large-cap Value	A	4806.3	31	No load ‡	1.00	35.3	33.7	0.2
SIFE TRUST A-I	B	Financial	C−	975.9	−7	5.00	1.25	5.0	2.5	1.0
SIT MID CAP GROWTH ⚖	C−	Mid-cap Growth	C	363.9	−5	No load	1.00	6.8	3.1	0.0
SKYLINE SPECIAL EQUITIES ⚖	C	Small-cap Value	C	445.8	−4	No load ‡	1.48	−7.2	−7.5	0.0
SMALLCAP WORLD	C−	Small-cap Growth	B+	8108.8	−6	5.75	1.06†	0.4	−0.8	0.4
SMITH BARNEY AGGR. GROWTH A ⚖	C−	Mid-cap Growth	C	418.2	23	5.00	1.21†	35.1	34.5	0.0
SMITH BARNEY APPRECIATION A	B+	Large-cap Blend	C	2853.2	15	5.00	0.95†	20.5	18.1	1.1
SMITH BARNEY BALANCED B (hhhh) ⚖	C	Domestic Hybrid	F	659.9	−25	5.00**	1.52†	11.4	2.8	2.7
SMITH BARNEY CONC. ALLOCATION BAL. B (iiii)		Domestic Hybrid		239.0	32	5.00**	1.35†	8.0	6.5	2.6
SMITH BARNEY CONC. ALLOCATION GRTH. B (jjjj)		Domestic Hybrid		418.2	31	5.00**	1.35†	12.7	11.8	0.9
SMITH BARNEY CONC. ALLOC. HIGH GR. A (kkkk)		Mid-cap Blend		328.0	34	5.00	0.60†	15.5	14.5	0.5
SMITH BARNEY CONC. ALLOC. SOCIAL A (llll)	B+	Domestic Hybrid	B+	251.9	27	5.00	1.28†	27.6	26.5	1.1
SMITH BARNEY CONTRARIAN B (mmmm) ⚖		Mid-cap Value		307.1	−44	5.00**	2.05†	−1.8	−2.4	0.0
SMITH BARNEY FUNDAMENTAL VALUE B	C	Large-cap Value	D	782.6	−11	5.00**	1.90†	15.0	13.4	0.0
SMITH BARNEY LARGE CAP. GROWTH B		Large-cap Growth		634.5	235	5.00**	NA†	53.7	53.7	0.0
SMITH BARNEY LARGE CAP. VALUE A (nnnn) ⚖	C	Large-cap Value	C−	804.2	14	5.00	0.92†	14.6	12.9	1.4
SMITH BARNEY PREM. TOT. RET. B	B+	Large-cap Value	B+	3178.1	2	5.00**	1.60†	5.7	3.3	1.3
SMITH BARNEY INTL. EQUITY A ⚖	D	Foreign	D	421.8	−3	5.00	1.31†	11.7	11.7	0.0
SOGEN INTERNATIONAL A ⚖	C	International Hybrid	B	2817.3	−30	3.75	1.19†	−0.3	−2.6	4.4
SOGEN OVERSEAS A	C	Foreign	A	679.8	−29	3.75	1.22†	2.5	−0.2	6.1
SOUND SHORE ⚖	B+	Mid-cap Value	A	1953.1	50	No load	1.08	4.4	4.2	0.7
SOUTHTRUST CORE EQUITY (oooo)	C	Large-cap Value	C−	379.8	9	4.50	0.94	12.6	10.1	0.5
SPECTRA ⚖	C	Large-cap Growth	C	224.2	132	No load	2.12	47.9	47.8	0.0
SSGA EMERGING MARKETS		Diversified Emerging Mkts.		236.4	−7	No load	1.25†	−15.9	−16.9	3.5
SSGA GROWTH & INCOME ⚖	A	Large-cap Blend	B+	204.1	154	No load	0.95†	34.7	29.7	0.4
SSGA MATRIX EQUITY ⚖	B	Large-cap Blend	C	566.5	20	No load	0.69†	21.7	15.6	0.7
SSGA S&P 500 INDEX	A	Large-cap Blend	B+	2250.1	55	No load	0.17†	28.4	23.4	1.3
SSGA SMALL CAP	C−	Small-cap Blend	B	453.3	61	No load ‡	1.04†	−7.6	−7.6	0.1
STAGECOACH ASSET ALLOCATION A	B+	Domestic Hybrid	B	1377.4	15	4.50	0.95†	25.6	22.7	1.6
STAGECOACH EQUITY INDEX A ⚖	B+	Large-cap Blend	B+	607.3	18	No load	0.89†	27.7	26.2	0.8
STAGECOACH GROWTH A	C	Large-cap Blend	C−	348.7	−2	5.25	1.12†	29.2	25.2	0.3

*Includes redemption fee. **Includes deferred sales charge. †12(b)-1 plan in effect. ‡Not currently accepting new accounts. §Less than 0.5% of assets. NA=Not available. NM=Not meaningful. (ffff) Formerly Schwab Asset Director-Balanced Growth. (gggg) Formerly Schwab Asset Director-High Growth. (hhhh) Formerly Smith Barney Utilities B. (iiii) Formerly Smith Barney Concert Balanced B. (jjjj) Formerly Smith Barney Concert Growth B. (kkkk) Formerly Smith Barney Concert High Growth A. (llll) Formerly Smith Barney Concert Social Aware A. (mmmm) Formerly Smith Barney Managed Growth B. (nnnn) Formerly Smith Barney Equity Income A. (oooo) Formerly SouthTrust Vulcan Stock.

AVERAGE ANNUAL TOTAL RETURNS (%) — HISTORY — PORTFOLIO DATA — RISK — TELEPHONE

3 YEARS PRETAX	3 YEARS AFTERTAX	5 YEARS PRETAX	5 YEARS AFTERTAX	10 YEARS PRETAX	10 YEARS AFTERTAX	RESULTS VS. ALL FUNDS	TURNOVER	CASH %	FOREIGN %	P-E RATIO	UNTAXED GAINS (%)	LARGEST HOLDING COMPANY (% ASSETS)	RISK LEVEL	BEST QTR	BEST %RET	WORST QTR	WORST %RET	TELEPHONE
24.7	21.9	21.7	18.8	19.8	16.9	2 1 1 1	Low	2	2	29	31	Chase Manhattan (3)	Low	IV 98	18.7	III 98	-7.8	800-426-6730
24.4	20.7	19.0	14.1	16.6	12.9	2 3 2 1	Average	1	3	26	10	Green Tree Financial (8)	High	IV 98	19.5	III 98	-25.4	800-426-6730
18.6	15.0	16.5	13.4	13.5	10.9	4 3 2 2	Average	2	2	27	25	CCA Prison Realty Trust (5)	Low	IV 98	14.6	III 98	-17.5	800-426-6730
23.9	20.3	20.6	16.8	16.6	12.7	3 2 1 1	Average	8	12	25	36	Viacom Cl. B (3)	Low	IV 98	17.4	III 98	-12.4	800-725-6666
18.6	16.9	17.8	16.0	14.5	12.8	4 2 2 2	Very low	19	12	20	63	Bank of New York (13)	Average	II 97	16.1	III 98	-14.7	800-725-6666
10.7	10.3	10.0	9.6	NA	NA	4 3	Very low	3	100	29	21	Royal Dutch Petroleum (2)	Average	IV 98	19.2	III 98	-14.9	800-435-4000
14.2	13.1	NA	NA	NA	NA	3	High	4	19	30	13	Schwab Long-Term Tax-Free (23)			NA		NA	800-435-4000
16.9	15.8	NA	NA	NA	NA	2	High	4	22	30	18	Schwab Small Cap Index (20)			NA		NA	800-435-4000
26.8	26.4	22.7	22.2	NA	NA	3 1 1	Very low	0	0	33	47	General Electric (3)	Average	IV 98	21.9	III 98	-10.7	800-435-4000
NA	NA	NA	NA	NA	NA	1	Very low	2	2	33	24	General Electric (3)			NA		NA	800-435-4000
11.9	11.3	11.6	11.2	NA	NA	2 3	Low	0	1	24	10	Ocean Energy (New) (§)	High	II 97	18.1	III 98	-20.9	800-435-4000
18.4	16.2	15.4	13.7	NA	NA	3 2	Low	5	NA	43	23	General Electric (3)	Low	IV 98	14.7	III 98	-6.3	800-225-2470
8.3	5.8	12.6	9.9	15.3	12.8	1 2 1 4	Average	4	1	38	41	Cintas (4)	High	IV 98	24.8	III 98	-19.9	800-225-2470
14.5	11.5	11.6	9.5	13.6	11.8	2 2 4 3	Average	2	67	27	22	USEC (2)	Average	II 97	13.6	III 98	-12.3	800-225-2470
28.0	27.0	NA	NA	NA	NA	1	Average	9	99	34	18	Telefonica (2)			NA		NA	800-225-2470
19.1	16.6	17.9	15.4	16.4	13.6	2 2 2 2	Low	3	14	25	22	Ford Motor (3)	Low	II 97	15.3	III 98	-13.4	800-225-2470
13.6	11.4	9.8	7.9	10.6	8.8	4 2 4 3	Average	10	99	32	24	Hoechst (3)	Average	IV 98	14.8	III 98	-14.4	800-225-2470
27.9	25.9	22.3	20.2	NA	NA	3 2 1	Average	5	NA	43	36	General Electric (5)	Average	IV 98	26.5	III 98	-12.3	800-225-2470
20.2	17.6	15.5	12.7	15.4	12.5	3 1 3 2	Low	3	6	21	29	IBM (4)	Average	IV 98	16.0	III 98	-14.2	800-225-2470
5.8	4.8	-0.7	-1.5	NA	NA	4 4	Low	5	99	16	-19	Telefonos de Mexico L ADR (10)	Very high	III 94	26.8	I 95	-23.2	800-225-2470
NA	NA	NA	NA	NA	NA			3	21	20	NA	Scudder Income (23)			NA		NA	800-225-2470
17.0	16.8	NA	NA	NA	NA	2	Low	3	NA	15	11	Black Hills (1)			NA		NA	800-225-2470
26.2	23.7	22.1	19.4	19.2	15.8	1 2 1 1	Average	13	4	33	44	Microsoft (2)	Low	IV 98	20.9	III 98	-11.2	800-888-2461
27.9	26.9	23.8	22.4	19.0	17.5	1 3 1 1	Very low	1	2	33	49	Microsoft (3)	Low	IV 98	21.3	III 98	-10.0	800-342-5734
31.9	30.4	NA	NA	NA	NA	1	Average	3	1	45	34	Dell Computer (5)			NA		NA	800-342-5734
22.4	19.5	19.4	17.1	14.4	12.1	3 4 2 1	Average	6	2	21	15	Dow Chemical (3)	Low	IV 98	16.6	III 98	-13.6	800-342-5734
10.9	8.2	14.2	11.2	NA	NA	1 4	High	5	2	33	8	S&P 500 Index (Fut.) (4)	Very high	IV 98	28.3	III 98	-24.1	800-342-5734
17.0	14.7	NA	NA	NA	NA	2	High	8	3	18	8	S&P 500 Index (Fut.) (5)			NA		NA	800-342-5734
27.8	25.9	22.8	21.0	18.0	15.2	2 4 2 1	Low	4	6	26	41	American Express (5)	Average	IV 98	22.2	III 98	-14.8	800-243-1575
19.4	16.8	16.8	13.5	18.1	14.8	1 2 1 2	High	10	NA	33	47	Liz Claiborne (4)	High	IV 98	31.0	III 98	-20.2	800-221-2783
18.8	15.1	16.1	12.7	15.0	11.7	2 3 2 2	High	3	3	27	31	Raytheon Cl. B (4)	Average	II 97	15.4	III 98	-7.8	800-221-2783
22.6	19.9	29.0	26.0	26.1	21.9	2 1 1 1	High	2	5	42	32	EMC/Mass (7)	Very high	IV 98	45.1	III 98	-16.6	800-221-2783
8.6	7.2	13.4	11.4	16.9	14.3	2 1 1 4	High	7	1	34	13	Total Renal Care Holdings (3)	High	II 97	20.3	III 98	-22.9	800-221-2783
24.6	21.8	19.0	15.9	17.4	13.9	1 3 2 1	Average	5	NA	39	47	Merck (4)	Average	IV 98	24.2	III 98	-9.6	800-221-2783
NA	NA	NA	NA	NA	NA	4	Average	2	57	28	1	CMG (3)			NA		NA	800-221-2450
18.6	16.8	NA	NA	NA	NA	1	Average	8	53	40	28	EMC/Mass. (4)			NA		NA	800-221-2450
9.8	7.1	8.6	6.1	11.0	8.2	4 1 4 3	High	1	2	27	8	GTE (1)	Very low	II 95	7.3	I 94	-4.0	800-221-2783
14.8	12.5	12.8	10.8	12.3	10.1	3 4 3 3	Average	2	1	27	28	IBM (2)	Very low	IV 98	9.9	III 98	-5.8	800-282-3863
20.8	17.7	18.5	15.5	15.9	13.3	2 3 2 2	Low	4	1	27	46	IBM (3)	Low	IV 98	16.5	III 98	-11.7	800-282-3863
33.1	31.5	28.1	27.0	21.8	19.8	1 2 1 1	Very low	18	NA	34	73	Berkshire Hathaway Cl. A (34)	Average	II 97	21.5	III 98	-12.6	800-686-6884
24.7	20.6	23.4	19.4	19.2	16.0	4 1 1 1	Average	12	NA	21	44	Fleet Financial Group (5)	Average	IV 98	19.6	III 98	-18.2	800-524-7433
15.3	11.1	15.3	11.5	16.9	14.4	1 3 1 3	Average	6	10	38	28	Elan ADR (5)	High	II 97	20.3	III 98	-19.1	800-332-5580
17.9	14.7	13.0	10.0	18.3	14.9	2 1 3 3	Average	5	1	18	8	Marquette Med. Sys. Cl. A (2)	Average	IV 98	17.8	III 98	-20.5	800-458-5222
10.4	8.1	9.9	7.4	NA	NA	1 2 4	Low	12	38	27	10	ISS Intl. Service Sys. Cl. B (1)	Average	IV 98	17.8	III 98	-19.9	800-421-4120
21.3	20.4	19.0	17.5	18.7	17.3	1 2 3 1	Very low	2	1	38	63	Intel (11)	High	IV 98	37.5	III 98	-12.2	800-451-2010
22.0	18.7	18.5	15.3	16.0	13.7	2 4 2 1	Average	18	3	29	38	Allstate (3)	Low	IV 98	17.9	III 98	-9.5	800-451-2010
11.0	6.4	9.9	6.4	11.3	8.2	3 3 4 3	Average	0	4	32	-26	MCI WorldCom (2)	Low	IV 98	14.4	III 98	-7.9	800-451-2010
NA	NA	NA	NA	NA	NA	3	Low	10	3	19	1	Smith Barney Diversified Str. (15)			NA		NA	800-451-2010
NA	NA	NA	NA	NA	NA	3	Low	1	6	25	3	Smith Barney Govt. Secs. (11)			NA		NA	800-451-2010
NA	NA	NA	NA	NA	NA	3	Low	1	10	27	0	Smith Barney Sm. Cap Blend (15)			NA		NA	800-451-2010
20.2	17.6	16.4	14.1	NA	NA	3 1	Average	0	5	33	35	EMC/Mass. (3)	Very low	IV 98	19.3	III 98	-7.5	800-451-2010
8.6	7.4	NA	NA	NA	NA	4	Low	2	6	25	16	Scholastic (3)			NA		NA	800-451-2010
16.0	14.4	14.9	12.5	NA	NA	2 3	Average	20	4	29	35	Wal-Mart Stores (4)	Average	IV 98	18.2	III 98	-10.1	800-451-2010
NA	NA	NA	NA	NA	NA			0	NA	41	NA	Intel (6)			NA		NA	800-451-2010
19.4	16.3	16.8	13.9	14.4	11.7	3 3 2 2	Low	3	4	28	34	American Home Products (4)	Low	II 97	15.3	III 98	-11.8	800-451-2010
16.5	14.0	14.7	12.1	14.4	11.6	2 3 3 2	Low	12	21	22	25	Loews (4)	Very low	II 97	10.2	III 98	-9.9	800-451-2010
9.0	9.0	3.9	3.7	11.5	10.9	2 1 4 4	Low	8	100	32	32	Nokia Cl. A (5)	High	I 98	16.5	III 98	-17.6	800-451-2010
7.2	4.7	7.8	5.7	10.5	8.4	3 2 3 4	Low	14	62	23	1	Buderus (2)	Very low	I 98	7.7	III 98	-11.0	800-334-2143
6.6	3.8	7.8	5.8	NA	NA	3 4	Low	1	96	23	-13	Secom (3)	Low	I 98	11.3	III 98	-13.8	800-334-2143
23.8	22.1	19.8	17.6	17.1	14.6	3 2 1 1	Average	10	6	21	11	First Union (4)	Low	IV 98	16.3	III 98	-14.5	800-551-1980
20.9	17.8	18.9	16.6	NA	NA	1 2	High	4	NA	25	24	Philip Morris (4)	Average	IV 98	23.9	III 98	-17.0	800-239-7470
30.1	30.0	27.5	21.6	25.8	20.3	1 1 1 1	High	10	3	47	28	America Online (4)	High	IV 98	33.7	III 98	-10.7	800-992-3863
-4.2	-4.9	NA	NA	NA	NA	4	Low	5	98	17	-39	Telefonos de Mexico L ADR (1)			NA		NA	800-647-7327
31.1	28.0	23.6	21.6	NA	NA	2 1	Average	2	NA	35	28	Philip Morris (4)	Average	IV 98	23.8	III 98	-8.1	800-647-7327
26.4	21.2	20.9	16.7	NA	NA	2 1	High	1	NA	28	18	IBM (3)	Average	IV 98	22.4	III 98	-13.9	800-647-7327
28.0	24.9	23.8	21.4	NA	NA	1 1	Low	1	2	33	28	S&P 500 Index (Fut.) (5)	Low	IV 98	21.3	III 98	-10.1	800-647-7327
13.8	12.2	15.6	14.1	NA	NA	1 3	Average	NA	NA	23	-5	Brightpoint (3)	High	IV 98	19.7	III 98	-27.2	800-647-7327
19.6	16.4	16.5	13.7	14.5	12.7	3 2 3 1	Average	0	3	32	29	General Electric (2)	Very low	IV 98	16.1	III 98	-5.6	800-222-8222
27.0	25.7	22.8	21.5	17.9	17.0	2 4 1 1	Very low	2	3	32	70	General Electric (3)	Low	IV 98	21.0	III 98	-10.1	800-222-8222
23.2	19.7	19.2	16.4	NA	NA	3 2 1	High	3	7	35	27	General Electric (5)	Average	IV 98	23.3	III 98	-10.7	800-222-8222

DATA: MORNINGSTAR, INC., CHICAGO, IL.

MUTUAL FUND SCOREBOARD

FUND	OVERALL RATING (COMPARES RISK-ADJUSTED PERFORMANCE OF EACH FUND AGAINST ALL FUNDS)	CATEGORY (COMPARES RISK-ADJUSTED PERFORMANCE OF FUND WITHIN CATEGORY)	RATING	SIZE ASSETS $MIL.	% CHG. 1997-98	FEES SALES CHARGE (%)	EXPENSE RATIO (%)	1997 RETURNS (%) PRE-TAX	AFTER-TAX	YIELD
STAGECOACH LIFEPATH 2040 A		Large-cap Blend		258.1	22	No load	1.20†	25.1	22.8	0.4
STAR RELATIVE VALUE Y (pppp) ♨		Large-cap Value		399.8	23	No load	NA	18.5	18.1	0.8
STATE ST. RESEARCH AURORA B		Small-cap Blend		213.3	−30	5.00**‡	2.15†	−15.8	−15.8	0.0
STATE ST. RESEARCH CAPITAL B ♨	D	Mid-cap Growth	D	380.0	−23	5.00**	1.98†	13.2	10.5	0.0
STATE ST. RESEARCH INVESTMENT B	B	Large-cap Blend	C	809.2	45	5.00**	1.51†	28.3	26.3	0.0
STATE ST. RESEARCH MGD. ASSET B	C	Domestic Hybrid	D	358.7	10	5.00**	2.03†	7.5	5.3	1.2
STEIN ROE BALANCED	B	Domestic Hybrid	C	268.8	−4	No load	1.05	12.2	9.8	2.7
STEIN ROE CAPITAL OPPORT.	D	Mid-Cap Growth	C−	710.7	−30	No load	1.17	−1.6	−1.6	0.0
STEIN ROE GROWTH & INCOME	A	Large-cap Blend	B+	416.3	22	No load	1.13	19.5	18.8	0.9
STEIN ROE GROWTH STOCK	B	Large-cap Growth	C	759.9	22	No load‡	1.07	25.5	25.5	0.0
STEIN ROE SPECIAL	C−	Mid-cap Blend	D	861.4	−32	No load	1.13	−11.3	−14.6	0.4
STEIN ROE YOUNG INVESTOR (qqqq)		Large-cap Growth		821.4	54	No load	1.31	17.7	17.1	0.0
STI CLASSIC CAPITAL GROWTH INVESTOR	B	Large-cap Blend	C	295.8	22	3.75	1.81†	27.3	23.6	0.0
STRONG AMERICAN UTILITIES	B+	Utilities	B+	245.6	31	No load	1.10	20.4	18.6	2.2
STRONG ASSET ALLOCATION	B+	Domestic Hybrid	C	319.7	15	No load	1.10	21.4	20.4	2.3
STRONG COMMON STOCK	C	Mid-cap Blend	C	1439.9	−8	No load‡	1.20	6.6	5.3	0.0
STRONG DISCOVERY ♨	D	Mid-cap Growth	C−	322.0	−16	No load	1.40	7.0	6.8	0.0
STRONG GROWTH	C	Mid-cap Growth	A	1834.7	15	No load	1.30	27.0	27.0	0.0
STRONG GROWTH & INCOME		Large-cap Blend		482.1	96	No load	1.20	33.0	32.9	0.1
STRONG OPPORTUNITY	B	Mid-cap Blend	B+	2037.9	6	No load	1.20	15.5	12.8	0.1
STRONG SCHAFER VALUE ♨	C	Mid-cap Value	D	1544.9	2	No load	1.20	−6.6	−6.8	0.6
STRONG TOTAL RETURN	C	Large-cap Blend	C	1022.5	20	No load	1.10	32.1	31.7	0.2
SUNAMERICA BALANCED ASSETS A	B	Domestic Hybrid	C−	221.8	28	5.75	1.50†	22.6	20.1	1.1
TCW/DW MID-CAP EQUITY B		Mid-cap Growth		253.9	40	5.00**	2.29†	62.7	62.7	0.0
TCW/DW SMALL CAP GROWTH B	D	Small-cap Growth	C−	340.9	2	5.00**	2.25†	19.4	19.4	0.0
TEMPLETON CAPITAL ACCUMULATOR	C−	World	C	214.9	18	9.00	1.00	8.6	7.2	1.6
TEMPLETON DEVELOPING MARKETS I	F	Diversified Emerging Mkts.	B+	2148.5	−38	5.75	1.96†	−18.7	−19.2	1.8
TEMPLETON FOREIGN I ♨	C−	Foreign	C	11509.8	−18	5.75	1.12†	−4.9	−7.5	2.8
TEMPLETON GLOBAL OPPORTUNITIES I	C−	World	D	676.1	−14	5.75	1.37†	−0.6	−1.6	2.1
TEMPLETON GLOBAL SMALL COMPANY I	C−	World	D	1294.0	−25	5.75	1.27†	−11.4	−12.3	1.5
TEMPLETON GROWTH I ♨	C−	World	C	12595.3	−1	5.75	1.08†	−2.5	−5.6	2.2
TEMPLETON WORLD I	C	World	B	8776.8	1	5.75	1.03†	6.0	3.5	2.1
THIRD AVENUE VALUE	B	Small-cap Value	B+	1600.1	−5	No load‡	1.13	3.9	3.5	1.3
THORNBURG VALUE A		Mid-cap Value		234.4	194	4.50	1.61†	22.3	22.0	0.6
TIAA-CREF GROWTH & INCOME		Large-cap Blend		209.3	239	No load	0.20	30.5	30.1	0.8
TIAA-CREF GROWTH EQUITY		Large-cap Growth		258.3	301	No load	NA	36.0	35.7	0.2
TORRAY	A	Large-cap Value	B+	1460.5	140	No load	1.13	8.2	8.1	0.4
TRANSAMERICA PREMIER EQUITY INVESTOR ♨		Large-cap Growth		289.7	163	No load	1.49†	33.9	33.8	0.1
TRANSAMERICA PREMIER SMALL CO. INVESTOR		Small-cap Growth		206.0	NM	No load	1.40†	80.3	79.4	0.0
TWEEDY, BROWNE AMERICAN VALUE	A	Mid-cap Value	A	1123.5	56	No load	1.39	9.6	9.1	0.6
TWEEDY, BROWNE GLOBAL VALUE	C	World	B+	2498.8	26	No load	1.42	11.0	8.9	2.1
UNITED ACCUMULATIVE A ♨	B	Large-cap Blend	C	1781.4	12	5.75	0.82†	22.6	18.0	1.1
UNITED CONTINENTAL INCOME A	B	Domestic Hybrid	C−	581.3	2	5.75	0.91†	10.4	8.4	2.7
UNITED INCOME A ♨	B	Large-cap Blend	C−	7211.1	16	5.75	0.84†	24.0	18.9	0.9
UNITED INTERNATIONAL GROWTH A	C−	Foreign	C	1179.5	16	5.75	1.23†	21.4	18.0	0.6
UNITED NEW CONCEPTS A	C	Mid-cap Growth	B	835.9	24	5.75	1.25†	38.6	35.0	0.0
UNITED RETIREMENT SHARES A	C	Domestic Hybrid	D	805.8	5	5.75	0.93†	9.7	8.0	2.5
UNITED SCIENCE & TECHNOLOGY A ♨	C−	Technology	C	1439.4	35	5.75	1.02†	59.3	57.0	0.0
UNITED VANGUARD A	C	Large-cap Growth	C−	1602.1	11	5.75	1.09†	31.2	30.8	0.1
USAA AGGRESSIVE GROWTH	D	Small-cap Growth	C	833.3	14	No load	0.71	22.2	18.4	0.0
USAA CORNERSTONE STRATEGY	C	Mid-cap Value	C	1367.0	−3	No load	1.01	2.0	−0.3	2.9
USAA EMERGING MARKETS		Diversified Emerging Mkts.		234.0	−24	No load	1.31	−26.1	−26.3	1.0
USAA GROWTH	C	Large-cap Blend	F	1546.7	14	No load	0.96	32.1	30.9	0.1
USAA GROWTH & INCOME	C	Large-cap Value	C−	1054.6	13	No load	0.85	6.5	4.9	1.0
USAA GROWTH & TAX STRATEGY	B+	Domestic Hybrid	B	237.7	12	No load	0.71	11.6	9.4	3.0
USAA GROWTH STRATEGY		Mid-cap Value		256.5	12	No load	1.25	15.0	13.7	0.5
USAA INCOME STOCK ♨	B	Large-cap Value	B	2490.7	4	No load	0.65	8.1	6.1	3.5
USAA INTERNATIONAL ♨	C−	Foreign	C	531.0	−8	No load	1.05	4.0	3.1	1.0
USAA S&P 500 INDEX		Large-cap Blend		1852.8	195	No load	0.18	28.6	28.2	1.1
USAA WORLD GROWTH	C−	World	C	327.8	1	No load	1.13	10.4	9.6	1.0
VALUE LINE	C	Mid-cap Growth	B+	417.6	9	No load	0.78	20.3	19.7	0.2
VALUE LINE LEVERAGED GROWTH INVESTOR	C	Large-cap Growth	C−	608.5	41	No load	0.86	39.6	38.9	0.0
VAN KAMPEN AMERICAN VALUE B (rrrr)		Small-cap Value		301.9	183	5.00**	2.25†	8.8	6.9	0.0
VAN KAMPEN COMSTOCK A (ssss)	B+	Large-cap Value	B	1756.1	15	5.75	0.94†	20.1	15.1	1.5
VAN KAMPEN EMERGING GROWTH A (tttt)	C−	Mid-cap Growth	C	2989.1	42	5.75	1.05†	34.7	33.2	0.0
VAN KAMPEN ENTERPRISE A (uuuu)	C	Large-cap Blend	D	2126.7	24	5.75	0.93†	23.6	22.5	0.2
VAN KAMPEN EQUITY-INCOME B (vvvv)	B+	Domestic Hybrid	B	1139.7	26	5.00**	1.64†	16.2	14.2	1.5
VAN KAMPEN GLOBAL EQUITY ALLOC. A (wwww)	C	World	B	241.7	224	5.75	1.61†	19.4	17.4	1.3
VAN KAMPEN GLOBAL EQUITY B (xxxx)		World		636.3	36	5.00**	2.45†	12.6	12.5	0.1
VAN KAMPEN GROWTH & INCOME A (yyyy)		Large-cap Blend	C	928.9	19	5.75	0.94†	18.4	16.7	1.0

*Includes redemption fee. **Includes deferred sales charge. †12(b)-1 plan in effect. ‡Not currently accepting new accounts. §Less than 0.5% of assets. NA=Not available. NM=Not meaningful. (pppp) Formerly Star Relative Value Tr. (qqqq) Formerly Stein Roe Young Investor. (rrrr) Formerly Morgan Stanley American Value B. (ssss) Formerly Van Kampen Amer. Cap Comstock A. (tttt) Formerly Van Kampen Amer. Cap Emerging Growth A. (uuuu) Formerly Van Kampen Amer. Cap Enterprise A. (vvvv) Formerly Van Kampen Amer. Cap Equity-Income B. (wwww) Formerly Morgan Stanley Global Equity Alloc. A. (xxxx) Formerly Morgan Stanley Global Equity B. (yyyy) Formerly Van Kampen Amer. Cap Growth & Income A.

AVERAGE ANNUAL TOTAL RETURNS (%)						HISTORY	PORTFOLIO DATA						RISK					TELEPHONE
3 YEARS		5 YEARS		10 YEARS		RESULTS VS.	TURNOVER	CASH %	FOREIGN %	P-E RATIO	UNTAXED GAINS (%)	LARGEST HOLDING	LEVEL	BEST		WORST		
PRETAX	AFTERTAX	PRETAX	AFTERTAX	PRETAX	AFTERTAX	ALL FUNDS						COMPANY (% ASSETS)		QTR	%RET	QTR	%RET	
23.3	20.8	NA	NA	NA	NA	1	Low	0	21	31	32	General Electric (3)			NA		NA	800-222-8222
NA	NA	NA	NA	NA	NA			2	8	27	NA	IBM (6)			NA		NA	800-677-3863
23.9	21.0	NA	NA	NA	NA	2	Average	5	5	16	-14	Exide (3)			NA		NA	800-882-0052
8.4	7.4	10.6	9.5	NA	NA	1 4	Very high	2	3	38	30	America Online (2)	High	IV 98	28.4	III 98	-22.2	800-882-0052
25.4	21.3	19.9	16.3	NA	NA	2 1	Average	6	8	33	36	General Electric (3)	Average	IV 98	20.3	III 98	-10.7	800-882-0052
13.9	10.7	11.0	8.7	NA	NA	4 3	High	6	29	31	8	ACE (1)	Low	III 97	9.9	III 98	-9.3	800-882-0052
15.5	12.7	12.7	10.1	12.9	10.1	2 3 3 3	Low	2	13	34	30	General Electric (4)	Very low	IV 98	12.5	III 98	-6.2	800-338-2550
7.9	7.9	13.6	13.3	14.6	13.6	4 1 1 4	Low	5	3	42	33	Papa John's International (4)	High	II 97	21.4	III 98	-25.1	800-338-2550
22.3	20.9	18.9	17.0	17.6	15.7	2 2 2 1	Very low	15	3	33	42	Wal-Mart Stores (3)	Low	IV 98	17.9	III 98	-11.7	800-338-2550
26.0	24.4	21.1	18.5	19.2	16.9	1 3 2 1	Very low	9	2	44	61	Cisco Systems (6)	Average	IV 98	24.8	III 98	-15.1	800-338-2550
9.9	6.9	8.8	6.0	13.8	10.9	1 1 3 4	Average	22	9	19	18	Carlisle (3)	Average	II 97	18.7	III 98	-18.1	800-338-2550
26.1	25.4	NA	NA	NA	NA	2	Average	9	4	38	27	Cisco Systems (3)			NA		NA	800-338-2550
25.6	20.2	18.9	15.1	NA	NA	3 1	Very high	11	3	31	24	General Electric (3)	Average	IV 98	22.8	III 98	-11.3	800-428-6970
18.5	16.1	17.3	15.3	NA	NA	2 2	Average	6	4	22	25	Ameritech (8)	Low	IV 97	12.2	I 94	-5.3	800-368-1030
16.1	12.9	13.4	10.6	11.8	9.0	4 3 4 2	Very high	1	2	37	21	General Electric (3)	Very low	IV 98	15.9	III 98	-8.2	800-368-1030
16.8	12.7	16.0	12.3	NA	NA	1 2 2	High	11	11	26	19	Tele-Comm. TCI Group Cl. A (2)	Average	IV 98	18.0	III 98	-16.5	800-368-1030
6.4	3.9	8.9	6.2	14.5	11.4	1 1 4 4	Very high	30	NA	31	7	Equity International (3)	High	IV 98	20.3	III 98	-17.4	800-368-1030
21.8	19.6	24.5	22.8	NA	NA	1 2	Very high	8	2	48	35	Microsoft (3)	High	IV 98	25.0	III 98	-12.7	800-368-1030
31.7	31.0	NA	NA	NA	NA	1	Very high	0	3	37	27	General Electric (3)			NA		NA	800-368-1030
19.0	15.2	17.2	14.2	15.8	13.8	4 1 2 2	Average	12	9	27	25	NIPSCO Industries (2)	Average	IV 98	17.5	III 98	-14.1	800-368-1030
14.1	13.3	13.8	12.7	16.6	14.3	2 1 2 3	Low	1	19	20	6	Western Resources (3)	Average	IV 98	19.7	III 98	-24.5	800-368-1030
23.2	18.3	18.6	15.2	13.9	11.6	4 2 3 1	Very high	9	1	43	25	MCI WorldCom (3)	Average	IV 98	22.2	III 98	-7.2	800-368-1030
18.4	15.2	15.8	12.8	NA	NA	3 2	High	10	2	35	21	General Electric (2)	Low	IV 98	15.6	III 98	-6.0	800-858-8850
NA	NA	NA	NA	NA	NA	1		3	2	45	43	Yahoo (13)			NA		NA	800-526-3143
14.5	14.5	18.1	18.1	NA	NA	1 4	Average	1	1	49	14	Citrix Systems (6)	Very high	IV 98	32.9	III 98	-22.1	800-526-3143
14.1	12.8	11.8	10.6	NA	NA	1 3 3	Very low	10	80	21	17	Nokia Cl. K (2)	Average	IV 98	17.4	III 98	-17.0	800-342-5236
-3.4	-4.4	-3.7	-4.8	NA	NA	4 4	Low	18	99	14	-46	Cemex Cl. B (3)	Very high	IV 98	24.0	IV 97	-24.9	800-342-5236
6.2	3.9	6.0	3.7	10.6	8.3	2 2 4 4	Low	3	100	17	-14	HSBC Holdings (HK) (2)	Average	IV 98	17.2	III 98	-17.2	800-342-5236
12.2	10.2	8.9	6.3	NA	NA	1 4 3	Low	29	69	22	18	British Energy 144A (3)	High	IV 98	12.8	III 98	-15.7	800-342-5236
5.0	2.9	5.4	3.1	9.4	6.5	3 2 3 4	Low	8	75	15	8	Gas y Electricidad Cl. 2 (2)	Average	II 95	10.5	III 98	-20.3	800-342-5236
10.9	7.7	10.5	7.3	12.8	9.6	3 1 3 3	Average	13	66	20	-3	General Motors (2)	Average	II 97	11.6	III 98	-15.2	800-342-5236
15.4	12.1	13.5	9.9	13.3	9.7	4 1 3 3	Low	5	67	19	11	Cheung Kong Holdings (2)	Average	IV 98	15.3	III 98	-14.1	800-342-5236
16.2	15.5	15.3	14.6	NA	NA	2 2 2	Very low	6	15	25	23	First American Financial (7)	Low	IV 98	16.7	III 98	-14.3	800-443-1021
31.1	29.4	NA	NA	NA	NA	1	High	2	16	29	16	Bank One (6)			NA		NA	800-847-0200
NA	NA	NA	NA	NA	NA		Very low	1	6	33	16	General Electric (3)			NA		NA	800-223-1200
NA	NA	NA	NA	NA	NA			3	5	38	NA	Tyco Intl. (5)			NA		NA	800-223-1200
24.2	23.6	24.2	23.1	NA	NA	3 1 1	Very low	5	NA	22	15	SLM Holding (8)	Average	IV 98	21.3	III 98	-21.3	800-443-3036
36.6	36.5	NA	NA	NA	NA	1	Very low	1	2	48	29	Dell Computer (8)			NA		NA	800-892-7587
NA	NA	NA	NA	NA	NA			14	NA	45	25	ENVOY (7)			NA		NA	800-892-7587
23.1	22.1	20.3	19.7	NA	NA	1 1	Very low	6	16	21	23	Pharmacia & Upjohn (Dep.) (4)	Low	II 97	15.7	III 98	-14.6	800-432-4789
18.0	15.5	13.7	12.0	NA	NA	3 3	Very low	4	81	25	13	Pharmacia & Upjohn (5)	Low	IV 98	16.2	III 98	-17.9	800-432-4789
21.2	15.5	19.1	14.2	15.5	11.5	3 3 2 1	Very high	8	7	31	13	Fannie Mae (6)	Low	II 97	14.2	III 98	-7.4	800-366-5465
12.4	9.3	12.0	9.4	12.4	10.2	3 3 3 3	Average	3	8	27	18	SBC Communications (3)	Low	II 97	9.5	III 98	-6.0	800-366-5465
23.9	20.5	19.4	16.8	17.2	14.8	2 2 2 1	Low	29	7	35	36	Warner-Lambert (3)	Average	III 97	18.7	III 98	-7.3	800-366-5465
19.0	15.6	13.1	9.9	12.1	9.8	4 1 4 2	High	18	95	32	19	Novartis (Reg) (4)	High	I 98	19.8	III 98	-17.3	800-366-5465
19.2	16.6	20.4	18.0	19.8	18.4	1 1 1 2	Low	19	4	44	40	America Online (5)	High	IV 98	31.7	III 98	-15.9	800-366-5465
12.5	9.5	12.0	9.3	13.1	10.7	2 2 3 3	Average	7	6	27	19	SBC Communications (2)	Low	II 97	9.8	III 98	-5.8	800-366-5465
22.8	19.9	25.9	23.3	20.8	18.3	1 2 1 2	Average	3	4	48	56	Yahoo (3)	High	IV 98	34.5	I 97	-15.2	800-366-5465
19.1	14.9	17.5	14.0	14.5	11.6	3 2 2 2	High	6	4	43	30	EMC/Mass. (6)	Average	IV 98	24.6	III 98	-9.5	800-366-5465
15.3	13.2	18.0	15.7	14.8	12.5	3 3 1 3	Average	2	4	41	30	Express Scripts Cl. A (3)	Very high	IV 98	38.0	III 98	-22.4	800-382-8722
11.6	9.2	10.3	8.0	10.7	8.9	4 2 4 3	Low	0	36	25	16	Bristol-Myers Squibb (2)	Low	II 97	8.5	III 98	-10.7	800-382-8722
-6.0	-6.6	NA	NA	NA	NA	4	Low	11	96	17	-53	Panamerican Beverages (2)			NA		NA	800-382-8722
17.3	13.8	17.1	13.5	15.5	12.9	2 3 1 2	Average	1	7	35	24	Cadbury Schweppes ADR (5)	Average	IV 98	26.1	IV 97	-16.1	800-382-8722
18.2	16.6	17.1	15.7	NA	NA	2 2	Low	3	1	30	21	Merck (3)	Average	IV 98	17.5	III 98	-17.5	800-382-8722
12.9	10.8	11.5	9.9	NA	NA	4 3 3	Average	1	0	35	22	Bristol-Myers Squibb (2)	Very low	IV 98	8.6	III 98	-3.9	800-382-8722
15.3	14.0	NA	NA	NA	NA	3	Average	2	23	32	15	AAR (3)			NA		NA	800-382-8722
17.7	14.9	15.8	13.2	14.9	12.4	2 3 2 2	Low	9	6	27	26	Bristol-Myers Squibb (5)	Low	IV 98	10.7	III 98	-8.1	800-382-8722
10.5	9.1	8.5	7.2	9.7	8.7	4 1 3 4	Low	6	99	22	17	Nokia Cl. A ADR (2)	Average	IV 98	16.8	III 98	-20.2	800-382-8722
NA	NA	NA	NA	NA	NA	1	Low	3	3	32	34	General Electric (3)			NA		NA	800-382-8722
14.1	12.4	11.0	9.7	NA	NA	3 3	Average	3	63	30	27	Nokia Cl. A ADR (1)	Average	IV 98	20.6	III 98	-19.0	800-382-8722
21.5	18.4	17.7	14.3	17.6	14.1	1 2 2 2	Average	12	NA	42	48	Compuware (3)	Average	IV 98	23.9	III 98	-13.2	800-223-0818
28.3	26.1	22.8	20.5	19.7	16.8	1 3 1 1	Low	4	NA	42	67	SunAmerica (5)	High	IV 98	31.0	III 98	-13.3	800-223-0818
21.4	19.2	NA	NA	NA	NA	2	Very high	-3	4	24	1	Safety-Kleen (2)			NA		NA	800-421-5666
24.1	18.3	20.2	14.1	17.1	12.6	2 3 2 1	High	3	8	25	18	Tenet Healthcare (4)	Low	IV 98	14.8	III 98	-6.0	800-421-5666
24.5	22.6	21.0	19.0	22.2	20.2	1 1 1 2	Average	6	1	48	37	Dell Computer (6)	High	IV 98	26.8	III 98	-12.8	800-421-5666
25.2	22.9	21.3	18.4	18.8	15.3	1 2 1 2	Average	2	1	36	37	S&P 500 Index (Fut.) (4)	Average	IV 98	24.6	III 98	-15.1	800-421-5666
17.9	15.0	16.0	13.4	NA	NA	3 2	Average	7	8	25	19	S&P 500 Index (Fut.) (3)	Low	II 97	12.6	III 98	-8.0	800-421-5666
16.3	13.6	13.5	11.4	NA	NA	3 3	High	19	47	28	12	CAC 40 Index (Fut.) (3)	Average	IV 98	16.0	III 98	-11.5	800-282-4404
NA	NA	NA	NA	NA	NA			0	61	23	8	American Stores (3)			NA		NA	800-282-4404
20.3	17.3	18.4	15.2	15.5	12.6	3 2 2 2	Average	6	9	26	19	S&P 500 Index (Fut.) (5)	Low	IV 98	15.9	III 98	-11.5	800-421-5666

DATA: MORNINGSTAR, INC., CHICAGO, IL.

MUTUAL FUND SCOREBOARD

FUND	OVERALL RATING (COMPARES RISK-ADJUSTED PERFORMANCE OF EACH FUND AGAINST ALL FUNDS)	CATEGORY (COMPARES RISK-ADJUSTED PERFORMANCE OF FUND WITHIN CATEGORY)	RATING	SIZE ASSETS $MIL.	% CHG. 1997-98	FEES SALES CHARGE (%)	FEES EXPENSE RATIO (%)	1997 RETURNS (%) PRE-TAX	1997 RETURNS (%) AFTER-TAX	1997 RETURNS (%) YIELD
VAN KAMPEN PACE A (zzzz)	C	Large-cap Blend	C–	3752.1	15	5.75	0.88†	22.0	19.3	0.7
VANGUARD AGGRESSIVE GROWTH (aaaaa)		Mid-cap Value		534.6	13	1.00*	0.40	0.5	0.2	1.0
VANGUARD ASSET ALLOCATION ⚓	A	Domestic Hybrid	A	6974.2	70	No load	0.49	25.4	22.7	3.0
VANGUARD BALANCED INDEX	A	Domestic Hybrid	B+	2003.6	60	No load	0.20	17.9	16.5	2.9
VANGUARD CAPITAL OPPORTUNITY (bbbbb) ⚓		Mid-cap Growth		206.5	226	1.00*	0.94	32.0	29.4	0.1
VANGUARD EMERG. MARKET STOCK INDEX (ccccc)		Diversified Emerging Mkts.		577.0	–15	1.00*	0.57	–18.2	–19.0	3.3
VANGUARD ENERGY (ddddd) ⚓	D	Natural Resources	C	819.9	–31	1.00*	0.38	–20.5	–21.3	1.9
VANGUARD EQUITY-INCOME ⚓	A	Large-cap Value	A	2938.5	40	No load	0.45	17.3	15.5	2.5
VANGUARD EUROPEAN STOCK INDEX (eeeee)	B	Europe	B+	4479.3	84	No load	0.31	28.9	27.9	2.1
VANGUARD EXPLORER	C–	Small-cap Blend	B	2463.6	–3	No load	0.62†	3.5	3.3	0.4
VANGUARD EXTEND MARKET INDEX (fffff) ⚓	C	Mid-cap Blend	C	2773.8	2	No load	0.23	8.3	6.4	1.1
VANGUARD 500 INDEX (ggggg) ⚓	A	Large-cap Blend	A	74228.5	50	No load	0.19	28.6	28.0	1.2
VANGUARD GOLD & PRECIOUS METALS (hhhhh)	F	Precious Metals	B	311.4	6	1.00*	0.62	–3.9	–4.3	1.4
VANGUARD GROWTH & INCOME ⚓	B+	Large-cap Value	B	5160.5	141	No load	0.36	23.9	22.5	1.0
VANGUARD GROWTH INDEX (iiiii)	A	Large-cap Growth		5721.0	142	No load	0.20	42.2	41.8	0.7
VANGUARD HEALTH CARE (jjjjj) ⚓	A	Health	B+	9268.4	108	1.00*	0.40	40.8	39.4	0.8
VANGUARD INTL. GROWTH ⚓	C–	Foreign	B	7723.2	13	No load	0.59	16.9	16.3	1.2
VANGUARD INTERNATIONAL VALUE	C–	Foreign	C	806.3	4	No load	0.49	19.5	17.1	4.1
VANGUARD LIFESTRATEGY CONS. GROWTH		Domestic Hybrid		1415.7	76	No load	0.00	15.9	14.1	4.0
VANGUARD LIFESTRATEGY GROWTH		Large-cap Blend		1924.1	70	No load	0.00	21.4	20.2	2.2
VANGUARD LIFESTRATEGY INCOME		Domestic Hybrid		448.9	80	No load	0.00	13.2	11.1	4.7
VANGUARD LIFESTRATEGY MOD. GROWTH		Domestic Hybrid		2201.9	62	No load	0.00	19.0	17.5	3.0
VANGUARD MORGAN GROWTH (kkkkk) ⚓	C	Large-cap Blend	C–	3555.2	27	No load	0.48	22.3	20.2	0.9
VANGUARD PACIFIC STOCK INDEX (lllll)	F	Japan		1032.8	25	No load	0.35	2.4	2.1	0.8
VANGUARD PRIMECAP (mmmmm) ⚓	B+	Large-cap Blend	B	11209.9	37	No load‡	0.51	25.4	24.2	0.7
VANGUARD REIT INDEX (nnnnn)		Real Estate		923.6	–28	1.00*	0.24	–16.3	–18.0	7.3
VANGUARD SMALL CAP INDEX (ooooo)	C–	Small-cap Blend	C	2643.8	0	No load	0.23	–2.6	–4.5	1.3
VANGUARD STAR	B+	Domestic Hybrid	B	8082.6	10	No load	0.00	12.4	10.1	3.1
VANGUARD TAX-MGD. BALANCED (ppppp)		Domestic Hybrid		206.9	73	2.00*	0.17	16.9	16.1	2.3
VANGUARD TAX-MGD. CAP. APPRECIATION (qqqqq)		Large-cap Growth		1478.8	66	2.00*	0.17	27.9	27.7	0.5
VANGUARD TAX-MGD. GROWTH & INCOME (rrrrr)		Large-cap Blend		1352.4	133	2.00*	0.17	28.7	28.2	1.1
VANGUARD TOTAL INTL. STK. IDX. (sssss)		Foreign		2445.4	152	No load	0.00	15.6	14.9	1.9
VANGUARD TOT. STOCK MARKET INDEX (ttttt)	B+	Large-cap Blend	B	8548.7	68	No load	0.20	23.3	22.6	1.2
VANGUARD U.S. GROWTH ⚓	A	Large-cap Growth	A	13623.6	69	No load	0.41	40.0	37.8	0.5
VANGUARD UTILITIES INCOME (uuuuu)	B+	Utilities	B+	951.0	39	No load	0.44	21.8	18.9	3.4
VANGUARD VALUE INDEX (vvvvv)	B	Large-cap Value	C	2328.7	30	No load	0.20	14.6	13.0	1.5
VANGUARD WELLESLEY INCOME (wwwww) ⚓	A	Domestic Hybrid	B+	8497.8	11	No load	0.31	11.8	9.0	4.9
VANGUARD WELLINGTON (xxxxx)	B+	Domestic Hybrid	B	25760.9	18	No load	0.29	12.1	9.1	3.6
VANGUARD WINDSOR (yyyyy)	C	Large-cap Value	D	18187.7	–13	No load‡	0.27	0.8	–1.2	1.5
VANGUARD WINDSOR II (zzzzz) ⚓	B+	Large-cap Value	B+	31538.2	29	No load	0.37	16.4	13.5	2.0
VICTORY BALANCED A	B+	Domestic Hybrid	B+	445.1	28	5.75	1.25	17.9	15.6	2.1
VICTORY DIVERSIFIED STOCK A	B+	Large-cap Blend	B	972.8	22	5.75	1.03	23.2	17.7	0.5
VICTORY GROWTH	B+	Large-cap Blend	B+	311.7	58	5.75	1.34	37.2	35.0	0.1
VICTORY SPECIAL VALUE A	C	Mid-cap Value	D	346.9	–22	5.75	1.37	–9.1	–10.0	0.6
VICTORY STOCK INDEX ⚓	B+	Large-cap Blend	B	712.8	41	5.75	0.56	27.7	24.5	1.6
VICTORY VALUE	B+	Large-cap Value	B	562.9	13	5.75	1.32	26.3	22.0	0.4
VINTAGE EQUITY S (aaaaaa)	B+	Large-cap Blend	B	210.3	–45	No load	1.31†	27.5	25.1	0.0
WADDELL & REED GROWTH B ⚓	C	Mid-cap Growth	A	354.3	32	3.00**	2.13†	44.6	40.0	0.0
WADDELL & REED TOTAL RET. B	B	Large-cap Blend	C–	478.7	15	3.00**	1.95†	20.7	17.7	0.1
WARBURG PINCUS CAP. APPR. COMM.	B+	Large-cap Blend	B	755.3	21	No load	1.01	25.8	24.7	0.0
WARBURG PINCUS EMERG. GROWTH COMM. ⚓	C–	Mid-cap Growth	C	1777.7	13	No load	1.22	5.8	5.8	0.0
WARBURG PINCUS GROWTH & INCOME COMM.	C	Large-cap Value	F	732.3	19	No load	1.15	12.7	11.7	0.7
WARBURG PINCUS INTL. EQUITY COMM.	D	Foreign	D	1172.1	–40	No load	1.33	4.6	4.6	0.0
WASHINGTON MUTUAL INVESTORS ⚓	A	Large-cap Value	A	51773.8	35	5.75	0.62†	19.4	16.9	1.7
WEBS INDEX JAPAN ⚓		Japan		299.1	66	No load	NA†	3.5	3.5	0.0
WEITZ PARTNERS VALUE	A	Mid-cap Value	A	263.7	97	No load	1.24	29.1	26.0	0.9
WEITZ HICKORY	B	Small-cap Blend	A	506.5	NM	No load‡	1.46	33.0	32.5	0.3
WEITZ VALUE ⚓	A	Mid-cap Value	A	1059.3	189	No load	1.27	29.0	26.1	0.5
WESTCORE MIDCO GROWTH ⚓	D	Mid-cap Growth	C–	491.3	–18	No load	1.14	10.4	7.6	0.0
WHITE OAK GROWTH STOCK	C	Large-cap Growth	C	1092.3	179	No load	0.98	39.5	39.5	0.0
WINTHROP SMALL COMPANY VALUE A	C–	Small-cap Value	B	246.8	–14	4.75	1.35†	–4.6	–4.7	0.3
WILLIAM BLAIR GROWTH	C	Mid-cap Growth	A	742.1	25	No load	0.84	27.2	25.1	0.4
WM BOND & STOCK A (bbbbbb)	B	Domestic Hybrid	C	304.3	–3	5.50	0.99†	6.9	5.0	2.8
WM GROWTH & INCOME A (cccccc)	B	Large-cap Blend	C–	541.4	75	5.50	1.05†	14.4	13.4	0.4
WM NORTHWEST A (dddddd)	C	Mid-cap Blend	C	304.0	18	5.50	1.05†	23.1	21.9	0.1
WRIGHT SELECTED BLUE CHIP EQUITY ⚓	C	Mid-cap Value	C	221.5	–15	No load	1.08†	0.1	–1.6	0.5
YACKTMAN	B	Mid-cap Blend	B+	307.4	–72	No load	0.86	0.6	–3.1	0.0
ZWEIG APPRECIATION A	C	Small-cap Value	B	239.9	–18	5.50	1.52†	–1.0	–3.1	0.4
ZWEIG MANAGED ASSETS C	B+	International Hybrid	B+	429.6	5	1.25**	2.29†	14.0	13.2	2.0
ZWEIG STRATEGY C	C	Mid-cap Value	C–	425.0	–28	1.25**	1.94†	–2.6	–3.3	0.2

*Includes redemption fee. **Includes deferred sales charge. †12(b)-1 plan in effect. ‡Not currently accepting new accounts. §Less than 0.5% of assets. NA=Not available. NM=Not meaningful. (zzzz) Formerly Van Kampen Amer. Cap. Pace A. (aaaaa) Formerly Vanguard Horizon Aggr. Gr. (bbbbb) Formerly Vanguard Horizon Cap. Opp. (ccccc) Formerly Vanguard Intl. Eq. Idx. Emg. Mkts. (ddddd) Formerly Vanguard Sp. Engy. (eeeee) Formerly Vanguard Intl. Eq. Idx. Euro. (fffff) Formerly Vanguard Idx. Ext. Mkt. (ggggg) Formerly Vanguard Idx. 500. (hhhhh) Formerly Vanguard Sp. Gold & Prec. Metals. (iiiii) Formerly Vanguard Idx. Growth. (jjjjj) Formerly Vanguard Sp. Health Care. (kkkkk) Formerly Vanguard/Morgan Gr. (lllll) Formerly Vanguard Intl. Eq. Id. Pac. (mmmmm) Formerly

3 YR PRETAX	3 YR AFTERTAX	5 YR PRETAX	5 YR AFTERTAX	10 YR PRETAX	10 YR AFTERTAX	RESULTS VS. ALL FUNDS	TURNOVER	CASH %	FOREIGN %	P-E RATIO	UNTAXED GAINS (%)	LARGEST HOLDING COMPANY (% ASSETS)	RISK LEVEL	BEST QTR	BEST %RET	WORST QTR	WORST %RET	TELEPHONE
24.2	20.1	19.6	15.2	16.3	12.3	2321	Average	2	3	30	29	Microsoft (3)	Average	IV 98	20.5	III 98	-12.6	800-421-5666
16.6	14.9	NA	NA	NA	NA	3	Average	0	NA	21	12	McKesson (3)			NA		NA	800-662-7447
22.7	19.8	19.6	17.0	16.7	14.3	2321	Average	0	2	33	23	Microsoft (1)	Very low	IV 98	14.3	I 94	-4.6	800-662-7447
18.0	16.5	15.8	14.3	NA	NA	32	Low	1	0	31	26	J. Ray McDermott (3)	Very low	IV 98	12.7	III 98	-5.6	800-662-7447
11.3	10.5	NA	NA	NA	NA	3	High	15	5	34	7	DeKalb Genetics Cl. B (5)			NA		NA	800-662-7447
-7.6	-8.3	NA	NA	NA	NA	4	Low	6	100	18	-49	Telefonos de Mexico Cl. L (3)			NA		NA	800-662-7447
7.0	5.7	8.6	7.3	11.1	9.3	1424	Low	3	33	24	2	Chevron (4)	High	III 97	16.1	III 98	-14.2	800-662-7447
21.8	19.6	19.6	17.5	15.6	13.5	3321	Low	1	3	26	36	Bell Atlantic (3)	Low	IV 98	13.2	I 94	-6.6	800-662-7447
24.7	23.8	19.3	18.4	NA	NA	231	Very low	0	100	29	37	Royal Dutch Petroleum (2)	Average	I 98	20.4	III 98	-14.4	800-662-7447
10.6	9.1	11.5	9.6	13.1	11.4	3124	Average	9	3	30	21	Genzyme-General Division (2)	High	IV 98	23.3	III 98	-18.5	800-662-7447
17.3	15.0	16.2	14.4	15.3	13.8	211	Very low	0	0	28	29	Berkshire Hathaway Cl. A (3)	Average	IV 98	22.1	III 98	-18.7	800-662-7447
28.2	27.4	24.0	23.1	19.0	17.9	1311	Very low	0	2	34	46	Microsoft (3)	Low	IV 98	21.4	III 98	-10.0	800-662-7447
-16.5	-17.0	-12.1	-12.6	-1.1	-1.8	4244	Low	3	75	32	-58	Anglogold ADR (9)	Very high	III 94	17.5	IV 97	-28.8	800-662-7447
27.4	24.1	22.8	20.1	19.0	16.6	1311	Average	1	1	29	22	Merck (3)	Average	IV 98	20.6	III 98	-13.0	800-662-7447
33.9	33.1	27.8	27.1	NA	NA	11	Low	0	1	40	32	Microsoft (7)	Low	IV 98	24.6	III 98	-7.3	800-662-7447
30.0	28.6	28.4	26.7	24.2	22.4	1311	Very low	11	18	42	31	Warner-Lambert (5)	Low	II 97	19.1	I 94	-5.3	800-662-7447
11.8	10.6	10.1	9.1	9.7	8.7	4333	Low	10	99	31	25	Novartis (Reg.) (5)	Average	IV 98	17.8	III 98	-12.8	800-662-7447
7.9	3.7	7.7	4.3	7.7	5.1	4444	Low	5	99	26	0	Nestle (Reg.) (5)	Average	IV 98	20.6	III 98	-15.7	800-662-7447
14.3	12.4	NA	NA	NA	NA	2	Very low	0	6	29	13	Vanguard Total Bond Mkt. Idx. (30)			NA		NA	800-662-7447
19.5	18.2	NA	NA	NA	NA	2	Very low	0	15	30	23	Vanguard Total Stk. Mkt. Idx. (49)			NA		NA	800-662-7447
11.7	9.5	NA	NA	NA	NA	3	Very low	0	1	28	8	Vanguard Total Bond Mkt. Idx. (50)			NA		NA	800-662-7447
17.1	15.5	NA	NA	NA	NA	2	Very low	0	11	29	19	Vanguard Total Stk. Mkt. Idx. (34)			NA		NA	800-662-7447
25.4	21.9	21.4	18.4	17.1	14.1	2411	Average	7	5	32	35	Home Depot (3)	Average	IV 98	25.9	III 98	-16.4	800-662-7447
-11.1	-11.4	-4.0	-4.3	NA	NA	444	Very low	0	99	33	-28	NT&T (5)	Very high	IV 98	26.5	IV 97	-20.7	800-662-7447
26.6	25.4	25.1	23.9	20.0	18.7	2211	Very low	9	11	31	44	Guidant (4)	Average	IV 98	28.8	III 98	-13.0	800-662-7447
NA	NA	NA	NA	NA	NA	3	Very low	2	NA	23	-5	Equity Office Properties Tr. (5)			NA		NA	800-662-7447
12.8	10.6	12.9	11.1	13.0	10.9	4123	Low	0	0	23	9	Reinsurance Grp. of America (§)	High	II 97	17.3	III 98	-20.1	800-662-7447
16.5	13.7	15.2	12.6	13.5	10.9	3322	Very low	12	4	25	23	Vanguard Windsor II (28)	Very low	IV 98	11.5	III 98	-8.1	800-662-7447
15.2	14.8	NA	NA	NA	NA	2	Very low	0	0	36	22	General Electric (1)			NA		NA	800-662-7447
25.3	25.1	NA	NA	NA	NA	1	Very low	0	0	36	40	General Electric (3)			NA		NA	800-662-7447
28.3	27.7	NA	NA	NA	NA	1	Very low	0	2	33	29	Microsoft (3)			NA		NA	800-662-7447
NA	NA	NA	NA	NA	NA	4	Very low	0	100	30	6	Vanguard Intl. Equity Index E (76)			NA		NA	800-662-7447
25.0	24.2	21.5	20.6	NA	NA	11	Very low	0	0	32	32	Microsoft (2)	Average	IV 98	21.5	III 98	-12.1	800-662-7447
30.5	28.4	26.2	24.5	21.2	20.1	1411	Average	3	2	43	44	Microsoft (5)	Low	IV 98	24.7	III 98	-9.4	800-662-7447
17.1	14.9	14.5	12.4	NA	NA	32	Low	0	8	24	27	Pinnacle West Capital (3)	Very low	IV 97	13.1	I 94	-7.0	800-662-7447
21.9	20.0	19.8	18.1	NA	NA	11	Low	0	4	24	27	Exxon (4)	Average	IV 98	17.5	III 98	-12.9	800-662-7447
13.7	10.6	12.6	9.8	13.2	10.3	2242	Low	3	5	25	16	Bell Atlantic (2)	Very low	II 95	8.5	I 94	-4.5	800-662-7447
17.1	14.2	16.2	13.8	14.3	11.9	3322	Low	1	9	26	21	Pharmacia & Upjohn (2)	Very low	II 97	12.2	III 98	-4.2	800-662-7447
15.8	12.4	15.1	11.6	13.4	9.9	4223	Average	0	12	21	10	Citicorp (6)	Average	III 98	13.5	III 98	-19.5	800-662-7447
24.1	21.3	21.3	18.7	17.3	14.8	3311	Low	2	2	25	27	Anheuser-Busch (3)	Low	IV 98	14.9	III 98	-11.8	800-662-7447
17.3	15.1	14.9	13.0	NA	NA	32	High	3	8	28	23	IBM (2)	Very low	IV 98	10.2	I 94	-4.1	800-539-3863
25.4	20.9	22.6	18.3	NA	NA	311	Average	2	4	28	14	American Home Products (3)	Average	IV 98	17.6	III 98	-7.8	800-539-3863
31.1	29.2	24.1	22.5	NA	NA	21	Low	2	1	36	43	General Electric (3)	Average	IV 98	22.8	III 98	-6.7	800-539-3863
11.5	9.6	12.2	10.7	NA	NA	23	Low	1	0	22	15	Everest Reinsurance Hldg. (2)	Average	IV 98	14.1	III 98	-20.9	800-539-3863
27.4	25.1	23.3	21.4	NA	NA	11	Very low	24	2	32	21	S&P 500 Index (Fut.) (16)	Average	IV 98	21.1	III 98	-10.0	800-539-3863
25.4	22.4	21.5	19.0	NA	NA	11	Low	1	NA	29	34	IBM (3)	Low	IV 98	18.2	III 98	-7.4	800-539-3863
26.3	24.1	22.8	21.2	NA	NA	11	Average	1	5	36	44	Warner-Lambert (3)	Average	IV 98	27.5	III 98	-15.2	800-438-6375
21.5	19.3	21.7	20.1	NA	NA	11	Low	15	4	39	57	America Online (5)	High	IV 98	28.8	III 98	-13.7	800-366-5465
21.1	19.7	17.7	16.8	NA	NA	22	Low	8	5	35	32	Warner-Lambert (3)	Average	II 97	17.1	III 98	-7.1	800-366-5465
26.8	22.9	22.3	18.5	17.8	15.2	3211	Very high	5	NA	41	27	Freddie Mac (4)	Average	IV 98	21.4	III 98	-11.4	800-927-2874
12.1	11.5	15.2	14.5	16.5	15.6	3113	Average	8	2	39	26	Citrix Systems (3)	High	IV 98	23.9	III 98	-23.0	800-927-2874
13.2	11.0	13.4	11.5	14.7	12.1	2133	High	10	10	23	17	IBM (3)	Average	IV 98	16.5	III 98	-14.4	800-927-2874
3.4	2.1	4.1	2.9	NA	NA	144	Average	5	99	28	-16	Suez Lyonnaise Des Eaux (2)	High	I 98	14.1	III 98	-17.8	800-927-2874
24.1	21.7	22.1	19.6	17.8	15.5	2311	Low	5	NA	28	35	AT&T (3)	Low	II 97	14.4	III 98	-7.0	800-421-4120
NA	NA	NA	NA	NA	NA	4		4	100	37	NA	NT&T (7)			NA		NA	800-810-9327
29.3	26.7	22.2	19.4	18.7	15.9	3121	Low	13	NA	27	34	Telephone & Data Systems (6)	Low	I 98	16.6	III 98	-9.0	800-232-4161
35.8	33.7	23.8	22.2	NA	NA	31	Low	17	NA	25	6	Centennial Cellular Cl. A (9)	Average	I 98	24.1	III 98	-15.6	800-232-4161
28.6	25.5	21.6	18.8	18.3	15.9	3221	Low	19	0	27	17	Telephone & Data Systems (6)	Low	I 98	16.5	III 98	-7.3	800-232-4161
14.1	10.4	13.4	10.7	18.1	14.9	1123	Average	2	2	43	26	MCI WorldCom (5)	High	IV 98	25.2	III 98	-18.8	800-392-2673
31.9	31.8	30.1	30.0	NA	NA	11	Very low	2	0	41	23	Eli Lilly (6)	High	IV 98	37.5	III 98	-19.1	888-462-5386
11.3	10.2	10.5	9.3	13.7	13.2	3133	Low	0	NA	20	29	Carlisle (3)	Average	IV 98	14.8	III 98	-18.2	800-225-8011
21.7	20.1	19.9	18.1	19.0	16.0	1212	Low	10	3	42	45	Automatic Data Processing (4)	Average	IV 98	23.7	III 98	-12.5	800-742-7272
13.4	10.4	13.3	10.8	11.9	9.5	3433	Average	1	5	24	16	Columbia/HCA Healthcare (1)	Very low	IV 98	12.9	III 98	-10.2	800-543-8072
21.9	19.8	19.9	17.9	14.7	12.5	3412	Average	1	6	31	24	Sprint (FON Group) (2)	Average	IV 98	21.3	III 98	-14.5	800-543-8072
26.1	23.3	20.1	18.4	18.0	16.8	1421	Low	2	0	31	43	Microsoft (3)	High	IV 98	45.3	III 98	-17.9	800-543-8072
16.4	12.3	14.7	11.5	13.3	10.1	2422	Average	2	NA	21	25	VF (3)	Average	IV 98	18.3	III 98	-19.2	800-888-9471
14.5	10.5	16.3	13.1	NA	NA	13	Average	4	1	21	36	Philip Morris (11)	Low	IV 98	16.1	III 98	-16.4	800-525-8258
12.3	9.3	11.5	9.1	NA	NA	33	Average	42	3	15	23	TR Financial (1)	Low	IV 98	15.0	III 98	-20.6	800-444-2706
12.4	9.9	9.5	7.5	NA	NA	43	High	15	52	27	18	Nokia Cl. A (1)	Very low	I 98	9.3	III 98	-4.3	800-444-2706
8.6	6.7	9.8	8.2	NA	NA	34	High	13	3	14	19	S&P 500 Index (Fut.) (4)	Low	IV 98		III 98	-20.1	800-444-2706

Vanguard/Primecap. (nnnnn) Formerly Vanguard Sp. REIT Idx. (ooooo) Formerly Vanguard Idx. Sm. Cap Stock. (ppppp) Formerly Vanguard T-M. Fund Bal. Port. (qqqqq) Formerly Vanguard T-M Fund Cap. Apprec. Port. (rrrrr) Formerly Vanguard T-M Fund Gr. & Inc. Port. (sssss) Formerly Vanguard STAR Tot. Intl. (ttttt) Formerly Vanguard Idx. Tot. Stk. Mkt. (uuuuu) Formerly Vanguard Sp. Util. Inc. (vvvvv) Formerly Vanguard Idx. Val. (wwwww) Formerly Vanguard/Wellesley Inc. (xxxxx) Formerly Vanguard/Wellington. (yyyyy) Formerly Vanguard/Windsor. (zzzzz) Formerly Vanguard/WIndsor II. (aaaaaa) Formerly Amcore Vintage Eq. (bbbbbb) Formerly Composite Bd. & Stk. A. (cccccc) Formerly Composite Gr. & Inc. A. (dddddd) Formerly Composite Northwest A. DATA: MORNINGSTAR, INC., CHICAGO, IL.

MUTUAL FUND SCOREBOARD

How to Use the Tables

BUSINESS WEEK RATING

Ratings measure risk-adjusted performance. This shows how well a fund performed relative to other funds and relative to the level of risk it took. Risk-adjusted performance is determined by subtracting a fund's risk-of-loss factor (see below) from its historic total return. Performance calculations are based on the five-year time period between Jan. 1, 1994, and Dec. 31, 1998. For BW ratings, funds are divided into taxable and tax-exempt funds. Funds are also rated against others in their category. Ratings are based on a normal statistical distribution within each group and awarded as follows:

A	SUPERIOR
B+	VERY GOOD
B	ABOVE AVERAGE
C	AVERAGE
C–	BELOW AVERAGE
D	POOR
F	VERY POOR

RISK

The risk-of-loss factor is the potential for losing money in a fund, calculated as follows: The monthly Treasury bill return is subtracted from the fund's total return for each of the 60 months in the rating period. When a fund has underperformed Treasury bills, the result is negative. The sum of these negative numbers is then divided by the number of months in the period. The result is a negative number, and the greater its magnitude, the higher the risk of loss.

PERFORMANCE COMPARISON

The tables provide performance data over three time periods. Here are equivalent total returns for the Lehman Brothers bond indexes during those periods:

	GOVT./CORP.	MUNI.
1998	9.5%	6.5%
3-year average (1996-98)	7.3%	6.7%
5-year average (1994-98)	7.3%	6.2%

FUND CATEGORIES

General bond funds are classified long-term (CL), intermediate-term (CI), short-term (CS), and ultrashort (UB); government, long (GL), intermediate (GI), and short (GS); municipal, national long (ML), national interm. (MI), single-state long (SL), single-state interm. (SI), Calif. long (MC), Calif. interm. (MF), New York long (MY), New York interm. (MN), and short-term (MS); specialized funds, convertible (CV), high-yield (HY), international (IB), emerging markets (EB), and multisector (MU).

SALES CHARGE

The cost of buying a fund, commonly called the "load." Many funds take loads out of initial investments, and for ratings purposes, performance is reduced by these charges. Loads on withdrawals can take two forms. Deferred charges decrease over time. Redemption fees are imposed whenever investors sell shares. Funds with none of these charges are called "no-load."

EXPENSE RATIO

Fund expenses for 1998 as a percentage of average net assets. The measures show how much shareholders pay for fund management. Footnotes indicate 12(b)-1 plans, which allocate shareholder money for marketing costs. The average expense ratio is 1.01% for taxable funds, 0.85% for tax-free funds.

TOTAL RETURN

A fund's net gain to investors, including reinvestment of dividends and capital gains at month-end prices.

YIELD

Income distributions during 1998 expressed as a percent of net asset value, adjusted for capital gains.

MATURITY

The average maturity of the securities in a fund's portfolio, weighted by market value.

HISTORY

A fund's relative performance during the five 12-month periods from Jan. 1, 1994, to Dec. 31, 1998. The numbers designate which quartile the fund was in during the period: **1** or the top quartile; **2** or the second quartile; **3** or the third quartile; **4** for the bottom quartile. No number indicates no data for that period.

TELEPHONE NUMBERS

See index on page 222.

FUND (COMPARES RISK-ADJUSTED PERFORMANCE OF EACH FUND AGAINST ALL FUNDS)	RATING	CATEGORY (RATING COMPARES FUND WITHIN CATEGORY)	RATING	SIZE ASSETS $MIL.	% CHG. 1997-98	FEES SALES CHARGE (%)	EXPENSE RATIO (%)	TOTAL RETURN (%) 1 YR.	3 YR.	5 YR.	YIELD (%)	MATURITY (YEARS)	HISTORY RESULTS VS. ALL FUNDS
TAXABLE													
AARP BOND FUND FOR INCOME		CI		196.7	143	No load	0.19	6.4	NA	NA	6.7	8.5	2
AARP GNMA & U.S. TREASURY	B+	GS	C	4535.2	0	No load	0.61	6.8	6.5	6.0	6.5	6.9	1 4 2 3 2
AARP HIGH-QUALITY SHORT TERM BOND (a)	C–	CS	F	440.1	–2	No load	0.90	5.5	5.4	5.6	5.7	2.9	2 2 4 3 3
ABN AMRO FIXED-INCOME COMM. (b)	C	CI	C	171.0	20	No load	0.71	7.1	6.6	6.5	5.6	13.2	2 2 3 2 1
ACCESSOR MORTGAGE SECURITIES	B+	GI	A	128.8	17	No load	0.84	6.4	7.0	6.9	5.5	9.1	1 3 1 1 2
ADVANCE CAPITAL I RETIREMENT INCOME	C	CL	B	220.7	10	No load	0.82 †	6.3	7.6	7.7	6.9	15.5	3 1 2 1 2
AIM EMERGING MARKETS DEBT B (c)	F	EB		116.7	–47	5.00 **	2.18 †	–29.3	2.2	0.5	13.4	11.7	4 1 1 1 4
AIM FLOATING RATE		UB		287.1	33	3.00 **	1.50	5.2	NA	NA	7.0	NA	3
AIM GLOBAL GOVT. INCOME A (d)	F	IB	D	119.4	–17	4.75	1.34 †	12.1	7.1	4.1	5.6	14.4	4 3 1 4 1
AIM HIGH-YIELD B	D	HY	C–	1813.0	10	5.00 **	1.65 †	–5.9	6.4	6.4	9.6	7.5	1 3 1 1 4
AIM INCOME A	C–	MU	C	398.1	17	4.75	0.94 †	4.9	8.4	7.7	6.6	14.4	4 1 1 1 4
AIM INTERMEDIATE GOVT. A	C	GI	C	244.4	47	4.75	1.00 †	8.2	6.5	6.3	6.6	7.4	2 3 4 2 1
AIM LTD. MATURITY TREASURY RET.	B+	GS	B+	408.1	6	1.00	0.54 †	6.1	5.6	5.4	5.0	1.5	1 4 1 4 2
AIM STRATEGIC INCOME B (e)	F	IB	F	183.5	–33	5.00 **	2.00 †	–2.5	7.6	2.7	6.9	14.7	4 3 1 4 4
ALLIANCE BOND CORP. BOND B	F	CL	F	678.4	18	3.00 **	1.75 †	–0.8	6.6	6.0	8.1	16.4	4 1 1 1 4
ALLIANCE BOND U.S. GOVT. B	D	GI	D	425.3	–2	3.00 **	1.76 †	7.8	5.2	5.0	6.3	NA	3 3 4 3 1
ALLIANCE GLOBAL DOLLAR GOVT. B		EB		114.6	22	3.00 **	2.26 †	–22.7	5.2	NA	13.6	16.4	1 1 2 4
ALLIANCE HIGH YIELD B		HY		371.1	361	4.00 **	2.13 †	–2.3	NA	NA	9.6	6.7	4
ALLIANCE MORTGAGE SECURITIES INC. A	C–	GS	F	462.3	24	4.25	1.41 †	5.8	6.3	5.4	6.5	NA	3 3 2 2 3
ALLIANCE NORTH AMER. GOVT. INCOME B	F	IB	F	1302.2	–7	3.00 **	2.09 †	5.7	14.4	6.1	11.8	8.2	4 1 1 1 3
AMERICAN CENT.-BENHAM BOND INV.	C	CI	C–	142.4	10	No load	0.80	6.6	5.9	6.4	5.9	10.6	2 1 4 2 2
AMERICAN CENT.-BENHAM GNMA INV.	B+	GI	A	1377.1	12	No load	0.58	6.4	6.8	6.7	6.1	NA	1 3 1 2 2
AMERICAN CENT.-BENHAM INTERM. TREAS. INV.	B	GI	B+	444.3	23	No load	0.51	10.3	7.5	6.7	6.4	6.9	1 4 2 3 1
AMERICAN CENT.-BENHAM INTL. BOND	D	IB	C	150.4	–9	No load	0.84	17.9	5.7	8.3	1.4	NA	1 1 1 4 1
AMERICAN CENT.-BENHAM L/T TREAS. INV.	D	GL	C–	163.0	26	No load	0.54	12.8	8.5	8.4	5.4	NA	4 1 4 1 1

* Includes redemption fee. ** Includes deferred sales charge. † 12(b)-1 plan in effect. ‡ Not currently accepting new accounts. NA = Not available. NM = Not meaningful.
(a) Formerly AARP High-Quality Bond. (b) Formerly Rembrandt Fixed-Income Comm. (c) Formerly GT Global High-Income B. (d) Formerly GT Global Government Income A. (e) Formerly GT Global Strategic Income B.

DATA: MORNINGSTAR, INC., CHICAGO, IL.

MUTUAL FUND SCOREBOARD — Bond Funds

FUND	RATING (COMPARES RISK-ADJUSTED PERFORMANCE OF EACH FUND AGAINST ALL FUNDS)	CATEGORY	RATING (RATING COMPARES FUND WITHIN CATEGORY)	SIZE ASSETS $MIL.	SIZE % CHG. 1997-98	FEES SALES CHARGE (%)	FEES EXPENSE RATIO (%)	TOTAL RETURN (%) 1 YR.	TOTAL RETURN (%) 3 YR.	TOTAL RETURN (%) 5 YR.	PORTFOLIO YIELD (%)	PORTFOLIO MATURITY (YEARS)	HISTORY RESULTS VS. ALL FUNDS
AMERICAN CENT.-BENHAM S/T GOVT. INV.	B+	GS	B	824.1	62	No load	0.59	6.1	5.4	5.2	5.3	NA	1 4 2 4 2
AMERICAN CENT.-BENHAM TARGET MAT. 2000	C-	GI	C-	221.3	-9	No load	0.59	7.4	5.3	5.5	6.3	NA	4 1 4 4 1
AMERICAN CENT.-BENHAM TARGET MAT. 2005	D	GL	C-	527.4	75	No load	0.59	12.9	7.2	8.1	4.7	NA	4 1 4 1 1
AMERICAN CENT.-BENHAM TARGET MAT. 2010	F	GL	D	246.1	56	No load	0.59	15.1	8.8	10.0	4.8	NA	4 1 4 1 1
AMERICAN CENT.-BENHAM TARGET MAT. 2015	F	GL	D	178.4	33	No load	0.59	14.7	9.7	11.6	4.5	NA	4 1 4 1 1
AMERICAN CENT.-BENHAM TARGET MAT. 2020	F	GL	F	423.7	-29	No load	0.59	16.8	11.1	12.7	6.1	NA	4 1 4 1 1
AMERICAN CENT.-BENHAM TARGET MAT. 2025		GL		303.4	57	No load	0.59	21.9	NA	NA	4.3	NA	1 1
AMERICAN HIGH-INCOME	C	HY	C	2573	17	4.75	0.81†	-1.6	9.1	8.2	9.0	7.3	3 1 1 1 4
AMSOUTH BOND PREMIER		CI		339.4	11	No load	NA	9.4	NA	NA	5.6	7.0	1
ARMADA BOND INSTITUTIONAL		CS		779.0	726	4.00	0.83†	8.5	6.6	NA	5.4	8.2	3 3 3 1
ARMADA INTERM. BOND INSTITUTIONAL	C	CS	D	311.2	109	No load	0.70†	7.9	6.0	5.6	5.3	5.2	2 3 3 1
ASSET MGMT. ADJUSTABLE RATE	A	UB	C	912.3	20	No load	0.50†	5.2	5.9	5.7	5.7	3.1	1 4 1 4 3
ASSET MGMT. SHORT U.S. GOVT. SECS.	B+	GS	B	121.2	15	No load	0.49†	6.7	5.5	5.6	5.8	2.4	1 4 3 4 2
ATLAS U.S. GOVT. & MORTGAGE A	B	GI	B	210.3	4	No load	1.03†	6.1	6.3	6.0	6.2	NA	2 3 2 3 2
BABSON BOND L	C	CI	B	128.0	-3	No load	0.97	7.4	6.6	6.3	5.9	8.0	2 3 3 2 1
BERNSTEIN GOVT. SHORT DURATION	B+	GS	B	145.0	0	No load	0.69	5.6	5.1	5.1	4.9	NA	1 4 2 4 3
BERNSTEIN INTERM. DURATION	B	CI	B	2532.1	19	No load	0.62	6.6	5.9	6.3	5.4	7.6	2 2 3 3 2
BERNSTEIN SHORT DURATION PLUS	B+	CS	B+	604.0	1	No load	0.64	5.9	5.4	5.3	5.2	1.9	1 4 1 4 3
WILLIAM BLAIR INCOME	B+	CS	C	188.1	17	No load	0.71	7.1	6.0	6.2	6.1	4.0	1 3 3 3 1
BOND FUND OF AMERICA	C	CI	C	9541.5	17	4.75	0.68†	5.2	7.0	6.6	6.9	9.2	3 1 1 2 3
BOSTON 1784 INCOME		CI		370.5	-2	No load	0.80†	7.4	5.9	NA	5.4	8.6	2 4 3 1
BOSTON 1784 SHORT-TERM INCOME		CS		185.4	-4	No load	0.64†	6.3	5.6	NA	5.4	2.6	4 2 4 2
BOSTON 1784 U.S. GOVT. MEDIUM-TERM	C	CI	C	277.0	15	No load	0.80†	8.0	6.0	5.8	5.3	7.2	2 3 4 3 1
BRINSON GLOBAL BOND I	B	IB	B+	119.5	113	No load	0.90	12.0	7.6	7.6	4.6	11.3	2 1 1 4 1
CAPITAL WORLD BOND	C-	IB	C	625.7	-12	4.75	1.06†	10.1	5.3	6.9	4.9	9.4	1 1 1 4 1
CHICAGO TRUST BOND	B	CI	B+	157.6	20	No load	0.80†	7.7	6.8	6.8	5.9	7.8	2 2 2 2 1
COLONIAL FEDERAL SECURITIES A	D	GI	D	803.8	-7	4.75	1.14†	9.1	6.6	6.6	5.9	11.4	2 1 3 2 1
COLONIAL HIGH-YIELD SECURITIES B	B	HY	B	573.0	12	5.00**	1.95†	1.2	8.4	8.0	8.4	8.4	1 2 1 1 4
COLONIAL INCOME A	C-	CI	C-	119.0	-1	4.75	1.11†	8.1	6.8	7.0	6.9	9.3	2 1 3 2 1
COLONIAL INTERM. U.S. GOVT. A	C	GI	C	630.0	-10	4.75	1.12†	8.2	6.4	6.3	5.7	8.2	1 3 4 3 1
COLONIAL STRATEGIC INCOME B	C	MU	C	919.2	10	5.00**	1.93†	4.4	7.2	7.0	7.3	9.8	2 1 1 3 4
COLUMBIA FIXED-INCOME SECURITIES	B	CI	B	426.0	12	No load	0.66	7.4	6.8	6.9	6.1	5.9	2 1 3 1 1
CONCERT INVESTMENT GOVERNMENT 1 (f)	D	GI	D	213.1	NM	6.75	0.84	6.3	5.8	5.6	6.2	NA	3 2 4 1 2
DAVIS CONVERTIBLE SECURITIES A	B	CV	B+	133.6	49	4.75	1.07†	-1.8	17.8	14.1	3.2	NA	4 1 1 1 4
DELAWARE DELCHESTER A	D	HY	C-	924.5	-10	4.75	1.06†	-1.9	7.8	6.4	10.5	7.7	2 3 1 1 4
DELAWARE LIMITED-TERM GOVT. A	C	GS	C-	317.4	-11	2.75	0.98†	7.4	5.4	4.5	6.2	2.8	1 4 3 4 1
DELAWARE U.S. GOVT. A	D	CI	F	138.4	-4	4.75	1.20†	7.1	6.0	5.0	6.5	11.1	3 4 4 3 1
DODGE & COX INCOME	B	CI	B+	953.9	35	No load	0.49	8.1	7.2	7.5	5.9	9.7	2 1 2 2 1
DREYFUS A BONDS PLUS	D	CI	F	596.1	-6	No load	0.95	2.7	4.9	5.4	6.0	14.3	3 1 4 2 4
DREYFUS DISCIPLINED INTERM. BOND RET.		CI		178.8	38	No load	0.55	8.5	6.7	NA	5.9	8.1	4 2 1
DREYFUS GNMA	B	CI	B	1107.1	-8	No load	0.96†	4.2	5.8	5.8	6.3	20.3	2 3 2 2 4
DREYFUS HIGH-YIELD SECURITIES		HY		141.0	1	1.00*	0.71	-15.8	NA	NA	15.3	6.5	1 4
DREYFUS PREMIER LTD.-TERM HIGH-INC. B		HY		550.8	180	4.00**	1.45†	-0.6	NA	NA	9.5	NA	4
DREYFUS SHORT-INTERM. GOVT.	B+	GS	C	483.6	1	No load	0.74	6.5	5.5	5.6	6.9	NA	1 4 2 4 2
DREYFUS SHORT-TERM HIGH-YIELD		HY		189.6	22	No load	1.09	-0.8	NA	NA	10.4	NA	1 4
DREYFUS SHORT-TERM INCOME	B+	CS	B	345.8	17	No load	0.87	4.3	6.2	5.9	6.8	NA	1 4 1 3 4
DREYFUS STRATEGIC INCOME	C	MU	C	285.1	3	No load	1.03	4.3	7.3	7.0	7.0	15.6	3 1 1 1 4
DREYFUS U.S. TREASURY INTERM. TERM (g)	C	GI	C	181.0	-4	No load	0.80	7.6	6.1	5.8	6.1	12.0	2 3 3 3 1
DREYFUS U.S. TREASURY LONG-TERM (h)	D	GL	C-	142.1	6	No load	0.80	10.8	7.7	7.2	5.0	20.6	4 1 4 1 1
DREYFUS U.S. TREASURY SHORT-TERM (i)	B+	GS		185.3	-5	No load	0.70	6.1	5.4	5.4	5.9	2.7	1 4 2 4 2
EATON VANCE GOVT. OBLIGATIONS A (j)	C	GS	D	251.9	-9	4.75	1.24†	5.6	5.8	5.7	7.7	4.0	1 3 2 3 3
EATON VANCE HIGH-INCOME B (k)	B	HY	B	647.1	-2	5.00**	1.73†	1.8	10.1	8.4	9.0	7.9	1 3 1 1 4
EATON VANCE INCOME OF BOSTON	B	HY	B	247.9	19	4.75	1.04†	2.7	10.8	9.1	9.5	7.9	1 3 1 1 4
EATON VANCE PRIME RATE RESERVES	A	UB	B+	2596.2	19	3.00**	1.31	6.9	6.9	7.0	6.8	NA	1 3 1 1 4
EATON VANCE STRATEGIC INCOME B	C-	MU		146.5	10	5.00**	2.08†	1.2	9.1	7.1	7.7	NA	3 3 1 2 4
EV CLASSIC SENIOR FLOATING RATE		UB		2979.9	23	1.00**	1.46	6.8	6.8	NA	6.7	NA	1 4 2
EVERGREEN INTERM.-TERM BOND A	C	CI	C	119.1	NM	3.25	1.11†	5.9	6.4	6.0	5.9	7.0	2 3 1 3 2
EVERGREEN STRATEGIC INCOME A	F	MU	D	165.7	168	4.75	1.26†	3.5	7.7	4.6	7.2	15.4	4 4 1 2 4
EVERGREEN U.S. GOVERNMENT B	C	GI	C	130.2	-8	5.00**	1.73†	7.4	5.8	5.7	5.1	8.6	2 3 4 3 1
EXCELSIOR INT.-TERM MGD. INCOME	C	CI	B	120.5	32	No load	0.61	8.5	6.3	6.6	5.3	10.4	2 1 4 3 1
EXCELSIOR MANAGED INCOME	C-	CL	C	218.1	10	No load	0.80	8.6	6.2	6.8	5.0	15.9	3 1 4 1 1
EXECUTIVE INVESTORS HIGH-YIELD	B	HY	C	218.5	0	4.75	1.22†	0.8	8.4	8.2	9.1	7.9	2 1 1 1 4
FEDERATED ADJ. RATE U.S. GOVT. F	B+	GS	C	142.9	-23	1.00**	1.10†	3.6	5.1	4.6	5.2	NA	1 4 1 4 4
FEDERATED BOND F	B	CI	B	411.7	17	2.00**	1.08	5.6	7.3	7.5	7.0	10.8	2 1 1 1 3
FEDERATED FUND FOR U.S. GOVT. A	C	GI	B	1073.5	-8	4.50	0.94	6.3	6.3	6.2	6.1	NA	1 3 2 3 2
FEDERATED GOVT. INCOME SECURITIES F	B	GI	B	1261.4	-15	2.00**	0.96	7.6	7.0	6.6	6.0	NA	1 3 2 2 1
FEDERATED HIGH-INCOME BOND B		HY		1130.8	32	5.50**	1.97†	1.3	8.7	NA	8.2	5.8	1 1 1 4
FEDERATED HIGH-YIELD	B+	HY	B	1099.8	-2	No load	0.88	1.1	9.1	8.5	9.4	6.6	1 1 1 1 4
FEDERATED INCOME INST.	B+	GI	A	697.3	-8	No load	0.58	6.6	6.7	6.7	6.0	NA	1 3 1 2 2
FEDERATED INTERM. INCOME INST.	B+	CI	B+	204.4	34	No load	0.55	7.2	6.6	7.3	5.9	NA	1 3 1 2 2

*Includes redemption fee. **Includes deferred sales charge. †12(b)-1 plan in effect. ‡Not currently accepting new accounts or deposits. NA=Not available. NM=Not meaningful.
(f) Formerly Common Sense Government. 1. (g) Formerly Dreyfus 100% U.S. Treasury Intermediate-Term. (h) Formerly Dreyfus 100% U.S. Treasury Long-Term. (i) Formerly Dreyfus 100% U.S. Treasury Short-Term. (j) Formerly EV Traditional Government Obligations. (k) Formerly EV Marathon High-Income.

DATA: MORNINGSTAR, INC., CHICAGO, IL.

FUND	RATING (COMPARES RISK-ADJUSTED PERFORMANCE OF EACH FUND AGAINST ALL FUNDS)	CATEGORY	RATING (RATING COMPARES FUND WITHIN CATEGORY)	SIZE ASSETS $MIL.	SIZE % CHG. 1997-98	FEES SALES CHARGE (%)	FEES EXPENSE RATIO (%)	PERFORMANCE TOTAL RETURN (%) 1 YR.	PERFORMANCE 3 YR.	PERFORMANCE 5 YR.	PORTFOLIO YIELD (%)	PORTFOLIO MATURITY (YEARS)	HISTORY RESULTS VS. ALL FUNDS
FEDERATED INTL. INCOME A	F	IB	C−	139.5	−19	4.50	1.30 †	14.5	6.4	6.2	3.7	7.3	2 2 1 4 1
FEDERATED SHORT-TERM INCOME INST.	B+	CS	B	187.2	−6	No load	0.56	5.7	5.9	5.5	6.0	NA	1 4 1 4 3
FEDERATED STRATEGIC INCOME B		MU		705.7	118	5.50 **	1.85 †	1.6	6.9	NA	8.2	5.3	1 3 4
FEDERATED U.S. GOVT.: 1-3 INST.	B+	GS	B+	595.7	−5	No load	0.54	6.4	5.7	5.4	4.9	1.7	1 4 2 4 2
FEDERATED U.S. GOVT.: 2-5 INST.	B	GS	C	722.7	3	No load	0.54	8.1	6.3	6.0	5.1	3.5	1 4 3 4 1
FFTW INTL FIXED-INCOME		IB		344.5	419	No load	0.60	18.4	NA	NA	8.2	NA	4 1
FFTW U.S. SHORT-TERM F/I	A	UB	C	837.4	73	No load	0.40	5.6	5.4	5.1	5.6	NA	1 4 1 4 3
FFTW WORLDWIDE F/I HEDGED	A	IB	A	181.0	135	No load	0.45	11.5	11.4	10.6	5.9	NA	1 4 1 1 1
FIDELITY ADV. GOVT. INVESTMENT T	C−	GI	C−	201.0	35	3.50	1.00 †	8.3	6.3	6.4	5.5	8.7	2 2 4 2 1
FIDELITY ADV. HIGH-YIELD T	C	HY	C	2550.4	12	3.50	1.07 †	−0.4	9.1	8.8	9.4	8.4	1 1 1 1 4
FIDELITY ADV. INTERMEDIATE BOND T	C	CS	D	287.7	23	2.75	0.98 †	7.0	5.8	5.3	5.3	5.9	1 4 3 4 1
FIDELITY ADV. SHORT FIXED-INCOME T	C	CS	C	313.1	−13	1.50	0.89 †	5.9	5.5	4.5	5.7	NA	2 4 2 4 3
FIDELITY ADV. STRATEGIC INCOME T		MU		190.2	65	3.50	1.19 †	2.3	8.1	NA	6.8	NA	1 1 2 4
FIDELITY CAPITAL & INCOME	C	HY	C−	2195.6	5	1.50 *	0.82	4.8	10.2	8.3	9.9	6.9	2 2 1 1 4
FIDELITY CONVERTIBLE SECURITIES	C−	CV	C	1035.6	3	No load	0.73	16.3	15.3	12.4	3.2	NA	1 1 1 1 1
FIDELITY GINNIE MAE	B+	GI	B+	1093.5	27	No load	0.72	6.4	6.6	6.7	6.2	5.5	1 2 1 2 2
FIDELITY GOVERNMENT INCOME (l)	C−	GI	C	1583.2	36	No load	0.68	8.6	6.5	6.2	5.9	8.9	3 2 4 2 1
FIDELITY HIGH-INCOME (m)	A	HY	A	2861.9	17	1.00 *	0.80	3.3	11.0	10.8	8.6	8.4	1 1 1 1 4
FIDELITY INTERMEDIATE BOND	B	CS	C	3443.8	8	No load	0.65	7.3	6.2	5.8	6.1	5.1	1 4 3 3 1
FIDELITY INTERMEDIATE GOVT. (n)	B+	GS	B	760.0	0	No load	0.38	7.5	6.4	6.3	6.5	4.7	1 3 2 3 1
FIDELITY INVESTMENT GRADE BOND	C	CI	C	2191.1	33	No load	0.71	7.9	6.6	5.8	5.7	8.2	3 3 3 2 1
FIDELITY MORTGAGE SECURITIES INITIAL (o)	A	GI	A	453.9	−6	No load ‡	0.71	5.9	6.8	7.8	6.3	4.9	1 2 1 2 3
FIDELITY NEW MARKETS INCOME	F	EB		206.9	−44	1.00 *	1.08	−22.4	8.9	3.1	13.5	16.3	4 4 1 1 4
FIDELITY SHORT-INTERMEDIATE GOVT.	B+	GS	C	132.6	5	No load ‡	0.78	6.5	5.7	5.4	6.3	3.4	1 4 2 4 2
FIDELITY SHORT-TERM BOND	C	CS	C−	841.7	−4	No load	0.70	6.2	5.7	4.5	5.9	2.4	2 4 1 4 2
FIDELITY SPARTAN GINNIE MAE	B+	GI	A	641.9	8	No load ‡	0.38	6.8	6.9	7.0	6.4	5.5	1 2 1 2 2
FIDELITY SPARTAN GOVT. INCOME		GI	B	642.8	130	No load	0.60	9.0	6.9	6.8	5.8	8.9	2 2 4 2 1
FIDELITY SPARTAN INVESTMENT GRADE BOND	C	CI	C	1261.4	92	No load ‡	0.38	8.8	7.0	6.6	6.0	7.8	3 1 3 2 1
FIDELITY SPARTAN SHORT-TERM BOND	B	CS	C−	302.9	7	No load ‡	0.38	6.6	6.1	4.6	6.2	2.4	2 4 1 4 2
FIDELITY U.S. BOND INDEX	B	CI	B+	1225.1	84	No load	0.31	8.9	7.2	7.2	6.3	7.9	1 2 3 1 1
FIRST AMERICAN ADJ. RATE MORT. A (p)	D	CS	F	121.4	−29	2.00	0.81 †	4.8	6.0	2.4	5.4	NA	3 4 1 4 4
FIRST AMERICAN FIXED-INCOME A	C	CI	C	171.1	NM	3.75	0.95 †	8.7	6.8	6.8	5.0	10.9	1 2 3 3 1
FIRST AMERICAN STRATEGIC INCOME		CI		113.9	67	No load	0.25	8.2	NA	NA	4.9	NA	1 1
FIRST INVESTORS FUND FOR INCOME A	B+	HY	B+	409.7	−9	6.25	1.27 †	4.1	9.7	9.5	9.9	7.3	1 1 1 1 4
FIRST INVESTORS GOVERNMENT A	C−	GI	C−	166.1	−2	6.25	1.28 †	6.5	6.1	5.8	5.9	NA	2 3 3 3 2
FIRST INVESTORS HIGH-YIELD A	B+	HY	B+	196.2	−6	6.25	1.36 †	3.6	9.5	9.2	9.4	7.4	1 2 1 1 4
FLAG INVESTORS TOTAL RET. U.S. TREASURY A	D	GL	B	126.6	5	4.50	0.83 †	10.8	7.1	7.5	6.0	14.4	2 1 4 1 1
FORTIS U.S. GOVT. SECURITIES E	C−	GI	C−	282.0	−7	4.50 ‡	0.79	8.5	6.9	6.0	5.3	7.7	3 3 3 2 1
FPA NEW INCOME	A	CI	A	591.6	5	4.50	0.59	3.9	6.4	6.9	7.8	NA	1 3 1 3 4
FRANKLIN ADJ. U.S. GOVT. SECURITIES	B	GS	C	304.4	−5	2.25	0.75 †	3.9	5.7	4.8	5.3	NA	1 4 1 4 4
FRANKLIN CONVERTIBLE SECURITIES A	D	CV	C−	170.2	−24	5.75	1.01 †	−7.0	9.2	9.7	5.2	NA	1 1 1 1 4
FRANKLIN SHORT-INTERM. GOVT. A (q)	B	GS	C−	211.8	13	2.25	0.78 †	6.6	5.5	5.0	5.4	2.0	1 4 2 4 2
FRANKLIN STRATEGIC INCOME		MU		197.6	94	4.25	0.25 †	4.1	10.2	NA	8.0	8.0	1 1 1 4
FRANKLIN U.S. GOVT. SECURITIES A (r)	B	GI	B+	8901.4	−4	4.25	0.64 †	6.6	6.9	6.8	6.5	4.9	2 2 2 2 2
FRANKLIN'S AGE HIGH INCOME A (s)	B	HY	B	3172.0	6	4.25	0.70 †	1.5	9.1	8.7	9.6	8.6	1 1 1 1 4
FREMONT BOND	B	CI	A	216.0	97	No load	0.61	9.5	8.1	8.0	6.3	8.0	2 1 1 1 1
GALAXY II U.S. TREASURY INDEX RET.	C	GI	B	190.6	65	No load	0.40	9.8	7.0	6.9	5.8	9.1	2 2 4 2 1
GE GOVERNMENT SECURITIES B	D	CI	F	371.9	−24	5.00 **	1.63 †	8.3	6.3	4.3	5.8	9.7	4 4 4 3 1
GLOBAL TOTAL RETURN A	B+	IB	B+	159.2	−13	4.00	1.39 †	8.9	8.8	8.6	6.6	7.0	4 1 1 4 1
GOLDMAN SACHS GLOBAL A	B+	IB	A	231.9	38	4.50	1.17 †	10.2	9.7	8.1	4.2	9.4	3 2 1 1 1
GOLDMAN SACHS HIGH YIELD A		HY		464.2	34	4.50	0.95 †	3.0	NA	NA	8.1	NA	4
GRADISON GOVT. INCOME	B	GI	B	159.8	3	No load	0.90 †	7.3	6.4	6.3	5.7	5.0	2 2 3 3 1
GREAT PLAINS INTERMEDIATE BOND		CI		134.9	1	3.00	0.79 †	9.1	NA	NA	5.6	7.9	1
GUARDIAN INVEST. QUALITY BOND A	C−	CI	D	142.0	44	4.50	0.75 †	7.9	6.3	5.9	5.2	10.6	3 2 4 3 1
HANCOCK BOND A (t)	B	CI	B	1343.1	−1	4.50	1.08 †	7.5	7.0	7.3	6.6	13.6	2 1 2 1 1
HANCOCK GOVERNMENT INCOME A		CI		624.6	78	4.50	1.13 †	8.8	6.8	NA	6.3	9.6	1 4 2 1
HANCOCK HIGH-YIELD BOND B	F	HY	F	756.2	25	5.00 **	1.80 †	−11.9	5.9	5.0	11.1	7.6	3 3 1 1 4
HANCOCK INTERM. MATURITY GOVT. A	B	GI	B+	171.9	1	3.00	1.09 †	8.6	6.9	6.4	6.1	7.7	1 4 3 2 1
HANCOCK STRATEGIC INCOME B	B+	MU	B+	571.0	44	5.00 **	1.62 †	4.7	9.1	8.1	7.3	10.9	2 2 1 1 4
HARBOR BOND	B+	CI	A	494.4	29	No load	0.67	9.6	7.9	7.6	5.4	9.7	2 1 1 2 1
HARBOR SHORT DURATION	A	CS	A	166.9	1	No load	0.36	6.4	6.3	5.8	5.6	4.4	1 4 1 4 2
HOMESTEAD SHORT-TERM BOND	A	CS	B+	143.7	32	No load	0.75	6.4	6.1	5.8	5.5	NA	1 4 1 4 2
HOTCHKIS & WILEY LOW DURATION	A	CS	A	387.2	99	No load	0.58	5.7	6.6	7.5	6.5	3.1	1 4 1 3 3
IDS BOND A	C	CI	C	2767.1	3	5.00	0.83	5.6	6.9	7.3	6.8	15.1	2 1 1 1 3
IDS EXTRA INCOME A	D	HY	D	2732.4	−6	5.00	0.89	−5.0	7.1	6.7	10.7	7.6	4 1 1 1 4
IDS FEDERAL INCOME A	B	GS	B	1619.2	20	5.00	0.86	6.8	6.3	6.4	5.6	6.2	1 3 2 3 2
IDS GLOBAL BOND A	D	IB	C	734.6	−1	5.00	1.16	8.1	6.3	6.4	4.5	11.4	3 1 1 4 1
IDS SELECTIVE A	C−	CI	C−	1230.0	−2	5.00	0.86	8.2	6.3	6.8	6.0	16.8	2 1 4 3 1
INTERMEDIATE BOND FUND AMERICA	C	CS	D	1587.9	20	4.75	0.76 †	6.7	6.0	5.6	6.0	4.3	2 4 2 4 2
INVESCO HIGH-YIELD	C	HY	C	829.0	41	No load	0.86 †	0.2	10.2	8.4	9.7	7.5	2 1 1 1 4

*Includes redemption fee. **Includes deferred sales charge. †12(b)-1 plan in effect. ‡Not currently accepting new accounts or deposits. NA=Not available. NM=Not meaningful. (l) Formerly /Fidelity Government Securities. (m) Formerly Fidelity Spartan High-Income. (n) Formerly Fidelity Spartan Limited Mat. Government. (o) Formerly Fidelity Advisor Mortgage Secs. Init. (p) Formerly Piper Adjustable Rate Mortgage Secs. (q) Formerly Franklin Short-Interm. U.S. Government I. (r) Formerly Franklin U.S. Government Securities. I. (s) Formerly Frankiln's AGE High Income I. (t) Formerly John Hancock Sovereign Bond A.

DATA: MORNINGSTAR, INC., CHICAGO, IL.

FUND (COMPARES RISK-ADJUSTED PERFORMANCE OF EACH FUND AGAINST ALL FUNDS)	RATING	CATEGORY	RATING (RATING COMPARES FUND WITHIN CATEGORY)	SIZE ASSETS $MIL.	% CHG. 1997-98	FEES SALES CHARGE (%)	EXPENSE RATIO (%)	1 YR.	3 YR.	5 YR.	YIELD (%)	MATURITY (YEARS)	HISTORY RESULTS VS. ALL FUNDS
INVESCO SELECT INCOME	A	CL	A	528.1	59	No load	1.06 †	7.1	7.9	8.4	6.4	8.9	1 1 1 1 1
ISG GOVERNMENT INCOME A (u)	C	CI	C	284.7	9	2.00	0.80 †	9.0	6.7	6.5	5.2	8.8	2 2 4 2 1
ISI TOTAL RETURN U.S. TREASURY	D	GL	B	300.0	2	4.45	0.83 †	10.8	7.1	7.5	6.0	14.7	2 1 4 1 1
JANUS FLEXIBLE INCOME	A	MU	B+	1169.4	53	No load	0.86	8.2	8.8	8.7	6.6	10.1	2 1 1 1 1
JANUS HIGH-YIELD		HY		295.2	−17	No load	1.00	1.0	13.1	NA	8.5	7.7	1 1 4
JANUS SHORT-TERM BOND	B+	CS	B	131.9	91	No load	0.65	6.8	6.5	5.5	5.9	2.9	1 4 1 4 2
KEMPER DIVERSIFIED INCOME A	C−	MU	C	578.1	1	4.50	1.03	3.8	6.9	7.1	8.4	7.3	2 1 1 3 4
KEMPER HIGH-YIELD A	C	HY	C	3472.4	−5	4.50	0.89	1.3	8.6	8.1	9.9	7.9	1 2 1 1 4
KEMPER INCOME & CAP. PRES. A	C	CI	C	575.1	10	4.50	0.97	7.9	6.1	7.0	6.2	9.0	2 1 4 2 1
KEMPER U.S. GOVT. SECURITIES A	C	GI	B	3223.0	−8	4.50	0.78	7.0	6.3	6.6	6.6	5.4	2 1 4 2 1
KEMPER U.S. MORTGAGE A	C	GI	C	1784.4	1	4.50	0.96	7.0	6.2	6.4	6.5	7.9	2 2 4 2 1
KEYPREMIER INTERM. INCOME		CI		296.0	28	4.50	0.37	7.8	NA	NA	6.0	NA	3 1
LEGG MASON GLOBAL GOVT. PRIM.	C−	IB	C	120.4	−12	No load	1.86 †	11.5	5.9	7.2	4.6	11.1	1 1 1 1 1
LEGG MASON HIGH-YIELD PRIM.		HY		431.7	13	No load	1.30 †	−2.1	9.3	NA	9.0	6.6	2 1 1 4
LEGG MASON INVESTMENT GRADE PRIM.	C	CI	B	164.7	35	No load	1.00 †	6.7	7.1	7.0	5.4	10.4	3 1 2 1 2
LEGG MASON U.S. GOVT. INTERM. PRIM.	B	CS	C	351.7	17	No load	1.00 †	6.4	5.9	5.9	5.1	7.0	1 3 2 4 2
LEXINGTON GNMA INCOME	A	GI	A	273.1	73	No load	1.01	7.5	7.8	7.3	5.7	NA	1 3 1 1 1
LOOMIS SAYLES BOND INST.	B	CL	B+	1495.6	19	No load	0.75	4.7	9.2	10.5	7.6	19.1	2 1 1 1 4
LORD ABBETT BOND-DEBENTURE A	B	HY	B	2320.2	12	4.75	0.89 †	4.8	9.5	8.2	8.0	NA	2 2 1 1 4
LORD ABBETT GLOBAL INCOME A	C	IB	B	119.5	−16	4.75	1.10 †	11.3	7.1	7.0	6.3	NA	2 2 1 4 1
LORD ABBETT U.S. GOVT. SECURITIES A	D	GI	D	1688.9	−18	4.75	0.92 †	7.9	6.4	5.9	6.4	NA	2 3 4 1 1
MAINSTAY CONVERTIBLE B	D	CV	C	657.7	−22	5.00 ** ‡	2.08 †	0.7	7.5	8.5	3.5	NA	1 1 1 1 4
MAINSTAY GOVERNMENT B	C−	GI	C	590.6	−7	5.00 **	1.65 †	7.5	5.7	5.8	4.9	8.8	2 3 4 2 1
MAINSTAY HIGH-YIELD CORP. BOND B	A	HY	A	3309.0	−2	5.00 **	1.62 †	1.3	9.3	9.7	9.1	6.4	1 1 1 1 4
MARSHALL GOVERNMENT INCOME	B	CI	B	288.3	32	No load	0.86	6.5	6.0	6.2	6.1	6.3	2 2 3 3 2
MARSHALL INTERMEDIATE BOND	C	CS	D	593.3	7	No load	0.72	6.3	5.3	5.5	6.0	4.3	2 3 4 4 2
MARSHALL SHORT-TERM INCOME	A	CS	B+	130.1	−13	No load	0.49	4.9	5.4	5.4	6.3	2.1	1 4 1 4 4
MAS FIXED-INCOME INST.	B	CI	B+	4672.4	29	No load	0.48	6.8	7.4	7.2	5.9	8.9	3 1 1 1 2
MAS HIGH-YIELD INST.	B	HY	C	817.3	47	No load	0.50	3.2	11.3	9.7	8.8	8.0	4 1 1 1 4
MAS LIMITED DURATION INST.	B+	CS	B	247.3	29	No load	0.42	5.6	5.7	5.4	5.4	NA	1 4 1 4 3
MAS SPECIAL PURPOSE F/I INST.	B	CI	B+	518.1	−1	No load	0.48	6.3	7.9	7.4	6.5	9.5	3 1 1 1 2
MCM INTERMEDIATE FIXED-INCOME		CI		136.2	23	No load	0.50	7.8	6.6	NA	5.5	4.4	3 2 3 1
MENTOR SHORT DURATION INCOME A		CS		114.2	160	1.00	0.86	6.1	5.3	NA	5.7	3.0	2 4 2
MERRILL LYNCH CORP. HIGH-INCOME B	D	HY	D	4161.1	−25	4.00 **	1.27 †	−3.7	5.9	6.1	9.9	7.7	2 2 1 1 4
MERRILL LYNCH CORP. INTERM.-TERM B	C	CI	C	188.3	26	1.00 **	1.18 †	6.8	5.6	5.8	5.7	NA	2 2 4 3 2
MERRILL LYNCH CORP. INVMT. GRADE B	C−	CI	F	756.4	32	4.00 **	1.34 †	7.3	5.4	5.6	5.4	NA	3 1 4 3 1
MERRILL LYNCH FEDERAL SECURITIES D	C	GI	C	854.3	−6	4.00	0.93 †	6.3	6.4	6.0	5.7	5.5	2 3 2 3 2
MERRILL LYNCH WORLD INCOME B	F	MU	F	283.0	−56	4.00 **	1.53 †	−24.2	−4.1	−0.8	10.9	6.7	3 3 1 4 4
METROPOLITAN WEST LOW DURATION		CS		210.0	169	No load	0.58 †	6.6	NA	NA	6.5	2.0	2
MFS BOND A	C−	CI	D	850.0	31	4.75	0.98 †	4.5	6.2	6.8	6.6	12.3	2 1 2 1 4
MFS GLOBAL GOVERNMENTS A (v)	F	IB	D	136.7	−22	4.75	1.35 †	4.1	3.3	3.5	6.9	11.0	4 3 1 4 4
MFS GOVERNMENT LTD. MATURITY B	C	GS	D	215.1	531	4.00 **	1.63 †	5.4	4.3	4.1	5.2	7.7	1 4 4 4 3
MFS GOVERNMENT MORTGAGE A	C	GI	C	628.9	1	4.75	0.97 †	6.1	5.9	6.2	6.3	24.3	1 2 3 2 1
MFS GOVERNMENT SECURITIES A	C−	GI	C	324.8	12	4.75	0.94 †	8.3	6.1	6.6	5.9	15.4	2 1 4 2 1
MFS HIGH-INCOME A	C	HY	C	742.1	3	4.75	1.01 †	1.0	8.7	7.9	9.2	8.3	1 2 1 1 4
MFS LIMITED MATURITY A	B	CS	C	116.3	24	2.50	0.89 †	5.2	5.1	5.4	6.3	NA	1 4 1 4 3
MFS STRATEGIC INCOME B	D	MU	C−	141.9	64	4.00 **	1.44 †	−1.4	5.8	5.8	9.2	9.9	3 1 1 1 4
MONTGOMERY SHORT DUR. GOVT. BOND R	A	GS	A	134.2	152	No load	0.28	7.4	6.5	6.4	5.5	NA	1 4 1 4 1
J.P. MORGAN BOND	B	CI	B	209.4	19	No load	0.68	7.4	6.5	6.7	6.0	12.1	2 2 3 2 1
MORGAN GRENFELL FIXED-INCOME	B+	CI	A	1273.4	13	No load	0.55	7.9	7.3	7.4	6.0	8.3	1 2 2 2 1
MSDW CONVERTIBLE B (w)	D	CV	C−	264.9	−16	5.00 **	1.84 †	−4.9	9.0	8.7	5.1	NA	2 1 1 1 4
MSDW DIVERSIFIED INCOME B (x)	B	MU	B	1035.3	10	5.00 **	1.40 †	2.5	5.6	5.6	7.4	5.5	1 4 1 4 4
MSDW FEDERAL SECURITIES B (y)	C−	GI	C−	627.0	2	5.00 **	1.52 †	9.1	6.3	6.2	5.9	NA	3 1 4 2 1
MSDW HIGH-YIELD SECURITIES B (z)		HY		1877.5	17	5.00 **	1.42 †	−3.4	NA	NA	12.0	NA	4
MSDW INTERMEDIATE INCOME B (aa)	C	CI	C	144.9	−6	5.00 **	1.63 †	6.9	5.4	5.3	5.0	NA	2 4 3 4 1
MSDW SHORT-TERM BOND (bb)		CS		211.0	162	No load	0.37	7.0	6.0	NA	6.2	NA	4 2 4 1
MSDW SHORT-TERM U.S. TREASURY (cc)	B	GS	C	369.1	32	No load	0.82 †	6.9	5.6	5.0	5.2	NA	1 4 2 4 1
MSDW U.S. GOVT. SECURITIES B (dd)	C	GI	B	4984.7	−8	5.00 **	1.26 †	7.3	6.3	6.2	5.9	5.0	2 2 3 2 1
NATIONWIDE BOND D (ee)	D	CL	D	137.4	9	4.50	0.72	8.3	6.3	6.5	5.8	7.6	4 1 4 2 1
NEUBERGER BERMAN LIMITED MATURITY	B+	CS	C	291.0	15	No load	0.70	4.7	5.3	5.2	6.0	2.4	1 4 2 4 4
NEW ENGLAND BOND INCOME A	C	CI	C	222.0	15	4.50	1.05 †	8.0	7.8	7.7	6.4	8.1	2 1 2 1 1
NEW ENGLAND LTD. TERM U.S. GOVT. A	C	GS	D	194.1	−13	3.00	1.28 †	6.5	5.3	5.2	5.7	NA	1 4 4 3 2
NEW ENGLAND STRATEGIC INCOME B		MU		134.2	−8	5.00 **	1.93 †	−2.4	6.4	NA	7.9	16.6	1 3 4
NICHOLAS INCOME	B+	HY	B+	239.4	−6	No load	0.50	0.5	8.5	8.2	9.3	7.1	1 3 1 1 4
NORTHEAST INVESTORS	A	HY	B+	2328.5	8	No load	0.61	−0.3	10.9	10.4	9.4	8.0	1 2 1 1 4
NORTHERN FIXED-INCOME		CI		251.3	53	No load	0.90	8.0	6.6	NA	5.1	12.0	1 4 2 1
NORTHERN INCOME EQUITY		CV		119.0	15	No load	1.00	9.2	16.5	NA	3.7	NA	1 1 1 1
NORTHERN U.S. GOVERNMENT		GS		261.2	22	No load	0.90	7.6	5.9	NA	4.8	4.3	4 3 3 1
NORTHSTAR HIGH TOTAL RET. B		HY		438.7	−21	5.00 ** ‡	2.12 †	−8.6	5.2	NA	11.1	7.9	1 1 1 4
NORTHSTAR HIGH TOTAL RET. II B		HY		181.2	163	5.00 ** ‡	1.95 †	−3.6	NA	NA	9.6	4.8	4

*Includes redemption fee. **Includes deferred sales charge. †12(b)-1 plan in effect. ‡Not currently accepting new accounts or deposits. NA=Not available. NM=Not meaningful. (u) Formerly DG Govt. Inc. (v) Formerly MFS World Govts. A. (w) Formerly Dean Witter Convertible Secs. B. (x) Formerly Dean Witter Diversified Income B. (y) Formerly Dean Witter Federal Securities B. (z) Formerly Dean Witter High-Yield Securities B. (aa) Formerly Dean Witter Interm. Income Secs. B. (bb) Formerly Dean Witter Short-Term Bond. (cc) Formerly Dean Witter Short-Term U.S. Treasury. (dd) Formerly Dean Witter U.S. Government Secs. B. (ee) Formerly Nationwide Bond.

DATA: MORNINGSTAR, INC., CHICAGO, IL.

FUND	RATING (COMPARES RISK-ADJUSTED PERFORMANCE OF EACH FUND AGAINST ALL FUNDS)	CATEGORY	RATING (RATING COMPARES FUND WITHIN CATEGORY)	SIZE ASSETS $MIL.	% CHG. 1997-98	FEES SALES CHARGE (%)	EXPENSE RATIO (%)	PERFORMANCE TOTAL RETURN (%) 1 YR.	3 YR.	5 YR.	PORTFOLIO YIELD (%)	MATURITY (YEARS)	HISTORY RESULTS VS. ALL FUNDS
NORTHSTAR HIGH-YIELD B		HY		139.8	29	5.00 **	1.91 †	1.3	8.4	NA	8.1	8.6	1 1 4
OPPENHEIMER BOND A	C	CI	C	247.2	30	4.75	1.27 †	5.6	6.8	6.5	6.5	6.8	2 2 1 1 3
OPPENHEIMER CHAMPION INCOME A	C	HY	C	606.9	15	4.75	1.06 †	0.4	8.4	7.9	8.9	6.0	1 3 1 1 4
OPPENHEIMER CONVERTIBLE SEC. B (ff)		CV		431.5	19	5.00 **	1.72 †	4.0	10.3	NA	4.5	5.5	1 1 4
OPPENHEIMER HIGH-YIELD A	C	HY	C-	1186.8	-3	4.75	1.00 †	0.1	8.6	7.5	9.4	NA	1 3 1 1 4
OPPENHEIMER INTERNATIONAL BOND B		IB		125.1	1	5.00 **	2.00 †	-5.1	4.6	NA	11.1	6.0	1 4 4
OPPENHEIMER LIMITED.-TERM GOVT. A	B+	GS	B	669.0	19	3.50	0.87 †	6.9	6.5	6.0	6.6	NA	1 4 1 3 2
OPPENHEIMER STRAT. INCOME B	C-	MU	C-	4080.0	12	5.00 **	1.67 †	0.9	6.6	5.7	8.0	5.8	3 3 1 3 4
OPPENHEIMER U.S. GOVT. A	B	GI	B	606.4	22	4.75	1.03 †	6.3	7.0	6.8	5.9	4.9	1 3 2 1 2
PACIFIC HORIZON CAPITAL INCOME A	C-	CV	C	367.4	-3	5.50	1.10	9.0	16.7	13.2	5.3	3.3	3 1 1 1 1
PAINEWEBBER GLOBAL INCOME A	C	IB	B	405.5	-13	4.00	1.21 †	10.7	7.2	6.0	5.8	6.2	2 4 1 4 1
PAINEWEBBER HIGH-INCOME A	F	HY	F	233.7	-16	4.00	0.98 †	-6.2	7.5	4.0	10.1	9.4	4 4 1 1 4
PAINEWEBBER INVT. GRADE INCOME A	C-	CL	C	215.4	1	4.00	1.03 †	4.8	6.9	6.6	6.6	17.8	3 1 2 1 4
PAINEWEBBER U.S. GOVT. INCOME A	D	GI	F	276.4	-5	4.00	0.94 †	7.9	5.9	4.5	5.6	10.2	4 2 4 2 1
PARKSTONE INTERM. GOVT. INVMT. A	C	GI	C	153.9	843	4.00	1.22 †	7.4	5.6	5.4	4.8	NA	1 4 4 4 1
PAYDEN & RYGEL TOTAL RET. R		CI		180.1	134	No load	0.45	8.9	NA	NA	6.3	6.2	2 1
PAYDEN & RYGEL GLOBAL FIXED-INCOME R	A	IB	A	526.6	7	No load	0.49	11.7	8.8	8.1	6.3	9.0	2 2 1 2 1
PAYDEN & RYGEL INVMT. QUALITY BOND R	C	CI	C	244.4	105	No load	0.45	8.1	6.2	6.5	5.9	6.2	2 1 4 2 1
PEGASUS BOND A	C	CI	C	226.3	80	4.50	0.86 †	7.9	7.5	7.4	5.8	6.0	4 1 1 1 1
PHOENIX HIGH-YIELD A	F	HY	D	473.4	-17	4.75	1.11 †	-6.7	7.5	6.1	10.4	7.3	4 2 1 1 4
PHOENIX MULTI-SECTOR FIXED-INCOME A	F	MU	D	154.3	-12	4.75	1.04 †	-6.9	4.9	5.2	9.5	15.9	4 1 1 2 4
PHOENIX U.S. GOVT. SECURITIES A	C-	CI	D	178.1	77	4.75	0.98 †	6.6	5.9	6.1	6.1	NA	2 2 4 2 2
PILGRIM HIGH-YIELD B (gg)		HY		216.3	178	5.00 **	1.75 †	-3.6	8.1	NA	9.3	7.9	1 1 4
PIMCO FOREIGN BOND INST.	A	IB	A	475.1	40	No load	0.50	10.0	12.8	10.0	5.9	10.0	4 1 1 1 1
PIMCO GLOBAL BOND INST.	B	IB	B+	253.9	-6	No load	0.56	12.4	7.1	8.2	5.3	10.9	1 1 1 4 1
PIMCO HIGH-YIELD INST.	A	HY	A	1733.3	49	No load	0.50	6.5	10.4	10.7	8.5	7.5	1 1 1 1 2
PIMCO LOW DURATION INST.	A	CS	A	3136.6	13	No load	0.43	7.2	7.2	6.8	6.5	2.4	1 4 1 3 1
PIMCO LOW DURATION II INST.	A	CS	B+	429.2	22	No load	0.51	6.6	6.5	6.2	5.8	2.9	1 4 1 3 2
PIMCO SHORT-TERM INST.	A	UB	B	377.7	103	No load	0.45	5.7	6.4	6.3	5.9	0.8	1 4 1 4 3
PIMCO TOTAL RETURN II INST.	B	CI	B+	857.8	81	No load	0.50	9.6	7.8	7.8	5.7	11.7	1 1 2 1 1
PIMCO TOTAL RETURN III INST.	B+	CI	A	430.5	29	No load	0.51	10.4	8.4	8.0	5.8	12.7	2 1 2 1 1
PIMCO TOTAL RETURN INST.	B+	CI	A	20125.7	36	No load	0.43	9.8	8.2	7.9	5.9	8.5	2 1 1 1 1
PIONEER AMERICA INCOME A	C-	GI	C-	127.8	-7	4.50	1.00 †	7.8	6.1	5.9	5.8	7.4	2 3 4 3 1
PIONEER BOND A	C-	CI	D	131.0	23	4.50	1.17 †	7.7	6.2	6.3	6.1	13.3	2 2 4 2 1
PREFERRED FIXED-INCOME	B	CI	B	162.1	10	No load	0.67	7.1	6.1	6.6	6.0	10.1	1 2 3 3 1
T. ROWE PRICE EMERG. MKTS. BOND		EB		146.1	29	No load	1.25	-23.1	7.1	NA	14.0	15.5	1 1 1 4
T. ROWE PRICE GNMA	B	GI	B+	1146.2	8	No load	0.70	6.6	6.4	6.9	6.5	6.6	1 2 3 2 2
T. ROWE PRICE HIGH-YIELD	C	HY	C	1704.0	8	1.00 *	0.81	4.5	10.1	7.3	9.1	8.8	4 3 1 1 4
T. ROWE PRICE INTERNATIONAL BOND	D	IB	C	926.5	12	No load	0.86	15.0	6.1	7.1	4.9	11.0	1 1 1 4 1
T. ROWE PRICE NEW INCOME	C	CI	C	2103.3	8	No load	0.71	5.0	5.6	6.4	6.3	13.7	1 1 4 2 4
T. ROWE PRICE SHORT-TERM BOND	C	CS	C-	346.9	1	No load	0.72	6.2	5.5	4.6	5.6	2.7	2 4 2 4 2
T. ROWE PRICE SHORT-TERM U.S.	B+	CS	B	136.3	34	No load	0.70	6.9	5.9	5.6	5.6	3.0	1 4 2 4 2
T. ROWE PRICE SPECTRUM INCOME	A	MU	A	2574.1	27	No load	0.00	6.6	8.8	8.6	6.2	11.5	1 1 1 1 2
T. ROWE PRICE U.S. TREAS. INTERM.	B	GI	B+	262.9	32	No load	0.61	10.2	6.9	6.7	5.2	5.9	1 3 4 3 1
T. ROWE PRICE U.S. TREAS. LONG-TERM	D	GL	C	309.8	50	No load	0.67	12.8	8.1	8.9	5.2	22.4	3 1 1 1 1
PRINCIPAL BOND A (hh)	C-	CL	C	148.1	14	4.75	0.95 †	7.1	6.7	7.3	6.1	10.7	2 1 4 1 1
PRINCIPAL GOVT. SECURITIES INCOME A (ii)	C-	GI	C-	251.5	1	4.75	0.84 †	7.2	6.9	6.7	6.1	NA	3 1 2 1 1
PRUDENTIAL DIVER. BOND B		MU		186.6	19	5.00 **	1.42 †	4.5	5.7	NA	5.8	11.0	1 3 4
PRUDENTIAL GOVT. INCOME A	C-	GI	C-	841.7	1	4.00	0.86 †	8.6	6.4	6.7	5.9	9.0	2 1 4 2 1
PRUDENTIAL GOVT. SHORT-INTERM. A	B	CS	C-	149.2	0	No load	0.97 †	6.0	5.7	5.4	5.5	4.0	1 4 2 4 2
PRUDENTIAL HIGH-YIELD B	C-	HY	C-	2379.4	-10	5.00 **	1.29 †	-0.7	7.6	7.3	9.2	7.0	2 2 1 1 4
PRUDENTIAL INTERM. GLOBAL INCOME A	B	IB	B+	126.2	-8	3.00	1.41 †	8.9	8.1	7.7	6.2	NA	4 1 1 4 1
PUTNAM AMERICAN GOVT. INCOME A	C	GI	C	1464.3	-4	4.75	0.97 †	8.5	6.6	6.9	5.9	NA	2 1 4 2 1
PUTNAM CONVERT. INCOME-GROWTH A	C	CV	B	1089.8	-8	5.75	1.03 †	4.9	13.9	12.4	4.5	NA	1 1 1 1 4
PUTNAM DIVERSIFIED INCOME B	D	MU	D	2145.1	-8	5.00 **	1.72 †	-2.6	4.1	4.5	9.4	9.6	3 2 1 3 4
PUTNAM GLOBAL GOVT. INCOME A	F	IB	D	250.6	-16	4.75	1.29 †	3.5	4.1	3.3	6.7	12.3	4 3 1 4 4
PUTNAM HIGH QUALITY BOND A (jj)	C-	CI	C-	340.4	-1	4.75	1.18 †	6.7	5.6	6.3	6.2	NA	2 1 4 3 2
PUTNAM HIGH YIELD ADV. A	F	HY	F	1262.6	-15	4.75 ‡	0.97 †	-9.5	4.3	5.0	11.5	NA	3 1 1 1 4
PUTNAM HIGH YIELD A	D	HY	D	2739.3	-16	4.75 ‡	0.95 †	-8.1	5.9	6.0	11.6	8.2	3 2 1 1 4
PUTNAM HIGH YIELD II B		HY		590.9	318	5.00 **	NA †	-0.2	NA	NA	8.3	NA	4
PUTNAM INCOME A	C-	CI	C-	1447.1	10	4.75	1.02 †	3.7	5.3	6.3	6.4	10.5	2 1 2 3 4
PUTNAM INTERM. U.S. GOVT. INCOME A	B	GS	C	237.5	76	3.25	1.15 †	7.6	6.2	6.4	5.6	NA	1 3 3 3 1
PUTNAM STRATEGIC INCOME B (kk)		MU		116.4	56	5.00 **	2.01 †	-2.7	NA	NA	7.8	NA	3 4
PUTNAM U.S. GOVT. INCOME A	C	GI	B	2096.7	0	4.75	0.87 †	6.8	6.4	6.5	6.3	5.1	1 3 2 2 2
REGIONS FIXED-INCOME INVMT. (ll)	C	CI	C	192.2	4	3.00 **	0.97 †	6.8	6.1	5.6	4.9	5.6	3 3 3 3 2
SALOMON BROS HIGH-YIELD BOND B		HY		326.8	0	5.00 **	1.99 †	-7.8	7.8	NA	9.9	8.1	1 1 4
SCHWAB SHORT-TERM BOND MKT. INDEX	B	CS	C	173.2	25	No load	0.46	7.0	6.0	5.1	5.4	NA	2 4 2 4 1
SCHWAB TOTAL BOND MKT. INDEX	C-	CI	D	327.1	247	No load	0.31	8.4	6.4	6.8	5.7	NA	3 1 4 1 1
SCUDDER EMERGING MKTS. INCOME	F	EB		208.4	-40	No load	1.49	-30.3	2.0	3.1	13.5	14.0	4 1 1 1 4
SCUDDER GNMA	B	GI	B	393.4	1	No load	1.02	6.6	6.4	6.9	5.9	6.6	2 2 2 3 2

*Includes redemption fee. **Includes deferred sales charge. †12(b)-1 plan in effect. ‡Not currently accepting new accounts or deposits. NA=Not available. NM=Not meaningful. (ff) Formerly Oppenheimer Bond Fund for Growth B. (gg) Formerly Pilgrim America High-Yield B. (hh) Formerly Princor Bond A. (ii) Formerly Princor Government Securities Inc. A. (jj) Formerly Putnam Federal Income A. (kk) Formerly Putnam Diversified Income II B. (ll) Formerly First Priority Fixed-Income Investment.

DATA: MORNINGSTAR, INC., CHICAGO, IL.

FUND (COMPARES RISK-ADJUSTED PERFORMANCE OF EACH FUND AGAINST ALL FUNDS)	RATING	CATEGORY	RATING (RATING COMPARES FUND WITHIN CATEGORY)	SIZE ASSETS $MIL.	% CHG. 1997-98	FEES SALES CHARGE (%)	EXPENSE RATIO (%)	PERFORMANCE TOTAL RETURN (%) 1 YR.	3 YR.	5 YR.	PORTFOLIO YIELD (%)	MATURITY (YEARS)	HISTORY RESULTS VS. ALL FUNDS
SCUDDER HIGH-YIELD BOND		HY		207.2	33	1.00 *	0.03	4.4	NA	NA	9.6	7.5	1 4
SCUDDER INCOME	C	CI	C	807.9	16	No load	1.18	6.1	6.0	6.2	5.8	9.0	2 1 3 2 2
SCUDDER INTERNATIONAL BOND	F	IB	D	145.5	-18	No load	1.36	12.6	3.8	2.1	5.3	7.1	4 4 3 4 1
SCUDDER SHORT-TERM BOND	C	CS	D	995.5	-15	No load	0.86	4.3	4.8	4.3	5.8	2.8	2 4 2 4 4
SEI DAILY INTERM.-DURATION GOVT. A	B	GI	B+	123.5	7	No load	0.49	8.5	6.5	6.4	5.5	6.8	2 3 3 3 1
SEI INST. CORE FIXED-INCOME A	B	CL	B+	1605.9	42	No load	0.60†	8.5	7.2	7.1	5.6	10.4	3 1 3 1 1
SEI INTERNATIONAL EMERG. MKT. DEBT A		EB		190.5	9	No load	1.35	-20.9	NA	NA	4.2	8.1	4
SEI INTERNATIONAL FIXED-INCOME A	C-	IB	C	592.7	73	No load	1.00	18.5	6.2	8.7	1.3	8.0	1 1 1 1 4
SELIGMAN HIGH-YIELD BOND A	B+	HY	B+	1050.5	40	4.75	1.14†	1.3	10.0	10.1	9.9	8.2	1 1 1 1 4
SIT U.S. GOVERNMENT SECURITIES	A	GS	A	141.9	53	No load	0.80	6.5	6.6	6.6	5.3	NA	1 4 1 3 2
SMITH BARNEY ADJ. RATE GOVT. A	B+	GS	B+	121.4	0	No load	1.58†	4.3	5.1	5.1	5.3	NA	1 4 1 4 4
SMITH BARNEY DIVERS. STRAT. INCOME B	B+	MU	B	2246.5	-6	4.50 **	1.50†	5.2	7.4	6.6	7.0	5.0	2 3 1 4 3
SMITH BARNEY GOVT. SECURITIES A	D	GI	D	351.4	-3	4.50	0.92†	8.1	7.0	6.1	5.5	NA	2 4 4 1 1
SMITH BARNEY HIGH-INCOME B	C	HY	C-	830.5	15	4.50 **	1.55†	-0.3	8.0	7.1	9.3	NA	3 2 1 1 4
SMITH BARNEY INVESTMENT GRADE B	F	CL	F	263.3	6	4.50 **	1.51†	7.7	7.5	8.7	5.4	NA	4 1 1 1 4
SMITH BARNEY MANAGED GOVT. A	C-	GI	C	365.1	-7	4.50	1.01†	5.7	6.3	5.9	6.1	NA	1 4 3 2 3
SMITH BARNEY U.S. GOVT. SECURITIES A	C	GI	C	257.5	-15	4.50	0.80†	6.0	6.5	6.8	6.1	NA	1 2 2 1 2
SOUTHTRUST BOND (mm)	C-	CI	D	128.3	22	3.50	0.84	9.3	7.0	6.3	5.3	9.0	2 3 4 1 1
SSGA BOND MARKET		CI		182.9	68	No load	0.48†	8.4	NA	NA	5.5	9.3	2 1
SSGA YIELD PLUS	A	UB	C	788.3	12	No load	0.41†	4.9	5.3	5.3	5.7	10.0	1 4 1 4 4
STAGECOACH U.S. GOVT. INCOME A	D	GI	D	179.3	-14	4.50	0.89†	7.4	5.2	5.7	5.3	NA	3 1 4 3 1
STAGECOACH VARIABLE RATE GOVT. A	C-	GS	F	130.4	-43	3.00	0.81†	3.6	4.5	3.4	5.1	NA	2 4 2 4 4
STAR STRATEGIC INCOME B		MU		200.9	13	5.00 **	1.26†	-3.2	3.7	NA	7.3	11.6	4 1 2 4
STAR U.S. GOVT. INCOME A	C-	CI	D	150.0	10	3.50	0.89†	7.9	6.2	6.0	5.4	10.8	2 3 4 2 1
STATE ST. RESEARCH GOVT. INCOME A	C	GI	B	517.2	-1	4.50	1.08†	9.1	7.1	7.0	6.0	10.7	2 2 3 2 1
STATE ST. RESEARCH HIGH-INCOME A	C	HY	C	649.3	-6	4.50	1.10†	-0.4	10.0	8.0	10.1	NA	1 4 1 1 4
STEIN ROE INCOME	C	CI	C	362.5	-15	No load	0.83	3.9	6.1	6.6	6.9	9.4	2 1 1 1 4
STEIN ROE INTERMEDIATE BOND	B	CI	B	454.9	16	No load	0.72	6.4	6.7	6.7	6.6	7.2	1 2 2 2 2
STRONG ADVANTAGE	A	UB	B	2631.9	29	No load	0.80	4.8	6.0	5.8	6.0	1.0	1 4 1 4 4
STRONG CORPORATE BOND	A	CI	A	844.5	51	No load	1.00	7.3	8.2	9.4	6.6	11.6	1 1 1 1 1
STRONG GOVERNMENT SECURITIES	B	CI	B+	1326.9	46	No load	0.80	8.1	6.6	7.0	5.6	NA	2 1 4 1 1
STRONG HIGH-YIELD BOND		HY		551.4	-3	No load	0.60	3.1	14.9	NA	9.5	9.5	1 1 4
STRONG SHORT-TERM BOND	B+	CS	B	1315.1	0	No load	0.90	4.9	6.2	5.7	6.9	2.2	1 4 1 4 4
STRONG SHORT-TERM HIGH-YIELD BOND		HY		135.3	-76	No load	1.00	8.4	NA	NA	7.4	2.9	1
SUNAMERICA HIGH-INCOME B	F	HY	D	119.3	11	4.00 **	2.13†	-6.2	6.7	4.4	10.1	7.9	4 4 1 1 4
SUNAMERICA U.S. GOVT. SECURITIES B	C	GI	B	148.3	-36	4.00 **	2.26†	6.1	5.1	5.6	4.4	13.5	1 3 4 4 2
TCW/DW NORTH AMERICA GOVT. INC.	F	IB	D	146.1	-27	No load	1.59†	6.8	6.2	3.3	5.4	NA	4 3 2 3 2
TEMPLETON GLOBAL BOND A (nn)	C	IB	B	181.5	-9	4.25	1.17†	5.4	6.1	6.3	5.6	5.1	2 1 1 4 3
THORNBURG LIMITED-TERM U.S. A	B	GS	C-	124.5	-5	2.50	0.97†	7.0	6.0	5.6	5.5	NA	1 4 2 4 1
TIAA-CREF BOND PLUS		CI		145.2	149	No load	NA	8.9	NA	NA	5.4	7.0	1
U.S. GOVERNMENT SECURITIES	C-	GI	C-	1307.0	17	4.75	0.79†	7.9	6.3	5.8	6.0	7.2	2 3 4 3 1
UNITED BOND A	C-	CI	D	547.5	5	5.75	0.77†	7.3	6.7	6.7	5.9	NA	3 1 3 1 1
UNITED GOVERNMENT SECURITIES A	C-	GI	D	137.6	7	4.25	0.89†	7.5	6.1	6.5	5.9	NA	3 1 3 1 1
UNITED HIGH-INCOME A	B	HY	B	1023.4	-5	5.75	0.84†	3.9	9.9	8.6	8.5	NA	2 2 1 1 4
UNITED HIGH-INCOME II A	C	HY	C	412.6	0	5.75	0.93†	2.7	9.8	8.2	8.8	NA	2 2 1 1 4
USAA GNMA	B+	GI	A	452.9	31	No load	0.30	8.2	6.9	7.3	6.3	10.5	1 2 4 1 1
USAA INCOME	C	CL	B	1768.6	3	No load	0.38	8.8	7.0	7.6	6.5	7.5	3 1 4 1 1
USAA SHORT-TERM BOND	B+	CS	B	204.6	41	No load	0.50	5.0	6.2	5.9	6.1	2.6	1 4 1 4 4
VALUE LINE AGGRESSIVE INCOME	C	HY	C	165.5	23	No load	0.95	-5.3	9.0	8.3	10.6	7.7	2 1 1 1 4
VALUE LINE U.S. GOVERNMENT	D	GI	D	182.4	-3	No load	0.66	7.7	6.9	4.6	5.8	5.8	4 3 2 2 1
VAN KAMPEN CORP. BOND A (oo)	C-	CI	C-	191.7	10	4.75	1.13†	7.3	6.8	7.2	6.6	13.9	2 1 4 1 1
VAN KAMPEN GOVT. SECURITIES A (pp)	C-	GI	C-	1876.1	-3	4.75	1.03†	8.3	6.4	6.1	6.2	6.4	2 2 4 2 1
VAN KAMPEN HARBOR A (qq)	D	CV	D	377.4	0	5.75	1.04†	7.5	12.1	10.1	3.4	7.8	3 1 1 1 1
VAN KAMPEN HIGH-INCOME CORP. B (rr)	C-	HY	C-	291.8	31	4.00 **	1.86†	-0.8	7.5	6.7	9.4	7.6	2 2 1 1 4
VAN KAMPEN HIGH-YIELD A (ss)	C-	HY	C-	270.1	-7	4.75	1.14†	-1.4	7.2	6.9	9.4	20.2	2 2 1 1 4
VAN KAMPEN PRIME RATE INCOME (tt)	A	UB	B+	7908.5	8	3.00 *	1.41	6.3	6.7	6.9	6.6	NA	1 4 1 4 2
VAN KAMPEN U.S. GOVT. A (uu)	C-	GI	C-	2077.9	-8	4.75	0.90†	5.8	6.1	5.9	6.8	4.9	3 2 2 3 3
VANGUARD CONVERTIBLE SECURITIES	F	CV	D	177.6	-5	No load	0.67	0.6	10.6	8.3	4.8	NA	3 2 1 1 4
VANGUARD GNMA (vv)	A	GI	A	10993.1	26	No load	0.31	7.1	7.3	7.4	6.6	5.6	1 2 1 2 1
VANGUARD HIGH-YIELD CORP. (ww)	A	HY	B+	5380.5	18	1.00 *	0.28	5.6	9.0	8.7	8.5	7.7	1 1 1 1 3
VANGUARD INTERM.-TERM U.S. TREASURY (xx)	C	GI	C	1863.7	24	No load	0.27	10.6	7.1	7.2	5.7	7.4	2 1 4 2 1
VANGUARD INTERM.-TERM BOND INDEX (yy)		CI		1102.4	61	No load	0.20	10.2	7.3	NA	6.1	7.0	1 4 2 1
VANGUARD INTERM.-TERM CORP. BOND (zz)	C	CI	C	1181.4	37	No load	0.26	8.3	6.6	7.1	6.2	7.0	2 1 4 2 1
VANGUARD LONG-TERM BOND INDEX (aaa)		CL		210.0	141	No load	0.20	12.0	8.5	NA	5.9	22.9	1 4 1 1
VANGUARD LONG-TERM CORP. BOND (bbb)	C-	CL	C	4152.9	15	No load	0.32	9.2	7.9	8.5	6.2	19.1	3 1 4 1 1
VANGUARD LONG-TERM U.S. TREASURY (ccc)	D	GL	D	1415.5	37	No load	0.27	13.1	8.3	9.0	5.6	18.5	4 1 4 1 1
VANGUARD PREFERRED STOCK	B+	CL	B+	372.8	13	No load	0.37	6.7	9.3	8.7	5.6	9.4	4 1 1 1 2
VANGUARD SHORT-TERM BOND INDEX (ddd)		CS		708.9	62	No load	0.20	7.6	6.4	NA	5.7	2.8	4 2 4 1
VANGUARD SHORT-TERM CORP. (eee)	A	CS	B+	5427.7	18	No load	0.28	6.6	6.1	6.1	6.1	2.8	1 4 1 4 2
VANGUARD SHORT-TERM FEDERAL (fff)	B+	GS	B	1634.9	16	No load	0.27	7.2	6.1	6.0	5.7	2.6	1 4 1 4 1

(mm) Form. SouthTrust Vulcan Bond. (nn) Form. Templeton Glob. Bond I. (oo) Form. Van Kampen Amer. Cap. Corp. Bond A. (pp) Form. Van Kampen Amer. Cap. Govt. Secs. A. (qq) Form. Van Kampen Amer. Cap. Harbor A. (rr) Form. Van Kampen Amer. Cap. H-I. Corp. Bond B. (ss) Form. Van Kampen Amer. Cap. H-Y A. (tt) Form. Van Kampen Amer. Cap. Prime Rate. (uu) Form. Van Kampen Amer. Cap. U.S. Govt. A. (w) Form. Vang. F/I GNMA. (ww) Form. Vang. F/I High-Yield Corp. (xx) Form. Vang. F/I I-T U.S. Treas. (yy) Form. Vang. Bond Index I-T. (zz) Form. Vang. F/I I-T Corp. (aaa) Form. Vang. Bond Index L-T. (bbb) Form. Vang. F/I L-T Corp. Bond. (ccc) Form. Vang. F/I L-T U.S. Treas. (ddd) Form. Vang. Bond Index S-T. (eee) Form. Vang. F/I S-T Corp. (fff) Form. Vang. F/I S-T Fed.   DATA: MORNINGSTAR, INC., CHICAGO, IL.

FUND (COMPARES RISK-ADJUSTED PERFORMANCE OF EACH FUND AGAINST ALL FUNDS)	RATING	CATEGORY	RATING (RATING COMPARES FUND WITHIN CATEGORY)	ASSETS $MIL.	% CHG. 1997-98	SALES CHARGE (%)	EXPENSE RATIO (%)	1 YR.	3 YR.	5 YR.	YIELD (%)	MATURITY (YEARS)	HISTORY RESULTS VS. ALL FUNDS
VANGUARD SHORT-TERM TREAS. (ggg)	B+	GS	B+	1184.1	19	No load	0.27	7.4	6.1	5.9	5.3	2.8	1 4 2 4 1
VANGUARD TOTAL BOND MKT. INDEX (hhh)	B	CI	B+	7764.6	55	No load	0.20	8.6	7.2	7.2	6.1	8.4	1 2 3 2 1
VICTORY INTERMEDIATE INCOME	C	CS	F	258.1	5	5.75	0.96	7.5	5.9	5.7	5.3	4.9	1 3 3 4 1
VICTORY INVESTMENT QUAL. BOND	C−	CI	C−	166.9	−10	5.75	1.04	7.5	6.1	6.3	5.3	7.2	1 2 4 3 1
WARBURG PINCUS FIXED INC. COMM.	B+	CI	A	415.0	33	No load	0.75	6.5	7.2	7.1	5.5	5.4	1 3 1 2 2
WARBURG PINCUS GLOBAL FIXED-INCOME	C	IB	B	156.0	−11	No load	0.96	8.4	6.8	6.0	5.9	10.2	3 3 1 4 1
WM INCOME A (iii)	C−	CL	C	209.3	169	4.50	1.03 †	7.2	7.0	7.2	6.6	11.4	3 1 3 1 1
WM U.S. GOVT. SECURITIES A (jjj)	C−	GI	C−	258.4	141	4.50	0.97 †	7.0	6.4	6.5	5.7	7.5	3 1 4 1 1
WPG CORE BOND (kkk)	D	CI	F	139.5	29	No load	0.86	9.3	6.8	4.7	5.6	10.1	4 4 2 3 1
WRIGHT TOTAL RETURN BOND	C−	CL	C	115.6	45	No load	0.90 †	9.5	6.5	6.6	5.1	8.5	4 1 4 2 1

TAX EXEMPT

FUND	RATING	CATEGORY	RATING	ASSETS $MIL.	% CHG. 1997-98	SALES CHARGE (%)	EXPENSE RATIO (%)	1 YR.	3 YR.	5 YR.	YIELD (%)	MATURITY (YEARS)	HISTORY
AARP INSURED T/F GENERAL BOND	C	ML	C	1713.5	0	No load	0.62	5.4	6.0	5.3	4.7	11.0	3 3 3 2 3
AIM MUNICIPAL BOND A	B	MI	C−	326.9	3	4.75	0.90 †	5.3	5.5	5.0	5.0	13.6	2 4 2 3 3
AIM TAX-FREE INTERMEDIATE	A	MS	C−	217.5	13	1.00	0.45	5.5	5.5	5.0	4.4	5.8	1 4 2 3 3
ALLIANCE MUNI. INCOME CALIF. A	C	MC	C	570.0	18	4.25	0.78 †	6.4	7.3	6.6	5.2	19.9	4 1 2 1 2
ALLIANCE MUNI. INSURED NATL. A	D	ML	D	177.5	1	4.25	1.02 †	5.6	6.7	6.2	4.6	18.7	4 1 2 1 3
ALLIANCE MUNI. INCOME NATL. A	C−	ML	C−	367.6	9	4.25	0.69 †	5.7	6.8	6.1	5.2	18.5	4 1 2 1 2
ALLIANCE MUNI. INCOME N.Y. A	C−	MY	C	214.0	13	4.25	0.65 †	5.9	7.2	6.1	5.1	21.4	4 1 2 1 2
AMERICAN CENT.-BENHAM CALIF. MUNI. HI-YLD.	A	MC	A	324.0	48	No load	0.50	6.8	7.7	6.9	5.1	21.9	3 1 1 1 2
AMERICAN CENT.-BENHAM CALIF. T/F INS.	C	MC	B	221.2	12	No load	0.48	6.1	6.4	6.0	4.8	18.4	4 1 3 2 2
AMERICAN CENT.-BENHAM CALIF. T/F INTERM.	B+	MF	B	480.0	10	No load	0.48	5.6	5.8	5.3	4.5	9.1	2 4 2 3 3
AMERICAN CENT.-BEN CALIF. T/F LONG	B	MC	B	340.2	9	No load	0.48	6.3	6.5	6.2	5.0	22.4	4 1 3 1 2
AMERICAN HIGH-INCOME MUNI. BOND		MI		521.2	43	4.75	0.79 †	4.9	7.2	NA	5.1	8.2	1 1 1 4
AMSOUTH MUNICIPAL BOND PREMIER		MI		320.3	−4	No load	NA	5.4	NA	NA	4.1	6.3	3
ATLAS CALIF. MUNICIPAL BOND A	C	MF	C−	211.6	9	No load	0.95 †	5.9	5.9	5.1	4.4	20.6	3 3 2 3 2
BERNSTEIN CALIF. MUNICIPAL	B+	MF	B	557.2	30	No load	0.67	5.1	5.1	5.0	4.0	5.8	2 4 3 4 3
BERNSTEIN DIVERSIFIED MUNI.	B+	MI	B	1407.7	19	No load	0.65	4.6	4.9	4.9	4.1	6.6	1 4 3 4 4
BERNSTEIN N.Y. MUNICIPAL	B+	MN	A	819.0	16	No load	0.65	5.2	5.1	5.0	4.2	6.0	1 4 3 4 3
BERNSTEIN SHORT DURATION DIV. MUNI.		MS		166.8	9	No load	0.72	3.9	3.7	NA	3.5	1.4	4 3 4 4
BOSTON 1784 CONN. T/E INCOME		SI		170.8	42	No load	0.80 †	6.7	6.3	NA	4.4	8.5	3 3 2 2
BOSTON 1784 MASS. T/E INCOME	B	SI	C	235.7	28	No load	0.80 †	5.8	6.0	5.1	4.4	9.8	3 4 3 2 3
BOSTON 1784 T/E MED.-TERM INCOME	A	MI	B+	326.7	14	No load	0.80 †	6.4	6.6	6.1	4.4	10.0	2 3 2 2 2
CALIFORNIA INVMT. TAX-FREE INCOME	C−	MC	C−	231.8	9	No load	0.61	6.3	6.2	5.7	4.4	13.0	4 1 3 2 2
CALVERT TAX-FREE RES. LTD.-TERM A	A	MS	B+	541.5	−4	1.00	0.69	3.9	4.0	4.0	3.7	0.7	1 4 2 4 4
CHURCHILL TAX-FREE OF KENTUCKY A	B+	SI	B+	229.3	1	4.00	0.72 †	5.0	5.8	5.4	4.9	17.2	2 4 2 3 4
CITIFUNDS NATL. TAX-FREE INCOME (a)		ML		246.5	NM	No load	0.14 †	10.1	8.2	NA	4.7	13.0	3 1 1
CITIFUNDS N.Y. TAX-FREE INCOME (b)	C	MY	B+	453.3	496	No load	0.80 †	6.9	6.5	5.7	4.3	11.5	4 2 3 1 2
COLONIAL CALIF. TAX-EXEMPT A	D	MC	D	247.7	−3	4.75	0.87 †	6.0	6.4	5.9	4.6	16.9	4 1 3 1 2
COLONIAL MASS. TAX-EXEMPT A	C−	SL	C	178.0	−2	4.75	0.90 †	6.0	6.0	5.8	4.7	15.4	3 1 4 2 2
COLONIAL TAX-EXEMPT A	C−	ML	C−	2459.8	−4	4.75	0.98 †	6.7	6.3	5.8	5.1	18.2	3 2 4 1 2
COLONIAL TAX-EXEMPT INSURED A	D	ML	D	168.6	−8	4.75	1.07 †	5.6	5.7	5.4	4.5	16.1	3 2 4 2 3
COLUMBIA MUNICIPAL BOND	B+	SI	B+	463.3	13	No load	0.57	5.6	5.9	5.3	4.6	12.0	2 3 3 2 3
DAVIS TAX-FREE HIGH INCOME B	A	MS	A	257.2	43	4.00 **	2.02 †	3.9	5.4	5.3	5.0	19.0	1 4 1 4 4
DELAWARE TAX-FREE PA. A	B	SI	C	876.2	−5	4.75	0.91 †	5.0	5.3	5.2	4.9	7.6	2 3 3 3 4
DELAWARE TAX-FREE U.S.A. A	C	MI	C−	565.8	−7	3.75	0.97 †	4.8	4.6	4.7	5.0	9.3	2 4 4 3 4
DELAWARE-VOYAGEUR MINN. INS. A	C	SL	C	285.9	−1	3.75	0.92 †	5.7	5.9	5.2	4.7	8.0	4 2 3 3 3
DELAWARE-VOYAGEUR T/F ARIZ. INS. A	C	SL	C	180.0	−4	3.75	0.82 †	5.7	6.2	5.7	4.6	6.6	4 1 2 2 3
DELAWARE-VOYAGEUR T/F COLO. A	C	SL	B	363.3	1	3.75	0.81 †	6.3	7.2	6.2	4.9	7.7	4 1 2 1 2 (66)
DELAWARE-VOYAGEUR T/F MINN. A	C	SL	B	418.2	0	3.75	0.89 †	6.1	6.3	5.6	4.9	7.4	4 2 3 1 2
DREYFUS BASIC MUNI. BOND		ML		209.8	51	No load	0.45	6.8	7.4	NA	4.8	21.0	1 2 1 2
DREYFUS CALIF. INTERMEDIATE MUNI.	C	MF	C−	202.6	0	No load	0.79	5.8	5.7	4.8	4.2	9.3	3 4 3 3 4
DREYFUS CALIF. TAX-EXEMPT BOND	C−	MC	C−	1290.0	−3	No load	0.71	5.8	5.8	4.7	4.6	17.2	4 3 3 3 3
DREYFUS FLA. INTERMEDIATE MUNI.	C	SI	C−	327.7	−6	1.00 *	0.80	5.0	4.9	4.6	4.4	7.9	3 3 3 3 4
DREYFUS INSURED MUNI. BOND	F	ML	F	186.7	−4	No load	0.85 †	5.8	5.5	4.4	4.6	24.1	4 3 4 4 4
DREYFUS INTERMEDIATE MUNI.	B+	MI	C	1320.5	−4	No load	0.74	5.5	5.6	5.2	4.8	8.9	2 3 2 3 3
DREYFUS MASS. TAX-EXEMPT BOND	C	SL	B	161.7	4	No load	0.81	6.1	6.4	5.5	4.8	21.8	3 3 2 2 2
DREYFUS MUNI. BOND	C	ML	C	3249.3	−5	No load	0.73	5.7	5.8	5.0	5.0	22.7	4 3 2 3 3
DREYFUS N.J. INTERM. MUNI. BOND	C	SI	C	217.5	1	No load	0.78	5.4	5.2	4.7	4.2	7.1	3 3 3 4 3
DREYFUS N.J. MUNI. BOND	B	SL	C	604.5	2	1.00 *	0.80 †	5.8	6.0	5.2	4.8	18.1	3 3 3 3 3
DREYFUS N.Y. TAX-EX. BOND	C	MY	C	1660.4	−1	1.00 *	0.73	6.7	6.1	5.3	4.7	17.4	4 3 4 2 2
DREYFUS N.Y. TAX-EX. INTERM. BOND	B	MN	C	375.6	3	1.00 *	0.80 †	6.0	6.1	5.3	4.3	8.3	3 3 2 3 3
DREYFUS PREMIER MUNI. BOND A	C	ML	C	442.1	−1	4.50	0.91	4.5	6.0	5.5	5.1	18.6	3 2 2 1 4
DREYFUS PREMIER ST. MUNI. CONN. A	C	SL	B	314.7	0	4.50	0.90	6.3	6.7	5.8	5.0	20.3	3 3 2 2 2
DREYFUS PREMIER ST. MUNI. MD. A	B+	SL	B+	263.1	−1	4.50	0.90	5.7	6.5	5.8	5.0	22.7	3 3 2 2 3
DREYFUS PREMIER ST. MUNI. OHIO A	B	SL	B+	238.3	−1	4.50	0.90	5.2	5.8	5.6	5.1	18.1	2 3 2 3 3
DREYFUS PREMIER ST. MUNI. PA. A	C	SL	B	191.2	−5	4.50	0.92	5.7	6.5	6.1	5.0	20.2	2 3 2 2 3
DREYFUS SHORT-INTERM. MUNI. BOND	A	MS	B	301.0	4	No load	0.76 †	4.5	4.6	4.1	4.2	2.4	1 4 2 4 4
DUPREE KENTUCKY TAX-FREE INCOME	B	SI	B	410.2	17	No load	0.62	5.6	5.8	5.6	5.0	17.6	2 3 3 3 3
EATON VANCE CALIF. MUNICIPALS B	C−	ML	B	294.3	−7	5.00 **	1.65 †	5.4	6.2	6.3	4.3	21.1	4 1 4 1 3

*Includes redemption fee. **Includes deferred sales charge. †12(b)-1 plan in effect. ‡Not currently accepting new accounts or deposits. NA=Not available. NM=Not meaningful. (ggg) Form. Vanguard F/I Short-Term U.S. Treas. (hhh) Form. Vanguard Bond Index Total Bond Mkt. (iii) Form. Composite Inc. A. (jjj) Form. Composite U.S. Government Secs. A. (kkk) Form. WPG Govt. Secs. (a) Form. Landmark Natl. Tax-Free Inc. A. (b) Form. Landmark N.Y. Tax Free Inc. A.

DATA: MORNINGSTAR, INC., CHICAGO, IL.

FUND (COMPARES RISK-ADJUSTED PERFORMANCE OF EACH FUND AGAINST ALL FUNDS)	RATING	CATEGORY (RATING COMPARES FUND WITHIN CATEGORY)	RATING	SIZE ASSETS $MIL.	SIZE % CHG. 1997-98	FEES SALES CHARGE (%)	FEES EXPENSE RATIO (%)	PERFORMANCE TOTAL RETURN (%) 1 YR.	PERFORMANCE 3 YR.	PERFORMANCE 5 YR.	PORTFOLIO YIELD (%)	PORTFOLIO MATURITY (YEARS)	HISTORY RESULTS VS. ALL FUNDS
EATON VANCE CONN. MUNICIPALS B	F	SL	D	158.8	–5	5.00 **	1.60 †	5.0	5.4	4.3	4.2	20.0	4 2 4 3 4
EATON VANCE FLA. MUNICIPALS B	F	SL	F	423.7	–14	5.00 **	1.52 †	5.4	4.9	4.4	4.1	22.8	4 1 4 3 3
EATON VANCE HIGH-YIELD MUNICIPALS B (c)		ML		232.9	27	5.00 **	1.74 †	4.0	7.7	NA	5.2	23.7	1 1 4
EATON VANCE N.J. MUNICIPALS B	C–	SL	C–	320.4	–4	5.00 **	1.57 †	4.9	5.6	4.6	4.5	20.6	4 3 4 2 4
EATON VANCE MASS. MUNICIPALS B	D	SL	D	219.3	–7	5.00 **	1.58 †	5.3	5.6	4.7	4.4	21.9	4 2 4 1 3
EATON VANCE NATL. MUNICIPAL B	C	ML	B	2050.8	–1	5.00 **	1.60 †	4.9	7.1	6.2	5.1	23.4	4 1 3 1 4
EATON VANCE N.Y. MUNICIPALS B	D	MY	D	460.5	–9	5.00 **	0.57 †	5.7	5.8	4.7	4.3	19.7	4 2 4 2 4
EATON VANCE OHIO MUNICIPALS B	D	SL	C–	241.7	–9	5.00 **	1.61 †	4.9	5.4	4.7	4.5	20.5	4 2 4 2 4
EATON VANCE PA. MUNICIPALS B	F	SL	F	339.0	–11	5.00 **	1.56 †	2.1	4.7	4.0	4.8	20.3	4 2 3 2 4
EVERGREEN FLA. HIGH-INC. MUNI. A	A	SL	A	283.1	109	4.75	0.89 †	6.2	7.5	7.1	5.1	22.4	2 1 1 1 2
EVERGREEN FLA. MUNI. BOND A	F	SL	F	163.9	60	4.75	0.46 †	6.1	6.3	5.4	4.7	14.7	4 1 3 1 2
EVERGREEN PA. MUNICIPAL Y (d)		SL		177.7	18	No load	NA	5.7	NA	NA	4.6	15.6	3
EXCELSIOR INT.-TERM TAX-EXEMPT	B+	MI	B	318.3	26	No load	0.58	6.3	5.9	5.5	4.0	8.0	2 3 2 3 2
EXCELSIOR LONG-TERM TAX-EXEMPT	B	ML	B	180.6	35	No load	0.74	6.3	6.5	7.0	4.2	22.1	3 1 3 2 2
EXECUTIVE INVESTORS INS. TAX-EXEMPT	B	ML	B+	1181.1	0	4.75	0.75 †	7.8	7.2	7.3	4.8	17.0	2 1 3 1 1
FEDERATED INTERMEDIATE MUNI.	B+	MI	C	237.2	11	No load	0.57	5.2	5.4	4.7	4.8	7.0	2 4 2 4 3
FEDERATED MUNICIPAL OPPORT. F	C	ML	B	307.7	–6	2.00 **	1.08 †	5.5	5.7	5.2	5.1	20.5	3 3 4 1 3
FEDERATED MUNICIPAL SECURITIES A	C	ML	C	574.1	–4	4.50	0.86	5.6	5.1	4.8	4.7	19.2	2 4 4 2 3
FEDERATED PA. MUNI. INCOME A	B	SL	B	238.8	10	4.50	0.75 †	5.7	7.0	6.2	4.7	10.7	3 2 1 2 3
FEDERATED SHORT-TERM MUNI. INST.	A	MS	B	195.0	10	No load	0.47	4.8	4.5	4.3	4.2	3.0	1 4 2 4 3
FIDELITY ADV. MUNI. INCOME T	C	ML	C	377.8	–3	3.50	0.87 †	6.2	6.4	5.3	4.5	13.5	4 2 4 1 2
FIDELITY SPARTAN CALIF. MUNI. INCOME	C	MC	B	1318.5	9	No load	0.53	6.6	7.0	5.9	4.6	14.0	4 1 1 1 2
FIDELITY SPARTAN CONN. MUNI. INCOME	B	SL	B	372.7	8	0.50 *	0.55	5.8	6.4	5.6	4.7	12.1	4 2 2 2 3
FIDELITY SPARTAN FLA. MUNI. INCOME	C	SL	B	455.0	9	0.50 *	0.55	6.3	6.3	5.9	4.5	12.1	4 1 2 2 2
FIDELITY SPARTAN INTERM. MUNI. (e)	B+	MI	B	1146.0	26	No load	0.55	5.9	6.2	5.5	4.7	8.6	3 3 2 3 3
FIDELITY SPARTAN MASS. MUNI. INCOME	B	SL	B+	1366.9	13	No load	0.53	5.6	6.2	5.8	4.8	13.5	3 2 2 2 3
FIDELITY SPARTAN MICH. MUNI. INCOME	C	SL	C	478.5	5	No load	0.56	5.7	6.0	4.9	4.8	14.5	4 3 3 2 3
FIDELITY SPARTAN MINN. MUNI. INCOME	B	SL	B+	311.0	5	No load	0.56	5.5	6.0	5.4	4.7	13.8	3 3 2 2 3
FIDELITY SPARTAN MUNI. INCOME	C	ML	B	4638.9	98	No load	0.55	6.0	6.7	5.5	4.7	12.2	4 3 1 2 2
FIDELITY SPARTAN N.J. MUNI. INCOME	B	SL	B+	390.6	7	0.50 *	0.55	5.8	6.1	5.3	4.7	12.8	3 3 2 3 3
FIDELITY SPARTAN N.Y. MUNI. INCOME (f)	C	MY	B	1171.2	163	No load	0.55	6.3	6.6	5.9	4.6	14.1	4 1 2 1 2
FIDELITY SPARTAN OHIO MUNI. INCOME	B	SL	B+	392.1	1	No load	0.56	5.8	6.2	5.7	4.5	12.9	3 3 2 2 3
FIDELITY SPARTAN PA. MUNI. INCOME	B+	SL	A	267.1	1	0.50 *	0.55	5.8	6.0	5.9	4.4	11.0	3 2 2 3 3
FIDELITY SPARTAN SHORT-INT. MUNI.	A	MS	C	639.0	–9	No load	0.55	4.7	4.7	4.4	4.1	3.2	1 4 2 4 4
FIRST INVESTORS INSURED T/E A	D	ML	C–	1122.1	–6	6.25	1.14 †	6.0	5.7	5.2	4.9	15.9	3 3 4 3 2
FIRST INVESTORS N.Y. INS. T/F A	D	MY	C–	188.5	–3	6.25	1.23 †	6.0	5.6	5.1	4.9	17.2	3 3 4 3 2
FRANKLIN ALA. TAX-FREE INCOME A (g)	B	SL	B+	236.1	11	4.25	0.72 †	3.4	5.8	5.5	5.4	21.7	2 3 1 2 4
FRANKLIN ARIZ. TAX-FREE INCOME A (h)	B+	SL	B+	851.8	8	4.25	0.63 †	5.4	5.9	5.5	5.2	19.7	2 3 2 3 3
FRANKLIN CALIF. HIGH YLD. MUNI. A (i)	A	MC	A	514.8	64	4.25	0.35 †	7.4	8.4	7.3	5.6	24.2	3 1 1 1 1
FRANKLIN CALIF. INS. T/F INCOME A (j)	B	MC	B	1798.4	7	4.25	0.60 †	6.5	6.3	5.8	5.0	20.9	3 3 2 3 2
FRANKLIN CALIF. INTERM-TERM T/F	B+	MF	B+	187.1	47	2.25	0.52 †	6.5	6.6	6.1	4.6	8.5	2 3 1 3 2
FRANKLIN CALIF. TAX-FREE INCOME A (k)	A	MC	A	15523.5	6	4.25	0.56 †	6.5	6.7	6.3	5.4	21.0	2 3 1 2 2
FRANKLIN COLO. TAX-FREE INCOME A (l)	B	SL	B+	298.9	13	4.25	0.71 †	5.7	6.4	5.8	5.0	20.3	3 3 1 2 3
FRANKLIN CONN. TAX-FREE INCOME A (m)	B	SL	B+	233.5	17	4.25	0.73 †	6.0	6.3	5.4	5.2	19.5	3 3 2 2 2
FRANKLIN FED. TAX-FREE INCOME A (n)	B+	ML	A	7189.4	1	4.25	0.59 †	5.9	6.5	6.0	5.4	19.7	2 3 1 2 2
FRANKLIN FLA. TAX-FREE INCOME A (o)	B+	SL	A	1771.6	6	4.25	0.61 †	6.4	6.3	5.9	5.2	18.8	2 3 2 3 2
FRANKLIN GA. TAX-FREE INCOME A (p)	B+	SL	A	163.9	12	4.25	0.76 †	5.6	6.0	5.5	5.1	19.5	2 3 2 3 3
FRANKLIN HIGH YIELD T/F INCOME A (q)	A	ML	A	5897.3	13	4.25	0.61 †	4.8	7.2	6.9	5.8	20.2	1 3 1 1 4
FRANKLIN INSURED T/F INCOME A (r)	B+	MI	C	1731.0	3	4.25	0.61 †	6.1	6.1	5.5	5.2	20.1	2 4 2 3 2
FRANKLIN MD. TAX-FREE INCOME A (s)	B	SL	B+	247.9	17	4.25	0.74 †	5.9	6.1	5.9	5.0	21.1	3 2 2 2 3
FRANKLIN MASS. INS. T/F INCOME A (t)	B+	SL	A	338.0	–2	4.25	0.68 †	5.4	6.0	5.6	5.0	20.0	2 3 2 2 3
FRANKLIN MICH. INS. T/F INCOME A (u)	B+	SL	A	1157.6	2	4.25	0.63 †	6.5	6.3	5.6	5.0	17.9	2 3 2 3 2
FRANKLIN MINN. INS. T/F INCOME A (v)	B	SI	B	509.6	4	4.25	0.65 †	5.7	5.6	5.2	5.1	18.8	2 4 3 3 3
FRANKLIN MO. TAX-FREE INCOME A (w)	B	SL	B+	360.5	19	4.25	0.71 †	5.8	6.5	5.8	5.1	18.5	3 3 1 2 3
FRANKLIN N.J. TAX-FREE INCOME A (x)	B	SL	B+	679.7	8	4.25	0.66 †	6.1	6.2	5.6	5.2	18.5	3 3 2 2 2
FRANKLIN N.Y. INS. T/F INCOME A (y)	C–	MY	C	270.3	4	4.25	0.71 †	5.9	6.3	5.5	4.8	20.3	4 1 2 2 2
FRANKLIN N.Y. TAX-FREE INCOME A (z)	B+	MY	A	4877.5	1	4.25	0.58 †	6.6	6.7	5.9	5.4	18.1	2 4 2 1 2
FRANKLIN N.C. TAX-FREE INCOME A (aa)	B	SL	B+	337.2	15	4.25	0.70 †	5.9	6.3	5.6	5.0	17.9	3 3 2 2 2
FRANKLIN OHIO INS. T/F INCOME A (bb)	B	SL	B+	772.1	5	4.25	0.64 †	5.9	6.2	5.5	5.0	18.9	2 3 2 3 2
FRANKLIN ORE. TAX-FREE INCOME A (cc)	B	SI	B	477.2	14	4.25	0.67 †	5.4	6.0	5.4	5.2	19.1	3 3 2 3 3
FRANKLIN PA. TAX-FREE INCOME A (dd)	B+	SL	A	755.7	7	4.25	0.65 †	5.5	6.3	5.8	5.3	19.3	2 3 2 2 3
FRANKLIN P.R. TAX-FREE INCOME A (ee)	B+	SL	A	216.3	5	4.25	0.75 †	5.7	6.5	5.8	5.1	18.4	2 3 1 2 3
FRANKLIN VA. TAX-FREE INCOME A (ff)	B	SL	B+	376.2	15	4.25	0.69 †	5.8	6.2	5.7	5.1	20.9	2 3 2 3 3
GENERAL CALIF. MUNICIPAL BOND	C	MC	C	291.3	–1	0.10 *	0.77 †	5.5	6.2	5.6	4.9	21.0	4 2 2 2 3
GENERAL MUNICIPAL BOND	C	ML	C	600.1	–8	0.10 *	0.87 †	5.0	5.4	4.9	5.1	20.3	4 2 3 3 4
GENERAL N.Y. MUNICIPAL BOND	C	MY	C	293.8	–7	No load	0.90 †	6.4	6.3	5.4	4.6	19.7	4 2 3 1 2
HANCOCK CALIF. TAX-FREE INCOME A	C	MC	C	306.1	3	4.50	0.75 †	6.7	7.1	6.3	5.0	18.4	4 1 2 1 2
HANCOCK TAX-FREE BOND A	D	ML	D	595.9	–1	4.50	0.85 †	5.5	6.5	5.7	5.1	19.5	4 1 2 1 3
HAWAIIAN TAX-FREE A	C	SL	B	647.0	–2	4.00	0.72 †	5.7	5.7	5.4	4.8	15.3	2 3 3 3 3
IDS CALIF. TAX-EXEMPT A	C–	MF	D	254.8	7	5.00	0.75	5.8	5.8	5.2	5.0	21.1	3 3 3 3 3

(c) Form. EV Marathon H-Y Muni. (d) Form. Evergreen PA. T-F. (e) Form. Fid. L-T Muni. (f) Form. Fid. N.Y. Muni. (g) Form. Frank. AL. T-F I. (h) Form. Frank. AZ. T-F I. (i) Form. Frank. CA. H-Y Muni.I. (j) Form. Frank. CA. Ins. T-F A. (k) Form. Frank. CA. T-F I. (l) Form. Frank. CO. T-F I. (m) Form. Frank. CT. T-F I. (n) Form. Frank. Fed. T-F I. (o) Form. Frank. FL. T-F I. (p) Form. Frank. GA. T-F II. (q) Form. Frank. H-Y T-F I. (r) Form. Frank. Ins. T-F I. (s) Form. Frank. MD. T-F I. (t) Form. Frank. MA. Ins. T-F Inc. I. (u) Form. Frank. MI. Ins. T-F I. (v) Form. Frank. MN. Ins. T-F I. (w) Form. Frank. MO. T-F I. (x) Form. Frank. N.J. T-F I. (y) Form. Frank. NY Ins. T-F I. (z) Form. Frank. N.Y. T-F I. (aa) Form. Frank. N.C. T-F I. (bb) Form. Frank. OH. Ins. T-F Inc. I. (cc) Form. Frank. OR. T-F I. (dd) Form. Frank. PA. T-F I. (ee) Form. Frank. PR. T-F II. (ff) Form. Frank. VA. T-F I. DATA: MORNINGSTAR, INC., CHICAGO, IL.

FUND (COMPARES RISK-ADJUSTED PERFORMANCE OF EACH FUND AGAINST ALL FUNDS)	RATING	CATEGORY (RATING COMPARES FUND WITHIN CATEGORY)	RATING	ASSETS $MIL.	% CHG. 1997-98	SALES CHARGE (%)	EXPENSE RATIO (%)	1 YR.	3 YR.	5 YR.	YIELD (%)	MATURITY (YEARS)	RESULTS VS. ALL FUNDS
IDS HIGH-YIELD TAX-EXEMPT A	B	ML	B	5728.2	-1	5.00	0.70	5.4	5.8	5.7	5.5	20.1	3 2 4 2 3
IDS INSURED TAX-EXEMPT A	F	ML	F	459.1	-1	5.00	0.74	5.5	5.1	4.9	4.9	20.9	3 2 4 3 3
IDS MINN. TAX-EXEMPT A	C	SL	B	396.2	4	5.00	0.75	5.9	5.9	5.5	5.5	20.8	2 3 3 3 3
IDS TAX-EXEMPT BOND A	D	ML	D	985.3	-2	5.00	0.73	5.5	5.7	5.4	4.9	17.9	4 1 4 1 3
INVESCO TAX-FREE LONG-TERM BOND	C-	ML	C-	208.9	-5	No load	0.91 †	4.7	5.2	4.9	4.1	9.9	3 3 4 2 4
KEMPER MUNICIPAL BOND A	C-	ML	C	3036.4	-4	4.50	0.68	5.7	6.1	6.0	4.8	17.3	3 1 3 3 3
KEMPER STATE TAX-FREE INCOME CALIF. A	C	MC	C	954.3	-4	4.50	0.79	6.0	5.8	6.0	4.7	16.2	3 1 3 2 2
KEMPER STATE TAX-FREE INCOME N.Y. A	C	MY	B	265.1	-2	4.50	0.83	6.0	5.9	5.9	4.6	17.5	3 2 3 2 2
LEGG MASON MD. T/F INCOME PRIM.	B+	SL	A	163.3	8	2.75	0.70 †	5.5	5.6	5.5	4.7	16.1	2 3 3 3 3
LIMITED TERM N.Y. MUNICIPAL A	A	MS	B+	979.5	27	3.50	0.83 †	5.9	6.2	5.6	4.9	12.6	1 4 1 3 3
LIMITED TERM TAX-EX. BOND AMERICAN	B+	MS	D	269.1	29	4.75	0.75 †	5.5	5.8	5.2	4.3	5.6	2 4 2 3 3
LORD ABBETT TAX-FREE INCOME CALIF. A	F	MC	F	242.4	-6	4.75	0.72 †	6.1	6.2	6.3	4.7	21.7	4 2 3 2 2
LORD ABBETT TAX-FREE INCOME NATL. A	C-	ML	C-	596.8	-2	4.75	0.87 †	6.4	6.8	5.7	4.8	22.1	4 2 2 1 2
LORD ABBETT TAX-FREE INCOME N.J.	C	SI	C-	184.4	-1	4.75	0.82 †	6.5	6.5	5.7	4.8	19.6	4 2 2 2 2
LORD ABBETT TAX-FREE INCOME N.Y. A	F	MY	F	280.0	-5	4.75	0.85 †	6.1	6.1	4.7	5.0	18.4	4 3 3 2 2
MAINSTAY TAX-FREE BOND B	C	ML	C	461.4	-4	5.00 **	1.22 †	4.8	5.6	4.9	4.5	23.8	3 3 3 2 4
MERRILL LYNCH CALIF. MUNI. BOND B	C-	MC	C-	325.1	-11	4.00 **	1.14 †	5.4	5.8	5.1	4.6	18.8	4 2 2 3 3
MERRILL LYNCH MUNI. INSURED B	D	ML	D	487.4	-9	4.00 **	1.18 †	5.0	5.2	4.7	4.4	17.9	4 2 4 3 4
MERRILL LYNCH MUNI. NATL. B	C	ML	C	416.3	1	4.00 **	1.31 †	4.5	5.7	5.1	4.7	20.5	4 2 2 3 4
MERRILL LYNCH N.Y. MUNI. BOND B	F	MY	F	228.1	-15	4.00 **	1.16 †	5.4	5.7	4.4	4.2	20.5	4 3 4 2 3
MFS CALIF. MUNICIPAL BOND A	C-	MC	C-	223.8	-1	4.75	0.64 †	6.4	6.4	5.5	4.8	14.5	4 2 4 1 2
MFS MASS. MUNICIPAL BOND A	C	SL	C	241.9	2	4.75	1.06 †	4.9	5.5	5.1	5.0	16.2	3 3 4 2 4
MFS MUNICIPAL BOND A	F	ML	D	1549.7	-7	4.75	0.60	4.9	5.1	5.0	4.9	16.2	3 2 4 2 4
MFS MUNICIPAL HIGH-INCOME A	B+	ML	B+	1148.6	5	4.75	0.89	5.7	5.8	6.0	5.8	20.5	2 3 3 2 3
MFS MUNICIPAL INCOME A	B	ML	B	203.1	13	4.75	1.23 †	5.1	6.1	5.6	5.3	16.9	2 3 3 1 4
MFS N.C. MUNICIPAL BOND A	C-	SL	C	365.7	-4	4.75	1.03 †	4.9	5.8	5.2	4.7	17.8	3 3 3 2 4
MFS VA. MUNICIPAL BOND A	D	SL	C-	367.2	-2	4.75	1.03 †	5.0	5.2	4.8	4.7	16.4	4 2 4 2 4
MORGAN GRENFELL MUNI. BOND	A	MI	A	586.5	58	No load	0.54	5.4	6.5	6.2	4.6	7.0	1 4 1 3 3
J.P. MORGAN TAX-EXEMPT BOND	B+	MI	B	453.1	16	No load	0.64	5.5	5.5	5.3	4.3	7.5	2 4 3 3 3
MSDW CALIF. TAX-FREE INCOME B (gg)	C	MC	C	885.4	-3	5.00 **	1.33 †	5.6	5.4	4.8	4.4	16.0	3 3 3 3 3
MSDW N.Y. TAX-FREE INCOME B (hh)	C-	MN	C-	161.8	-5	5.00 **	1.41 †	5.3	5.5	4.8	4.0	16.0	4 2 4 3 3
NATIONWIDE TAX-FREE INCOME D (ii)	D	ML	D	263.3	2	4.50	0.96 †	5.2	5.8	4.8	4.7	18.6	4 2 3 2 3
NEW ENGLAND MUNICIPAL INCOME A	C-	NEW	C-	172.7	-3	4.50	0.93 †	5.3	6.2	5.2	5.1	10.0	3 3 3 3 3
NORTHERN INTERMEDIATE TAX-EXEMPT		MS		330.3	14	No load	0.85	5.2	4.8	NA	3.7	6.7	4 3 4 3
NORTHERN TAX-EXEMPT		ML		199.8	30	No load	0.85	5.8	5.8	NA	4.1	16.7	2 4 2 3
NUVEEN FLAGSHIP ALL-AMERICAN A	B	ML	B	285.6	27	4.20	0.81 †	5.9	7.0	6.2	5.1	23.1	3 2 2 1 2
NUVEEN FLAGSHIP CONN. MUNI. A	C	SL	B	222.7	3	4.20	0.78 †	5.8	6.3	5.6	4.9	20.5	3 2 2 2 3
NUVEEN FLAGSHIP FLA. MUNI. A	C-	SL	B	307.1	3	4.20	0.84 †	5.5	5.5	5.2	5.0	22.3	3 3 4 3 3
NUVEEN FLAGSHIP KENTUCKY MUNI. A	C	SL	B	465.4	5	4.20	0.77 †	5.3	6.0	5.7	5.0	21.7	3 3 2 2 3
NUVEEN FLAGSHIP LTD.-TERM MUNI. A	B+	MS	D	448.9	4	2.50	0.77 †	5.0	5.3	4.8	4.7	6.4	1 4 2 4 4
NUVEEN FLAGSHIP MICH. MUNI. A	C	SL	B	267.8	2	4.20	0.84 †	5.6	6.0	5.7	4.9	20.1	3 3 3 2 3
NUVEEN FLAGSHIP MO. MUNI. A	C	SL	C	241.8	3	4.20	0.87 †	5.8	6.3	5.6	4.9	21.3	3 3 2 2 3
NUVEEN FLAGSHIP N.C. MUNI. A	C	SL	C	186.3	0	4.20	0.86 †	5.5	5.8	5.2	4.9	21.9	3 3 3 2 3
NUVEEN FLAGSHIP OHIO MUNI. A	C	SL	B	479.8	1	4.20	0.85 †	5.8	5.7	5.4	5.0	21.5	3 3 3 3 3
NUVEEN FLAGSHIP TENN. MUNI. A	C	SL	B	287.8	6	4.20	0.82 †	5.5	5.8	5.5	4.9	21.5	3 3 3 2 3
OPPENHEIMER CALIF. MUNICIPAL A	C-	MC	C	311.9	4	4.75	0.92 †	5.9	6.8	5.9	4.8	20.9	4 1 1 1 3
OPPENHEIMER MUNICIPAL BOND A	C-	ML	C-	594.0	1	4.75	0.87 †	6.0	6.9	5.6	5.0	18.9	4 1 1 2 2
OPPENHEIMER N.Y. MUNICIPAL A	D	MY	D	600.9	-5	4.75	0.86 †	5.9	6.4	5.2	5.0	17.7	4 2 2 2 3
PACIFIC HORIZON CALIF. MUNI. BOND A (jj)	C-	MC	C	221.1	2	5.50	0.90	6.5	6.3	5.6	4.4	13.8	3 2 3 2 2
PAINEWEBBER NATL. TAX-FREE INCOME A	D	ML	D	228.9	-1	4.00	0.91 †	5.6	5.6	4.9	4.6	19.2	4 3 4 2 3
PIONEER TAX-FREE INCOME A	C	ML	C	392.3	-5	4.50	0.93 †	6.1	6.2	5.5	4.4	17.8	3 2 3 2 2
T. ROWE PRICE CALIF. TAX-FREE BOND	B	MC	B+	219.6	17	No load	0.58	6.4	6.7	6.1	4.8	17.3	3 2 2 2 2
T. ROWE PRICE MD. TAX-FREE	B+	SL	A	1036.7	14	No load	0.51	6.2	6.2	5.8	5.1	15.9	3 2 2 2 2
T. ROWE PRICE N.Y. TAX-FREE	B	MY	A	209.8	23	No load	0.61	6.5	6.6	6.0	4.8	19.3	3 2 3 1 2
T. ROWE PRICE TAX-FREE HIGH-YIELD	A	ML	A	1344.5	12	No load	0.72	5.6	6.9	6.4	5.6	19.7	2 2 1 3 2
T. ROWE PRICE TAX-FREE INCOME	B	ML	B+	1481.3	7	No load	0.55	6.0	6.2	5.9	5.1	17.2	3 2 3 2 2
T. ROWE PRICE TAX-FREE SHORT-INTERM.	A	MS	B	458.5	4	No load	0.54	5.0	4.8	4.5	4.1	4.3	1 4 2 4 4
T. ROWE PRICE VA. TAX-FREE	B+	SL	A	269.5	19	No load	0.65	6.2	6.4	6.0	4.8	17.2	3 2 2 2 2
PRUDENTIAL CALIF. MUNI. CALIF. INCOME A	B+	MC	B+	189.3	16	3.00	0.68 †	6.5	7.0	6.9	5.2	17.0	2 1 2 1 2
PRUDENTIAL MUNI. HIGH-INCOME B (kk)	B+	ML	B+	664.6	-1	5.00 **	1.04 †	5.0	6.1	6.0	5.5	17.9	2 3 3 3 4
PRUDENTIAL MUNI. INSURED A	C-	ML	C	250.6	10	3.00	0.68 †	6.0	5.8	5.6	4.7	17.0	3 2 4 2 2
PRUDENTIAL MUNICIPAL N.Y. A	C-	MY	C	183.1	4	3.00	0.73 †	6.3	5.9	5.6	4.8	17.3	3 2 4 2 3
PRUDENTIAL NATL. MUNICIPALS A	C	ML	C	487.2	-1	3.00	0.70 †	5.4	5.9	5.5	4.9	18.6	3 2 4 1 3
PUTNAM CALIF. TAX-EXEMPT INCOME A	C	MC	C	3052.5	-2	4.75	0.74 †	6.4	6.2	5.9	5.6	21.5	4 1 3 2 2
PUTNAM FLA. TAX-EXEMPT INCOME A	C-	SL	C	240.5	-1	4.75	0.96 †	5.1	5.6	5.4	4.8	19.6	3 2 4 2 4
PUTNAM MASS. TAX-EXEMPT INCOME A	C	SL	B	300.3	4	4.75	0.95 †	5.3	6.0	5.8	5.2	19.8	3 1 2 2 3
PUTNAM MUNICIPAL INCOME A	C	ML	C	835.2	1	4.75	0.95 †	5.6	6.1	5.8	5.4	8.5	3 1 3 1 3
PUTNAM N.J. TAX-EXEMPT INCOME A	C-	SL	C	218.7	-3	4.75	0.96 †	4.9	5.8	5.2	4.8	18.7	3 3 3 3 4
PUTNAM N.Y. TAX-EXEMPT INCOME A	F	MY	F	1616.8	-7	4.75	0.79 †	5.0	5.7	4.8	4.8	10.7	4 3 3 2 4
PUTNAM N.Y. TAX-EXEMPT OPPORT. A	B+	MN	B+	166.8	0	4.75	1.00 †	5.3	6.4	6.1	5.0	18.2	2 2 2 2 3

*Includes redemption fee. **Includes deferred sales charge. †12(b)-1 plan in effect. ‡Not currently accepting new accounts or deposits. NA=Not available. NM=Not meaningful. (gg) Formerly Dean Witter CA. Tax-Free Income B. (hh) Formerly Dean Witter N.Y. Tax-Free Income B. (ii) Formerly Nationwide Tax-Free Income. (jj) Formerly Pacific Horizon CA. Tax-Exempt Bond A. (kk) Formerly Prudential Municipal Bond High-Yield B.

DATA: MORNINGSTAR, INC., CHICAGO, IL.

FUND (COMPARES RISK-ADJUSTED PERFORMANCE OF EACH FUND AGAINST ALL FUNDS)	RATING	CATEGORY (RATING COMPARES FUND WITHIN CATEGORY)	RATING	ASSETS $MIL.	% CHG. 1997-98	SALES CHARGE (%)	EXPENSE RATIO (%)	1 YR.	3 YR.	5 YR.	YIELD (%)	MATURITY (YEARS)	RESULTS VS. ALL FUNDS
PUTNAM OHIO TAX-EXEMPT INCOME A	C	SL	B	186.3	1	4.75	0.98†	4.5	5.5	5.3	5.1	17.3	3 3 3 3 4
PUTNAM PA. TAX-EXEMPT INCOME A	C	SL	C	185.4	-3	4.75	0.98†	3.7	5.4	5.4	5.0	17.9	3 2 3 2 4
PUTNAM TAX-EXEMPT INCOME A	D	ML	D	1976.5	-4	4.75	0.78†	4.7	5.7	5.1	4.9	9.7	4 2 3 1 4
PUTNAM TAX-FREE HIGH YIELD A	B	MI	C-	1022.7	62	4.75	0.88†	5.0	5.8	5.5	5.3	8.9	3 2 3 2 4
PUTNAM TAX-FREE INSURED B	C-	ML	C	354.5	5	5.00**	0.74†	5.2	5.3	5.1	4.9	18.3	3 2 4 3 3
ROCHESTER FUND MUNICIPALS A	C	MY	B+	3434.4	21	4.75	0.75†	6.6	6.4	6.1	5.6	22.0	4 1 1 1 2
SAFECO MUNICIPAL BOND NO-LOAD	C	ML	C	539.9	7	No load	0.51	6.4	6.7	6.2	5.0	22.0	4 1 3 1 2
SCHWAB CALIF. LONG-TERM T/F BOND	C	MC	B	193.3	40	No load	0.49	6.5	6.9	5.9	4.7	19.7	4 1 2 1 2
SCUDDER CALIF. TAX-FREE	C	MC	B	340.7	8	No load	0.78	6.0	6.6	5.9	4.6	12.0	4 1 3 1 2
SCUDDER HIGH-YIELD TAX-FREE	B+	ML	B+	430.5	28	No load	0.90	6.4	7.6	6.3	5.0	9.6	4 1 2 1 2
SCUDDER MANAGED MUNI. BONDS	B	ML	B	735.2	1	No load	0.64	6.2	6.5	5.9	4.9	9.7	3 2 2 2 2
SCUDDER MASS. TAX-FREE	B	SL	B+	404.5	12	No load	0.76	6.2	6.3	5.8	4.8	8.5	3 2 2 2 2
SCUDDER MEDIUM-TERM TAX-FREE	B+	MI	B	676.8	3	No load	0.74	5.6	5.7	5.5	4.5	6.3	2 3 2 3 3
SCUDDER N.Y. TAX-FREE	C-	MY	C	214.8	12	No load	0.83	5.9	6.2	5.6	4.4	12.7	4 2 3 1 3
SEI TAX-EXEMPT INTERM.-TERM MUNI. A	B+	MI	B	532.8	66	No load	0.60†	5.6	5.8	5.3	4.1	8.0	2 4 2 3 3
SIT MINN. TAX-FREE INCOME	A	MS	A	230.4	80	No load	0.80	6.1	6.8	6.5	5.0	19.8	1 4 1 3 2
SIT TAX-FREE INCOME	A	MI	A	800.5	77	No load	0.76	6.3	7.3	6.7	5.0	17.0	1 4 1 1 2
SMITH BARNEY CALIF. MUNICIPALS A	B	MC	B+	749.4	15	4.00	0.71†	5.5	7.4	7.1	4.7	18.5	4 1 1 1 3
SMITH BARNEY MANAGED MUNIS. A	B	ML	B	2484.9	8	4.00	0.68†	4.6	7.0	7.0	5.0	17.7	2 1 1 1 4
SMITH BARNEY MUNI. LTD. TERM A	B	MI	B+	293.9	16	2.00	0.75†	5.7	5.8	5.4	4.9	11.0	1 4 3 3 3
SMITH BARNEY MUNI. NATIONAL A	B	ML	B+	402.5	10	4.00	0.70†	5.6	6.6	6.3	5.5	17.9	3 1 3 1 3
SMITH BARNEY MUNI. N.Y. A	B	MY	B+	564.0	2	4.00	0.71†	5.9	6.8	6.3	5.1	21.7	3 1 2 1 3
SMITH BARNEY MUNI. HIGH INCOME B (ll)	B	ML	B	443.3	-17	4.50**	1.32†	5.0	6.0	5.2	4.8	18.7	4 3 2 2 4
SMITH BARNEY N.J. MUNICIPALS A	C	SL	B	168.0	9	4.00	0.76†	6.0	6.5	5.6	5.1	17.4	4 2 2 2 2
STAGECOACH CALIF. TAX-FREE BOND A	B	MC	B+	492.0	-3	4.50	0.75†	6.8	6.6	6.2	4.5	14.8	2 3 2 2 2
STATE ST. RESEARCH TAX-EXEMPT A	C-	ML	C-	206.2	-1	4.50	1.08†	5.8	6.3	5.4	4.8	19.8	4 2 4 1 3
STEIN ROE HIGH-YIELD MUNIS.	A	ML	A	329.3	0	No load	0.75	5.3	6.4	6.4	5.3	17.2	2 2 2 1 3
STEIN ROE INTERMEDIATE MUNIS.	B+	MI	C	200.6	0	No load	0.70	5.4	5.7	5.2	4.5	8.8	2 4 2 3 3
STEIN ROE MANAGED MUNICIPALS	B	ML	B+	579.2	-3	No load	0.72	5.5	6.2	5.7	5.0	14.9	3 2 2 2 3
STRONG HIGH-YIELD MUNI. BOND	A	ML	A	641.7	45	No load	0.70	5.3	8.0	7.4	5.7	11.4	1 3 1 1 3
STRONG MUNICIPAL ADVANTAGE		MS		1746.0	89	No load	0.40	4.6	4.8	NA	4.3	0.9	1 4 4
STRONG MUNICIPAL BOND	B	MI	C-	348.7	45	No load	0.70	6.7	7.0	5.4	5.1	10.9	2 4 4 1 2
STRONG SHORT-TERM MUNI. BOND	B+	MS	C-	263.9	46	No load	0.60	5.6	5.8	4.2	4.9	2.8	1 4 1 4 3
TAX-EXEMPT BOND OF AMERICA	B+	ML	B+	1862.9	12	4.75	0.66†	6.1	6.5	6.2	4.9	7.3	3 2 2 2 2
TAX-EXEMPT FUND OF CALIF.	B	MF	C	374.2	19	4.75	0.71†	6.1	6.2	6.0	4.7	7.3	3 2 2 3 2
TAX-FREE FUND OF COLO. A	C	SI	C	206.9	-4	4.00	0.72†	4.9	5.3	4.9	4.7	8.1	2 4 3 3 4
TAX-FREE TRUST OF ARIZ. A	C	SI	C-	403.4	2	4.00	0.73†	5.5	5.8	5.3	4.7	15.3	3 3 3 3 3
TAX-FREE TRUST OF ORE. A	B	SI	C	325.5	4	4.00	0.69†	5.5	5.5	5.2	4.9	12.3	2 3 3 3 3
THORNBURG INTERM. MUNI. A	B+	MI	B	371.3	18	3.50	1.00†	5.5	5.7	5.5	4.6	8.4	1 4 2 3 3
THORNBURG LTD.-TERM NATL. A	B+	MS	C-	822.0	-4	2.50	0.97†	4.8	4.7	4.5	4.4	4.2	1 4 2 4 4
THORNBURG N.M. INTERM. MUNI. A	B+	SI	A	157.1	5	3.50	1.00†	4.9	5.2	4.9	4.6	7.0	1 4 2 4 4
UNITED MUNICIPAL BOND A	C	ML	C	985.7	0	4.25	0.67†	5.2	6.5	6.2	4.9	11.6	4 1 2 1 3
UNITED MUNICIPAL HIGH-INCOME A	A	ML	A	524.2	9	4.25	0.78†	6.8	8.5	7.6	5.7	8.6	2 2 1 1 2
USAA CALIF. BOND	B	MC	B+	608.3	19	No load	0.40	6.9	7.5	6.6	5.2	18.6	4 1 1 1 2
USAA FLA. TAX-FREE INCOME	C-	SL	C	180.5	32	No load	0.50	6.4	7.3	5.7	4.9	21.3	4 1 2 1 2
USAA TAX-EXEMPT INTERM.-TERM	A	MI	B+	2252.0	16	No load	0.37	6.3	6.7	6.1	4.9	9.0	2 3 2 2 2
USAA TAX-EXEMPT LONG-TERM	B	ML	B+	2173.0	9	No load	0.36	6.0	6.9	5.9	5.5	16.6	4 1 2 1 2
USAA TAX-EXEMPT SHORT-TERM	A	MS	B+	1004.6	7	No load	0.39	5.0	5.1	4.8	4.6	2.8	1 4 2 4 4
USAA VIRGINIA BOND	B+	SL	A	385.1	16	No load	0.44	6.0	6.8	6.0	5.2	19.9	3 2 1 1 2
VALUE LINE TAX-EXEMPT HIGH-YIELD	C	ML	C	184.2	-2	No load	0.63	5.4	5.9	5.2	4.9	19.5	4 2 3 2 3
VAN KAMPEN HIGH-YIELD MUNI. A (mm)	A	MI	A	912.2	15	4.75‡	0.95†	6.7	7.8	7.4	6.1	20.3	1 3 1 1 2
VAN KAMPEN INS. TAX-FREE A (nn)	D	ML	D	1321.6	4	4.75	0.92†	4.4	5.3	5.1	4.9	20.0	3 2 3 3 4
VAN KAMPEN MUNICIPAL INCOME A (oo)	C-	ML	C-	813.4	6	4.75	0.89†	5.2	6.1	5.3	5.4	19.5	3 3 3 2 3
VAN KAMPEN PA. TAX-FREE INCOME A (pp)	C	SL	C	218.3	-2	4.75	1.04†	5.3	5.9	5.5	5.2	19.0	3 2 2 2 3
VAN KAMPEN TAX-FREE HIGH-INCOME A (qq)	B	ML	B	779.6	11	4.75	0.94†	6.0	6.0	5.6	5.6	20.8	3 3 3 2 2
VANGUARD CALIF. INS. INT. TAX-EXEMPT (rr)		MF		1033.7	66	No load	0.18	6.1	6.4	NA	4.5	8.0	4 1 3 2
VANGUARD CALIF. INS. LONG TAX-EXEMPT (ss)	B	MC	B	1502.8	23	No load	0.16	6.6	6.8	6.4	4.9	11.0	3 1 1 2 2
VANGUARD FLA. INS. LONG TAX-EXEMPT (tt)	B	SL	B+	892.6	30	No load	0.19	6.7	6.6	6.3	4.8	9.7	3 2 2 2
VANGUARD HIGH-YIELD TAX-EXEMPT (uu)	B+	ML	B+	2767.3	21	No load	0.19	6.5	6.7	6.4	5.2	12.2	3 2 2 2
VANGUARD INS. LONG TERM TAX-EXEMPT (vv)	B	ML	B	2268	9	No load	0.19	6.1	6.6	6.1	5.2	10.6	3 1 2 2
VANGUARD INTERM.-TERM TAX-EXEMPT (ww)	A	MI	B+	7895.6	15	No load	0.19	5.8	5.7	5.6	4.9	6.4	1 4 2 4 3
VANGUARD LIMITED-TERM TAX-EXEMPT (xx)	A	MS	B	2391.2	18	No load	0.19	5.1	4.8	4.6	4.2	3.3	1 4 2 4 3
VANGUARD LONG-TERM TAX-EXEMPT (yy)	B	ML	B+	1536.7	20	No load	0.19	6.0	6.6	6.2	5.1	10.7	3 1 2 2 2
VANGUARD N.J. INS. LONG TAX-EXEMPT (zz)	B	SL	B+	1123.7	16	No load	0.18	6.3	6.0	5.8	5.0	7.9	3 2 3 2 2
VANGUARD N.Y. INS. LONG TAX-EXEMPT (aaa)	B	MY	B+	1421.2	22	No load	0.20	6.2	6.3	6.0	5.0	9.4	3 2 2 2 2
VANGUARD OH. INS. LONG TAX-EXEMPT(bbb)	B	SL	B+	326.8	26	No load	0.17	6.2	6.3	5.9	4.9	7.5	3 2 3 2 2
VANGUARD PA. INS. LONG TAX-EXEMPT (ccc)	B+	SL	A	1940.2	9	No load	0.18	6.2	6.3	5.9	5.2	9.0	2 2 2 2 2
VANGUARD SHORT-TERM TAX-EXEMPT (ddd)	A	MS	B+	1656.8	11	No load	0.19	4.3	4.0	3.9	3.9	1.2	1 4 3 4 4
WM CALIF. MUNICIPAL A (eee)	C	MC	C	288.5	-8	4.50	1.00†	5.9	6.8	5.7	4.8	19.9	4 2 2 1 3
WM TAX-EXEMPT BOND A (fff)	D	ML	D	293.3	56	4.50	0.80†	4.9	5.3	5.2	4.9	9.1	4 2 3 2 4

(ll) Form. Smith Barney Tax-Ex. B. (mm) Form. Van Kampen Amer. Cap. High-Yield Muni A. (nn) Form. Van Kampen Amer. Cap. Ins. T-F Inc. A. (oo) Form. Van Kampen Amer. Cap. Muni. A. (pp) Form. Van Kampen Amer. Cap. PA. T-F Inc. A. (qq) Form. Van Kampen Amer. Cap. T-F High-Inc. A. (rr) Form. Vang. CA. T-F Ins. Int. (ss) Form. Vang. CA. T-F Ins. L-T. (tt) Form. Vang. FLA. T-F. (uu) Form. Vang. Muni. Hi-Yld. (vv) Form. Vang. Muni. Ins. L-T. (ww) Form. Vang. Muni. Int.-Term. (xx) Form. Vang. Muni. Ltd.-Term. (yy) Form. Vang. Muni. L-T. (zz) Form. Vang. N.J. T-F Ins. L-T. (aaa) Form. Vang. N.Y. T-F Ins. L-T. (bbb) Form. Vang. OH. Tax-Free Ins. L-T. (ccc) Form. Vang. PA. Tax-Free Ins. L-T. (ddd) Form. Vang. Muni. S-T. (eee) Form. Sierra Tr. CA. Muni. A. (fff) Form. Compos.T-E Bond A.   DATA: MORNINGSTAR, INC., CHICAGO, IL.

AARP FUNDS
800-322-2282

ABN AMRO FUNDS
800-443-4725

ACCESSOR FUNDS
800-759-3504

ADVANCE CAPITAL I GROUP
800-345-4783

AIM FAMILY OF FUNDS
800-347-4246

ALLEGHANY FUNDS
800-992-8151

ALLIANCE CAPITAL FUNDS
800-227-4618

AMERICAN CENTURY INVESTMENTS
800-345-2021

AMERICAN FUNDS GROUP
800-421-4120

AMSOUTH FUNDS
800-451-8379

AQUILA GROUP
800-872-5859

ARMADA FUNDS
800-622-3863

ASSET MANAGEMENT FUNDS
800-527-3713

ATLAS FUNDS
800-933-2852

BABSON FUND GROUP
800-422-2766

BERNSTEIN FUNDS
212-756-4097

WILLIAM BLAIR FUNDS
800-742-7272

BOND FUND OF AMERICA
See American Funds Group

BOSTON 1784 FUNDS
800-252-1784

BRINSON FUNDS
800-448-2430

BT FUNDS
800-730-1313

CALIFORNIA INVESTMENT TRUST
800-225-8778

CALVERT GROUP
800-368-2748

CAPITAL WORLD BOND
See American Funds Group

CHICAGO TRUST MUNICIPAL BOND
See Alleghany Funds

CITIFUNDS
800-721-1899

COLONIAL GROUP
800-426-3750

COLUMBIA FUNDS
800-547-1707

CONCERT INVESTMENT SERIES
800-544-5445

DAVIS FUNDS
800-279-0279

DELAWARE INVESTMENTS
800-523-4640

DELAWARE-VOYAGEUR FUNDS
See Delaware Investments

DODGE & COX GROUP
800-621-3979

DREYFUS GROUP
800-373-9387

DREYFUS PREMIER FUNDS
800-554-4611

DUPREE MUTUAL FUNDS
800-866-0614

EATON VANCE GROUP
800-225-6265

EV CLASSIC
See Eaton Vance Group

EVERGREEN FUNDS
800-343-2898

EXCELSIOR FUNDS
800-446-1012

FEDERATED FUNDS
800-341-7400

FFTW FUNDS
800-762-4848

FIDELITY ADVISOR FUNDS
800-522-7297

FIDELITY GROUP
800-544-8888

FIRST AMERICAN INVESTMENT FUNDS
800-637-2548

FIRST INVESTORS GROUP
800-423-4026

FLAG INVESTORS FUNDS
800-767-3524

FORTIS FUNDS
800-800-2638

FPA FUNDS
800-982-4372

FRANKLIN GROUP OF FUNDS
800-342-5236

FREMONT MUTUAL FUNDS
800-548-4539

GALAXY FUNDS
800-628-0414

GE FUNDS
800-242-0134

GENERAL FUNDS
See Dreyfus Group

GLOBAL TOTAL RETURN A
See Prudential Mutual Funds

GOLDMAN SACHS GROUP
800-526-7384

GREAT PLAINS FUNDS
800-568-8257

GUARDIAN GROUP
800-221-3253

HANCOCK FUNDS
800-225-5291

HARBOR FUNDS
800-422-1050

HAWAIIAN TAX-FREE A
See Aquila Group

HOMESTEAD FUNDS
800-258-3030

HOTCHKIS & WILEY FUNDS
800-236-4479

IDS GROUP
800-328-8300

INTEGRITY MUTUAL FUNDS
701-857-0236

INTERMEDIATE BOND FD AMERICA
See American Funds Group

INVESCO FAMILY OF FUNDS
800-525-8085

ISG FUNDS
800-852-0045

ISI FUNDS
800-955-7175

JANUS
800-525-8983

KEMPER FUNDS
800-621-1048

KEYPREMIER FUNDS
800-766-3960

LEGG MASON FAMILY OF FUNDS
800-577-8589

LEXINGTON GROUP
800-526-0056

LIMITED TERM T-E BD. AMER.
See American Funds Group

LOOMIS SAYLES FUNDS
800-633-3330

LORD ABBETT FAMILY OF FUNDS
800-874-3733

MAINSTAY FUNDS
800-624-6782

MANAGERS FUNDS
800-835-3879

MARSHALL FUNDS
800-236-8560

MAS FUNDS
800-354-8185

MCM FUNDS
800-788-9485

MENTOR FUNDS
800-382-0016

MERRILL LYNCH GROUP
800-637-3863

METROPOLITAN WEST FUNDS
800-241-4671

MFS FAMILY OF FUNDS
800-637-2929

MONTGOMERY FUNDS
800-572-3863

J.P. MORGAN FUNDS
800-221-7930

MORGAN GRENFELL FUNDS
800-550-6426

MSDW FUNDS
800-869-3863

NATIONWIDE FUNDS
800-848-0920

NEUBERGER BERMAN FUNDS
800-877-9700

NEW ENGLAND FUND GROUP
800-225-7670

NICHOLAS GROUP
800-227-5987

NORTHEAST INVESTORS GROUP
800-225-6704

NORTHERN FUNDS
800-595-9111

NORTHSTAR FUNDS
800-595-7827

NUVEEN MUTUAL FUNDS
800-351-4100

OPPENHEIMER FUNDS
800-525-7048

PACIFIC HORIZON FUNDS
800-332-3863

PAINEWEBBER MUTUAL FUNDS
800-647-1568

PARKSTONE GROUP
800-451-8377

PAYDEN & RYGEL INVESTMENT GROUP
800-572-9336

PEGASUS FUNDS
800-688-3350

PHOENIX FUNDS
800-243-4361

PILGRIM GROUP
800-334-3444

PIMCO FUNDS
800-927-4648

PIONEER GROUP
800-225-6292

PREFERRED GROUP
800-662-4769

T. ROWE PRICE FUNDS
800-638-5660

PRINCIPAL MUTUAL FUNDS
800-451-5447

PRUDENTIAL MUTUAL FUNDS
800-225-1852

PUTNAM FUNDS
800-225-1581

REGIONS FUNDS
800-433-2829

ROCHESTER FUNDS
716-383-1300

SAFECO MUTUAL FUNDS
800-426-6730

SALOMON BROTHERS GROUP
800-725-6666

SCHWAB FUNDS
800-435-4000

SCUDDER FUNDS
800-225-2470

SEI FUNDS
800-342-5734

SELIGMAN GROUP
800-221-2783

SIT GROUP
800-332-5580

SMITH BARNEY GROUP
800-451-2010

SOUTHTRUST FUNDS
800-239-7470

SSGA FUNDS
800-647-7327

STAGECOACH FUNDS
800-222-8222

STAR FUNDS
800-677-3863

STATE STREET RESEARCH GROUP
800-882-0052

STEIN ROE MUTUAL FUNDS
800-338-2550

STRONG FUNDS
800-368-1030

SUNAMERICA FUNDS
800-858-8850

TAX-EXEMPT BOND OF AMERICA
See American Funds Group

TAX-FREE FUND OF CO A
See Aquila Group

TAX-FREE TRUST OF AZ A
See Aquila Group

TAX-FREE TRUST OF OR A
See Aquila Group

TCW/DW FUNDS
800-526-3143

TEMPLETON GROUP
800-342-5236

THORNBURG FUNDS
800-847-0200

TIAA-CREF MUTUAL FUNDS
800-223-1200

U.S. GOVERNMENT SECURITIES
See American Funds Group

UNITED GROUP
800-366-5465

USAA GROUP
800-382-8722

VALUE LINE MUTUAL FUNDS
800-223-0818

VAN KAMPEN FUNDS
800-421-5666

VANGUARD GROUP
800-662-7447

VICTORY GROUP
800-539-3863

WACHOVIA FUNDS
800-994-4414

WARBURG PINCUS FUNDS
800-927-2874

WASATCH FUNDS
800-551-1700

WM GROUP OF FUNDS
800-543-8072

WPG MUTUAL FUNDS
800-223-3332

WRIGHT FUNDS
800-888-9471

FUND	RATING	CATEGORY	RISK	SIZE ASSETS $MIL.	FEES EXPENSE RATIO (%)	NAV. RET. (%) 1 YR.	NAV. RET. (%) 3 YRS.	SHARES RET. (%) 1 YR.	SHARES RET. (%) 3 YRS.	YIELD (%)	HISTORY RESULTS VS. ALL FUNDS	1998 HIGH	LOW	1/29/99
ADAMS EXPRESS	B+	Large-cap Blend	Low	1687.6	0.39	23.4	25.0	19.0	22.6	1.8	1 1 1	-13.0	-18.0	-18.4
AIM EASTERN EUROPE	C-	Europe	High	47.1	1.88	-45.5	-6.3	-51.5	-8.2	0.0	1 1 4	-6.1	-34.5	-20.7
ALLIANCE ALL-MARKET ADVANTAGE	B+	Large-cap Growth	Average	94.9	2.43	54.6	39.9	61.5	44.6	1.8	1 1 1	15.4	-7.0	0.6
ARGENTINA	C	Latin America	Average	125.5	NA	-19.5	4.4	-27.3	-4.9	5.0	1 1 4	-16.5	-30.0	-22.8
ASA LIMITED	D	Precious Metals	High	151.1	0.71	-21.6	-21.7	-21.0	-22.2	5.1	4 4 4	20.7	-1.8	3.0
ASIA PACIFIC	D	Pacific ex-Japan	High	153.9	1.57	-4.4	-14.5	-8.7	-19.2	0.6	2 4 4	7.6	-27.6	-18.1
ASIA TIGERS	C-	Pacific ex-Japan	High	163.3	1.60	-11.1	-13.5	-12.4	-16.0	0.2	2 4 4	3.5	-27.9	-20.0
AUSTRIA	C	Europe	Average	127.9	1.71	16.8	12.9	18.1	15.7	3.2	1 4 1	-8.6	-22.1	-14.0
AVALON CAPITAL	B	Large-cap Growth	Low	11.4	NA	16.8	21.4	20.6	NA	0.0	1 1 1	33.7	-41.6	1.2
BAKER FENTRESS	B	Large-cap Value	Very Low	771.3	0.74	11.9	14.2	3.6	14.4	2.8	1 1 1	-12.4	-21.4	-21.7
BERGSTROM CAPITAL	B	Large-cap Growth	Low	183.2	NA	38.4	24.5	28.6	24.6	0.2	1 1 1	-6.6	-15.2	-15.6
BLUE CHIP VALUE	B	Large-cap Value	Low	171.5	0.94	17.4	23.1	1.4	25.7	0.5	1 1 1	12.9	-5.5	-3.8
BRAZIL	C-	Latin America	Average	333.7	1.46	-28.0	3.6	-34.0	-7.4	5.7	1 1 4	-17.3	-34.4	-15.3
BRAZILIAN EQUITY	D	Latin America	High	33.0	NA	-50.1	-8.4	-53.4	-19.3	3.3	1 2 4	-12.8	-32.8	-4.6
CENTRAL EUROPEAN EQUITY	C	Europe	Average	183.1	1.10	-25.2	6.6	-26.4	7.1	1.1	1 1 4	-12.9	-29.7	-20.6
CENTRAL EUROPEAN VALUE	C	Europe	Average	75.7	2.00	-5.8	5.9	-5.7	-2.9	3.0	1 4 4	-14.4	-33.6	-21.9
CENTRAL FUND OF CANADA	C	Precious Metals	Average	72.2	NA	-10.0	-6.9	-11.1	-8.4	0.3	4 4 4	7.7	-9.7	-5.7
CENTRAL SECURITIES	B	Mid-cap Value	Low	467.5	0.53	15.2	22.3	-10.5	14.3	3.7	1 1 1	10.4	-19.9	-16.0
CHILE	C-	Latin America	High	180.4	3.34	-24.5	-7.9	-33.8	-16.9	2.8	4 1 4	-15.3	-29.9	-23.6
CHINA	D	Pacific ex-Japan	High	108.7	2.15	-27.8	-3.3	-32.0	-9.2	1.0	1 4 4	-1.7	-34.9	-22.7
CLEMENTE GLOBAL GROWTH	C	World	Average	78.8	NA	26.3	18.7	36.4	23.4	0.0	2 1 1	-7.8	-18.1	-9.2
COHEN & STEERS REALTY INCOME	B	Real Estate	Low	22.2	NA	-15.7	11.6	-16.5	10.5	6.7	1 1 4	19.9	-2.9	20.3
COHEN & STEERS TOTAL RETURN REALTY	B	Real Estate	Low	91.4	NA	-12.7	12.5	-10.6	14.1	8.0	1 1 4	11.7	-8.2	10.7
DELAWARE DIVIDEND & INCOME	B+	Dom. Hybrid	Very Low	233.5	0.82	-4.2	14.8	7.8	21.6	6.5	1 1 4	19.9	-5.7	13.5
DELAWARE GLOBAL DIVIDEND & INCOME	B	Dom. Hybrid	Very Low	104.9	NA	1.3	13.9	-7.5	15.2	7.7	1 1 3	10.1	-9.1	-1.2
DUFF & PHELPS UTILS. INCOME	B	Utilities	Low	2131.7	1.13	12.9	14.3	19.5	16.8	6.9	4 1 1	13.5	-0.8	8.8
EMERGING GERMANY	B	Europe	Average	212.5	NA	38.5	26.5	43.9	33.3	9.0	1 1 1	-5.4	-18.0	-5.9
EMERGING MARKETS INFRASTRUCTURE	C	Div. Emg. Mkts.	Average	154.4	2.02	-30.9	-4.5	-35.3	-9.6	0.0	1 3 4	-14.5	-30.5	-21.0
EMERGING MARKETS TELECOM.	C	Div. Emg. Mkts.	Average	94.3	1.90	-16.7	3.0	-18.5	0.1	0.0	2 1 4	-11.7	-28.1	-18.0
EMERGING MEXICO	D	Latin America	High	67.4	1.64	-52.0	-2.1	-45.3	-1.4	0.0	1 1 4	-6.9	-28.3	-11.6
EQUUS II	C	Dom. Hybrid	Average	113.4	3.98	-18.7	12.3	-26.7	12.8	0.0	1 1 4	-7.4	-33.3	-24.3
EUROPEAN WARRANT	B+	Europe	Average	223.2	1.65	29.8	49.6	42.5	55.2	0.0	1 1 1	-1.8	-24.8	-10.0
FIDELITY ADVISOR EMERGING ASIA	C-	Pacific ex-Japan	Average	72.5	1.71	-1.6	-7.7	2.8	-8.6	0.0	1 4 4	-3.7	-19.8	-12.3
FIDELITY ADVISOR KOREA	F	Pacific ex-Japan	Very High	42.7	1.88	145.2	-15.0	49.2	-16.8	0.0	4 4 1	47.8	-19.0	-16.3
FIRST AUSTRALIA	C	Pacific ex-Japan	Average	151.6	1.39	5.7	1.6	2.5	-0.6	3.2	2 4 3	-12.9	-28.9	-23.4
FIRST FINANCIAL	C	Financial	Average	177.5	1.04	-33.4	9.6	-42.1	9.2	0.4	1 1 4	19.5	-6.9	1.2
FIRST ISRAEL	C	Foreign	Average	70.1	2.26	-3.6	10.0	-5.2	6.8	1.7	2 1 4	-12.9	-27.7	-17.9
FIRST PHILIPPINE	D	Pacific ex-Japan	Very High	89.8	1.75	-1.5	-22.4	-13.8	-22.5	0.0	1 1 4	18.9	-20.6	-13.0
FOREIGN & COLONIAL EMG. MID. EAST	C	Foreign	Average	43.7	2.89	-16.8	11.3	-15.9	13.3	0.0	1 1 4	-8.3	-28.0	-17.8
FRANCE GROWTH	B	Europe	Low	251.9	1.48	35.4	25.2	40.3	24.2	5.0	1 1 1	-14.6	-22.9	-16.6
GABELLI EQUITY	B+	Mid-cap Blend	Low	1206.5	1.14	13.1	17.2	12.1	19.6	9.8	2 1 1	6.0	-9.1	1.0
GABELLI GLOBAL MULTIMEDIA	B+	Communication	Low	132.6	NA	33.2	25.3	35.3	26.9	0.0	2 1 1	-9.4	-19.0	-13.7
GENERAL AMERICAN INVESTORS	A	Large-cap Blend	Very Low	755.3	0.98	34.6	28.4	30.7	30.3	1.4	1 1 1	-6.3	-14.5	-11.2
GERMANY	B	Europe	Average	505.1	1.19	25.6	26.6	24.6	28.1	13.6	1 1 1	-4.2	-22.5	-8.3
GLOBAL SMALL CAP	C	World	Average	58.1	1.53	5.1	14.9	0.9	14.6	5.4	1 3 3	-9.8	-27.1	-18.8
GREATER CHINA	D	Pacific ex-Japan	High	67.3	1.88	-28.5	-0.5	-35.0	-10.6	0.8	1 4 4	1.5	-31.8	-25.7
H&Q HEALTHCARE INVESTORS	C	Health	Average	190.6	1.57	3.2	7.4	-5.6	-1.2	0.0	2 2 3	-13.8	-26.5	-24.9
H&Q LIFE SCIENCES INVESTORS	C	Health	Average	121.3	1.67	4.3	3.4	-9.0	-2.4	0.0	4 4 3	-11.3	-25.5	-24.2
HANCOCK BANK & THRIFT OPPORTUNITY	A	Financial	Low	1013.1	1.45	1.1	28.8	-17.3	30.2	1.2	1 1 1	13.6	-16.5	-10.5
HANCOCK PATRIOT GLOBAL DIVIDEND	A	Mid-cap Value	Very Low	128.5	1.27	9.2	12.1	12.2	9.7	7.6	2 1 1	-9.3	-17.3	-10.5

NA = Not available.

DATA: MORNINGSTAR, INC., CHICAGO, IL.

How to Use the Tables

Closed-end funds are publicly traded investment companies. Their results are measured two ways: one, by the change in net asset value (NAV), which is generated by the fund's manager; the other, by the change in the shares' market price. Total returns, which include dividends and capital gains, are shown for one- and three-year periods. The three-year figure is an average annual return. All returns are pretax.

BUSINESS WEEK RATING
Ratings are based on three-year risk-adjusted performance of the fund's portfolio. A rating is calcu-

lated by subtracting a fund's risk-of-loss factor from total return. Equity funds are rated against each other, and to earn an above-average rating, must beat the S&P 500 on a risk-adjusted basis. For ratings, municipal bond funds are separated from other bond funds.

A	SUPERIOR
B+	VERY GOOD
B	ABOVE AVERAGE
C	AVERAGE
C-	BELOW AVERAGE
D	POOR
F	VERY POOR

RISK
For each fund, the monthly Treasury bill return is subtracted from

the monthly NAV return in each month of the rating period. When a fund has underperformed Treasury bills, this monthly result is negative. The sum of these negative numbers is then divided by the number of months. The result is a negative number, and the greater its magnitude, the higher the risk of loss.

EXPENSE RATIO
Fund expenses for 1998 as a percent of average net assets. Ratio may include interest expense.

YIELD
Income earned during 1998, as a percentage of yearend NAV per share, adjusted for capital gains.

MATURITY
The average maturity of the securities in a bond fund, weighted according to their market value.

HISTORY
A fund's relative performance during 1996, 1997, and 1998. From left to right, the numbers designate which quartile the fund was in for each period: 1 for the top quartile; 2 for the second quartile; 3 for the third quartile; and 4 for the bottom quartile.

PREMIUM/DISCOUNT
The market price of closed-end funds is either less than the value of their securities, a discount, or more, a premium, to their NAVs.

FUND	RATING	CATEGORY	RISK	SIZE ASSETS $MIL.	FEES EXPENSE RATIO (%)	NAV. RET. (%) 1 YR.	3 YRS.	SHARES RET. (%) 1 YR.	3 YRS.	YIELD (%)	HISTORY RESULTS VS. ALL FUNDS	1998 HIGH	LOW	1/29/99
HANCOCK PATRIOT PREFERRED DIV.	A	Mid-cap Value	Very Low	104.1	1.27	8.6	11.2	−4.8	8.2	9.1	2 1 1	5.1	−0.5	−13.1
HANCOCK PATRIOT PREMIUM DIV. I	A	Mid-cap Value	Very Low	163.8	1.26	10.7	12.6	10.1	10.2	7.0	2 1 1	−2.8	−10.7	−6.5
INDIA	C−	Pacific ex-Japan	High	300.5	NA	9.1	−0.3	−14.4	−10.7	0.0	4 4 1	−5.3	−31.7	−27.4
INDIA GROWTH	C−	Pacific ex-Japan	Average	98.6	2.23	2.1	−3.2	−16.2	−15.4	0.0	4 4 3	0.8	−36.3	−21.3
INDONESIA	F	Pacific ex-Japan	Very High	12.5	1.89	−24.1	−33.8	−25.7	−30.2	0.0	1 4 4	260.7	36.3	46.3
INVESCO GLOBAL HEALTH SCIENCES	C	Health	Average	499.2	1.22	37.2	22.9	42.5	28.6	2.3	1 1 1	−5.7	−14.7	−7.8
IRISH INVESTMENT	B+	Europe	Low	126.7	1.54	22.5	23.7	19.8	26.1	0.0	1 1 1	−5.5	−28.8	−5.1
ITALY		Europe	Average	170.9	1.29	42.5	28.5	43.8	27.4	1.4	1 1 1	−13.8	−25.6	−17.4
JAKARTA GROWTH	F	Pacific ex-Japan	Very High	10.7	NA	−24.4	−37.0	−26.3	−33.3	0.0	2 4 4	106.0	10.0	14.8
JAPAN EQUITY	C−	Japan	Average	67.6	1.03	14.5	−15.0	8.7	−17.3	0.0	4 4 1	40.1	−0.1	20.4
JAPAN OVER-THE-COUNTER EQUITY	D	Japan	High	57.6	NA	19.7	−13.2	9.3	−15.3	0.1	4 4 1	42.4	−0.1	17.3
JARDINE FLEMING CHINA REGION	D	Pacific ex-Japan	High	68.3	NA	−36.5	−12.3	−43.6	−17.9	0.0	4 4 4	1.7	−31.0	−20.8
JARDINE FLEMING INDIA	C−	Pacific ex-Japan	High	74.5	NA	−13.6	−5.7	−28.3	−17.8	0.0	4 2 4	−5.5	−33.4	−28.7
KOREA	F	Pacific ex-Japan	Very High	392.5	1.63	116.7	−20.5	40.9	−23.1	0.0	4 4 1	57.0	−7.8	−2.3
KOREA EQUITY	F	Pacific ex-Japan	Very High	32.5	NA	88.3	−24.8	17.0	−25.3	0.0	4 4 1	54.8	−13.0	−3.4
KOREAN INVESTMENT	F	Pacific ex-Japan	Very High	30.6	2.11	85.3	−23.8	11.8	−25.9	0.0	4 4 1	48.5	−16.8	−10.7
LATIN AMERICA EQUITY	C−	Latin America	High	86.7	1.89	−40.9	−8.3	−46.9	−13.8	1.1	2 1 4	−15.2	−32.4	−25.7
LATIN AMERICA INVESTMENT	C−	Latin America	Average	91.1	NA	−33.4	−5.0	−38.7	−10.4	5.4	2 2 4	−15.0	−31.9	−26.5
LATIN AMERICA SMALLER COMPANIES	D	Latin America	High	49.1	2.30	−51.1	−17.2	−41.8	−14.8	0.9	2 4 4	−0.9	−34.7	−1.6
LATIN AMERICAN DISCOVERY	C	Latin America	High	111.1	1.82	−33.0	12.2	−42.6	5.8	0.7	1 1 4	53.6	−29.8	−21.5
LIBERTY ALL-STAR EQUITY	B	Large-cap Blend	Low	1350.7	1.01	19.7	22.6	8.7	19.3	0.4	1 1 1	2.0	−8.9	−9.8
LIBERTY ALL-STAR GROWTH	B	Large-cap Blend	Average	198.5	NA	15.0	20.1	7.7	19.1	0.0	1 1 1	−0.5	−14.5	−14.1
MALAYSIA	F	Pacific ex-Japan	Very High	26.3	1.35	−39.4	−42.0	−38.7	−34.4	0.9	1 4 4	108.4	29.8	51.1
MEXICO	C−	Latin America	High	790.6	0.91	−39.2	4.8	−43.6	−0.5	4.5	1 1 4	−17.0	−30.5	−26.2
MEXICO EQUITY AND INCOME	C	Latin America	Average	129.4	1.49	−40.0	7.3	−43.2	2.4	17.9	1 1 4	−14.5	−29.0	−19.5
MFS SPECIAL VALUE	B	Small-cap Blend	Low	101.5	NA	16.0	17.3	−9.3	15.0	10.2	1 1 1	40.5	11.6	0.8
MORGAN GRENFELL SMALLCAP	C	Small-cap Growth	Average	114.0	1.42	0.7	13.0	−12.4	9.5	0.0	1 1 4	0.4	−16.2	−17.2
MORGAN STANLEY AFRICA INVESTMENT	C	Foreign	Average	180.9	1.77	−11.7	−0.5	−20.6	−2.3	1.5	2 4 4	−13.9	−29.5	−29.4
MORGAN STANLEY ASIA-PACIFIC	C	Div. Pacific	Average	508.7	1.34	−0.3	−11.1	−5.8	−16.7	0.1	4 4 4	−5.0	−25.9	−13.4
MORGAN STANLEY EMG. MKTS.	C−	Div. Emg. Mkts.	Average	225.6	1.84	−19.7	−3.2	−24.9	−12.3	1.1	2 4 4	3.3	−26.3	−19.6
MORGAN STANLEY INDIA INVESTMENT	C−	Pacific ex-Japan	High	306.8	2.06	4.8	1.3	−19.4	−9.6	0.0	4 4 3	9.0	−32.2	−24.1
MORGAN STANLEY RUSSIA & NEW EUROPE		Europe		58.8	2.50	−50.6	NA	−57.4	NA	0.0	1 4	0.3	−28.1	−23.2
NAIC GROWTH	B+	Large-cap Blend	Low	19.5	NA	19.7	22.8	−24.9	19.2	1.2	1 1 1	46.9	−17.2	−17.1
NATIONS BALANCED TARGET MATURITY		Dom. Hybrid	Very Low	55.9	1.18	9.7	12.7	7.8	14.5	3.8	2 1 1	−0.1	−11.8	−11.3
NEW GERMANY	B	Europe	Low	233.0	0.99	28.1	21.2	21.4	22.3	6.5	1 2 1	−13.8	−25.9	−17.8
NEW SOUTH AFRICA	D	Foreign	High	41.9	2.35	−26.1	−16.1	−17.9	−11.7	0.0	4 4 4	−5.1	−31.7	−6.2
PAKISTAN INVESTMENT	D	Pacific ex-Japan	Very High	32.5	NA	−56.9	−26.6	−58.0	−26.9	8.7	4 1 4	−13.1	−37.0	−22.5
PETROLEUM AND RESOURCES	C	Nat. Resources	Average	474.8	0.47	−11.1	9.8	−9.8	9.7	2.7	1 1 4	5.5	−12.7	−9.5
PORTUGAL	B	Europe	Average	98.1	1.56	21.6	30.6	27.5	31.4	0.2	1 1 1	−5.6	−23.9	−10.8
ROC TAIWAN	C−	Pacific ex-Japan	Average	246.3	1.51	−17.9	6.0	−20.4	−4.7	4.7	1 1 4	−7.0	−28.5	−15.7
ROYCE GLOBAL	C	Small-cap Value	Average	47.4	0.94	1.0	8.6	4.3	11.6	9.6	3 1 4	−9.2	−21.9	−17.0
ROYCE MICRO-CAP	C	Small-cap Value	Low	135.5	0.83	−4.0	12.5	−9.3	11.7	0.8	1 1 4	−4.2	−16.0	−16.2
ROYCE VALUE	C	Small-cap Value	Low	516.9	0.67	0.9	14.1	−1.0	14.0	5.5	1 1 4	−3.4	−13.6	−12.3
SALOMON BROTHERS	A	Large-cap Blend	Low	1696.2	NA	19.1	24.4	20.9	29.2	0.8	1 1 1	1.0	−13.4	−6.0
SCUDDER NEW ASIA	C	Div. Pacific	Average	102.8	1.90	3.8	−6.0	−3.9	−11.3	0.0	4 4 3	3.0	−26.7	−15.2
SCUDDER NEW EUROPE	A	Europe	Low	374.0	NA	34.9	29.6	36.6	28.3	0.1	1 1 1	−13.7	−27.3	−8.0
SCUDDER SPAIN AND PORTUGAL	B+	Europe	Average	22.3	1.74	33.6	32.9	38.0	43.7	3.8	1 1 1	15.5	−15.4	−1.5
SINGAPORE	D	Pacific ex-Japan	High	72.6	1.87	8.8	−14.8	−6.4	−19.9	1.6	4 4 1	20.5	−16.9	−4.5
SOURCE CAPITAL	B	Mid-cap Value	Low	363.6	0.87	5.4	17.5	5.4	18.8	9.4	1 1 3	14.3	−2.3	6.4
SOUTHEASTERN THRIFT & BANK	B+	Financial	Low	100.2	1.06	−4.8	24.8	−18.0	23.8	1.3	1 1 1	12.6	−17.6	−13.8
SOUTHERN AFRICA	C−	Foreign	High	73.3	2.05	−24.3	−6.6	−23.6	−4.5	4.1	4 2 4	−14.5	−28.5	−22.1
SPAIN	A	Europe	Low	203.6	1.55	56.0	40.4	53.0	44.8	2.6	1 1 1	−10.4	−20.5	−10.0
SWISS HELVETIA	C	Europe	Average	469.9	1.17	23.0	20.8	24.0	19.6	0.4	4 1 1	−15.6	−25.2	−17.1
TAIWAN EQUITY	C−	Pacific ex-Japan	High	59.2	NA	−9.5	8.6	−14.4	−2.9	0.0	1 2 4	−13.9	−32.2	−20.5
TAIWAN	C−	Pacific ex-Japan	High	259.6	NA	−14.0	5.5	−18.4	−5.1	0.0	1 4 4	−6.3	−29.1	−21.4
TEMPLETON CHINA WORLD	D	Pacific ex-Japan	High	156.1	NA	−18.5	−6.7	−26.7	−12.6	3.5	1 4 4	−0.0	−29.4	−20.6
TEMPLETON DRAGON	C−	Pacific ex-Japan	High	528.5	1.53	−18.0	−4.5	−25.7	−11.2	7.7	1 4 4	1.7	−28.0	−19.8
TEMPLETON EMERGING MARKETS	C	Div. Emg. Mkts.	Average	159.9	1.67	−15.6	2.2	−19.2	−3.4	2.1	1 4 4	67.5	−12.6	17.4
TEMPLETON EMERGING MARKETS APPREC.	C	Int. Hybrid	Average	48.4	1.88	−12.0	5.6	−24.9	−3.4	4.5	1 4 4	4.6	−20.7	−12.0
TEMPLETON RUSSIA	F	Europe	Very High	41.4	1.99	−70.9	−5.0	−74.8	−5.9	0.0	1 1 4	78.3	−2.1	24.8
TEMPLETON VIETNAM & S.E. ASIA	C−	Pacific ex-Japan	High	42.5	NA	14.5	−10.5	−7.6	−14.0	0.0	2 4 1	1.3	−24.4	−19.5
THAI	F	Pacific ex-Japan	Very High	52.5	1.44	11.1	−45.3	14.9	−34.4	3.2	4 4 1	155.4	44.3	84.9
THERMO OPPORTUNITY		Technology		15.3	NA	−31.2	NA	−37.8	NA	0.0	4 4	−11.7	−30.5	−27.9
TRI-CONTINENTAL	B+	Large-cap Blend	Low	3915.2	0.60	25.9	24.3	26.3	25.1	1.6	1 1 1	−13.9	−20.7	−17.4
TURKISH INVESTMENT	C−	Foreign	High	41.2	1.91	−33.0	9.2	−39.0	−4.4	2.7	1 1 4	−8.9	−25.2	−16.0
TUXIS CORPORATION	B	Dom. Hybrid	Very Low	12.4	NA	7.3	5.3	19.6	NA	8.2	4 4 2	1.1	−11.3	−6.1
UNITED KINGDOM	B+	Europe	Very Low	71.4	NA	10.3	15.3	15.2	20.3	2.2	1 3 1	−6.2	−17.1	−5.5
Z-SEVEN	C	World	Average	19.9	NA	7.4	8.8	−24.4	1.1	0.7	2 2 2	31.1	−6.3	−1.1
ZWEIG	B	Dom. Hybrid	Low	723.5	1.16	5.9	13.9	−8.7	9.5	11.2	1 1 3	13.5	−9.1	−10.3
ZWEIG TOTAL RETURN	B+	Dom. Hybrid	Very Low	757.2	1.04	8.0	9.4	4.4	12.1	9.5	2 2 1	12.4	−1.3	2.6

NA=Not available.

DATA: MORNINGSTAR, INC., CHICAGO, IL.

FUND	RATING	CATEGORY	RISK	SIZE ASSETS $MIL.	FEES EXPENSE RATIO (%)	NAV RET. (%) 1 YR.	NAV RET. (%) 3 YRS.	SHARES RET. (%) 1 YR.	SHARES RET. (%) 3 YRS.	YIELD (%)	MAT. (YRS.)	TREND 3-YEAR ANALYSIS	1996 HIGH	LOW	1/31/97
ACM GOVERNMENT INCOME	F	Multisector	Very High	517.2	NA	−9.3	6.8	−10.1	10.6	8.9	20.5	1 1 4	18.0	−5.2	3.7
ACM GOVERNMENT OPPORTUNITY	D	Multisector	High	111.0	1.27	4.9	7.6	6.0	11.3	7.2	11.0	2 3 3	−3.4	−9.6	−5.7
ACM GOVERNMENT SECURITIES	F	Multisector	Very High	690.2	1.08	−8.3	7.5	−10.1	10.3	9.5	16.6	1 1 4	4.8	−7.8	−1.8
ACM GOVERNMENT SPECTRUM	C−	Multisector	High	263.8	NA	5.4	7.4	0.9	6.9	8.1	10.9	2 3 3	−6.5	−12.6	−12.0
ACM MANAGED DOLLAR INCOME	F	International	Very High	100.1	1.01	−29.4	5.7	−30.5	9.2	15.2	13.2	1 1 4	22.5	−5.4	7.8
ACM MANAGED INCOME	D	Multisector	Very High	198.3	1.05	−2.1	8.7	1.7	11.8	9.7	10.5	2 1 4	9.9	−6.0	8.0
ACM MUNICIPAL SECURITIES INCOME	B+	Muni. Ntl. Long	Low	144.9	0.94	4.9	8.2	2.0	10.7	5.7	24.0	2 2 3	10.1	−0.1	4.5
ALL AMERICAN TERM	C	Interm. (Gen.)	Average	190.3	1.10	−0.2	7.0	1.7	9.1	7.6	6.2	2 3 4	−1.9	−9.0	−5.6
ALLIANCE WORLD DOLLAR GOVT.	F	Emerg. Mkts.	Very High	88.9	1.43	−25.1	6.0	−19.8	10.8	12.3	15.1	1 1 4	23.8	−2.6	21.3
ALLIANCE WORLD DOLLAR GOVT. II	F	Emerg. Mkts.	Very High	694.4	1.26	−27.8	3.8	−30.0	5.3	13.7	20.9	1 1 4	17.8	−6.7	9.0
ALLMERICA SECURITIES	B	Interm. (Gen.)	Average	104.4	NA	9.1	8.6	11.0	9.9	7.5	12.2	3 2 1	−4.8	−12.5	−6.9
AMERICAN MUNICIPAL INCOME	D	Muni. Ntl. Long	High	71.7	0.78	8.6	8.4	13.6	12.3	5.3	17.7	3 2 1	−4.8	−12.6	−9.1
AMERICAN MUNICIPAL TERM	C	Muni. Ntl. Interm.	Low	97.0	NA	5.4	5.2	7.2	8.3	5.6	11.7	4 4 3	2.4	−2.9	−0.8
AMERICAN MUNICIPAL TERM II	C	Muni. Ntl. Interm.	Low	83.9	NA	5.5	5.8	7.7	9.3	5.4	13.5	3 4 3	0.7	−5.6	−0.8
AMERICAN MUNICIPAL TERM III	C−	Muni. Ntl. Long	Average	58.4	NA	6.5	7.0	8.9	9.7	5.0	13.5	3 3 2	−1.0	−7.3	−2.9
AMERICAN SELECT	A	Interm. (Gen.)	Low	154.5	NA	11.4	10.5	8.4	12.5	8.9	5.1	2 2 1	−5.2	−10.1	−8.8
AMERICAN STRATEGIC INCOME	A	Interm. (Gen.)	Low	61.3	NA	9.6	9.4	8.5	10.3	8.3	12.6	2 2 1	−6.7	−10.9	−8.7
AMERICAN STRATEGIC INCOME II	A	Interm. (Gen.)	Very Low	234.6	NA	10.1	9.3	8.8	12.2	8.6	13.7	2 3 1	−7.6	−11.6	−9.8
AMERICAN STRATEGIC INCOME III	B+	Interm. (Gen.)	Average	299.5	1.34	10.4	10.0	12.6	12.6	8.7	12.5	2 2 1	−3.9	−10.7	−6.2
APEX MUNICIPAL	A	Muni. Ntl. Long	Very Low	208.3	NA	6.1	8.5	6.3	13.5	6.1	21.5	2 2 3	1.8	−6.1	−4.4
BANCROFT CONVERTIBLE	B+	Convertibles	Very High	87.0	1.20	12.6	18.0	9.0	16.9	3.4	5.9	1 1 1	1.4	−16.1	−16.1
BEA INCOME	C−	High Yield	High	265.3	0.84	0.5	8.0	−5.7	9.6	9.5	9.0	2 2 1	4.1	−5.7	0.2
BEA STRATEGIC INCOME	D	Multisector	High	92.9	NA	−5.0	6.5	−5.4	8.2	11.0	9.7	2 2 4	−3.3	−12.5	−5.7
BLACKROCK 1999	B	Short (Gen.)	Very Low	217.6	NA	6.5	7.3	8.8	11.0	4.4	4.9	2 4 2	−3.0	−5.8	−2.7
BLACKROCK 2001	B	Short (Gen.)	Low	1371.5	0.63	7.1	7.3	10.0	11.1	4.4	10.9	3 3 2	−6.1	−9.1	−6.8
BLACKROCK ADVANTAGE	B	Interm. (Gen.)	High	106.2	NA	10.7	9.0	11.6	11.7	6.4	9.3	3 2 1	−8.7	−13.7	−11.2
BLACKROCK BROAD INVMT. GR. 2009	B+	Multisector	High	43.6	NA	7.8	9.7	12.0	13.3	6.9	16.0	3 1 1	−9.3	−16.1	−11.3
BLACKROCK CALIF. INS. MUNI. 2008	B	Muni. Calif. Long	Low	178.7	NA	7.8	7.8	9.8	10.9	4.9	10.4	3 3 1	−5.9	−10.0	−9.0
BLACKROCK CALIF. INVMT. QUAL. MUNI.	B+	Muni. Calif. Long	Average	8.1	NA	7.6	8.4	11.7	15.3	5.4	13.2	2 2 2	9.0	−0.6	3.5
BLACKROCK FLA. INS. MUNI. 2008	C	Muni. S.S. Long	Low	144.0	NA	6.4	6.7	10.3	9.8	5.1	10.7	3 3 2	2.3	−3.5	−2.4
BLACKROCK FLA. INVMT. QUAL. MUNI.	C−	Muni. S.S. Long	Average	9.2	NA	8.3	8.4	21.8	14.6	4.8	17.0	4 2 1	0.9	−11.5	−3.4
BLACKROCK INCOME	B+	Long (Gen.)	Average	502.3	1.02	6.7	9.6	6.5	11.7	8.1	23.4	2 1 2	−9.8	−16.0	−13.7
BLACKROCK INSURED MUNICIPAL 2008	C	Muni. Ntl. Long	Average	464.5	NA	6.9	7.6	11.3	11.9	4.9	10.2	3 3 2	−5.1	−10.1	−9.9
BLACKROCK INSURED MUNICIPAL	B	Muni. Ntl. Long	Low	161.4	NA	5.9	6.6	10.5	11.0	5.4	12.3	3 3 3	5.4	−5.4	−4.5
BLACKROCK INVESTMENT QUALITY MUNI.	C	Muni. Ntl. Long	Average	263.0	NA	7.2	8.8	23.1	17.1	5.1	15.8	2 2 2	2.6	−10.9	−2.1
BLACKROCK INVESTMENT QUALITY	C	Interm. (Gen.)	High	358.0	0.89	7.4	7.6	12.1	11.4	6.2	13.8	4 2 2	−7.6	−12.8	−7.5
BLACKROCK MUNICIPAL TARGET	C	Muni. Ntl. Long	Low	285.8	0.88	5.6	6.1	9.3	10.1	5.4	8.7	3 4 3	4.0	−6.6	−4.3
BLACKROCK N.J. INVMT. QUAL. MUNI.	C	Muni. S.S. Long	Average	7.5	NA	8.1	8.0	16.3	11.7	4.9	17.4	4 2 1	−1.1	−10.7	−3.1
BLACKROCK N.Y. INS. MUNI. 2008	C	Muni. N.Y. Long	Average	103.6	NA	6.7	7.0	10.8	10.4	5.1	10.7	4 3 2	0.5	−5.4	−5.9
BLACKROCK N.Y. INVESTMENT QUALITY	C	Muni. N.Y. Long	Average	10.6	NA	8.0	8.9	10.0	14.9	5.2	14.3	3 1 1	1.3	−5.7	0.4
BLACKROCK NO. AMER. GOVT. INCOME	B	International	High	437.5	0.93	7.7	10.4	4.0	10.8	8.3	16.3	2 3 1	−13.3	−20.3	−16.9
BLACKROCK STRATEGIC	B+	Interm. (Gen.)	Low	580.4	NA	11.3	8.8	14.0	12.8	5.2	12.5	3 3 1	−8.1	−12.3	−8.8
BLACKROCK TARGET	C	Interm. (Gen.)	Low	975.1	NA	8.4	6.7	10.8	10.1	5.5	13.8	3 4 1	−4.2	−7.2	−3.6
BULL & BEAR GLOBAL INCOME	F	International	Very High	29.8	NA	−3.9	2.3	−20.4	NA	14.2	NA	2 4 4	11.4	−17.7	−11.3
BULL & BEAR U.S. GOVERNMENT SECS.	F	Interm. Govt.	High	11.2	NA	6.3	4.1	16.1	NA	8.7	NA	4 4 2	−5.6	−13.7	−11.2
CASTLE CONVERTIBLE	C	Convertibles	High	54.4	1.00	1.0	9.9	−10.8	6.0	6.4	6.5	1 2 4	−3.2	−15.7	−15.1
CIGNA HIGH-INCOME SHARES	D	High Yield	Very High	337.1	1.06	−9.1	7.3	−3.7	9.2	12.2	7.8	1 1 4	20.3	−3.6	19.3
CIM HIGH-YIELD SECURITIES	C−	High Yield	High	46.4	NA	−5.1	8.1	−5.6	6.9	9.6	7.5	1 2 4	9.9	−9.3	−3.6
CIRCLE INCOME SHARES	C	Interm. (Gen.)	Average	33.6	0.89	7.5	7.4	3.9	7.9	7.0	10.3	3 3 2	1.7	−15.1	−7.7
CNA INCOME SHARES	B	Interm. (Gen.)	High	83.8	NA	−1.4	9.5	−7.2	9.4	9.4	13.4	1 1 4	16.5	0.6	5.9
COLONIAL HIGH-INCOME MUNICIPAL	B+	Muni. Ntl. Long	Very Low	263.6	0.96	6.0	6.5	2.5	11.1	6.3	22.4	3 3 3	4.0	−5.6	0.1
COLONIAL INTERMARKET INCOME I	B	Multisector	Average	121.2	0.96	5.6	8.4	8.7	10.2	8.8	9.2	2 3 3	−3.2	−14.0	−7.4
COLONIAL INTERM. HIGH-INCOME	B	High Yield	High	103.2	0.89	−0.2	10.0	−7.6	8.2	11.0	7.9	1 1 4	9.5	−7.0	−1.9
COLONIAL INVMT. GRADE MUNICIPAL	C	Muni. Ntl. Long	Average	132.2	NA	6.4	7.5	12.0	10.6	5.5	19.2	3 2 2	1.7	−8.8	−7.2
COLONIAL MUNICIPAL INCOME	A	Muni. Ntl. Long	Very Low	208.7	NA	7.8	7.1	13.6	13.5	6.1	21.3	3 4 1	9.1	−2.2	6.2
CORPORATE HIGH-YIELD	D	High Yield	High	286.0	NA	−3.5	6.8	−8.7	7.2	10.6	7.6	2 2 4	9.3	−8.0	2.3
CORPORATE HIGH-YIELD II	D	High Yield	High	103.7	NA	−4.7	6.4	−0.1	9.9	10.7	9.6	2 2 4	12.7	−3.0	2.5
CURRENT INCOME SHARES	C−	Long (Gen.)	High	49.5	NA	7.5	7.1	8.0	8.8	6.7	13.0	4 3 2	−5.4	−14.2	−10.9
DREYFUS CALIF. MUNICIPAL INCOME	A	Muni. Calif. Interm.	Very Low	44.0	0.98	4.9	6.6	7.0	16.6	5.4	23.5	2 4 3	8.8	0.9	6.8
DREYFUS MUNICIPAL INCOME	B	Muni. Ntl. Interm.	Very Low	195.7	NA	6.1	5.4	−3.9	7.7	6.1	21.9	3 4 3	11.1	−6.0	−6.5
DREYFUS N.Y. MUNICIPAL INCOME	B+	Muni. N.Y. Interm.	Very Low	37.9	1.03	5.3	5.5	2.2	7.1	5.5	21.9	4 4 3	11.8	1.3	−2.2
DREYFUS STRATEGIC GOVTS. INCOME	B	Multisector	Average	148.8	NA	5.5	8.3	4.0	10.2	8.2	9.0	2 2 3	−7.7	−13.0	−10.5
DREYFUS STRATEGIC MUNICIPAL BOND	B+	Muni. Ntl. Interm.	Very Low	453.3	NA	5.9	6.1	−2.3	9.1	6.3	20.5	3 4 3	13.5	−3.5	−2.1
DREYFUS STRATEGIC MUNICIPAL	B+	Muni. Ntl. Interm.	Very Low	590.8	NA	6.2	6.5	−2.9	8.3	6.2	23.3	3 4 3	9.4	−3.7	−6.9
DUFF AND PHELPS UTILITIES T-F INC.	D	Muni. Ntl. Long	Average	73.9	NA	5.1	6.0	5.9	8.3	5.8	19.5	4 3 3	5.2	−0.4	−1.9
DUFF AND PHELPS UTIL. & CORP. BOND	D	Long (Gen.)	Very High	526.3	0.92	10.7	8.5	15.4	12.3	7.7	20.8	4 2 1	7.0	−4.9	1.0
1838 BOND-DEBENTURE TRADING	B	Long (Gen.)	High	83.6	NA	10.4	8.7	12.1	8.3	7.6	22.3	4 2 1	−2.3	−10.2	−7.2
ELLSWORTH CONVERTIBLE GR. & INC.	A	Convertibles	High	83.3	1.20	13.2	19.0	9.2	18.5	3.2	5.6	1 1 1	−3.8	−14.5	−15.1
EMERGING MARKETS FLOATING RATE	F	Emerg. Mkts.	Very High	62.8	1.49	−20.8	6.4	−20.9	8.9	14.3	12.3	1 2 4	22.5	−2.9	6.2
EMERGING MARKETS INCOME	F	Emerg. Mkts.	Very High	38.3	NA	−26.9	9.8	−19.6	15.3	22.4	13.1	1 1 4	42.2	−1.6	7.7

NA=Not available.

DATA: MORNINGSTAR, INC., CHICAGO, IL.

MUTUAL FUND SCOREBOARD — Closed-End Bond Funds

FUND	RATING	CATEGORY	RISK	SIZE ASSETS $MIL.	FEES EXPENSE RATIO (%)	NAV. RET. (%) 1 YR.	3 YRS.	SHARES RET. (%) 1 YR.	3 YRS.	YIELD (%)	MAT. (YRS.)	TREND 3-YEAR ANALYSIS	1998 HIGH	LOW	1/29/99
EMERGING MARKETS INCOME II	F	Emerg. Mkts.	Very High	207.4	1.35	-27.1	7.9	-18.0	11.1	17.2	13.5	1 1 4	43.0	-2.1	10.6
EXCELSIOR INCOME SHARES	C	Interm. (Gen.)	Low	40.1	NA	7.9	7.0	5.1	8.4	6.2	10.4	4 3 1	-7.9	-13.7	-11.3
FIRST AUSTRALIA PRIME INCOME	F	International	Very High	1211.3	1.25	-0.1	1.8	-12.5	-5.8	12.8	6.1	1 4 4	-1.8	-27.5	-13.0
FIRST COMMONWEALTH	C-	International	High	124.2	NA	8.0	8.6	-3.5	6.6	8.9	8.5	1 4 1	-7.0	-21.6	-18.7
FORT DEARBORN INCOME SECURITIES	C-	Long (Gen.)	High	143.8	0.75	8.6	8.3	14.0	12.3	6.2	15.9	4 2 1	-0.5	-10.9	-4.5
FORTIS SECURITIES	B	Interm. (Gen.)	Average	116.2	0.76	4.1	8.4	4.6	11.5	8.1	17.8	2 2 3	2.3	-10.7	-5.3
FRANKLIN MULTI-INCOME	B	Multisector	Very High	57.9	NA	3.7	12.3	4.2	13.5	7.6	8.3	2 1 3	-5.3	-11.4	-10.9
FRANKLIN UNIVERSAL	C	Multisector	High	259.2	1.12	1.2	10.2	5.7	13.2	8.7	8.2	2 1 3	2.0	-12.9	-2.0
GABELLI CONVERTIBLE SECURITIES	B	Convertibles	Average	90.7	1.67	11.5	11.1	22.0	11.4	8.0	8.0	2 2 1	-1.9	-14.8	-3.1
GLOBAL HIGH INCOME DOLLAR	D	Emerg. Mkts.	Very High	295.0	1.42	-5.2	9.5	-11.5	7.7	11.0	17.4	1 2 4	-6.4	-19.9	-18.0
GLOBAL PARTNERS INCOME	D	International	Very High	143.4	1.31	-13.7	12.2	-18.1	11.2	16.4	10.5	1 1 4	10.0	-7.7	-2.3
GREENWICH STREET CALIF. MUNICIPAL	C-	Muni. Calif. Long	Average	51.9	NA	6.2	7.4	6.0	10.1	4.8	22.8	3 2 3	-3.6	-11.4	-10.5
GREENWICH STREET MUNICIPAL	F	Muni. Ntl. Long	High	233.2	NA	5.7	4.5	1.5	3.6	5.5	21.6	4 4 3	-0.9	-14.2	-9.6
HANCOCK INCOME SECURITIES	C	Interm. (Gen.)	Average	176.8	0.84	7.9	7.7	1.7	8.2	7.2	14.2	3 3 1	1.6	-9.9	-4.6
HANCOCK INVESTORS	C	Interm. (Gen.)	Average	169.5	NA	7.7	7.6	6.7	10.4	6.9	12.4	3 3 1	3.5	-6.2	-3.0
HATTERAS INCOME SECURITIES	C-	Interm. (Gen.)	Average	54.7	NA	8.0	6.8	10.5	5.9	7.3	14.4	4 3 1	-5.0	-14.1	-9.3
HERITAGE U.S. GOVERNMENT INCOME	C-	Interm. Govt.	High	38.1	1.00	9.0	7.2	-0.2	6.7	7.8	16.7	4 3 1	-3.5	-16.6	-15.5
HIGH INCOME OPPORTUNITY	C	High Yield	High	768.9	1.21	1.0	8.8	-8.3	9.7	10.4	9.0	2 2 4	3.6	-8.4	-8.6
HIGH-YIELD INCOME	C	High Yield	High	79.1	1.20	0.8	9.5	-3.1	6.4	10.4	7.6	2 1 4	8.3	-14.8	2.5
HIGH-YIELD PLUS	F	High Yield	Very High	85.3	1.08	-6.7	5.8	-10.4	6.1	11.4	8.0	2 2 4	17.4	-2.7	-1.8
HYPERION 1999	D	Interm. Govt.	Average	454.5	NA	6.4	5.5	10.0	10.0	5.9	11.2	4 3 2	-2.2	-6.2	-1.6
HYPERION 2002	C	Long Govt.	High	281.2	NA	7.8	8.5	12.3	11.9	6.1	11.7	4 2 1	-8.3	-12.9	-9.0
HYPERION 2005 INVMT. GR. OPPORT.	B	Interm. (Gen.)	High	88.4	NA	6.3	9.5	9.0	12.3	6.4	12.6	3 1 2	-9.5	-14.1	-11.1
HYPERION TOTAL RETURN	C-	Multisector	High	240.5	NA	2.0	7.2	-1.3	7.8	8.7	13.2	2 2 3	-9.5	-15.6	-14.4
INA INVESTMENT SECURITIES	C-	Interm. (Gen.)	Average	92.0	NA	7.7	6.5	6.8	6.9	7.1	12.8	4 3 1	-6.2	-15.6	-10.9
INCOME OPPORTUNITIES 1999	B	Short Govt.	Low	424.1	NA	5.3	7.3	7.6	11.7	5.4	9.2	2 4 3	-1.7	-4.4	-1.5
INCOME OPPORTUNITIES 2000	C	Short Govt.	Average	111.3	NA	6.5	7.4	6.6	10.2	5.8	13.1	2 4 2	-2.9	-6.0	-2.6
INDEPENDENCE SQUARE INCOME SECS.	C-	Interm. (Gen.)	High	33.6	NA	7.0	7.1	10.0	9.0	6.9	19.8	4 3 2	4.6	-8.9	-7.2
INSURED MUNICIPAL INCOME	D	Muni. Ntl. Long	High	323.3	NA	7.3	7.7	13.9	12.3	5.3	22.0	4 2 2	0.0	-13.6	-10.1
INVESTMENT GRADE MUNICIPAL	B+	Muni. Ntl. Long	Low	175.9	NA	6.2	7.5	9.4	11.7	5.7	22.5	2 3 3	-3.9	-12.0	-7.0
KEMPER HIGH-INCOME	B	High Yield	High	209.6	1.01	1.1	9.6	6.7	13.0	8.2	7.7	1 2 3	16.8	3.0	12.5
KEMPER INTERM. GOVERNMENT	C-	Short Govt.	Average	266.8	0.95	8.1	6.5	8.2	10.3	7.8	18.1	4 4 1	-0.2	-7.7	-4.3
KEMPER MULTI-MARKET INCOME	C-	Multisector	High	207.6	1.01	3.1	6.9	-2.4	3.0	8.8	12.7	3 4 3	-5.5	-17.7	-9.5
KEMPER MUNICIPAL INCOME	B	Muni. Ntl. Interm.	Low	476.3	1.01	5.6	6.6	6.5	10.7	6.1	21.9	3 4 3	20.0	5.4	-0.4
KEMPER STRATEGIC INCOME	F	Multisector	Very High	45.4	1.24	-6.8	9.3	-12.5	12.4	10.7	15.1	1 2 4	37.3	4.8	18.2
KEMPER STRATEGIC MUNICIPAL INC.	A	Muni. Ntl. Interm.	Very Low	130.5	0.76	4.7	6.7	1.7	7.4	6.0	19.1	2 3 3	9.2	-1.8	0.9
KLEINWORT BENSON AUSTRALIAN INC.	F	International	Very High	95.8	1.14	2.9	3.5	-5.6	-0.7	7.7	5.7	1 4 3	-9.1	-22.0	-18.0
LIBERTY TERM 1999	B	Interm. Govt.	Low	39.1	NA	7.0	7.1	9.7	11.3	4.1	2.7	3 3 2	-2.8	-6.0	-2.7
LINCOLN NATL. CONVERTIBLE SECS.	D	Convertibles	Very High	117.1	1.05	-4.6	9.5	-16.6	7.8	6.9	6.4	1 2 4	0.5	-13.0	-14.1
LINCOLN NATIONAL INCOME	B	Interm. (Gen.)	Average	96.1	NA	7.8	8.5	17.4	12.2	7.3	11.7	2 3 1	6.8	-4.9	3.8
MANAGED HIGH-INCOME	C	High Yield	High	454.3	1.20	0.7	8.8	-8.7	9.1	10.2	9.4	2 2 4	5.1	-8.9	-6.3
MANAGED HIGH-YIELD	D	High Yield	High	73.2	NA	-6.4	7.8	-10.1	8.9	10.8	8.5	1 2 4	5.4	-8.7	-3.4
MANAGED MUNICIPALS	D	Muni. Ntl. Long	Average	426.8	1.00	5.4	6.4	-2.2	4.5	4.9	21.1	4 3 3	-2.0	-12.7	-9.8
MANAGED MUNICIPALS II	D	Muni. Ntl. Long	Average	137.9	1.10	5.3	5.8	2.0	3.7	4.9	21.0	4 4 3	-2.0	-13.4	-9.9
MASS. HEALTH AND ED. TAX-EXEMPT	B	Muni. S.S. Long	Average	32.8	NA	6.5	7.9	12.4	16.5	5.0	20.1	3 2 2	8.3	-0.6	2.7
MENTOR INCOME	C-	Interm. (Gen.)	High	117.4	NA	7.1	7.3	-0.5	9.0	8.6	21.0	2 3 2	-1.5	-16.5	-14.0
MFS CHARTER INCOME	C	Multisector	Average	722.9	0.86	4.6	7.8	8.4	11.9	8.4	11.3	2 3 3	-1.8	-10.2	-4.1
MFS GOVERNMENT MARKETS INCOME	C-	Multisector	Average	517.1	NA	7.7	6.5	5.0	8.5	7.1	11.9	3 4 1	-6.8	-13.5	-14.0
MFS INTERMEDIATE INCOME	C	Multisector	Low	1091.4	0.90	6.7	6.7	4.5	8.8	7.5	13.0	2 4 2	-4.1	-12.9	-11.6
MFS MULTIMARKET INCOME	D	Multisector	High	731.2	0.77	0.7	6.7	-1.1	8.2	9.1	10.9	2 3 4	-5.5	-12.2	-11.8
MFS MUNICIPAL INCOME	B+	Muni. Ntl. Long	Very Low	333.1	1.18	5.5	5.7	-1.4	2.8	6.8	19.8	4 4 3	11.3	1.7	1.4
MINNESOTA MUNICIPAL INCOME	C-	Muni. S.S. Long	High	61.9	NA	8.3	8.1	13.7	12.3	5.2	17.0	2 4 1	-0.1	-9.2	-5.4
MINNESOTA MUNICIPAL TERM	B+	Muni. S.S. Long	Very Low	65.5	NA	5.1	5.7	9.6	8.9	5.3	13.9	3 4 3	3.5	-6.4	-1.1
MINNESOTA MUNICIPAL TERM II	B	Muni. S.S. Long	Low	37.9	NA	6.0	6.3	12.6	9.3	5.2	13.4	3 4 3	5.0	-7.1	0.7
MONTGOMERY STREET INCOME SECS.	C	Interm. (Gen.)	Average	210.2	NA	5.4	7.9	8.8	11.3	6.9	15.3	2 2 3	-0.2	-7.7	-2.8
MSDW MUNICIPAL INCOME II	B+	Muni. Ntl. Long	Low	270.3	NA	6.9	6.9	6.1	5.2	5.4	21.3	3 3 2	-5.6	-12.9	-9.2
MSDW CALIFORNIA INSURED MUNICIPAL	C	Muni. Calif. Long	Average	191.4	NA	8.0	8.3	15.7	15.2	5.1	20.5	3 2 1	0.6	-8.3	-5.1
MSDW CALIFORNIA QUALITY MUNICIPAL	C-	Muni. Calif. Long	High	161.5	NA	8.5	8.9	16.8	15.9	5.1	19.7	3 2 1	-1.2	-9.8	-5.4
MSDW GOVERNMENT INCOME	B+	Interm. Govt.	Low	406.0	0.73	8.9	8.3	10.1	9.3	6.8	17.3	2 3 1	-6.1	-9.4	-8.1
MSDW HIGH INCOME ADVANTAGE II	F	High Yield	High	162.0	NA	-8.8	3.2	-11.2	4.9	13.6	6.1	2 3 4	20.3	3.3	7.1
MSDW HIGH INCOME ADVANTAGE III	F	High Yield	High	64.0	0.98	-10.2	2.4	-10.6	5.5	11.2	5.9	2 3 4	29.1	4.4	18.3
MSDW HIGH INCOME ADVANTAGE	F	High Yield	High	122.1	0.92	-9.3	2.6	-4.0	7.9	11.8	7.1	2 4 4	32.8	5.7	18.3
MSDW INCOME SECURITIES	B	Long (Gen.)	High	218.7	NA	7.8	9.2	15.0	12.5	7.2	20.7	2 2 1	-0.1	-11.5	-1.5
MSDW INSURED CALIF. MUNICIPAL	B	Muni. Calif. Long	Low	253.2	NA	6.4	6.9	9.4	12.9	5.0	22.3	3 3 2	-1.7	-7.5	-4.9
MSDW INSURED MUNICIPAL BOND	B	Muni. Ntl. Long	Low	79.9	NA	5.4	6.2	4.5	12.6	6.1	21.4	3 4 3	5.9	2.1	2.0
MSDW INSURED MUNICIPAL INCOME	C	Muni. Ntl. Long	Average	437.7	NA	8.2	9.0	17.5	15.8	5.3	20.9	3 2 1	-1.4	-11.9	-3.5
MSDW INSUREED MUNICIPAL SECURITIES	C	Muni. Ntl. Long	Low	140.1	NA	6.8	7.3	9.9	11.9	5.3	22.1	3 3 2	-2.3	-9.0	-5.6
MSDW INSURED MUNICIPAL	C	Muni. Ntl. Long	Low	357.6	NA	6.2	6.2	9.3	9.5	5.9	19.9	3 4 3	1.7	-4.0	-3.9
MSDW MUNICIPAL INCOME	B	Muni. Ntl. Long	Low	300.1	0.63	6.4	6.8	0.1	6.3	5.7	20.9	3 3 2	-4.1	-13.2	-12.0
MSDW MUNICIPAL INCOME III	C	Muni. Ntl. Long	Low	63.1	NA	6.0	5.9	2.6	3.9	5.5	21.6	4 4 3	-4.2	-13.6	-12.1

NA=Not available.

DATA: MORNINGSTAR, INC., CHICAGO, IL.

MUTUAL FUND SCOREBOARD — Closed-End Bond Funds

FUND	RATING	CATEGORY	RISK	SIZE ASSETS $MIL.	FEES EXPENSE RATIO (%)	NAV RET. (%) 1 YR.	NAV RET. (%) 3 YRS.	SHARES RET. (%) 1 YR.	SHARES RET. (%) 3 YRS.	YIELD (%)	MAT. (YRS.)	TREND 3-YEAR ANALYSIS	1998 HIGH	LOW	1/29/99
MSDW MUNI. INCOME OPPORTUNITY	A	Muni. Ntl. Long	Very Low	186.4	1.04	7.3	8.2	18.5	12.2	5.9	19.0	2 3 2	11.4	−2.7	7.2
MSDW MUNI. INCOME OPPORTUNITY II	A	Muni. Ntl. Long	Very Low	181.5	NA	6.6	7.7	7.0	8.2	6.0	20.8	2 3 2	−0.1	−5.9	−4.0
MSDW MUNI. INCOME OPPORTUNITY III	A	Muni. Ntl. Long	Very Low	106.0	NA	6.6	7.5	−0.9	10.1	6.4	19.2	2 3 2	6.0	−7.1	−6.3
MSDW MUNICIPAL PREMIUM INCOME	B	Muni. Ntl. Long	Low	145.1	1.14	6.9	7.1	2.5	9.0	6.0	21.7	3 3 2	−2.4	−12.3	−11.2
MSDW NEW YORK QUALITY MUNICIPAL	C	Muni. N.Y. Long	High	74.8	NA	8.3	9.2	14.2	13.8	5.1	18.7	3 1 1	−4.2	−13.8	−9.0
MSDW QUALITY MUNICIPAL INCOME	B+	Muni. Ntl. Long	Low	538.0	0.70	7.1	7.7	9.0	11.9	5.8	19.6	3 3 2	−0.5	−8.4	−3.3
MSDW QUALITY MUNICIPAL INVESTMENT	B	Muni. Ntl. Long	Low	279.5	NA	6.1	6.9	6.2	9.8	6.0	22.6	3 3 3	1.4	−4.5	−1.7
MSDW QUALITY MUNICIPAL SECURITIES	C	Muni. Ntl. Long	Average	272.9	NA	8.4	9.4	16.6	15.2	5.3	19.4	3 1 1	−3.8	−12.7	−7.2
MORGAN STANLEY EMG. MKTS. DEBT	F	Emerg. Mkts.	Very High	164.3	1.51	−32.9	7.2	−31.9	7.9	13.9	13.5	1 1 4	26.5	−4.7	7.5
MORGAN STANLEY GLOBAL OPP. BOND	F	Emerg. Mkts.	Very High	42.1	NA	−21.4	6.9	−29.0	3.1	14.1	10.1	1 1 4	12.1	−12.7	−7.9
MORGAN STANLEY HIGH-YIELD	A	High Yield	High	152.8	1.06	4.0	13.1	11.0	20.1	8.8	9.4	1 1 3	9.8	−11.5	12.0
MUNIASSETS	A	Muni. Ntl. Long	Very Low	152.6	NA	4.9	7.7	8.4	12.0	5.8	19.3	2 2 3	0.4	−9.2	−1.5
MUNICIPAL ADVANTAGE	C−	Muni. Ntl. Long	Average	106.8	NA	7.6	8.4	10.2	13.4	5.6	21.4	3 2 2	−5.4	−12.0	−8.5
MUNICIPAL HIGH-INCOME	A	Muni. Ntl. Long	Very Low	197.2	0.74	5.0	7.1	4.4	12.2	6.3	21.9	2 3 3	6.9	−4.9	−1.2
MUNICIPAL PARTNERS	B	Muni. Ntl. Long	Average	84.2	NA	6.5	8.2	11.4	13.6	5.6	22.8	3 2 2	−4.6	−13.0	−9.5
MUNICIPAL PARTNERS II	C	Muni. Ntl. Long	Average	85.0	NA	6.6	8.2	10.5	12.6	5.6	18.0	3 2 2	−6.8	−13.3	−11.0
MUNIENHANCED	D	Muni. Ntl. Long	Average	348.9	NA	6.3	6.6	9.7	12.0	5.4	23.0	4 3 2	1.5	−9.0	−0.5
MUNIINSURED	C	Muni. Ntl. Long	Low	40.8	NA	6.6	7.0	14.5	12.6	4.9	21.4	3 3 2	−1.5	−10.4	−4.4
MUNIVEST	C	Muni. Ntl. Long	Average	619.6	0.93	6.3	7.4	9.8	12.6	5.8	19.2	3 3 2	2.2	−55.9	−0.5
MUNIVEST II	C	Muni. Ntl. Long	Average	294.3	NA	6.0	7.4	8.8	12.7	5.7	21.2	3 3 3	−0.7	−8.1	−3.1
MUNIVEST FLORIDA	C−	Muni. S.S. Long	Average	84.6	NA	6.3	7.4	9.0	11.2	5.4	22.1	3 3 3	1.8	−4.6	−3.5
MUNIVEST MICHIGAN INSURED	C−	Muni. S.S. Long	Average	106.4	NA	7.4	6.6	11.6	12.2	5.3	17.6	4 3 2	1.1	−10.3	−4.8
MUNIVEST NEW JERSEY	C−	Muni. S.S. Long	Average	81.0	NA	7.5	7.0	14.8	13.9	5.2	20.3	4 3 2	2.6	−6.2	−3.1
MUNIVEST PENNSYLVANIA INSURED	D	Muni. S.S. Long	High	55.0	NA	6.5	6.6	14.9	12.6	5.2	22.4	4 2 2	3.6	−8.6	−1.7
MUNIYIELD	B	Muni. Ntl. Long	Average	591.3	0.91	6.4	8.2	12.4	14.1	5.7	21.8	2 2 2	7.7	−3.9	3.6
MUNIYIELD ARIZONA	D	Muni. S.S. Long	Average	62.4	NA	6.6	6.7	18.8	12.4	5.0	17.2	4 2 2	3.6	−7.6	−1.5
MUNIYIELD CALIFORNIA	B	Muni. Calif. Interm.	Average	327.4	0.67	6.0	7.5	12.5	16.4	5.3	19.8	2 3 3	7.7	−2.4	3.8
MUNIYIELD CALIFORNIA INSURED	C−	Muni. Calif. Long	High	248.1	NA	6.4	7.2	17.5	16.1	4.9	21.6	4 2 2	10.7	−6.4	4.0
MUNIYIELD CALIFORNIA INSURED II	D	Muni. Calif. Long	High	282.4	NA	6.7	7.1	18.2	16.0	5.1	21.7	4 2 2	9.6	−5.5	5.6
MUNIYIELD FLORIDA	D	Muni. S.S. Long	Average	120.9	NA	5.7	6.7	13.1	14.6	5.1	18.8	3 3 3	9.0	−3.3	3.7
MUNIYIELD FLORIDA INSURED	D	Muni. S.S. Long	Average	128.5	NA	6.2	6.9	14.8	14.8	5.0	21.1	3 3 3	7.8	−5.1	2.3
MUNIYIELD INSURED	C−	Muni. Ntl. Long	Average	972.2	NA	6.9	7.5	13.6	14.3	5.4	22.4	4 3 2	5.6	−8.9	0.3
MUNIYIELD MICHIGAN	C	Muni. S.S. Long	Average	120.0	NA	6.0	6.4	17.0	14.3	5.3	15.3	3 3 3	9.3	−4.8	4.4
MUNIYIELD MICHIGAN INSURED	C−	Muni. S.S. Long	Average	106.4	NA	6.8	6.4	16.2	12.5	5.2	17.2	4 3 2	4.8	−8.9	−0.6
MUNIYIELD NEW JERSEY	C	Muni. S.S. Long	Average	140.7	NA	6.6	6.3	12.3	13.7	5.3	21.4	4 4 2	8.6	−4.1	3.7
MUNIYIELD NEW JERSEY INSURED	C−	Muni. S.S. Long	Average	133.9	NA	7.1	6.6	13.0	14.7	5.1	17.7	4 3 2	9.0	−2.1	4.8
MUNIYIELD NEW YORK INSURED	D	Muni. N.Y. Long	Average	194.1	NA	7.4	6.5	13.3	12.7	5.2	20.2	4 3 2	7.1	−3.5	3.4
MUNIYIELD NEW YORK INSURED II	C−	Muni. N.Y. Long	Average	416.6	NA	7.6	7.3	10.5	12.3	5.4	18.2	4 2 2	0.5	−8.2	−2.1
MUNIYIELD PENNSYLVANIA	C	Muni. S.S. Long	Average	90.5	NA	6.4	7.1	21.6	16.0	5.2	23.1	4 2 2	8.6	−4.1	3.3
MUNIYIELD QUALITY	C	Muni. Ntl. Long	Average	472.3	NA	6.8	7.5	11.0	13.8	5.7	19.5	4 2 2	1.4	−7.5	−3.0
MUNIYIELD QUALITY II	C	Muni. Ntl. Long	Average	522.3	NA	5.1	7.6	15.0	15.1	5.6	23.8	2 2 3	5.5	−6.4	1.7
NATIONS GOVERNMENT INCOME 2003	A	Long Govt.	Average	147.3	NA	9.2	11.9	13.5	13.1	6.2	10.0	2 2 1	0.0	−10.9	−8.1
NATIONS GOVERNMENT INCOME 2004	A	Interm. Govt.	Average	124.8	NA	9.9	11.9	14.4	13.6	6.4	10.1	2 2 1	−0.1	−12.0	−6.6
NEW AMERICA HIGH-INCOME	D	High Yield	Very High	283.6	NA	−6.8	8.0	−11.1	9.9	11.0	8.2	1 1 4	13.9	−1.6	9.0
NEW YORK TAX-EXEMPT INCOME	B+	Muni. N.Y. Interm.	Very Low	2.4	NA	5.5	5.8	−12.2	2.3	5.2	22.6	3 4 3	17.4	−8.9	−5.7
NUVEEN ARIZ. PREM. INC. MUNI.	C−	Muni. S.S. Long	Average	67.6	NA	6.2	6.6	13.6	13.9	4.9	17.9	4 3 3	9.8	−2.8	3.7
NUVEEN CALIF. INVMT. QUALITY	B+	Muni. Calif. Interm.	Low	213.3	NA	6.3	6.5	9.9	10.0	5.5	20.8	3 4 2	12.3	4.5	3.0
NUVEEN CALIF. MUNI. MKT. OPPORT.	B	Muni. Calif. Interm.	Low	130.1	NA	5.9	6.3	10.8	11.6	5.6	20.7	4 3 3	11.6	3.3	6.5
NUVEEN CALIF. MUNI. VALUE	A	Muni. Calif. Interm.	Very Low	260.6	0.74	7.8	7.0	11.1	5.6	5.0	21.2	3 4 1	5.4	−6.2	−7.4
NUVEEN CALIF. PERF. PLUS MUNI.	B+	Muni. Calif. Interm.	Low	201.9	NA	6.1	6.4	11.8	13.1	5.6	19.9	3 4 3	17.3	9.4	7.6
NUVEEN CALIF. PREM. INC. MUNI.	C	Muni. Calif. Long	Average	82.3	NA	7.8	7.9	12.1	14.9	5.1	17.8	3 2 1	4.4	−3.7	−2.9
NUVEEN CALIF. QUAL. INC. MUNI.	B+	Muni. Calif. Interm.	Low	353.1	0.79	6.8	7.5	12.2	12.7	5.5	21.0	2 3 2	10.1	2.8	1.2
NUVEEN CALIF. SELECT QUAL. MUNI.	B+	Muni. Calif. Interm.	Low	359.9	NA	6.2	6.7	11.7	11.6	5.5	21.5	3 3 3	9.1	3.2	1.8
NUVEEN CONN. PREM. INC. MUNI.	D	Muni. S.S. Long	Average	76.7	NA	7.1	7.7	13.4	13.8	4.9	19.7	4 2 2	14.1	3.4	5.2
NUVEEN FLA. INVMT. QUAL. MUNI.	C	Muni. S.S. Interm.	Low	255.7	NA	5.2	5.7	5.1	9.9	5.5	18.3	3 4 3	17.1	8.0	6.9
NUVEEN FLA. QUALITY INCOME MUNI.	C	Muni. S.S. Long	Low	226.5	NA	5.6	6.4	8.4	10.9	5.3	20.7	3 4 3	8.2	0.7	−2.4
NUVEEN GA. PREMIUM INCOME MUNI.	C−	Muni. S.S. Long	Average	55.2	NA	7.0	7.5	14.1	14.8	4.9	21.2	4 2 2	13.1	−1.7	6.8
NUVEEN INS. CALIF. PREM. INC. MUNI.	D	Muni. Calif. Long	High	104.7	NA	6.9	7.0	11.7	13.1	5.0	19.1	4 2 2	2.2	−6.9	−5.9
NUVEEN INS. CALIF. PREM. INC. MUNI. 2	C	Muni. Calif. Long	Average	188.2	NA	7.9	7.9	15.4	12.9	5.0	18.7	3 2 1	2.9	−6.5	−3.8
NUVEEN INS. CALIF. SEL. TAX-FREE INC.	B+	Muni. Calif. Interm.	Low	95.8	0.39	5.8	6.5	13.7	11.9	5.0	18.2	3 4 3	4.4	−4.5	−1.3
NUVEEN INS. FLA. PREM. INC. MUNI.	D	Muni. S.S. Long	High	225.8	NA	7.4	7.2	11.9	12.7	4.8	17.9	4 2 2	−0.0	−8.6	−8.3
NUVEEN INS. MUNICIPAL OPPORTUNITY	C	Muni. Ntl. Long	Low	1283	NA	6.0	6.4	7.1	10.2	5.8	22.4	3 4 3	6.3	−1.2	2.3
NUVEEN INS. N.Y. PREM. INC. MUNI.	D	Muni. N.Y. Long	High	128.0	NA	6.9	7.2	11.9	13.9	5.1	21.2	4 3 2	6.0	−3.7	0.7
NUVEEN INS. N.Y. SEL. TAX-FREE INC.	B	Muni. N.Y. Interm.	Low	58.7	0.42	5.9	6.3	9.3	11.0	5.1	16.9	3 4 3	5.3	−2.4	−2.6
NUVEEN INS. PREM. INC. MUNI. 2	D	Muni. Ntl. Long	Average	523.3	NA	7.2	7.2	11.7	11.7	5.3	17.8	4 2 2	−1.2	−8.0	−4.9
NUVEEN INSURED QUALITY MUNI.	C	Muni. Ntl. Long	Low	595.5	NA	6.3	6.4	5.2	9.6	5.7	23.3	3 4 2	3.4	−3.4	−2.9
NUVEEN INVMT. QUALITY MUNI.	B	Muni. Ntl. Interm.	Low	567.6	NA	6.1	6.6	5.9	8.8	6.1	20.3	4 3 3	3.8	−3.5	−1.6
NUVEEN MD. PREMIUM INCOME MUNI.	C−	Muni. S.S. Long	Average	154.1	NA	6.8	7.2	15.4	15.2	4.8	18.8	4 3 2	10.7	0.8	4.0
NUVEEN MASS. PREMIUM INCOME MUNI.	B	Muni. S.S. Long	Average	69.9	NA	6.4	7.4	8.2	12.5	5.1	19.7	3 2 2	14.3	7.2	5.3
NUVEEN MICH. PREMIUM INCOME MUNI.	C	Muni. S.S. Long	Average	119.1	NA	7.0	7.5	11.8	14.4	5.2	17.0	4 2 2	2.5	−5.9	−5.3

NA=Not available.

DATA: MORNINGSTAR, INC., CHICAGO, IL.

FUND	RATING	CATEGORY	RISK	SIZE ASSETS $MIL.	FEES EXPENSE RATIO (%)	NAV. RET. (%) 1 YR.	3 YRS.	SHARES RET. (%) 1 YR.	3 YRS.	YIELD (%)	MAT. (YRS.)	TREND 3-YEAR ANALYSIS	1998 HIGH	DIFFERENCE FROM NAV LOW	1/29/99
NUVEEN MICHIGAN QUALITY INC. MUNI.	C	Muni. S.S. Long	Low	182.4	NA	5.8	6.3	7.2	10.7	5.4	21.4	4 3 3	10.7	-0.0	2.4
NUVEEN MISSOURI PREMIUM INC. MUNI.	C-	Muni. S.S. Long	Average	31.5	NA	6.6	7.0	14.6	14.1	4.9	16.7	4 3 2	6.6	-2.9	-1.8
NUVEEN MUNICIPAL ADVANTAGE	B	Muni. Ntl. Interm.	Low	673.5	NA	6.0	6.5	9.3	7.9	6.1	20.7	3 4 3	4.4	-0.8	0.9
NUVEEN MUNICIPAL INCOME	A	Muni. Ntl. Interm.	Very Low	95.8	0.83	6.0	6.5	8.7	7.8	5.7	21.2	3 4 3	6.2	-1.8	0.2
NUVEEN MUNICIPAL MARKET OPPORT.	B+	Muni. Ntl. Interm.	Very Low	717.7	NA	6.1	6.5	8.1	8.2	6.1	20.8	3 4 3	5.0	-1.7	1.4
NUVEEN MUNICIPAL VALUE	B+	Muni. Ntl. Long	Very Low	1999.5	0.68	6.6	6.9	8.6	7.0	5.3	20.8	3 3 2	-2.0	-8.0	-4.7
NUVEEN N.J. INVMT. QUAL. MUNI.	B+	Muni. S.S. Long	Low	310.6	NA	5.4	6.2	7.8	9.0	5.6	17.0	3 4 3	15.1	2.8	3.8
NUVEEN N.J. PREMIUM INCOME MUNI.	C	Muni. S.S. Long	Average	185.3	NA	6.6	7.2	14.6	14.3	5.2	18.2	4 2 2	8.1	-2.1	-0.8
NUVEEN N.Y. INVMT. QUAL. MUNI.	B	Muni. N.Y. Interm.	Very Low	274.5	0.82	5.0	4.7	7.0	9.3	5.8	22.6	4 4 3	15.7	9.4	9.8
NUVEEN N.Y. MUNICIPAL VALUE	B+	Muni. N.Y. Interm.	Very Low	154.2	NA	5.8	5.6	2.0	2.5	5.3	23.3	4 4 3	4.0	-7.2	-2.3
NUVEEN N.Y. PERF. PLUS MUNICIPAL	B+	Muni. N.Y. Interm.	Very Low	238.5	NA	5.3	5.1	0.2	7.3	6.1	20.7	4 4 3	16.0	6.2	7.3
NUVEEN N.Y. QUAL. INCOME MUNI.	C	Muni. N.Y. Interm.	Low	373.6	0.80	5.1	5.9	4.9	8.8	5.6	21.7	3 4 3	7.6	1.4	4.0
NUVEEN N.Y. SELECT QUALITY MUNI.	B	Muni. N.Y. Interm.	Low	363.9	NA	4.6	5.0	6.7	8.3	5.7	19.8	4 4 3	10.9	1.9	5.8
NUVEEN N.C. PREMIUM INCOME	D	Muni. S.S. Long	High	91.7	NA	6.7	7.8	16.7	17.9	4.8	20.1	4 2 2	13.8	2.1	8.1
NUVEEN OHIO QUALITY INCOME MUNI.	C	Muni. S.S. Long	Average	158.2	NA	6.5	6.9	13.0	14.3	5.0	19.5	3 3 2	17.5	3.7	7.3
NUVEEN PA. INVMT. QUALITY MUNI.	B	Muni. S.S. Long	Low	254.1	NA	4.9	5.5	11.3	8.2	5.6	18.9	3 4 3	12.9	6.9	5.7
NUVEEN PA. PREMIUM INCOME MUNI. 2	B	Muni. S.S. Long	Average	237.2	NA	7.3	8.0	5.1	10.9	5.3	20.4	3 3 2	-3.8	-9.5	-8.9
NUVEEN PERFORMANCE PLUS MUNI.	B+	Muni. Ntl. Interm.	Low	918.1	0.77	6.4	6.7	4.3	5.9	6.2	21.7	3 4 2	3.8	-4.7	-4.8
NUVEEN PREMIER INSURED MUNI. INC.	C	Muni. Ntl. Long	Low	308.2	NA	6.5	6.4	7.3	10.2	5.6	19.5	4 3 2	4.3	-1.7	0.2
NUVEEN PREMIER MUNICIPAL INCOME	B+	Muni. Ntl. Long	Low	313.0	NA	5.8	6.9	5.8	10.4	5.9	17.7	2 3 3	11.4	-0.5	3.4
NUVEEN PREMIUM INCOME MUNICIPAL	B	Muni. Ntl. Long	Low	998.8	NA	7.2	7.3	9.2	8.4	5.8	22.4	3 3 2	-1.0	-6.8	-2.6
NUVEEN PREMIUM INCOME MUNICIPAL 2	B	Muni. Ntl. Long	Low	656.3	NA	7.0	8.0	11.1	13.9	5.5	20.3	2 3 2	5.1	-3.6	1.1
NUVEEN PREMIUM INCOME MUNICIPAL 4	B	Muni. Ntl. Long	Average	612.9	NA	6.7	7.8	10.0	12.3	5.6	18.8	3 2 2	0.6	-8.6	-3.2
NUVEEN QUALITY INCOME MUNICIPAL	B+	Muni. Ntl. Interm.	Very Low	848.7	0.78	5.8	6.7	9.1	11.5	6.0	21.3	3 3 3	9.3	1.4	3.9
NUVEEN SELECT MATURITIES MUNICIPAL	B	Muni. Ntl. Long	Low	148.3	NA	5.7	6.1	8.6	6.9	5.1	13.6	3 4 3	1.0	-5.2	-4.6
NUVEEN SEL. QUALITY MUNICIPAL	B+	Muni. Ntl. Interm.	Low	527.8	NA	6.1	6.8	6.2	10.4	5.9	21.3	3 3 3	6.3	0.1	0.8
NUVEEN SEL. TAX-FREE INCOME	B+	Muni. Ntl. Long	Very Low	265.5	0.44	5.4	6.5	12.0	9.4	5.4	16.5	3 3 3	8.3	-1.0	0.7
NUVEEN SEL. TAX-FREE INCOME 2	B+	Muni. Ntl. Long	Very Low	272.8	0.45	5.9	6.5	12.1	8.9	5.3	16.6	3 4 3	6.2	-2.9	-1.9
NUVEEN SEL. TAX-FREE INCOME 3	B+	Muni. Ntl. Long	Very Low	195.2	0.51	6.2	7.0	10.5	10.6	5.3	17.4	3 3 3	5.4	-3.9	-2.0
NUVEEN TEXAS QUALITY INCOME MUNI.	C	Muni. S.S. Long	Low	150.2	NA	6.0	7.0	6.8	9.8	5.7	21.3	3 3 3	3.8	-3.5	-2.1
NUVEEN VA. PREM. INC. MUNI.	C-	Muni. S.S. Long	Average	130.6	NA	6.9	7.8	11.4	14.3	4.9	22.6	3 2 2	12.4	3.0	3.8
NUVEEN WASH. PREMIUM INCOME MUNI.	C-	Muni. S.S. Long	Average	35.5	NA	7.3	8.1	12.3	12.7	5.2	19.1	4 2 2	-2.7	-10.2	-7.2
OPPENHEIMER MULTI-SECTOR INCOME	C	Multisector	Average	311.9	0.99	2.2	7.9	-4.8	6.6	9.2	10.6	2 4 3	-0.8	-13.4	-13.6
PACHOLDER	C	High Yield	High	110.7	1.47	-3.7	10.2	-0.6	8.8	10.4	7.4	1 1 4	11.8	-3.2	4.6
PACIFIC AMERICAN INCOME SHARES	C-	Interm. (Gen.)	High	147.0	0.71	5.5	7.6	5.9	10.4	5.4	16.8	2 3 3	6.5	-1.6	3.0
PILGRIM PRIME RATE	B+	Ultrashort	Very Low	1751.3	1.39	7.7	7.7	-2.5	9.2	8.8	5.6	2 4 1	12.2	-1.2	3.2
PIMCO COMMERCIAL MORTGAGE SECS.	B+	Interm. (Gen.)	Average	212	0.97	7.5	9.2	9.9	13.0	8.9	19.5	2 3 2	1.6	-10.3	-0.5
PIONEER INTEREST SHARES	C	Interm. (Gen.)	Average	101.7	NA	7.0	8.0	4.6	8.3	7.7	14.1	2 3 2	8.2	-8.0	0.1
PREFERRED INCOME	A	Long (Gen.)	Low	159.6	1.34	6.2	11.6	7.4	16.5	6.9	32.4	2 1 3	-0.1	-7.8	-5.6
PREFERRED INCOME MGT.	A	Long (Gen.)	Low	149.5	1.60	6.4	12.6	-7.3	12.4	7.3	32.8	1 1 2	-0.5	-17.8	-21.3
PREFERRED INCOME OPPORT.	A	Long (Gen.)	Low	148.8	NA	6.9	12.5	8.5	17.8	7.3	NA	2 1 2	-1.3	-9.5	-6.8
PROSPECT STREET HIGH-INCOME	F	High Yield	Very High	207.8	NA	-23.0	1.2	-8.6	5.6	12.8	6.1	1 2 4	30.4	0.2	12.4
PUTNAM CALIF. INVMT. GR. MUNI.	B	Muni. Calif. Long	Low	72.6	1.15	5.8	6.7	5.6	9.7	5.4	20.5	3 3 3	4.7	-2.1	0.4
PUTNAM CONV. OPPORTS. AND INCOME	C-	Convertibles	Very High	85.7	NA	-3.7	9.3	-0.9	15.4	7.7	6.7	1 1 4	3.9	-10.0	-1.0
PUTNAM DIVIDEND INCOME	A	Long (Gen.)	Low	65.7	1.46	5.8	9.9	11.0	12.5	6.3	NA	2 2 3	-4.9	-12.2	-8.3
PUTNAM HIGH INCOME CONV. & BOND	C-	Convertibles	High	113.7	0.97	-4.2	7.0	-6.4	9.3	8.8	6.4	2 2 4	21.6	3.3	8.2
PUTNAM HIGH YIELD MUNICIPAL	A	Muni. Ntl. Long	Very Low	202.9	1.12	5.2	6.5	9.6	12.1	6.1	22.1	2 4 3	26.0	11.9	17.0
PUTNAM INVMT. GRADE MUNICIPAL	C	Muni. Ntl. Long	Low	249.9	1.41	4.9	5.8	8.7	11.1	6.4	20.1	4 3 3	27.2	10.4	12.0
PUTNAM INVMT. GRADE MUNICIPAL II	C-	Muni. Ntl. Long	Low	190.0	1.23	4.4	5.6	5.7	10.2	6.2	20.5	4 3 3	9.4	0.9	5.4
PUTNAM INVMT. GRADE MUNICIPAL III	B	Muni. Ntl. Long	Low	54.1	1.23	5.7	6.2	8.7	11.0	6.0	21.8	4 3 3	3.1	-5.8	-0.1
PUTNAM MANAGED HIGH YIELD	D	High Yield	High	92.2	NA	-6.7	7.2	3.8	12.7	9.4	8.5	1 1 4	18.4	-0.5	16.3
PUTNAM MANAGED MUNI. INCOME	C	Muni. Ntl. Long	Low	453.6	1.18	4.3	5.4	5.8	10.1	6.5	20.1	4 4 3	23.1	4.4	9.7
PUTNAM MASTER INCOME	D	Multisector	High	439.5	0.93	-0.9	5.9	-1.6	9.2	9.4	11.5	2 4 4	0.9	-9.9	-2.2
PUTNAM MASTER INTERM. INCOME	C-	Multisector	Average	797.5	1.01	1.7	6.3	5.2	11.4	8.7	7.8	2 4 3	0.8	-10.4	0.3
PUTNAM MUNICIPAL OPPORTUNITIES	C	Muni. Ntl. Long	Average	230.1	NA	6.6	7.1	8.2	11.1	6.1	22.8	3 3 2	11.0	-1.2	6.3
PUTNAM N.Y. INVMT. GR. MUNICIPAL	B	Muni. N.Y. Long	Low	40.6	1.28	5.7	6.0	9.6	10.0	5.6	22.9	4 3 3	5.7	-3.9	-2.7
PUTNAM PREMIER INCOME	D	Multisector	High	1113.7	0.82	-0.5	6.1	5.3	11.9	9.0	13.1	2 4 4	5.0	-9.4	3.5
PUTNAM TAX-FREE HEALTH CARE	A	Muni. Ntl. Long	Very Low	206	0.89	5.3	7.7	11.9	14.3	5.8	19.8	2 3 3	6.5	-4.4	-3.6
RCM STRAT. GLOBAL GOVT. INC.	C-	International	High	353.3	1.25	5.3	8.0	-4.0	8.5	8.8	16.5	2 3 3	-5.5	-18.4	-13.8
SALOMON BROS. 2008 WLD. DOL.	C	International	Very High	361.6	NA	-5.3	13.9	-1.4	14.8	9.9	21.9	1 1 4	4.0	-10.8	2.9
SALOMON BROTHERS HIGH INCOME	C-	High Yield	High	71.6	NA	-6.0	8.8	-2.2	12.1	10.3	10.2	1 2 4	23.5	1.6	15.6
SALOMON BROTHERS WLD. INCOME	F	Emerg. Mkts.	Very High	182.2	NA	-24.5	10.5	-20.7	10.0	18.8	14.2	1 1 4	32.0	-8.6	6.2
SCUDDER GLOBAL HIGH INCOME	F	Emerg. Mkts.	Very High	58.4	1.85	-53.3	-8.0	-57.4	-8.5	24.3	14.7	1 2 4	52.4	-3.1	-10.7
SELIGMAN QUALITY MUNICIPAL	C	Muni. Ntl. Long	Average	72.5	NA	6.6	7.0	7.0	11.2	5.8	24.8	3 3 2	3.8	-3.7	-11.0
SELIGMAN SELECT MUNICIPAL	B	Muni. Ntl. Long	Low	165.0	NA	7.0	7.0	-3.3	7.8	6.1	25.4	3 3 2	13.0	-2.3	-3.9
SENIOR HIGH-INCOME	C-	High Yield	High	330.4	0.75	-0.1	7.3	-11.6	5.8	10.1	6.7	2 2 4	10.8	-4.0	-3.4
SMITH BARNEY INTERM. MUNICIPAL	B	Muni. Ntl. Interm.	Very Low	88.6	0.76	5.1	5.6	6.7	6.8	5.1	10.3	3 4 3	2.3	-8.0	-7.6
SMITH BARNEY MUNICIPAL	B	Muni. Ntl. Long	Low	63.6	0.85	5.4	6.0	6.5	9.0	5.4	12.6	4 4 3	-3.2	-9.6	-9.1
STRATEGIC GLOBAL INCOME	A	International	Average	265.4	1.20	9.2	10.5	6.2	11.8	9.2	13.6	1 4 1	-9.7	-20.1	-13.0
TCW CONVERTIBLE SECURITIES	B	Convertibles	Very High	393.6	0.74	13.2	15.4	11.2	12.6	10.7	6.4	2 1 1	16.1	-1.6	-1.4

NA=Not available.

DATA: MORNINGSTAR, INC., CHICAGO, IL.

MUTUAL FUND SCOREBOARD — Closed-End Bond Funds

FUND	RATING	CATEGORY	RISK	SIZE ASSETS $MIL.	FEES EXPENSE RATIO (%)	NAV.RET.(%) 1 YR.	NAV.RET.(%) 3 YRS.	SHARES RET.(%) 1 YR.	SHARES RET.(%) 3 YRS.	YIELD (%)	MAT. (YRS.)	TREND 3-YEAR ANALYSIS	1998 HIGH	LOW	1/29/99
TCW/DW TERM TRUST 2000	B	Short-Term	High	455.3	NA	9.3	9.5	9.0	13.8	5.9	15.0	2 2 1	-3.8	-7.4	-3.8
TCW/DW TERM TRUST 2002	B+	Short-Term	High	419.7	NA	11.2	10.9	11.1	14.4	6.3	15.0	2 1 1	-5.4	-9.8	-6.0
TCW/DW TERM TRUST 2003	B+	Long (Gen.)	High	921.7	0.74	11.5	11.6	12.3	15.4	6.1	14.0	2 1 1	-8.1	-12.4	-8.9
TEMPLETON EMG. MKTS. INCOME	F	Emerg. Mkts.	Very High	529.1	1.19	-8.8	8.4	-14.0	4.8	13.1	10.8	1 3 4	-0.7	-12.9	-14.8
TEMPLETON GLOBAL GOVT. INCOME	C-	International	High	173.4	NA	5.7	6.6	-1.4	4.6	8.6	6.2	2 4 3	-4.2	-16.2	-12.1
TEMPLETON GLOBAL INCOME	C-	International	Average	942.8	0.75	6.4	7.2	2.4	8.6	8.5	6.3	2 4 2	-7.4	-14.8	-12.9
TRANSAMERICA INCOME SHARES	C-	Long (Gen.)	High	160.1	0.62	8.2	7.6	13.9	11.3	7.0	16.1	4 3 1	9.4	-0.7	6.1
2002 TARGET	C	Long Govt.	Average	118.5	NA	6.6	7.8	10.6	9.9	6.0	14.8	2 3 2	-5.1	-10.0	-6.3
USLIFE INCOME	B	Long (Gen.)	High	59.8	NA	7.0	9.4	12.1	9.3	7.6	19.8	2 1 2	-1.3	-11.3	-6.9
VAN KAMP. ADVANTAGE MUNI. INCOME	C	Muni. Ntl. Long	Average	322.3	NA	7.3	8.0	14.2	10.9	5.5	20.8	3 2 2	-1.4	-10.8	-9.4
VAN KAMP. ADV. MUNI. INCOME II	C	Muni. Ntl. Long	Average	119.7	NA	7.6	8.1	13.1	12.9	5.5	18.8	3 2 1	-4.3	-16.6	-10.8
VAN KAMP. ADV. PA. MUNI. INCOME	C-	Muni. S.S. Long	Average	76.7	NA	6.7	6.8	10.9	10.9	5.5	18.7	4 3 2	0.6	-6.7	-6.9
VAN KAMP. BOND	C	Interm. (Gen.)	Average	230.1	0.68	9.2	8.0	3.6	8.8	7.2	17.5	4 3 1	0.2	-9.3	-5.0
VAN KAMP. CALIF. MUNI. INCOME	C	Muni. Calif. Interm.	Average	34.0	1.58	6.8	7.1	1.5	8.9	5.6	21.6	4 3 2	17.2	4.7	2.9
VAN KAMP. CALIF. QUALITY MUNICIPAL	B+	Muni. Calif. Interm.	Low	170.0	1.61	6.9	8.3	15.4	13.4	5.3	20.6	3 2 2	6.1	-2.6	-1.9
VAN KAMP. CALIF. VALUE MUNI. INCOME	C	Muni. Calif. Long	Average	100.5	NA	7.7	8.5	15.0	16.3	5.0	16.7	3 2 1	-1.7	-9.1	-7.2
VAN KAMP. CONVERTIBLE SECS.	C	Convertibles	Very High	74.2	NA	7.2	13.2	2.4	10.8	4.2	7.5	2 1 2	-6.6	-15.4	-18.0
VAN KAMP. FLORIDA MUNI. OPPORT.	D	Muni. S.S. Long	High	25.5	NA	5.9	6.9	14.4	13.7	4.9	19.6	4 2 3	-1.6	-10.5	-7.6
VAN KAMP. FLORIDA QUALITY MUNI.	C-	Muni. S.S. Long	Low	111.4	1.64	5.6	5.7	11.9	8.1	5.3	20.3	4 4 3	5.0	-3.2	-1.3
VAN KAMP. INCOME	B+	Long (Gen.)	Average	120.0	0.91	5.7	8.6	5.1	11.6	8.3	12.1	2 2 3	3.0	-5.7	-7.4
VAN KAMP. INTERM.-TERM HIGH-INCOME	C	High Yield	High	80.4	NA	0.3	8.6	-4.2	10.6	11.0	6.9	2 2 4	19.7	4.3	9.7
VAN KAMP. INVMT. GRADE MUNI.	D	Muni. Ntl. Long	Average	51.1	NA	5.4	4.9	8.3	8.7	6.2	20.4	4 3 2	5.8	-1.2	2.9
VAN KAMP. LTD.-TERM HIGH-INCOME	C-	High Yield	High	61.6	NA	-0.3	8.3	-2.6	10.2	11.1	6.2	2 2 4	22.3	0.4	15.1
VAN KAMP. MASS. VALUE MUNI. INCOME	B	Muni. S.S. Long	Average	42.0	NA	6.9	7.9	14.2	15.6	4.9	16.4	3 2 2	2.8	-6.7	-4.7
VAN KAMP. MUNICIPAL INCOME	C	Muni. Ntl. Long	Average	296.6	1.28	6.7	7.4	6.4	8.0	6.2	21.1	3 3 2	10.3	0.0	1.9
VAN KAMP. MUNICIPAL OPPORT.	C-	Muni. Ntl. Long	Average	269.3	NA	7.0	8.2	13.9	14.0	5.4	18.6	3 2 2	-4.7	-11.1	-7.3
VAN KAMP. MUNICIPAL OPPORT. II	C-	Muni. Ntl. Long	Average	175.6	NA	7.4	8.0	13.6	14.7	5.4	18.6	3 2 2	-2.7	-9.5	-7.7
VAN KAMP. MUNICIPAL	B	Muni. Ntl. Long	Low	610.0	1.61	7.0	7.9	13.7	14.1	5.5	21.2	3 2 2	1.0	-7.8	-4.3
VAN KAMP. N.J. VALUE MUNI. INC.	C	Muni. S.S. Long	Average	39.5	NA	7.7	8.1	12.8	14.6	5.0	17.6	3 2 1	-3.4	-10.7	-8.3
VAN KAMP. N.Y. QUALITY MUNI.	C	Muni. N.Y. Interm.	Average	97.9	1.68	6.5	6.5	9.7	7.7	5.4	17.8	4 3 2	-1.5	-6.9	-7.1
VAN KAMP. N.Y. VALUE MUNI. INC.	D	Muni. N.Y. Long	High	69.3	NA	8.1	8.7	11.9	15.0	5.2	16.1	4 1 1	-5.0	-11.2	-9.5
VAN KAMP. OHIO QUALITY MUNI.	B	Muni. S.S. Long	Low	74.0	1.78	5.0	6.2	7.7	11.3	5.3	15.6	3 4 3	11.4	2.4	4.5
VAN KAMP. OHIO VALUE MUNI. INC.	C-	Muni. S.S. Long	Average	26.3	NA	6.4	7.4	10.9	12.3	4.9	17.0	3 2 2	-7.2	-13.8	-9.5
VAN KAMP. PA. QUALITY MUNI.	B	Muni. S.S. Long	Low	140.7	NA	5.3	6.1	11.4	8.3	5.6	16.1	4 3 3	5.3	-0.3	-1.8
VAN KAMP. PA. VALUE MUNI. INC.	C-	Muni. S.S. Long	Average	71.1	NA	6.5	7.6	15.2	12.5	5.2	15.5	3 2 2	-5.2	-13.7	-9.8
VAN KAMP. SELECT SECTOR MUNI.	C	Muni. Ntl. Long	Average	57.0	NA	7.6	8.1	14.4	12.9	5.4	19.1	3 2 1	-4.6	-13.0	-9.8
VAN KAMP. STRATEGIC SECTOR MUNI.	C-	Muni. Ntl. Long	Average	159.4	NA	6.8	7.8	12.5	11.8	5.6	17.5	4 2 2	-1.7	-11.6	-8.3
VAN KAMP. TRUST INSURED MUNIS.	C	Muni. Ntl. Long	Average	166.7	NA	7.0	7.0	9.3	11.3	5.6	20.6	4 3 2	2.5	-4.2	0.7
VAN KAMP. TRUST INVMT. GR. MUNIS.	C	Muni. Ntl. Long	Average	472.3	NA	6.3	7.8	13.1	10.6	5.7	20.6	3 2 2	-0.2	-9.8	-7.1
VAN KAMP. TRUST INVMT. GR. CA. MUNIS.	C	Muni. Calif. Interm.	Average	79.2	NA	6.9	7.9	14.9	12.9	5.3	21.0	3 2 2	6.9	-2.3	1.0
VAN KAMP. TRUST INVMT. GR. FL. MUNIS.	D	Muni. S.S. Long	Average	73.4	NA	5.4	6.0	11.2	12.5	5.3	19.7	4 3 3	7.2	-5.0	-1.3
VAN KAMP. TRUST INVMT. GR. N.J. MUNIS.	D	Muni. S.S. Long	Average	70.7	NA	6.9	7.0	13.7	12.2	5.2	16.9	4 3 2	2.3	-6.6	-2.5
VAN KAMP. TRUST INVMT. GR. N.Y. MUNIS.	C	Muni. N.Y. Long	Average	110.1	NA	6.8	7.4	11.2	13.3	5.4	18.4	4 2 2	1.0	-5.4	-4.8
VAN KAMP. TRUST INVMT. GR. PA. MUNIS.	C	Muni. S.S. Long	Average	131.9	NA	6.7	6.8	10.3	11.0	5.6	18.9	4 2 2	-1.1	-7.5	-8.2
VAN KAMP. VALUE MUNI. INCOME	C-	Muni. Ntl. Long	Average	367.4	1.70	7.0	7.8	12.0	12.3	5.5	19.3	3 2 2	-3.4	-10.8	-8.8
VESTAUR SECURITIES	C-	Interm. (Gen.)	High	98.3	0.90	6.7	6.9	6.8	11.1	7.1	16.2	4 3 2	3.2	-6.3	0.0
VOYAGEUR ARIZ. MUNI. INCOME	C-	Muni. S.S. Long	Average	44.9	NA	7.5	7.5	13.5	14.1	5.0	18.8	4 2 2	2.0	-6.8	-0.5
VOYAGEUR COLO. INS. MUNI. INCOME	D	Muni. S.S. Long	High	33.9	NA	6.7	7.4	15.1	13.8	4.8	20.2	4 2 2	-0.6	-8.1	-5.3
VOYAGEUR FLA. INS. MUNI. INCOME	F	Muni. S.S. Long	High	37.2	NA	8.6	8.1	12.2	14.0	5.0	23.5	4 3 2	-2.6	-8.4	-6.7
VOYAGEUR MINN. MUNICIPAL INCOME	B	Muni. S.S. Long	Low	40.0	NA	7.0	7.1	15.4	11.3	5.6	19.9	4 3 2	8.7	-0.4	5.8
VOYAGEUR MINN. MUNICIPAL INCOME II	B	Muni. S.S. Long	Average	107.8	NA	7.2	7.8	14.9	12.0	5.5	22.5	4 2 2	0.1	-7.8	-1.3
VOYAGEUR MINN. MUNICIPAL INCOME III	C	Muni. S.S. Long	Average	25.4	NA	7.7	8.3	13.9	12.1	5.5	22.7	3 2 1	0.4	-6.7	-1.9
WORLDWIDE DOLLARVEST	F	Emerg. Mkts.	Very High	39.5	0.82	-50.0	-5.3	-52.3	-6.7	19.9	17.9	1 4 4	45.8	-8.8	-16.4
ZENIX INCOME	C-	High Yield	High	105.9	NA	-3.1	9.3	-19.4	7.5	12.0	9.2	1 1 4	21.1	-9.6	-1.6

NA=Not available.

DATA: MORNINGSTAR, INC., CHICAGO, IL.

About the Author

Jeffrey M. Laderman is a senior writer at BUSINESS WEEK specializing in finance. He helped launch the annual BUSINESS WEEK Mutual Fund Scoreboard, writes the accompanying cover stories, and reports on the stock market and mutual funds. He also helped create the Interactive Mutual Fund Scoreboard and is a regular contributor to BUSINESS WEEK Online. Mr. Laderman is a graduate of Rutgers University and has a master's degree in journalism from Columbia University. He is a Chartered Financial Analyst and a member of the New York Society of Security Analysts and the Association for Investment Management and Research.